D1519156

TRAVEL SURVEY METHODS

Related Books

AXHAUSEN (ed.)	Travel Behaviour Research
ETTEMA & TIMMERMANS (eds.)	Activity-based Approaches to Travel Analysis
HENSHER & BUTTON (eds.)	Handbooks in Transport Series
MAHMASSANI (ed.)	In Perpetual Motion
TAYLOR (ed.)	Transportation and Traffic Theory in 21st Century
STOPHER & JONES (eds.)	Transport Survey, Quality and Innovation

Related Journals

Journal of Transport Geography
Editor: R. D. Knowles

Transport Policy
Editor: M. Ben-Akiva

Transportation Research Part A: Policy and Practice
Editor: P.B. Goodwin

Transportation Research Part B: Methodological
Editor: F. Mannering

Transportation Research C: Emerging Technologies
Editor: M. Papageorgiou

TRAVEL SURVEY METHODS
QUALITY AND FUTURE DIRECTIONS

Edited by

PETER STOPHER
The University of Sydney, New South Wales, Australia

and

CHERYL STECHER
Franklin Hill Group, Santa Monica, USA

ELSEVIER

Amsterdam – Boston – Heidelberg – London – New York – Oxford – Paris
San Diego – San Francisco – Singapore – Sydney – Tokyo

Elsevier
The Boulevard, Langford Lane, Kidlington, Oxford OX5 1GB, UK
Radarweg 29, PO Box 211, 1000 AE Amsterdam, The Netherlands

First edition 2006

Copyright © 2006 Elsevier Ltd. All rights reserved

British Library Cataloguing in Publication Data
A catalogue record for this book is available from the British Library

Library of Congress Cataloging-in-Publication Data
A catalog record for this book is available from the Library of Congress

ISBN-13: 978-0-08-044662-2
ISBN-10: 0-08-044662-0

For information on all Elsevier publications
visit our website at books.elsevier.com

Printed and bound in The United Kingdom

06 07 08 09 10   10 9 8 7 6 5 4 3 2 1

FOREWORD

This book is a new chapter in the ISCTSC's continuing focus on maintaining and improving the quality of data collection in transport surveys. The papers extend discourse on broad topic areas that have been addressed by the ISCTSC in previous gatherings, update us on travel survey initiatives currently under way in many countries, and provide a glimpse into the future in the form of changing contexts, new topics, new technologies, and new standards. However, what these papers really tell us is that there are many ways to improve the quality of transport surveys; too many to be covered in a single book or conference proceedings. There is no set of absolute standards that, if observed, will automatically ensure the quality of a particular research effort or product. However, there are general (and generally measurable) guidelines for high-quality research that are widely appreciated in the ISCTSC community and beyond.

As we pick up the baton as ISCTSC chairs, reading this book reminds us of the importance of the fundamentals of *good* survey design. No survey fully satisfies the theoretical ideals of scientific inquiry. Every survey represents a collection of compromises between the ideal and the possible. For us, the primary goal of the ISCTSC is to help the international community of transport survey researchers arrive at the best possible compromises by facilitating communication among those conducting transport survey research, opening new lines of communication with those conducting related research in different disciplines, and extending information dissemination about survey practice and methods research. *Perfect* transport surveys may never be possible, but *good* surveys can and should be done.

We would like to thank the authors who participated in this volume, particularly those of you who are long-standing contributors to ISCTSC programs. We look forward to working with you over the next several years and commit to stimulating and expanding the ISCTSC roles in collaboration and dissemination. We would particularly like to acknowledge the solid foundation that has been provided for our upcoming tenure by Peter Stopher, Cheryl Stecher, and Peter Jones, and all the Chairpersons of the previous International Conferences on Transport Survey Methods. We would also like to thank Chester Wilmot for his unwavering behind-the-scenes support as Secretary/Treasurer of ISCTSC. We thank them for their diligence in support of the goal of transport survey quality, and hope to carry on that tradition.

Johanna Zmud
Tony Richardson

FOREWORD

PREFACE

It is hoped that this book will move the practice of Travel Surveys forward again, as a follow on to the earlier book *Transport Survey Quality and Innovation* (Stopher and Jones, 2003a), published three years ago. It is the goal of this book to make further progress in establishing ways in which the quality of transport surveys can be assessed and improved, as well as to set out some future directions for research in improving travel survey methods. Since the earlier book was published, a significant research effort has drawn to its conclusion, sponsored by the US National Cooperative Highway Research Program (NCHRP), through the Transportation Research Board of the National Academies of Science and Engineering in the US. This research effort was aimed at establishing standardised procedures for personal travel surveys in the US, and the work accomplished in that research forms the basis of the second chapter of this book, which was also used as a keynote paper in the 7th International Conference on Travel Survey Methods, held in Costa Rica in August 2004.

This book is not a conference proceedings. However, the various chapters of the book have been developed from papers that were a part of the 7th International Conference on Travel Survey Methods. All of the papers written for and as a consequence of the conference were reviewed by three referees. Only those papers that achieved the highest ratings from the referees were selected for inclusion in this book. Prior to the conference, a call for abstracts yielded a total of more than forty abstracts. Following a review of all the abstracts, twenty three papers were eventually selected for inclusion in the conference. Seventeen resource papers were commissioned. Following review of these and modification by the authors, sixteen were included in the conference. Three keynote papers were also commissioned, and all three were included in the conference, following extensive reviews of each. Thus, in the conference itself, forty two papers were presented either to plenary sessions or to workshops. Of these, twenty two were selected for revision and inclusion in this book. In addition, the chairs of the fifteen workshops were asked to write papers that summarised the deliberations of those workshops and that could be included as chapters of this book. These papers were also reviewed before being included. Final versions of most of the chapters were completed in May-June of 2005, almost a year after the conference was held.

GOALS OF THIS BOOK

The goals of this book are twofold. First, this book seeks to extend the discussions of the Costa Rica Conference and its two predecessor conferences on the topic of survey quality. Second, it sets out to create a research agenda for travel surveys for the coming years, recognising where some of the most critical areas are for future developments and innovations. To set the stage for these goals, the first chapter of the book presents an overview of travel surveys in South and Central America. The second chapter offers a series of proposals for possible standards and guidelines that could be considered for adoption on a national or global basis.

In the area of survey quality, discussions began with the 5th International Conference on *Transport Surveys: Raising the Standard* in 1997, held in Germany. While that conference raised many issues relating to survey quality, no consensus was reached on measures of quality, nor the applicability of those measures to the global transport survey community. The debate continued in 2001 in the 6th International Conference on *Transport Survey Quality and Innovation* that was held in South Africa. While the sixth conference began with a more concrete list of possible areas of standardisation, it was noted that 'Few recommendations of specific standards emerged from the conference, although many of the proposals for standards...appear to be supported by various workshops' (Stopher and Jones, 2003b). In the meantime in the US, a research project was undertaken under the funding of the NCHRP to develop standardised procedures for personal travel surveys, as noted above. The list of possible areas for global standards that was put before the 2001 Conference came from the early work on this project. For the 2004 conference, the set of proposed standards, detailed in chapter 2 of this book (Stopher *et al.*, 2006), was developed from the findings of this research project and put forward as a starting point for consideration.

Chapters 3 to 18 cover this area of survey quality, standards, and guidelines. The chapters address various broad areas of survey design and implementation. The six broad areas covered by this part of the book are:

- Survey Design;
- Sample Design;
- Instrument Design;
- Survey Implementation;
- Processing, Analysing, and Archiving Survey Data; and
- Quality Assessment.

With respect to a research agenda, the International Steering Committee for Travel Survey Conferences (ISCTSC) developed a list of topic areas that appear to be among the most pressing research areas for the continued development of travel surveys in the beginning of the 21st century, to assist in the guidance of transport policy and investment in the next few years. A subset of topic areas were selected for the conference to consider. Each area was described in a one-paragraph synopsis, and the workshops in the 7th International Conference were asked to consider these topics and to develop a research agenda for these areas. Chapters 19 to 37 cover these topics, which are:

- Stated Preference (SP) surveys;

- Panel surveys;
- Freight surveys;
- Investment Quality surveys;
- Process data;
- New technologies (not web based);
- New technologies (web based);
- Emergency events surveys; and
- Simulated travel survey data.

Several of these topics have not appeared before in one of these conferences, while others have appeared frequently but often without resulting in a clear forward direction. This is particularly the case with the area of freight data, which, like freight modelling, appears to suffer from some considerable lack of clear direction within the profession. New topics to this conference include those of panel surveys, investment quality surveys, emergency events surveys, and simulated travel survey data.

The final chapter of this book consists of a summary of the conference and of the chapters of this book, and is intended to provide a quick overview of the overarching conclusions that can be drawn from the various chapters of this book. The final chapter also provides one paragraph descriptions of each of the workshops, which readers may find to be a useful starting point for selecting those portions of this book to read. In addition, the reader will find it helpful to refer to the previous books in this series (Stopher and Jones, 2000; Stopher and Jones, 2003a), to gain the greatest benefit from the material herein.

Cheryl Stecher
Peter Stopher

January, 2006

REFERENCES

Stopher, P.R. and P.M. Jones (eds) (2003a). *Transport Survey Quality and Innovation*, Pergamon Press, Oxford, 646 pp.

Stopher, P.R. and P.M. Jones (2003b). Summary and Future Directions. In: *Transport Survey Quality and Innovation* (P.R. Stopher and P.M. Jones, eds), 635-646, Pergamon Press, Oxford.

Stopher, P.R., C.G. Wilmot, C.C. Stecher and R. Alsnih (2006). Household Travel Surveys: Proposed Standards and Guidelines. In: *Travel Survey Methods – Quality and Future Directions* (P.R. Stopher and C.C. Stecher, eds), 19-74, Elsevier, Oxford.

Stopher, P.R. and P.M. Jones (eds) (2000). *Transport Surveys: Raising the Standard*, Transportation Research Circular E-C008, Transportation Research Board, Washington, DC.

ACKNOWLEDGEMENTS

The chapters in this book were originally prepared either for or as a result of a conference that was held in Costa Rica in August 2004. That conference was conceived and directed by the ISCTSC, under the co-chairmanship of Cheryl Stecher and Peter Stopher. The ISCTSC was set up in 1997 to '...organise periodic international conferences dealing with research subjects relevant to the conduct of transport surveys that support planning, policy, modelling, monitoring, and related issues for urban, rural, regional, intercity, and international person, vehicle, and commodity movements'. The ISCTSC was assisted in organising the local arrangements and logistics by a Local Organising Committee in the US and Costa Rica, under the co-chairmanship of Carlos Arce and Carlos Contreras Montoya. The conference co-chairs would like to acknowledge the hard work put in by these two committees, the members of which are shown in Tables 1 and 2.

Table 1: Members of the International Steering Committee for Travel Survey Conferences for the Costa Rica Conference

Name	Affiliation	Country
Carlos Arce	NuStats	USA
Patrick Bonnel	ENTPE	France
Werner Brög	Socialdata, GmbH	Germany
Carlos Contreras Montoya	Ministerio de Obras Publicas y Transportes	Costa Rica
Lee Geisbrecht	Bureau of Transportation Statistics, USDOT	USA
Peter Jones	UCL	UK
Ryuichi Kitamura	Kyoto University	Japan
Martin Lee-Gosselin	University of Laval	Canada
Jean-Loup Madre	INRETS	France
Arnim Meyburg	Cornell University	USA
Elaine Murakami	US Department of Transportation, FHWA	USA
Juan de Dios Ortúzar	Pontificia Universidad Católica de Chile	Chile
Tom Palmerlee	Transportation Research Board	USA
Alan Pisarski	Consultant	USA
Tony Richardson	The Urban Transport Institute	Australia
Gerd Sammer	Universitat für Bodenkultur	Austria
Cheryl Stecher (co-chair)	The Franklin Hill Group	USA
Peter Stopher (co-chair)	The University of Sydney	Australia
Orlando Strambi	Escola Politecnica da Universidade Sao Paulo	Brazil
Harry Timmermans	Eindhoven University of Technology	The Netherlands
Mary Lynn Tischer	Virginia Department of Transportation	USA
Klaas van Zyl	Stewart Scott	South Africa
Manfred Wermuth	Technische Universitat Braunschweig	Germany
Chester Wilmot (Secretary)	Louisiana State University	USA

Table 2: Members of the Local Organising Committee for the Costa Rica Conference

Name	Affiliation	Country
Carlos Arce (co-chair)	NuStats	USA
Carlos Contreras Montoya (co-chair)	Ministerio de Obras Publicas y Transportes	Costa Rica
Rafael Chan Jaen	Ministerio de Obras Publicas y Transportes	Costa Rica
Jose Manuel Hernandez Monge	Ministerio de Obras Publicas y Transportes	Costa Rica
Minor Rodriguez Barrantes	Ministerio de Obras Publicas y Transportes	Costa Rica
Juan de Dios Ortúzar	Pontificia Universidad Católica de Chile	Chile
Juan Carlos Soto Vindas	Eurobus, SA	Costa Rica
Orlando Strambi	Escola Politecnica da Universidade Sao Paulo	Brazil
Olman Vargas Zeledon	Colegio Federado de Ingenieros y Arquitectos	Costa Rica

We would also like to acknowledge the workshop chairs and rapporteurs, who contributed substantially to the success of the conference as well as contributing to chapters in this book and to the refereeing process for various chapters. We would also like to acknowledge Andrea Hernandez Torres and Adriana Hernandez Torres of the University of Costa Rica and Olman Vargas Benavides and Samanta Solorio Murillo of the Colegio Federado de Ingenieros y Arquitectos who assisted the LOC and staffed the conference registration desk throughout the conference.

We are also grateful to the following organisations that provided financial support and sponsorships for the conference, without which this book would not exist:

- The US Department of Transportation, Federal Highway Administration;
- AVV Transport Research Centre, Dutch Ministry of Transport;
- NuStats of Texas;
- Ministerio de Obras Publicas y Transporte, Costa Rica ;
- Colegio Federado de Ingenieros y Arquitectos, Costa Rica;
- Morpace, Inc. of Michigan;
- Resource Systems Group, Inc. of Vermont; and
- Eurobus, S.A. of Costa Rica.

The sponsorship of these organisations enabled a number of scholarships to be awarded to delegates, primarily from South and Central America, but also to Africa, the latter also using funds that were generated by the previous conference held in South Africa in 2000. None of these delegates would have been able to attend without this assistance. Their presence in the conference enriched the conference discussions greatly, and has also contributed to the dissemination of good practice in travel surveys in a number of countries.

We would also like to acknowledge the assistance provided by Carmen Stopher in reading and checking the manuscript for this book. Her help has been invaluable. We would also like to thank the publishers, Elsevier Science, and especially Chris Pringle, for their encouragement and support of this venture.

DEDICATION – PATRICIA VAN DER REIS

This book is dedicated to the memory of Patricia van der Reis, who died unexpectedly in October 2005. Pat had been associated with the International Travel Survey Conferences for more than twenty years. During this time, she made major contributions to the profession, as well as providing strong representation of the African subcontinent in this international setting. In the Second International Conference on New Survey Methods, held at Hungerford Hill in Australia in September 1983, Pat contributed a chapter on 'The transferability of rating scale techniques to transport research in a developing country'[1], which drew the attention of the conference delegates to special issues in asking people in Africa to use rating scales to assess aspects of transport service. At the Third International Conference on Survey Methods in Transportation, held in Washington, D.C. in January 1990, Pat chaired one of the workshops on the topic of New Technologies in Surveys, where the primary new technologies seen then as applying to transport surveys were lap-top computers, use of computer assisted telephone interviewing, audio and video taping, and the potential for obtaining data from vehicle on-board computers.

The next in this series of conferences that Pat attended was the Fifth International Conference that was held in Eibsee, Germany in May, 1997. In this conference, Pat presented a landmark paper on issues of illiteracy and semi-literacy in travel surveys[2], as well as contributing to the two workshops she attended during the conference. When it became apparent that there would be further conferences in this series, Pat proposed that the next conference should be held on the African continent and volunteered herself as the chair of the Local Organising Committee. Over the next three years, she worked tirelessly to ensure that the conference that would be held in 2001 in the Kruger Park in South Africa would be an even greater success than its predecessors. She formed a Local Organising Committee, helped obtain local sponsorship funds, organised the location of the conference, and assisted in a vast number of ways to ensure that conference participants would have a rewarding and also enjoyable conference. For many of those who attended, this was their first visit to Africa, and Pat made it a memorable one for all those who attended. She also worked extremely hard to ensure that various professionals from all over sub-Saharan Africa would have an opportunity

---

[1] Van der Reis, P. (1985). The transferability of rating scale techniques to transport research in a developing country. In *New Survey Methods in Transport*, (Ampt, E.S., Richardson, A.J., and Brög, W. eds), 273-287, VNU Science Press, Utrecht, Netherlands.

[2] Van der Reis, P. (2000). Transportation surveys among illiterate and semiliterate households in South Africa. In: *Transport Surveys: Raising the Standard*, III-G/1-11, Transportation Research Circular E-C008, Transportation Research Board, Washington, DC.

to attend the conference. She did this both by finding ways to publicise the conference and also in helping to find funds that could be used to provide scholarships for those who would otherwise be unable to attend. In total, of 106 delegates to the conference, forty one were from thirteen African countries, with the remaining delegates coming from Europe, the US, Australia, Japan, and South America. This afforded these African delegates an opportunity to interact with an international group that they would rarely have the opportunity to meet. Pat also arranged for a keynote address from a prominent survey specialist in Africa, which added immeasurably to the success of the conference and to setting an appropriate stage for the balance of the conference. Notwithstanding all of the work involved in organising the conference, Pat still found the time to contribute, with her friend and colleague Marina Lombard, an important resource paper on multi-cultural and multi-language transport surveys[3]. Pat took part in the deliberations of the two series of workshops, while also continuing to ensure that the conference ran smoothly and that all delegates' needs were met.

After the conference was over, it was decided by the International Steering Committee to purchase fifty copies of the resulting conference book and to distribute these to delegates and universities in sub-Saharan Africa. Again, Pat provided addresses of many universities in Africa, to which books were subsequently sent, as well as ensuring that all delegates from Africa received a copy of the book.

The next conference in the series was held in Costa Rica. Pat assisted from the outset, first by documenting carefully what she had done as Local Organising Committee chair and sharing this with the incoming Local Organising Committee chair, and then in accepting a role as a workshop chair of the workshop on Survey Implementation Standards and Guidelines. In her inimitable fashion, she was one of the first workshop chairs to submit her workshop report, which appears as a chapter in this book[4], as well as getting reviews done promptly of the papers in her workshop and providing recommendations to the editors.

Pat will be remembered by the many international delegates to these various conferences as a gentle, self-effacing, and highly professional contributor. She showed remarkable ability in the area of travel survey design and implementation and led the way in innovations to allow such surveys to be done in the very different contexts to be found in Africa, from where most travel survey techniques have been developed in Western Europe and North America. Pat contributed in more ways than most of us are probably aware, not only in innovation in travel surveys, but also in championing the

---

[3] Van der Reis, P. and M. Lombard (2003). Multi-cultural and multi-language transport surveys, with special reference to the African experience. In: *Transport Survey Quality and Innovation*, (P. Stopher and P. Jones eds), 191-208, Pergamon Press, Oxford.

[4] Van der Reis, P. and A.S. Harvey (2006). Survey implementation. In: *Travel Survey Methods – Quality and Future Directions*, (P. Stopher and C.C. Stecher eds), 213-222, Elsevier Science, Oxford.

development of her fellow Africans and assisting the international community of transport and travel survey professionals.

On a personal note, I had the privilege to work with Pat in the organising of the past three conferences. I came to depend upon her in many ways. She was always responsive, providing replies to questions and solutions to problems more rapidly than any of us had a right to expect. She was extraordinarily diligent in all that she took on to do, and was always cheerful in the execution of whatever task was before her. I also had the pleasure of getting to know Pat personally, and enjoyed enormously a trek into Kruger Park with Pat and her husband Gunther, where we saw many fabulous sightings of African wildlife. We also spent pleasant African evenings talking in the moonlight, and planning the conference, and talking of other matters of mutual interest.

Pat's presence in and contribution to her profession and to these conferences will be greatly missed.

Peter Stopher
Sydney, Australia

CONTENTS

Foreword v

Preface vii

Acknowledgements...xi

Dedication..xiii

Contents...xvii

Chapter 1
Travel Survey Methods in Latin America
Juan de Dios Ortúzar 1

Chapter 2
Household Travel Surveys: Proposed Standards and Guidelines
Peter R. Stopher, Chester G. Wilmot, Cheryl C. Stecher, and Rahaf Alsnih....................19

Chapter 3
Survey Design: The Past, the Present and the Future
Henk van Evert, Werner Brög and Erhard Erl 75

Chapter 4
Survey Design
David Kurth and Nancy McGuckin 95

Chapter 5
Sample Design and Total Survey Error
Mira Paskota..111

Chapter 6
Sample Design
Rosella Picardo 139

Chapter 7
Instrument Design: Decisions and Procedures
Johanna Zmud..143

Chapter 8
Instrument Design Standards and Guidelines
Tom Cohen 161

Chapter 9
Scheduling Considerations in Household Travel Surveys
Stacey Bricka *175*

Chapter 10
Proxy Respondents in Household Travel Surveys
Laurie Wargelin and Lidia Kostyniuk...*201*

Chapter 11
Survey Implementation
A. Pat van der Reis and Andrew S. Harvey..*213*

Chapter 12
The Metropolitan Travel Survey Archive: A Case Study in Archiving
David Levinson and Eva Zofka *223*

Chapter 13
Processing, Analysis, and Archiving of Travel Survey Data
Gerd Sammer...*239*

Chapter 14
Processing, Analysing, and Archiving Standards and Guidelines
Orlando Strambi and Rodrigo Garrido *271*

Chapter 15
Quality Assessment
Peter Bonsall...*279*

Chapter 16
Possible Explanations for an Increasing Share of No-Trip Respondents
Linda Christensen *303*

Chapter 17
Quality Assessment
Barbara Noble and Simon Holroyd *317*

Chapter 18
Handling Individual Specific Availability of Alternatives in Stated Choice Experiments
John M. Rose and David A. Hensher...*325*

Chapter 19
Stated Preference Surveys: An Assessment
Peter M. Jones and Mark A. Bradley...*347*

Chapter 20
Panel Surveys
Dirk Zumkeller, Jean-Loup Madre, Bastian Chlond, and Jimmy Armoogum *363*

Chapter 21
Moving Panel Surveys from Concept to Implementation
Elaine Murakami, Stephen Greaves, and Tomás Ruiz *399*

Chapter 22
Energy Consumption Estimation with a Shipper and Transport Chain Survey
Christophe Rizet, Jimmy Armoogum, and Philippe Marchal *413*

Chapter 23
Goods and Business Traffic in Germany
Manfred Wermuth, Christian Neef, and Imke Steinmeyer........................*427*

Chapter 24
Issues Related to Freight Transport Data Collection
Arnim H. Meyburg and Rodrigo Garrido..*451*

Chapter 25
In Search of the Value of Time: From South Africa to India
N.J.W. van Zyl and M. Raza...*457*

Chapter 26
Investment-Grade Surveys
Johanna Zmud...*485*

Chapter 27
Process Data for Understanding and Modelling Travel Behaviour
Mark Bradley *491*

Chapter 28
Collection and Analysis of Behavioural Process Data: Challenges and Opportunities
Ram Pendyala and Stacey Bricka *511*

Chapter 29
Application of New Technologies in Travel Surveys
Jean Wolf...*531*

Chapter 30
Using Combined GPS and GSM Tracking Information for Interactive Electronic Questionnaires
Matthias Kracht *545*

Chapter 31
Non-Web Technologies
Martin E.H. Lee-Gosselin and Andrew S. Harvey *561*

Chapter 32
Characteristics of Web Based Surveys and Applications in Travel Research
Rahaf Alsnih *569*

Chapter 33
New Technology: Web-Based
Patrick Bonnel and Jean-Loup Madre *593*

Chapter 34
Data Collection Related to Emergency Events
Chester G. Wilmot *605*

Chapter 35
Emerging Issues in Emergency Event Transport
Carlos Arce *619*

Chapter 36
Simulating Household Travel Survey Data
Stephen P. Greaves *625*

Chapter 37
Using Microsimulation to Generate Activity-Travel Data Under Conditions of Insufficient Data
Harry J.P. Timmermans *651*

Chapter 38
Transport Survey Standards and Futures
Peter R. Stopher and Cheryl C. Stecher *659*

Glossary of Abbreviations *681*

1

TRAVEL SURVEY METHODS IN LATIN AMERICA

Juan de Dios Ortúzar, Pontificia Universidad Católica de Chile, Santiago, Chile

REGIONAL ENQUIRY ABOUT TRAVEL SURVEY METHODS

Because practically no publications about official travel survey guidelines or reports of experiences and/or results are available in the majority of countries in the region, we had to resort to an Internet-based enquiry. This took the form of a simple request for information sent to a large number of scholars and officials in most of Latin America[5]. In some cases, this produced minimal information, whilst in others it produced a sizeable amount of information, in yet others a link to another person who was known to be knowledgeable in this subject, and so on. At the end (the enquiry lasted for some two months), we obtained fourteen responses from eight countries; in addition, published data from Chile was obviously available. In what follows, we summarise this information in the simplest possible way.

Argentina

This country has a fairly long tradition of conducting medium-scale origin-destination (O-D) surveys for the purposes of direct transport planning. However, the main efforts seem to have occurred in the past decade, with one-off household O-D surveys con-

---

[5] The e-mail request was sent to all professionals known to have been involved in the design, analysis or commissioning of a large scale travel survey in eleven countries; a similar request but emphasising the need to get names of people with experience in large travel surveys was also sent to active academics and consultants in the same countries. A total of forty five messages were finally sent.

ducted in several cities between 1994 and 1999 using the standard methodology at the time (Richardson *et al*, 1995). However, we could only obtain one survey report, for the city of Rosario in 2002 (Adjiman, 2004), where three percent of the city's households were interviewed. In general, the surveys have been conducted by professionals typically working at a university centre. Although sample and questionnaire design follow usual practice, in some cases the zoning systems defined have been too aggregate (i.e., forty five zones for a city of over one million inhabitants). The surveys have included socioeconomic and travel information; in some cases, respondents' opinions about public transport service quality, transport needs for the physically handicapped, and willingness-to-use alternative transport modes, such as the bicycle, have also been asked (Petrone, 2004). Interestingly, in this period, no survey was done in Buenos Aires although one, to be conducted by foreign consultants in 2001 with World Bank support, was aborted mid-way due to financial and legal difficulties.

Brazil

Brazil has a long tradition in this area and, apart from Chile, it is the country in Latin America where most care and interest has been put into transport survey methods. Many cities have conducted large-scale household surveys in recent years. These are usually conventional one-off O-D surveys, with face-to-face interviewing and asking about trips the day before. Generally, walking trips of less than 400 metres are not recorded (except in the case of compulsory trips which are recorded irrespective of distance). Trips by children under five have been recorded in some cases and validation seems to be more an exception than a rule. Finally, in most cases intercept surveys at cordon and screen lines are also conducted. Some further details are as follows (Strambi, 2004):

- Since 1967, São Paulo has conducted large-scale household O-D surveys every ten years and the methodology has been almost the same since 1977; large samples (i.e., 20,000 to 30,000 households) have been selected, based on some sort of stratification; the more recent by energy consumption levels, in addition to the conventional stratification by zone. In 2002, a smaller complementary survey, with a sample of just 6,000 households, was conducted using the same approach (DM, 2003).
- The most recent survey in Brazil was completed in May 2004 for the southern city of Porto Alegre. The project was undertaken by a pool of firms including TIS, from Portugal; this is expected to have added quality to the traditional O-D survey approach in the country, because TIS has much experience in Europe in this field, but no details were available when this chapter was written.
- Rio de Janeiro has also conducted two or three surveys since the 1970s and the last one concluded in early 2004. At the time of writing this chapter, consultants were discussing the processes of correction and expansion.

- Although several other cities have embarked on surveys of this type, it is interesting to mention an important and sobering exception: Curitiba, universally considered an example of good land use and transport planning practice, has never conducted a household O-D survey.

Costa Rica

The most recent household O-D survey in this country was carried out by the Ministry of Public Works and Transport between 1989 and 1991, for the Greater Metropolitan Area (GMA). This area is in the centre of the country and comprises some 1,967 sq. km. (roughly 3.8 percent of Costa Rica's land area); the GMA integrates four provincial capitals: Alajuela, Cartago, Heredia, and San José, and, at the time of the survey, had about 1.5 million inhabitants (about fifty percent of the country's population). Almost 13,000 households were interviewed and the zone system consisted of 388 zones. The only previous O-D survey had been conducted in the 1970s in San José. Unfortunately, it was not possible to obtain further details and no reports seem to be available.

Ecuador

According to our sources, the most recent household O-D survey in the country was done in Guayaquil in 2000, by the university, but no report is available, and it is fairly obvious that it was conducted by a team of non-specialists. The most recent O-D survey for Quito was conducted in 1977. It is interesting to mention that the prevalent approach in this country is to use intercept rather than household surveys; subsequent transport modelling is based on rather simplistic assumptions. For example, the interesting and successful bus development projects in Quito and Guayaquil were both based on simple on-bus surveys, and used the local knowledge, experience and ingenuity of seasoned planners.

Colombia

In spite of the difficulties associated with the general perception of insecurity, it has been customary in Colombia to conduct urban mobility surveys in the main cities of the country. Notwithstanding, it is not easy to get access to data; in particular, there seems to be no recent mobility data for the capital Bogotá. In the old days, the procedures used in each case were defined by the local administrations who would hire consultants to do the job, but, since 2000, local governments are supposed to follow the official guidelines set up by the Ministry of Transport (MTC, 1999). However, this manual has been heavily criticised on items such as sample size, questionnaire design, and for the requirement to collect seemingly redundant information (Cárdenas and Colomer, 2003). Although we could not obtain official reports, it is obvious that current methodology is not in line with the state of practice in the developed world.

Mexico

According to a mission from the Massachusetts Institute of Technology (MIT), Mexico City's most recent O-D survey was conducted in 1994 as part of a national effort (INEGI, 1994) and the city lacks a strategic urban transport model; in fact, they are building a rather precarious one with 1994 data (Gamas *et al*, 2004). Apart from the scarcity of resources, the reason for lacking proper data would be that the authorities do not understand fully the nature and gravity of the environmental and transport problems faced by the city. In fact, there seems to be money available only for relatively short-term interventions, such as building new road capacity, which only help to exacerbate the problems. Also, the city is so big that the authorities (and consultants) have apparently ceased to try and work with it as a whole system and work instead with parts of it, ignoring the potential interactions with the rest (Gamas, 2004).

On the other hand, it appears that, in the past ten years, the majority of the main urban areas of the country and some medium-sized cities have conducted some kind of O-D survey. These have used both household (the minority) or intercept surveys; a few have used a mixture of the two. The surveys have been commissioned by the local authorities and conducted by consultants with a very short-term view (i.e., use the data in a specific project). Consultants have traditionally lacked a technical counterpart, so data quality is definitively an issue. This is compounded by the fact that, in most cases, there are no official reports available to the public, so that it is not easy to ascertain the state-of-practice (Sánchez, 2004). In recent years, household surveys have been undertaken also by educational institutions; in particular, the reputable El Colegio de Mexico is conducting a survey to determine mobility habits in several districts of Mexico City, but, to our knowledge, they do not have experts in this area.

Peru

The case study that follows is used as an example of how bad things can go when large surveys and/or transport studies are undertaken with inadequate technical participation. In the early 1990s, an expensive but, as it turned out, almost useless large-scale household O-D survey was conducted by a firm called Transurb Consult, as part of a larger study for the Municipality of Lima. To solve a financial dispute involving doubts about the quality of the data and models, the Municipality hired the Pontificia Universidad Católica del Perú, who in turn contacted the author's university, and eventually brought in the author as an expert witness, who spent a week in Lima examining the study reports. To let the reader understand how badly the author felt it had been done, the following is a quote from the author's final report to the Municipality:

> 'This study would had been qualified as "not pass" if it had been presented as one of the student group assignments for my *Introduction to Transport Engineering* course in Santiago'.

Intrigued by the amazing lack of expertise of the consultants, the author made enquiries and was informed that Transurb Consult was a façade in Brussels, a one-man operation, the *modus operandi* of which was to scan for potential studies in the Third World, hire some mercenaries (obviously not too well-qualified) and get a cut of the profits.

Between 1997 and 1998, with a few resources provided by the World Bank in the context of a light rail study and design of a peripheral highway for Lima, a brave effort was made to correct and update the aforementioned data, apparently with the help of the same firm. Soon enough, they realized there was not much that could be done and resorted to intercept and on-board surveys to try to estimate some models for the city (Gutierrez, 2004). More recently, there have been several attempts to start the ground work for a properly conducted and much needed O-D survey for Lima, and it seems that, with the cooperation of the Japanese International Cooperation Agency (JICA), this may bear fruit in the near future. One important problem, the author envisages, is that, once again, the clients for such work lack technical personnel who are sufficiently knowledgeable to be able to review proposals to undertake the work, and assess the final products of the selected consultants.

Venezuela

Information here was very scant although this country has well-prepared professionals and several universities where transport engineering and urbanism have been taught for many years. The author was able to obtain a report, specially prepared at his request, concerning a 1995 study done in Mérida by Spanish consultants ALG (Pérez, 2004). The study was conducted professionally, albeit using the traditional methodology of the 1990s. The study area of some 150,000 inhabitants was divided into eighty zones, later aggregated into thirty one to achieve a 'better statistical representation'. Eventually some 1,800 household interviews were conducted. The questionnaire design and the survey method on site were properly done and documented. Interestingly a twenty percent validation sample, taking care of checking data by all interviewers, was implemented and data are available on sampling errors at the level of the survey zone.

THE CASE OF CHILE

This country has been blessed by an unique relation between university and government in the transport field. When the main academic transport centres were founded in 1970, they established close links with the then Ministry of Public Works and Transport. The good rapport continued when the Ministry of Transport was created as a separate entity in the mid 1970s, and good links were also established with the Planning Ministry. But most importantly, the university was instrumental in the creation in 1980 of what is now SECTRA, the executive and technical secretariat of an inter-ministerial commission for urban transport planning. The agency is in charge of strategic transport modelling and project evaluation for urban areas in the whole country, and is directed and staffed mainly by former students of the two main transport academic and research centres in the country.

A Brief History of Travel Survey Methods

There was some experience with data collection and strategic travel demand model estimation in Santiago in the 1960s, due to the development of the Santiago underground which involved French consultants. But the first large-scale household O-D survey, properly designed, conducted and analysed took place in 1977 (DICTUC, 1978). In the 1980s, well designed O-D surveys – in the sense that a specialist study was commissioned for the design task, two years prior to the actual survey – were also undertaken in Valparaíso (1986) and Concepción (1989), the two major conurbations outside the capital Santiago. Also, smaller-scale surveys were conducted using an *ad-hoc* methodology in several medium-sized cities.

The 1990s saw a radical change. In 1991 the last traditional large-scale O-D survey was conducted in Santiago (Ortúzar *et al*, 1993). This involved a sample of some 31,000 households, plus a travel diary sample of another 500 families to correct for non-reported trips and gather appropriate data for modal choice. The whole exercise lasted more than a year and included intercept surveys, traffic counts, matrix estimation, and network calibration, at a cost of approximately US$1,000,000.

In 1998 a study was commissioned to propose a new methodology consistent with the state-of-the art in the most advanced nations (DICTUC, 1998). This was followed by a one-year pilot study which examined several methods to conduct household interviews, established new questionnaire design principles, and data correction and validation methods (DICTUC, 2001). Finally, in 2001 a new era started, the Santiago 2001 O-D study was conceived as an on-going survey, with a first wave of 15,000 households and subsequent waves of 5,000 households (apart from intercept surveys, traffic counts, etc.). Results of the first wave, together with a description of the methodology can be found in Ampt and Ortúzar (2004). The second wave, which suffered a delay of almost two years for political reasons, is currently under way. Since 2001, also, household O-D surveys at some fifteen medium-sized cities have been undertaken, at a rate of approximately four cities per year. In all cases the sample size has been 1,500 households and the same methodology has been applied (DICTUC, 2001).

The State of Practice in the Region

In what follows, the main components of the Santiago 2001 O-D Survey are described, as it can justly be labelled the state of practice in the region. The technical detail will not be dwelt on, because readers can usefully check the comprehensive paper by Stopher *et al*. (2006) for standards and guidelines.

An Ongoing Data Collection Process

Data are gathered for each day of the week throughout the year and over several years. This allows the capture of seasonal variations, as well as weekend-weekday differences. The government can always have updated data available, changes in demand over time can be measured and, in particular, these changes can be correlated with changes in the supply system. Because respondents only report data for one day it makes their task easy and reliable, at the same time giving data over a longer period. Finally, the approach results in lower operational costs and allows for better quality control.

Issues to be addressed include the need to keep interviewers motivated over a longer period (including high quality re-training), the development of weighting processes to take account of seasonal variations, and special methods for post-weighting annual data, if it is combined with ongoing survey data.

GIS Basis of Recording Origin and Destination Data

Geocoding the origin and destination information allows using the data at any level of aggregation, and liberates the analyst from the need for a standard zoning system. This has become a standard in major metropolitan surveys (NCHRP, 2002).

Periodic Updating of Matrices and Models

The periodic updating of matrices and models to match the ongoing data collection system is of particular significance to maximise the benefit of the continuous information. Trip tables for the whole urban area will be updated only every twelve to eighteen months in Santiago. We strongly believe in the need for updating models periodically (Ortúzar and Willumsen, 2001), but this is likely to have an effect on the data collected. For example, which information is most sensitive to updating? We believe that elements worthy of periodic updating include, trip generation and attraction models, O-D trip tables, mode shares, including the market shares of non-motorised modes (in developing countries, the number of trips made on foot is typically over twenty percent possibly reflecting an income effect), traffic levels in the whole network, and car ownership and household formation trends in various municipalities.

Sample Size

The essence of sample size calculations is one of trade-offs. Too large a sample means that the survey will be too costly for its stated objectives and associated degree of precision. Too small a sample will mean that results may have a large degree of variability jeopardising decision making. Somewhere in between lies the most cost-effective sample size for the stated survey objectives. On the other hand, the scope of mobility surveys should include all travellers in the area (see Figure 1); i.e., not only residents but also visitors, people in hotels and in non-private dwellings (such as hospitals), and travellers that pass through the area on survey days. Once the scope has been defined, the sampling frame needs to be determined, that is, a list providing information on all residents, visitors, and people who pass through the area.

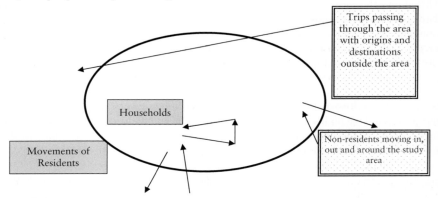

Figure 1: Data Collection Scope of a Metropolitan O-D Survey

In Santiago it was decided to concentrate on households ignoring travellers staying at hotels, etc. The sample frame was provided by the Tax Registry; its main problem was that it contains data from the previous year and, in fast changing areas such as cities of the Second and Third Worlds, inevitably some of the listed addresses may cease to be residential in one year (i.e., they can be demolished or be transformed into an office or a commercial establishment). Use of the most typical frame in industrialised nations, the telephone listings (Stopher and Metcalf, 1996), was rejected because telephone ownership is still far from universal in Chile.

There are well-documented procedures for estimating the sample size of household surveys so that it is possible to satisfy different objectives; for example, estimation of trip generation rates by categories, levels of car ownership, and even of mode choice variables for different income strata (Smith, 1979; Stopher, 1982). Given reasonable budget limitations, the analyst can check that all these objectives can be achieved with a reasonably small sample (see Purvis, 1989). The situation changes, however, if it is necessary to estimate origin-destination (O-D) matrices. For example, Ortúzar *et al.* (1998) analysed the number of trips by O-D cell in Santiago for a group of only thirty four zones (e.g., at the municipality level) using data from the 1991 O-D survey. They observed that even at that large level of aggregation (and using data from 33,000 households) only fifty eight percent of the O-D cells contained more than 1,000 trips. Smith (1979) shows that in this case a sample size of four percent would be needed to estimate an O-D matrix with a twenty five percent standard error and ninety percent confidence limits. So, as there were about 1,400,000 households in Santiago, this would imply a huge sample size (i.e., 56,000 households) to accomplish a really meagre objective. It is obvious to conclude that trip matrices should not be the object of the household survey;

for this purpose intercept data is key. Ampt and Ortúzar (2004) discuss methods to design for more reasonable sample sizes, and conclude that a sample of some 5,000 households in a city the size of Santiago ought to be sufficient for most purposes.

Notwithstanding, a sample of 15,000 responding households was required to satisfy the modelling needs of the government, including the 'entry cost' to a radically new system. This was the number of households interviewed in the first year of the ongoing Santiago 2001 O-D survey; but in subsequent years more reasonable numbers were defined for updating purposes, namely 5,000 for each of the next three years.

Further advantages of the approach are that, with a small and well-trained field force and proper administrative procedures, in year 2 and beyond we will be able to ensure high quality data with minimal effort; also, a financial commitment for three years was made in year 2, reducing the risk of difficulties of receiving repeat funding later. However, the method requires the development of an easy-to-use and robust annual weighting and integration system, to ensure that data are readily useable for modelling purposes at the end of each year (wave). Such a method will help to provide an up-to-date representation of existing travel behaviour for modelling and other purposes. In cities like Santiago, where rapid changes occur in car ownership, land-use spread and distribution, this will mean a more accurate modelling capability than was ever possible in the past. It will also provide a larger sample size for use in second and subsequent years enabling more detailed questions to be asked of the data in those years. Ampt and Ortúzar (2004) discuss these issues in more detail.

Survey Methodology and Survey Instrument

After extensive piloting in Santiago, we decided to use a personal interview-based system (which has the advantages of highest response and greater response efficiencies per contacted household), combined with a self-completion regime for households that cannot be accessed other than by remote security-bell systems and for which attempts at personal interview result in low response rates. The self-completion form was used by less than four percent of households.

The main characteristics of the data needed, given its subsequent use in the calibration of strategic transport models for the city were the following:

- Availability of *stage-based trip data* (i.e., all movements on a public street, e.g., separating walk to the bus from travelling on the bus) to ensure that analyses can relate specific modes to specific locations/times of day/trip lengths, etc.;
- Because of the growth of non-car modes, the data should incorporate *all modes of travel*, including non-motorised travel;
- Due to the growing importance of independent trips by children and of non-motorised modes, the data should consider the movements made by *all* people in

the household (including non-family members such as maids/servants, who are more prevalent in less developed countries);

- To facilitate the individual's task of recording all travel, an activity-recall framework is used; in this case, people record travel in the context of activities they have undertaken rather than simply the trips they have made; this results in more accurate travel measurement (Stopher, 1998);
- Because people have difficulty recalling infrequent and discretionary activities, even when they are recent, we assign a 'travel day' to each household and each member is given a brief memory jogger in advance of these days; the information in the jogger is transcribed (adding the full details needed by the survey) to the self-completion form or reported to the interviewer at the end of the day (or as soon as possible thereafter); and
- Data are collected at the maximum level of disaggregation (x-y co-ordinate level) with a geographical information system (GIS) forming the basis of this.

The survey instrument was designed for minimum respondent burden (Ampt, 2003), maximum response rate (CASRO, 1982), and, hence, maximum robustness of the data. The form was divided into two parts – one for household variables (e.g., age, gender, occupation, and vehicle details), and another for personal information (work patterns, income) and trip making by each individual; the collection of household details at the first stage makes the main interview shorter for each individual respondent, and has the advantage of providing sociodemographic details if nonresponse occurs at a later stage.

Data correction procedures

Correction and weighting are essential in any travel survey (Stopher and Jones, 2003); the Santiago 2001 O-D Survey considers the following elements:

- Corrections by household size and sociodemographic characteristics, to guarantee that the household size, age and sex, housing type, and vehicle ownership distributions of the sampled data represent the population (based on census data). Multi-proportional fitting (Ortúzar and Willumsen, 2001), also known as 'racking ratio' (Armoogum and Madre, 1998), guarantees convergence in very few iterations.
- Corrections for non-reported data: these are needed when certain elements of the survey have not been answered (item nonresponse). In self-completion surveys this can be addressed by interviewing a validation sample of people using personal interviews and then weighting the data accordingly. On the other hand, if interviewers are well trained and supervised, the incidence of item nonresponse should be minimal in personal interviews (Stopher and Jones, 2003).
- Corrections for nonresponse: these are needed when a household or individual does not respond, i.e., does not return the survey instrument or refuses verbally or by mail to respond to the survey. This can be attributed to a variety of causes,

and it is important to differentiate between genuine nonresponse and sample loss (e.g., vacant dwellings that do not generate travel should be ineligible), and refusals (where the person could be travelling, but not responding, clearly eligible). In the case of personal interviews corrections can be based on the number of visits necessary to achieve a response, because it has been shown that this is associated to potential differences in travel behaviour.

Integration Weighting

It is important to consider the weighting procedures required to integrate the continuous data set. This should be done annually to unite each wave of the survey. As the second year of the Santiago survey was still in progress at the time this chapter was written, the process had not yet been tested. However, Ampt and Ortúzar (2004) give a good example of how this can be done.

Income Imputation

In the first wave of the Santiago 2001 O-D Survey only 543 households out of 15,537 did not answer the family income question. Due to the strong asymmetry of the income distribution, a logarithmic transformation of the data was used which allowed us to centre the distribution and achieve a better resemblance to a Normal distribution. Multiple imputations were successfully produced using a linear model based on the Student t-distribution with five degrees of freedom, estimated using Gibbs sampling (Geman and Geman, 1984). Outliers were detected and removed from the estimation process; as it turned out, they were found to be wrongly coded which meant that the process had the secondary advantage of allowing for further checks on the quality of the data. Interested readers can find more details in DICTUC (2002).

Some Lessons From the Santiago Mobility Survey

In what follows we summarise some of the most important conclusions from the 2000 pilot study and also present a brief review of the main characteristics of the first wave of the 2001 survey that took place between August 2001 and March 2002. As may be typical of a developing country, the study ran for less than a year (a mixture of delayed start and data required with urgency), stopped for more than a year, but has started again in 2004 for a further three years.

Pilot Study

During the pilot stage, five survey methods were tested: two for mail back questionnaires (delivered and collected by hand, and delivered and returned by mail), two for personal interviews (on paper and on laptop computers) and one mixed-mode method, where part of the interview was carried out by an interviewer (typically collecting household data) and the remainder was completed by the respondent and returned by mail. In all cases the survey forms were carefully designed (employing the services of both an editor and a graphic designer), printed in attractive colours and initially tested in several focus groups. This led to a significant simplification of the design for both personal and mail-back forms; the originals had been based on the VATS survey forms (Richardson and Ampt, 1993), where data was needed for estimating not only strategic models, but also disaggregate choice models. This required a level of complexity that greatly burdened the typical Chilean and was not a must for the Chilean government.

After the initial pilot the new forms were tested first in focus groups and then in the field. Information was collected for 150 households in three income strata for each of the five methods, i.e., a total sample of 750 households. The results of these tests led to abandoning the laptop computer interviews and the full mail-back method, and to concentrating on personal interviews (with the possibility of mail-back for those preferring to fill in their own diaries). Mail-back forms were delivered and collected by hand for those houses/flats where it was too difficult or impossible to get eye-contact with the dwellers. These were tested in a second pilot leading to various minor improvements that were incorporated into the full survey (DICTUC, 2001). The idea of collecting data from non-residents was also abandoned at this stage, because it turned out to be a very complex task.

During this preliminary study, a heuristic was designed to obtain the minimum set of intercept stations in the strategic network that would allow the detection of a given number of trips between O-D pairs in the area (say one hundred per time period), at the same time as being less than a maximum allowed error level between the observed and estimated O-D matrix with data from those points. This was done for car and public transport trips, yielding one hundred stations (in the car case) and less than fifty (in the public transport case) for the whole of Santiago (DICTUC, 2001). Special software was also designed to aid survey coding and validation. Among its many features were the automatic production of a validated list of streets and places in the city, to minimise digitising errors for addresses. The software also detects missing data and does on-line validation using more than 300 checks and reports. There is no limit to the number of data coding stations that can work concurrently on the data base.

First Wave of the Final Survey

A complete field-work system was developed for the final survey. The study area was divided into five districts and offices were strategically located at the centre of each district – each housing a professional in charge, a supervisor, two coders/validators and up to fifteen interviewers. All these personnel were coordinated from the main office at the university.

A large marketing/information campaign was designed by a specialist firm and launched just prior to the start of the survey effort. It involved newspapers and radio, road and bus signs, and leaflets that were distributed to houses, malls and at special events. It included a monthly raffle of Ch$100,000 (around US$200) for households that had been surveyed and returned complete forms for all their household members. The campaign continued at a decreasing level during the whole survey period and special focus groups conducted during and after it suggested that it had been an important element in the success of the data collection exercise. These results convinced the government of the need to stage a new campaign and raffle for the second wave of the survey, two years later.

Personnel selection and training was a complex task; a specialist consulting firm was hired and given appropriate specifications to find and recruit the staff needed. Part-time actresses were recruited, because they obtained very high responses in the pilot; we also hired salesmen (e.g., insurance) who had shown that they were very resilient (having the capacity to handle rejection is a key attribute of a good interviewer). More than 750 people were interviewed to fill the eighty plus initial interviewer positions. It is interesting to mention that the rate of progress was slower during the Chilean winter period with shorter daylight hours than in the pilot phase, which had taken place during the spring.

The training activities took a full week and involved tests on the comprehension of the survey forms, role playing and tests on detecting faulty or missing data, work with psychologists on how to handle rejection, discussions on innovative ways to contact people, supervised work in the field, etc. Personnel loss was around twenty percent during the first two months of the survey but it stabilised after that.

Work in the field proceeded as follows: every week a set of addresses was generated for each office (i.e., a random process in space and time). The interviewers visited these addresses, collected the general information, assigned a travel day, and left a 'memory jogger' for each household member. They came back the day after the travel day (or at most, two days later), filled in the travel information for each respondent (making heavy use of the jogger) and returned the survey forms to the office (two days later at the most). Here the data were given a preliminary check by hand by the supervisor and all obvious errors and missing data were detected. These were corrected immediately either by phone or by a special visit to the household.

The 'apparently complete' data were then sent to headquarters to be digitised. Here the special software allowed the validators to do their work more efficiently by activating special fields to fill in the data. This process ended with a final report on the status of the household; if some information was missing or was apparently faulty, the survey forms were returned to the local office for correction. After this step, the new data (if it was obtained) was entered into the database and a final summary made of the status of each survey form (i.e., complete, incomplete and, in this case, grouped in one of several categories). Finally, the data were physically archived (there is a librarian in charge) to assist speedy retrieval. The database is backed up twice a day on two computer servers and also copied onto a CD once per week, thus ensuring a secure system.

In parallel to the data collection process, a validation system consisting of a visit to approximately ten percent of the households interviewed was implemented (the figure was higher in the case of interviewers with unusually high efficiency, or with unusually low household sizes or trip rates by household). The process used a especially designed form that enquired, first, if the interviewer had really visited the home; after that, a check was made on the veracity of the information registered in the survey instrument, and finally questions were made about the interviewer behaviour (i.e., serious, helpful, and respectful) and survey process (i.e., the number of days before the 'travel day' that the survey material was received). At the end of this stage, 1,582 households were re-interviewed; this allowed detection of 101 false interviews (that were eliminated) and correction of minor errors in another 298 cases. Obviously the interviewers that had invented data were made redundant, and this was widely publicised among the interviewer staff. A stick and carrot approach was used as also the best interviewers were recognised each month.

As mentioned above, the data collection stage for the first set of 15,000 households began in August 2001. Data were collected for the 'normal period' (August-December 2001; March-April 2002) and for the 'summer' period (January-February 2002). Thus, by May 2002 the process was completed with the totals shown in Table 1 achieved.

It is important to mention that the overwhelming majority of households (96.8%) was contacted using the personal interview-based system. In only 490 cases were self-completion forms eventually needed (i.e., when it was not possible to contact the household personally). In some cases, particularly when the household had many members, the opportunity was given (and some members, particularly students, asked for it with no prompts) to fill out the form personally with a later check by the interviewer. This sped up the process considerably in these cases.

Table 1: Sample Achievement by Method and Day of the Week

Day of Week	Normal Period	Summer Period	Total
Weekday	9,048	2,290	11,338
Saturday	1,575	432	2,007
Sunday	1,723	469	2,192
Total	12,346	3,191	15,537

Table 2 presents information about response rates. As can be seen, the figures (around seventy percent) are very high, suggesting that the careful methodology described works properly in a non-industrialised country. Of the 15,537 'complete' households, 14,383 (i.e., 92.6 percent) are absolutely complete; 606 have one or more items missing from the household (e.g., income, vehicle data, or information about mortgage or rent paid;

only in ten cases were data missing about a complete household member), 509 have one or more items of trip data missing (e.g., trip time, fare paid, incomplete destination), and 39 have items missing in both categories. Finally, it is worth repeating that only 543 (3.5 percent) of all the complete households lacked income information. This percentage was higher (3.8 percent against 2.3 percent) for the normal (non-summer) period.

Table 2: Response Rates by Survey Period

Status	Normal Period	Summer Period	Total
Complete household	12,346	3,191	15,537
Incomplete household	338	3	341
Refusals	2,653	633	3,286
False (discarded)	101	-	101
Forms received but not returned	0	4	4
Forms returned unanswered	0	1	1
No contacts*	2,679	924	3,603
Response Rate (%)	68.15	67.09	67.93

* Note that many of these might be non-eligible, so the real response rate is probably higher.

Intercept Survey Results for the First Wave

During the first year more than 475,000 valid intercept surveys were also conducted on buses and shared taxis, and by intercepting cars, taxis, lorries, bicycles, and pedestrians at some 150 intercept stations distributed throughout the city, as shown in Table 2. The stations were selected, as mentioned, to maximise the likelihood of observing numbers of trips greater than 100 between all O-D pairs in the city, for the final system of 775 zones. We did not intercept trips in the underground as the company (Metro) conducts its own intercept O-D surveys every year.

Table 3: Intercept Survey Results by Transport Mode

Mode of Transport	Period					
	Normal			Summer		
	Weekday	Weekend	Total	Weekday	Weekend	Total
Bus	53,195	17,991	71,186	56,954	15,931	72,885
Private transport	107,317	19,952	127,269	41,471	25,598	67,069
Lorry	9,327	845	10,172	3,266	725	3,991
Non motorised	38,819	22,797	61,616	34,764	26,542	61,306
Total	208,658	61,585	270,243	136,455	68,796	205,251

In conclusion, the early results from the Santiago 2001 continuous O-D survey clearly show that the state-of-practice methodology described here is capable of giving high response rates and hence valid data for the purpose of estimating state-of-the-art strategic transport planning models not only in the First World but also in developing countries. Data is currently being used for that purposes.

ACKNOWLEDGEMENTS

Many friends and acquaintances spared some of their time freely to help the author collect information about the state of practice in travel survey methods in the region. In particular, I wish to thank the following individuals: José Marcos Adjiman, César Arias, Patricia Brennan, David Briggs, Carlos Contreras, Victor Cantillo, Daniel Cárdenas, Julia Gamas, Luis Gutierrez, María Consuelo López, José Enrique Pérez, Leonardo Petrone, Luis Ignacio Rizzi, Oscar Sánchez, Orlando Strambi, Ian Thomson, and Christopher Zegras. Thanks are also due to the National Fund for Scientific and Technological Development (FONDECYT), for having helped my research activities during many years, and to the Research and Postgraduate Direction of the School of Engineering, Pontificia Universidad Católica de Chile, for having supplemented the funds to attend the conference.

REFERENCES

Adjiman, J.M. (2004). Síntesis Metodológica Encuesta Origen-Destino de Rosario, Mimeo, Instituto de Estudios de Transporte, Universidad Nacional de Rosario, Argentina, May 2004 (in Spanish).

Ampt, E.S. (2003), Respondent Burden. In: *Transport Survey Quality and Innovation*, (P.R. Stopher and P.M. Jones, eds.),Pergamon, Oxford, 507-521.

Ampt, E.S. and J. de D. Ortúzar (2004). On Best Practice in Continuous Large-Scale Mobility Surveys, *Transport Reviews*, 24, 337-363.

Armoogum, J. and J.L. Madre (1998). Weighting or Imputations? The Example of Nonresponses for Daily Trips in the French NPTS, *Journal of Transport Statistics*, 1, 53-63.

Cárdenas, D.H. and J.V. Colomer (2003). Justificación de la Agregación Modal en la Encuesta Domiciliaria de Movilidad, Considerada en el Método Oficial Colombiano para Estudios Urbanos, *VI Simposio de Ingeniería de Tránsito y Transporte*, Universidad del Cauca, Popayán, Colombia, March 2003 (in Spanish).

CASRO (1982). On the Definition of Response Rates, *Special Report Task Force on Completion Rates*, Council of American Survey Research Organisations, New York, USA, July.

DICTUC (1978). *Encuesta Origen-Destino de Viajes para el Gran Santiago*, Final Report to the Ministry of Public Works, Department of Transport Engineering, Pontificia Universidad Católica de Chile, Santiago, Chile, July 1978 (in Spanish).

DICTUC (1998). *Actualización de Encuestas Origen-Destino de Viaje*, Final Report to the Ministry of Planning, Department of Transport Engineering, Pontificia Universidad Católica de Chile, Santiago, Chile, December (in Spanish).

DICTUC (2001). *Análisis de la Encuesta Piloto EOD-2001*, Final Report to the Ministry of Planning, Department of Transport Engineering, Pontificia Universidad Católica de Chile, Santiago, Chile, March (in Spanish).

DICTUC (2002). *Encuesta Origen-Destino de Viajes Santiago 2001*, Executive Report to SECTRA, Department of Transport Engineering, Pontificia Universidad Católica de Chile, September (in Spanish).

DM (2003). *Afericao da Pesquisa Origem e Destino na Regiao Metropolitana de Sao Paulo em 2003*, Diretoria de Planejamento e Expansao dos Transportes Metropolitanos, Gerencia de Tecnologia e Concepcao de Transportes, Departamento de Planejamento de Transportes, Sao Paulo, Brasil, August (in Portuguese).

Gamas, J.A. (2004). *Private communication.* Massachusetts Institute of Technology (jgamas@mit.edu)

Gamas, J.A., D. Amano, W. Anderson, R. Dezzani, and J. Sussman (2004). Improving Emission Estimates in the Mexico City Metropolitan Area, *Proceedings XIII Pan-American Conference on Traffic and Transportation Engineering*, Albany, USA, September.

Geman, S. and D. Geman (1984). Stochastic Relaxation, Gibbs Distribution and the Bayesian Restoration of Images, *IEEE Transactions on Pattern Analysis and Machine Intelligence*, 6, 721-741.

Gutierrez, L.R. (2004). *Private communication.* World Resources Institute (lgutierrez@wri.org).

INEGI (1994). *Encuesta Nacional de Origen-Destino 1994*, Instituto Nacional de Estadística Geografía e Informática, Aguascalientes (in Spanish).

MTC (1999). *Manual para Estudios de Origen y Destino de Transporte de Pasajeros y Mixto en Áreas Municipales Distritales y Metropolitanas*, Ministerio de Transporte de Colombia, Bogotá, Colombia, October (in Spanish).

NCHRP (2002). The Case for Standardising Household Travel Surveys, *Research Results Digest*, **261**, Transportation Research Board, Washington, DC.

Ortúzar, J. de D., A.M. Ivelic, H. Malbrán and A. Thomas (1993). The 1991 Great Santiago Origin-Destination Survey: Methodological Design and Main Results, *Traffic Engineering and Control*, 34, 362-368.

Ortúzar, J. de D., P.M. Armstrong, A.M. Ivelic and C. Valeze (1998). Tamaño Muestral y Estabilidad Temporal en Modelos de Generación de Viajes, *Actas X Congreso Panamericano de Ingeniería de Tránsito y Transporte*, Santander, Spain, September (in Spanish).

Ortúzar, J. de D. and L.G. Willumsen (2001). *Modelling Transport*, Third Edition, John Wiley and Sons, Chichester.

Pérez, J.E. (2004). Apuntes Sobre Encuesta Domiciliaria de Mérida-1994, Mimeo, ALG, Barcelona, Spain, June (in Spanish).

Petrone, L. (2004). *Private communication.* Universidad Nacional de Córdoba (lpetrone@eco.unc.edu.ar)

Purvis, C.L. (1989). *Sample Design for the 1990 Bay Area Household Travel Survey*, Working Paper 1, Bay Area Metropolitan Transport Commission, San Francisco, USA.

Richardson A.J. and E.S. Ampt (1993). *The Victoria Integrated Travel, Activities and Land-Use Toolkit*, Vital Working Paper VWP93/1, Transport Research Centre, Melbourne, Australia.

Richardson A.J., E.S. Ampt and A.H. Meyburg (1995). *Survey Methods for Transport Planning*, Eucalyptus Press, University of Melbourne, Parkville, Australia.

Sánchez, O. (2004). *Private communication*. Universidad Autónoma del Estado de México (osanchez@uaemex.mx).

Smith, M.E. (1979). Design of Small Sample Home Interview Travel Surveys, *Transportation Research Record No. 701*, 29-35.

Stopher, P.R. (1982). Small-Sample Home-Interview Travel Surveys: Application and Suggested Modifications, *Transportation Research Record No. 886*, 41-47.

Stopher, P.R. (1998). Household Travel Surveys: New Perspectives and Old Problems. In: *Theoretical Foundations of Travel Choice Modelling* (T. Gärling, T. Laitila and K. Westin, eds), Pergamon, Oxford, 399-419.

Stopher, P.R. and P.M. Jones (2003). Developing Standards of Transport Survey Quality. In: *Transport Survey Quality and Innovation* (P.R. Stopher and P.M. Jones, eds), Pergamon Press, Oxford, 1-38.

Stopher, P.R. and H.M.A. Metcalf (1996). *Methods for Household Travel Surveys*, NCHRP Synthesis of Highway Practice No. 236, Transportation Research Board, Washington, DC.

Stopher, P.R., C.G. Wilmot, C.C. Stecher and R. Alsnih (2006). Household Travel Surveys: Proposed Standards and Guidelines. In: *Transport Survey Methods – Quality and Future Directions* (P.R. Stopher and C.C. Stecher eds), Elsevier, Oxford, 19-74.

Strambi, O. (2004), *Private communication*. Universidade de Sao Paulo (ostrambi@usp.br).

Travel Survey Methods: Quality and Future Directions
Peter Stopher and Cheryl Stecher (Editors)
© 2006 Published by Elsevier Ltd.

2

HOUSEHOLD TRAVEL SURVEYS: PROPOSED STANDARDS AND GUIDELINES

Peter R. Stopher, Institute of Transport and Logistics Studies, The University of Sydney, NSW, Australia
Chester G. Wilmot, Department of Civil and Environmental Engineering and Louisiana Transportation Research Centre, Louisiana State University, Baton Rouge, LA, USA
Cheryl Stecher, The Franklin Hill Group, Santa Monica, CA, USA
and
Rahaf Alsnih, Institute of Transport and Logistics Studies, The University of Sydney, NSW, Australia

INTRODUCTION

Household travel surveys continue to be an essential component of transport planning and modelling efforts. However, with rising costs of many surveys, and the critical need for good quality data, how best to obtain a quality survey that also provides comparable data to other household travel surveys is a question that constantly arises. Standards for household travel surveys are non-existent, while those for any type of social survey are uncommon, and deal with only a few aspects of surveys.

A number of potential standards are discussed in this chapter. This chapter is divided into seven sections. The first looks at the design of survey instruments; the second is concerned with the design of data collection procedures; the third looks at pilot surveys and pretests; the fourth looks at survey implementation; the fifth is concerned with data coding and geo-coding; the sixth deals with data analysis and expansion; and the final section is concerned with the assessment of data quality.

It was not always possible to develop specific standardised procedures for the areas investigated either because there was insufficient information, or the resources available were too limited. With this in mind, some areas have only recommended guidelines.

DESIGN OF SURVEY INSTRUMENTS

Minimum Question Specification

This item is concerned with establishing the minimum question content of a household travel survey, whether it is time-use, activity, or trip based, to obtain essential information about travel, activity, demographic, and vehicular attributes of the household. Achieving a set of minimum questions or a list of core survey questions (Pratt, 2003) will enable the development of standard variables and categories and allow for uniformity and, hence, comparability across data sets. Another benefit is that the value of data already collected will increase, while the cost of implementing the standardised procedure remains minimal. Table 1 shows the recommended minimum question content of a household travel survey. These questions are relevant for time-use, activity or trip based surveys.

Standardisation of Categories

This item is concerned with establishing standards for the categories, used to describe the variables that evolved from minimum question specification. There appears to be considerable merit in setting standards for categories of those questions that are included in the minimum specifications, as well as also considering standard categories for some of the questions that are not specified within the minimum, but which may be included in many surveys. Probably, the most important of these are income, race (in place of ethnicity), employment status, building/dwelling type, relationships among household members, travel modes, mobility handicaps, education levels, and activities.

To devise standard categories, seven international statistical agencies' definitions, for the specific variables, were looked at and compared with the seven data sets examined as well as two other survey definitions. The results are shown in Table 2.

Standard Question Wordings

To permit comparisons across surveys conducted in different locations, at different times, it is essential that certain key questions be asked in the same manner. It is also important that the question wording or response definitions in a local survey be consistent with the wording (and definitions) used in a national survey or census, especially for variables that may serve as the basis for sampling, expansion, and checking for bias.

Again, the focus of this issue is the minimum questions, but with the addition of some other questions that are frequently used in travel surveys, such as income. Only those questions where the wording is not necessarily self-evident, and where variations that could affect the responses given are offered for standardisation in Table 3.

Table 1: Recommended Minimum Question Specifications

Category	Ref.	Item	Description
Household	H1	Location	Home address or home position in geographic terms
	H2	Type of Building	Detached, semi-detached, terraced, flat, etc.
	H3	Household Size	Number of household members
	H4	Relationships	Matrix of relationships between all members of the household
	H6	Number of Vehicles	Summary of number of vehicles from vehicle data
	H7	Housing tenure	Own or rent status
	H8	Re-contact	Willingness to be contacted again for further surveys, etc.
Personal	P1	Gender	
	P2	Year of Birth	(Preferable to requesting age)
	P4	Paid Jobs	Number of paid positions and hours worked at each in the past week
	P6	Job Classification	Employee, self-employed, student, unemployed, retired, not employed, etc.
	P7	Driving License	Whether or not a current drivers license is held
	P8	Non-mobility	Indication of why no out-of-home activity was performed on a survey day including work-at-home days
	P10	Education Level	Highest level of education achieved
	P11	Disability	Types of mobility disability, both temporary and permanent
	P12	Race[6]	Defined as currently measured in the US Census
Vehicle	V3	Body Type	E.g., car, van, RV, SUV, etc.
	V4	Year of Production	
	V5	Ownership of Vehicle	Household/person, lease, institution
	V6	Use of Vehicle	Main user of vehicle
Activity	A1	Start Time[7]	
	A2	Activity or Purpose	
	A3	Location	Where the activity was performed, unless travelling
	A4	Means of Travel	If activity is travel, what mode(s) was used (including specifying if a car passenger or driver)
	A5	Mode Sequence	Unless collected as fully segmented data
	A6	Group Size	Number of persons travelling with respondent as a group
	A7	Group Membership	Number of persons in the group who live in respondent's household
	A8	Costs	Total amount spent on tolls, fares and respondent's share
	A9	Parking	Amount spent to park

Table 2: Recommended Category Standards

Variable	Primary Category	Code	Secondary Category	Code
Type of Dwelling (H2)	Single family house detached	1	Single family house detached	10
	Single family house attached	2	Townhouse	21
			Row house	22
			Duplex	23
			Triplex/fourplex	24
			Apartment/Mother-in-law suite	25

---

[6] All surveys should use the US Census Bureau definition of Race.

[7] Only start time needs to be ascertained in a time-use or activity survey, because, by definition, the start time of an activity is the end time of the previous activity. Only the last activity should need an end time. In a trip-based survey, start and end time should be included.

Variable	Primary Category	Code	Secondary Category	Code
	Apartment/condominium	3	Condominium	31
			Rented apartment	32
	Mobile home/trailer	4	Mobile home	41
			Trailer/camper	42
	Dorm/group quarters	5	Dormitory	51
			Hostel	52
			Nursing home	53
			Military barracks	54
	Hotel/motel	6	Hotel/motel	60
	Other	9	Other	90
Relationship (H4)	Self	1	Self	10
	Spouse/partner	2	Husband/wife	21
			De facto husband/de facto wife	22
	Son/daughter	3	Natural son/daughter	31
			Adopted son/daughter	32
			Stepson/stepdaughter	33
			Son-in-law/daughter-in-law	34
	Father/mother	4	Natural father/mother	41
			Adopted father/mother	42
			Stepfather/stepmother	43
			Father-in-law/mother-in-law	44
	Brother/sister	5	Natural brother/sister	51
			Adopted brother/sister	52
			Stepbrother/stepsister	53
			Brother-in-law/sister-in-law	54
	Grandfather/grandmother	6	Paternal grandfather/grandmother	61
			Maternal grandfather/grandmother	62
	Grandchild	7	Grandson	71
			Granddaughter	72
	Other relative	8	Male	81
			Female	82
	Not related	9	Boarder	91
			Housemate/ room mate	92
			Other non-relative	93
Housing Tenure (H7)	Own	1	Owned with mortgage	11
			Owned without mortgage	12
	Rent	2	Rent paid	21
			Occupied without rent	22
	Provided by job/military	3	Provided by job	31
			Provided by military	32
Education Level (P10)	No school completed	1	No school completed	10
	Elementary school	2	Preschool/nursery	21
			Kindergarten- 4th grade	22
	High school	3	5th-8th grade (junior high)	31
			9th-12th grade (no diploma)	32
			High school diploma	33
	College/university	4	Some college but no degree	41
			Associate degree in college	42
			Bachelor's degree	43
	Post graduate studies	5	Some graduate school, no degree	51
			Master's degree	52
			Professional school degree	53
			Doctorate degree	54
Disability (P11)	Difficulty standing	1	Difficulty standing	10
	Difficulty climbing	2	Difficulty climbing	20

Variable	Primary Category	Code	Secondary Category	Code
	Visually impaired/blind	3	Visually impaired/blind	30
	Hearing impaired/deaf	4	Hearing impaired/deaf	40
	Require wheelchair	5	Require wheelchair	50
	Require cane/walker	6	Require cane/walker	60
	Other (specify)	9	Other (specify)	90
Race (P12)	White (alone)	1	White (alone)	10
	Black/African American (alone)	2	Black/African American (alone)	20
	American Indian/Alaskan Native (alone)	3	American Indian	31
			Alaskan Native	32
	Asian (alone)	4	Asian Indian	41
			Chinese	42
			Filipino	43
			Japanese	44
			Korean	45
			Vietnamese	46
			Other Asian	47
	Native Hawaiian or Pacific Islander (alone)	5	Native Hawaiian	51
			Guamanian or Chamorro	52
			Samoan	53
			Other Pacific Islander	54
	Some other race (alone)	6	Some other race (alone)	60
	Two or more races	7	Two or more races	70
Vehicle Body Type (V1)	Auto	1	Auto	10
	Van	2	Van	20
	Recreational Vehicle (RV)	3	Recreational Vehicle (RV)	30
	Utility Vehicle	4	Utility Vehicle	40
	Pick up Truck	5	Pick up Truck	50
	Other Truck	6	Other Truck	60
	Motorcycle	7	Motorcycle	70
	Other (specify)	9	Other (specify)	90
Vehicle Ownership (V5)	Household member owned or leased	1	Household member owned or leased	10
	Employer owned or leased	2	Employer owned or leased	20
	Other (specify)	3	Other (specify)	30
Trip Purpose (A2)	Home	1	Home – domestic activity	10
			Home – paid work	11
	Work and Work Related	2	Main job	21
			Other job	22
			Volunteer work and community services	23
			Looking for work	24
	Education/Childcare	3	Attendance at childcare	31
			Attendance at school	32
			Attendance at college	33
	Eating Out	4	Restaurant/Café	41
			Fast food	42
			At friends' home	43
	Personal Business/Medical	5	Availing of/shopping for administrative services	51
			Availing of/shopping for professional services	52
			Availing of/shopping for government/public services	53
			Availing of/shopping for personal services	54

Variable	Primary Category	Code	Secondary Category	Code
			Availing of/shopping for medical and health care services	55
	Shopping	6	Purchasing food and household supplies (groceries)	61
			Purchasing clothes, shoes, personal items	62
			Purchasing household appliances, articles, equipment	63
			Purchasing capital goods (cars, houses etc.)	64
			Comparison shopping	65
			Window shopping	66
	Social/Recreational	7	Communication/ correspondence	71
			Socializing activities	72
			Participating in religious/community/cultural events/activities	73
			Visiting entertainment and cultural venues	74
			Indoor and outdoor sporting activities	75
			Games/hobbies/arts/ crafts	76
			Print/audio/visual media	77
	Accompanying others/travel related	8	Accompanying children to places	81
			Accompanying adults to places	82
			Pick up or drop off other people/get picked up or dropped off (private car, car/van pool, shuttle/limousine)	83
			Activities related to bus, public transit and group rides (except car/van pool and shuttle/limousine)	84
			Change travel mode	85
	Other (specify)	9	Not further defined (n.f.d.)	90
Means of Travel (A4)	Car/van/truck driver	1	Car driver	11
			Van driver	12
			Truck driver	13
	Car/van/truck passenger	2	Car passenger	21
			Van passenger	22
			Truck passenger	23
	Motorcycle/Moped	3	Motorcycle	31
			Moped	32
			Scooter	33
	Bicycle	4	Bicycle	40
	Walk/Wheelchair	5	Walk	51
			Skate/Roller skate/ Roller board	52
			Motorized Wheelchair	53
			Non-motorized wheelchair	54
	Bus/School Bus	6	Regular bus	61
			Intercity bus	62
			Express bus	63
			School Bus	64
	Train	7	Train	71
			Trolley/streetcar	72
	Taxi/Shuttle	8	Taxi	81
			Shared-ride taxi/jitney	82
			Commuter van/shuttle bus: employer paid	83

Variable	Primary Category	Code	Secondary Category	Code
			Commuter van/shuttle bus: pay fare	84
			Dial-a-Ride	85
			Shuttle/Limousine	86
	Other (specify)	9	Other (specify)	90
Fuel Type	Gasoline	1	Gasoline	10
	Diesel	2	Diesel	20
	LPG/LNG	3	LPG/LNG	30
	Dual Fuel	4	Dual Fuel	40
	Other (specify)	9	Other (specify)	90
Employment Status	Full-time	1	35-45 hours	11
			46-55 hours	12
			Greater than 56 hours	13
	Part-time	2	Less than 20 hours per week	21
			Greater than 20 hours per week	22
	Retired	3	Retired	31
			Semi-retired	32
	Full-time homemaker	4	Full-time homemaker	40
	Unemployed seeking employ-ment	5	Unemployed seeking employment	50
	Unemployed not seeking em-ployment	6	Unemployed not seeking employment	60
	Full-time Student	7	Full-time Student	70
	Child not in school/infant*to be specified if skip mechanism not in place	8	Child not in school/infant*to be speci-fied if skip mechanism not in place	80
	Volunteer work (unpaid)	9	Volunteer work (unpaid)	90

Table 3: Recommended Standard Question Wordings

Question	Recommended Standard for Question Wording
Household size (H3)	'Including yourself, how many people live at this address? Please do not include anyone who usually lives somewhere else or is just visiting, such as a college student away at school. (If further clarification is needed--include infants and children, live-in domestic help, housemates, roomers)'
Number of Vehicles (H6)	'How many vehicles are owned, leased, or available for regular use by the people who currently live at this address? Please be sure to include motorcycles, mopeds and RVs'. (As clarification, regular use means 'are in working order'.) **As an advanced practice**, it is recommended that travel surveys include a separate question regarding the availability of bicycles for daily travel: 'How many bicycles in working condition are available to members of your household for use in their daily travel?'
Owner or Renter Status (H7)	'Do you own or rent your home? 1 Own/buying (e.g. paying off a mortgage) 2 Rent/lease or 3 Provided by job or military'
Gender (P1)	'Are you (is this person) male or female?'
Disability (P11)	A question asking about disabilities that impact travel should be asked. 'Do you have a disability or condition that has lasted 6 or more months and which makes it difficult to go outside the home alone, for example to shop or visit a doctor's office?'
Activity or Trip Purpose (A2)	For work or work-related activities: • Volunteer work should be specifically excluded from the definition; • The clarification should be added that work means work for pay or profit; and,

Question	Recommended Standard for Question Wording
	• Questions should be asked about a second job. When asking for activities, at a minimum include a category 'Other at-home activities'. Advanced practice is to ask separately for activities that could be performed either at or away from home, such as meals, work, shopping (using the Internet).
Number in Travelling Party (A6)	'Including yourself, how many people were travelling with you? How many of these were household members?' If CATI is used, it is suggested that the follow-up question regarding number of household members only be asked when the household size is greater than one. At a minimum, the number in the travelling party should be asked whenever a private car, van or truck is the mode of travel.
Income	'Please stop me when I get to the category that best describes the total combined income for everyone living at this address for last year': Income response categories should match the start and end points used by the US Census, although collapsing across income categories is acceptable.

DESIGN OF DATA COLLECTION PROCEDURES

Number and Type of Contacts

In terms of recruitment, the question arises as to the number of times a household should be contacted to obtain a complete recruitment response, especially if initial contact results in the household requesting to be called back, or simply a non-contact (answering machine, busy, and modem/fax). Analysis and results from previous studies indicate that there is no significant reduction in nonresponse bias if more than six attempts are made to call a household during either recruitment or retrieval. There are also no real changes in the conversion to complete interviews for households that requested to be called back, or that were not contacted initially.

The following standardised procedures are recommended to be followed:

1. A survey should include the use of reminders, which should be planned and programmed in the initial stages of the survey. The form of the reminders will depend on the methods used for the survey. However, some mix of telephone, mail, and e-mail reminders would normally be appropriate.
2. A schedule of contacts and reminders, based on Table 4, should be put in place for a household travel survey, at least up to step 6, with use of the reminders to step 11 being recommended except where response rates have already fallen below the point of cost effectiveness for further reminders.
3. The number of attempts to call back to a household that is not reached on the first call, or where a request is made for a call back should be limited to five (i.e., a maximum of a total of 6 calls made to a household). These call-

back attempts should be made at different times on different days of the week. This would apply separately to the initial attempt at recruitment and to the attempt to retrieve data.

Table 4: Proposed Schedule of Contact and Reminders

Step	Day	Contact Type	Content	Received by Household
1	Advance letter	Mail	Pre-Notification letter	R-7
2	Recruitment (R)	Telephone	Recruitment interview	R
3	R+1	Mail	Survey package sent out	R+3 to R+5
4	Day before Diary Day (D – 1)	Telephone	Pre-Diary Day Reminder (motivation call)	D-1
5	D+1	Telephone	Reminder to return completed survey (motivation call)	D+1
6	D+2	Mail	Postcard reminder/reset of Diary Day to D+7	D+4 to D+6
7	D+6	Telephone	Reminder and check on second opportunity for Diary Day	D+6
8	D+9	Mail	Postcard reminder and reset of Diary Day to D+14	D+11 to D+13
9	D+13	Telephone	Reminder and check on third opportunity for Diary Day	D+13
10	D+15	Mail	Re-mailing of Survey Package and reset of Diary Day to D+21	D+17 to D+19
11	D+20	Telephone	Reminder and check on fourth opportunity for Diary Day	D+20

Proxy Reporting

In surveys that use telephone or personal interviews as the method to retrieve completed data, there is a continual issue regarding who provides the activity or travel information: the person performing the activity or travel (direct respondent) or someone else. Those instances in which the activities or travel are reported by someone other than the person who actually performed the activity are referred to as having been reported by 'proxy'. There is a relatively large body of research that concurs that the number of trips is lower when reported by proxies. It is recommended that all surveys, at a minimum, establish the following policies with regard to proxy reporting:

1. For all responses, include a code for whether the activity/travel report was provided directly by the respondent, or by a proxy;
2. For persons aged fourteen and under, require adult proxy reporting;
3. For persons aged fifteen to seventeen, permit proxy reporting unless the individual is available to report their activities directly with parental permission;
4. All persons aged eighteen or older should be asked directly for their activities or travel;

5.   The survey methods report should include the percent of adult respondents (persons aged eighteen or older) whose activities or travel were reported by proxies (regardless of whether a completed diary was available or not), excluding persons who were physically or mentally unable to provide direct reporting at the time of retrieval (illness, incapacity, etc.); and

6.   Establish a calling protocol that requires at least one call back attempt to obtain a direct report from each adult household member aged eighteen or older.

Once sufficient surveys have been conducted using these guidelines, it may be possible to develop factors by trip type to adjust for under- or over-reporting by proxies.

Complete Household Definition

A complete household response is generally defined as a household in which complete information is obtained from all eligible household members (Stopher and Metcalf, 1996; Ampt and Ortúzar, 2004; Nustats International, 2000). The definition of what is a complete household is important because it determines when the sample size specified for a survey is met. There is considerable variability in what has been used as the definition in past household travel surveys, with some surveys specifying that every member of the household must complete travel information and personal details for the household to be considered complete, while others specify that only fifty percent of household members have to complete the survey for the household to be considered complete. There are important trade-offs in this. The more stringent definitions will lead to many households being excluded, especially large households, with potential sample biases arising. On the other hand, too lenient a definition will likely result in poor estimation of household travel.

The following standardised procedures are recommended:

1.   At least key household, person, and vehicle information be obtained. In other words, the minimum set of questions outlined in Table 1 of this chapter should be answered for a household response to be considered acceptable or valid. Other key information may also be required for the response to be considered complete, but this is dependent on the specific objectives of the survey.

2.   At least an adult from every age group represented in the household, as well as younger household members if eligible, should complete the trip/activity data items. These age groups may be the following:

a.   15-17 (if household members under the age of 18 are eligible);

b.   18-64 years;

c.   65-74 years; and

d.   over 74 years.

3.   For the last three age groups, proxy reports should not count towards determining completeness of the household.

4.   Partial responses should not be eliminated from the data set. Partial responses can be useful and these households may be re-contacted in various follow-up exercises. Complete person information from incomplete households can be used in various applications. Also, it is a waste of resources to remove households from the data set. This is important given increasing survey costs.

Sample Replacement

Refusals result in lost sample and require sample replacement. Procedures for sample replacement are critical in preserving the integrity of the sample. Two questions arise:

1.   When should a sampled household or person be considered nonresponsive and when should a replacement household or person be selected; and

2.   How should replacements for the sample be provided?

Quite frequently, the decision to make up sample is not seriously considered and additional samples are added after a relatively minor attempt to gain the original sample. This leads to serious potential biases in the sample and is a practice that should be avoided. The following standards are recommended:

1.   A pilot survey should be conducted to enable the estimation of the expected nonresponse rate. This will help with developing the required sample size.

2.   To overcome unanticipated sample loss, it is suggested that the initial sample that is drawn be much larger than the final required sample, taking into account the expected nonresponse rate, and then increasing beyond this to allow for unforeseen problems.

3.   The order in which numbers are drawn needs to be preserved and contact made strictly in that order. For example, for a Random Digit Dialing (RDD) list, numbers listed later in the list should not be recruited before numbers listed earlier in the list have either been recruited or discarded.

4.   If using RAND (RAND Corporation, 1955) random numbers, additional sample may be created and drawn after the intitial sample has been exhausted. If using RDD lists, this should not be done because the two random samples will not be related and bias may be introduced.

5.   Refusal conversion should be conducted, with a maximum of five attempts to convert initial soft refusals. This recommendation is also stated for initially non-contactable households.

Obviously, the rate of refusal will also be a function of other important factors such as the survey instrument and content, the recruitment and data retrieval methods employed, whether incentives are offered, and the data collection period.

Item Nonresponse

Item nonresponse has been defined as 'the failure to obtain a specific piece of data from a responding member of the sample' (Zimowski *et al.*, 1997), or the 'failure to obtain 'true' and complete data from each respondent' (Zmud and Arce, 2002). Thus, item nonresponse occurs not only as a result of data being missing, but also when incorrect data are provided.

The need for standards in the identification and measurement of item nonresponse in travel surveys is motivated by the desire to achieve two features of future travel surveys; consistency among surveys so that meaningful comparisons can be made, and the potential to use item nonresponse as a measure of data quality. Item nonresponse must be minimized by good survey design and good survey execution. To achieve this, the following basic practice standards are recommended:

1. For Computer Assisted Telephone Interviews (CATI), Computer Assisted Personal Interviews (CAPI) and Internet surveys, administration of the survey should be programmed to require that a response is obtained on each item.
2. Mail-back surveys should be edited immediately upon receipt so that respondents can be re-contacted to query missing or incorrect data items while the survey is still fresh in their memory.
3. Item nonresponse should be considered to include items where values are missing, where the respondent has indicated that they 'don't know' and where the respondent has refused to answer.
4. An overall estimate of item nonresponse should be obtained from the level of nonresponse on each of the following items:
    a. Travel mode;
    b. Driver license status;
    c. Start time and end time of trip OR travel time of trip (if only travel time of trip is reported); and
    d. Vehicle occupancy.

A statistic – the average item nonresponse among the above items – should be used as the overall measure of nonresponse in the data, expressed as a percentage.

Unit Nonresponse

A definition of unit nonresponse is the absence of information from some part of the target population of the survey sample (Black and Safir, 2000; Harpuder and Stec, 1999). There are two broad categories for unit nonresponse. These are refusals (hard refusals, soft refusals, and terminations) and non-contacts (for CATI surveys, these are busy, no reply, and answering machines). High rates of unit nonresponse are generally associated with nonresponse error. Nonresponse error is a function of the nonresponse rate and the difference between respondents and non-respondents on the statistic of interest (Keeter *et al.*, 2000). For example, characteristics of non-respondents to travel surveys are that they are more likely to be low and high income households and households with low or high mobility rates (Richardson, 2000; De Heer and Moritz, 2000). A lower unit nonresponse rate is desired because this reduces the incidence of nonresponse bias. Nonresponse rates are influenced by the survey topic, the number of call backs, the sponsor of the research, incentives, the number of follow-ups and the survey environment (Ettema *et al.*, 1996; Melevin *et al.*, 1998; Schneider and Johnson, 1994).

Unit nonresponse is a significant and growing problem in household travel surveys. A number of standardised procedures and guidelines are recommended as a means to attempt to reduce this phenomenon:

1.   Use pre-survey monetary incentives. The effect of incentives has been clearly demonstrated in the research reviewed and undertaken. It appears that larger incentives may be required to convince those who usually refuse or terminate the survey to complete it. This may require a second round of attempts to convert non-responders to responders, in which a higher incentive is offered to induce conversion.

2.   Use a pre-notification letter and reminders. Special care is required in formulating the pre-notification letter, so that it is simple in language, appealing to a wide range of people, and clearly sets forth the importance of responding. Care must also be taken in determining who should sign the letter, and the affiliations shown in the letterhead used.

3.   Where interviewers are used, special training of interviewers has been shown to have substantial effects on response. Therefore, considerable effort should be paid to developing thorough and complete training of interviewers.

4.   Increase efforts to contact households that are difficult to contact. This may be done by increasing the number of calls for non-contacted units, designating specific times to call non-contacted units, expanding the data collection period, and conducting face-to-face interviews.

5.   Nonresponse surveys should be undertaken as a standard element of all household travel surveys, rather than as the exception that is the present situation.

The following guidance is also offered, based on our research on this topic:

1.   Efforts should always be undertaken to reduce respondent burden in the design of any survey. This often has more to do with the ease with which people can complete the survey task than the actual length of the survey, *per se*.

2.   Shorter surveys should be used wherever possible. This raises difficult issues as the need for more detailed data emerges in the transportation profession. Pilot surveys offer a useful mechanism for testing alternative designs, and fo-

cus groups should also be used in the design process, to determine how to make a survey design shorter, while still being effective.

3.   Providing options on how and when to respond appear likely to increase the number of terminators who will complete the survey. However, more research is needed on the effect of mixed-mode surveys.

Initial Non-Contacts

The first contact made with a potential respondent in a survey can be by telephone, mail, e-mail, or possibly, even personal interview. In telephone surveys and personal interviews, it involves the very first few words uttered following contact with a prospective respondent. When the initial contact is by post, it is the envelope in which the material is posted, the documentation in the envelope, and the opening sentence of the cover letter.

The primary need is to design the introduction to surveys in such a fashion that refusals are avoided as much as possible. Currently, the proportion of refusals that occur during initial contact is surprisingly high. The factors that influence the rate at which people hang up seems to have received relatively little research attention in the past. One study experimented with different opening scripts and observed a 'cooperation rate' that varied between fifty three and sixty four percent (Vaden-Kiernan *et al.*, 1997). Cooperation rate was defined as the percentage of the calls in which the person picking up the phone listened to the entire opening message and permitted the interviewer to determine the eligibility of the household.

A pretest was conducted using sample sizes varying between 100 and 200 observations per changed feature in the introductory message. The conclusions of the experiment were that the introduction should be brief, should state the purpose of the study, identify official sponsorship of the survey, and make it clear no funds were being solicited. In addition, changes to the experimental pretest were made such as using the word 'study' instead of 'survey', changing the opening to state 'this is [person name] calling from' as a more neutral statement, and using a text that assures the person being called that no money will be solicited. This last item distinguishes the call from telemarketing.

Standardised procedures on script formulation would be advantageous in limiting the growing trend in hang ups with telephone surveys. However, further research is required before any standardised procedures or guidelines can be recommended in this area. It is suggested, however, as an interim procedure that the opening statement on the telephone should be:

1.   As brief as possible
2.   State as early as possible that it is not a marketing call

3. Start with the words 'Hello, this is _____...' rather than 'Hello, my name is _____ ...', the latter of which seems to signal that it is probably a marketing call.

Incentives

Incentives have ranged from a gift to a significant payment of money (US$10 and more per household, particularly for GPS surveys, where incentives as high as US$50 have been offered), and some are offered only to those completing the survey, while others are offered to all potential respondents. The only extensive review of the use of incentives in transportation surveys was performed in the mid-1990s by Tooley (1996), who concluded that '...general survey literature supports the use of monetary pre-incentives as being the most effective incentive method'. She also noted that the general survey literature also supported non-monetary incentives, but found them less effective than money, while the same literature is not supportive of post-incentives of any form. In general, one could conclude from this that the general survey literature would rank monetary pre-incentives as the most effective, followed by non-monetary pre-incentives, and then, as least effective, by any form of post-incentive. The transportation profession appears to remain generally unaware of this and post-1995 surveys have still offered post-incentives, and also offered non-monetary incentives.

Several recommendations are offered for standardised procedures on this topic.

1. Incentives should be offered in all personal travel surveys, unless a pilot survey is able to demonstrate clearly that a final response rate in excess of 70 percent can be achieved without any incentive.
2. Incentives should be offered only as pre-completion incentives, i.e., they are offered to all recruited units of the sample, and are not offered in return for respondents returning a completed survey.
3. Incentives should be indicated as being provided for completing the survey task, but not conditioned on a return being received.
4. Incentives should be monetary in form, except where local laws or ordinances prohibit offering money. In such cases, a small gift should be offered.
5. Monetary incentives should generally be small and on the order of US$1-US$2 per person, except in cases where attempts are being made to obtain responses from those who typically fail to respond to a survey. In the latter case, a larger incentive may be worthwhile.
6. Incentives should be offered to each individual rather than to the entire household.
7. Entry into a sweepstakes, provision of lottery tickets, and other similar forms of incentives are not recommended. The literature does not provide support that such incentives are effective.

It is recommended that alternative incentives be tested in a pilot survey, whenever possible, to establish whether a particular population will be responsive to specific incentives. Such tests may compare alternative monetary levels, as well as compare between a gift and money, although existing tests of gifts versus money have clearly shown the supremacy of money.

Respondent Burden

Respondent burden is both tangible and intangible. In tangible terms, it can be measured as the amount of time, cost, etc. that is involved in a respondent complying with the requests of a survey. It could also be measured in terms of the number of times a respondent is contacted and asked to provide information. The intangible aspects of respondent burden are much less easily measured, and may be subsumed under the general title of perceived burden.

According to the US Office of Management and Budget guidelines, respondent burden is defined as the 'time, effort, or financial resources' expended by the public to provide information to or for a federal agency, including:

- 'Reviewing instructions;
- Using technology to collect, process, and disclose information;
- Adjusting existing practices to comply with requirements;
- Searching data sources; completing and reviewing the response; and
- Transmitting or disclosing information'.

Burden is estimated in terms of the 'hour burden' that individuals expend in filling out forms, and in terms of the 'cost burden' in terms of electronic recordkeeping and reporting. Ampt (2000) has suggested that respondent burden is more than just the measured burden in terms of minutes but that it depends on the 'perceived difficulty' of a survey and, as a perception, can vary for different people. She suggests that response burden is perceived as being less when:

- The respondent has greater influence in choosing the time (and perhaps the place) to complete the survey;
- The survey topic or theme is important or relevant to them and/or their community;
- The questionnaire design is as simple as possible, to minimize perceived difficulties (physical, intellectual, and/or emotional);
- Negative external influences (other people) are avoided, and/or positive external influences are enhanced; and,
- The survey appeals to the respondent's sense of altruism.

Table 5 presents the average duration (in minutes) of the telephone calls in some of the more recent travel surveys that have used telephone for both recruitment and travel diary retrieval.

Table 5: Measured Respondent Burden in Terms of Average Call Duration, for Telephone Recruitment and Retrieval

Survey	Recruitment/ Screener Call (minutes/ household)	Reminder Call (mins/hh)	Retrieval Call (minutes/household)	Total Call Duration per Household (minutes)
2001 NHTS	7.8	Not Reported	34.0	41.8 [8] [9]
2001 California Statewide Survey	15.6	Not reported	17.0	32.6 [4]
2002 Regional Transportation Survey, Greater Buffalo-Niagara Reg. Trans. Council	21.2	Not reported	25.5	46.7 [4]
1996 Dallas-Ft. Worth Household Travel Survey	8	3.6	65.5	77.1

As basic practice it is recommended that an estimate of measured respondent burden be routinely reported as part of any travel survey method documentation. This estimate should include the actual or estimated time in minutes for:

- Review of printed materials, including instructions;
- Record keeping (as applicable to survey design);
- Use of 'memory jogger' to record trips;
- Recording odometer readings from household vehicles;
- Actual average call time for (as applicable);
- Recruitment;
- Reminder;
- Retrieval; and
- Other calls (verification, re-contact for incomplete data, odometer readings, etc.);
- Completing diaries and other requested data (mail-back or Internet);
- Gathering the completed surveys from responding household members; and
- Mailing the surveys back to the survey firm/sponsoring organisation (if applicable).

To permit comparisons across surveys, it is recommended that the measured respondent burden be reported at the household level, using the average number of persons per household to factor person-level response times to an estimate for the entire household.

---

[8] Does not include reminder call average duration.

[9] Does not include separate calls to household to collect odometer readings.

PILOT SURVEYS AND PRETESTS

Requirements For Pretests And Pilots

Pretests and pilot surveys are the process of testing various aspects of the survey design, protocol, instruments, analysis, etc. on a small sample of the population, prior to fielding the main survey. The intention of pretests and pilot surveys is to determine whether or not everything in the intended survey will work and produce the expected results. In some instances, pretests or pilot surveys may be conducted to compare two or more methods for some element of the survey process, and to determine which to choose. In other cases, there is no comparison test involved, although it may be anticipated that some refinements to elements of the survey process will result.

It is recommended that the terms *pilot survey* and *pretest* be defined as follows:

- *Pilot Survey* – a complete run through or dress rehearsal of the entire survey process, including drawing the sample, conducting the survey, coding the data, and performing basic analysis of the data. A pilot survey is conducted on a small sample of the same population that will be sampled for the main survey. As distinct from a *pretest*, the pilot survey involves a test of every element of the main survey, conducted in exactly the same way as is planned for the main survey. A pilot survey may also be used to test two or more different survey procedures and compare the results, to assist in selection of one for the main survey. In such a case, each version to be tested is subjected to every step of the main survey.
- *Pretest* – a test of any element, or sequence of elements of a survey, but comprising less than the full survey execution. For example, the instrument may be pretested by having a small subsample of respondents complete the instrument and then reviewing limited aspects of the completed instruments to determine if any design changes are warranted. Any aspect of survey design and implementation may be subjected to a pretest. Pretests may also be used to compare alternatives for an element or elements of a survey. The main distinction between a pretest and a pilot survey is that pretests do not involve testing all aspects of the planned main survey, but may be limited to subsets of the protocol, instrument, sampling, etc. During the design phase, several sequential pretests could be conducted to test various refinements of the instrument, protocol, sampling, etc.

Second, it is recommended that one or more pretests and/or one or more pilot surveys should be an essential step in ALL transport surveys, unless there are specific circumstances that render such a step unnecessary and unlikely to produce useful information.

It is further recommended that the following guidelines with respect to pilot surveys and pretests be adopted:

- In any survey in which interviewers will interact with respondents, the pilot survey or pretest should include listening in to interviewers to determine how they interact with potential respondents, how well they keep to the script of the survey, and whether the script causes difficulties in conversational style.
- In any survey that uses interviewers or observers, there should be a debriefing with those used in the pilot survey or pretest, to determine whether or not difficulties were experienced in handling survey procedures, questionnaires or other materials, scripts, etc.
- If it has been ten years or more since the last time a survey as done, a pilot survey should always be undertaken, because the changes in population that will have occurred will render any past experience irrelevant.

Sample Sizes For Pretests and Pilot Surveys

There are no clear statistical procedures for determining the sizes of samples for pretests and pilot surveys. Clearly, the first issue must be one of what is desired from conducting the pretest or pilot survey. Because this will vary from survey to survey, it is possible that no standard can be set, but only guidance offered. However, some fundamentals can be considered here. Kish (1967) notes that 'If the pilot study is too small, its results are useless, because they are less dependable than the expert guesses we can obtain without it'. (p.51). Dillman (2000) suggests that a pilot survey should have a sample size of 100 to 200 respondents in general, and notes that the size may be larger than this, if resources allow. He also states that '…entering data from 100-150 respondents allows one to make reasonably precise estimates as to whether respondents are clustering into certain categories of questions'. (p.147).

Another important area to consider is how the samples are to be drawn for pilot surveys and pretests. It is clear that we do not wish to survey the same households in the main survey as were surveyed in the pretests or pilot survey. Therefore, those households that are used in the pilot survey and/or pretests should be excluded from the main survey. If, however, these samples are drawn at the outset of the study, and are then excluded for the drawing of the main sample, a bias has been introduced. Random sampling which is essential for representativeness of the sample, requires that all households have an equal probability of being sampled. If households used in the pilot survey or pretest are excluded, then representativeness is compromised, even if only slightly.

It is recommended as basic practice that:

1. Whenever possible, the main sample should be drawn first, and the pilot survey or pretest sample drawn only from those households or persons who were not drawn for the main sample. When the pilot survey or pretest is being conducted to determine the sample size required for the main survey, two

options are possible: first, a main sample can be drawn that is expected to be more than sufficient in size. The pilot survey or pretest sample can then still be drawn subsequently from those households or persons who will not be included in the main sample under any likely circumstances. The second alternative is to draw the pilot survey or pretest sample at random from the total population, and then be sure to exclude all such drawings from the population for drawing the main sample. The former of these two is the preferred method.

2. No pretest or pilot survey should use a sample of less than thirty completed households or respondents. Exercises using smaller samples than this should be regarded as preliminary tests and pre-pilot surveys, and should always be followed by a pretest or pilot survey with a sample size of at least thirty.

3. The minimum sample sizes shown in Table 6 should be used in all pilot surveys and appropriate pretests.

Table 6: Sample Sizes Required for Specified Levels of Accuracy

Measure	Assumed Value	Desired Accuracy	Sample Size	Measure	Assumed Value	Desired Accuracy	Assumed Variance	Sample Size
Response Rate	50%	±5%	384	Household or	10	±1	100	384
	50%	±10%	96	Person Trip	10	±2	100	96
	50%	±15%	43	Rate	10	±3	100	43
	50%	±20%	24		10	±4	100	24
	60% or 40%	±5%	369		10	±1	50	192
	60% or 40%	±10%	92		10	±2	50	48
	60% or 40%	±15%	41		10	±3	50	21
	60% or 40%	±20%	23		10	±4	50	12
	75% or 25%	±5%	288		7	±0.5	70	1076
	75% or 25%	±10%	72		7	±1	70	269
	75% or 25%	±15%	32		7	±1.5	70	120
	75% or 25%	±20%	18		7	±2	70	67
Nonresponse	10%	±3%	384		7	±0.5	50	768
to a Question	10%	±5%	138		7	±1	50	192
	10%	±8%	54		7	±1.5	50	85
	10%	±10%	35		7	±2	50	48
	20%	±3%	683		4	±0.4	40	960
	20%	±5%	246		4	±0.8	40	240
	20%	±8%	96		4	±1	40	154
	20%	±10%	61		4	±1.5	40	68
	30%	±3%	896		4	±0.4	16	384
	30%	±5%	323		4	±0.8	16	96
	30%	±8%	126		4	±1	16	61
	30%	±10%	81		4	±1.5	16	27

The minimum sample sizes required for different possible outcomes from a pilot survey or pretest are shown in Table 6. These sample sizes are all based on the assumption that the relevant statistic of concern to the pretest or pilot survey is to be known with the specified level of accuracy at a ninety five percent confidence level. If the confidence level is lowered to ninety percent, the sample sizes reduce, while they increase if the confidence level is raised to ninety nine percent or higher.

To use Table 6, the following example is provided. Suppose a pilot survey is to be done in which it is desired to determine the response rate to within ±10 percent accuracy, where it is expected to be 40 percent, to determine the nonresponse rate to the income question to ±5 percent, when it is assumed that the level will be 20 percent, and to estimate the household trip rate, expected to be around 10 with a variance of 100, to within ±2 trips per household per day. Entering the table first for the response rate, this shows the need for a pilot survey sample of 92 completed households. Entering the table for the income nonresponse yields a sample size of 246 households, and for the trip rate, a sample size of 96. The critical element proves to be the nonresponse to income, which requires a sample size of 246 households. If we now suppose that, based on this, and the scarcity of resources, it is decided instead to reduce the desired accuracy on the nonresponse to income to ±8 percent, then the sample size for this is seen to be 96, which is the same as that for the trip rate, and only slightly larger than that required for the response rate. Based on this, the decision would be to obtain a completed sample of 100 households, which, assuming the response rate to be forty percent, would require contacting and attempting to recruit a total of 250 households.

SURVEY IMPLEMENTATION

Ethics

The development of ethical standards for travel surveys must be comprehensive enough to ensure that desired codes of behaviour are maintained, and yet are not unduly extensive or restrictive. After reviewing documents prepared by various associations on different aspects of ethical conduct in the execution of travel surveys, it is recommended that the following ethical conduct be observed in all future travel surveys:

- The anonymity of the persons surveyed, and the confidentiality of the information they provide, must be protected at all times;
- A survey respondent may not be sold anything or asked for money as part of the survey;
- Persons must be contacted at reasonable times to participate in the survey and must be allowed to reschedule participation in the survey to a different time if that is more convenient for them;
- Survey personnel must be prepared to divulge their own name, the identity of the research company they represent, the identity of the agency that commissioned the study, and the nature of the survey being conducted, if requested by a respondent;
- Children under the age of 14 may not be interviewed without the consent of a parent or responsible adult;

- A respondent's decision to refuse participation in a survey, not answer specific questions in the survey, or terminate an interview while in progress, must be respected if that is the respondents' firm decision;
- Respondents may not be surveyed or observed without their knowledge. Methods of data collection such as the use of hidden tape recorders, cameras, one-way mirrors, or invisible identifiers on mail questionnaires, may only be used in a survey if the method has been fully disclosed to the respondent and the respondent agrees to its use.
- A research agency may not release research findings prior to the public release of the findings by the organization that commissioned the study, unless approval of the client organization is obtained to do so; and
- A research agency must ensure the reasonable safety of its fieldworkers during the execution of a survey.

Mailing Materials

Most surveys involve some mailing of materials to respondents, whether this is just an initial contact letter telling about the survey to be done, the recruitment materials, or the full survey form. There is evidence to suggest that the materials used to mail to households, as well as materials for households to mail back, have an effect on response rates. Some survey practitioners maintain that the appearance of mailing materials is of considerable importance for households to take a survey seriously (Dillman, 2000).

It is recommended that the following procedures be adopted with regard to format and appearance of mailing materials for travel surveys:

- The use of a *stamped return envelope*, ideally with instructions on which materials need to be mailed back;
- The use of a *large white envelope* (4" x 9½" or larger), with the *address printed directly onto the envelope*, rather than the use of address labels;
- Print a *recognizable return address* on the envelope and *indicate the contents* of the envelope – at least the survey name; and
- Affix *postage stamps*, especially commemorative stamps, rather than using a franking machine or pre-printed bulk mail.

Respondent Questions

In virtually any travel survey, respondents have concerns regarding the legitimacy of the survey and those conducting it. While some of these concerns may be addressed in a cover letter, the typical survey has more nuances than may be explained in a single (or even double) page letter. The state of the practice has evolved three methods for respondents to verify the survey, and obtain answers to frequently asked questions. These include the use of a:

- Telephone Contact Number;
- Informational Brochure, with Frequently Asked Questions (FAQs); and
- Internet Web Site.

In relation to these methods, the following are recommended as basic practice in the execution of travel surveys:

- A telephone contact within the sponsoring agency;
- A toll-free telephone contact within the data collection entity (if different from sponsoring agency); and
- Detailed instructions in the form of an informational brochure or fact sheet. Care should be taken to ensure that the information is presented in an easy to read manner, with appropriate use of graphics where possible.

It is recommended as an advanced practice standard that the execution of a travel survey include an Internet web site with information about the survey, links to sponsoring agencies, answers to frequently asked questions, email and telephone contact for assistance or further information, and the ability to download survey materials.

If non-respondents to household interview surveys tend to travel more than respondents (Richardson, 2000), then providing an additional alternative that permits responding, when convenient to the respondent, may increase the response rate. Accordingly, providing respondents with on-line response capabilities is encouraged.

Caller ID

Caller ID, Caller Line Identification, and Caller Display are different names for the service provided by many telephone companies that allows the customer to see the telephone number, and sometimes the directory listing, of the person who is calling. With the addition of Call Blocking, telephone customers may automatically block incoming telephone calls that do not permit the display of a telephone number.

In light of the general decline in telephone survey response rates, it is incumbent upon legitimate survey researchers to provide any information that may encourage responses from the full range of households. One of the primary uses of Caller ID is for households to screen out unwanted telephone calls by simply ignoring calls that do not display a known number or identify the caller.

As basic practice, it is recommended that Caller ID be provided by the entity conducting the telephone calls, whether a contracted survey firm, university, or government agency, because existing data indicate that providing any ID at all may assist response rates more than being unrecognised. However, after careful review, we have concluded that there are no standards that can be recommended regarding Caller ID listings.

Answering Machines and Repeated Call-Back Requests

There are two related issues encountered by every telephone-based survey: First, when an answering machine is reached, does it assist completion rates if a message is left? Second, when a household requests an interviewer call them back at another time, is there a point beyond which repeated call backs do not increase completion rates? There are several points in the typical telephone-based survey in which a potential household maybe contacted:

- During initial screening/recruitment;
- As a reminder in advance of their assigned travel day; and,
- During the process of retrieving travel information.

Unless or until there is clear evidence that leaving a message when an answering machine is reached does more harm than good, messages should be left. Similarly, survey researchers should treat call back requests as a standard part of the survey process. Treating each request as if it was genuine, and honouring the request, does appear to encourage potential respondents to participate. It is recommended that messages be left on answering machines, as follows:

1.   When an answering machine is reached on the initial recruitment/screening call, a message should be left at least once in the call rotation before classifying the number as non-responding. The message should identify the client organization, the nature of the survey and provide a toll-free number for the household to contact should they desire to participate. The message should be short (no more than 15 seconds), and preferably provided by a 'live' interviewer as opposed to a recorded message.
2.   When an answering machine is reached on a reminder telephone call, a message should always be left.
3.   When an answering machine is reached during telephone retrieval of travel information, a message should always be left.

It is also recommended that:

1.   Telephone survey protocols include a process for complying with call back requests, whether they occur in the recruitment or retrieval activities.
2.   After the fifth or sixth request for a call back from the same household, the household should be categorized as a 'soft' refusal and, therefore, eligible for any 'soft refusal' conversion techniques in use.

Incorrect Reporting of Non-Mobility

Users of travel survey data frequently assume that a high percentage of non-mobility is an indicator of poor survey technique. In order to use the percent of non-mobiles reliably as an indicator of survey quality, a standard set of questions must be asked and, at a minimum, the percent of non-mobile persons must be routinely reported. Standardisation is recommended in three portions of the travel survey process:

In Data Collection: It is recommended as a minimum standard that a question to verify reported non-mobility be asked of all persons who report they did not travel (stayed in one place/did not leave home) during the entire travel period. The question wording in the 2001 NHTS, (NHTS, 2001), (see Table 3) should suffice. For those who want to explore the issue of non-mobility further, it is recommended as an advanced standard to include questions that gently challenge persons who report non-mobility by asking for the reason(s) why no travel was made during that day.

In Data Coding: At a minimum, it is recommended that the data set include an indicator to distinguish between cases where a person indicated that he or she did not travel, and those where a person refused to provide travel data.

In Reporting: As a minimum requirement, it is recommended that the survey results report include the percent of non-mobile person days. In single day surveys, this would be determined by the number of persons reporting that they did not travel, divided by the total number of persons reporting. If questions regarding the reasons why no travel was asked, as an advanced requirement the report should include analyses of these reasons and the characteristics of persons who reported no travel.

Recording Time of Day

This item relates to coding time of day values for database entry and how data are recorded and stored, rather than how respondents provide the information. Travel or activity diaries tend to start at 3 a.m. or 4 a.m., and end at the same time one or more days later, depending on the design of the survey. Standard practice in most travel surveys is to transform a.m. and p.m. times into military time. This is an appropriate practice, and should, theoretically, allow elapsed durations to be obtained by subtracting the start time from the end time. However, a problem arises with a diary that starts at 3 a.m. on one day and ends at 3 a.m. on the second day. By using military time alone, the first day runs from 03:00 to 24:00 hours, and the second day runs from 00:01 hours to 02:59 hours. While this means there is no duplication of hours, it results in a problem for any activity that spans midnight, where the subtraction of a time before midnight, such as 23:30, from a time after midnight, such as 00:30, results in a negative time. Using a format such as elapsed time in minutes would alleviate this problem, but the time of day would not be easily apparent from looking at the raw data. The same applies to a modified military time that adds 24 hours to the times on each additional day (e.g., 01:30 on the second survey day would be written as 25:30).

It is recommended that time of day for data entry and storage be undertaken using two fields: one for the day number, and one for the time in military time (00:00 – 23:59). The day number is intended to indicate the day of the diary. In the case of a diary that starts and ends at midnight and runs for twenty four hours, no day number would be required. In all other cases, the day number is required. For a twenty four hour diary beginning in the early hours of the morning, the day on which the diary is commenced is coded as day 1, and the day on which it ends is coded as day 2. For a forty eight hour diary, beginning an hour or more after midnight, the starting day is day 1, the following day is day 2, and the day on which the diary ends is day 3. Thus, a diary that starts at 3 a.m. on one day and ends at 3 a.m. on the next day would record a time of, say, 6:00 a.m. on the first day as 1, 06:00, and 2.30 a.m. on the following day as 2, 02:30.

Time of Day To Begin and End Reporting

Surveys use various different times at which to start and end the time for a twenty four hour (or longer) travel or activity diary. The aim is usually to choose a time that is expected to interrupt relatively little travel, so that respondents will not be put in the awkward situation of trying to respond about travel that had started before the start time of the diary. However, there is wide discrepancy in the selection of this time, which appears to range anywhere from midnight to 5 a.m.

Ideally, start and end times should be selected so that there is little likelihood of beginning and ending in the middle of travel, or any other activity other than sleeping. Average hourly traffic volumes from highways and roads in North America, as well as in Great Britain and Australia suggest that the lowest volumes consistently occur between 3 a.m. and before 4 a.m. A review of recent data sets in the US generally confirms that the optimal time to start a travel or activity diary is between 2 a.m. and 4 a.m. Table 7 provides a summary of the information for the hours from midnight to 4 a.m.

Table 7: Percentages of Trips Starting and Ending in the Early Morning Hours

Trip Times	NYC		Phoenix		DFW		OKI		SEF		SLC		Merged	
	Start	End	Start	End	Start	End	Start	End	Start	End	Start	End	Start	End
12:01-1:00am	0.5	0.6	0.2	0.2	0.5	0.7	0.2	0.1	0.4	0.3	0.3	0.4	0.3	0.4
1:01-2:00am	0.2	0.2	0.1	0.2	0.2	0.2	0.1	0.1	0.1	0.1	0.1	0.2	0.1	0.2
2:01-3:00am	0	0.1	0.1	0.1	0.1	0.2	0.3	0.1	0.1	0.1	0.03	0.1	0.1	0.1
3:01-4:00am	0.1	0.1	0.3	0.2	0.1	0.1	0.3	0.1	0.2	0.1	0.1	0.1	0.2	0.1
Total	0.8	1.0	0.7	0.7	0.9	1.2	0.9	0.4	0.8	0.6	0.5	0.8	0.7	0.8

It is recommended that start and end times for twenty four hour diaries should be 03:00 a.m. to 02:59 a.m. In the case of diaries that cover more than one day, end times are extended by twenty four hours for each additional day.

Creation of Identification Numbers

The primary issue with respect to identification numbers is that the numbers should permit ready retrieval of specific records, and should provide an unique identifier for each unit in the survey. In addition, there is the potential to provide some additional information through the identification number, such as the membership in a specific sampling category, thereby permitting easy checking of the sampling progress during the survey and ready identification for purposes of expansion and weighting after the survey is completed.

It would be helpful if all personal travel surveys used the same procedures for assigning identification numbers to survey units, because this would mean, first, that complete and incomplete households were always handled identically, and second, that if information is encoded into the ID number, this would be done consistently in all surveys. Such consistency would allow standard processing software to be set up that would utilize the information in the ID number.

It is recommended that:

- An ID number should be assigned at the outset to each eligible address or telephone number in the contact list which should remain attached to the person or household for the duration of the survey. Telephone numbers or addresses that are established to be non-household numbers should not be assigned an ID number. While it could be argued that an ID number should be assigned to every telephone number, it seems unlikely that there would generally be a desire to retain a data entry for ineligible units. It should be noted that this may not be achievable with some commercially-available CATI software, and such software should probably be avoided for use with personal travel surveys.
- A stratification-based ID number be used for all stratified samples, while date-based ID numbering should be used for surveys where sampling is performed by simple random sampling or systematic sampling. It should be noted that, if the RDD software generates a sequential ID number, the additional information can be added in post-processing.

DATA CODING INCLUDING GEOCODING

Geocoding Standards

Geocoding is the process of identifying the geographic location of a trip end and coding a number, such as a traffic analysis zone (TAZ), census tract or block, or latitude and longitude, to represent that location (Cambridge Systematics, 1996). Despite advances in technology, geocoding continues to be an expensive and problematic activity in most Household Travel Surveys. Until quite recently, most geocoding was done manually. This would generally involve a team of coders looking at maps to find address information recorded in surveys, and then transcribing this information into a corresponding trip file. The shortcomings of this approach have been well documented by Cambridge Systematics (1996) and Greaves (1998, 2003).

The problems associated with using zonal spatial units, the availability of address matching programs within standard desktop GIS packages and continued improvements being made to the quality of reference databases lead to the following recommended standardised practices:

1.   All travel surveys should geocode to latitude/longitude;
2.   US State Plane and other North American Datum coordinate systems (e.g., NAD27, NAD83) are default formats adopted in most standard GIS packages and GPS receivers. In light of this, it is recommended that these be adopted in geocoding unless there is a specific need to use another format;
3.   TIGER/Line files should be used as reference databases for address matching;
4.   Information about frequently visited locations should be collected and geocoded in the recruitment stages of a survey to maximise the opportunity to re-contact households to check addresses that cannot be matched;
5.   Geocoding for non-household and non-habitually visited locations should be performed within a few days of data retrieval, also to allow households to be re-contacted if necessary;
6.   Respondents should be asked for the names of cross streets and/or landmarks during data retrieval;
7.   Interviewers should have a good knowledge of the survey area, or have access to gazetteers containing accurate addresses for shopping centres and schools. On-line address directories (e.g., www.infoseek.com , www.usps.com), should be used to locate addresses in situations where supplementary information is not available;
8.   Pretests and evaluations should always be performed to assess the success of geocoding using one, or all of the following methods outlined by Greaves (2003):
     a. Aggregation checks on the location of geocodes;

b. Checking addresses against other information such as telephone exchanges;

c. Verifying that one trip starts where the other finishes; and

d. Cross checking reported distances and times with those calculated from geocoded points.

Level of Geocoding To Be Performed

The success of geocoding depends on the quality of reference and target databases and the technique used to match addresses, and as such, a problem in one of these areas will result in a less than perfect match rate. Although the quality of TIGER/Line files and commercially available address databases appears to be improving, it is unlikely that these sources of information will ever be completely free of errors. In addition to this, it will probably never be possible to have all addresses reported accurately by respondents. In any survey, there will always be a certain number of addresses reported incorrectly, either because respondents genuinely do not know the right address, or because they may deliberately choose not to report it.

It is recommended that:

1. Surveys should successfully geocode no less than 99 percent of household addresses, 95 percent of school and workplace addresses and 90 percent of other locations to latitude/longitude.

2. Any locations that cannot be geocoded to latitude/longitude should be referenced at least to a TAZ to avoid systematic bias.

3. Where it is not possible to match out of region locations with a TAZ, it is suggested they be assigned to a representative point outside the study area.

Missing Values, Use of Zero, Etc.

There is no agreement among recent household surveys on what to use for flagging missing values, and other aspects of setting coded values for non-numeric data. It is not uncommon to find that codes are left blank if the response is missing. This is unfortunate when zero is a legitimate response, because it becomes impossible in most computer analyses to distinguish between a blank and a zero in a numeric field. In statistical packages, missing values can be declared and are replaced in internal data sets with the missing data code of the package. However, in ASCII data files that are usually the ones stored for archives and provided to other agencies and individuals, these missing data codes may vary from variable to variable within one survey.

Several issues arise from the coding of missing values. The first is to address the appropriate use of blanks in data fields. The second issue is to specify standard codes that should be used to indicate missing data. The codes need to distinguish between a respondent refusal, a lack of knowledge by the respondent, and non-applicability or legitimate skips. The third issue is to specify as a standard that there should be correspondence between the numeric values of a categorical variable and the codes.

A fourth issue is the inclusion of the number of trips reported in the diary. This is seen as necessary, where it is otherwise difficult to determine if a respondent refused to return a travel diary, returned a blank travel diary, or indicated that no travel was performed on the diary day. The fifth issue is to establish standard codes for binary variables, such as questions to which the answer is 'yes' or 'no', or 'male' or 'female', etc.

It is recommended that the following practice be adopted together as a group, because adoption of some without others will actually increase ambiguities in the data:

1. *No blanks standard* – Blanks should never be a legitimate code, and all data fields must contain alphanumeric data.
2. *Missing data standard* – Missing data, whether as the result of a respondent refusal, an indication that the respondent does not know the answer, or a legitimate skip of the question, must receive a coded numeric value. These values should be negative values (because negative values will not normally occur in a data set), and it should be -99 for a refusal. For 'don't know' responses, it should be set as -98. For legitimate skips or non-applicability of a question, it should be -97.
3. *Correspondence between numeric values and codes standard* – In any question where a legitimate response could be zero, the code for that response will be the number zero (0). This will normally apply to any question requesting a count of elements, where a count of zero is possible, e.g., number of workers in the household, number of children in the household, number of infants in the household, number of cars available to the household, etc. In like manner, the count that is the response will be the coded value in all cases.
4. *Coding the number of person trips reported* – In all personal travel surveys that seek to ascertain trip-making behaviour of individuals, the person record must contain a count of the number of trips reported by the individual. In this variable, a count of 0 is to be used only to indicate the response that the person did not travel on the diary day. If no travel information was provided, then the value coded should be all 9s.
5. *Coding binary variables* – The principal binary variables in personal travel surveys are yes/no responses, and responses to gender. For questions to which the response is either 'yes' or 'no', the response of 'yes' is coded as 1 and the response of 'no' is coded as 2. For response to the gender question, 'male' is 1 and 'female' is 2.

Coding Complex Variables

There are a number of complex variables, where it would be useful to adopt a standard for the values used to report the data. This would enhance comparability of surveys and remove potential ambiguities. Standard categories have been proposed for the following: relationship, race, disability, employment status, education level, type of dwelling, housing tenure, obtained vehicle, fuel type, vehicle ownership, body type, Internet and cell phone use, and means of travel.

It is recommended that:

1. Multi-digit codes for complex variables, similar to the codes shown in Table 8, be adopted in all future travel surveys. For income, the codes specified in Table 8 are recommended to be used as the standard categories.

Table 8: Possible Coding for Varying Income Detail

Minimum Detail for Income Categories	Minimum Coding	More Detailed Categories	More Detailed Coding
Under $10,000	00	Under $5,000	000
		$5,000-$9,999	005
$10,000-$19,999	01	$10,000 -$14,999	010
		$15,000-$19,999	015
$20,000-$29,999	02	$20,000-$24,999	020
		$25,000-$29,999	025
$30,000-$39,999	03	$30,000-$34,999	030
		$35,000-$39,999	035
$40,000-$49,999	04	$40,000-$44,999	040
		$45,000-$49,999	045
$50,000-$59,999	05	$50,000-$54,999	050
		$55,000-$59,999	055
$60,000-$69,999	06	$60,000-$64,999	060
		$65,000-$69,999	065
$70,000-$79,999	07	$70,000-$74,999	070
		$75,000-$79,999	075
$80,000-$89,999	08	$80,000-$84,999	080
		$85,000-$89,999	085
$90,000-$99,999	09	$90,000-$94,999	090
		$95,000-$99,999	095
$100,000-$109,999	10	$100,000-$104,999	100
		$105,000-$109,999	105
$110,000-$119,999	11	$110,000-$114,999	110
		$115,000-$119,999	115
$120,000-$129,999	12	$120,000-$124,999	120
		$125,000-$129,999	125
$130,000-$139,999	13	$130,000-$134,999	130
		$135,000-$139,999	135
$140,000-$149,999	14	$140,000-$144,999	140
		$145,000-$149,999	145
$150,000 and over	15	$150,000 and over	150
Legitimate skip	97	Legitimate skip	997
Don't Know	98	Don't Know	998
Refused	99	Refused	999

2.   The activity categories shown in Table 9 be adopted for general use in future travel surveys. These categories are based on more or less commonly used trip purpose categories, but provide for a much more detailed breakdown into activity types that can be used in activity surveys.

Table 9: Guidelines for Trip Purpose/Activity Categories

Primary Category	Code	Secondary Categories	Code	Tertiary Categories	Code
Home	01	Sleeping/napping	011	Sleeping	0110
		Preparing/eating meals/snack/drinks	012	Preparing a meal/snack	0121
				Eating a meal/snack	0122
				Other specified food related activities	0129
		Home mainte-nance/cleaning	013	Indoor cleaning	0131
				Outdoor cleaning	0132
				Gardening/ tending plants	0134
				Care of textiles and footwear	0138
				Other specified home maintenance and cleaning	0139
		Household management	014	Paying household bills	0141
				Budgeting, organizing, planning	0142
				Selling, disposing of household assets	0143
				Other specified household management	0149
		Personal care activities	015	Showering, bathing, personal grooming	0151
				Health/medical care to oneself	0152
				Receiving personal care from others	0153
				Other specified personal care activities	0159
		Using com-puter/telephone	016	Using telephone (fixed line) (not incl. telephone shopping)	0161
				Using cell phone (not incl. telephone shopping)	0162
				Sending/reading/receiving email	0163
				Internet browsing (not incl. on-line shopping)	0164
				Shopping for goods and services using telephone (fixed line)	0165
				Shopping for goods and services using cell phone	0166
				Shopping for goods and services using Internet	0167
				Other specified use of computer/telephone	0169
		Caring for others	017	Caring for children	0171
				Teaching, training, helping children	0172
				Caring for adults	0173
				Other specified caring for others	0179
		Paid work	018	Paid work – main job	0181
				Paid work – other job	0182
				Other specified at home paid work	0189
		Other specified at home activities	019	Not further defined (n.f.d.)	0190
Work	02	Main job	021	Regular hours	0211
				Overtime hours	0212
				Extra hours (not paid as overtime)	0213
				Other specified main job activities	0219
		Other job	022	Regular hours	0221
				Overtime hours	0222
				Extra hours (not paid as overtime)	0223
				Other specified other job activities	0229
		Work in internship, ap-prenticeship etc.	023	Regular hours	0231
				Overtime hours	0232

Primary Category	Code	Secondary Categories	Code	Tertiary Categories	Code
				Extra hours (not paid as overtime)	0233
				Other specified internship/apprenticeship activities	0239
		Unpaid work in family business	024	n.f.d.	0240
		Breaks and interruptions from work	025	n.f.d.	0250
		Training and studies in relation to work	026	n.f.d.	0260
		Volunteer work and community services	027	n.f.d.	0270
		Looking for work/setting up business	028	Looking for work	0281
				Looking for/setting up business	0282
		Other specified work related activities	029	n.f.d.	0290
Education/ Childcare Activities	03	Attendance at childcare	031	n.f.d.	0310
		Attendance at school	032	n.f.d.	0320
		Attendance at college	033	n.f.d.	0330
		Breaks/waiting at place of general education	034	n.f.d.	0340
		Self study for distance education course work	035	n.f.d.	0350
		Homework, study, research	036	n.f.d.	0360
		Career/professional development training and studies	037	n.f.d.	0370
		Other specified activities relating to education/childcare	039	n.f.d.	0390
Eating Out	04	Restaurant/Café	041	Restaurant	0411
				Café/Snack Bar/Cafeteria	0412
		Fast food	042	Take out	0421
				Eat in	0422
		At friends' home	043	n.f.d.	0430
		Picnicking	044	n.f.d.	0440
		Other specified eating out	049	n.f.d.	0490
Personal Business	05	Availing of/shopping for administrative services	051	Post Office	0511
				Other specified administrative service	0519
		Availing of/shopping for educational services	052	n.f.d.	0520
		Availing of/shopping for professional services	053	Banking/Credit Union	0531
				Insurance	0532
				Real Estate	0533
				Tax or Accountant	0534
				Legal services	0535
				Other specified professional services	0539
		Availing of/shopping for government/public services	054	n.f.d.	0540
		Availing of/shopping for personal services	055	Hairdresser/barber/beautician	0551
				Other specified personal service	0559
		Availing of/shopping for medical and health care services	056	Medical	0561
				Dental	0562
				Eyecare	0563
				Physiotherapy	0564
				Other specified healthcare service	0569

Primary Category	Code	Secondary Categories	Code	Tertiary Categories	Code
		Availing of/shopping for rental services	057	n.f.d.	0570
		Availing of/shopping for repair and maintenance services	058	n.f.d.	0580
		Other specified activities relating to personal business	059	n.f.d.	0590
Shopping	06	Purchasing food and household supplies (groceries)	061	n.f.d.	0610
		Purchasing clothes, shoes, personal items	062	n.f.d.	0620
		Purchasing school supplies	063	n.f.d.	0630
		Purchasing medical supplies	064	n.f.d.	0640
		Purchasing household appliances, articles, equipment	065	n.f.d.	0650
		Purchasing capital goods (cars, houses etc.)	066	n.f.d.	0660
		Comparison shopping	067	n.f.d.	0670
		Window shopping	068	n.f.d.	0680
		Purchasing other specified goods.	069	n.f.d.	0690
Social and Recreational Activities	07	Communication/ correspondence	071	n.f.d.	0710
		Socializing activities	072	Doing activities/going to places and events together	0721
				Receiving visitors	0722
				Visiting friends and relatives	0723
				Other specified socializing activities	0729
		Participating in religious/community/cultural events/activities	073	Participating in community celebration of historical/cultural events	0731
				Participation in non-religious community rites of weddings, funerals, births etc	0732
				Participating in community social functions	0733
				Participating in religious activities	0734
				Participating in other specified religious/community/cultural activities.	0739
		Visiting entertainment and cultural venues	074	Attendance at movies/cinema	0741
				Attendance at concerts	0742
				Attendance at sporting events	0743
				Attendance at library	0744
				Attendance at amusement park	0745
				Attendance at museum/exhibition/art gallery	0746
				Attendance at zoo/animal park	0747
				Attendance at other specified entertainment and cultural venues	0749
		Indoor and outdoor sporting activities	075	Organized sport	0751
				Informal sport	0752
				Exercise (excludes walking)	0753
				Walking, hiking, bushwalking	0754
				Fishing, hunting	0755
				Driving for pleasure	0756
				Participation in other specified indoor and outdoor sporting activities	0759

Primary Category	Code	Secondary Categories	Code	Tertiary Categories	Code
		Games/hobbies/arts/crafts	076	Card, paper, board games, crosswords	0761
				Gambling	0762
				Arcade games	0763
				Home computer games	0764
				Hobbies, handwork, crafts	0765
				Other specified activities relating to games/hobbies/arts/crafts	0769
		Print/audio/visual media	077	Reading	0771
				Watching/listening to television/video programs/radio	0774
				Other specified activities using print, audio or visual media	0779
		Other specified social and recreational activities	079	n.f.d.	0790
Accompanying/helping others and travel related	08	Accompanying children to places	081	Accompanying children to receive personal services	0811
				Accompanying children to receive medical/health services	0812
				Accompanying children to school, daycare centres	0813
				Accompanying children to sports lessons etc.	0814
				Accompanying children to other specified places	0819
		Accompanying adults to places	082	Accompanying adults to receive personal services	0821
				Accompanying adults to receive medical/health services	0822
				Accompanying adults for shopping	0823
				Accompanying adults for social activities	0824
				Accompanying adults to cultural, sports and entertainment venues	0825
				Accompanying adults to other specified places	0829
		Pick up or drop off other people/get picked up or dropped off (private car, car/van pool, shuttle/limousine)	083	Pick up someone or get picked up	0831
				Drop off someone or get dropped off	0832
		Activities related to bus, public transit and group rides (except car/van pool and shuttle/limousine)	084	Wait for/get on vehicle	0841
				Leave/get off vehicle	0842
		Change travel mode	085	n.f.d.	0850
		Other specified activity related to accompanying others or travel related	089	n.f.d.	0890
No activity	09	No activity	091	n.f.d.	0910
		No recorded activity	092	n.f.d.	0920
		No further activity recorded	093	n.f.d.	0930
Other	99	n.f.d.	990	n.f.d.	9900

DATA ANALYSIS AND EXPANSION

Assessing Sample Biases

Sample bias is a systematic error in survey sample data. It reflects a consistent deviation of sample values from true values in the population. Bias can occur within individual observations when, for example, a faulty measurement device is used and a consistent error is introduced into each observation.

The establishment of standards in the assessment of bias in travel surveys would be useful because it would permit the identification, measurement, and interpretation of bias in a uniform manner. This would allow bias in individual data sets to be used as a measure of data quality and the extent of bias to be compared among data sets. It is recommended that the following basic practice standards be adopted with respect to bias in travel surveys:

1. Each travel survey test for bias;
2. The following variables be used to test for bias:
    a. household size;
    b. vehicle availability;
    c. household income;
    d. age of each person in the household; and
    e. gender of each person in the household.
3. The variables be measured as follows:
    a. household size: mean value;
    b. vehicle availability: categories of 0,1,2, and 3+;
    c. household income: categories corresponding to those in Table 8;
    d. age: categories: 0-5, 6-10, 11-14, ...76-80, 80+; and
    e. gender: male and female.

Total error should be measured using the Percentage RMSE statistic defined in equation (1).

$$Percent\ RMSE = \sqrt{\frac{1}{n_i}\sum_{i}^{n_i}\frac{1}{n_{ji}}\sum_{j}^{n_{ji}}(\frac{r_{ij}-s_{ij}}{r_{ij}})^2}\ x\ 100 \quad \text{.. (1)}$$

where,

n_i = number of variables i;
n_{ji} = number of categories j in variable i;
r_{ji} = reference value of variable i in category j;
s_{ji} = sample value of variable i in category j.

Weighting and Expansion of Data

Weighting is the process of assigning weights to observations in a sample so that the weighted sample accurately represents the population. Expansion is the multiplication applied to each observation in a sample so that the expanded sample is an estimate of the population.

Several authors have called for standardising the weighting process in travel surveys (Purvis, 1990; Stopher and Metcalf, 1996). This has been motivated by the need to improve the comparability of values among surveys and reduce variability in the process followed in estimating weights. Weighting reduces bias in survey values and, therefore, provides more accurate estimates of the true underlying values obtained in a survey. Requiring that all future travel surveys use a common weighting process would improve consistency among surveys and remove uncertainty among users as to whether or not weighting was performed on the data.

It is recommended that:

1. Each travel survey be required to conduct a weighting and expansion exercise, to include the weights in the data set, and to include a description of the weighting process in the metadata;
2. The weights include expansion factors, so that the sum of the weights match population estimates; and
3. The two-stage procedure, described below, should be adopted as the standard method of calculating weights.

Calculating weights

Stage 1. To establish household weights, stage 1 of the weighting and expansion process must include the following steps:

1. Estimate an initial weight equal to the inverse of the design sampling rate. If disproportional sampling is used then weights must be estimated for each stratum separately. The initial weight of household i in stratum h is:

$$w_{i,\exp} = \frac{1}{s_{h,i\in h}}$$

where,

$w_{i,\exp}$ = initial weight (or expansion factor) for household i.
$s_{h,i\in h}$ = design sampling rate in stratum h of which i is an element.

2. If knowledge is available on levels of nonresponse in the survey at geographic or demographic subdivision level, establish a weight to account for differen-

tial nonresponse. If nonresponse is not known at a level which subdivides the sample, assume the weight for this step is 1 and proceed to the next step. If the response rate is known at a level that subdivides the sample, the response weight for household i in subdivision j is:

$$w_{i,resp} = \frac{1}{r_{j,i \in j}}$$

where,

$w_{i,resp}$ = response weight for household i.
$r_{j,i \in j}$ = response rate in subdivision j of which i is an element.

3. Weight for difference in selection probabilities. This is necessary when the sample frame and the sampling unit do not coincide as, for example, when the sample frame is residential telephone numbers and the sampling unit is households. In such a case, households with multiple telephone lines are more likely to be selected than households with one. The same applies if the sample frame is dwelling units and multiple households occupy some dwelling units. To account for these differential selection probabilities, the following weight should be applied to the households, where a one-to-one relationship between the sample frame and the households does not exist:

$$w_{i,sel} = \frac{1}{u_i}$$

where,

$w_{i,sel}$ = selection weight for observation i.
u_i = number of times household i is represented in the sample frame[10].

4. Obtain a composite weight for each household by multiplying the weights from the equations in steps a, b, and c together:

$$w_i = w_{i,exp} \times w_{i,resp} \times w_{i,sel}$$

The weights identified for households in stage 1 are also assigned to the persons and trips in the household.

Stage 2. Separate weighting is conducted for households and persons. While the procedure used is similar, different variables are used in each weighting process. Final weights for households are identified by conducting the following steps:

---

[10] Note that u_i can range from a fraction for those households who share a dwelling or telephone line (or are episodic telephone owners) to values in excess of 1 when a household owns multiple telephone lines or inhabits more than one dwelling in the study area.

1. Identify household variables for which population values are available (from external sources) and which also occur within the sample. The choice of variables should be dictated by the purpose of the survey, where bias is most expected, and the reliability of population values.

2. Each variable must be broken into a manageable number of categories. The categories must be selected so as to ensure that the multidimensional 'cells' that are produced by simultaneously cross-classifying all variables, all contain at least some sample values, because empty cells cannot be adjusted by weights and are, therefore, redundant. Individual cells can be collapsed into single larger cells to eliminate empty cells.

3. Households weights, established in stage 1, must be summed in each cell.

4. Iterative proportional fitting should be applied to the cell weights identified above. The order in which the variables are considered in each iterative cycle is irrelevant because an unique solution is guaranteed irrespective of the order of the variables. A closing error of no more than one percent on any marginal value is recommended.

5. Final weights are identified by dividing the final cell weights above by the sum of the households in each cell. This is effectively dividing the weighted sum of households in each cell by the unweighted sum to produce a common weight for all households that belong in each cell. Note that while individual households had different weights at the end of stage 1, households in the same cell now have the same weight. However, the effect of those individual weights did have an impact in structuring the seed n-dimensional matrix used in the iterative proportional fitting process employed here. The adjustments in stage 2 represent a further improvement in stage 1 weights, but, because cell totals are used in the process, individual weights are lost.

6. Transfer the final household weights to the data and include a description of the expansion and weighting process in the metadata.

7. Person weights are established in the same manner as was accomplished with household weights with the exception that person variables are used in the process and person weights from stage 1 are used in the initial (seed) n-dimensional matrix. Final person weights are established by dividing the final cell values by the number of persons in each cell.

8. Trip weights are established by applying person weights to each trip. The sum of all trip weights in the sample will then represent the total number of trips made in the study area during the survey period although trip underreporting will tend to result in this estimate being lower than the true number of trips conducted. Separate trip weights cannot be established because the true number of trips made in an area is unknown.

Missing Data Imputation

Imputation is the substitution of values for missing data items, or for values of data items that are known to be faulty. Data values are known to be faulty if they are infeasible (e.g., a five-year old with a drivers license) or are inconsistent with other information known of an individual or their household.

For imputation to work most effectively, collected data must first be subjected to editing. Editing involves reviewing data values for reasonableness, consistency, and completeness. The reasonableness of values is determined by establishing permissible or feasible ranges of values and testing whether the collected data falls within those ranges. Where possible, cases in which variable values fall outside the feasible range of values are identified, and the persons re-contacted to establish the correct value. Where the correct value cannot be obtained, the value should be identified as a candidate for inference or imputation. Consistency checks are verification that information on an individual or household is consistent among variables. For example, a consistency check could include verification that a walk-access transit trip does not include a parking cost, that persons under fifteen are not recorded as having a drivers license, or that persons travelling between the same two locations, report similar travel time.

A variety of imputation methods are available for use in travel surveys (NCES, 2002). While the assessment of the accuracy of the different methods of imputation in travel surveys is limited, there is a consensus among users of imputation in general that the method of overall mean imputation is inferior to other methods. Therefore, it seems reasonable that any imputation method be used in travel surveys with the exception of the method of overall mean imputation.

It is recommended that:

1. Data editing must be conducted in all travel surveys.
2. Inference must always precede imputation.
3. Any imputation procedure with the exception of overall mean imputation may be used.
4. If hot-deck imputation is employed, it should be conducted without replacement.
5. Every inferred and imputed value should be flagged in the data to clearly indicate its nature.

Data Archiving

There is little information available as to how best to preserve transport data. This makes it very difficult to propose a list of standards but importantly, highlights the need for more work to be done in this area. However, the following is a list of things to consider when archiving data:

1. How to describe the system;
2. How to describe the property;
3. Description of text -- how data were generated, analysed, variables created and why;
4. Descriptions of changes over time;
5. How to save and store database management systems (size, version, propriety software, etc.);
6. Make sure that all relevant documentation is incorporated in the archive;
7. How should changes to databases be saved; should data be saved at every point in time or just archive the important results;
8. How to preserve operating systems, hardware, and storage media; and
9. Who pays for data preservation and storage (CODATA, 2003).

The Inter-university Consortium of Political and Social Research (ICPSR) proposed the following guidelines for the deposition of any social science database into an archive:

1. Databases to be in ASCII format; as portable SPSS or SAS files. However, privacy of respondents must be maintained, therefore, it is recommended that any personal information be removed from the data base before it is deposited;
2. If the archive contains two or more related files, such as for travel data bases, variables that link the files together should be included in each file;
3. Despite having a different definition of a codebook to that used by transport professionals, the documentation to be included in the archive is almost identical to that suggested by Sharp (2003). However, an important inclusion in this archive is the archival of call history documentation part of the process involved in CATI surveys. The documentation should be in the DDI format - extended markup language; and
4. The ICPSR also has a data deposit form that must be completed by the data producer.

Given the guidelines proposed by the ICPSR (2002) and literature consulted, the following are recommendations as to how best to archive transport data:

1. The sponsoring agency should be the primary organization responsible for archiving the data, associated metadata, and any relevant archiving auxiliary data.
2. Maps of zones, locations and networks should be included in the archive. The recognised standard for storing travel behaviour data is the ASCII format to overcome problems associated with archived spatial data networks due to rapidly changing software.

3. Adequate documentation of the data should be archived. Any changes made to the data should be documented and codebooks and documentation of sampling and weighting procedures need to be archived with the data.
4. Transportation documentation, preservation metadata, and archives should utilize the document type definition (DTD) such as extended markup language (XML).
5. Raw data should be archived. Modified data sets do not need to be stored as long as statistical tests and modifications made to the data are thoroughly documented.
6. Telephone recruitment and telephone or mail-back data retrieval and call history files describing call dispositions of sampled households during the recruitment process should also be archived.

Clearly more research is needed to devise some formal guidelines, let alone standards, for the archiving of transport data. The inevitable increase in use of GPS devices to record travel data in the future, warrants investigations to be carried out that specifically look at how best to preserve and maintain this data.

Documentation

Very little has been written about documentation of travel data. The term 'metadata' in European literature is what is generally referred to in US transportation literature as 'data documentation' (Axhausen and Wigan, 2003). Data documentation is generally defined as descriptive information or documentation about statistical data that describes specific information about data sets and allows for the understanding of the elements and structure of a given dataset (Wigan *et al.*, 2002; Gillman *et al.*, 1996; Spreche, 1997; McKemmish *et al.*, 2001; National Archives of Australia, 1999; Sharp, 2003). *Preservation metadata* is the documentation of elements included in a data archive.

Due to the varying time horizons for the use of transport and travel data, it is essential that data collected, and all relevant documentation, are not lost (Wigan *et al.*, 2002). Any loss of information will result in a loss of knowledge. This reinforces the need for standards on data archiving and documentation.

The following is a comprehensive list of the ideal requirements for travel survey documentation, and is recommended for adoption as a consistent procedure for household travel survey documentation:

1. Sponsorship for the survey – name of the agency, ministry, or organisation sponsoring the travel survey and, if relevant, the name of the survey firm.
2. Survey purpose and objectives – description of why the survey is being conducted, what it hopes to achieve and expected results.

3. Questionnaire and other survey documents – wording of all questions including specific interviewer and respondent instructions. It also includes aids such as recruitment scripts, interview script (telephone and personal interview), maps, travel diaries, memory joggers, etc. These should be provided as an Appendix.
4. Other useful survey materials such as interviewer instruction manuals, validation of results (techniques employed), codebooks, incentive descriptions (pre or post, type of incentive, if monetary, the level offered).
5. Population and sampling frame – a description of the population that the survey is intended to represent as well as why this population was selected, and a description of the sampling frame used to identify this population.
6. Sample design – a complete description of the sample design: sample size, sampling frame, information on eligibility criteria, screening procedures.
7. Sample selection procedures – methods by which respondents were selected by the researcher, details of how the sample was drawn, the levels of proxy reporting tolerated, what constituted a complete household and the sample size.
8. Sample disposition – refusals, terminations, ineligibles, completed interviews, and non-contacts. Also a description of the level of item nonresponse accepted for key variables and why.
9. Response rates – how the eligibility rate for the unknown sample units was determined, a description of the response rate formula used, as well as the calculation of the overall response rate for a two or more stage survey.
10. Processing description – editing, data adjustment, and imputing procedures used.
11. Precision of estimates – sampling error and include other possible sources of error to inform user of accuracy or precision, description of weighting, or estimating procedures.
12. Basic statistics – a description of all base estimates from which conclusions are drawn.
13. Data collection methods – survey mode and procedures.
14. Survey period dates of interviews of fieldwork or data collection and reference dates for reporting, e.g., time, day and date when calls, or other forms of contact, were made.
15. Interviewer characteristics – number and background of fieldwork staff.
16. Quality indicators – results of internal validity checks and any other relevant information such as external research.
17. Contextual information – any other information required to make a reasonable assessment of the findings and data.
18. A description of how geocoding was conducted – this also includes the level of data imputation and inference and how these values are flagged, etc.

It is also important to include organisational documentation, such as the request for proposals and proposal submission, contracts and modifications, all progress reports, key meetings results, costs, key personnel, and information about situations that occurred during the period of the survey. This may include both positive and negative information. Preserving this information will allow agencies to improve on future research projects and proposal submissions because staff writing such documents may consult older examples of these types of documents (Sharp, 2003).

ASSESSMENT OF QUALITY

Computing Response Rates

Proper calculation of response rates is important because response rates are used by analysts to assess survey quality. Higher response rates are usually desired to reduce the likely incidence of nonresponse bias. Until recently, the Council of American Survey Research Organizations, CASRO, was the only organisation with its own method for calculating response rates. However, some years after the development of the CASRO method, the American Association of Public Opinion Research (AAPOR) developed another method for calculating response rates. Both the CASRO and AAPOR formulas are commonly used by survey practitioners.

Standardised procedures are proposed regarding the definitions of the components used in the calculation of response rates. Final disposition codes should be divided into four major groups, regardless of the survey modes to be used:

1.   Complete interviews;
2.   Eligible cases that were not interviewed (non-respondents);
3.   Cases of unknown eligibility; and
4.   Ineligible cases.

These categories can be sub-classified further, depending on the level required by the survey firm and the survey execution method employed. Final disposition codes, adapted from the AAPOR standards, suggested for consistency among transportation surveys, are shown in Table 10.

We recommend that the AAPOR (RR3A) formula be adopted for the calculation of response rates for all household and personal travel surveys.

$$RR3A = \frac{SR}{(SR+PI)+(RB+O)+e_A(UH+UO+NC)} \quad \ldots\ldots\ldots(2)$$

where
SR = number of complete interviews/questionnaires

PI = number of partial interviews/questionnaires
RB = number of refusals and terminations
O = other
NC = number of non-contacts
UH = unknown if household occupied
UO = unknown other
e_A = estimated proportion of cases of unknown eligibility that are eligible (AAPOR eligibility rate: the same formula for calculating the eligibility rate is used).

Table 10: Final Disposition Codes for RDD Telephone Surveys

Eligibility	Eligibility Code	Disposition	Disposition Code
Eligible Interview	1.0	Complete	1.1
		Partial	1.2
Eligible Non-Interview	2.0	Refusal and termination	2.10
		Refusal 2.11 Household-level refusal	2.111
		Termination	2.12
		Respondent never available after call back request	2.21
		Telephone answering device (message confirms residential household)	2.22
		Miscellaneous	2.35
Unknown Eligibility, Non Interview	3.0	Unknown if housing unit	3.10
		Not attempted or worked	3.11
		Always busy	3.12
		No answer	3.13
		Telephone answering device (don't know if housing unit)	3.14
		Telecommunication technological barriers, e.g., call blocking	3.15
		Technical phone problems	3.16
		Housing unit, unknown if eligible respondent	3.20
		No screener completed	3.21
		Other	3.90
Not Eligible	4.0	Out of sample	4.10
		Fax/data line	4.20
		Non-working number	4.31
		Disconnected number	4.32
		Temporarily out of service	4.33
		Special technological circumstances	4.40
		Number changed	4.41
		Cell phone	4.42
		Cell forwarding	4.43
		Business, government office, other organization	4.51
		Institution	4.52
		Group quarters[1]	4.53
		No eligible respondent	4.70
		Quota filled	4.80

[1] If specified as ineligible in the survey design
Source: adapted from AAPOR (2004).

We recommend that the AAPOR (RR3A) formula be adopted for the calculation of re-sponse rates for all household and personal travel surveys.

$$RR3A = \frac{SR}{(SR+PI)+(RB+O)+e_A(UH+UO+NC)} \quad \ldots\ldots(2)$$

where
SR = number of complete interviews/questionnaires
PI = number of partial interviews/questionnaires
RB = number of refusals and terminations
O = other
NC = number of non-contacts
UH = unknown if household occupied
UO = unknown other
e_A = estimated proportion of cases of unknown eligibility that are eligible
(AAPOR eligibility rate: the same formula for calculating the eligibility rate is used).

The eligibility rate for the unknown sample units will vary from survey to survey. It is recommended that careful consideration is given to disposition codes, that the bounds of the research are clearly defined, and that the eligibility rate for the unknown sample units should be defined from this analysis. In transport surveys (as recommended as a standard by AAPOR), it is recommended that:

1.   The estimation of the eligibility rate be left to the discretion of the organiza-tion(s) and individual(s) undertaking the research;
2.   The estimate for eligibility from unknown cases should be based on the best available scientific information; and
3.   The basis of the estimate should be stated explicitly and explained.

It is recommended not to use the terms resolved and known, and unresolved and un-known, interchangeably. Depending on the bounds of the study conducted, cases la-belled as eligible may not be resolved. This arises when call backs are given eligible status. Clearly, however, these calls have not been resolved; therefore, using the terms interchangeably in this situation would be incorrect.

Transportation Measures of Quality

A variety of data quality measures are proposed in this chapter but, in this section, we consider variables that have not been used elsewhere. The type of variables considered are those that are temporally and spatially stable and, therefore, should exhibit similar values among surveys. Special circumstances may cause values to deviate from the norm but, generally, deviations from standard values are an indication that the data are not of the expected quality.

Past studies suggest that typical non-mobile rates are twenty percent at the person level and one percent at the household level. It is recommended that these values serve as reference values against which new surveys are measured. Person non-mobile rates less than twenty percent and household non-mobile rates of less than one percent, suggest data quality that is better than average although no clear interpretation of data quality *vis-à-vis* the non-mobile rate is available at this time. Similarly, person non-mobile rates in excess of twenty percent, and household non-mobile rates in excess of one percent, indicate below average data quality.

Because of the lack of standardisation of activity classification and the variety of activity classification schemes used in transportation at this stage, it is not recommended that activity rates be used to measure data quality. If future travel surveys adopt consistent definitions of activities, as proposed elsewhere in this chapter, activity rates could be re-considered as an indicator of data quality.

Trip rates from numerous studies show reasonable stability among studies. As expected, trip rates at the person level demonstrate less variability than trip rates at the household level due to the influence of household size. However, household trip rates are frequently quoted and have formed the basis of validation checks in the past. Therefore, it is recommended that the trip rates in Table 11, which include household trip rates, serve as reference values for future travel surveys. Deviations from these values must be interpreted by the analyst, because the specific relationship between trip rates and data quality has not been established. Note that the trip rates shown in Table 11 are linked, unweighted trip rates per day.

Table 11: Recommended Reference Trip Rates for Travel Surveys

Unit of Analysis	Purpose	Mean Value	Range
	All	9.2	8 – 11
Household	Home-based Work (HBW)	1.7	-
	Home-based Other (HBO)	4.7	-
	None-Home-Based (NHB)	2.8	-
Person	All	3.4	-

Coverage Error

Coverage error in surveys is the error incurred by having a sampling frame that deviates from the survey population. It is usually considered to represent the failure to include all the units of the target population. However, in addition to the 'under-coverage' that results from exclusion of valid units in the sampling frame, it is also the unintentional inclusion of units in the survey sample (including duplication of units) that do not belong there. This 'over-coverage' can occur, for example, when telephone numbers are used as a sampling frame in a random digit dialling (RDD) sampling process and, as a consequence, households with multiple telephone lines are sampled at a higher rate than those with a single line. Similarly, 'under-coverage' occurs in the same type of survey because some households do not own a telephone or have interrupted telephone service.

Coverage error is traditionally measured by the extent to which the population is accurately measured by the sample frame (US Census, 2000). A statistic which achieves this is a formulation that measures the percentage error in population estimation resulting from deviation of the sampling frame from the true population (Kish, 1995). Coverage error is distinct from nonresponse error although both result from not obtaining information from units in the survey population. Coverage error results from not having some units in the sampling frame, or from having units in the sampling frame that do not belong there. Nonresponse is failing to obtain a response from units that are within the sampling frame.

It is recommended that:

1.   Coverage error should be estimated in each future travel survey, using equation (3):

$$CE = (1 - \frac{F_x}{X})100 \quad \dots\dots\dots\dots\dots\dots\dots\dots\dots\dots\dots\dots\dots\dots\dots\dots\dots\dots\dots\dots\dots\dots\dots \quad (3)$$

where,

CE = coverage error in percent
F_x = sample population multiplied by the inverse of the sampling rate
X = population from an external source.

2.   Coverage error must be estimated as the percentage deviation of the population of the study area estimated using the planned sample, from that of the population of the same area using a reliable external source. That is, coverage error must be estimated using the definition of coverage error in equation (3) above.

3.   Each future survey must include descriptions of the survey population and the sampling frame, and coverage error must be reported.

Proxy Reporting as a Quality Indicator

Proxy reporting in a travel survey is the reporting of one person on behalf of another, as discussed earlier in this chapter. While proxy reporting is unavoidable in some cases, it is also influenced by survey design and the method of survey execution. Because proxy reporting affects the accuracy of the data, it is reasonable to suggest that more proxy reporting is likely to lead to less accuracy in the data. Accuracy is an important component of data quality and, therefore, it is suggested that the incidence of proxy reporting can be used as a measure of data quality of the data set.

It is recommended as a standardised procedure that:

1. Each travel survey should include questions on the age of each person in the household (see also earlier in this chapter), as well as the capability of each member over the age of fourteen to complete the survey.
2. Only those individuals fifteen years of age or older, and those capable of completing the survey should be included in estimating the level of proxy reporting in the data.
3. For each individual in the household, it should be established whether the information being reported for that individual was:
    a. Prepared by the individual; and
    b. Reported by the individual.
4. Each travel survey should report the percentage of proxy reports in the data, based on the above conditions relating to what represents a proxy report for this purpose.

Validation Statistics

Validation is the process of verifying the authenticity of collected data by recontacting a sample of households. It is used in interview-based surveys to determine whether the interviewer actually conducted the interview and whether the information obtained is accurate (Cambridge Systematics, 1996). It can also be used in self-administered questionnaires where the validation survey then usually involves a face-to-face or telephone interview to check the quality and completeness of data (Richardson *et al.*, 1995).

Validation surveys typically involve a limited set of key questions only. These usually include identifying and trying to make contact with the person involved in the original survey, and verifying a few trips reported by the respondent. Validation surveys are conducted to ensure the authenticity and integrity of the data.

The following recommendations are proposed with respect to validation surveys:

1. Each travel survey should conduct a validation survey;
2. The validation survey should use the following three questions:
    a. Did you complete the initial survey? (yes or no). If 'yes', go to question 3 below. If 'no', go to the second question below.
    b. Did someone else in your household complete the survey? (yes or no). If 'yes' go to question 3 below. If 'no' terminate the validation survey.

    c. Select a trip that the respondent is likely to remember from among the trips reported in the initial survey and note the time spent at the destination. Ask the respondent to recall the trip in question and to report the approximate time spent at the destination.

3. A statistic should be prepared indicating the percent of validated surveys that provided a negative answer to each of the first two questions or a mismatch on the third question; and

4. The commissioning agency should establish at the outset what is considered to be a tolerable level of failure on validation.

Acceptance of a one percent failure on the first two questions and five percent on the third might be considered to represent a reasonably good quality.

Data Cleaning Statistics

Data cleaning or data checking is an activity that is conducted almost routinely in travel surveys. It involves checking and, where possible, correcting data values that can be identified as being incorrect. It is usually performed as soon after the data are retrieved as possible. Ideally, error checking should be conducted at the time of data collection by the interviewer (Richardson *et al.*, 1995). CATI and CAPI surveys can help achieve this by incorporating range, logic and consistency checks in the program, as well as procedures that detect missing information beyond merely missing information on a data item. For example, if the travel portion of the survey does not include travel on every person in the household, the interviewer should be prompted to verify that the person or persons who reported no trips were indeed immobile during the survey period. In self-administered surveys, illegible writing, incorrectly spelt street names, and illogical or inconsistent statements, must be addressed by the reviewer as soon after self-administered surveys are returned as possible.

The number of variables vary from survey to survey. In addition, the potential to generate missing values or erroneous responses differs from variable to variable. For these reasons, it is recommended that the estimation of data quality from the data cleaning process be restricted to the data cleaning required among the set of core questions recommended for a travel survey (Minimum Question Specifications). Using a fixed set of variables allows a consistent comparison among data sets.

The following Data Cleaning Statistic (DCS) provides a mechanism to measure the incidence of cleaned data items in a data set. It is recommended that:

1. All transportation surveys compute and report the DCS statistic; and
2. Based on experience with this statistic, future ranges be established to indicate the quality of the data, based on the amount of cleaning required.

$$DCS = \frac{\sum_{n=1}^{N} \sum_{i=1}^{I} count(x_{i,n})}{N \times I}$$

where:

$x_{i,n} = i^{th}$ data item of respondent n

$$count(x_{i,n}) = \left\{ \begin{array}{l} 1 \text{ if } i^{th} \text{ data item of respondent } n \text{ was cleaned} \\ 0 \text{ otherwise} \end{array} \right\}$$

N = number of respondents in survey

I = number of minimum (core) questions

Number of Missing Values

The number of missing values in a data set is a measure of how much information was not collected. If expressed as a proportion of the total number of data items in the data set, it serves as a measure of the relative information content of the data. Thus, it could be used as a measure of data quality. The need for standards arises from the fact that no common practice exists with respect to the definition of missing values and how they may be measured to give an overall assessment of missing information in a data set. Standardising these aspects of missing data measurement would establish a common missing value statistic that would promote understanding within the travel survey profession and would allow comparison among data sets using a common measure of assessment.

Missing values can be defined as data items where respondents have:

- Failed to provide a response because they refuse to divulge the information, or
- Are unable to provide an answer to the question because they do not know the correct answer.

Given this definition of missing values, a missing value index can be calculated that is the proportion of missing data items among all the data items in the data set. That is, the following missing data index can be calculated. It is recommended that:

1. The definition of missing data provided be adopted as a standard definition in travel surveys;
2. The MVI be computed for all travel survey data sets; and
3. Values representing various levels of data quality be established, based on experience with the MVI over time.

$$MVI = \frac{\sum\limits_{n=1}^{N} \sum\limits_{i=1}^{I} x_{i,n}^{*}}{\sum\limits_{n=1}^{N} \sum\limits_{i=1}^{I} x_{i,n}}$$

where,

MVI = Missing Value Index

$$x_{i,n}^{*} = \begin{cases} 1 \text{ if data item i of respondent n is missing} \\ 0 \text{ otherwise} \end{cases}$$

$$x_{i,n} = \begin{cases} 1 \text{ if a response to variable i is applicable to respondent n} \\ 0 \text{ if a response is not applicable} \end{cases}$$

I = number of variables

N = number of respondents in data set

Adherence to Quality Guidelines

One of the ways to improve the quality of data is to have a checklist of actions that must be performed or standards that must be met in each survey. Such a checklist is not currently accepted or used in reporting on household and personal travel surveys. The items identified by Richardson and Pisarski (1997) form the basis of the items included in this measure, but rather than including all items in that list, it is suggested that a sub-set of relatively easily-collected items be used in the analysis. From the original fifty-five items identified by Richardson and Pisarski (1997), ten questions have been compiled to assess the quality of the survey process. It is recommended that the following questions be answered for each travel survey:

1.   Has the survey agency an active quality control program in operation?
2.   Is a senior, independent staff member responsible for quality control in the organisation?
3.   Have pretests been conducted?
4.   Has a pilot survey (or surveys) been conducted?
5.   Have validation surveys been conducted?
6.   Have data reported by proxy been flagged to indicate they were obtained by proxy reporting?
7.   Have data values obtained through imputation been flagged to indicate the nature of their origin?
8.   Has the survey report been prepared and submitted to the client?
9.   Has a coding manual and other metadata that accompanies the data, been prepared and submitted to the client?
10. Has the survey data been adequately archived in a safe, accessible, and well-recognised data storage location?

Answers in the affirmative are favourable and if they are allowed to each count one point, then a score out of ten would indicate the level of adherence to principles of good survey practice. This statistic should be produced for all future travel surveys.

CONCLUSION

Clearly some sort of guidance needs to be given in relation to design phases of travel surveys, travel survey instrument design, conducting travel surveys, and the coding and assessment of the data obtained. The benefits of these standards far outweigh the costs involved in implementation. In addition, these issues may apply equally to surveys in general; thus, demonstrating the usefulness of these standards.

In this chapter, forty items in travel surveys were described. Recommendations for each item were listed along with justifications for the recommendations. Standardisation in other areas in survey research still needs to be conducted; thus, further research efforts are required. It is also recognised that a number of the items discussed in this chapter are applicable to surveys in the US and are not necessarily directly applicable in other countries or contexts. However, one of the challenges to the profession is to determine what of these standards can be adopted in other countries, and what needs adaptation to specific circumstances and contexts.

Overall, standardisation will not only make travel survey results comparable, but will enable the collection of higher quality data, by developing better survey instruments. Good survey design should lead to a reduction in the number of nonresponses, a problematic issue across all fields in social science and behavioural research.

REFERENCES

American Association for Public Opinion Research (2000). *Standard Definitions: Final Dispositions of Case Codes and Outcome Rates for Survey*s. Lenexa, Kansas: AAPOR, www.aapor.org/default.asp?page=survey_methods/standards_best_practices Accessed on 04/07/03.

Ampt, E.S. (2000). Understanding the People We Survey. In: *Transport Surveys: Raising the Standard*. Transportation Research Circular No. E-C008, Transportation Research Board, Washington, DC, II-G/1-13.

Ampt, E. and J.D. Ortúzar (2004). On Best Practice in Continuous Large-Scale Mobility Surveys, *Transport Reviews*, **24**, (3), 337-364.

Axhausen, K.W. and M.R. Wigan (2004). The Public Use of Travel Surveys: The Metadata Perspective. In: *Transport Survey Quality and Innovation* (P.R. Stopher and P.M. Jones, eds), Pergamon Press, Oxford, 605-628.

Black, T., and A. Safir (2000). Assessing Nonresponse Bias in the National Survey of America's Families, www.amstat.org/sections/SRMS/proceedings/paper/2000.pdf Accessed on 12/01/03.

Cambridge Systematics, Inc. (1996). *Scan of Recent Travel Surveys*, Report DOT T-97-08, Federal Highway Administration, US Department of Transportation, 110 pages.

CASRO (1982). *On the Definition of Response Rates: A Special Report of the CASRO Task Force on Completion Rates*, Council of American Survey Research Organizations www.casro.org Accessed on 6/11/02.

CODATA (2003). *Working Group on Archiving Scientific Data*, from http://www.codata.org, Accessed on 18/08/03

De Heer, W.F. and G. Moritz (2000). Data Quality Problems in Travel Surveys, An International Overview. In: *Transport Surveys: Raising the Standard.* Transportation Research Circular No. E-C008, Transportation Research Board, Washington, DC, II-C/1-21.

Dillman, D.A.. (2000). *Mail and Internet Surveys; The Tailored Design Method*, Second Edition, John Wiley and Sons, New York.

Ettema, D, Timmermans, H., and L. van Veghel (1996). *Effects of Data Collection Methods in Travel and Activity Research*, European Institute of Retailing and Services Studies Report, www.bwk.tue.nl/urb/eirass/report.htm , Accessed on 22 January, 2003.

Gillman, D.W., M.V. Appel, and W.P. LaPlant (1996). Statistical Metadata Management: A Standards Based Approach, www.amstat.org/sections/SRMS/proceedings/paper/1996.pdf   Accessed   on 30/08/03.

Greaves, S. (1998). *Applications of GIS Technology in Recent Travel Survey Methodologies,* Report prepared for the Travel Model Improvement Program, Federal Highway Administration, Washington, DC, June.

Greaves, S. (2003). GIS and the Collection of Travel Survey Data. In *Handbook of Transport Geography and Spatial Systems* (D. A. Hensher, K.J. Button, K.E. Haynes and P. R. Stopher eds), 375-390, Elsevier, Oxford.

Harpuder, B.E. and J.A. Stec (1999). Achieving An Optimum Number of Callbacks Attempts: Cost Savings Versus Nonresponse Error Due To Non-Contacts in RDD Surveys, www.amstat.org/sections/SRMS/proceedings/paper/1999.pdf Accessed on 12/01/03.

ICPSR (2003). Inter-university Consortium for Political and Social Research, http://www.ispcr.umich.edu/DDI/glossary.html#dtd Accessed on 21/10/02.

Keeter, S., C. Miller, A. Kohut, R.M. Groves, and S. Presser (2000). Consequences of reducing nonresponse in a national telephone survey, *Public Opinion Quarterly*, 64, (2), 125-148.

Kish, L. (1967). *Survey Sampling*, John Wiley & Sons, New York.

Melevin, P.T., D.A. Dillman, R. Baxter, and C.E. Lamiman (1998). *Personal Delivery of Mail Questionnaires for Household Surveys: A Test of Four Retrieval Methods,*

Research Papers, http://survey.sesrc.wsu.edu/dillman/papers.htm Accessed on 5/11/02.

McKemmish, S., G. Acland, N. Ward, and B. Reed (2001). Describing Records in Context in the Continuum: the Australian Recordkeeping Metadata Schema, http://rcrg.dstc.edu.au/publications/archiv01.htm Accessed on 29/08/03.

NCES (2002). *NCES Statistical Standards*, National Centre for Education Statistics, September. http://nces.ed.gov/pubs2003/2003601.pdf Accessed on 11/05/03.

National Archives of Australia (1999). *Archives Advice 41: Recordkeeping Metadata Standard for Commonwealth Agencies*, http://www.naa.gov.au/recordkeeping/rkpubs/advices/index.html, Accessed on 2/09/03.

NHTS (2001). *Users Guide, Chapter 5: Weight Calculations*, National Household Travel Survey, http://nhts.ornl.gov/2001/usersguide Accessed on 06/25/03.

NPTS (2001). *Documentation for the 1990 NPTS Datasets*, Derived from the 1990 NPTS User's Guide for the Public Use Tape and the 1990 Public Use Tapes http://www-cta.ornl.gov/npts/1990/index.html Accessed on 30/10/01.

NuStats International (2000). *Regional Travel – Household Interview Survey: Data Users Manual*, Report prepared for the New York Metropolitan Council (NYMTC) and the North Jersey Transportation Planning Authority (NJTPA) in association with Parsons Brinckerhoff Quade & Douglas, Inc., February.

Pratt, J.H. (2003). Survey Instrument Design. In: *Transport Survey Quality and Innovation* (P.R. Stopher and P.M. Jones eds), Pergamon Press, Oxford, 137-150.

Purvis, C. L. (1990). Survey of Travel Surveys II, *Transportation Research Record No. 1271*, Transportation Research Board, Washington, DC, 23-32.

RAND Corporation (1955). *A Million Random Digits with 100,000 Normal Deviates*, The Free Press, New York.

Richardson, A.J. (2000). Behavioural Mechanisms of Nonresponse in Mailback Travel Surveys, paper presented to the Transportation Research Board, 79th Annual Meeting, January 9-13, Washington, D.C.

Richardson, A.J., E.S. Ampt and A.H. Meyburg (1995). *Survey Methods for Transport Planning*. Eucalyptus Press, University of Melbourne, Parkville, Australia.

Richardson, A. J., and A. Pisarski (1997). Guidelines for Quality Assurance in Travel & Activity Surveys. International Conference on Transport Survey Quality and Innovation, *Transport Surveys: Raising the Standard*, Grainau, Germany, 30 pp.

Schneider, K.C. and J.C. Johnson (1994). Link Between Response-Inducing Strategies and Uninformed Response, *Marketing Intelligence and Planning*, 12, (1), 29-36.

Sharp, J. (2003). Data Interrogation and Management. In: *Transport Survey Quality and Innovation* (P.R. Stopher and P.M. Jones eds), Pergamon Press, Oxford, 629-634.

Sprehe, J.T. (1997). The US Census Bureau's Data Access and Dissemination System (DADS), *Government Information Quarterly*, 14, (1).

Stopher, P.R., and H.M.A. Metcalf (1996). *Methods for Household Travel Surveys*. NCHRP Synthesis of Highway Practice 236, Transportation Research Board, Washington DC, 57 pp.

Tooley, M. (1996). Incentives and Rates of Return for Travel Surveys, *Transportation Research Record No.1551*, 67-73.

US Bureau of the Census (2000a). *Design and Methodology, Current Population Survey*, Technical Paper 63, US Department of Commerce, Washington DC, (http://www.census.gov/prod/2000pubs/tp63.pdf , Accessed on 11 Sept. 2003.

US Bureau of the Census (2000b). *Historical Census of Housing Tables*, http://www.census.gov/hhes/www/housing/census/historic/phone.html , Accessed on 02/11/04

Vaden-Kiernan, N., D. Cantor, P. Cunningham, S. Dipko, K. Malloy, P. Warren (1997). *1997 NSAF Telephone Survey Methods, Report No. 9*, NSAF Methodology Reports, Urban Institute, Washington, DC.

Wigan, M., M. Grieco, and J. Hine (2002). Enabling and Managing Greater Access to Transport Data Through Metadata, Paper presented at the 81st Annual Transportation Research Board Meeting, Washington, DC, January.

Zimowski, M., R. Tourangeau, R. Ghadialy, and S. Pedlow (1997). *Nonresponse in Household Travel Surveys*, prepared for Federal highway Administration (http://tmip.fhwa.dot.gov/clearinghouse/docs/surveys/nonresponse/glossary.stm) Accessed on 19/10/01.

Zimowski, M., R. Tourangeau and R. Ghadialy (1997). *An Introduction To Panel Surveys in Transportation Studies*, prepared for Federal Highway Administration http://tmip.fhwa.dot.gov/clearinghouse/docs/surveys/panel_surveys/ Accessed on 9/10/01.

Zmud, J.P. and C.H. Arce (2002). Item Nonresponse in Travel Surveys: Causes and Solutions. In: *Transport Surveys: Raising the Standard*, Transportation Research Circular E-C008, Transportation Research Board, Washington, DC, II-D/20-34.

3

SURVEY DESIGN: THE PAST, THE PRESENT AND THE FUTURE

Henk van Evert, AVV Transport Research Centre, Rotterdam, The Netherlands
Werner Brög, Socialdata Institut für Verkehrs- und Infrastrukturforschung, München, Germany
Erhard Erl, Socialdata Institut für Verkehrs- und Infrastrukturforschung, München, Germany

INTRODUCTION

In the world of travel surveys three main types can be found:

- Face-to-face surveys;
- Telephone surveys; and
- Self-administered surveys.

These surveys can be enriched by computer tools leading to prominent contractions like CAPI (Computer-assisted personal interviewing) or CATI (Computer-assisted telephone interviewing). In the last few years surveys using GPS (Global Positioning System) and GSM (Global System for Mobile Communication) have been implemented. Internet and e-mail surveys are developments of the self-administered survey type.

Two remarks are necessary prior to a further description of survey designs. The first is that types are often mixed. The second is that a survey design consists of very many elements, starting from the sampling, comprising the administration of the survey process, and ending with the data preparation.

Face-to-face interviews are a direct personal communication between interviewer and respondent. This situation generates the advantages and disadvantages of this method.

Information can be collected in a personal interview with a chance for further enquiries and direct validation of answers. However, this survey type requires a lot of time, costs and personnel. Also in many societies the 'visit at home' is becoming more and more difficult in practice. So personal interviews are still being carried out in some countries, but are no longer an option in many other countries.

Telephone surveys are often seen as a quick and cost-effective option. They were discovered as a means of interviewing when the network density and registration of telephone numbers were still high. The new telephone technologies, e.g., mobile phones, different providers, caller ID, and answering machines, have led to increasing problems for such types of surveys and to the need to supplement them with other forms of survey – mainly mail-back – to include non-listed households. In addition, this combination has major disadvantages – there is no longer any control about survey effects and only a minor chance to make corrections.

Self-administered surveys are mainly implemented as mail-back surveys. This form of survey can be combined with telephone motivational calls, telephone interviewing of genuine non-respondents, or even personal interviewing, when the survey forms are collected from the households directly. This survey type has reached a high degree of standardisation in the KONTIV design (Brög, 2000); which even gives other survey types the questionnaire structure. The main disadvantage of self-administered surveys seems to be that they need a special expertise. Their main advantage is the solidity of the data collected and the possibility to control and validate methodological effects either by telephone explorations or the known response speed.

All these survey designs were applied within the Dutch Travel Survey. Thus, the history of this survey gives an unique opportunity for describing both the advantages and disadvantages of the design and all its elements in a practical case study.

The Dutch Government has investigated the mobility of the Dutch population on a yearly basis since 1978. The objective of the Dutch Travel Survey is to describe the travel patterns of the Dutch population by collecting information on origins and destinations, time of day, mode of transport, purpose, and the distance and time travelled of trips; in addition, ample attention is paid to the factors explaining the various discernible travel patterns. The survey population encompasses the resident population of the Netherlands. The sampling unit is the household. The special attention to be paid to explanatory factors calls for the collection of data on households and the persons within the households. Therefore, the survey has a hierarchical structure (see Figure 1).

Household data are gathered for each household in the sample, and personal data for each person in the household. From each person trip and stage, (Axhausen, 2000) data are gathered for every trip made during a specified period.

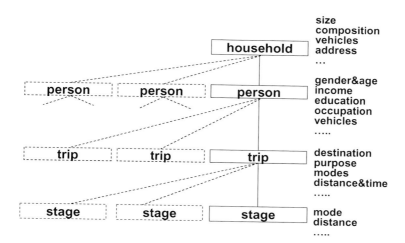

Figure 1: Levels in Data Collected (example variables) in the Dutch Travel Survey

The large number of variables included in the survey can provide data which reveal a great variety of interrelations, even at various levels. Important output variables are number of trips and distance travelled per person per day, the average distance per trip, and the total distance travelled by the Dutch population by mode of transport and purpose.

During a long history spanning twenty-six years, several projects have been carried out to find more efficient methods of observation for the Dutch Travel Survey and to reduce survey costs. In this chapter, we use the history of the Dutch Travel Survey as a guide to describe the evolution of survey designs in the past decades.

THE PAST

The Start

Statistics Netherlands (the Dutch Statistical Office, CBS) started the investigation of the mobility of the Dutch population in 1978. This survey is known as the Onderzoek Verplaatsingsgedrag (OVG). The OVG met the long existing need for recent data about the whole field of passenger transport.

Until 1984, the survey was conducted with personal interviews. Each month around 1,500 households were visited. The sample was equally divided over all days. Two visits took place for every participating household. During the first visit the household data were gathered on paper and a travel diary was left behind for each household member of twelve years and older. Household members had to fill in the personal data and the data on the trips they made over a two-day period. The diaries were collected during a second visit.

Anticipating the possible need to lower costs, alternative survey designs were tried out in the early 1980s. In September 1980 a mail-back survey was tested. This experiment led to the following conclusions:

- The results were comparable with the standard face-to-face survey;
- Significant differences may have been caused partly by the interview instruments;
- The interview instruments employed could be refined;
- Savings in financial terms amounted to about thirty percent; and
- The response rate was, however, only fifty percent.

Before the telephone/postal method was introduced in 1985, two pilot studies were carried out in June 1983 and June 1984 to test the method. The objectives of these pilot studies were, *inter alia*:

- To measure the response;
- To determine the extent of zero-travel of people; and
- To compare the trips thus measured with those from the method used at that time.

A number of comparisons between the results of the two methods were possible because the pilot studies were both carried out simultaneously with the then used method of interviewers visiting people's homes:

- More trips and greater total distances were measured using the telephone/postal method;
- The number of people with zero-travel was more or less the same;
- There was a relationship between the amount of travel and the number of telephone calls before initial contact was made: the number of phone calls was positively correlated with greater amounts of travel;
- Households with unlisted telephone numbers as well as those without a telephone were different from households with listed telephone numbers as far as the amount of travel was concerned. Those households with unlisted numbers travelled eight percent more kilometres and those without a telephone travelled twelve percent fewer kilometres than those with listed telephone numbers. It was assumed that the overall effect on the amount of travel was of no consequence;
- The response at the household level was higher;

- The response with regard to trip data was about the same;
- Nonresponse was higher than average among older people and those without their own means of transport;
- Non-responding households were smaller on average; and
- Car ownership was lower among the non-responding households.

The First Redesign

To reduce costs, telephone interviewing was introduced in 1985, combined with a mail-out/mail-back survey with self-completion questionnaires. Statistics Netherlands announced the telephone call in advance by an introductory letter. The data collected during the telephone interview (CATI) included household details, the composition of the household, and vehicle ownership. After that, the travel diaries were sent by post to the household. Each individual (aged twelve years and older) in the household was asked to keep a record of all his or her trips for one day. Besides the information about travel, some personal information was asked such as personal income, education, and occupation. If the respondent did not return a completed diary within five days after the survey day, a first recall with a new diary was sent. The respondent was asked again to keep a record of all his trips on a new predetermined interview day (seven days after the first interview day). If the respondent refused again to return a completed diary, a second recall was sent with the request to fill in a new diary on a new predetermined interview day (fourteen days after the first day).

The various steps taken and the means of communication of the 1985 survey and those of the survey in the period 1978-1984 are described in Table 1.

Table 1: OVG (1978-1984) and OVG 1985 Procedures

Steps	1985	1978-84
Introduction of survey	Letter	Letter
Household data	Telephone	First interviewer visit
Distribution of trip diaries	Post	First interviewer visit
Personal data	Written by respondent	Written by respondent
Completing trip diaries	Written by respondent	Written by respondent
Return trip diaries	Post	Second interviewer visit

The method used had advantages in the sphere of the sample distribution in terms of time and space. Furthermore the costs per unit of data gathered (per survey day) were much less than those for interviewers visiting homes. Because the data obtained during the telephone call were immediately entered to a computer, it was possible to check for and rectify mistakes from the respondent and/or the interviewer during the telephone data collection step.

The sample was drawn as a stratified sample from the so-called Geographic Basic Register (GBR). The stratification variables were Province and Urbanisation. Each address had an equal chance of being drawn. The Dutch telephone company added telephone numbers to the addresses where possible. The sample was spread randomly over all days of the year. The date thus allotted to each address was the date for which the respondent was requested to complete a travel diary. The telephone approach meant that households with unlisted telephone numbers as well as those without a telephone were excluded from the survey. Because of this redesign, the results of the OVG 1978-1984 are not comparable with those of the OVG for 1985 and after.

The Extension

In 1993, an inventory of the data needs of the regional authorities and the Ministry of Transport, Public Works, and Water Management (which is hereafter referred to as the Ministry of Transport) showed the need for additional information on travel behaviour in three closely connected aspects:

- Public transport;
- Being able to derive regional transport trends; and
- Improve availability of regional data for use with regional transport models.

To answer these data needs AVV Transport Research Centre of the Ministry of Transport asked Statistics Netherlands to investigate whether the OVG could be extended in such a way that these needs would be met.

In 1994, the sample size of the OVG was tripled compared to 1993: a doubling of the number of addresses for the national sample and one extra element for the transport regions of Arnhem-Nijmegen and Utrecht. At that time, transport regions were an important policy item within the Ministry of Transport.

When the OVG was set up in 1978, it did not cover children aged under twelve. The reason for this was a purely methodological one: the participation of all the members of a household was considered too much of a burden. There was still insufficient insight into the methodological aspects of surveying children. Nevertheless, measuring the mobility of under-twelves was of great importance in the context of road safety. Because the survey design was changed drastically in 1985, new possibilities were created for the participation of children as respondents at relatively low costs. A pilot survey to this end was conducted in February 1986. The pilot survey was assigned to find out whether the mobility of children and adults could be measured in a similar way. The travel diaries were adapted to the language used by children and the situations in which they often find themselves. The structure and layout of the diary, however, were not very different from those used in the regular survey. Within each household, only the children under twelve participated in this pilot survey. On the basis of the results, this method was expected to enable the measurement of the mobility of the under-twelves. The survey was received very positively. There was an eighty percent response (i.e., the proportion of households willing to cooperate); more than ninety-seven percent of the diaries were completed and sent back.

In October 1991 a follow-up pilot survey was conducted. On the whole, the same diary was used for the under-twelves as in the pilot survey from 1986. In the follow-up, all the members of households with children under twelve were asked to participate in the survey. The parents were asked to fill in the diaries of their children. The respondents aged twelve and above were asked to keep a record of all their travel with the same diary used in the regular survey. Comparing the results of the pilot with the results of the households with children under twelve from the regular survey, the proportion of households willing to cooperate was the same. The response for under-twelves was ninety percent. Of the persons aged twelve and above, eighty-six percent sent back completed diaries. In the regular survey the response rate was eighty percent for households with children under twelve. Thus, in spite of the increased effort for respondents, the response rate increased significantly. The hypothesis that participation of all the members of the household would cause a decrease in the response rate was rejected. In view of the positive results, the incorporation of the measurement of the mobility of children in the normal survey started in 1994.

With this addition the entire Dutch population was covered from that date. The total number of respondents thus increased from over 20,000 in 1993 (people aged twelve and over) to over 80,000 in 1994 (extension and children under the age of twelve included). The tripling of the sample size added over 40,000 people and the addition of children under twelve added about 20,000 people.

On the basis of a study in which the best expansion option was determined, Statistics Netherlands advised that the OVG be sextupled in 1995 (to around 60,000 households) as compared to 1993 (around 10,000 households) and that the survey techniques not be altered. Thus, since 1994 the yearly sample size has been expanded. The Ministry of Transport has financed the expansion since 1995.

The Second Redesign

From 1985 to 1998, there was a significant decline in response to the OVG, as shown in Figure 2. The decline of overall response rates stemmed partly from an increasing proportion of unlisted telephone numbers and, therefore, a declining accessibility to households. However, there was also a tendency toward increasing unwillingness to participate. These combined factors resulted in a drop of overall response rates from fifty-one percent in 1985 to thirty-five percent in 1998. Because only about eighty-five percent of the responding households provided complete data, the 1998 response result at household level was, in fact, less than thirty percent of the original sample.

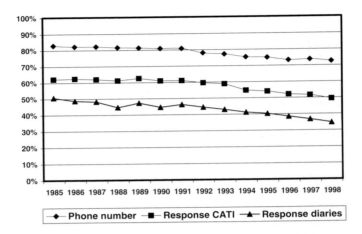

Figure 2: Accessibility and Response Rates Dutch Travel Survey 1985-1998

The declining accessibility and rapidly falling response rates gave rise to serious and increasing doubts with respect to the representativeness of the sample and the comparability of survey results (de Heer and Moritz, 2000). These developments coincided with a growing demand from policy-makers for information about transport and mobility. This situation prompted Statistics Netherlands, in co-operation with the AVV, to look for an alternative design that would combine significantly improved response results with enhanced research flexibility.

Preliminary investigations for a new design of the Dutch National Travel Survey resulted in a choice of the German New KONTIV® Design (Brög, 2000), developed by the institute *Socialdata* in Munich. The NKD has been developed over a number of years, applied in many local and regional surveys and implemented successfully in several countries.

The NKD is set up as a normal self-administered survey, with telephone motivation of respondents and (possible) subsequent follow-up surveys for more detailed data per subgroup, see Figure 3. An important advantage of a written survey is that this method of data collection is generally the least burdensome for respondents. The respondents are phoned when they have received the survey material and are encouraged to fill in the questionnaire and the diary. The telephone is not used actually to carry out the survey, but merely as an instrument to motivate the respondents. Only if the required information cannot be obtained otherwise are data collected by telephone (for example, if a respondent asks for help).

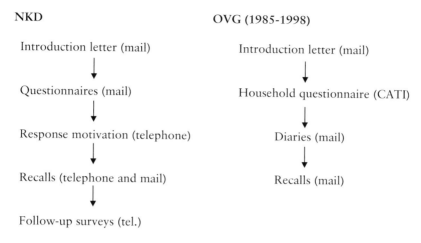

Figure 3: NKD and OVG (1985-1998) Procedures

The basic NKD survey consists of a questionnaire for the household and a questionnaire for each individual within the household. In the latter questionnaire, respondents are asked to report their trips (activity based) for a specified travel day. The questionnaire itself is kept as user-friendly as possible, i.e., as simple as possible. The respondents are not burdened with definitions or questions that would only apply to a small part of the population. The idea is that respondents can answer questions in their own words. Categories are given only for mode and trip purpose, and are clear and understandable. For example, the NKD questionnaire gives four purposes (work, education, work-related business and shopping plus return home) and an open space for respondents to self-report trip purpose. From these questions, a total of forty five categories for purpose are coded. Furthermore, this procedure avoids misunderstandings by respondents (Brög and Erl, 1999). Pre-coded answers, explanations or definitions may lead to confusion. The design aims to place the burden on the surveyor rather than the respondent. If the data from the received questionnaires are incomplete or require clarification, correct or additional data are collected by telephone.

If necessary the basic NKD survey is followed up by several 'satellite' surveys, as shown in Figure 4, to obtain additional data for specific subgroups (for example, children under six years of age) and research topics (for example, use of public transport). These satellite surveys are mostly carried out by telephone, but other methods of data collection can also be used.

In contrast to the OVG design, it can be said that the NKD makes it easy for respondents to co-operate and makes it more difficult to refuse. The NKD starts from the premise that the researchers must adjust to the respondents, not the respondents to the researchers. The diary is designed in such a way that a trip is defined by the individual activity performed at an out-of-home destination. The basic idea behind the diary design is to obtain all information concerning the out-of-home activities performed, not simply those which reflect the researcher's *a priori* views on what are 'formally correct' answers. Correspondingly, the possibility for respondents to report in their own words is regarded as more important than the provision of unclear and therefore confusing concept explanations. The consistent respondent-orientation also requires a certain graphic design in terms of comprehensibility and readability and avoids code symbols in the questionnaire.

New Kontiv Design

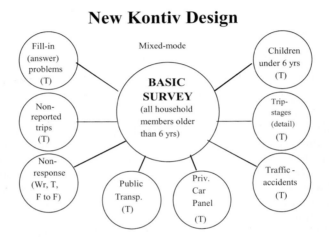

Figure 4:New KONTIV Design

To test the possibilities of the NKD, Statistics Netherlands conducted a pilot project in September 1997. The complete survey process of the NKD was carried out at the office of Statistics Netherlands in Heerlen, supervised by a field coordinator from *Socialdata*. All details of the NKD survey process, a wholly new approach, were made available to Statistics Netherlands staff. The results of the NKD pilot were compared with the results from a control group taken from the ongoing OVG. The overall response in the NKD pilot was significantly higher. The number of useful diaries (responding individuals) was seventy percent higher in the NKD pilot compared to the OVG control group. In spite of the use of simplified questionnaires, no loss of data quality could be detected. Spread, rounding errors, and item nonresponse in the NKD pilot were not essentially different from the data collected with the OVG design.

As a result of the NKD pilot, Statistics Netherlands redesigned the National Travel Survey using the NKD. The goal of this redesign (*Nieuw Onderzoek Verplaatsingsgedrag-*

NOVG) was to improve the quality of the data and to create a more flexible design. The NOVG was tested in the first three months of 1998 and ran parallel with the old OVG for the last nine months of 1998. Again, the results were very good. The pilot study (organisation and results) and the NOVG (the test and parallel survey in 1998) are described in detail in the chapter by van Evert and Moritz (2000).

The NOVG started on January 1, 1999. The response rates since 1999 are around seventy percent (Figure 5). The overall costs of the old OVG design and the NOVG design are about the same.

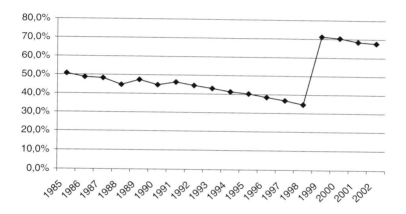

Figure 5: Response Rates Dutch Travel Survey 1985-2002

Because of the parallel run of the old and the new OVG in the last nine months of 1998, the results of OVG 1985-1998 could be corrected and are comparable with those of the NOVG after 1998.

THE PRESENT

New Challenges

In recent years, budget constraints have precluded the funding of the full sample extension by the AVV. As a result of this, the sample size diminished as shown in Table 2 and the reliability of the data at the regional level decreased. At the same time, CBS strategies changed in such a way that they were not able to use the flexibility of the survey design to answer current policy questions. As a result, the AVV decided to start their own travel survey in 2004. This survey is called Mobiliteitsonderzoek Nederland (MON). This new survey is an opportunity to introduce new subjects into the investigation of the mobility of the Dutch population. This opportunity for AVV to use the flexibility of the survey design is a service innovation. More specifically it is a new service concept.

Table 2: Response of Dutch Travel Surveys 1985-2002 in Households and Persons

Year	Households	Persons[11]
1985	9,287	21,201
1986	10,154	22,516
1987	10,170	22,109
1988	10,024	21,294
1989	10,270	21,927
1990	10,139	21,390
1991	9,659	19,852
1992	10,235	21,203
1993	10,029	20,504
1994	34,454	82,835
1995	68,433	167,923
1996	62,785	152,547
1997	60,124	143,979
1998	58,082	137,991
1999	63,336	146,348
2000	64,240	146,528
2001	57,491	130,146
2002	44,058	100,266

In the (N)OVG the data that are sent to end-users are supply-dominated. End-users select desired data from a list of available data. In the new survey, MON, the data are demand-dominated. End-users are able to ask for specific topics or a regional extension of the sample size which satisfies their needs. AVV interacts with the end-users in a more facilitating way. Furthermore, there is an organizational change because AVV will carry out the MON and is, therefore, now responsible for the survey. More information about the MON concept and organisation can be found in van Evert (2004).

The MON differs from its predecessor in the possibilities offered by the extension and follow-up options. There will be no trend break as a result of the transition from the OVG to the MON. The MON will use the same survey design as the OVG since 1999. As an extra, AVV has added two standard follow-up surveys on nonresponse and non-

---

[11] Since 1994 persons younger than 12 years are included.

reported trips. These follow-up surveys are standard in the New KONTIV design, but were not implemented in the OVG.

Fieldwork for the MON started on 1st January 2004. Delivery of the definitive basic survey data file is planned for 1st March 2005. Completion dates for extension and follow-up surveys will be agreed per assignment. MON is now the 'official' Dutch National Travel survey which replaced the OVG.

MON Quality Principles

The new design applied in the MON survey follows nine quality principles which were newly developed for the MON following a new 'quality philosophy'. Such principles were not explicitly used for the OVG before.

Respondents Are 'Customers'

This principle implicitly means that the survey design has to be as respondent-friendly as possible. Respondents must be treated as if they were customers, who can elect to buy or not to buy a product. (In this case, the 'product' is the completion of the travel survey.)

Continuous Improvements

The sections above show clearly that a survey design has to adjust to the times over the years. In three decades, there were three different designs. There is no reason to believe that this has come to an end now.

Fit for the Foreseeable Future

With the need for continuous improvements in mind it is particularly important to have a methodology in place which will withstand foreseeable future developments. Examples of such developments are:

- More reluctance to let strangers (the interviewers) into your home
- Fewer detectable phone numbers and growing resistance to telephone contact;
- Increasing concerns about privacy related to the implementation of 'Orwell-like' IT-technologies; and
- Increasing demand for non-intrusive methods and customer focus in public dealings and surveys.

An attempt has been made to address all of these concerns in the development of the MON-design.

High Response Rates

In every survey the response rate reflects the readiness of the respondents to participate. Thus, the response rate is an excellent indicator of the total quality of the design, and, of all quality indicators, it is the easiest to understand and among the easiest to measure.

Response rates of seventy percent or more of usable returns are achievable; we need to set a lower limit of at least sixty percent. It has to be noted, however, that for a given survey design, a higher response will result in lower travel figures. This is not because late respondents are using the answer 'immobile' as an excuse for not filling in many trips (this effect can be controlled), but because people with difficulties, illnesses, few social contacts, etc. are over-represented in respondents beyond the fifty to sixty percent return rate (Brög and Meyburg, 1981).

Immanent Validation

Every measurement produces its own errors; one hundred percent accurate measurement is not possible. This means that in every survey a mechanism has to be established that controls the most common errors produced by the survey design. In transport research, these are the item nonresponse and unit nonresponse. If it is true that every measurement (e.g., every survey design) produces its own errors, then it is desirable to measure item and unit nonresponse with the same method and not with a different one. In the latter case, it might happen that one compares the artefacts of method A with those of method B instead of the mobility of respondents and non-respondents. Therefore, the MON uses existing tools (self-administered diaries) for specific non-reported trip explorations and for further mailings until a response rate in the vicinity of ninety percent is achieved. It is of great assistance that in a well-controlled self-administered survey the speed of response is an invaluable tool to learn more about early and late respondents and how to project this onto non-respondents. (Brög and Meyburg, 1981).

Total Households

For numerous reasons, the MON design aims to include all household members of all ages. There were reservations about the value of such a concept for a long time, but now it seems to find much greater acceptance with the increasing need for mobility data on children and the elderly.

A number of recent mobility surveys conducted by phone have suffered from the fact that it is impossible to collect mobility information from all household members for the same sample day with a reasonable recall rule. As a consequence, they applied a 'fifty percent rule', meaning that a household is then 'complete' when information on fifty percent of its (adult) members has been collected. Needless to say, this rule introduces selectivity, which seriously affects the quality of these surveys.

In the third phase of the 'MON history', information for children under six was collected separately in a later telephone call. This design has now been further developed and the information about children is collected directly together with the other diaries.

Linked and Unlinked Trips

The question of how to define a trip has occupied transport researchers all over the world. This has resulted in numerous confusing trip definitions presented to respondents. A respondent-orientated survey would use a different approach (and so does the MON). It would determine the respondents' understanding of a trip and if this understanding fits with the aim of the survey. If this understanding fits, it can be used without the need to bother the respondents with a specific definition. It so happens that by 'trip' most respondents understand the so-called 'linked trip' and it is this linked trip that is exactly what the MON wants to collect in its standard part.

That leaves the question open for 'unlinked trips' (stages). Of course there are research and policy needs which could be addressed much better if data on stages were available. Most surveys would now change their design and ask questions about stages. This increases the burden for the respondents, makes it much more difficult for them to understand (because it violates their 'natural' thinking) and leaves the decision on what a stage is to the individual respondents. That results in many different definitions (e.g., in most cases, respondents do not report short stages, or in telephone surveys the interviewer is overwhelmed by the task of deciding on the spot which stages are involved, etc.)

Therefore the MON has a different solution: because stages are only really important when public transport is used, there is a follow-up survey on stages for all respondents with public transport trips. For the other diaries, stage information is collected in a sub-sample.

Attitudes and behaviour

It is a 'golden rule' of behaviour research not to collect attitudes and behaviour in the same stage of a survey or even with the same questionnaire (Brög and Erl, 1985). The New KONTIV®-Design has a specifically designed module for follow-up, in-depth interviews. This is available to MON and will be used in the future. It has numerous advantages, e.g.,

- The filled-in diaries can be taken back to the respondents and used for more realistic questioning;
- In-depth survey methods can be applied which provide better and more valid results than simplified methods; and

- It is possible to ask respondents about their level of information and then to crosscheck with secondary data. This is the only way to get a realistic measure of people's actual information level.

Human beings desperately needed

Data on behaviour for all household members are rather complex. If they are collected in a respondent-friendly way they are in a format which is not directly usable in a computer. The link that is needed is data editing and entering. There have been many attempts to automate the process of editing and entering. To be sure that the data that form the basis of all the complex analyses, models, and forecasts are correct, it is not only unavoidable, but strongly desirable, that this last phase of transforming real life information into computer data files be controlled by well-trained human beings.

THE FUTURE

When, how, where, and why do Dutch people travel? Information about travel behaviour is, and will continue to be, of key importance for policy-makers and researchers. Over the past few years, a trend for more specific and up-to-date information has emerged. Furthermore, policy-makers are attaching progressively more value to the speed and flexibility with which this information can be made available. These developments are set to continue in the years to come and MON, the Dutch Travel Survey has been designed as a response to this trend.

The MON already incorporates three principles, which will be of general importance in the future:

- Flexibility;
- Quality standards; and
- Respondent-orientation.

Flexibility means that there is a survey design that is able to react to demands of the users. In the MON concept, an extension of the sample of the basic survey is possible at any time during the survey, as are special follow-up surveys about transport-related topics, where the basic survey gives a baseline or screening reference (e. g., accidents, mobility-impaired people, etc.).

The MON uses a quality scheme that is specific to it, but is also based on principles that constitute useful general guidelines. The elements of this scheme are:

- Households will be surveyed each day of the year;
- The households are selected randomly;

- Only members of the household living at the sample address are interviewed;
- All members of the household living at the sample address are interviewed;
- The net response rate must be sixty percent for each month. The net response is defined as quotient from:
  - number of usable returned household forms; and
  - number of sample of selected households;
- The share of households responding by phone rather than returning complete surveys via mail must be a maximum of twenty percent of all responding households per month;
- Validation surveys are part of the basic survey for:
  - public transport trips (collecting of stages);
  - problems of completing the forms;
  - nonresponse; and
  - validation of non-reported trips;
- The response rate for the public transport follow-up is at least eighty percent of the respective sample per month (usable returns); and
- The respondents of the survey do not get any incentives.

Some remarks should be added about computer-assisted data collection. 'Computer-assistance' can be found for each of the general survey types mentioned at the beginning. It is appropriate to mention that, even if the computer is not used in the process of interviewing, it can back up other parts of the survey process like sampling, survey administration, data entry, and data control. Thus, the differentiation between computer-assisted and other types of surveys is misleading. New survey technologies, such as Internet-based surveys or surveys employing GSM or GPS technologies, should be considered carefully to determine if they can provide additional information on the total mobility of the population (FGSV, 2003).

Surveys using the Internet (or electronic mail) are again self-administered surveys. They are widespread in market research, but are seldom found in travel behaviour research. A broad application for collecting individual travel behaviour is still missing. The use of a portable computer for collecting travel behaviour requires a high input, in terms of costs and techniques, and provides valid data, but is limited to small samples and respondents who are highly motivated to participate.

Survey methods based on GSM (Global System for Mobile Communication) or GPS (Global Positioning System) can provide information about origin, destination and routing of a trip. They can be combined with separately asked information about the purpose or mode of a trip, which again could be an electronic questionnaire using SMS (Short Message Service), for example. GPS-applications can be found in the travel survey literature, but have been mainly used for collecting information about travel in autos (e.g., vehicle stops, fuel consumption, and emissions by measuring speed, distance and time). The availability and use of personal GPS (not only vehicle-based GPS) is increasing, so GPS applications for personal travel are becoming more feasible. With these systems, once again investment costs for the survey organisation are quite high, the validity of the data is good, but the range of the data is very limited.

In summary, it can be said that, looking into the future, we do not see a technical solution, but the ongoing need to communicate with respondents and treat them as individuals and be as customer-orientated as possible This is the pre-condition for achieving quality and reliability of the data collected.

CLOSING REMARKS

Independently from all available technical advice, the survey remains a communication process. This process will only be successful when it is designed for the respondents; the 'right' motivation of respondents is needed for all respondents in all types of surveys.

Measuring the success of a survey and the reliability of the collected data will become more and more important. The criterion is not standardisation but quality. The key elements concerning quality include the following:

- The response rate achieved;
- The completeness and accuracy of the data;
- The inclusion of all persons in the selected households;
- A control about the results; and
- The validation of the reported travel patterns.

These elements have to be embedded in flexible survey architectures, orientated toward the needs of the data-users and policy-makers, to provide reliable and useful results.

REFERENCES

Axhausen, K. (2000). Definition of Movement and Activity for Transport Modelling. In: *Handbook of Transport Modelling* (D.A. Hensher and K.J. Button, eds) , 271-283, Elsevier Press, Oxford.

Brög, W. and A.H. Meyburg (1981). Consideration of Nonresponse Effects in Large-Scale Mobility Surveys, *Transportation Research Record No. 807*, 39-46.

Brög, W. and E. Erl (1985). The Application of Interactive Measurement Techniques as a Basis for the Forecast of Complex Behavioural Reactions. In: *New Survey Methods in Transport* (E.S. Ampt, A.J. Richardson, and W. Brög eds), 289-307, VNU Science Press BV, Utrecht.

Brög, W. and Winter (1990). *Untersuchung zum Problem der 'non-reported trips' zum Personen-Wirtschaftsverkehr bei Haushaltsbefragungen, Forschung Straßenbau und Straßenverkehrstechnik*, Heft 593, Bonn-Bad Godesberg

Brög, W. (1997). Raising the Standard! Transport Survey Quality and Innovation. In: *Transport Surveys: Raising the Standard* (P.R. Stopher and P.M. Jones, eds), I-A/1-9, Transportation Research Circular Number E-C008, Transportation Research Board, Washington, DC.

Brög, W. and E. Erl (1999). Systematic Errors in Mobility Surveys. Paper presented at the ATRF Conference, Perth.

Brög, W. (2000). The new KONTIV design. Paper for the International Conference on Establishment Surveys, Buffalo, New York, June.

Dillman, D.A. (2000), *Mail and Internet Surveys. The Tailored Design Method,* John Wiley& Sons, Inc., New York.

Evert, H.C. van and G. Moritz (2000). The New Dutch Travel Survey. Paper for the 9th International Association for Travel Behaviour Conference, Gold Coast, Queensland, Australia.

Evert, H.C. van (2004). The Respondent as Customer and the Customer as Respondent, Keynote paper for the International Conference on Travel Survey Methods, Costa Rica, 2004

Ettema, D., H. Timmermans, and L. van Veghel (1996). *Effects of Data Collection Method in Travel and Activity Research,* EIRASS, Eindhoven.

FGSV (2003). *Methoden computergestützter Erhebungen zum individuellen Verkehrsverhalten,* Forschungsgesellschaft für Straßen- und Verkehrswesen, Köln.

Heer, de, W. and G. Moritz (1997). Sampling, Response and Weighting. Data-quality problems in Travel Surveys, an international Overview, *Transport Surveys: Raisign the Standard* (P.R. Stopher and P.M. Jones, eds), II-C/1-21, Transportation Research Circular Number E-C008, Transportation Research Board, Washington, DC.

Madre, J-L., K.W. Axhausen and W. Brög (2004). *Immobility in travel diary surveys: An overview,* Arbeitsbericht Verkehrs- und Raumplanung 207, Institut für Verkehrsplanung und Transportsysteme (IVT), Eidgenössische Technische Hochschule Zürich (ETH), March.

Mangione, T.W. (1995). *Mail Surveys: Improving the Quality,* Sage, Thousand Oaks, CA.

Moritz, G. (1992). *The National Travel Survey in the Netherlands,* Heerlen, July.

Snijkers, G. and M. Luppes (2003). The best of two worlds: Total Design Method and New Kontiv Design. An operational model to improve respondent co-operation, *Netherlands Official Statistics,* **15,** 4 – 10.

4

SURVEY DESIGN

David Kurth, Parsons, Denver, CO, USA
and
Nancy McGuckin, Washington, DC, USA

OVERVIEW

In this chapter, a range of issues in the area of survey design are discussed. This chapter represents the discussions undertaken in a workshop[12] on Survey Design, which was part of the 7th International Conference on Travel Survey Methods, held in Costa Rica in 2004. Specific survey design topics considered include:

1. The number and type of contacts made with potential survey respondents;
2. The applicability of proxy reporting for trips or activities;
3. How to define 'complete' in terms of an individual household survey acceptance;
4. How to properly replace samples lost to non-contact or nonresponse prior to the completion of a household survey;
5. How to adjust or correct for item nonresponse;
6. How to adjust or correct for unit (i.e. entire household) nonresponse;
7. Methods and advice on initial contacts;
8. The use of incentives in household surveys;
9. Methods to measure respondent burden; and
10. The use of survey translations for minority populations.

---

[12] Workshop members were: Alfonzo Castro (Peru), Laverne Dimitrov (South Africa), Henk van Evert (Netherlands), David Kurth (USA), Nancy McGuckin (USA), Marcela Munizaga (Chile), Sharon O'Connor (USA), Christophe Rizet (France), Dorothy Salathiel (UK), Imke Stenmeyer (Germany).

The first nine topics were assigned as part of the charge to the workshop. The tenth topic was added by the workshop members in response to comments from workshop members regarding the challenges posed by different populations with different languages.

Guidance for the workshop deliberations were provided by the conference plenary paper on survey standards and guidelines for travel surveys in the US (Stopher *et al.*, 2006) along with the commissioned workshop resource paper on the history of the Dutch National Travel Survey (van Evert *et al.*, 2006). Those two papers were supplemented by four offered workshop papers. Brief summaries of all six papers are provided in a subsequent section of this chapter.

Contributions of Workshop Papers to Survey Design Discussions

This section provides a brief overview of the commissioned workshop papers along with offered workshop papers that provided important background information for the workshop discussions. The commissioned workshop paper comprises the preceding chapter of this book (chapter 3); the reader is urged to review this chapter in more detail for its contribution both to the workshop and to travel survey design and application in general.

Keynote Paper – 'Household Travel Surveys: Proposed Standards and Guidelines'

The keynote paper summarised proposed standards and guidelines being developed as part of a National Cooperative Highway Research Program (NCHRP) study. Based on this paper, specific questions were presented for consideration by all conference workshops:

- Can there be an agreed upon set of standards and guidelines listed in the draft NCHRP study?
- Are the standards applicable multi-nationally and, if not, how should they be changed to be more generally applicable?
- Are there other standards and guidelines that should be considered?

Commissioned Workshop Paper – 'Survey Design: The Past, the Present and the Future'

The commissioned paper for the Survey Design Workshop described the evolution of the Dutch National Travel Survey from its inception in 1978 to present. In response to increasing costs and decreasing response rates, the survey has evolved over the past twenty-six years in the following manner:

- 1978-1984: Face-to-face surveys requiring two interviewer visits to each participating household were conducted. Household and two-day travel diaries were distributed on the first visit and collected on the second visit.
- 1985-1998: Telephone-based recruiting coupled with mail-out/mail-back surveys were performed. Household data were collected during the telephone portion of the survey. Self-enumeration travel diaries were then mailed to respondents. Respondents mailed completed diaries back to the survey administrators.
- 1999-2004: The German New KONTIV® Design (NKD) was employed as the survey method. The NKD survey consists of simple, user-friendly written questionnaires for households and individual household members with few predetermined response categories. This design places the burden for interpretation on the surveyor, not the respondent. The telephone is used in the NKD survey as an instrument to motivate respondents.
- 2004: The NKD design was enhanced to provide more opportunities for extension and follow-up surveys. The new survey is called Mobiliteitsonderzoek Nederland (MON).

The MON survey uses nine quality principles:

- Respondents are 'customers', so the surveys should be as respondent friendly as possible.
- Continuous improvement must be made to surveys to adjust to the times over the years.
- Flexibility for the future must be provided, with an eye towards new technologies to improve surveys.
- High response rates are required to maintain quality; response rates of at least sixty percent are set as the lower limit with response rates of seventy percent or higher being the goal.
- Validation is included in the design of the survey to monitor and reduce item and unit nonresponse.
- All members of the household are included in the survey to reduce nonresponse and account for all travel.
- As a respondent-orientated survey, respondents are allowed to use their own understanding of a 'trip'. Typically, this understanding parallels a 'linked' trip. Information on unlinked trips as defined by transportation planners is collected in follow-up surveys.
- In accordance with the 'golden rule' of behavioural research, attitudes and behaviour are not collected in the same survey. In-depth, follow-up surveys are used to collect attitudes.
- The use of well-trained interviewers and coders is crucial to the design since complex travel data are collected in a respondent-friendly manner. Thus, data editing and data entry by well-trained individuals provides the mechanism for consistent recording of travel.

Offered Workshop Paper – 'The Santiago TASTI Survey (Time Assignment Travel And Income)'

This workshop paper by Jara-Diaz *et al.* (2004) described a detailed survey of Santiago workers used for detailed analyses of worker activity patterns. Specifically, this 322-person survey focused on middle income Central Business District (CBD) workers who travelled in a specific corridor. The self-administered diary survey was designed to obtain detailed information on how workers allocated time to work and other 'unpleasant' activities versus pleasurable and utilitarian activities for a detailed analysis of value of time.

A review of documented international experience in travel surveys was undertaken prior to the design of the TASTI survey. The review was useful for the design of a survey that obtained a high response rate (valid information was obtained for 290 individuals for a response rate of over ninety percent) and a detailed and reliable experimental database that included disaggregated and detailed income data. The direct cost for the survey was only about US$10 per respondent.

The authors concluded that the creative combination of different survey methods, that considered previous experience, allowed for the collection of all required information for the study. The data collection had seemed overly ambitious at the beginning stages of the study.

Offered Workshop Paper – 'The Effects of Monetary Incentives on Response Rates and Sample Bias'

This workshop paper by Salathiel and Nicolaas (2004) described the results of a six-month experiment to test the impact of monetary incentives on response rates for the British National Travel Survey (British NTS). Like many large scale surveys, response rates for the British NTS have been falling in recent years. The British NTS is a seven-day travel diary that all household members must complete for a survey to be considered complete. The experiment tested two different levels of incentive payments (£5 and £10).

The following conclusions were reached:

- There was a significant and large rise in response rates using the £5 incentive, caused by a reduction in refusals and a shift from partial responses;
- The additional increase in response rates resulting from the payment of the £10 incentive was not significant;
- Incentives improved the representativeness of the survey in terms of average household size, single-parent families, age, ethnicity, and marital status;
- Incentives led to significant shifts in the distributions of personal mileage, travel purpose, and travel mode; and

- Increasing the sample size to match the increase in completed samples was estimated to be about twice the cost of using a £5 incentive.

Offered Workshop Paper – 'Sources and Impacts of Nonresponse in Household Travel Surveys: Three Case Studies'

This paper by Contrino and Liss (2004) also addressed the problem of declining survey response rates by reviewing recent US surveys conducted in Ohio, Atlanta, and Phoenix. The paper focused on the populations under-represented (due to low response rates) and the impacts caused by that under-representation. The review of the surveys suggested that African-American, Hispanic, and Native American populations were typically under-represented in travel surveys along with fifteen to nineteen and thirty four to forty four year old age groups.

The under-representation of the various populations tended to cause the under-representation of trips made on transit, by walking and by bicycle. The under-represented populations also, in general, tended to have lower trip rates.

The paper suggested several techniques to combat the problem of nonresponse, including:

- Over-sampling of selected population groups that are typically under-represented in travel surveys;
- The use of alternative strategies for recruitment and retrieval of data from selected population groups; and
- Employment of post-survey stratified weighting techniques to account for the under-representativeness of different population groups.

Offered Workshop Paper – 'South Africa's First National Travel Survey '

This workshop paper by Lombard and Dimitrov (2004) describes the first South African National Travel Survey (South African NTS) performed in 2002. The call for and planning for a South African NTS started in 1986. However, due to the diverse populations that needed to be included in the survey and the associated costs with surveying those populations, substantial planning and pilot testing took place between 1988 and 1999.

Any data collection in South Africa is challenging:

'…It has to cater for the wide diversity within South Africa's population that constitutes its rainbow nation. Life circumstances, educational and employment opportunities, living conditions and access to infrastructure differ greatly within the country by race, gender and urban or rural place of residence'. (Hirschowitz, 2003)

The challenge of developing a survey for South Africa might be best understood simply by considering the language requirements. There are eleven official languages in South Africa and interviewers had to be fluent in English, because the questionnaire was developed in English. In addition to having the ability to translate the questionnaire into an official language, interviewers had to have the ability to translate the questionnaire into the vernacular used by the population group being surveyed. Transport terms such as 'mode of travel' do not exist in most of the African languages.

Other General Survey Background

A number of countries were represented in the survey design workshop. Workshop members provided background on the surveys performed in their home countries. The summaries below are very brief and are only meant to provide some basis for understanding the recommendations of the workshop regarding the three questions posed to all workshops in the keynote paper (Stopher *et al.*, 2006).

Chile

One of the biggest problems encountered in travel surveys in Chile is nonresponse by high income households. High income citizens are more likely to live in gated communities making the acquisition of a full sample frame of addresses for face-to-face interviews difficult.

France

The French NTS design includes a large-scale household survey every five years combined with a continuous small-sample panel survey.

Germany

The design of German National Travel Survey (German NTS) is under review. Specifically, questions regarding the continued use of the KONTIV design or changing to a design that makes increased use of the telephone is being debated. The German NTS tested a mixed method of calling and mail-back of surveys in 2001. Concerns regarding data quality and response rates are being investigated.

Netherlands

The Dutch NTS is described in van Evert *et al.*(2004). One of the difficulties encountered with the Dutch NTS is nonresponse in large cities, especially among non-Dutch nationalities and ethnic groups. The Dutch NTS is administered only in Dutch. The need for surveys in Turkish, Arabic, French and other languages has been identified.

In addition to the response issues with non-Dutch nationalities and ethnic groups, the Dutch NTS is working to reduce item nonresponse. As with many surveys, the collection of income information has been problematic. An attempt has been made to obtain the income information through tax records but privacy issues have precluded the use of this method to obtain income data.

Peru

Sample design is difficult in Peru. Peru does not have a regular census and the most recent census is more than ten years old. The fourth Metro area survey was conducted for Lima in 2004. The first Peru NTS was also scheduled for 2004.

United Kingdom

As mentioned in the workshop paper by Salathiel and Nicolaas (2004), response rates and unit nonresponse have been issues being addressed in the British NTS. Response rates are problems at both ends of the income spectrum, especially in London and other metropolitan areas. Similar to the experience reported in Chile, completing surveys of high income households, living in housing estates requiring the use of security phones for visitor access, presents a problem. Also, as in the Netherlands and South Africa, language barriers often present problems to surveyors. Quite frequently, children living in the household are called upon to translate the surveys for adult members of the household.

United States

One of the biggest problems with the US National Household Travel Survey (NHTS) is nonresponse of specific groups of people. As in other countries, nonresponse from low- and high-income households presents a particular problem. Nonresponse from specific groups of people such as American Indians living on reservations and new immigrants also poses a problem. The design of the US NHTS does not reflect the practices suggested by the KONTIV design used in Germany and the Netherlands since the US NHTS is not respondent-orientated. However, some KONTIV design techniques are used; trained telephone interviewers fit survey responses into categories and definitions (such as the definition of a 'trip'). The Spanish language version of the US NHTS was used for the first time in 2001.

SYNOPSIS OF WORKSHOP DELIBERATIONS

The workshop used the three questions, discussed above, to guide its deliberations. It must be recognised that the deliberations were based on the assumption that telephone-based or mail-out/mail-back surveys define standard survey procedures – at least for the

NCHRP project to set standards for surveys in the US that formed the basis for the key-note paper. Thus, obvious overarching questions for all of the workshop deliberations were whether or not US survey standards could be used in international settings and, in fact, whether or not standards can be set for other survey-types that are used in international settings.

With the above background in mind, summaries of discussions regarding each of the nine specific survey design questions listed in the overview of this workshop report are presented below.

The Number and Type of Contacts Made With Potential Survey Respondents

Guiding Principle for Discussions: Many contacts of potential survey respondents in different forms for reminders and motivation is a good survey practice.

As a reference, the potential NCHRP standards suggest five to seven contacts starting with an advance letter being sent to potential respondents at least one week prior to recruitment. Final contacts are dependent upon the survey method. For mail-back surveys, they include a post-card reminder to mail completed surveys two days after the assigned survey day and a telephone reminder six days after the assigned survey. For telephone collection surveys, the final contact is the initial contact to collect the survey data one day after the assigned survey day.

Workshop members agreed that making numerous contacts in different forms for reminders and motivation was a good guideline to follow. The ideal of multiple contacts is built into a number of survey designs, especially well established survey designs such as those based on the German KONTIV design. The KONTIV design is a mail-out/mail-back type of survey that stresses customer (respondent) support and motivation. Nevertheless, even with the KONTIV design, strict standards are not set. Rather, since the design focuses on treating the respondent as a customer, the number of contacts is determined to some degree by respondent needs. The NHTS (US) has a standard of nine attempts for first contact of sample numbers, but, once the sample has been determined to be an eligible household, a larger number of contacts may be required to obtain a survey.

Other stumbling blocks to establishing a specific set of standards were identified. In those countries where surveys were administered or, at least, distributed face-to-face, limited numbers of contacts were made. For example, in the South Africa NTS, the planned Peru NTS, the British NTS, and the Santiago TASTI survey, a pamphlet or brochure was left with households, or an introductory letter was mailed prior to the initial contact by the surveyor. After the initial introductory contact, all remaining contacts are those required by the interviewer to collect the travel survey data.

Thus, while there was much agreement regarding the importance of multiple contacts, the need to develop a set of standards, let alone specific sets of standards, was not clear. The numbers and types of contacts must consider the type of survey being performed along with the needs of the customers.

The Applicability of Proxy Reporting for Trips or Activities

Guiding Principles for Discussions: Ensure that researchers can identify whether or not a survey is self-reported or reported by a proxy. Self-reporting is desired but flexibility is necessary based upon the situation.

Workshop members reported that proxy reporting of trips for certain populations was standard practice for travel surveys in their countries. Some groups listed as being acceptable for proxy reporting include the young, the elderly, and the mentally or physically disabled. Different minimum ages were identified for allowable proxy reporting in the various countries represented. For example, in South Africa, proxy reports were not accepted for respondents of age fifteen or older. In the UK, children aged eleven or older were assumed to be capable of completing their own travel diaries, while in the US the assumption was thirteen years and older. In Germany, special survey questionnaires were developed for children aged six or older; proxy reporting was used only for children under the age of six.

It was agreed that local mores and customs must be considered in determinations regarding the use of proxy reporting. The use of self-reporting should be encouraged.

How to Define 'Complete' In Terms of Individual Household Survey Acceptance

Guiding Principles for Discussions: Standards regarding this issue are closely related to those for proxy reporting. The objective for surveys should be to have every household member respond and every survey question to be completed.

The issue of 'complete' households is greatly impacted by standards regarding the imputation of missing data for household members, trips, or activities. Imputation of missing data to complete households was a subject that could not be discussed adequately within the time limits of the survey workshop. Different countries permit different levels of data imputation. One primary area of discussion was whether data imputation provided a net gain or a net loss for the survey. In other words, did the imputation of data to save more partially complete households add more bias to the survey than losing households due to a one hundred percent reporting requirement?

Standards defining complete household surveys varied by country. In the United Kingdom, Germany, and the Netherlands, one hundred percent of all household members are required to report for a survey to be complete. In contrast, the US NHTS requires only fifty percent of adult household members to report for a survey to be considered to be complete. Analysis of past surveys in the US found limiting a complete household to one hundred percent of household members biased the resulting sample by including fewer large, (e.g., Hispanic), households.

In France and Denmark, sample selection is based on individuals. In France, one, two, or three people are selected from each household for the survey. In Denmark, individuals are selected as the survey participant and household information for other household members is collected from the selected individual. Because of the widely varying practices regarding survey completion criteria, proxy reporting, and the imputation of data, no recommendations regarding completion standards could be made. However, there was general agreement that efforts should be made to obtain one hundred percent reporting and limit proxy reports.

How to Replace Samples Lost to Non-Contact or Nonresponse Properly Prior to the Completion of a Household Survey

Guiding Principle for Discussions: Sample replacement is a survey concern that must be addressed for surveys with quotas.

Proper sample replacement is an issue in surveys that are not performed on a regular basis. In the US, regional household surveys performed every ten to fifteen years for major metropolitan areas are examples of these types of surveys. A key issue to address in these types of surveys is the selection of a sufficiently large sample of households to produce the desired sample size considering anticipated sample loss through nonresponse and non-contact. In the US NHTS, sample lists are updated quarterly (in a one-year collection period), and the sample is managed closely to balance response rates and to obtain the full number of attempts for each listing.

Sample replacement was not a major concern in countries where continuous surveys are administered. In the UK and the Netherlands, surveys are administered continually. In the UK, an annual sample is selected and surveyors receive twenty two addresses to contact each month. In the Netherlands, sample addresses are drawn monthly to keep the addresses up-to-date and minimize sample loss.

Sample replacement was not a major concern of the workshop members. No recommendations or guidelines were suggested.

How to Adjust or Correct for Item Nonresponse

Guiding Principle for Discussions: All data items should be appropriately coded (response, skipped, don't know, refused) with no blanks. Item nonresponse should be meas-

ured in a consistent manner, either by singular items (income) and/or by an index of key questions that are vital as inputs to the models or vital to stakeholders.

Item nonresponse is also a quality assurance-quality control (QA/QC) issue for travel surveys. Two commonly used measures of quality used for comparisons across surveys are the proportion of people (or households) reporting no travel on the survey day and the proportion of households not reporting income.

In the short-term, the impact of item nonresponse might be subjective based on the issues of importance to the survey. For example, if the survey data will be used to estimate cross-classification trip generation models based on car ownership and household size, item nonresponse for income might not be a major concern. However, in the long-term, all item nonresponse can be an issue in travel surveys, because future topics that may be addressed using the data cannot always be identified at the time of the survey.

The Netherlands provides an example of the importance that should be placed on reducing item nonresponse. As has been mentioned previously, the Netherlands uses an extension of the NKD survey which employs simple, user-friendly written questionnaires with few predetermined response categories for households and individual household members. The NKD survey places the burden for interpretation on the surveyor, not the respondent, and the telephone is used as an instrument to motivate respondents. Yet, even with the emphasis on a user-friendly survey design that places much of the burden on the surveyor, item nonresponse is a concern and is monitored. As is typical with survey designs in many countries, households are re-contacted to complete missing information.

While there was much agreement regarding the importance of reducing item nonresponse, no consensus on the development of a set of standards was reached. International survey efforts vary from well established surveys such as those performed in the Netherlands to first-time efforts such as the South African NTS. Standards for item nonresponse vary based on the type of survey being performed, the proposed use of the data being collected, and the needs of the customers.

How to Adjust or Correct for Unit (Entire Household) Nonresponse

Guiding Principle for Discussions: Unit nonresponse is a significant and growing problem in household travel surveys. Nonresponse error is a function of the nonresponse rate and the difference between respondents and nonrespondents on the statistic of interest. A lower unit nonresponse rate is desired because this reduces the incidence of nonresponse bias.

Unit nonresponse was not explicitly addressed other than through the discussions on proxy reporting, the definition of complete households, and sample replacement.

Methods and Advice on Initial Contacts

Guiding Principle for Discussions: The success of the first contact of potential respondents is crucial to the reduction of unit nonresponse. The primary need for initial contacts is to design an introduction to surveys in such a fashion that refusals are avoided as much as possible.

The issue of initial contacts was addressed as part of the discussion of the number and types of contacts that should be made with potential survey respondents. Due to the different methods used for surveys, no consensus was reached on standards for initial contacts in an international setting. In developed countries where surveys are well established such as Germany, the Netherlands, the UK, and the US, initial contact procedures are also relatively well developed, especially for NTS type surveys.

However, in countries where travel surveys are not well established such as South Africa and Peru, the initial contact is just one of many issues that must be addressed in conducting a travel survey. In those two countries, the importance of the initial contact has been recognised and attempts have been made to get survey information to potential respondents prior to the initial contact by a surveyor.

The Use of Incentives in Household Surveys

Guiding Principle for Discussions: Incentives provide a means to reduce nonresponse to travel surveys. Types of incentives, payment methods, and effectiveness of incentives in reducing nonresponse vary.

The workshop paper by Salathiel and Nicolaas showed that cash incentives were quite effective in increasing response rates in the United Kingdom. Small, non-monetary incentives were used for the Santiago TASTI survey. The use of a larger non-monetary incentive, an entry in a lottery to win a trip, was rejected by a focus group as too frivolous for academic research. Incentives were not used in either the South African NTS or the Dutch NTS. The use of incentives has been a generally accepted procedure for increasing response rates in the US.

While the use of incentives in household surveys was discussed, no conclusions were reached regarding their general applicability and standards for their use in surveys. The impact of incentive use varied from being instrumental in increasing response rates to not being required for increasing response rates.

Methods to Measure Respondent Burden

Guiding Principle for Discussions: Respondent burden is both tangible and intangible. The US Office of Management and Budget (OMB) defines respondent burden as the 'time, effort, or financial resources' expended by the public to provide information to or for a federal agency. At a minimum, respondent burden should be reported at the household level to permit comparison across alternatives.

In the Netherlands, the measurement of respondent burden would need to be linked to interest in the statistic. Other measures, such as unit nonresponse and complaints received, are used to evaluate the 'burden' of the travel surveys on the respondent. The expenditure of time and effort measuring respondent burden was deemed to out-weigh any benefit from measuring the statistic. In addition, one of the bases of the KONTIV design is the minimisation of respondent burden.

In the UK, the CAPI techniques automatically recorded interview time, but respondent burden for completing travel diaries was not recorded. The average time for completing the main interview is maintained at about one hour by removing some questions whenever new questions are added. In the US, the time to complete the survey is frequently recorded by survey firms as a method for budgeting surveys. However, these measurements ignore the respondent burden for completing travel diaries. Respondent burden was, however, measured and reported in the US NHTS at the behest of the US OMB.

The measurement of respondent burden could provide information for analysing whether respondents under-report travel or change their travel behaviour to reduce the amount of burden. In one US survey, monitoring of the telephone collection of travel information yielded a startling report from one respondent. In the course of the survey collection, the respondent reported that she decided to postpone an activity to the day after her survey day since she was tired of filling out the travel diary. Thus, it is possible that some decreased amount of travel typically attributed to nonresponse or under-reporting is actually suppressed travel caused by respondent burden. The general measurement of respondent burden for different travel surveys might provide the data necessary to determine whether response rates are affected by respondent burden.

While the measurement of respondent burden could provide some interesting information to researchers, there was no consensus that the data should be collected. Basic arguments against expending the time and effort to collect respondent burden data were:

- It is difficult to measure;
- Other measures, such as unit nonresponse and complaints, can be used to determine whether the survey design is too burdensome; and
- It is unclear whether or not there is an interest in the data by the users of the travel survey data. Decision makers are interested in statistics such as trip rates, time spent travelling, modes used, not the amount of time spent completing the survey.

The Use of Survey Translations for Minority Populations

Guiding Principle for Discussions: Potential respondents cannot participate in a travel survey if they cannot understand the survey. Survey nonresponse can be greatly affected by the availability of survey forms in the respondent's native language. However, the costs associated with translating surveys into multiple languages might preclude the translations.

Language is a basic problem in travel surveys. The South African NTS is indicative of the complications caused by multiple languages in some countries. The South African NTS was printed only in English but was translated by surveyors as necessary to survey respondents. This was deemed to be more effective and efficient than attempting to translate the written survey instrument into each of eleven official languages, especially because terms such as 'mode of travel' do not exist in many of the languages.

Similar difficulties are reported in most countries represented in the workshop:

- In the Netherlands, surveys are printed only in Dutch even though the need has been identified for surveys in Turkish, Arabic, and French;
- In Peru, the NTS will be printed only in Spanish. As in South Africa, bilingual interviewers will be used to administer the survey in languages other than Spanish; and
- In the US, the NTS included a Spanish version for the first time in 2001. However, in some regions, there is a need for French or Southeast Asian versions of the survey.

The translation of survey instruments can be overwhelming in some countries. In other countries, only a small number of translations would be required to enhance response rates for some population groups. No standards regarding, say, sizes of population groups triggering the need for a special translation, have been set.

RECOMMENDATIONS

At the present time, the international adoption of survey standards and guidelines is unlikely. In the international setting, large differences exist in survey methods and the cultures being surveyed. At the same time, many of the standards proposed for the conference keynote paper are very method and culture specific. Thus, the specification of international survey standards is a long-term goal.

While international survey standards are not currently recommended, the publication of international survey 'principles' should be considered. The standards suggested in the conference keynote paper provide a starting point for the development of international survey principles. However, they must be supplemented with principles guiding other survey designs such as face-to-face interviews and the KONTIV design.

REFERENCES

Contrino, H. and S. Liss (2004). Sources and Impacts of Nonresponse in Household Travel Surveys: Three Case Studies. Paper presented at the ISCTSC Seventh International Conference on Travel Survey Methods, Costa Rica, August.

Hirschowitz, R. (2003). Planning and Managing a Household Survey and a Population Census in a Multicultural and Multilingual Context. In: *Transport Survey Quality and Innovation* (P.R. Stopher and P.M. Jones eds), Pergamon Press, Oxford, 39-47.

Jara-Diaz, S.R., M.A. Munizaga, and C. Palma (2004). The Santiago TASTI Survey (Time Assignment Travel and Income). Paper presented at the ISCTSC Seventh International Conference on Travel Survey Methods, Costa Rica, August.

Lombard, M. and L. Dimitrov (2004). South Africa's First National Travel Survey. Paper presented at the ISCTSC Seventh International Conference on Travel Survey Methods, Costa Rica, August.

Salathiel, D. and G. Nicolaas (2004). The Effects of Monetary Incentives on Response Rates and Sample Bias. Paper presented at the ISCTSC Seventh International Conference on Travel Survey Methods, Costa Rica, August.

Stopher, P.R., C.G. Wilmot, C.C. Stecher, and R. Alsnih (2006). Household Travel Surveys: Proposed Standards and Guidelines. In: *Transport Survey Methods – Quality and Future Directions* (P.R. Stopher and C.C. Stecher eds), 19-74, Elsevier, Oxford.

van Evert, H., W. Brög, and E. Erl (2004). Survey Design: The Past, the Present and the Future. In: *Transport Survey Methods – Quality and Future Directions* (P.R. Stopher and C.C. Stecher eds), 75-93, Elsevier, Oxford.

5

SAMPLE DESIGN AND TOTAL SURVEY ERROR

Mira Paskota, University of Belgrade, Belgrade, Serbia

INTRODUCTION

All phases of survey research are closely related and in a way subordinated to the re-search goal. The same goes for the sample. We can easily say that survey results and the quality of collected data depend directly on the quality of the sample; we can also say that sample design must be co-ordinated with the type of survey for a specific study; again, this depends largely on research goals.

Every survey is basically a very complex process. Travel surveys are even more complex than public opinion surveys, or surveys in marketing, or other areas. What makes travel surveys so complex is the larger number of dimensions than in other survey areas. For example, in non-transport surveys, spatial information is used mainly to define geo-graphic areas, within which subpopulations do not have to be homogenous based on relevant indicators. On the other hand, in travel surveys, spatial information is given a new, essentially different meaning. Traffic circulates in the study area; hence, differ-ently defined geographic areas or urban zones, as well as modes of their interconnec-tions, become the subject of the survey.

However, let us go back to the beginning and ask why we need a sample. What interests every researcher the most is to find out something new about the population, not about the sample. And yet, the sample is discussed much more than the population. There are very few cases where the researcher has the opportunity to analyse the whole popula-tion, and such a survey is called a census. In travel surveys, total population analysis is rarely required and truly justified.

One should constantly keep in mind that every researcher, no matter what she or he does with the sample, actually wants to draw conclusions about the population. If the population were entirely homogeneous, it would be irrelevant as to which part of it we are examining, we would always get the same results. However, all real populations are far from being homogeneous, and it is of great importance for us that the part we are examining adequately describes the totality about which we want to talk, draw conclusions, and perhaps make decisions. When we say adequate, we mean that the diversity of the total population should be represented to the same degree in one selected part of it – the sample. The sample that reaches this goal we call representative.

The sample is always a compromise between the wish or need for the data to be as accurate as possible, and the costs of collecting them. During sampling, a statistician cannot be guided by purely theoretical reasons, but must take reality and the limitations of various kind into account. The smallest possible sample error, which typically requires large samples, is of supreme importance for every survey. On the other hand, the budget available tends to limit the size of the sample.

SAMPLE DESIGN AND OTHER ASPECTS OF TRAVEL SURVEYS

Influence of Survey Mode on the Sample

Sample design is closely connected with the way researchers intend to collect data, that is, with the chosen survey mode. Choice of survey mode is mainly influenced by the goals of the survey, target population characteristics, size and complexity of the questionnaire, as well as limited resources, whether measured in money, staff, time, or equipment. Various forms of surveys are sensitive to different kinds of errors that can occur in the course of taking a survey, and they are discussed in the next sections of this chapter. All this has direct effects on the sample.

Traditional methods of interviewing are:

- Mail survey;
- Telephone survey; and
- Face-to-face survey.

Due to the rapid development of computers, there have been significant changes in this field during the past twenty five years. Some new methods of interviewing have been developed, and traditional methods have suffered significant changes. First to appear was CATI as a modification of the telephone survey and CAPI as a modification of the face-to-face survey. Then came CASI (Computer-Assisted Self-Interviewing) and ACASI

(Audio Computer-Assisted Self-Interviewing). Internet surveys have been very popular lately, and some experts claim them to be the survey method of the future. Also, a large number of various combinations of different interviewing types have appeared. All of them, along with other factors, have influenced sample design.

From a sampling viewpoint, what is crucial is the first contact and the motivation for respondents to participate in the survey. Of course, the possibility of communication between the interviewer and the respondent depends directly on the type of survey. Mail as a type of interviewing is highly impersonal, so the communication possibility is minimal. As a consequence, with mail surveys the response rate is lowest. Face-to-face surveys provide the interviewer with the best possibilities for communication, but only under the condition that the contact has been made. This problem cannot be discussed without mentioning huge differences that exist among particular countries.

Advantages and Disadvantages of Some Survey Modes

When listing advantages and disadvantages of the best-known survey modes, we have paid special attention to the huge differences that exist among countries, relative to this.

Mail Survey

This was the dominant survey mode at the very beginning of survey research, and has maintained the leading position for a long time. This was probably a consequence of the fact that people had more time, and their mailboxes were less occupied with junk mail than today.

The sole advantage of mail surveys is that they are relatively cheap and do not require a large number of trained staff. However, a great disadvantage is the possibility of coverage error and low response rate. Address lists are difficult to obtain and often unreliable. These problems occur in many countries to a varying extent and for various reasons; however, they are significant everywhere. Lists of the general population with addresses are publicly available in no country, so researchers manage in various ways, by using phone books, electoral rolls, membership lists from all sorts of associations, and similar sources. These sorts of lists miss a large part of the population as a rule, and usually are out of date.

Some other flaws of mail surveys are: the degree of interest of respondents for the survey topic strongly influences the response rate, and this introduces a large bias that is uncontrollable. There is no control about who fills in the questionnaire, if it is the person it was addressed to, or someone else. It is not possible to control whether the questionnaire is filled in correctly and completely. Also, one should not forget that, in some countries, there still exists the problem of illiteracy.

Telephone Survey

In highly developed countries, where telephone penetration is extremely high, for years this has been, and still to a great extent is, a dominant survey mode. It is convenient for a number of reasons. These surveys are much faster than face-to-face and mail surveys. Use of RDD (Random Digit Dialling) enables design of a high quality sample for the given frame, as well as anonymity. The participation of interviewers brings significant control into the interviewing process. Use of CATI systems enables simultaneous control of the course of the survey, data entry, data control, and immediate accessibility in the desired format.

The general limitation of telephone surveys lies in the fact that it is not practical for very long questionnaires or diary surveys, which are both relatively common in travel surveys. Other problems with telephone surveys vary between developed and less developed countries. In less developed countries there is still the problem of noncoverage due to low telephone penetration, especially in rural areas – a problem long since forgotten in developed countries. However, in developed countries, the non-coverage problem is now coming back, but for different reasons and in quite a different form. In the past few years, an interesting phenomenon has been observed in highly developed countries – a growing number of households, mainly young couples and individuals, do not use land lines at home, but only mobile phones. Since these individuals are much more mobile than the average population, this kind of noncoverage could cause serious problems when travel surveys are considered. Experience in some countries has shown that surveys on mobile phones are not practical, making this an issue of high current interest which has not been solved in a satisfactory manner.

Face-to Face Survey

The face-to-face (FTF) survey was and remains the traditional and still unsurpassed mode of survey. This is the only way to take a survey among a non-listed population. It enables completion of the longest and most complex questionnaires, possibly demanding some additional material to display to respondents (visual aids and similar). The presence of the interviewer ensures correct filling in. The application of CAPI methodology and lap-top computers bring all the advantages of telephone CATI surveys to the face-to-face survey. It is extremely convenient for general population surveys and multistage samples.

One serious disadvantage of this survey mode is its high cost. The most common form of this survey mode is the FTF household survey. This survey mode demands that the interviewer strictly observes the rules of household selection and selection of individuals within it, as well as rigorous control of field work. Some of the well-known problems related to FTF household surveys are that nonresponse differs drastically in urban and rural areas, and that smaller households are undersampled as a rule. There are huge differences among countries about the possibility of entering the household and establishing first contact. In highly developed countries, especially in urban and exclusive residential parts, it is very difficult to enter the household, unlike less developed countries in which this problem rarely exists.

Internet Surveys

The majority of so-called 'surveys' one often sees on the Internet have no sample control whatsoever, and cannot be regarded as suitable for serious research. This, of course, does not mean that it would be impossible to organise a serious survey on the Internet, but such a project would take much more planning, rigorous control, and much, much more work than is currently typical. Internet surveys call for extreme caution. At the moment, high quality Internet surveys are possible only for very narrow and specific populations, for whom an appropriate frame is available, and for which there is confidence about their having regular access to Internet, such as a university population or the population of employees in a company.

For general population surveys, and travel surveys belong to these, the Internet in general is still not an appropriate survey method. However, in the cases when frame choice and sampling are done without the Internet, then among others, Internet could be offered to the respondent as a completion method. In that case, as usual with combinations of the data collection methods, one should take care of the measurement error because of the differences between self-administered questionnaires and questionnaires completed by the interviewer.

Convenient Combinations of Survey Modes

In less developed countries, due to the low penetration of the telephone network, relatively low nonresponse with FTF surveys and easy access to households, face-to-face is typically the best survey mode for the general population, provided that there is enough professional staff at disposal. In developed countries, the situation is quite different, and it is difficult to give general recommendations for an ideal survey mode. Because of the disadvantages listed for the best-known survey modes, the decision has to be made individually for each study. One of the options, which is most often resorted to, is combining various modes of data collection in one survey.

Combinations of survey modes take advantage of the strengths of two or more survey modes, while reducing their disadvantages. For instance, with the telephone survey, the problem of non-coverage can be resolved by FTF interviewing of the respondents that have no telephone. Telephone is also often used to reduce nonresponse in mail surveys. After a while, respondents that have not returned surveys are reminded by phone and asked to do so. Other combinations are also possible, such as mail invitation to participate in a web survey, telephone announcement and scheduling of FTF interviews, among others.

The survey mode is directly related to the available sample frame. For telephone surveys, the most natural choice of frame is random digit dialling, the telephone directory being an unsuitable sampling frame. Face-to-face household surveys require an address listing. In multimode surveys, caution is advised in cases when the same questionnaire is used in one way on one part of the population, and in another way on the rest of the population, because measurement error could differ significantly and bring in significant bias.

IMPORTANCE OF THE SAMPLE FRAME

The sample frame is a group of elements (households or persons) that qualify for being chosen for the sample. The sample can be representative only if the frame equals the population, i.e., if there is no coverage error. Such ideal frames are seldom available. Probability sampling, and that is the only kind we are dealing with in this chapter, implies that each element (household or person) has a known probability to be included in the sample. With simple random sampling, those probabilities are equal for each element; however, with some other samples, as we are about to see, those probabilities are not necessarily equal. Therefore, the sampling frame consists only of the elements with known probabilities to be chosen for a sample.

Although all the surveys begin with an idea that the sample should represent the population, one should bear in mind that the sample can represent only the sample frame, and that those elements that are outside the frame cannot be found in the sample either. When general populations are considered, such as populations for household surveys, the persons who are usually left outside the frame are: soldiers, individuals living in dormitories, prisons, nursing homes, or some other social institution, and homeless people.

The frame usually represents the list of population elements. In order to make a list good enough to be used as a sample frame, several conditions have to be met. The sample frame must:

- Cover the population as well as possible;
- Exclude duplicates; and
- Exclude non-population elements (meaning that all the elements of the list are population elements).

The frame could also be a geographic map or city map. If, along with geographically defined entities, there is also a list containing information about them, we are talking about a standard frame. If information about the entity is not given, only an area probability sample is applicable.

In many cases, lists are formed based on several sources, by combining a larger number of lists, containing similar information on different elements. This occurs as a result of efforts to reduce non-coverage, but could easily introduce another problem – duplicates and elements that do not belong in the population existing in the list. Duplicates can be eliminated through a process of careful examination of the list, whereas elements that do not belong in the target population can be identified and removed using screening during the field work.

In some surveys, phone books of different areas, electoral lists, home ownership lists, some club membership lists, and similar could be used as the frame. However, for general populations, such frames are basically wrong, because they leave a large part of the population uncovered and are often out of date. This is especially the case with phone books and various membership lists, where a large number of population elements are missing and some of them are duplicated or entered multiple times. This is the reason why they are not recommended as frames for travel surveys. In some cases, the aim of the first part of the survey is to produce a reliable list of households from fieldwork, that would form the frame used for the subsequent sampling. However, surveys that do this are very rare, due to the high costs of such fieldwork.

It is very important to list everything that has been used as the frame when producing a sample design for each individual sample, thus focusing attention on possible causes of coverage error. For the final sample estimate, details of the process are necessary, as well as the response rate.

As described above, obtaining an appropriate list for the frame could prove challenging; therefore, on some occasions it would make sense to ask if it would be better to choose a frame without the list. One alternative to a frame-based sample is an area probability sample. With this type of sample, geographically defined areas are used as the basis, which are, due to the lack of other sorts of data, chosen with probabilities that are proportional to their area size.

Survey Process and the Possibility of Error

One of the first steps in designing a survey, right after the survey goals are defined, is to determine the target population, i.e., the population of interest for a specific survey. In this chapter we assume that the target population has been defined previously and clearly.

Because the survey is, as already mentioned, a very complex process consisting of several phases, each of these phases opens up the possibility for errors to occur. Some of these errors are not related to the sample design, and are not the subject of interest in this chapter. However, sample design is closely related to some of the phases of the survey; therefore, all the errors that can arise in those phases of the survey process will be of interest to us.

In the literature, four types of errors occurring in surveys are most frequently mentioned: coverage error, sampling error, nonresponse error, and measurement error (Fowler, 2002, Salant and Dillman, 1994). Classification into sampling and non-sampling errors is standard, and coverage error, nonresponse error, and measurement error are usually listed under non-sampling errors. However, it is quite clear that only one of them – measurement error – is completely unrelated to the process of sample design and realisation. From the viewpoint of the sample statistician, as well as for the purpose of this chapter, it would be useful to make a somewhat different yet more complete classification of survey errors, which would include some errors that are rarely mentioned in the survey literature. Such a survey error classification is given in Figure 1. Two basic groups of errors are those that are (directly or indirectly) dependent on sampling, and those that are completely independent. In this chapter, only those errors that are sample dependent are discussed.

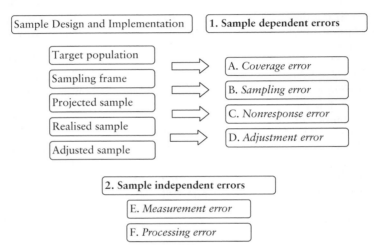

Figure 1: Classification of Sampling and Survey Errors

Coverage Error

The first issue we have to face in drawing the sample is the issue of the frame. This is also the first opportunity for an error to occur. We need to determine how well the frame covers the population, and how big is the discrepancy between them. We have seen that even the best frame does not cover the population entirely; the discrepancy between the target population and the sampling frame is called the coverage error. We may have an idea about the maximum allowable coverage error in a specific survey, but it is highly questionable as to how reliable our estimation of the error will be. Estimation of coverage error represents a problem for numerous surveys; one of the goals should be to reduce it as much as possible. If the discrepancy between the target population and the sample frame is too large, the intended sample frame will frequently be abandoned completely and another type of frame chosen, or possibly another solution.

Sampling Error

Sampling error occurs because, instead of drawing conclusions about the population based on all its elements, we use only a sample of the population. The reason for error lies in the random nature of sampling; it is calculated from probability theory. Sampling error is the only error that can be estimated, and is discussed at length in this chapter.

One of the most common misleading notions related to surveys is that it is possible to calculate error for every survey. Unfortunately, this is not the case. This is possible only with sampling error, and only with probability samples. It is a common practice for researchers to mention estimated error along with their survey results. But it is very seldom that they note that the mentioned error estimate is only a sampling error, and that is not the only source of error in a survey. Even more rarely do they specify the type of sample used. Quota sampling is often used in travel surveys, which is nonprobabilistic, so that sampling error cannot be estimated for it. However, this does not seem to bother some 'researchers', who specify errors even for quota samples.

Another misleading notion that has spread among non-experts is that 'the bigger the sample, the smaller the error', and that the size of the sample should be proportional to the size of the population. This is partly true, because smaller samples always possess larger errors than large samples. However, very large samples are usually not needed, and are basically not rational. Increasing the sample above a certain limit only increases costs, whereas the data quality increase is negligible. A sample size of 500 will provide practically the same error both for a population size of 10,000 and for a population size of 1,000,000. This 'paradox' is caused by the fact that the relationship between error and sample size is not linear, but quadratic. As a consequence, if we would want to reduce error k times, we would have to increase sample size k^2 times. One useful consequence of this insight is that, with nationwide surveys, the same sample size is sufficient both for, say, Austria and the US. Regardless of the fact that the US is several times bigger than Austria, the error would be almost the same. This opens the possibility of conducting the same type of surveys in various countries, using a sample of the same total size. However, everyday experience shows that in large countries larger samples are still more common. The reason for this is not related to the size of the total population, but to the number of entities for which the conclusions are drawn (number of strata).

Sampling error cannot be discussed in an abstract manner. Actually, sampling error is not completely a precise expression, and it is often incorrectly believed that it is possible to calculate sampling error *per se*, which is not the case. The error can be determined only for a specific measure or statistic calculated from the sample, and is different for each of such measure. This is the reason why, among other things, it is necessary to know, when determining sample size, the expected uses of the collected data. The type of survey (descriptive or analytical) will dictate the requested level of precision and, consequently, the sample size.

Nonresponse Error

The actual sample is always different from the one that has initially been drawn. This difference is called the nonresponse error. Keeter *et al.* (2000) suggest that nonresponse error is a function of both the nonresponse rate and the differences between respondents and nonrespondents based on the variable of interest. Nonresponse can take place for a number of reasons, and it is common practise in surveys that diaries of nonresponse are kept in during the course of the fieldwork, to obtain information on the nonresponse rate. Unfortunately, heterogeneity between respondents and nonrespondents remains generally unknown.

It is common knowledge that some populations are harder to reach than others. For instance, nonresponse is much higher in urban than in rural areas in all countries. For household surveys, it is much harder to find smaller, especially one person households. If the behaviour of these subpopulations relative to the survey subject were the same, the nonresponse problem would not exist; however, there are usually significant differences between those who are easy to reach and those who are hard to reach in the population, and significant attention should be focused on the nonresponse problem. Nonresponse error could have greater impact on data quality and the reliability of travel surveys than on the quality of other types of surveys. Younger populations and members of smaller households, regularly underestimated in household surveys, are probably an extremely mobile part of the population, and are, therefore, the persons who move around and travel the most, and are very relevant for any travel survey.

Experienced professionals can evaluate the nonresponse rate subjectively, based on the characteristics of the defined population and the proposed questionnaire, and the sample drawn is as large as possible, to make the size of the realised sample sufficiently large. The only way to reduce nonresponse error is to obey strictly the procedure of respondent selection, and execute strict control of the fieldwork. If, after that, a significant error still arises, the usual way to remove it is by weighting.

Adjustment Error

After the data have been collected, and prior to their final analysis, there is always an effort to remove the errors that could have arisen in the process: coverage, sampling, and nonresponse error. By performing analysis of the actual sample and its relationship to the population structure, it would be possible to establish which groups of the population are overrepresented, and which are underrepresented. Then, the underrepresented elements are given more weight, and those that are overrepresented are given smaller weights. This procedure is called weighting, post-stratification, or sample adjustment. Basically, the idea for adjustment is to improve sample quality; however, the effect is not always the desired one. Choice of appropriate weights is a critical point, where a mistake is easily made, and in such cases the consequences are significant. For the weights to be adequately determined, good knowledge of the population structure is required and, if the secondary data are not sufficient or not precise enough, sometimes professional heuristic expertise is used.

SAMPLING

Some Sample Classifications

In the literature, various sample classifications, based on various criteria, can be found. A common sample classification is between probability samples and nonprobabilistic samples. Error is present in all types of samples, but only with probability samples is it possible to speak about estimation of error, or at least a part of it.

Probability samples are classified as follows:

- *Simple random sample.* In the case of a simple random sample, an enumerated list of the total population is needed. Elements are chosen completely at random, independent from one another and without replacement. In the past, random number tables were used for simple random samples; today computer random number generators are used almost exclusively.
- *Systematic sample.* Some authors consider systematic sampling to be a variation of simple random sampling, although it could be considered as a special case of cluster sampling, or even as a special case of stratified sampling. By dividing the population size by the sample size, we get a value called the step. It is sufficient to generate one random number smaller than the step; this value is called the start and represents the ordinal number of the first element chosen for the sample. Then, the step value is added to the start value and the next sample element is determined. The procedure continues in this way, systematically determining the following elements all the way to the end, i.e., to the last sample element.
- *Complex random samples* (Stratified sample, cluster sample, multistage sample).

Depending on whether an appropriate list of all sample elements exists, sample frames can be classified into those that are based on an exhaustive list of all elements, and those without a list. If there are clearly defined subpopulations (strata) in a population, the sample is created to reflect each of those strata and is called stratified sampling. Stratified samples can be drawn with proportional probabilities, or with different probabilities of selection.

Depending on the number of stages by which the sample is drawn, the standard classification is of one-stage and multistage samples. Multistage samples are those for which the first stage involves no sampling of the final sample elements, but only groupings of final elements, defined in various ways. In the practice of travel surveys, two-stage and three-stage samples are usually used.

Samples that do not reflect properly the population from which they have been selected are biased. Anyone who deals with surveys is aiming for an unbiased sample. An unbiased sample is also called a representative sample. Representativeness is a necessary condition for drawing conclusions about the population based on the sample.

What is Necessary to Know Before Starting with Sample Design

Each of the phases in the survey could be called critical for the process development, and that certainly goes for sampling. One reasons that sample design is often perceived as a mystery or an unknown in survey methodology is its statistical nature. On the one hand, many researchers use surveys on a regular basis, without sufficient formal knowledge of statistics. On the other hand, statisticians dealing with samples have shown a lasting tendency to stay within the limits of their own area, without explaining sample design to users. Both approaches, extreme as they are, are bound to be wrong. Anyone dealing with survey design or with analysis of the collected data, has to be acquainted with all the phases in the survey, and the degree of knowledge in statistics that is required for understanding basic principles of sample design is not too high. Also, with some good will, statisticians could adapt their terminology and explain in a simple manner the rationale for their sample design processes.

As already stated, the aim of the survey is a starting point for all the phases of the survey, including sample design. Clearly, a defined target population and the instrument to be applied (questionnaire) also have to be known before sampling begins. Every researcher would like to know the sample size as soon as possible, and try to fit it in the budget, or vice versa. However, sample size is a very complex issue. Generally, sample size is influenced by:

- The maximum error allowed;
- The population size (influences significantly when small populations are in question);
- The variance in the data;
- The identity of the smallest group (and its exact size) in the population for which we want an estimate based on the sample; and
- What we intend to do with the collected data.

When asking data users about the permitted error level, one should check how clear they are about the concept of total survey error. This should include if they can tell the difference between sampling and non-sampling errors, and whether they are capable of determining the exact level of precision needed.

Before starting the process of sample design, it is necessary to define sampling units. Sampling units are elementary units or groups of them, clearly defined, easily identifiable, and suitable for sampling. Groups consisting of a large number of elementary sampling units are usually called primary sampling units. In travel surveys, elementary sampling units are usually households or persons. With multistage samples, on higher sample levels, primary sampling units are always groups of elementary units. With households samples, we are usually talking about city blocks, local community centres, census areas or electoral districts.

Before starting sample design, data availability is examined for the population structure, according to variables which influence the survey subject. At the very beginning, one should know if there are sufficient data for stratification and, potentially, for weighting.

Other information which is less often discussed, and which is directly implied by the goals of the survey, is necessary before starting sample design. We need to know what purpose the data will serve, how they will be analysed, and what statistical methods will be applied. It would be useful to know, at least generally, what the final report tables should look like and whether multivariate statistics will be applied and, if so, which methods will be used. If the data are to serve as input to transport planning models, this has to be known at the outset of sample design.

Sample design is always a compromise, aiming to achieve maximum final sample efficiency – achieving optimal precision by using all available means and taking the existing limitations into account.

Because travel surveys are mainly conducted with the general population, or some differently defined large populations, this chapter assumes that the population is large enough that a finite population correction (fpc) can be disregarded. In practice, a population is considered to be large if its size is ten thousand units or more. Other indicators that should be evaluated, such as error, variance, and minimal population groups for which an estimate is desired, are always important when creating sample designs for travel surveys.

Choosing Respondents in Households

In some travel surveys, households are the final sampling units. In such cases, information on the whole household and all household members are gathered (a sort of census at the household level). However, in other cases, the final sample element in travel surveys is an individual and, in such cases, only one person is chosen from a household. In travel surveys, as well as in other household-based surveys of persons, two methods for respondent selection in households are most common: Kish tables and first birthday. Both methods, provided they are consistently applied, generate a uniform distribution, thus preserving population structure by sex and age. Some researchers prefer one method, some the other, but the choice of method is largely immaterial; the crucial issue for selecting one or the other is not related to the differences in the results they produce. Rather it is an issue of ensuring the accurate realisation of the desired sample, i.e., it is a matter of deciding which method interviewers will conduct more successfully in the field, and to which method they will find least resistance by respondents. Years of experience of this author indicate that both methods give very similar results, and that, if consistently applied, in neither case is posterior weighting by sex or age needed.

Hoffmeyer-Zlotnik (2003) describes and criticises the practise that has recently appeared in Germany. A change is introduced in the last stage of probability sampling – selection of the household member. Instead of traditional Kish tables or first birthday methods, interviewers get the list of households and quotas with detailed instructions on how to follow them. When creating this new hybrid, the idea was to reduce interviewer fieldwork, thus reducing the total cost of survey implementation, and to achieve better results than with standard quota samples. Unfortunately, this last stage makes an otherwise appropriate sample into a nonprobability sample, for which error estimation is not possible. According to Hoffmeyer-Zlotnik (2003), this attempt did not succeed in removing flaws from standard quota samples, and samples drawn in this way differed significantly in structure from the population.

SAMPLE SIZE AND ESTIMATION OF ERROR

It is often the case that the survey client's first question related to how large a sample is needed for the survey the client wishes to have done. Alternatively, the client may ask if a particular sample is large enough. A definitive answer cannot be given to either question. Sample size is a complex problem that cannot be solved easily, and the answer to this question depends on many things. When dealing with a defined target population, to determine the necessary size sample, the things we need to know are:

- What is to be measured?
- How precisely should it be measured?
- Is it reasonable to assume that the population is homogenous relative to the desired measures?
- Are sample elements to be chosen individually or in groups?

As we are about to see, even this is not enough.

Error and sample size are closely related to each other. The standard procedure is to have an idea about the allowable error for a specific survey. Then, taking this error into account, as well as numerous other parameters, the sample is drawn. Only after the interviewing and data collection are over is it possible to give a final estimation of the sampling error.

Simple Random Samples

A simple random sample (SRS) is an ideal sample, we could even say prototype of all other samples; however, we seldom have the opportunity to use it in practice. A SRS gives each element of the sample frame an equal chance of being selected. Theoretically speaking, when designing a SRS, one should determine all possible samples without replacement[1] of the size *n*, and than chose one of them randomly. This is never done in practice, because it is too time consuming for large populations.

The sample size of a SRS depends on the type of statistics we would like to calculate, or, to be precise, to estimate. The statistics that are most often estimated are the mean and proportion.

Sample Size and Estimation of Mean

The mean carries a smaller error than the proportion, and it takes a smaller sample for its estimation than for the estimation of a proportion. In travel surveys, we encounter continuous variables more often than in other survey types. An example of such a variable would be the following question:

> *How long did your home to work trip last yesterday?*

Assume that the researcher wants to know the mean of the trip duration. The question is how big a sample is needed. In order to determine sample size we need to know maximum allowed absolute error, variance, and confidence level. One of these values is usually unknown – the variance. To determine sample size for the mean of a variable, such as travel time, we should know the variance of that variable. We do not know the variance in advance and we can estimate it only after the data are collected. This is a serious problem. We need to ascertain if there is any other information that could be of help, or if similar surveys been done somewhere before, the results of which could provide guidelines on an approximate variance size.

Based on Table 1, one can get an impression of the influence of variance on sample size and about the importance of the correct estimation of its approximate size. If we underestimate the variance and choose a smaller sample, we shall find ourselves in the position to be unable to estimate the mean accurately enough. If, on the other hand, we overestimate the variance, the sample size will be bigger than we really need, therefore putting us in the position of spending money needlessly.

---

[1] Samples may be drawn without replacement, meaning that once an element is sampled, it cannot be sampled again; or with replacement, meaning that an element can be sampled more than once.

Table 1: Sample Size Required for 95% Confidence Interval of the Mean Depending on Error and Standard Deviation

Standard deviation (s)	Error			
	±4 minutes	±3 minutes	±2 minutes	±1 minute
10 minutes	25	44	98	392
15 minutes	56	98	221	882
20 minutes	98	175	392	1568

Sample Size and Proportion Estimation

Although they contain more continuous variables than other surveys, travel surveys also contain a large number of extremely important variables from which proportions are estimated. This means that for the final decision on sample size, proportions are crucial, not the mean.

Let us consider the following, relatively simple question:

Did you use public transport yesterday?

We shall assume that the population is large enough that we do not have to use the finite population correction. As with the mean, the standard deviation of the proportion depends on the value we are trying to estimate. This problem is inevitable when we are talking about the sample, and is usually resolved by relying on data from some other source (from the past, or someone else's data). The question the user must answer is whether there are some previous data, results of some prior surveys, secondary data and similar, that could provide information about what this proportion could be, at least roughly speaking. If such information is not available, the most conservative value of $p=q=0.5$ must be used, this being the value of the proportion with the highest variance.

The next thing one must know is the level of error that is acceptable for the user. It is important to stress that no one can guarantee that the true population value is within the limits from the calculated value of the proportion, but it can be stated with high confidence. If we choose a confidence level of ninety-five percent, then the error we can tolerate is approximately two standard deviations. In Table 2, the required sample sizes for various error values and proportions are listed. Sometimes, in practice, confidence levels different from ninety five percent are used. Sample sizes required for some other confidence levels are not given in Table 2, but are easy to calculate.

In estimating proportions, we need a bigger sample than for estimating the mean. In all surveys, there is at least one variable of great interest that is presented in the form of a proportion. That is the reason why, in some books on survey methodology, when discussing determining sample size, the mean is not even mentioned, and only proportions are discussed. In textbooks on sampling (Cochran, 1977, Murthy, 1967), the mean, its error, and determining the size of the required sample always have their own chapter, but are, unfortunately, treated separately from the proportion.

Table 2: The Required Sample Size for 95.46% Confidence Interval for Proportion ($\pm 2\sigma_{\bar{p}}$), Depending on the Error and the Expected Proportion

Proportion p	Error e		
	±5%	±3%	±1%
0.1	144	400	3,600
0.2	256	712	6,400
0.3	336	934	8,400
0.4	384	1,067	9,600
0.5	400	1,112	10,000

If the results collected in the survey are analysed using one of the advanced statistical methods, numerous other methods that have remained unmentioned above will appear as a result, e.g., the variance and covariance, the difference between two values, the correlation coefficient, a regression coefficient, canonical correlation, and similar. Methods of estimating the standard error of those parameters can always be found in the relevant statistics literature (Cochran, 1977, Murthy, 1967, etc.).

Stratified Sample

Everything mentioned in the previous section of this chapter is related exclusively to simple random samples. When it comes to household surveys, this type of sample is almost never used. Household surveys almost always require a stratified sample.

Often we can divide the population into easily distinctive groups we call subpopulations. The general population is naturally divided into male and female, and older and younger subpopulations. When subpopulations are mutually exclusive they are called strata. The variable used to divide the population into strata is called the stratification variable. Examples of stratification variables, besides sex and age, are race, religion, mother tongue, state or municipality of permanent stay, socioeconomic status, etc. Also, in cases where we are interested in travel phenomena, stratified variables can be defined in various other ways. At the household level, we separate those that own at least one motor vehicle from those who do not, households living in their own apartment/house from those living in rented dwellings, urban and rural populations, etc. Individuals could be classified into those who have driver licences and those who do not, whether they travel from home to work/school on a daily basis, whether they have travelled abroad during the previous year or not, or in many other different ways.

For stratified sample design, it is necessary to know the size of the stratum in the population. To obtain such information, external and secondary sources are used. For example, demographic variables can be obtained from a census; the number of registered motor vehicles or drivers can be obtained from appropriate official data bases, etc.

There are many reasons for stratification. Stratification is needed if conclusions are to be drawn about each subpopulation independently. One of the most common reasons for stratification is reduction of the total variance, which also represents an attempt to reduce the sample size. Sometimes, reasons for stratification are solely administrative.

If a simple random sample is taken from each stratum, such a sample is called a stratified random sample. Appropriate stratification can reduce the variance compared to a random sample, thus increasing the precision of the estimate of statistics for the total population. Of course, a good stratification that accomplishes this effect is only the one that manages to separate strata that are essentially different from one another, and rather homogenous within themselves.

After the strata in a population have been defined, and information about their size obtained, the next step in designing a stratified sample is allocation. Allocation represents the distribution of total sample size into strata. The most common and simplest allocation is the one in which every stratum is allocated a sample that is proportional to its size. Such allocation is called allocation with probabilities proportional to size (PPS).

In sample design and statistics in general, it is usual to denote the population size with N, and the sample size with n. The ratio between those two values n/N is called the sampling fraction and is denoted f. If we assume that there is a total of k strata, we shall denote the size of each of them as N_i, and the size of an appropriate sample as n_i. With proportional (PPS) allocation, we can see that

$$\frac{N_i}{N} = \frac{n_i}{n} = w_i, \ i=1, \ ..., \ k. \tag{1}$$

Quotients w_i are called stratum weights. Equation 1 could also be expressed as shown in equation 2.

$$\frac{n_i}{N_i} = \frac{n}{N} = f, \ i=1, \ ..., \ k. \tag{2}$$

Samples with a constant n_i/N_i ratio are called self-weighting samples. With samples where this is not the case, if the allocation is not proportional, posterior data weighting is needed, to bring back each stratum to a probability proportional to its size. This kind of weighting procedure is called post-stratification.

Variance with Non-Proportional Allocations

Many authors have dealt with the problem of variance estimation with stratified samples in detail (Golder and Yeomans 1973, Cochran, 1977, Kish and Anderson, 1978,

Jolliffe, 2003). For the purpose of understanding the variance estimation issue better and determining sample size in the case of complex samples, in this chapter only the basic concepts are given.

In the case of a stratified sample, the mean of the whole set could be calculated based on strata means as a weighted mean. The variance of the mean with a stratified sample, for very large populations ($n<<N$), when finite population correction does not have to be used, is given by equation 3.

$$\sigma_{\bar{x}}^2 = \sum_{i=1}^{k} \frac{w_i^2 \sigma_i^2}{n_i} = \frac{1}{n}\sum_{i=1}^{k} w_i \sigma_i^2 \, , \tag{3}$$

where k stands for the number of strata; n_i for sample size in each stratum; w_i for the weights of each stratum and σ_i^2 for the variance within each stratum.

Based on (3), determining the size of stratified sample is simple, $n = \dfrac{\sum_{i=1}^{k} w_i \sigma_i^2}{\sigma_{\bar{x}}^2}$, yet im-

plies that variances of all subsamples are known, which is a theoretical assumption in most cases. The situation is similar with a proportion, where the variance is shown in equation 4.

$$\sigma_p^2 = \sum_{i=1}^{k} \frac{w_i^2}{n_i} p_i q_i = \frac{1}{n}\sum_{i=1}^{k} w_i p_i q_i \, . \tag{4}$$

In cases of non-proportional allocation, the formula to calculate the mean and variance is even more complicated, but since all these formulae can be found in relevant literature (Cochran, 1977, Kish and Anderson, 1978), this chapter will not be needlessly burdened with the addition of more equations.

Optimal allocation is a procedure for determining subsample sizes that minimise the total variance of the mean, for a given total sample size. For each stratum, the subsample size is determined as shown in equation 5.

$$n_i = n \frac{w_i \sigma_i}{\sum w_i \sigma_i} = n \frac{N_i \sigma_i}{\sum N_i \sigma_i} \, . \tag{5}$$

This type of allocation is also called Neyman allocation, and provides a stratified sample with the lowest variance. If we denote the variance of the mean as σ_{sr}^2 in the case of a simple random sample, as σ_{pps}^2 in the case of a stratified sample with probabilities proportional to size (PPS) and as σ_{opt}^2 in the case of a stratified sample with optimal (Neyman) allocation, then equation 6 holds.

$$\sigma_{opt}^2 \leq \sigma_{pps}^2 \leq \sigma_{sr}^2 \, . \tag{6}$$

As Golder and Yeomans (1973) explain, the contribution of proportional stratification relative to a simple random sample can be measured accurately as shown in equation 7.

$$\sigma_{sr}^2 = \sigma_{pps}^2 + \frac{\sigma_{bs}^2}{n},$$ (7)

where σ_{bs}^2 denotes the between-strata variance. Thus, the variance with proportional stratification is always σ_{bs}^2/n smaller than the simple random sample variance.

Optimal allocation is optimal in the matter of the variance; however, in the matter of allocation, it may possess a serious problem. In some cases (small stratum and large total sample size), optimal allocation could produce a sample size for a stratum bigger than the population size in that stratum. Of course, such allocation is not possible, and in such cases one hundred percent allocation is used in that stratum.

Theoretically the ideal variable for stratification is precisely the variable we are measuring, that is, the one of special interest for the survey, because stratification according to it would produce a very small variance. Of course, stratification according to that variable is not possible, because we have no prior knowledge about it. Because of this, it is common practice, when choosing among variables for which we have data about the population, to pick for stratification those we assume to be in most ways related to the measuring subject. This introduces an amount of subjectivity into the stratification process. However, it would be impossible to avoid subjectivity with this sample design. Because a well-chosen stratified variable significantly improves the quality of estimation, the choice of it made by an experienced researcher is completely justified.

DETERMINING THE SAMPLE SIZE BASED ON MULTIPLE VARIABLES

As Žarković (1961) claims, the reality is even more complicated than the examples given in textbooks. In most surveys, there is more than one variable of interest for the study; therefore, another problem arises, that of determining the optimal sample size that would take all of them into account. If all the variables had the same variance, and if that variance were known to us, there would be no problem and sample size could be determined in a very simple formula. However, variables that are of interest to us have various distributions and various variances. Applying the procedure as described above would be hard work and mostly a waste of time, because we would get a large number of different values for sample size, from extremely small to extremely large, and again we wouldn't know which one to choose.

Common practice has found a compromise solution. In most cases, the first step is to narrow down the number of variables on which sample size is determined. It is necessary to choose several, but not too many variables, which are of the greatest importance for the study. If their variances are similar, sample sizes attained for each of them will also be similar. It would suffice to choose one convenient number of a suitable size. This procedure means that a small number of variables, but the ones of highest interest for the study, get to be measured with the desired precision. The precision of other variables will be lower or higher than this one, depending on their variances.

However, if sample sizes that are determined by this narrower set of variables differ significantly from one another, we are forced to accept a conservative approach and take the highest value for the sample size, thus providing sufficient precision even for the variable with an extreme variance. Of course, in that case other variables will be measured with a higher precision than actually required. If this is the case, then we are in the position of having to drastically increase sample size because of one variable, which automatically increases the costs. In such cases perhaps it would be wise to re-consider the importance of that variable, and its role in the survey. A final decision cannot be made without consulting the ultimate user of the data.

One kind of sample that is commonly used in travel surveys is a stratified cluster sample. Cluster sampling basically increases intergroup correlation. Also, correlation between the stratifying variable and the variable we are examining is larger in cluster samples than in simple random samples. Because of this, when using cluster sampling, to avoid increase of the variance due to interclass correlation and design effects, the number of elements in one cluster should usually not be too large.

Stratification is typically undertaken with the primary goal of reducing the total sample variance. A gain from stratifying variables depends on their correlation with the variable we are studying, as well as their interclass correlation. Perhaps it would be better for the discussion, relative to introducing potential default variances and choosing typical variables to determine sample size, to be directed to the problem of improving stratification. Stratification deals with both issues and successfully unites them. Thus, it would be wise to see what others have done to date in this area.

In solving problems of stratification, multivariate statistics have been used by a number of authors in different ways. The simplest and, probably because of that, the first that has been used for these purposes, is principal components analysis (PCA). Principal components analysis is applied on a set of stratifying variables, and then stratification is done according to the first component, or according to the first and the second principal components. The procedure is simple and quite attractive, but has some shortcomings. Kish and Anderson (1978) state the following:

- Principal components are not suitable for categorical (especially nominal) stratifying variables;
- Quantitative stratifying variables that are not linear will not contribute to variance reduction;
- Strata obtained in this manner are difficult to interpret; and

- The method refers more to the internal structure of variables, and not so much on their effect on survey variables.

The same authors also state that bivariate stratification is always better than stratification across only the first principal component.

Another interesting idea that has caused a lot of comment and discussion is stratification by cluster analysis. Golder and Yeomans (1973) have used cluster analysis for sample stratification in a survey on the use of seat belts in cars. Taking a large number of stratifying variables as a starting point, cluster analysis is used to reveal latent, otherwise undetectable, clusters in the population. Then, the stratification is done across the clusters thus obtained. Unlike principal components, in this type of statistical analysis, the variables are not of primary importance, but the elements or objects are. In some cases of cluster analysis, it is possible to set in advance the number of clusters/strata, whereas in other cases this number does not have to be fixed.

Heeler and Day (1975) do not criticise the idea of applying cluster analysis in stratification, but criticise the choice of measure used by Golder and Yeomans. Because it is generally known that cluster analysis results depend on the choice of metrics, as well as on the choice of grouping algorithm – and both of these are usually determined subjectively based on the researcher's previous experience – clearly this method of stratification is extremely flexible, and not subject to standardisation. For each specific case of a travel survey, it is possible to find at least one suitable metric out of various possibilities, that, if combined with an appropriate grouping algorithm, could provide good results.

An interesting viewpoint about multivariate and multipurpose stratification was presented by Kish and Anderson (1978). The emphasis of their work is on multipurpose stratification. Although they criticise both principal components analysis and cluster analysis, these two, and even some other multivariate statistical methods, certainly deserve attention when it comes to multivariate stratification. Probably, most stratification problems related to travel surveys are, to some degree, possible to standardise. Certainly, results of only one survey would not suffice for something like that. However, it would make sense to consider the idea of making such an attempt, based on the same survey conducted in several countries. The same multivariate statistical methods should be applied to the data collected in this way. Comparative analysis of the results of such a complex survey could provide us with an idea about a suitable stratification mode.

Another idea worth considering is applying other multivariate statistical methods in stratification. The usual situation in travel surveys is to have secondary data only on demographic characteristics of population, whereas data on travel variables stay unknown as a rule. Use of canonical correlation or discriminant analysis of the results of previous travel surveys could solve the problem of determining the set of demographic variables that are most closely related to travel variables, and could be used for stratification in some future travel survey.

In some cases of stratification, the primary goal is not variance reduction, but the creation of a domain for analysis, i.e., appropriately defined subpopulations from which we can draw conclusions about the phenomena with which we are dealing. This is especially the case with multivariate stratification. A large number of stratifying variables are especially convenient in multipurpose surveys. Each of the variables we are analysing has a different best stratifying variable, and stratification across several of them could be a good idea. Of course, with this multivariate stratification, there is always a limitation in the total number of strata allowed for the sample. Depending on the survey goal, the type of population, and the budget, the total sample size could vary, but the number of strata, even for the largest sample, is seldom over ten, and is often much smaller.

As already mentioned, in sample design all the elements need not necessarily have the same probability of selection. Whether these probabilities are going to be the same or not often depends on the survey goal – whether we are interested in the general population, or want to find out more about its mobile members, i.e., about those who travel more frequently than others. If, for example, the sample of passengers to be drawn is based on a list of tickets an airline has sold during the previous year, the probability of selection is higher for passengers that have travelled more often and bought more tickets – the more mobile passengers. If we do not want different choice probabilities, then we shall allocate equal probabilities to all elements in a posterior weighting process.

SAMPLE DESIGN FOR THE BELGRADE 2002 SURVEY

In the autumn of 2002, a very complex travel survey was conducted in the city of Belgrade, Serbia (Paskota, 2002). The survey goal was to collect sufficient data to study problems of public transport and city traffic in general. The whole survey was multipurpose and took place on multiple levels and, because of that, a specially created composite measurement instrument was used – a questionnaire with questions addressing different target groups. Apart from the demographic data, information was collected on habits, ownership of motorised and non-motorised vehicles, parking problems, public transport use, all daily trips in the city, attitudes to traffic and public transport, etc.

The first group of questions was related to the household as a whole, the second to all the household members aged six years or over, whereas the third group of questions was answered by only one chosen member of each household, aged fifteen or over. The data collected were analysed on five levels:

- Households;
- All household members six years of age or older;
- Daily trips;
- Daily trip segments (trip legs); and
- The selected individuals over fifteen years of age.

For each level, a different sample was drawn. From a common basis, different samples were designed for each of the three levels:

- On the household level, a two-stage stratified household sample;
- On the individual level, for questions on daily trips, a three-stage stratified cluster sample of persons; and
- On the individual level, for questions on attitudes to traffic and public transport, a three-stage stratified random sample of persons.

Target Population and Population Structure

For the part of the survey about daily trips, the target population was defined as the urban population of Belgrade, aged six or over. For the part about attitudes to traffic and public transport, the target population was defined as the urban population of Belgrade, aged fifteen or over. The population structure in terms of age and sex was taken from the last population census, dated 31st March, 2002.

Frame

Because a reliable list of all households was not available, the list of electoral units from the urban city territory was taken. Each electoral unit in the city consists of around 200 households or around 600 persons.

Stratification

Administrative areas were used for stratification. Out of ten municipalities belonging to the city centre, eight are inhabited by exclusively urban populations, whereas a small part of the population is rural in two municipalities. Because only urban populations were of interest to this study, for the two municipalities with rural inhabitants, strata were defined as the urban part only. Allocation of the number of primary sampling units (PSU) across strata was proportional to the size of their urban parts. To reduce interclass correlation as much as possible, the number of sampling units (households) in one PSU (electoral unit) was ten. The projected size was 2,600 households or 260 PSU, but, based on previous experiences with problems arising during fieldwork, a sample of 2,750 (275 PSU) was drawn.

Two-Stage Stratified Household Sample

For the first stage, sampling units were the electoral units, defined by street and house number. PSUs were chosen with probabilities proportional to the number of voters. For the second stage, the sampling unit was the household. In this stage, a systematic sample was used, with given start, step and direction.

Three-Stage Stratified Cluster Sample of Persons (Questions on Daily Trips).

The first two stages are the same as for the household sample. In the third phase, all household members satisfying the criterion of being over six years old were listed.

Three-Stage Stratified Random Sample of Persons (Questions on Attitudes on City Traffic and Public Transport)

The first two stages were the same as for the household sample. In the third stage, only one person aged fifteen or over was selected from the household. For the selection of respondents within the household, Kish tables were used.

Possible Sources of Error

Bias caused by non-coverage could appear for two reasons: out of date electoral lists and the difference between voters and the over-6-year-old population. In the autumn of 2002, lists of voters in Belgrade were significantly updated from those of two years earlier, including:

- The removal of deceased persons;
- Adding new listed voters; and
- Removing people who have left the country.

The biggest problem with this list was not the lack of persons, but the surplus. A certain number of people are on it because they are registered at their old addresses, but left the country years ago (economic emigration from Serbia has been significant since the beginning of the 1990s). Because the emigrants tend to be young people, mostly single or couples without their own apartments and living with their parents, the assumption was that emigration has not significantly affected the total number of households, but it changed the age structure of the central city parts. The new age structure, different from the 1991 census, was known from the results of the 2002 census. Through control of the age structure and household sizes in the strata, it has been established that there were differences in the representativeness of the six to eighteen years old population, but not to the extent of affecting the decision about the choice of lists of electoral units for the sample frame. Household size in municipalities varied from 2.24 to 2.71, not too big a deviation from the city mean, which is 2.62.

Fieldwork and Actual Sample Size

Fieldwork was performed during a two-week period, on Tuesday to Friday afternoons and evenings, and for the whole day on Saturday. Questions about daily trips always referred to the previous, necessarily, working day. One hundred and five interviewers took part, with ten percent of the sample being subject to random control. Households with problematic or incomplete questionnaires were also controlled. Data entry lasted for ten days, and forty four persons took part in doing it. The actual sample size was 2,650 households, consisting of 7,852 household members over six, 16,181 daily trips, 28,272 trip legs, and 2,650 persons over fourteen.

Post-Stratification

The actual sample changed the strata sample size slightly; in the post stratification process weights varying from 0.8 to 1.11 were used.

Sampling Error Estimate

The simple random sample error for a proportion does not exceed two percent for households and 1.2 percent for all household members, and in most cases is much lower. Values for these estimated errors for different proportions are shown in Table 3.

Table 3: Estimation of SRS error for 95.46 percent confidence level, depending on sample size and the proportion

Proportion p	Sample size	
	2650	7852
0.5	1.94%	1.13%
0.2	1.55%	0.90%
0.05	0.85%	0.49%

Because we used administrative stratification, not some variable that is significant for travel, the stratification only reduced the variance and, thus, the sampling error of the proportions for variables related to traffic slightly. For example, the number of households with at least one motor vehicle (whose proportion estimated from the sample is 0.541 or 54.1 percent), in the case of a SRS sample size of 2,650 would have an error of 1.94 percent, and the estimated error in the actual stratified sample for the same variable would be 1.92 percent. Therefore, with confidence higher than 95 percent, we could state that in urban parts of Belgrade, the number of households that own at least one motor vehicle equals 54±4 percent, that is, somewhere between 50 and 58 percent. From the example shown, we can see that, in case of this survey, as upper error limit we can freely take values for the SRS.

CONCLUSIONS

Sample error is historically the first error from various survey errors to be identified. Many authors, dealing with this issue using a solid statistical basis, have stated that this sort of error is explained most easily and can be quantified precisely. For a number of years, researchers have known that the main cause of error in surveys is not sampling error at all. The problem of sample design is mainly solved in a satisfying, though not always standard, manner. If, in some surveys, the sampling error is extremely high, the reason for this should not be looked for in poor methodology, but rather in a lack of will to pursue it consistently in practice. Travel survey practice in most countries shows that non-sampling errors, primary among them being nonresponse error, are a much more common source of error. Although from year to year growing attention has been paid to such sources of error, it seems that, for a number of reasons, these errors have a tendency to grow constantly.

As for travel survey sample design, standards make sense only in limited circumstances. If we wish to conduct the same survey in a number of countries, gather the same kind of data, use the same or similar questionnaire, and define the population in the same manner, then it would be necessary to consider standardisation of the sample design. Before that, we have to be sure that we are measuring the same things on the same objects in the same way. Even if we use different types of survey modes to collect the same data (face to face, telephone, or mail), this alone could cause problems.

The information that is collected in the course of most travel surveys is most commonly used for travel modelling and planning, which is the reason why the precision of these data is of much greater importance than is true for other surveys. One should bear in mind that the error propagated through the process of modelling traffic is the total survey error. A well drawn sample with a low sampling error is necessary, but it still does not guarantee high data precision. For data precision, good quality sampling implementation is just as important. We should not forget that non-sampling errors generally behave conversely from sampling errors: they increase with sample size. Because of this, an unnecessary increase in sample size, besides increasing total survey cost, could also lead to an increase in total survey error.

In weighing all these reasons, a measure of subjectivity must be used. Many things are done subjectively in survey research, and even in statistics. The very selection of the subject of measurement is subjective. The same can be said for the maximum allowed error – some will think that five percent is acceptable, while others will demand three percent or even less. One could speculate as to the reasons for this. Possibly, the acceptable error is defined on the basis of what has been read in reports from other surveys, or because colleagues are known to have specified this level of error. One also has to wonder whether the person demanding no more than a 1.5 percent sampling error is aware of the size of the other types of error he cannot measure, but which are almost certainly higher than this? The usual phrase that is met in the literature is that, in numerous situations like this, we rely on expert knowledge. This does not seem to be an unreasonable position to take.

REFERENCES

BTS (1997). *1995 American Travel Survey Technical Documentation*, Bureau of Transportation Statistics, US Department of Transportation, Washington, DC.

Cochran, W.G. (1977). *Sampling Techniques*, 3rd edition, John Wiley & Sons, New York.

Fowler, F.J. Jr. (2002). *Survey Research Methods*, 3rd edition, Sage Publications, Thousand Oaks, CA.

Golder, P.A. and K.A. Yeomans (1973). The Use of Cluster Analysis for Stratification, *Applied Statistics*, **22**, 213-219.

Heeler, R.M. and G.S. Day (1975). A Supplementary Note on the Use of Cluster Analysis for Stratification, *Applied Statistics*, **24**, 342-344.

Hoffmeyer-Zlotnik, J.H.P. (2003). New Sampling Designs and the Quality of Data. In: *Developments in Applied Statistics* (A. Ferligoj and A. Mrvar eds), FDV, Ljubljana, Slovenia.

Jolliffe, D. (2003). Estimating Sample Variance From the Current population survey: A Synthetic Design Approach to Correcting Standard Errors, *Journal of Economic and Social Measurement*, **28**, 239-261.

Keeter, S., C. Miller, A. Kohut, R.M. Groves, S. Presser (2000). Consequences of Reducing Nonresponse in a National Telephone Survey, *Public Opinion Quarterly*, **64**,125-148.

Kish, L. and D.W. Anderson (1978). Multivariate and Multipurpose Stratification, *Journal of the American Statistical Association*, **73**, 24-34,

Murthy, M.N. (1967). *Sampling Theory and Methods*, Statistical Publishing Society, Calcutta, India.

Paskota, M. (2002). *Citizens' Daily Trips and Attitudes on Traffic and Public Transport, Belgrade 2002*, SYSTRA and SMMRI, Belgrade, Serbia.

Salant, P. and D A. Dillman (1994). *How to Conduct Your Own Survey*, John Wiley & Sons, New York.

Žarković, S.S. (1961). *Sampling Methods and Censuses – Volume I: Collecting data and Tabulation*, FAO, UN.

6

SAMPLE DESIGN

Rosella Picardo, PB Consult, Seattle, WA, USA

INTRODUCTION

The Sample Design workshop[14] was tasked with discussing two general sets of questions, the first dealing with sample design *per se*, and the second dealing with the recommendations for standardising pilot surveys and pretests. Discussions were assisted by the workshop resource paper (Paskota, 2006).

SAMPLE DESIGN

The specific questions posed to the workshop were:

- Would the establishment of typical variances of data items be worthwhile and useful?
- What variables should be considered in establishing sample size?
- How should the sample sizes needed for each variable be combined to establish a common sample size?
- Is there a need for sensitivity analysis to study how input variable errors affect estimation errors?
- Is there a need for a standardised procedure for establishing sample sizes?

---

[14] Members of the workshop were: Rosella Picardo (USA), Mira Paskota (Serbia), Arnim Meyburg (USA), Lidia Kostyniuk (USA), Carlos Arce (USA), Manfred Wermuth (Germany), Carlos Contreras (Costa Rica).

These questions were examined in the broad context of transport surveys, rather than the narrower context of household surveys. In addition to household surveys, transport-related surveys include on-board surveys, road-side intercept surveys, and commodity flow surveys. An effort was also made to consider an international dimension in the discussion, and not just to focus on what may be applicable only to the US.

Much of the discussion centred on the errors that may occur in surveys, regardless of the survey stage in which they occur. To the extent possible, the sample design should be such as to minimise total survey error, and not just sampling error. The questions posed to the workshop imply that sample design is only concerned with minimising, or at least measuring, sampling error for probabilistic samples. The workshop participants instead concluded that it is important to identify all sources of error related to the sample, not just those that can be measured. Undue emphasis should not be placed on reducing sampling error, when other sample-dependent errors, such as coverage error or non-respondent error can be much larger than sampling error. The latter errors are related to the sample design in that they are wholly or partially dependent on the choice of frame, which is an important step in designing the sample. While these errors cannot be measured, every attempt should be made to identify potential sources of error and their likely magnitude, both *a priori* (before the sample is drawn) and *a posteriori* (after the sample is implemented).

Sample Dependent Errors

The resource paper identifies four types of sample-dependent errors: coverage error, sampling error, nonresponse error and adjustment error. Of these, coverage error is increasingly a concern, particularly where face-to-face interviewing combined with a telephone-based frame is prohibitively expensive. This type of survey is at least partially infeasible in several relatively common circumstances:

- In communities where telephone penetration is low (typically either very low or very high income neighbourhoods);
- In societies where mobile telephones are increasingly substituting for household (land-line) telephones; and
- In countries where *a priori* information about households, individuals and carriers is becoming less available due to privacy concerns, as seems to be the trend in Europe.

Two possible solutions to at least some of these problems were discussed: the use of multiple-frame samples, and the use of the Internet as a sampling frame. It was agreed that the Internet, even in countries with high usage, remains a largely unproven and untested choice of frame, and that multiple obstacles remain to be overcome before Internet access can be used as a frame. Among these are the lack of a comprehensive and publicly available list of users, the need to identify minors and other populations to whom access is generally not granted, the need to ensure that the survey respondent is in fact the intended survey target, and the lack of a geographic reference (street address), which is often an important stratifying variable. Internet-based surveys are also likely to exhibit very large nonresponse errors. Dual or multiple-frame samples, on the other hand, appear quite feasible. The challenge, of course, is in identifying mutually exclusive frames. When this is not possible, care should be taken to compute the likelihood of appearing in multiple frames, and to design and weight the sample accordingly.

Nonresponse error was also identified by workshop participants as a concern, and an area where better documentation of the sample design and its implementation would help to understand and quantify the error. Two types of nonresponse errors were discussed: genuine and non-genuine. The latter occurs when a population member has zero chance of being sampled; this is often the result of an incomplete frame or a poorly-designed (or executed) sample. When the frame is known to miss certain members of the population, every effort should be made at least to qualitatively characterise these cohorts as well as their behaviour (in terms of what the survey is trying to measure). Genuine nonresponse also needs to be thoroughly documented. Follow up surveys of non-responders, whether through secondary data or in-depth face-to-face interviewing should be a standard procedure for all household surveys.

The workshop participants identified choice of frame and sample stratification as the critical aspects of sample design. Yet options for both of these sample design aspects are typically limited, and sometimes largely determined by available data. To the extent that available data allow, the choice of frame and stratification should be driven by the objective of the study, more so than by the specific methods that will be used to analyse the data. Problems may arise when the survey has multiple objectives, in which case a compromise between the various objectives and the survey cost often needs to be achieved. It is also not uncommon that some uses and methods of analysis of the data will become clear only after the survey has been designed and conducted. Hence, it is of critical importance to document the entire sample design process. Often missing from typical documentation are errors in the frame and unit nonresponse.

CONCLUSIONS AND RECOMMENDATIONS

To address specifically the questions posed to the workshop, its participants offered various conclusions and observations, as detailed below.

First, the choice of variables for sample design is driven by the objectives of the study; hence, the question of which variables to consider in establishing sample sizes cannot be answered generically. Even within the general category of household surveys, and assuming the data would be used to develop travel demand models, ideally the model specification (trip-based, tour-based, micro-simulation, market segmentation, etc.) would dictate the choice of sample design variables. In more practical terms, the variables that are typically available are few, either because of the lack of a reliable and informative census, previous surveys, privacy concerns, and other restrictions placed on access to existing population or vehicle databases.

Second, methods to combine the sample sizes needed for different variables are already well-documented in the literature. Acceptable error limits for each variable, and for the survey as a whole, are often the result of tradeoffs between variable error and survey cost, which is directly related to sample size. Establishment of typical variances alone is unlikely to be useful, given the differences that are likely to exist across different countries. However, to the extent that these differences can be explained or at least related to population characteristics, it may prove useful to guide preliminary survey designs where no local information is available. The researcher is likely to be better off conducting a small scale survey to obtain guidance on variable variances, rather than to rely solely on information of dubious transferability. The study of input variable error propagation should be pursued as needed on a case-by-case basis; whether and how extensively this is done is solely the purview and responsibility of those using the survey data. The responsibility of the survey designer and, therefore, of the sample designer is to provide sufficient information to allow others to qualify and quantify the survey errors adequately.

Third and finally, the workshop discussed the recommendations presented at the conference for the standardisation of pilot surveys and pretests. In general, there was agreement with the recommendations. The workshop participants recommend, however, that the minimum sample sizes suggested for pilot surveys and pretests be considered guidelines, not standards. Secondly, that verification, whether call back or respondent debriefing, also be considered as a standard tool to complement pilot surveys and pretests.

REFERENCES

Paskota, M. (2006). Sample Design and Total Survey Error. In: *Travel Survey Methods – Quality and Future Directions* (P.R. Stopher and C.C. Stecher eds), 111-138, Elsevier, Oxford.

Travel Survey Methods: Quality and Future Directions
Peter Stopher and Cheryl Stecher (Editors)
© 2006 Published by Elsevier Ltd.

7

INSTRUMENT DESIGN: DECISIONS AND PROCEDURES

Johanna Zmud, NuStats, Austin, TX, USA

INTRODUCTION

Instrument design is a complex process not a simple task. It requires decision-making and cognitive effort at three distinct process points. First, the target population and survey both affect significantly the range of instruments that can be used effectively. Second, the instrument designer needs to write questions. Third, the instrument designer needs to construct the instrument. Fortunately, both the travel behaviour and survey methods disciplines have extensive research literatures to provide guidance on specific elements of the instrument design process. This chapter 'mines' these two literatures to identify design principles related to each of these process points that have proved their worth over time and under various circumstances. Hence, these principles could be considered as the state-of-the-practice. This discussion is neither exhaustive nor perfect, because instrument design for travel surveys is complex, entailing many different aspects. However, it identifies those principles that appear to be most useful in developing effective travel survey instruments. At the same time, it recognises that reconciling principles for instrument design with any one particular survey situation sometimes brings principles into conflict with reality. While the theory and principles of instrument design could be viewed as science, adapting these to a particular survey situation continues to be an art.

THE SURVEY MODE

The survey mode (or data collection methodology) is important because it affects the way in which questions are written or questionnaires are constructed. For example, mail or Internet surveys rely more on principles of visual design and layout than do telephone surveys, which place more significance on the verbal language used in questionnaire design. Mixed-mode designs (discussed further in this section) place a greater burden on the instrument designer, because an effective and consistent, yet independent, questionnaire needs to be developed for each mode.

Types of Survey Modes

Travel survey researchers are currently using a plethora of survey modes for data collection. There are at least five data collection modes in common use today: face-to-face (or intercept), telephone, mail, Internet, and global positioning system (GPS). But this list only begins to scratch the surface of the options available for capturing travel behaviour data. There are not only various survey modes to consider, but also sub-modes to consider as well. Telephone and face-to-face surveys can be conducted either by paper-and-pencil or computer. Even computer-based applications have their options: desktop computers, laptops, handheld-devices, or Pen Tablet PCs. While standards for the selection of a particular survey mode might be welcomed, the reality is that survey mode selection is dependent on the survey situation. In addition, the survey situation can best be defined as encompassing the target population, eligible respondents, data needs, and available budget.

Dillman (2002) points out that the 'future of surveying is far more likely to evolve toward the use of different survey modes for different studies than it is to be the disappearance of older modes in favour of only one or two new ones'. For example, in the 1970s, telephone surveys were expected to replace face-to-face methods because of their greater cost-efficiencies and sampling efficiencies (Massey, 1988). For the past five years, some people have been talking about Internet surveys replacing all other modes, because of the greater cost-efficiencies and respondent reporting improvements (Adler *et al.*, 2002). GPS is also highly appreciated for its passive, real-time data capture capabilities, leading to improved data quality (Wolf *et al.*, 2001). Leveraging technology is important for dealing with the conflicting pressures related to response rate and respondent burden. However, technological solutions run the risk of fitting the survey situation to the survey mode instead of the reverse.

Related to this latter point is the fact that there is a dynamic relationship between contact method (survey mode), sample composition (who responds), and sample attitude (how they feel about being involved in the survey). Groves *et al.* (1992) suggested that most potential respondents take a heuristic approach to the decision to participate in a survey. By heuristic, they meant that the act of survey participation was typically based on one or two highly prominent messages in the survey introduction that appealed to the respondent's individual motivation for survey participation. The decision to participate was rarely of sufficient personal relevance to cause respondents to systematically process all available information into their decision. They make the decision without thinking, without processing.

Mixed-Mode Designs

In the 1990s, household travel surveys in the US gravitated toward designs that are best described as 'mixed-mode'. Simply defined, a mixed-mode survey is one that uses two or more methods to collect data for a single data set. Commonly, US household travel surveys have been executed using telephone recruitment of households to complete a travel diary, mail-out of a travel diary for recording travel, and telephone retrieval of data recorded in the diary. Recruiting households by telephone became easier than mail or face-to-face due to the completeness and lower cost of the sampling frames. Retrieving travel data by telephone produced higher quality data because trained interviewers were available to help the respondents provide complete information (Schultz *et al.*, 1990). Now telephone call-blocking technologies and busy household lifestyles are combining to degrade the response rates of telephone surveys. In addition, the change in connectedness of telephone numbers from households to individuals has led to concerns of coverage bias in random digit dialling (RDD) sampling frames.

In the true sense of tailoring the survey mode to the survey situation, survey researchers need reconsider the 'standard' methodology for conducting household travel surveys in the US. This is not a simple task. The availability of complete sampling frames is not concomitant with the number of survey modes from which to select. For example, the use of GPS requires the consideration of another mode (e.g., telephone, mail, face-to-face, or Internet) for recruitment. The availability of a sampling frame from which to draw a probability sample for Internet surveys is virtually non-existent. The same restrictions exist for mail surveys, unless one has access to a complete address database or is able to use a 'block-listing' method. For most household survey situations in the US, RDD sampling frames, while problematic, still provide the most consistent population coverage, but they are wrought with response bias.

Mixed-mode designs for the collection of travel survey data will increase due to the move toward matching survey modes to survey situations, the lack of availability of appropriate sampling frames, and increasing concerns about response bias and respondent burden. However, the trend will be in the use of more varied types of mixed-mode designs. Dillman and Tarnai (1988) developed a useful typology of mixed-mode designs that can be used as guidance for future designs (see Table 1). The mixed-mode design in use in US household travel surveys most closely resembles type four – to collect different data from the same respondents during a single data collection period. However, as the table indicates there are many more ways in which mixed-mode designs could be used for personal travel surveys. For example, the methodology for the Sydney Household Travel Survey fits category six. While its core collection method is face-to-face, telephone interviews are used to collect person and trip data from a straggling household member. If all but one member of the household has responded by face-to-face, the remaining household member is allowed to respond by telephone (Battelino and Peachman, 2003).

Table 1: Six Types of Mixed-mode Surveys

Mode	Example
1. To collect same data from different respondents within a sample	Mail for early respondents; telephone and/or face-to-face interviews for respondents who could not be contacted
2. To collect follow-up panel data from same respondents at a later time	Face-to-face interview for initial survey; telephone for panel study follow-up interview
3. To collect same data from different sample frames in the same population for combined analysis	Dual frame survey using area probability sample for face-to-face interview and RDD sample for telephone
4. To collect different data from same respondents during a single data collection period	Mail questionnaire administered to respondents immediately after completing a telephone interview
5. To collect data from different populations for comparison purposes	GPS data capture used to validate trip information from diaries
6. To increase response rate for another mode	Option given to respondents to respond by several modes – telephone, Internet, mail

Challenges in Implementing Mixed-Mode Designs

If future travel behaviour surveys will be done with a mix of modes, there are a number of issues that affect data quality that must be considered and addressed. Morris and Adler (2003) and Bonnel (2003) provide a preliminary list of such issues. Below, the issues they raised have been enhanced with information from other sources to create areas for future research. First, the availability and adequacy of sampling frames are becoming more difficult due to privacy concerns at the individual, household, and corporate (agency) levels, so that sampling will become a critical determinant in the selection of survey mode. For example, at the agency level, utility operators, cellular operators, or Internet providers have resisted offering directories of subscribers' numbers so there is not a way to generate a complete sampling frame. At the individual or household level, privacy concerns have lead to incomplete frames, wherein persons or households have unlisted telephone numbers, or have registered with do-not-call lists (telephone) or do-not-contact lists (Internet). These same concerns about individual privacy have caused some individuals to house themselves in 'gated' or 'walled' communities, so even if their address can be found within a listing, they are off-limits to face-to-face surveyors. These issues will continue to impact coverage and ultimate choice of survey mode in the coming decade.

Second, the survey mode affects the type of data that can and should be collected. How does one synchronise trip data from the GPS, collected in a steady stream, with data from a travel diary that is collected as discrete trips? Such concerns about compatibility of data derived from different survey modes are far from trivial. These concerns will require not only new methods and tools for analysing data, but also greater care in the survey design and budgeting stages to ensure that they have been considered fully. Third, one must consider the measurement consequences of mixed-modes used within a single travel behaviour survey or across several different travel surveys. Past research has indicated that different survey modes sometimes produce different responses, leading to questions of data compatibility (Bradburn and Sudman, 1979; Sudman and Bradburn, 1987; Holbrook *et al.*, 2003). For example, Zmud *et al.* (2003) found that trip rate reports were higher among households who reported their information via the Internet than via the telephone, when controlling for household demographics, even though the Internet did not reach a different 'type' of survey respondent than the telephone.

Fourth, researchers tend to ask questions differently when using different modes. Whereas face-to-face interviewers and mail surveys often use long, fully labelled scales, telephone interviews tend to use fewer scale categories (Dillman, 2000). Internet surveys often rely on check-all-that-apply formats, where telephone surveys would use a yes/no format. Most importantly, the ease with which a second or third survey mode can be added to a survey design, sometimes overcomes the designer's diligence about how consistent the modes are in presenting the same question to respondents that comprise the same sample.

Fifth, the trajectory of survey methodology is toward diversity rather than unity. Perhaps, the future is one of fragmentation on mode choices and their uneven application to a variety of survey situations. Methodologists have to be concerned about the threats that such a future holds for quality surveying. The more modes that are available, and the more options that are available for tailoring the survey to the situation, the more difficult it is then to achieve standardisation. Our response might be the need for greater cross-communication among survey methodologists, so that best practices, regardless of mode or survey situation, can be widely disseminated.

WRITING QUESTIONS

Survey questions are queries with nouns, verbs, and modifiers. Sometimes these queries are open-ended (i.e., the statement of a question with no explicit answer choices) and, at other times, they are closed-ended (i.e., the statement of the question and the response categories). Asking questions and giving answers are such commonplace habits of everyday life that both can and are done carelessly. To be done right, the question writer needs to have a clear idea of why the study is being done, the proposed analyses, and the specific data inputs for the analyses. As Lazarsfeld (1986) states in his seminal essay written in 1934, *The Art of Asking Why*, 'we cannot leave it up to the respondent to tell us whatever they are inclined'. We need to frame the question so that the respondent tells us what we want to know. At best, our queries should be unadorned and uncomplicated, as explicit and single-minded as a lawyer's interrogation.

The question writer must have an understanding of who the answer provider will be. Lazarsfeld (1986) called this 'fitting questions to the experience of the respondents'. Gendall (1998) summed up this relationship with a single sentence. 'If there is a single, fundamental principal of question design, it is that the respondent defines what you can do: the types of questions you can reasonably ask; the types of words you can reasonably use; the concepts you can explore'. Well-written questions are designed by focusing on the characteristics, perceptions, and motivations of respondents. Although the focus is primarily on the respondents, for interviewer-mediated surveys, the requirements placed on interviewers cannot be overlooked. Interviewers have to be able to read the questions smoothly, pronounce the words clearly and unambiguously, read questions and record answers in an unbiased and non-leading manner, and have clear instructions for recording the responses.

Guidance for Writing Survey Questions

There are numerous guides for writing survey questions and each approaches the subject of question writing a bit differently (Sudman and Bradburn, 1987; Dillman, 2000; Converse and Presser, 1986; Czada and Blair, 1996; Richardson *et al.*, 1995). For example, Sudman and Bradburn (1987) focus on types of questions (e.g., threatening or non-threatening behaviour questions, attitude questions, knowledge questions), whereas Dillman (2000) focuses on principles for making question structure and wording decisions. What these various guidebooks have in common, though, is that their goal is to help question writers *develop questions that every potential respondent will interpret in the same way, be able to respond to accurately, and be willing to answer*. As such, there are common points:

- Use simple structure for the instrument;
- Use simple, familiar words (avoid slang, jargon, and technical terms);
- Use complete sentences but choose as few words as possible to ask the question;
- Ask specific questions and provide concrete answer choices;
- Avoid questions that contain two ideas (i.e., double barrelled);
- Ask questions to which respondents will have a ready-made answer, avoid unnecessary calculations;
- Use cognitive designs to improve recall; and
- Pretest question wording with actual respondents.

Question Types

In personal travel surveys, questions typically fall into two main types: classification questions and behaviour questions. Attitude and opinion questions are not yet a common occurrence in most personal travel surveys. A lot of the issues that can affect responses, such as order effects, are related more to attitude and opinion type questions (e.g., subjective measurements) than classification and behaviour questions, which are more objective. Classification questions are asked to obtain a basic description of the respondent (or the respondent's household, its members, or its property). Such questions usually relate to socio-economic and demographic characteristics (Richardson *et al.*, 1995). Behaviour questions relate to activities (past, present, or future) conducted by the respondent. Sudman and Bradburn (1987) point out that while behaviour questions are the most direct and probably the most common that are asked of respondents, they are not as simple and straightforward as they might first appear.[15]

With both classification and behaviour questions, the two key variables that impact respondents answering truthfully and accurately are the perceived level of threat in the question and the presence of memory (recall) error. This is not intended to suggest that principles of good question design are not important with these two question types. Major points of question writing, such as making the question as specific as possible or using words that virtually all respondents will understand, are critical. There are numerous guides for writing for survey questions, as mentioned previously; however, there are fewer guides for determining whether a question would be considered threatening to a potential respondent or whether a respondent might be able to recall a particular type of behaviour.

A respondent's perceived level of threat in a question affects the degree to which the question is answered truthfully or whether it is answered at all.[16] Not all respondents will find a particular question threatening. In focus groups the author conducted in November 2003 with potential respondents in a household travel diary survey for the Kansas City (US) region, individuals were asked if they had 'concerns' about answering specific questions. These questions were:

- Number of people in your household;
- Number of vehicles;
- Types of vehicles (make, model, year);
- Where you live;
- Where you work;
- Where your children go to school;
- Who you work for;
- Owner/renter status;
- Household income;
- Length of residence;
- Race/ethnicity; and
- Ages of people in the household.

Three focus groups were conducted, one each with African Americans, English-speaking (assimilated) Hispanics, and Spanish-speaking (recent immigrant) Hispanics. The findings across the three focus groups revealed some surprising outcomes. For example, the number of vehicles owned by the household was not threatening but the types of vehi-

---

[15] It should be noted that Sudman and Bradburn (1987) categorised classification (or demographic) questions under the rubric of behaviour questions.

[16] Another phenomenon not discussed fully here is the concept of social desirability (the degree to which respondents feel the need to present themselves in a socially desirable light to the interviewer (e.g., appearing 'green'). The interviewer's approach to questioning is a key to controlling this tendency of respondents.

cles were. 'Where you work' (address location) was not threatening but 'who you work for' was. 'Where you live' and owner/renter status were threatening to recent immigrants. Household income and race/ethnicity were threatening to African Americans. More important than these specific findings was the fact that the level of threat inherent in these questions was diminished when the reasons for asking the specific question was justified to the respondents. Once they understood why the question was being asked and how it related to the topic of the survey (i.e., understanding travel patterns in the Kansas City region), the threatening aspect of the question was mitigated. The latter experience is only one of many reasons why it is necessary to pretest questions with the target population. As questions become threatening, over- or under-statements of behaviour will occur. Threatening questions need special care in wording. Tactics for doing so include the use of open questions with familiar words, the use of an appropriate time frame (asking about 'last' rather than 'usual' behaviour), and embedding the threatening topic among non-threatening questions to reduce the perceived importance of the question.

Mitigating Item Nonresponse

Sudman and Bradburn (1987) state that the most serious problem with non-threatening behavioural questions is that 'human memory is fallible and depends on the length and recency of the time period and saliency of the topic'. One of the key pieces of information sought via personal travel surveys are reports of travel for 24- or 48-hours, or longer, of individual household members. Richardson *et al.* (1995) report that past studies of the results of travel behaviour surveys indicate consistently that the number of trips reported in household travel surveys is less than the number that actually occurred. They point out that such underreporting of trips could not be due to ignorance *per se,* because the respondent actually took part in his/her own travel. Thus, it must be due to the fallibility of human memory. From experience, we know that many reporting errors have a definitional cause – respondents are not aware of what the interviewer means by a 'trip'. Recently, through the validation of trip making afforded by GPS technology, the author has studied characteristics associated with underreporting of trips (Zmud and Wolf, 2003; Zmud, 2004). The characteristics of persons and trips that appear to be associated with underreporting are age of the respondent, the number of household members, and the length of the trip, all of which influence whether or not a trip will be reported – the younger the adult respondent, the larger his/her household, and the shorter the trip, the more likely that the trip will not be reported. This list is of variables that were available for analysis within the data elements collected in a typical household travel survey.

What is important in this type of analysis, but often overlooked, is the fact that a healthy percentage of respondents (between thirty and forty percent) are perfect reporters of the trips that they make. The majority of respondents, if they do forget to report a trip, miss only one. The continued use of GPS technology for validation studies will enable us to define further the conditions that are associated with underreporting of trips and to write better questions or design instruments with such conditions in mind.

Whether underreporting of trips is due to memory error or carelessness, there are ways to write questions to make it easier for respondents to answer accurately. Richardson *et al.* (1995) discuss the benefits of an 'announce-in-advance' technique for reporting travel outside the home when compared to a recall technique. In the recall technique, respondents are asked to report travel for a period of time in the past. In the announce-in-advance technique, respondents are contacted prior to the travel day and alerted to the fact that they will have to report their travel. The most thorough method of collecting travel data uses the announce-in-advance technique and provides respondents a diary. Dillman (2000) emphasises that getting people to record activities in the diary at the time they occur is essential for obtaining quality data. In addition, a minimum of six contacts with the household via various modes (e.g., mail, telephone) is necessary to improve the accuracy of the information recorded in the diary and lower nonresponse.

Aided-recall procedures can also be used to provide one or more memory cues to the respondent as part of the question to improve respondent reports of behaviour. Examples of aided-recall procedures in common use in personal travel surveys include providing a list of activities or travel modes to respondents in the travel diary or asking the respondent, 'did you make any stops as you travelled to "x" location?'. When aided recall is used, certain precautions must be observed. First, the list or examples provided must be as exhaustive as possible. Behaviours not mentioned in the question or mentioned only as 'other specify' will be substantially under-reported relative to items that are mentioned specifically (Sudman and Bradburn, 1987). Second, once a list becomes large, the order of the list becomes important. For this reason, it may be important to place frequently under-reported activities, travel purposes, or travel modes at the top of lists provided to respondents.

Pretesting Questions

The goal of question writers is to develop questions that all potential respondents can and will answer. Pretesting questions is essential to ensure that respondents provide answers that are valid and reliable.[17] Generally, questions should be tested for four characteristics: (1) an acceptable level of variation in the target population; (2) whether the meaning intended by the writer was shared by respondents; (3) the level of cognitive effort required to answer the question; and (4) respondent interest and attention. The first characteristic affects the statistical analyses that can be done with the data. The second affects measurement error, and the latter two impact respondent burden and nonresponse.

---

[17] It is important to note that pretesting questions does not preclude a pilot test of the entire survey process (i.e., sampling, interviewing, data capture, analysis) as is discussed in the next section. The context in which the questions appear does influence how respondents interpret the question and provide their responses.

There are several pretesting methodologies in common use today. One-on-one or cognitive interviews are done to determine respondents' comprehension. Usually cognitive interviews follow a procedure called the 'think-aloud' from cognitive psychology, in which respondents are instructed to think out loud as they answer each question. The idea is to determine what things respondents consider in answering the question. Interaction coding is a pretesting method developed by Cannell *et al.*, (1968) to assess quantitatively how well a question works. In the procedure, the interviewer reads the question verbatim and the respondent replies with an answer. A third party uses a simple set of codes to indicate such things as respondents' requests for clarification, requests to re-read the question, or inadequate answers. Then the percentage of times a problem occurs for each question is calculated. As another pretesting method, an expert panel can be used to identify potential problems with a questionnaire. The participants are subject-matter experts and/or survey professionals. In an expert panel session, the panel reviews the questionnaire item-by-item.

Identifying Problem Questions

Because item testing can become quite elaborate, time-consuming, and costly, it is always advisable to borrow existing questions whenever possible – if they have been shown to work. Thus, it would be helpful to have a database of standard questions that can be used in personal travel surveys. The database should contain survey items that have gained a particular 'survey pedigree' through testing and use in many different surveys or in longitudinal replications. In the personal travel survey realm, there are no known principles or criteria for determining that a question has attained a 'survey pedigree'. There is guidance to be gleaned from the survey research literature. Graesser *et al.*, (1999) identified 12 potential problems with questions that they say handle 96 percent of all problems identified in the questionnaire design literature. This list (or something like it) could be used as a checklist for diagnosing specific flaws with the questions in personal travel surveys and as a filter for identifying questions that might attain a survey pedigree. The ten most relevant of their items are shown in Table 2.

It should be noted, as Graesser *et al.*, (1999) do, that while the types of problems are conceptually distinct they are sometimes interdependent or correlated. For example, a question might suffer from having an unclear purpose (category 10), if there is an unfamiliar technical term (category 4), or if the respondent is unlikely to know an answer (category 9). Question writers can use the problem types to check their own questions or it can be used to guide think-aloud protocols during question pretesting from a sample of respondents. However, more importantly, the problem types can be used as the filter to weed out problem questions. The residual items from such a process could be used as the foundation for a database of 'pedigreed' travel survey questions.

Table 2: Checklist to Identify Problems with Questions

Problem Type	Problem Definition	Problem Example
1. Complex syntax	Grammatical structure is embedded, dense, or structurally ambiguous	For each of the modes of travel shown below, please specify which of the remaining modes you think are most similar with respect to the comfort experienced whilst using each mode.
2. Working memory overload	Words, phrases or clauses impose a high load on immediate memory	Has anyone in your immediate household – you, your spouse, children, mother, father, brothers, and sisters – used a public bus or train in the past month? *Respondent must keep track of long list of family members and recall if each used either a bus or a train.*
3. Vague or ambiguous noun	The referent of a noun or pronoun is unclear	What is your household income? *The word 'your' can be singular or plural and is confusing.*
4. Unfamiliar technical term	Few persons would know the meaning of word or expression	What was your mode of travel?
5. Vague or imprecise predicate	The predicate (main verb, adjective, or adverb) is not specified on an underlying continuum	Where did you go next? *What distance is prescribed by 'go' – next door, downstairs, change in location?*
6. Misleading or incorrect presupposition	Question assumes something about person that may or may not be true	Please select the feature (A or B), which you would most prefer to be included in a public transit service for your journey to work. *Assumes that respondent would prefer something related to public transit.*
7. Mismatch between question category and answer option	Question invites answers that are not included in the response categories	What was the purpose of this ferry ride? [Work, Education, Shopping, Personal Business, Social Activity] *Sightseeing not an option.*
8. Difficult to access specific knowledge	Typical person would have difficulty recalling the information requested	How many times in the past year have you taken public transit?
9. Unlikely to know answer	Not reasonable to expect person to answer accurately	What was the distance of this trip?
10. Unclear purpose	Information sought does not appear relevant	What is the name of [your, his, her] employer?

If such a database were to be developed, there are a number of issues that affect data quality that must be considered and addressed. First, the issue of whether such a database(s) should be national or international needs to be addressed. If national, the question arises of whether and how one adapts the question wording for specific population subgroups. If international, the question needs to be answered as to whether the item is adopted then translated, or is selected then adapted to another language and culture.[18] Cross-cultural research still harbours the myth that questionnaire design in cross-cultural (or multi-national) studies is a matter of choosing and translating a questionnaire with a good (Western) pedigree. On the contrary, it is important that travel survey researchers identify those questions that stand as is (meaning the question only needs to be translated into the host country language, *etic* questions) and those questions that need to be rewritten as culture-specific questions (*emic* questions). Second, the criteria for inclusion of the item in the database should be established. Potential criteria might

---

[18] Harkness *et al.* (2003) identify five different approaches for developing cross-cultural questions. Existing source questions can either be adopted (translated as is) or adapted (translated and evaluated for cultural context suitability). Or, new questions can be developed for the other cultural context. The new questions can be developed sequentially (after the source questions are developed), in parallel (source questions developed by a multicultural group to be appropriate for all target cultures), or simultaneously (development moves between languages and cultures).

address the level and type of pretesting or the number of 'validated' replications the item has undergone. Third, recommended wording changes for use in different survey modes should be addressed. For example, how would a standard household income question be worded if the item were administered via telephone versus via the Internet?

CONSTRUCTING QUESTIONNAIRES

Questionnaires are constructed by placing questions in the desired order, with instructions as necessary for the respondent or interviewer, and an opening that provides an introduction to the questioning itself. Questionnaires can be constructed in ways that make them easy to understand and answer, or they can be designed with features that result in questions being misread and items, or even pages, being answered carelessly or skipped altogether. These problems have little to do with question wording, but are the result of unfortunate decisions about questionnaire format, question order, and, in the case of web or paper and pencil self-administered surveys, the appearance of individual pages

Typically, the questionnaire is constructed with only the respondent in mind. However, an important source of non-sampling error in surveys – one that is often overlooked – is interviewer error. Telephone and in-person surveys, whether constructed on paper or on a computer, need to consider the interviewer who is administering the questionnaire. The characteristics of simplicity, regularity, and symmetry that Dillman (2000) espouses to make the respondents task easier are just as important for making the interviewing task easier. For example, changing the codes of answer categories (from 'yes' = 1, to 'yes' = 0) for different questions in different sections of the questionnaire requires additional learning and cognitive effort by the interviewer. The maintenance of simplicity and regularity gives the questionnaire page a look that allows the interviewer, or the respondent in self-administered surveys, to know exactly how to ask and code or answer each question after only a quick glance.

Question Order

While some principles about constructing questionnaires are specific to the survey mode, this chapter seeks to present principles that are relevant regardless of mode. The first decision that one makes in constructing a questionnaire (regardless of mode) is how to order the questions. Most researchers agree that the question topics (and questions within topics) should be grouped from most salient to least salient to the respondent. Threatening questions should be placed near the end of the questionnaire, if possible, because respondents may find threatening questions less objectionable in light of previously answered questions. The beginning is not the place for a question that has numerous response choices, concerns an unexpected topic, requires a long answer, or is confusing in any way.

Dillman (2000) recommends that the question order take into account what the respondent has been told in the cover letter as the 'argument' for responding to the questionnaire. A questionnaire should start with questions that are topically related to what the respondent already knows the interview is about and then should move to subjects that may seem less related. In personal travel surveys, a typical argument for participating in the survey is to improve transport infrastructure or services in the region. However, the first questions often asked are screener type questions, such as household size or number of vehicles. While these questions are highly relevant to the study objectives and easy to answer, the respondents may not see the obvious relevance to the topic. It may be useful to ask some attitude or opinion questions about necessary transport improvements or perceptions about traffic congestion so that respondents will find the questionnaire interesting and salient. Attitude and opinion questions work well for the first questions because they apply to everyone, and if well written, are easy for respondents to comprehend and answer.

After the introductory questions, decisions have to be made about how to group or order the remaining questions. Czada and Blair (1996) suggest this be done according to the characteristics of relevance, ease, interest, internal logic, and smooth flow through the questionnaire. Because most terminations occur early in the interview, it is important to progress from questions that the respondent will perceive as most relevant and interesting to those that are less so. At the same time, the respondent should have a sense of progressing smoothly through the questionnaire without the sense that questions on a particular topic are scattered through the questionnaire. Questions on the same topic should be grouped, as well as similarly structured questions within topic areas.

Physical Layout

For a self-administered questionnaire, the physical format of the self-administered questionnaire pages is as important a consideration as the order of the questions. It should follow the typical reading pattern, which in western cultures is from upper left-hand corner to bottom right-hand corner. The most important information for the respondent or the interviewers should be placed in the upper left-hand corner and less important information in the lower right quadrant (Dillman, 2000).

It is important that the questionnaire delivers the same stimulus for all respondents. While this principle of questionnaire construction goes against the notion of tailoring[19], it is still considered by most survey researchers as essential for obtaining quality survey data. However, it is probably not really possible to get each respondent to hear or read

---

[19] Tailoring is a relatively new concept that is being tested in light of diminishing response rates. With tailoring, interviewers are instructed to alter question wording as they feel necessary for respondents to be able to comprehend and answer specific questionnaire items.

and comprehend every word of every question in a particular order, but there are aids that can be used to ensure success more often than not.

The questionnaire designer needs to define a desired navigational path for the questionnaire. Well-designed mail and telephone questionnaires look very different because they are not intended for the same audience. Self-administered surveys, whether on paper or the Web, rely on both verbal and visual information to communicate with respondents, whereas telephone or face-to-face surveys rely only on verbal information. As Salant and Dillman, (1994) point out, in a mail questionnaire, the goal is to create a format in which the questions look and are easy to answer. With telephone interviews, the goal is to use good graphical design and consistency to make the interviewers' job routine, so that they can concentrate on listening to respondents. Page design for both self-administered and interviewer-mediated instruments should err on the side of consistency – consistent type style, use of font for special purposes, question formats, answer formats, placement of answer categories, and a numbering system for questions.

Questionnaire Instructions

Instructions whether read by the respondent or by the interviewer to the respondent need to be placed where that information is needed and not at the beginning of the questionnaire or in a separate instruction booklet. At best instruction books are used unevenly by respondents, resulting in some respondents being subjected to different stimuli than others (Dillman, 2000). Respondents start answering questions and revert to instruction booklets when they run into problems. Instructions should be provided at the point that respondents are ready to act on them. Visual components, such as colour, graphics, typography, and animation, should be used to guide respondents or interviewers (in the case of telephone or CATI scripts) through the words and sentences in the desired order. Furthermore, the effects of such design on respondents (or on interviewers) are in need of research attention. For example, Couper *et al.*, (2001) point out that visual features designed to maintain respondent interest in doing a survey (like a graphic progress indicator) might have deleterious effects on data quality, because they require additional download time.

Transitions are an important part of surveys and should be considered an important part of questionnaire construction. In interviewer-mediated surveys, they improve the tone and pace of the interview. For self-administered surveys, they signal a change in topic for the respondent. Transitions give people a sense of where the interview is headed and make it easier to understand the questions when they are asked. For example, Salant and Dillman (1994) found that it was helpful to signal the end of one subject in a telephone interview and the beginning of another, 'that's all the questions about where you live, and now I'd like to ask to a few questions about where you work'. The transitions in self-administered questionnaires can be achieved via graphical elements.

Pilot Surveys

Pilot surveys need to be done. A pilot survey is a 'dress rehearsal' of the survey as a whole. In a pilot survey, a relatively large number of interviews are conducted using the exact procedures planned for the study. The pilot survey is used not only to detect flaws in the questionnaire but also to assess contact, cooperation, and response rates. Is the questionnaire length appropriate? Where do terminations take place? As Converse and Presser (1986) point out, a pilot survey is not a time to make new explorations, rather it is a time for cutting, trimming, re-arranging, and formatting for clarity – i.e., for polishing. A systematic procedure should be used to evaluate the pilot survey, including oral debriefing with interviewers or respondents, field observation of the questionnaire in action, as well as coding of answers and tallying of marginal frequencies. The desired outcome of the questionnaire construction process is a document that has been tested and retested, and is ready to be turned over to the respondent (in a self-administered survey) or to the interviewer (if the survey situation is interviewer-mediated) for full implementation of the survey.

CONCLUSION

While questionnaires must be custom-built to the specifications of given survey situations, there are guidelines that inform instrument design. Even so there are still unresolved issues and basic methodological questions about the instrument design process. A few issues are identified in this conclusion that stem from issues that arose previously in this chapter.

While this chapter attempts to accommodate both self-administered and interviewer-mediated questionnaires, it is apparent that the task of questionnaire construction is very much tied to the survey mode. Furthermore, research issues related to questionnaire construction are also mode-specific. For example, with Internet surveys, researchers are attempting to understand principles that underlie visual processing of information, such as the effects of relative size, colour, brightness, or the location of information on questionnaire pages (Dillman, 2002). On the other hand, with CATI questionnaires, researchers are more concerned with interviewer performance, because it is a crucial part of the data quality (Czada and Blair, 1996). Researchers are focusing on how to reduce the level of interviewer effort. Future research should focus on identifying these mode-specific instrument problems and their potential solutions.

This latter idea is important within the context of mixed-mode designs, and underlies the additional level of effort required for their application. The instrument designer needs to be aware of the decisions and problems associated with each individual mode and to design instruments accordingly. Ensuring the conceptual equivalence of the mixed-mode instruments is challenging at best. Also, empirical research needs to be done on evaluating the potential mode affects specific to personal travel surveys and their impact on data quality.

A pressing issue is how travel survey questions (and instruments) could be designed better to capture more accurate reports of trip making. As validation studies using GPS have indicated, trip under-reporting is an ongoing threat to data quality. The move from trip reporting to activity reporting was done under the assumption that asking for trips reports as a part of a coherent activity pattern would provide more accurate recall of those trips and their characteristics. However, little systematic research has been done that actually tests this hypothesis. Qualitative research techniques could be used for this purpose. A potential research activity would be to conduct an ethnography of the travel survey interview to examine how responses are affected by respondents' understandings of the larger survey context. This research activity would address such issues as: why people think they are being interviewed, what they think will be done with the answers, and how these considerations impact their reports of travel.

Standardisation is a concept that needs additional research. At issue is whether, how much, and what kinds of, flexibility ought to be permitted to interviewers in personal travel surveys. It is necessary to answer the question of how standardisation undermines the communication process between interviewers and respondents, thereby making it more difficult for them to reach a shared understanding of the questions and, thus, reducing data quality. One possible research activity would be to analyse transcripts of interviews to identify interviewer and respondent behaviours that are likely to be associated with travel data quality. Such analysis might identify 'flexible' or 'tailored' scripts that some interviewers use to capture more accurate trip information from respondents.

Research on effective diary designs is important. Whereas diaries are known to increase recall, there has been little systematic research on which diary formats or designs have the greatest possible effect on recall of travel information. In some cases, conflicting empirical results have been found. For instance, Dillman, (2000) states that matrix type designs are too difficult for respondents; that the ability to relate rows to columns is a literacy skill much more difficult than simply reading and answering individual questions. However, in focus groups over the course of designing instruments for personal travel surveys in Southern California, St. Louis, and Kansas City, respondents preferred the matrix design to one in which they were asked to answer individual questions. Whether a diary should contain all the questions that would subsequently be asked in retrieval of travel information or only those most susceptible to memory loss is another fundamental research question.

Related to this latter issue is the need for improved measures of data quality to evaluate improvements achieved by different questioning strategies. For example, to decide which of two ways of collecting trip information results in better data, travel researchers need a better criterion for improvement than the common rule of thumb that more is better. One idea is to build in cognitive assessments to measure and test the effects of factors that may influence respondents' performance on trip-related survey items.

One final area of research is to test strategies for developing comparative measures of travel behaviour across countries. This relates to the ways in which questions are adopted or adapted for use in different countries. Blind reliance on questions (or instruments) not tested for cross-cultural suitability is a mistake. Future research activities in this area should include careful documentation of design decisions that will enable cross-cultural researchers to begin accumulating a knowledge base of question use and instrument design experience that promotes awareness of particularly 'good' measures across languages or cultures. Such documentation would include details of how instrument (or questions) were translated or pretested.

REFERENCES

Adler, T., L. Rimmer and D. Carpenter (2002). Use of Internet-Based Household Travel Diary Survey Instrument, *Transportation Research Record No. 1804*, 134-143.

Battellino, H. and J. Peachman (2003). The Joys and Tribulations of a Continuous Survey. In: *Transport Survey Quality and Innovation* (P.R. Stopher and P.M. Jones eds), Pergamon, Oxford, 49-68.

Bonnel, P. (2003). Postal, Telephone, and Face-to-Face Surveys: How Comparable are They? In: *Transport Survey Quality and Innovation*, (P.R. Stopher and P.M. Jones eds), Pergamon, Oxford, 215-238.

Bradburn, N. and S. Sudman (1979). *Improving Interview Method and Questionnaire Design*, Jossey-Bass Publishers, San Francisco, California, chapter 1, 1-13.

Cannell, C., F. Fowler and K. Marquis. (1968). The Influence of Interviewer and Respondent Psychological and Behavioral Variables in the Reporting in Household Interviews? *Vital and Health Statistics*, 2, (26), US Government Printing Office, Washington, DC.

Converse, J. and S. Presser (1986). *Survey Questions: Handcrafting the Standardized Questionnaire*, Sage Publications, Beverly Hills, California.

Couper, M., M. Traugott and M. Lamias (2001). Web Survey Design and Administration, *Public Opinion Quarterly*, 65, (2), 230-253.

Czada, R. and J. Blair (1996). *Designing Surveys*, Pine Forge Press, Thousand Oaks, CA.

Dillman, D. (2000). *Mail and Internet Surveys: The Tailored Design Method*, John Wiley & Sons, New York.

Dillman, D. (2002). Navigating the Rapids of Change: Some Observations on Survey Methodology in the Early Twenty-First Century, *Public Opinion Quarterly*, 66, (3), 473-494.

Dillman, D. and J. Tarnai (1988). Administration Issues in Mixed-mode Surveys, *Telephone Survey Methodology,* John Wiley & Sons, New York, 509-528.

Gendall, P. (1998). A Framework for Questionnaire Design: Labaw Revisited, *Marketing Bulletin* 9, 28-39

Graesser, A., T. Kennedy, P. Wiemer-Hastings and V. Ottati (1999). The Use of Computational Cognitive Models to Improve Questions on Surveys and Questionnaires, *Cognition and Survey Research,* John Wiley & Sons, New York, 199-218.

Groves, R., R. Cialdini and M. Couper (1992). Understanding the Decision to Participate in a Survey, *Public Opinion Quarterly*, 56, (4), 475 -95.

Harkness, J., F. Van de Vijver and T. Jonson (2003). Questionnaire Design in Comparative Research, *Cross-Cultural Survey Methods*, John Wiley & Sons, Hoboken, New Jersey, chapter 2, 19-34.

Holbrook, A., M. Green and J. Krosnick (2003). Telephone versus Face-to-Face Interviewing of National Probability Samples with Long Questionnaires, *Public Opinion Quarterly*, 67, (1), 79-125.

Lazarsfeld, P. (1986). *The Art of Asking Why*. Advertising Research Foundation, New York (original work produced in 1934 in *The National Marketing Review*).

Massey, J. (1988). An Overview of Telephone Coverage, *Telephone Survey Methodology*, John Wiley & Sons, New York, 3-8.

Morris, J. and T. Adler (2003). Mixed-Mode Surveys. In: *Transport Survey Quality and Innovation* (P.R. Stopher and P.M. Jones, eds), Pergamon, Oxford, 239-253.

Richardson, A., E. Ampt and A. Meyburg (1995). *Survey Methods for Transport Planning*, Eucalyptus Press, Australia.

Salant, P. and D. Dillman (1994). *How to Conduct your Own Survey*, John Wiley & Sons, New York.

Schultz, G., M. Douglas and K. Manges (1990). Mail versus Telephone Travel Diary Retrieval. Paper presented at Conference on the Application of Transportation Planning Methods, Dallas, Texas, April 1990.

Sudman, S. and N. Bradburn (1987). *Asking Questions: A Practical Guide to Questionnaire Design*, Jossey-Bass Publishers, San Francisco, California, 261-280.

Wolf, J., R. Guensler and W. Bachman (2001). Elimination of the Travel Diary: Experiment to Derive Trip Purpose from Global Positioning System Travel Data, Transportation Data and Information Technology, *Transportation Research Record No. 1768*, 125-134.

Zmud, J. (2004). *Technical Report of Methods for the GPS Study for Southern California*, Report prepared for the Southern California Association of Governments, in cooperation with Battelle, January.

Zmud, J. and J. Wolf (2003). Analysis of Trip-Reporting in the California Statewide Travel Survey. Paper presented at the International Association of Travel Behaviour Research Conference, Lucerne, Switzerland, August 2003.

8

INSTRUMENT DESIGN STANDARDS AND GUIDELINES

Tom Cohen, Steer Davies Gleave, London, UK

INTRODUCTION

Workshop Charge

The workshop[20] entitled 'instrument design' was set the following task by the conference organisers:

> 'Because survey instruments, and the manner in which they are used, may vary from one part of the world to the other, aspects of instrument design that are significant may vary. Issues that will form the subject of discussion include guidelines on good practice in the design of a self-administered questionnaire (e.g., layout, font, colour, etc.) or the structure and content of a telephone-administered survey, the desirability of identifying a core set of questions to be included in all travel surveys, the value of establishing standard wording for some questions, standardisation of categories on items such as education level, job classification, or income, and whether there is a desirable ordering of questions in a survey. These issues need to be discussed in the context of different international settings.

---

[20] The following were the members of this workshop: Davy Janssens (Belgium), Felipe Targa (USA), Jean Wolf (USA), Johanna Zmud (USA), Rahaf Alsnih (Australia), Rami Noah (Israel), and Tom Cohen (UK).

'Consider the standards on slides 5 to 8 of the Standards Keynote Paper (Stopher *et al.*, 2006). Is there agreement on these standards and guidelines? Can they be applied multi-nationally? If not, how should they be modified? Are there other standards and guidelines that should be developed?'

Because the second paragraph of the charge was quite specific in its instructions, the contents of the four slides referred to are reproduced here for reference.

- Design of Survey Instruments:
    o Minimum question specification;
    o Standardisation of categories; and
    o Standard question wordings.
- Minimum specification questions as shown in Table 1.

Table 1: Minimum Question Specifications

Category	Item	Category	Item
Household	Location	Vehicle	Body Type
	Type of Building		Year of Production
	Household Size		Ownership of Vehicle
	Relationships		Use of Vehicle
	Income		Fuel Used in Vehicle
	Number of Vehicles	Activity	Start Time
	Housing Tenure		Activity or Purpose
	Re-contact		Location
Personal	Gender		Means of Travel
	Year of Birth		Mode Sequence
	Paid Jobs		Group Size
	Job Classification		Group Membership
	Driving License		Costs
	Non-mobility		Parking
	Education Level		
	Handicap		
	Race		

- Standardisation of categories:
    o Relationship;
    o Race;
    o Disability;
    o Employment Status;
    o Educational Level Attained;
    o Type of Dwelling;
    o Housing Tenure;
    o Year of Production;
    o Obtained Vehicle;
    o Fuel Type;
    o Vehicle Ownership;

  - o Body Type;
  - o Trip Purpose; and
  - o Means of Travel.
- Standard question wordings should be provided for:
  - o Number of Persons in Household;
  - o Number of Vehicles;
  - o Income;
  - o Owner or Renter Status;
  - o Gender;
  - o Disability; and
  - o Number in Travelling Party

As is seen in this chapter, the workshop did not consistently adhere to the letter of the charge.

Discussion of Charge

The participants in the workshop began by discussing the charge and this led to the approach adopted for the remainder of the sessions spent on the subject. In addition, participants were invited to consider the priorities for further research as set out by the author of the workshop resource paper (Zmud, 2006).

As a result of considering these two sets of propositions, the participants agreed upon a distinct approach to the workshop. It was felt that this would enable the exploration of some of the elements of the workshop charge without allowing the discussion to be hide-bound by a point-wise consideration of each element of the Standards Keynote Paper. As set out later, however, the participants did examine the recommendations of that paper with regard to topics for universal use in household surveys.

AGREEING AND SPREADING STANDARDS

Feasibility

The first question considered in detail was that of the feasibility of applying the standards from the Keynote Paper. Workshop participants represented five countries of origin and had experience of conducting surveys for quite different purposes – some to provide parameters for modelling and others to test the effectiveness of an intervention. Various issues were raised concerning feasibility:

- Clients typically set the parameters for data collection and may not be open to the addition or modification of elements;

- Time and budget constraints frequently limit what can be done;
- Surveys are conducted for very different purposes across nations and regions, making the creation of a uniform set of principles difficult; and
- Cultural differences may actually militate against the creation of standards.

This last point is taken up in the final section of this chapter.

Desirability

The discussion moved on to the question of how desirable it would be to have international standards. It was agreed that standardised survey data is very welcome when comparisons across datasets are being made.

There followed a debate concerning the relative merits of standards: would they be enforced? If so, by whom? If not, would they have any potency? Was there a risk that the establishment of standards would be seen as imperious? It was also noted that several sets of guidelines relating to survey work already exist and concern was voiced over adding to them.

A GOOD PRACTICE RESOURCE

The workshop participants concluded that they preferred the concept of a 'good practice resource'. Rather than dictate that a given approach was the right one, the resource would provide tested tools and proven advice on which those designing and conducting surveys could draw. It would, as a consequence, lack the unified nature of a set of standards or guidelines. However, it would avoid the risk of alienating users or promoting a method that, because of the specific characteristics of the location or the task in hand, might be inappropriate.

Having defined this as the workshop's goal, the participants set out to list topics for which they felt support would be most welcome. The items mentioned are set out in Table 2. To provide the workshop participants with a tractable task, a vote was held on the possible constituents and two topics were selected for detailed examination:

- How to achieve equivalence when working across survey modes; and
- Translation across locations, cultures, languages.

METHOD

A consistent method was developed to enable the topics to be explored thoroughly and methodically. For each topic, the participants started by setting out relevant 'framing questions' to which they felt it would be helpful to develop answers. For each framing question, a set of 'conjectures' (plausible answers) was developed as a means of moving from the questions to a set of practical suggestions. On the assumption that the conjectures were accurate, a set of 'practical responses' leading from each was formulated.

Table 2: Possible Constituents of a Good Practice Resource

Topic	Notes
How to achieve equivalence when working across survey modes	If a survey is being conducted using both telephone interviewing and Internet self-completion, say, how can the intrinsic differences between those methods of collection best be handled to maximise the quality of the data collected?
Translation across locations, cultures, languages	When wishing to apply a survey in multiple locations or with multiple groups, how should the differences between the audiences and settings be catered for in the survey instrument?
Data maintenance and dissemination	(It was conceded that this subject was being handled in another workshop)
Handling sensitive topics	How can survey instruments (and the survey approach itself) be designed to minimise offence and refusals or unreliable answers?
Multi-disciplinary team advice on surveying	When provided with the assistance of experts from different fields, how can surveyors make best use of their expertise in designing and executing their surveys?
Demographic bias due to survey mode	Because the demographic profile of respondents differs with the survey mode used, what can be done to compensate for this and to avoid biased results when using a single mode or mixed modes?
Rationalisation with mixed mode	Can the use of more than one survey mode (telephone interview and GPS tracking, say) enable us to save resources by collecting data only once, using the mode best suited to the job, rather than using a second mode as a checking mechanism?
Definitions	Given the critical role of terms such as 'trip', 'household' in the collection of data, would it be helpful to arrive at some shared view of how each should be defined?

The result of this approach was that, rather than simply setting out a list of future research wants, the workshop produced some outputs which will hopefully be of immediate value to practitioners. In addition to the practical responses, discussion also threw up some suggestions of further research which might help to elucidate the subject in question. These research topics are listed after the responses.

In the following summary, conjectures have been paired with the research questions that prompted them. For example, the first framing question articulated in discussions of the *equivalence across survey modes* topic was 'how does survey mode influence data accuracy and completeness?'. In answer to this, six plausible conjectures were arrived at, the first of which was 'interview-based surveys provide skilled interviewers with the opportunity to detect incomplete answers and to follow up'. As explained later, responses for this topic are presented in a single list for simplicity and to allow for the fact that one response may be relevant to more than one conjecture. The research questions which arose from the discussion of the topic are listed beneath the responses.

EQUIVALENCE ACROSS SURVEY MODES

Problem definition

Survey mode is chosen in response to a range of considerations – survey purpose, audience profile, budget, and timescale. Each of these modes has strengths and weaknesses, in terms of:

- Cost per completed interview/questionnaire;
- Typical accuracy of data collected;
- Proportion of interviews/questionnaires completed in full; and
- Capacity to ask difficult questions and/or follow up on initial answers.

As a consequence, any exercise that involves data collected using one or more modes (be that a mixed mode survey or a comparative study of two or more surveys of different types) presents a challenge, in that the sets of data are likely to be different in terms of their quality (and therefore value). As a corollary, if there is a qualitative difference between the datasets gathered using different modes, it is reasonable to posit that some modes typically produce *better* data than others.

These considerations led to a shared desire to explore ways in which to compensate for the inherent weaknesses of given modes. Hence, this topic was selected for more detailed scrutiny.

Framing Questions and Conjectures

The following research questions were developed by the workshop members. The conjectures which were subsequently proposed in answer to them are set out after each.

How Does Survey Mode Influence Data Accuracy and Completeness?

Implicit in this question is the way in which the mode is used: the data derived from the use of a telephone interview, for example, is dependent both on the method and the approach taken to its use. In response to this research question, the workshop participants proposed the following conjectures:

- Interview-based surveys provide skilled interviewers with the opportunity to detect incomplete answers and to follow up;
- Interview-based surveys are stressful for the respondent, leading to brevity in answers;

- Some survey modes provide more information to the respondent, prompting more accurate responses;
- Certain survey modes provide a clear indication of the time and effort required to complete an interview/questionnaire and thus reduce abandonment rates (but also, possibly, absolute rate of response);
- If a 'mental map' is provided, completion is easier, leading to better data. This 'mental map' could take several forms – it could be a geographic representation of the area in question or a clear indication of the survey structure;
- People differ in the way they think (visual versus verbal, for example) and in their degree of comfort with geography and mapping and will respond accordingly; and
- Certain modes explicitly offer a 'don't know' option for questions, leading this to be chosen more frequently than in other modes.

What Are the Effects of the Constraints that Different Modes Impose on Data Collection?

This question reflected the observation that Internet-based surveys, for example, generally collect data from individuals and therefore lack the breadth of interviewer-administered surveys which target all members of a household. In response to this research question, the workshop participants proposed the following conjectures:

- Where the mode does not enable data collection from all household members and where the selection method within the household is not random, sample bias can result;
- Where only one household member is interviewed, the dataset will lack the interactions between household members, perhaps leading to the need to synthesise data;
- Recall methods (respondents reporting actions historically) may produce data of different quality from methods requiring the near simultaneous recording of data, because recall methods are limited by the accuracy of the respondent's memory; and
- GPS-collected movement data is unconstrained by the accuracy of the respondent's memory and so produces fuller and more accurate data, but it lacks the context provided by interviews/questionnaires because there is no interrogative element.

What Are the Different Mental States Associated with the Various Modes?

This question arose from the assertion that different survey modes engender a range of emotional responses in respondents – people may feel more pressured when interviewed at the doorstep than when completing a questionnaire at their kitchen table in their own time – and that this may be significant in understanding how to compensate for differences. In response to this research question, the workshop participants proposed the following conjectures:

- Interview-based surveys can lead respondents to be defensive because they feel they are being judged; it is suggested that, as a result, respondents may give the answers which they think the interviewer wishes to hear;
- Self-completion surveys place the respondent under less perceived or actual pressure, leading to more honest and, perhaps, fuller answers;
- (In contradiction of the conjecture above) self-completion surveys provide respondents with complete freedom, leading to dishonest responses; and
- Survey methods which give advance warning (a letter advising of forthcoming contact, say) can help to reduce distrust or stress.

Are there Survey Questions that Transcend Mode?

Reverting to the workshop charge, participants were keen to explore whether certain questions could be asked in the same way across survey modes with the expectation that data of similar accuracy would result. The assumption was that some subjects are sufficiently clear and free of emotional association for this to be at least a possibility. In response to this research question, the workshop participants proposed the following conjectures:

- There are certain topics that are sensitive (e.g., age) irrespective of survey mode and therefore present equal challenges to the surveyor who is attempting to collect accurate data; and
- Some purely factual information types can be collected effectively by any mode (e.g., purpose of trip, type of transport used).

Responses

Whilst participants examined each conjecture in turn in developing practical responses, the suggestions produced in this exercise are presented in a single list because a given responses may help to compensate for the effects of more than one mode-related bias, making the strict association of conjecture and response dubious.

- Where data are collected without an interview, provide more context (what the survey is for) and explanation (how to complete the questionnaire) in situations where respondent misunderstanding is suspected.
- In Internet surveys, use automatic sense checks as far as possible to identify anomalies in data, thus emulating the natural sense check of the interviewer-survey.
- Train all interviewers rigorously to ensure that they all perform consistently.

- Train interviewers to justify the research exercise thoroughly (why it is being done, who will do what with the data), if necessary.
- Provide clear guidance in all surveys (irrespective of mode) concerning the level of commitment involved in complying.
- Use a database of locations in the respondents' vicinity to ease the task of identifying where journeys started and ended and to improve accuracy of the data collected.
- In telephone surveys, provide a structure for the respondent by explaining movement between sections of questions. For example, use phrases such as 'these next ten questions are about you and your family; then we'll talk about the cars you use before getting on to the trips you make'.
- In telephone surveys, circulate visual materials (such as a map) by post before calling.
- Where interviewing just one member of the household, ensure that her/his selection is random.
- If synthesising household data, ensure that a robust method is used.
- Give advance warning to respondents of the information that is going to be sought. (Some debate was had as to level of detail which would be desirable – should respondents know in advance all the questions they will be asked?)
- When using GPS to provide movement data, develop effective methods to enable raw geographic/temporal information to be enriched with supposed mode and the identity of origin and destination.
- When collecting trip data, prompt respondents to think of missed trips by asking about regular destinations or trip purposes and possible stop-offs, and use logic checks to identify anomalies that may conceal further trip detail.
- In surveys where social conformity is suspected, use test questions in the interview/questionnaire to identify likely subjects. Certain established questions in social research can help to identify individuals who might conceal their real actions and opinions in a desire to appear a certain way.
- For sensitive questions, use answer bands to avoid obliging the respondent to give a precise answer and, in face-to-face interviews, use show cards with lettered bands to introduce a perceived layer of privacy.

Research Questions

As explained above, research questions arose during the course of discussion. They are set out below.

- In long interviews, does telling the respondent how long it will take improve or degrade the quality of data collected?
- If, as was mooted by participants, there is a 'quality hierarchy' of survey modes – some simply produce less rich data than others – do the benefits of adopting a

lowest common denominator approach (adapting tools to match the least rich mode in use) outweigh the costs?

- Does saying 'we're not judging and there are no right/wrong answers' have any impact on respondent candour?
- Do some questions transcend mode effectively? (This could be tackled by conducting content analysis on datasets derived using different modes or by carrying out new targeted research.)

TRANSLATION ACROSS LOCATIONS, CULTURES, AND LANGUAGES

Problem Definition

For reasons of efficiency and comparability, it is desirable to be able to use survey tools in different settings. However, this is made difficult by differences of many types, the most significant being:

- Language;
- Background (the cultural and ethical setting of the respondents); and
- Nationality.

It is noted that the mere translation of a tool from one language to another may well fail to remove the possible sources of misunderstanding. The goal is to find ways of converting tools so that their use in settings other than their 'native' environment will not lead to either bias or unreliable data. The timing of the workshop was such that this subject was explored in less detail than that of equivalence across survey modes.

Framing Questions and Conjectures

The following research questions were developed by the workshop members. The conjectures which were subsequently proposed in answer to them are set out after each.

Which Topics Are Universal and Which Are Not?

Of the various subjects handled in transport-related surveys, which, if any, would apply in all settings? In answering this question, we would both establish which aspects of a survey tool required least attention in preparing for its use elsewhere and identify the elements which would require detailed consideration. Responses to this question are implied by the contents of Table 3.

Table 3: Applicability of Minimum Question Specification

Topic	Category	Applicability of Topic	Applicability of Categories
Household	Location	✓ (NB 'colonias' lacking address, i.e., there may be no locally established means of determining location)	-
	Type of building	✓	!
	Size	? (some societies have much looser definitions of households than in the West)	!
	Relationships	✓	!
	Income	? (Barter/informal economies, college students with no real income)	!
	No of vehicles	✓ (subject to definition including human- and animal-powered vehicles and checks that they are used for travel)	!
	Housing tenure	✓ (possibly null if location has uniform housing arrangements)	!
Personal	Gender	✓	✓
	Year of birth	✓ (some people do not know)	✓
	Paid jobs	X (e.g., agrarian societies with informal arrangements for remuneration)	
	Job classification	✓	!
	Driving licence	X	
	Non-mobility	✓	!
	Education level	X	
	Handicap (disability)	✓	✓
	Race	X (certain nations do not acknowledge race as a characteristic)	
Vehicle	Body type	✓	!
	Year of production	✓ (only relevant to motorised)	✓
	Ownership of vehicle	✓	!
	Use of vehicle	✓	✓
	Fuel used in vehicle	✓	!
Activity	Start time	✓	✓
	Activity or purpose	✓	!
	Location	✓ (see comment on household location)	-
	Means of travel, mode sequence	✓	!
	Group size	✓	✓
	Group membership	? (depends on definition of household – see above)	
	Cost (including parking)	✓	✓

Where and Why Does Translation Fail?

In response to this research question, the workshop participants proposed the following conjectures:

- The local consultation carried out is not sufficient;

- Local consultation conducted is not relevant (i.e., is conducted with people who do not have the desired understanding of the individuals to be interviewed); and
- Travel concepts do not apply in the secondary setting or do not apply in the same way.

Examples mooted in this context were *reliability* and *commuting*.

Which Concepts Are Not Universal?

In contrast to the question on topics, this question tackles the 'meta-survey' – the fundamental basis on which travel surveying sits. For example, do the concepts of trip and household apply universally? In response to this research question, the workshop participants proposed the following conjectures:

- Distinctions between household and trip may not hold for members of the Roma community (a European group which lives in movable dwellings and therefore 'moves home' more frequently than most other groups); and
- The concept of household does not apply to homeless people.

Within a Given (Universal) Topic, Which Categories Are Not Universal?

If journey purpose is a universal topic (i.e., if all journeys can be said to have a purpose of some sort), then is it necessary to define a specific set of possible responses to questions of journey purpose, depending on the setting? Responses to this question are implied by the contents of Table 3.

Responses

Because of shortness of time, it was not possible to cover this subject. There follow two suggestions which were voiced in passing during discussion.

- Design surveys in teams rather than alone, to pick up possible failures of translation; and
- Pilot translated tools in detail before roll-out.

Research Topics

No suggested research topics resulted from the brief discussions held on this subject.

Review of Stopher *et al.* (2006) Recommended Minimum Question Specifications

The workshop participants examined the list of items set out in Table 1 of Stopher *et al.* (2006) and repeated as Table 1 in this chapter. This table presents a set of items which, it was proposed, should feature in household surveys in general. For each item, the following questions were asked:

- Would the topic apply universally? That is, would it be appropriate and meaningful to attempt to ascertain a household or individual's status in respect of the topic, regardless of the location of the survey and its target audience?
- (If the answer to the previous question was positive) would a single set of categories serve for all circumstances or would the set need to be adapted to fit the survey location and target audience?

The results of this examination are set out in Table 3. In the 'Applicability of Topic' column, a tick indicates that participants were content that the topic would be universally applicable. A query (?) indicates doubt and a cross (X) a conclusion that the topic is not universal. Brief notes are given where relevant. In the 'Applicability of Categories' column, a hyphen (-) indicates that categories do not apply for the topic in question, a tick indicates that the categories applicable in the US would be appropriate throughout the world and an exclamation mark indicates that the US categories would require adjustment for different settings.

REFERENCES

Stopher, P. R., C. G. Wilmot, C.C. Stecher and R. Alsnih (2006). Household travel surveys: proposed standards and guidelines. In: *Travel Survey Methods – Quality and Future Directions* (P.R. Stopher and C.C. Stecher, eds), Elsevier, Oxford, 19-74.

Zmud, J (2006). Instrument design: decisions and procedures. In: *Travel Survey Methods – Quality and Future Directions* (P.R. Stopher and C.C. Stecher, eds), Elsevier, Oxford, 143-160.

9

SCHEDULING CONSIDERATIONS IN HOUSEHOLD TRAVEL SURVEYS

Stacey Bricka, NuStats, Austin, Texas, USA

INTRODUCTION

Household travel surveys fulfil an important need in the documentation of regional travel behaviour and determination of trip rates and other inputs into regional travel demand models. Many factors influence the design and conduct of these surveys, including contractual requirements, available funding, and contractor processes and procedures. Although generally agreed upon as important, the lack of standards in this area result in inter-project variations that ultimately affect the comparability of the resulting data sets (Stopher *et al.*, 2004). In addition, some contractual specifications and contractor practices may affect the reliability of the survey data. The purpose of this chapter is to present a discussion of the planning and administration activities necessary to minimise error that might be introduced from the fielding of household travel surveys. Given this focus, the chapter does not address design or pilot testing issues, nor post-collection issues such as validation or imputation.

The chapter is organised about two sections. In the first section, the basic activities that are common to most household travel surveys are presented, along with a discussion of the factors that influence scheduling those activities. This includes the planning and scheduling of events, training of project staff, quality control, and preparing/documenting the final data files. Details regarding potential standardisation of these activities are presented. The second section focuses specifically on interviewer selection, training and assignment to respondents. While not a scheduling issue *per se*, this section of the chapter argues for interviewer training to be more than a one-time event at the start of the project. To improve data quality, continuous feedback to the interviewers over the life of the project should be considered.

Finally, this chapter draws from the US perspective and experience in conducting household travel surveys. The schedule approach outlined herein reflects a process integral to more than sixty household travel surveys conducted by NuStats over the past twenty years. While the questions being asked of the respondents and the methods used to collect the data vary greatly from study to study, this chapter approaches the scheduling of survey administration tasks from the perspective of 'just in time' contact with respondents. This 'just in time' approach has been shown to increase response rates and allow for cost efficiencies in data collection.

SCHEDULING CONSIDERATIONS

The purpose of this portion of the chapter is to outline the planning and scheduling considerations necessary for successful execution of a household travel survey. The customary multi-stage survey method employed in household travel surveys is used as the foundation of this effort and is accepted as a given, to focus on the planning and scheduling aspects of conducting the survey. Ten specific areas are considered:

1. Training;
2. Advance Notification;
3. Recruitment;
4. Placement of Materials;
5. Reminder Call;
6. Travel Period;
7. Retrieval;
8. Quality Control;
9. Geocoding; and
10. Data File Construction.

These activities form the standard scope of work for most household travel surveys conducted in the US today, which rely primarily on telephone interviewing. It is recognised that household travel surveys conducted elsewhere may use a different approach. In addition, some projects may receive additional funding to perform additional activities, such as those associated with equipping households with GPS devices, administering follow-up stated preference surveys based on the revealed travel behaviour in the travel logs, or conducting follow-up surveys with non-responders. Given that limited funding often restricts the extent to which these supplemental activities take place, the scheduling and integration of these additional activities is not addressed in this chapter.

From a process point of view, the activities listed above take place sequentially. First, the study is designed, then interviewers are trained and advance notification materials sent to sampled households. Households are recruited into the survey and packets with respondent materials are sent to the households. The day prior to the start of the travel day, a reminder call is placed. Retrieval begins immediately following the travel day. The travel data are processed, subjected to quality control and geocoding activities, then assembled in a final data file for use in travel demand modelling and other analyses along with the appropriate documentation.

From a scheduling viewpoint, however, the key event is the travel period. All activities are timed to commence in relation to when the travel period will be for a participating household. For any given travel period, the reminder call is placed the day prior, the packets are mailed to arrive two days prior, and the recruitment call takes place in such a time as to allow for timely arrival of the packet. Once the travel data have been obtained ('retrieved') from the participating household, they are typically processed, geocoded, and subjected to quality control standards in a timely manner such that follow-up calls with participating households to clarify responses can be made as needed. When the time needed to perform all activities is taken into account, it takes approximately twenty one days for each participating household to complete the process.

Given that the focus of this chapter is on the scheduling aspects of survey implementation, the contents are arranged from that perspective. First, a discussion of why activities centre about the travel period is presented, followed by timing issues for those activities that take place before the travel period, followed by those that occur afterwards. Within each sub-section, the activities are presented and discussed in 'scheduling order' to allow the discussion to focus on the logistics. At the conclusion of the section, the entire schedule is summarised in the sequential process perspective. As each activity is presented, recommendations for viable standardisation of tasks are provided.

THE TRAVEL PERIOD

In terms of scheduling the activities and tasks associated with household travel survey administration, the travel period is the central point. This is the specified time period for which the household members have been asked to record their travel. It is the key event and all other activities are timed carefully to make this task as easy as possible for the participating respondents. Three important factors about the travel period that affect the rest of the survey schedule include the length of the travel period, the starting point for the travel period, and the valid travel periods.

Length of Travel Period

The length of the travel period varies across studies and seems to be dictated as much by available budget as data needs. The twenty four hour travel period is most prevalent in the US, while extended travel periods are more common in Europe. Two-day (forty eight hour) studies have been conducted in the Bay Area (1996 and 2000) and Phoenix (2001). In addition, for several studies, including Los Angeles 2002 and Statewide California 2001, the majority of participating households were assigned to a twenty four hour period, but subsets of the sample were asked to record travel for forty eight hour periods (Friday/Saturday and Sunday/Monday pairs).

The pros and cons of single- versus multi-day travel periods were the focus of a workshop at the 2001 Conference on Transport Survey Quality and Innovations. As documented by Madre (2003), the data produced by single versus multi-day travel surveys serve different purposes. The focus of household travel surveys using twenty four hour travel periods is the provision of data sufficient for infrastructure planning. Given the shift in interest from 'designing infrastructures to enhancing communities' (Madre, 2003), however, travel periods of more than twenty four hours are needed to provide a 'better understanding of individual behaviour, not only during one day but all over the year' (Madre, 2003).

From a survey implementation perspective, the advantage to a twenty four hour travel period is better respondent participation (measured in terms of the response rate) compared to multi-day studies. As discussed in the workshop at the 1997 Conference on Transport Survey Quality and Innovations, striking a balance between data needs and respondent burden continues to be a challenge (Murakami, 2000). Both the data needs and the respondent burden (reflected in response rates) impact the survey budget. Reducing respondent burden includes consideration of when the telephone calls are scheduled, and, as is discussed later in this chapter, scheduling calls based on the type of respondent will be important, regardless of how much data has been requested from the respondent (Ampt, 2000).

While the length of the travel period may vary across studies, the timing of the other related activities is based on when the travel period will take place for each household. For example, whether respondents are asked to record travel for twenty four hours, forty eight hours, or a more extended time period, the reminder call usually is made on the day prior to the start of the travel period and retrieval should begin as close to the end of the travel period as possible. For purposes of this chapter, a twenty four hour travel period is used for illustrative purposes. However, the same scheduling logic applies whether the travel period is twenty four hours, forty eight hours, or longer.

Travel Period Start Time

The travel period usually begins in the early morning hours, when few respondents are travelling but the actual starting time varies across studies. The Kansas City study anchors its twenty four hour travel period at 3 am, as do most recent household travel surveys, including those in Los Angeles, Phoenix, and Little Rock. Other studies, such as Denver's 1997 survey and the 2001 National Household Travel Survey, began the travel period at 4 am. The actual start time is not as important as the need to designate a starting point for the travel period, preferably one at which time most respondents would not be travelling.

Valid Travel Periods

As part of the survey scheduling process, it is both important and necessary to identify early in the project the calendar dates for which respondents will be assigned to record travel. Because data collected to date have mostly been used to support traditional four-step travel demand models, travel days have been determined with the objective of capturing 'typical' travel. Requests for proposals routinely specify that travel be recorded only for Tuesday through Thursday, or Monday through Thursday. With the evolution of regional models from a traditional four-step model to more disaggregate focus, the need for data throughout the week, including Fridays and potentially weekends, is becoming more important and should be considered in the scheduling of travel periods.

This desire for 'typical' travel often results in travel days that occur in March/April or September/October. For larger metropolitan areas in the US, the travel period schedule might range from February through the end of school (mid-May) or between Labor Day (early September) and Thanksgiving. Very little travel is documented during the holiday season (Thanksgiving through New Year) or in the summer (June through August). This is unfortunate, particularly given air quality conformity analyses that focus on travel during the months of January and July. The NHTS (and its predecessor the NPTS) provides data on travel throughout the year and for all seven days of the week.

Once the window of travel days has been determined, the next step is to finalise the valid calendar dates for recording travel within that window. For example, if the study calls for travel days of Monday through Thursday only during the months of September through November, all thirteen Fridays occurring during this time period would be excluded from the master list of travel days.

In addition to considering the specific days of the week, federal and regional calendars need to be consulted to determine holidays or special events that might result in the collection of 'atypical' travel. Again, this is the current practice given the focus of regional travel demand models on aggregate travel behaviour – as the focus of the models change, there will be a shift in the notion of 'typical' travel. In this case, atypical travel refers to workers not going to work and students not attending school. Examples of holidays that would be considered as 'invalid' in the US include:

- New Year's Day;
- Martin Luther King Jr.'s Birthday;
- Presidents Day;

- Good Friday/Passover (and sometimes the Monday after Easter, depending on school schedules);
- Memorial Day;
- Independence Day;
- Labor Day;
- Columbus Day;
- Halloween;
- Veteran's Day;
- Thanksgiving and the day after;
- Christmas Eve and Christmas Day; and
- New Year's Eve.

Examples of regional holidays include the Azalea Festival in Wilmington, NC (which has activities Friday-Monday across the first weekend in April) and 'March Vacation' in the Kansas City region (a school break that results in a long weekend). Other examples include major sporting events (such as the Superbowl) and unforeseen emergencies such as bad weather days, hurricanes, etc. Consideration is usually also given to when school breaks are scheduled in the region. Sometimes they are scheduled to take place at the same time across all regional schools. At other times, they will vary. Because not all households have students, it is reasonable to assign households with students to record their travel on days outside school breaks, while still collecting data from households without students. If weekend travel is desired, the consideration of regional events is more important, because many events are scheduled for a Saturday or Sunday.

Standardisation Considerations

Although the execution date of the household travel survey contract drives the master schedule or window of time in which travel will be recorded, there is a need for additional research to help document the changing definition of a 'typical' travel day. On the plus side, establishing a standard that calls for travel throughout the week will help to ensure that future household travel survey data sets contain the variation in travel necessary to support the changing modelling paradigm, even if the region may only currently use the traditional four-step model. The drawback is that regional variations (both dates and types) preclude setting standard 'holidays' or non-travel days. Also, until funding becomes more stable, standards should not be recommended for the travel period (twenty-four hours versus forty-eight hours or longer). If this were to be considered, agencies would be forced to consider reduced sample sizes to accomplish the survey within a given budget. Depending on the model requirements, that may result in too few data observations for critical modelling functions.

PRE-TRAVEL ACTIVITIES

Once the travel period has been defined and mapped out with regard to when respondents will be asked to record travel, the scheduling of the other activities can take place. Many tasks associated with the conduct of travel surveys are time sensitive and scheduling about the travel period ensures the activities take place at the optimal time, both from the respondents' perspective as well as from an efficiency viewpoint. This section addresses the pre-travel period activities of advance notification, recruitment, placement of materials and reminder calls, as well as training considerations. The next section addresses post-travel activities. As listed previously, the pre-travel period activities include training, advance notification, recruitment, placement of materials, and a reminder call.

The recruitment, placement of materials, and reminder call activities are linked directly to the travel period, while the timing of the advance notification is based on the recruitment interview. Thus, the discussion in this section is presented in reverse order, to discuss the scheduling aspects. A complete summary and discussion of the activities in sequential order is included later in this chapter.

As shown in Table 1, the pre-travel activities need to be scheduled to take place along a continuum of one to fourteen days prior to the start of the travel period. This means that if travel is scheduled for Wednesday, 4th February, 2004, then the reminder call would be made the day prior (Tuesday, 3rd February), the packet mailed a week prior (Tuesday, 27th January), and so on. The advance notification mailing, which is the first activity in the process or sequence of household travel survey activities, would actually take place approximately fourteen days prior to travel (Tuesday, 20th January).

Table 1: General Scheduling of Pre-Travel Activities

Activity	Timing	Example Dates
Travel Period	Day 0	Wednesday, 4th February, 2004
Reminder Call	1 day prior	Tuesday, 3rd February, 2004
Mailing of Packet	7 days prior*	Tuesday, 27th January, 2004
Recruitment Interview	9 days prior	Sunday, 25th January, 2004
Advance notification	14 days prior*	Tuesday, 20th January, 2004

*Will vary in each region based on mail lead-times

The discussion of scheduling the pre-travel activities would be straightforward if mail were delivered daily and processing and fulfilment staff were working every day. Unfortunately, mail in the US is only delivered Monday to Saturday (federal holidays excluded). In addition, from an efficiency point of view, processing and fulfilment staff typically are scheduled Monday to Friday as they may perform other duties that require their weekday presence. Thus, the actual timing of activities will vary based on the day of week for which travel will be recorded. Table 2 shows how the schedule varies based on the day of week for which travel is scheduled. As shown in that table, the reminder call always takes place the day prior to travel, but all other activities vary in timing.

To understand variation in scheduling pre-travel activities better, the calendar dates listed in Table 2 were translated into the number of calendar days prior to travel and are shown in Table 3. As shown in Table 3, the activities necessary to support travel on Tuesday or Wednesday follow the same timing cycle. Travel days on Thursday and Friday share the same timing cycle, except for when the advance notification needs to be mailed. Travel on Monday has a different timing cycle entirely.

Table 2: Scheduling of Pre-Travel Activities by Day of Week

Activity	Timing (Calendar Dates)				
Travel Period	Monday 2nd February	Tuesday 3rd February	Wednesday 4th February	Thursday 5th February	Friday 6th February
Reminder Call	Sunday 1st February	Monday 2nd February	Tuesday 3rd February	Wednesday 4th February	Thursday 5th February
Mailing of Packet	Friday 23rd January	Monday 26th January	Tuesday 27th January	Wednesday 28th January	Thursday 29th January
Recruitment Interview	Wednesday 21st January	Saturday 24th January	Sunday 25th January	Monday 26th January	Tuesday 27th January
Advance notification	Friday 16th January	Tuesday 20th January	Wednesday 21st January	Wednesday 21st January	Thursday 22nd January

Table 3: Scheduling of Pre-Travel Activities by Day of Week

Activity	Timing (# of Calendar Days Prior to Travel)				
Travel Period	Monday 2nd February	Tuesday 3rd February	Wednesday 4th February	Thursday 5th February	Friday 6th February
Reminder Call	-1	-1	-1	-1	-1
Mailing of Packet	-10	-8	-8	-8	-8
Recruitment Interview	-12	-10	-10	-10	-10
Advance notification	-17	-14	-14	-15	-15

As mentioned earlier, the scheduling of these pre-travel activities is usually timed to make participation in the survey as easy as possible for the respondent. All scheduling contacts should be made in a timely manner – similar to the 'just in time' concept in the manufacturing industry. 'Just in time' refers to scheduling an event (in this case the reminder) to occur at the best possible moment, such that 'returns' are maximised at a minimal cost. In a travel survey, this means maximising respondent retention and participation in the survey through a well timed reminder, either via mail or telephone. Timing these reminders appropriately in the overall survey schedule is a cost-effective way of retaining the respondent in the survey process, thereby minimising the need to reschedule a respondent's travel day because he/she forgot or replacing him/her entirely because he/she felt 'harassed' by multiple reminders that were made at the wrong time. Similarly, several of the pre-travel activities are linked together in terms of timing. The advance notification refers to an upcoming recruitment interview. The survey packet refers to the retrieval interview. In each case, the length of time between the two events should be carefully scheduled. An advance notification that refers to an upcoming recruitment interview should arrive a day or two before the contact, because the document leads the respondent to anticipate such a contact. Similarly, once the respondent has completed the travel log or diary, they are anticipating the opportunity to report their travel. Delays in contacting the respondent reduce this sense of anticipation and may result in lower participation rates or completion rates.

Reminder Call

The ultimate purpose of this call is to remind the household of its commitment to participate in the survey by recording their travel for the time period commencing the next calendar day. The call can also be used for other purposes, such as to confirm receipt of the packet, answer questions, obtain odometer readings, and confirm demographic information about the household. Little empirical evidence exists, within the travel survey literature, to justify a particular timing for the call. Convention dictates that the call take place the day prior to the start of the travel period. This allows the interviewers to confirm that the packet has been received, answer questions, and reiterate the importance of the household's participation in the survey.

For most US household travel surveys, the reminder call is typically scheduled to take place the day prior to the start of the travel period. If no one answers the telephone, but an answering machine picks up, a message is left in order to fulfil the objective of the call. Phase I findings from the NCHRP Project 8-37 (NCHRP, 2002) credited the need for reminder calls to the change in survey method from a retrospective survey to one that required the completion of a travel diary. In a review of recent studies, it was found that eighty percent of the surveys employed a reminder (the majority of which took place via telephone). Of the studies employing a reminder call, sixty percent made one call on the day prior to the start of the travel period, twenty percent made two or three reminders, and twenty percent used four or more reminders. However, 'most of these reminders were to get survey responses and not on the eve of the survey day'.

In the spring of 2003, 1,366 households were recruited to participate in a household travel survey for the Central Arkansas/Little Rock metropolitan area. Of the 1,366 households, reminder calls were completed with 696 (51 percent), while answering machine reminders were left with 331 households (24 percent). Although reminder calls were attempted with the remaining 339 households, no contact (either in person or via machine) was made. A total of 1,029 households completed the survey, providing travel information for all household members for assigned 24-hour travel periods.

The relationship between the reminder call and survey completion is shown in Table 4. As indicated in that table, eighty two percent of the households where a reminder call was completed with a live person also completed the retrieval interview. There was no statistical difference in completion rates between those households that were left a message and those for whom no reminder contact could be made (sixty eight percent and sixty nine percent completion rates, respectively).

Table 4: Relationship Between Reminder Call Completion and Retrieval Completion

Retrieval Survey Completion Status	Reminder Call Outcome			Total
	Household Member Reached (n=696)	Left Message (n=331)	No Contact (n=339)	
Completed Survey (n=1029)	81.8%	68.3%	69.0%	75.3%
Did Not Complete Survey (n=337)	18.2%	31.7%	31.0%	24.7%
Total	100.0%	100.0%	100.0%	100.0%

Standardisation Considerations

The information available about reminder calls supports the need for this respondent contact and also confirms the implicit standard already in place today of making that call on the day prior to the start of the travel period. Although variations in the timing of this call have yet to be tested empirically, preliminary evidence from the Little Rock survey as shown in Table 4 supports the benefits from making this pre-travel contact. It is recommended that this step be a standard part of any household travel survey.

Placement of Materials

As with the reminder calls, the survey packets (containing the travel diaries and other respondent communications) should be mailed sufficiently in advance to reach the household in time for use in the travel period. Packets mailed too early may be misplaced and not available when needed. Those mailed too late result in a need to re-schedule the household or risk the household participating without the diaries. The packet should be mailed in adequate time to arrive 'just in time' for the participating household to use on the travel day. (The 'just in time' concept is used often in manufacturing and refers to the flow of parts such that inventory is minimised and manufacturers have the necessary parts just as they are needed.)

The final report for the 1997 Denver Household Travel Survey (DRCOG, 2000) documents adjusting the length of time between the mailing of the packet and the start of the travel period. 'Travel survey packets were mailed one to two weeks in advance of the scheduled travel day. Initial packets were sent with longer lead times. However, it was discovered that most of the packets were delivered three to five days after being mailed. As a result, the lead-time for mailings was reduced to about one week as the survey progressed' (DRCOG, 2000).

Standardisation Considerations

Although the mail-out timeframe cannot be standardised (because it will vary based on where the mailings take place in relation to the region being studied), testing of the typical mailing time between the mail point and the region of study is strongly recommended and should be standard in the conduct of any household travel survey. Subsequent to testing mail lead-times, the standard should be to schedule any mail-outs such that they arrive 1-2 days prior to when the respondent needs those materials.

Recruitment

The purpose of the recruitment call is to secure the participation of the household in the travel survey. The timing of the recruitment call is closely linked to the mail lead-time issue addressed above. However, there are several important considerations that may affect when the recruitment call is made. First, recruitment calls can be made throughout the week, while the US Postal Service only provides mail services Monday through Saturday. In addition, processing and fulfilment staff may not be scheduled to work every day of the week, concentrating on Monday through Friday schedules instead. Thus, a Friday recruitment call may not be mailed until Monday. If that Monday is a federal holiday, the mail-out could conceivably not take place until Tuesday (four days after the recruitment call).

Second, the largest portion of the survey budget is expended on the actual collection of data during both the recruitment and retrieval interviews. Interviewer productivity is the measure used to monitor budget performance. It is a reflection of survey length, contact rates, and response rates. Survey length and response rates are reflective of the survey design elements. Contact rates (the rate at which respondents actually answer the telephone), however, are based on the quality of the sample and the probability of reaching a respondent at home at the time the recruitment call is placed (as compared to response rates, which are reflective of design and method choices that influence a household's decision to participate in the survey after they have answered the phone). Although survey research is not subject to recent Federal legislation regarding appropriate calling hours, generally accepted telephone etiquette translates into calling households only between the hours of 9 a.m. and 9 p.m., unless the respondent specifically requests contact at a different time.

The timing of the recruitment call in relation to the travel period was discussed earlier. In this section, a summary of prior research regarding the best time of day to make the recruitment call is presented. Weeks *et al.* (1980) found that 'the chances of finding a household respondent at home on a weekday generally improved the later in the day and were best in the late afternoon and early evening'. Dillman (1978) found that the best time to call depended on the population being studied – traditional workers cannot be found at home during the day, while shift workers will not be home in the evenings.

Others, such as students and homemakers, can be found at home throughout the day. Dillman's total design method calls for varied calling times, beginning with weekday evenings then followed by weekend calls on Saturday and Sunday afternoons. 'Those households for which no answers are received throughout the week and weekend are made the subject of weekday afternoon calls'. The last resort is weekday morning calls.

Lavrakas (1993) recommends that, 'for surveys of the general public, Sunday through Thursday evenings and Saturday afternoons are the best time to reach potential respondents'. He recognises the variations in 'best time to call' based on the region of the US being studied. In addition, contact on Monday nights during the autumn football season may be lower than during the rest of the year. Indeed, even more so after the events of 11th September, 2001 and with the US at war, interviewing schedules need to be sensitive to national events, broadcasts, and other current events.

In a workshop resource paper for the 1997 Transport Quality and Innovations Conference, Ampt (2000) discusses the 'appropriate moment' for conducting the survey. As shown in Table 5, this moment varies based on different types of respondents.

Table 5: Appropriate Moment for Interview

Type of Respondent	Appropriate Moment
Shift workers	Early morning (just after returning home from work) or late at night (before work)
Pensioners and other people who spend the entire day at home (except parents of younger children)	During the day – evening calls are considered inappropriate
Parents who stay at home with children	Either during free time (between hours of 10 am and 3 pm) or after dinner
Workers who work from home	Although the worker can be found at home during the day, they prefer not to be interrupted until after normal business hours.

Care should be taken in scheduling daytime interviewing hours. Because the literature supports evening hours as the most productive, more interviewer hours are usually scheduled during that time period. Too many daytime hours in a region without considerable shift worker presence can introduce too many elderly respondents into the data set, which affects the overall trip rate calculations. Too few daytime hours will exclude those 'stay-at-home' mothers who are generating considerable travel in the early evening hours in support of children activities.

Standardisation Considerations

The ultimate timing of when the recruitment call is made is a sequential issue – in sufficient time to allow for mailing the respondent materials to arrive at the participating household's location. The scheduling of the recruitment call on the given day, however, is variable and critical to the budgetary success of the project. Depending on the day of the week, interviewers should be scheduled to make calls at the time they have the highest probability of reaching a respondent. Once contact is made, the survey design elements take over in securing participation. Because the 'best time to call' is largely dependent upon the demographic characteristics of the region being studied, no standardisation is recommended with regard to when the recruitment call should be made.

Advance Notification

The first activity sequentially, but the last to be scheduled, is the advance notification mailing. The purpose of this mailing is to alert the sampled households that they were (randomly) selected for inclusion in the household travel survey. Although the format and content vary, most advance notification pieces detail the study name and purpose, sponsor, and the name of the survey research organisation. As documented in Dillman's total design method, the advance notification 'not only eliminates the element of surprise, but it also provides tangible evidence that the interviewer is legitimate and that the telephone call is neither a sales gimmick nor a practical joke' (Dillman, 1978). His research found the use of a 'prior letter' to influence positively the quality of data obtained through household surveys. Specifically, by providing this tangible evidence of the legitimacy of the survey, households are more likely to participate in the survey. This increased likelihood of participation results in a more representative sample then might otherwise be achieved if the notification were not sent. Dillman recommends that the advance letter be sent three to five days in advance of the telephone call. In cases where a large amount of sample has been drawn to support the survey effort, such as in a large-scale household travel survey, 'the sample should be split and the advance letters sent according to the dates on which the first calls to each portion of the sample are anticipated' (Dillman, 1978).

Standardisation Considerations.

The actual number of days between the advance mailing and the recruitment interview is a function of the mail service between the fulfilment site and the survey region, so it should not be standardised. However, testing the mailing time should be considered a standard pilot survey activity.

POST-TRAVEL ACTIVITIES

Household travel survey activities that take place once the travel period has ended have evolved over the past decade through technological improvements in data collection. For the most part, pen-and-paper retrieval instruments have been replaced by CATI, data processing is made more efficient through software advances, geocoding accuracy has increased with improved coverage files, and quality control activities have been enhanced as well. While the post-travel activities in household travel surveys conducted through the mid-1990s took months to complete (due mainly to the volume of hand-editing and data entry required), they now can and should be completed within a week of the retrieval interview. The main benefit to the faster and more frequent movement of data is a higher quality of data, achieved both with timely feedback to interviewers as well as a greater probability of reaching the respondent in a timely manner for clarifying any data issues that may have arisen in processing or geocoding the travel data.

The purpose of this section is to discuss the scheduling of five post-travel period activities, with a focus on the benefits of daily movement of small amounts of data, rather than processing periodic larger batches. This includes the retrieval interview, quality control, geocoding, data file construction, and documentation. The discussion of these activities is sequential, because both when they take place and how they are scheduled are complementary.

Retrieval Interview

The purpose of the retrieval interview is to collect the travel data recorded by participating households in the diaries. In the US, this is typically conducted using CATI. The household is contacted and the interviewer attempts to speak with each household member age twelve and over about their travel, relying on proxy interviews where the household members are not available. The retrieval interviewing process is usually scheduled to begin as close to the end of the travel period as possible. If a specific retrieval 'appointment' was not made during recruitment or the reminder call, then applying the calling rules discussed in the earlier recruitment interview section would maximise retrieval rates.

The largest issue regarding retrieval interviews is in setting the number of post-diary days for which the household is eligible for retrieval. Often referred to as the 'data freshness' window, household travel survey contracts vary greatly in specifying the length of the window. In the 2002 Laredo Household Travel Survey (TxDOT, 2001), the Texas Department of Transportation required that retrieval commence within three days after diary completion, or the household had to be rescheduled or replaced. The recent Kansas City regional household travel survey had a six-day freshness window, which is the same amount of time allowed for retrieval as in the 2001 NHTS. Although not explicitly stated, households that completed their travel diaries on the assigned day and returned them through a mailback option were exempted from the data freshness window requirement.

At the heart of the matter is a concern for the ability of the respondents to recall properly all travel and the desire to control for this through a requirement that forces retrieval of data as close to the travel day as possible. From a survey administration point of view, the data freshness window helps to bound the time period of retrieval and prioritise the retrieval sample properly to reach all households as quickly as possible. Thus, while having a data freshness window is not controversial, and actually is a good data quality indicator, the length of that window is something that should be considered for standardisation. For example, the short three-day freshness window may introduce a bias in the data set that would be reflected through lower trip rates, because only those households who travel little are more likely to be reached.

To illustrate the danger of restricting data freshness windows too narrowly, a preliminary analysis of mean reported trip rates by retrieval date was conducted using administrative data from the 2003 Wilmington, NC household travel survey. This study, which obtained travel data only from household members age sixteen and over, allowed retrievals within a seven to ten day window of travel, with the goal of retrieving from most households within the first seven days. As shown in Table 6, the average number of reported trips on the first day of retrieval was 7.23 per household. This increased slightly to 7.69 average trips reported by households that had travelled two days prior, then decreased to 6.55 for households that had travelled three days prior. There was then a significant increase to 8.33 average trips reported by households retrieved four days after the travel period. This increase in average number of trips reported corresponds to an increase in the average household size for those households reporting. The trip rates decline slightly for those households retrieved between six and eight days past retrieval (even though household size remains relatively constant). However, on the ninth and tenth days after travel, the household size declines slightly but the trip rate increases, suggesting that in this latter portion of the retrieval window, contact was finally made with highly mobile households.

Table 6: Retrieval Statistics by Number of Days Past Travel Day

Number of Days Past Travel Day	N	Average Trip Rate	SE of Mean Trip Rate	Average HH Size	SE of Mean HH Size
1	369	7.23	0.24	2.05	0.06
2	133	7.69	0.45	2.20	0.09
3	60	6.55*	0.61	2.05	0.15
4	45	8.33	0.87	2.20	0.19
5	52	8.15	0.77	2.54	0.19
6	31	8.16	0.98	2.39	0.25
7	33	7.70	1.02	2.48	0.27
8	48	7.83	0.74	2.54	0.21
9	32	8.19	0.93	2.13**	0.15
10	86	8.27	0.47	2.16	0.10

*The Day 3 average trip rate is statistically different (lower) than the trip rates for days 2 and 4.
**The Day 9 average household size is statistically lower than the day 8 average household size. This difference is significant, as the trip rates are not statistically different between days 8 and 9, so these smaller households travel more.

While the argument for data freshness windows of longer than three days seems reasonable, many practitioners are concerned about retrieving data after about six days from the travel period, despite the fact that travel diaries are provided for use by respondents. The main issue, as stated in the NHTS User's Guide (USDOT, 2003), is that recall would be too difficult after about six days in cases where the travel diary was not used. While the recall of travel data is not directly addressed in the literature, several articles have addressed the issue of respondent recall that aid in the consideration of this issue when travel diaries are not used.

According to Sudman (2003), 'the basic idea in determining a time period is that forgetting is related to time elapsed and saliency. The more important the event, the easier it is for the respondent to remember'. Three dimensions define saliency: the uniqueness of the event, the economic and social costs or benefits, and the continuing consequences. Thus, activities at the time of major events are more clearly remembered than those of daily events (and might be recalled each time a car payment is made). The activities on the day a new car was purchased are easier to remember than those on the day grocery shopping occurred (assuming that new car purchases are infrequent and grocery shopping routine).

Sudman suggests that highly salient events can be recalled for periods of two or three years (historical events for even longer), while periods of two weeks to a month seem to be appropriate for low salience events. He cautions against time periods that are too short, because 'telescoping' may occur. 'Telescoping results when the respondent remembers the event occurring but forgets the exact date. The respondent, in response to an implied request from the interviewer, remembers the event as having occurred in the period mentioned in the question' (Sudman, 2003). Telescoping is particularly an issue with a retrieval data freshness window that is too short, because Sudman (2003) found that 'telescoping biases increase as the time period becomes shorter. The worst problems with telescoping are for very short periods yesterday, the last three days, last week'. This suggests that a data freshness window of seven to ten days, particularly when aided with a completed travel diary, may be the most appropriate for obtaining travel data.

Standardisation Considerations

In Wilmington, as in other studies, the larger households took longer to reach for retrieval, but reported more trips. Standards regarding data freshness windows should be considered by workshop participants, particularly as the data suggest that freshness windows that are too short can introduce bias and result in a lower trip rate simply from the exclusion of the larger, harder to reach households.

Although most data freshness windows close six days after the end of the travel period, preliminary data suggest that allowing a data freshness window of up to ten days may actually increase the probability that those highly mobile households would be included in the data set. The benefit of such a standard is a more representative survey data set. The main drawback is the potential for increased error to be introduced based on the ability of the respondent to properly recall his or her travel. Literature regarding respondent recall suggests that a seven to ten day freshness window is reasonable.

Processing, Quality Control, and Geocoding

The retrieved survey data is usually processed as soon after retrieval as possible. This not only ensures that loss of data is minimised (through the creation of a back-up file in the case of CATI retrieval), but also allows for quality checks and geocoding to take place within a reasonable time frame. Most large-scale non-CATI household travel surveys required an extensive period of time for editing the paper forms, entering the data, processing it into a master database, then subsequent quality control and geocoding. With the advances in technology, combined with sufficient staffing, it is possible and more efficient to perform quality checks and geocoding activities on the data as they are being collected rather than waiting until the survey has been completed. It is rapidly becoming the norm, even among agencies such as the Bureau of the Census in conducting its establishment survey (US Bureau of the Census, 2003). It is recommended that processing take place on a daily basis, and that quality checks and initial geocoding sessions with the retrieved travel data begin within a few days after data collection. There are several reasons for this, most notably consideration for the respondent and the ability to improve the quality of the next day's data through timely feedback to the interviewers.

The ultimate outcome of the quality control and geocoding process, and the level of resources necessary to carry out this work in a timely manner are a function and reflection of the initial design work. The questionnaires and materials designed to obtain the required data affect the level of nonresponse and respondent burden, which in turn determine the level of editing required for item nonresponse. The method used to administer the survey (paper and pencil vs. CATI) affects the quality of the data collected, because CATI allows for built-in quality checks as the data are being collected. All things considered, the ability to perform quality control and geocoding in a timely and efficient manner is determined at the survey design phase of the project. Given the limited resources available to conduct household travel surveys, the editing, quality control and geocoding activities form the second largest portion of the budget, after data collection.

In addition to design considerations, as Brög (2000) indicates, 'as a rule, surveys in the transport field deal with various aspects of the mobility of people, and therefore, with a type of behaviour that only appears to be simple and easily explained but is, in reality, very complex and sophisticated'. As discussed in the retrieval section, the desire is to collect the travel data as quickly as possible after the travel period, within a seven to ten day window at most, due to saliency and recall issues associated with the complexity of data being collected. Out of respect for the respondents who willingly participated and made themselves available to record then report the travel data, a timely review of the consistency and completeness of their responses is warranted. To repeatedly stress the importance of the need for their travel information, then to not review the data until collection has been completed for the entire study, suggests a disregard for the respondent's time. In addition, the ability to re-contact respondents to clarify or complete complex travel patterns diminishes as the length of time since the retrieval interview increases.

The other side of the argument for reviewing the completed interviews as close to the retrieval interview as possible, and the one that most directly impacts the survey budget, is the ability to provide timely feedback to the interviewing staff and thereby increase the efficiency of these tasks. As the Centers for Disease Control (2005) aptly state, 'if not caught early, data collection problems can be very costly and time consuming to fix'. If an interviewer is consistently but incorrectly obtaining bus transfer locations, data quality and geocoding activities can be performed more efficiently if that interviewer is retrained within a few days, thereby limiting a higher level of effort by the data staff to a few days effort rather than an entire data collection session's worth of incorrectly obtained bus stop locations.

Standardisation Considerations

Timely quality control and geocoding requires the dedication of sufficient staff in these areas throughout the project. However, the cost of providing continuous review of the data, comparable to that of performing a large-scale quality control and geocoding effort at the conclusion of the data collection effort, may be more cost effective due to the potential to identify and reduce interviewer error early in the process. It also has the added benefit of reducing the length of time between data collection and delivery of the final data set. The extent to which this activity takes place throughout the project rather than just at the end is not widely reported in household travel survey documentation, thus the prevalence of the approach is unknown. If it is indeed common practice (and has just not been documented), there is no need for considering standards.

File Creation

In line with the approach described above, it is possible to begin final data file creation within a week after the travel data for the first participating household is retrieved (assuming the data file specifications were clearly delineated in the survey design stage). Subsequent completed households can be appended to the final data set as they complete the quality control and geocoding stages. The advantage to assembling the final data file at the start of the retrieval effort is the ability to manage data collection efficiently through definitive documentation of the composition of completed households.

Because some households that have been retrieved may not pass the quality standards or achieve the required level of geocoding, the number and type of retrieved surveys is often used as a proxy for what the final data set will look like. The danger in relying on the counts of retrieved surveys versus completed or acceptable surveys is that the actual number of complete and usable surveys before quality work may appear to be adequate, but, after checking, may then fall short of the contractual requirements due to the post-collection identification of unusable households.

Standardisation Considerations

None are recommended.

SCHEDULE OVERVIEW

If the activities are properly timed and sufficient resources available, it is possible to produce a final data set within one month of the completion of data collection activities. A sample schedule, using the timing detailed above and assuming a desired sample size of 3,000 households, is shown in Table 7. In cases where less frequent post-travel activity is performed, the length of time between completion of data collection and data file delivery can take three to six months. Once the final data set has been delivered, there is typically a length of time for review and comments on the contents of the final data set. This may range from one to three months, depending on the scale of the household travel survey in terms of participating households.

Table 7: Sample Survey Schedule

Activity	Timing (Calendar Dates)
Begin Advance Notification	Friday, 16th January
Begin Recruitment Interviews	Wednesday, 21st January
Mail 1st Batch of Packets	Friday, 23rd January
Begin Reminder Calls	Sunday, 1st February
First Travel Day	Monday, 2nd February
Begin Retrieval	Tuesday, 3rd February
Begin Processing	Wednesday, 4th February
Begin QC and Geocoding	Thursday, 5th February
Begin Data File Construction	Thursday, 12th February
Final Advance Notification	Thursday, 15th April
Final Recruitment Interviews	Tuesday, 20th April
Mail Final Batch of Packets	Thursday, 22nd April
Final Reminder Calls	Thursday, 29th April
Final Travel Day	Friday, 30th April
Final Retrieval Interviews	Monday, 10th May
Last Processing	Tuesday, 11th May
End QC and Geocoding	Friday, 21st May
Final Cases Added to Data Set	Monday, 24th May
Data Delivery	Wednesday, 25th May

INTERVIEWER SELECTION, TRAINING, AND ASSIGNMENT

Much of the work on a household travel survey data collection effort is designed to ensure timely contact with respondents. The purpose of this section is to present guidelines for interviewer selection, the focus of their training, and differing approaches for how interviewers may be assigned to respondents. The goal is to maximize participation rates through proper selection, training, and assignment.

Interviewer Selection

The role of the interviewer is a critical one in conducting any survey, but particularly household travel surveys where the questions are aimed at obtaining detailed information about how respondents spent their day, address information for where they and their children went, and exact times that these travel-related activities took place. The importance of interviewer selection extends beyond simply looking presentable (for in-person interviews) or sounding pleasant (for telephone interviews), because interviewers can introduce bias into the survey data through how they interact with the respondents and how they elicit responses to the survey questions (Boyd and Westfall, 1955).

The most basic criteria are the ability to read questions fluently, followed closely by physical appearance (if in-person interviewing), and voice quality (Wiggins, 2000). Interviewers that are friendly, objective, able to guide the interview back on course, and not take respondent refusals personally perform the best during the actual fielding of the survey. Similarly, potential interviewers who sound like salespersons, dislike certain groups of people, are shy, or are too empathetic should be avoided (Losh, 2000).

Quantitative studies focusing on the issue of interviewer selection and assignment confirm these recommendations and provide more direction in this area. Blair (1980) strongly recommends screening interviewers through the use of a practice interview, focusing on non-fluencies (stumbling over the interview questions), reading errors (skipping or adding a word), handling of probes, and how well they receive feedback. Carton (1998) found that good reading and writing skills were important, as well as the ability to balance the rules of interviewing with the need to take initiative such that rapport can be established. For Carton (1998), the interviewer's level of education was positively correlated with better performance (although she does note that this is also positively correlated with higher pay). Finally, Boyd and Westfield (1970) indicate that self-confidence, dominance, and attention to detail have been positively correlated with good interviewer performance.

Standardisation Considerations

Although the actual survey mode varies across countries, the core competencies of fluency, reading without errors, handling of probes and the ability to receive feedback are essential for good household travel survey interviewers. Physical appearance criteria are more important for in-person interviewing than telephone interviewing. However, voice quality is also important.

Interviewer Training

Equally important to interviewer selection is interviewer training. According to the American Association of Public Opinion Research (AAPOR), training should cover both the techniques of interviewing and the subject matter of the research. Techniques include how to make the initial contact, how to deal with reluctant respondents, and most importantly, how to administer the survey in a way that does not influence or cause biased results. AAPOR (2002) strongly recommends that interviewers be trained on the survey instruments as well. 'Time should be spent going over survey concepts, definitions, and procedures, include a question-by-question approach to be sure that interviewers can deal with any misunderstandings that may arise' (AAPOR, 2002).

In household travel surveys, the ideal approach is to plan for interviewer training that lasts the life of the project. At the start of the project, the focus is typically on the project specifications and study area, the questionnaire items and the objective of each item, and other project specifics. Training for each telephone contact (before the recruitment interview, reminder call, and retrieval interview) should take place at least two days prior to the start of each activity. This allows time for the interviewers to become familiar with the project and CATI programs. It also allows for a second round of training and practice interviews to confirm interviewers are ready to begin the interviewing process. As the project progresses, regular training sessions can focus on the provision of feedback regarding data quality, discussions of the project's performance and progress, and answering questions that have arisen in the course of conducting the interviews. These frequent training sessions can be kept short, but the communication will ensure successful completion of the project.

Standardisation Considerations

Household travel survey standards should address the need to have training that addresses both interviewing technique and instruction on the survey instruments themselves. The highest quality data are obtained through short but frequent re-briefings during the life of the project and these should be encouraged.

Interviewer Assignment

Several studies recently have investigated the assignment of interviewers to particular respondents, based on gender or ethnicity. In addition, there is a greater question in multi-stage surveys as to whether it is better to have one interviewer assigned to make all contacts with a respondent. Both of these issues are addressed in this section.

First, in terms of gender, Huddy *et al.* (1997) examined gender-of-interviewer effects in two surveys. They found that small but consistent effects were noted when the survey questions related to gender issues, with female interviewers eliciting stronger responses from women. They also found that these effects were more pronounced and consistent when the survey focused on controversial political topics. Their general conclusion is that gender-of-interviewer effects were most pronounced when the respondents were younger and less educated, compared to older and better-educated respondents.

With regard to ethnicity, Webster (1996) found that response quality was affected by the interaction of respondent and interviewer ethnicity. Her study suggests that the highest quality data are obtained when the interviewer is of the same ethnic group, but the opposite gender. This type of interviewer assignment, according to her findings, is most important when culturally sensitive questions are asked.

The third area of interviewer assignment addressed in this chapter is that of 'tailoring' the respondent/interviewer contact by assigning a single interviewer to a respondent for all respondent contacts. Under the tailored approach, all respondent contact would be initiated and managed by a single point of contact – the same interviewer conducts the recruitment interview, reminder call, and retrieval interview for a given household. This is in contrast to the typical practice of having interviewers that specialise in a particular interview, resulting in the respondent dealing with at least three different interviewers throughout the survey process. The theory is that the single point of contact for the re-spondent will make the process easier and ensure higher cooperation rates.

Proponents of the tailored interview feel that the one interviewer is able to establish a stronger rapport through the multiple contacts as compared to three interviewers estab-lishing lower levels of rapport (enough to complete that stage of the survey but poten-tially not enough to engender a full buy-in on the complete survey process). Respondent rapport is an important element in the successful completion of household travel sur-veys. Although never completely defined, rapport involves 'a spirit of cooperation and respect between the interviewer and respondent' (Beatty, 2003). In the tailored ap-proach, it would be built up through multiple contacts or interactions between the in-terviewer and the respondent.

The notion of establishing rapport with the respondent is a well-established component of survey research. However, for Likert and other modern survey research pioneers in the US, there is a direct and inverse relationship between rapport and open-ended questions: the greater the structure of the interview, the weaker the level of rapport established (Beatty 2003). Thus, to establish rapport firmly, interviewers must be 'released' from the standardised/structured approach to survey administration that entails strict adherence to the questions as worded and neutral re-reading of questions in response to requests for clarifications by respondents and freed to pursue a less formal interview process. The freer approach would result in the same data items being collected, but interviewers would rely on previous responses provided to guide the interview process.

For example, when asking for household size, the respondent may reply, 'its just me and my husband'. Later, when collecting person information, instead of reading the script exactly, the interviewer might say, 'I need to collect your information first, then that of your husband', but never reconfirm that there were only two household members the way the questionnaire was structured to be read. The danger in releasing interviewers from the structured interview approach is that response bias can be introduced into the survey data through unintentional interviewer leading or the respondent 'agreeing with perceived interviewer opinions' (Beatty, 2003).

With experienced household travel survey interviewers, the ability to interview in a less structured environment may be plausible. However, the benefits of standardised interviewing – each respondent being presented with the questions in the same manner and all responses being recorded the same rather than to allow the interpretation of differing responses to reflect differences between respondents (Fowler 1990) – would not be realized and the possibility of introducing interviewer-related error into the survey data is a strong possibility.

Standardisation Considerations

Interviewer assignment based on gender and ethnicity should be considered, particularly in areas that can be described as younger and lower educated. When considering whether to employ a tailored interview approach, the agency should determine whether the higher cooperation rates and potential for more complete trip reporting outweighs the potential for the introduction of biases from a more open interview process.

CONCLUSIONS

Prior Survey Methods Conferences have addressed many design issues that impact the execution of household travel surveys. From properly designed questionnaires that collect data elements that have been properly balanced against respondent burden to details about why those questions are being asked as a standard element of interviewer training, combined with carefully scripted and well-timed respondent interactions, the successful administration of household travel surveys can be an efficient process.

The timing issues considered in this chapter are based on the concept of 'just in time', from the perspective of both providing respondents with the information and survey materials at the appropriate time and performing quality control and geocoding on the data as retrieval takes place rather than waiting until data collection has been completed. The benefits can be seen in both higher cooperation rates as well as higher quality data collection, focused through timely interviewer feedback. These benefits translate into real cost-efficiencies as well.

Conversely, surveys that are not timed properly suffer from low response rates, increased costs, and the potential for lower quality data. While it is not possible to provide a remedy or correction for travel surveys that are not properly timed, this chapter presents details for each stage of the data collection process and the elements that impact how and when they are scheduled. Fieldworkers who have encountered timing issues can get back on track by focusing first on ensuring sufficient retrieval interviews, because it helps to maximise the number of completed retrieval interviews. From there, it is recommended that the project team revisit the timing between recruitment and the travel period, then follow the general recommendations for all other stages.

Several areas have been presented for consideration in terms of establishing survey standards. These include the days of week for which travel should be recorded, the testing of mail-lead times necessary to ensure 'just in time' delivery of survey materials, the length of the 'data freshness window' for retrieval interviews, and the timely review of retrieved data. Ultimately, the decisions supported by the workshop participants will help in both the scope development for future household travel surveys and standard responses by survey practitioners, allowing for making the most of the limited resources available for most surveys today.

REFERENCES

AAPOR (2002). *Standards and Best Practice,* American Association of Public Opinion Research, http://www.aapor.org/default.asp?page=survey_methods/standards_and_best_pr actices/best_practices_for_survey_and_public_opinion_research#best7, last accessed 5/8/2005.

Ampt, E. (2000). Understanding the People We Survey. In: *Transport Surveys: Raising the Standard,* Transportation Research Circular, Number E-C008, Transportation Research Board, Washington, DC, II-G 1-13.

Beatty, P. (2003). *Understanding the Standardized/Non-Standardized Interviewing Controversy. Interviewing.* Sage Publications, 109-123.

Blair, E. (1980). Using Practice Interviews to Predict Interviewer Behaviors, *Public Opinion Quarterly*, 44, (2), 257-260.

Brog, W. (2000). Raising the Standard! Transport Survey Quality and Innovation. In: *Transport Surveys: Raising the Standard*, Transportation Research Circular, Number E-C008, Transportation Research Board, Washington, DC, I-A 1-9.

Boyd, H. and R. Westfall (1955). Interviewers as a Source of Errors in Surveys, *The Journal of Marketing*, **XIX**, (4), 311-324.

Boyd, H. and R. Westfall (1970). Interviewer Bias once More Revisited. *Journal of Marketing Research*, 7, (2), 249-253.

Carton, A. (2000). *Interviewer Selection and Data Quality in Survey Research*. http://www.amstat.org/sections/srms/Proceedings/papers/1998_161.pdf, last accessed 5/8/2005.

Centers for Disease Control (2005). *Behavioral Risk Factor Surveillance System Operational and Users Guide*, http://www.cdc.gov/brfss/pdf/userguide.pdf, last accessed 9/10/2005.

DRCOG (2000). *Denver Regional Travel Behaviour Inventory: Household Survey Report*. Denver Regional Councils of Government and Parsons Transportation Group.

Dillman, D.A. (1978). *Mail and Telephone Surveys: The Total Design Method*. John Wiley & Sons, New York.

Fowler, F.J. and T.W. Mangione (1990). *Standardized Survey Interviewing: Minimizing Interviewer-Related Error*. Sage Publications: Newbury Park, CA.

Huddy, L., J. Billig, J. Bracciodieta, L. Hoeffler, P. Myonihan, and P. Pugliani (1997). The Effect of Interviewer Gender on The Survey Response. *Political Behaviour*, **19**, (3), 197-220.

Lavrakas, P.J. (1993). *Telephone Survey Methods: Sampling, Selection, and Supervision*. Sage Publications, Newbury Park, CA.

Losh, S.C. (2000). *A Survey Research Timetable*. http://edf5481-01.su00.fsu.edu/SurveyResearchTimetable.html, last accessed 5/8/2005.

Madre, J-L. (2003). Multi-day and Multi-period Data. In: *Transport Survey Quality and Innovation* (P.R. Stopher and P.M. Jones, eds), Pergamon Press, Oxford, 253-269.

Murakami, E. (2000). Summary of Workshop on Respondent Burden. In: *Transport Surveys: Raising the Standard*, Transportation Research Circular, Number E-C008, Transportation Research Board, Washington, DC, II-G 14-17.

NCHRP (2002). *The Case for Standardizing Household Travel Surveys*. National Cooperative Highway Research Program Research Results Digest, Number 261.

NHTS (2001). *Users Guide, Chapter 5: Weight Calculations*, http://nhts.ornl.gov/2001/usersguide

Stopher, P. R., C. G. Wilmot, C.C. Stecher and R. Alsnih (2006). Household travel surveys: proposed standards and guidelines. In: *Travel Survey Methods – Quality and Future Directions* (P.R. Stopher and C.C. Stecher, eds), Elsevier, Oxford, 19-75.

Sudman, S. (2003). Reducing Response Error in Surveys. *Interviewing*. Sage Publications, 231-267.

TxDOT (2001). *Request for Bids to Conduct the Laredo Household Travel Survey.* Texas Department of Transportation, Austin, TX, November.

US Bureau of the Census (2003). *Changes to Data Editing Strategies When Establishment Survey Data Collection Moves to the Web.* March 6, http://www.bls.gov/bls/fesacp2032103.pdf, last accessed 9/10/2005.

USDOT (2003). *2001 National Household Travel Survey User's Guide.* US Department of Transportation, Federal Highway Administration, Washington, DC.

Webster, C. (1996). Hispanic and Anglo Interviewer and Respondent Ethnicity and Gender: The Impact on Survey Response Quality. *Journal of Marketing Research*, **XXXIII**, 62-72.

Weeks, M. F., B. L. Jones, R.E. Folsom Jr, and C.H. Benrud (1980). Optimal Times to Contact Sample Households. *Public Opinion Quarterly*, **44**, (1), 101-114.

Wiggins, B.B. (2000). *Conducting Telephone Surveys.* http://www2.irss.unc.edu/irss/bwiggins/shortcourses/telephonehandout.pdf, last accessed 5/8/2005.

10

PROXY RESPONDENTS IN HOUSEHOLD TRAVEL SURVEYS

Laurie Wargelin, MORPACE International, Farmington Hills, Michigan, USA
and
Lidia Kostyniuk, University of Michigan Transportation Research Institute, Ann Arbor, Michigan, USA

INTRODUCTION

Most current transportation planning models use household travel/activity data that are collected through household travel/activity surveys. These surveys collect travel and activity information from each person in the sampled households. Because data from complete households are desired, travel/activity information about a household member who is unable or unwilling to cooperate is sometimes accepted from another person, i.e., a proxy response. A problem with proxy responses in surveys is that there may be differences in the types of people who are likely to respond for themselves and those who have some other person respond for them. If proxy respondents answer differently from self respondents, and the proportion of proxy respondents is large, or concentrated in particular subgroups of respondents, then the travel estimates based on these data may be biased. Knowledge of the accuracy of proxy records is important because, if records obtained by proxy differ significantly from records that are self reported, transportation planners need to be aware of, and adjust for these differences when using these data in modelling and planning applications.

Questions about proxy-response bias and accuracy in surveys are not new. The US Census uses proxy information supplied by neighbours and others when a response cannot be obtained otherwise, and recently conducted a study to identify characteristics of people likely to be proxy respondents in the decennial census (Wolfgang *et al.*, 2003). The extent of errors and reliability associated with proxy reports relative to self reports has been examined in many fields, among them: survey research (e.g., Maclean and Genn, 1979; Hill, 1983; Moore, 1988), epidemiology (e.g., Nelson *et al.*, 1990), health behaviour (Todorov, 2003), mental health studies (e.g., Bassett *et al.*, 1990; Stancliffe, 2000), and marketing (e.g., Menon and Bickert, 1995). In examining the reliability between proxy and self responses in epidemiological studies (which by their nature often have to rely on proxy responses), Nelson *et al.*, (1994) found high reliability for demographic information and less reliability for information about people's activities. Nelson *et al.* (1994) also report that the relationship between the person providing the proxy report and the proxy respondent affects the reliability of the information. Studies of agreement between spousal reports of household behaviours (Menon and Bickert, 1995), in the context of marketing survey research, show that as the level of discussion or joint participation in an event between a couple increases, the convergence between self-and proxy reports increases. While these studies offer some insights into the differences between information obtained by proxy and self-report, their comparison indicates that the quality of proxy reporting varies considerably over surveys, and appears to depend on the substance area of the survey.

What constitutes a proxy response differs substantially between travel/activity surveys and most surveys in epidemiological, public health, or marketing studies, because most travel/activity surveys utilise diaries, on which respondents record their trips and activities, and on which they rely when reporting these in the retrieval telephone interview. In conducting the retrieval interview, interviewers ask for the diary information, and also prompt respondents for any additional trips or activities that might not have been recorded in the diary. A proxy respondent in a travel/activity survey usually has completed (or partially completed) a diary, but someone else reads from the diary in the retrieval interview. The proxy respondent does not benefit from the additional prompts in the retrieval interview and, thus, some trips or activities might not be reported. However, if the diary was filled out carefully, and/or if the person who is participating in the retrieval interview is familiar with that person's trips and activities, then there should be little difference between a self and proxy report. The question that needs to be answered is whether or not there is an under reporting bias associated with proxy interviews in household travel/activity surveys? The objective of the study reported in this chapter is to determine if there is under reporting of trips by proxy respondents and to identify the characteristics of individuals who are likely to be proxy respondents in household/activity surveys.

DATA AND METHODS

Data from four National Household Transportation Survey (NHTS) 'add-on surveys' were used in this study. The NHTS is conducted by the United States Department of Transportation (USDOT) to obtain information on the travel of the US population. The most recent wave of this survey was initiated in 2001 and sampled approximately 25,000 households nationwide. The add-on surveys are conducted for regional governments interested in using NHTS data for local transport planning. Because the NHTS sample for local regions is not large enough for this purpose, regional government agencies enter into cooperation agreements with the USDOT for additional samples in their regions. In this study, data from NHTS add-on surveys from the Baltimore Metropolitan Area, Lancaster County in Pennsylvania, the Des Moines Metropolitan Area, and Carter, Edmonson, Pulaski, and Scott counties in the state of Kentucky were used. All data were collected from June 2001 through July 2002.

Survey methods, protocols, procedures, and instruments used in the add-on surveys are the same as those used in the national NHTS (Federal Highway Administration, 2003). Households were randomly selected for participation in the NHTS add-on surveys. Prenotification letters were sent to the sample household informing them that they had been selected, and providing more information about the survey. The households were then contacted by telephone for a short recruitment interview in which demographic information about the household and individuals was also collected. Recruited households were sent a trip diary for each member of the household to keep track of their travel for one assigned travel day. Travel information for the 24 hours of the travel day was retrieved from each person through a retrieval telephone interview. All telephone interviews were computer assisted (CATI). The resulting data contain person-level travel data, such as the number, length, and purpose of trips, as well as other trip details including mode of transportation and the time of day each trip was made by all members of sample households during their travel day. The final data from the four NHTS add-on surveys used in this study contain information on individuals from 1,003 households in Lancaster County Pennsylvania, 3,519 households in the Baltimore Metropolitan Area, 1,231 households in the Des Moines Metropolitan Area, and 1,154 households in the Kentucky four-county region.

In each of the four surveys, records were kept whether the person responded for him- or her-self (self report) in the retrieval interview or whether another person reported for that individual (proxy report). If an individual 18 years of age or older was not available to self report their diary information during the first four days following the travel period, with few exceptions, a proxy was not accepted, and the individual was called back. However, if a self report could not be obtained within this time period, the survey protocol allowed the acceptance of a proxy report for the final two interview days. There were no protocols for reviewing responses from persons or households that reported no trips. Unlike the national NHTS where household interviews were considered complete if at least 50% of adults (18 years or older) in the household reported (by self or proxy) their diary information, for regional NHTS add-on samples, all members of the household had to report their diary information by either method, for the household interview to be considered complete.

To determine if the frequency of proxy response varies by socio-economic characteristics, the proportions of proxy respondents within socio-demographic groups (men, women, age groups, education levels, income categories, household size, car-ownership

204 Travel Survey Methods – Quality and Future Directions

groups) were compared for respondents across the four surveys. Because of the possibility that a person reporting for someone else could easily end the interview by reporting that the proxy respondent made no trips on the travel day, this comparison was carried out for respondents with reported trips on the travel day and for respondents with no reported trips on the travel day. Only respondents age 18 and older were included in this study. The reason for this is that parental permission was required to interview children under age 18, and proxy responses from individuals under age 18 did not necessarily represent a choice of that individual not to self report. To determine if there was a systematic bias in the number of trips reported by proxy report, the average number of trips per day for respondents who reported trips were compared and tested for statistical significance for respondents grouped by age and sex in each of the four surveys.

RESULTS

Table 1 shows the number of adult respondents from each of the four surveys included in this study, the number and proportion of proxy respondents, and the number and proportion of respondents who reported no trips on the travel day. Overall, the proportion of proxy respondents ranged from thirty four to thirty eight percent in these four surveys, and the proportion of respondents reporting no trips ranged from twelve to fifteen percent.

Table 1: Number of Respondents, Proxy Respondents, and Respondents with No Trips

Survey	All Adult Respondents	Proxy Respondents (Percent of all)	Respondents Reporting No Trips (Percent of all)
Lancaster	1,390	529 (38.1%)	220 (15.8%)
Baltimore	6,019	2,047 (34.0%)	744 (12.4%)
Des Moines	2,244	785 (35.0%)	342 (15.2%)
Kentucky	2,071	787 (38.0%)	287 (13.9%)

Table 2 shows the number and proportion of proxy respondents from among adult respondents who reported at least at least one trip on the travel day, and among those who reported no trips on the travel day. About one-third of respondents who reported at least one trip in all four surveys were proxy respondents. Of respondents who reported no trips on the travel day, approximately one-half responded by proxy. The dichotomous classification of respondents by whether or not any trips were reported for the travel day is denoted as trip/no trip in subsequent tables.

Comparing the proportion of proxy respondents among men and women (Table 3) shows that men were more likely to be proxy respondents than women. In all four surveys, the proportion of proxy respondents among men was consistently higher than among women. This was true for the respondents with reported trips as well as those with no reported trips. The proportion of proxy respondents among men ranged from thirty five to forty nine percent across the four surveys for those with trips on the travel day, and from sixty to sixty five percent for those with no trips. The proportion of proxy respondents among women ranged from twenty three to thirty two percent for those with trips, and from thirty two to forty nine percent for those with no trips.

Table 2: Number and Proportion of Proxy Respondents by Trip/No Trip

Survey	Proxy Respondents with Trips (Percent of N) N (Respondents with Trips)	Proxy Respondents with No Trips (Percent of N) N (Respondents with No Trips)
Lancaster	412 (33.4%) N=1,170	117 (53.2%) N=220
Baltimore	1,681 (31.9%) N=5,275	366 (49.2%) N=744
Des Moines	622 (32.7%) N=1,902	163 (47.7%) N=342
Kentucky	659 (36.9%) N=1,784	128 (44.6%) N=287

Table 3: Number and Proportion of Male and Female Proxy Respondents by Trip/No Trip

Survey	Male Proxy Respondents Percent of N N=Male Respondents		Female Proxy Respondents Percent of N N=Female Respondents	
	Trip	No trip	Trip	No trip
Lancaster	218 (35.1%) N=621	53 (59.6%) N=89	194 (31.6%) N=612	64 (48.9%) N=131
Baltimore	970 (40.0%) N=2,427	179 (62.4%) N=287	711 (25.0%) N=2,848	184 (40.5%) N=454
Des Moines	386 (43.1%) N=895	96 (64.9%) N=148	236 (23.4%) N=1,007	67 (43.5%) N=194
Kentucky	423 (48.6%) N=871	72 (63.7%) N=113	236 (26.8%) N=913	56 (32.2%) N=174

Table 4 shows the number and proportion of proxy respondents within each of three age categories (eighteen to thirty four years, thirty five to fifty four years, and fifty five years and older). Examination of the table shows that overall, the youngest respondents (eighteen to thirty four) were more likely to respond by proxy than older respondents. The highest proportion of proxy respondents was in the youngest age group in all four surveys among respondents with trips, and in three of the surveys among respondents with no trips. Although the lowest proportion of proxy respondents with trips was in the oldest age group in all four surveys, this pattern was not evident among respondents with no trips.

The pattern in the proportions of proxy respondents by educational levels (Table 5) was not as clear as the patterns by sex and age. Among respondents with trips, the highest proportions of proxy respondents were consistently among those with less than a high-school education, but no pattern was discerned at the higher education levels. Among respondents with no trips, no trends or patterns in proportion of proxy responses by education level were evident.

Table 4: Number and Proportion of Proxy Respondents in Each Age Category (N) by Trip/No Trip

Age	Lancaster		Baltimore		Des Moines		Kentucky	
	Trip	No Trip	Trip	No Trip	Trip	No Trip	Trip	No Trip
18-34	153	28	451	67	153	29	210	21
	(48.0%)	(57.1%)	(38.3%)	(63.2%)	(41.7%)	(50.9%)	(46.1%)	(44.7%)
	N=319	N=49	N=1,186	N=106	N=369	N=57	N=456	N=47
35-54	242	28	723	88	294	58	266	45
	(36.3%)	(45.9%)	(32.2%)	(44.4%)	(33.2%)	(46.0%)	(34.2%)	(52.3%)
	N=666	N=61	N=2,245	N=198	N=886	N=126	N=778	N=86
55+	146	61	491	197	174	76	183	61
	(28.1%)	(56.0%)	(27.6%)	(46.9%)	(26.9%)	(48.4%)	(33.3%)	(39.9%)
	N=519	N=109	N=1,778	N=420	N=648	N=157	N=550	N=153
Total	541	117	1,665	352	622	163	659	127
	(36.0%)	(53.2%)	(32.0%)	(47.3%)	(32.7%)	(47.7%)	(36.9%)	(44.4%)
	N=1504	N=220	N=5,209	N=744	N=1,902	N=342	N=1,784	N=286

Table 5: Number and Proportion of Proxy Respondents in Each Educational Level (N) by Trip/No Trip

Education Level	Lancaster		Baltimore		Des Moines		Kentucky	
	Trip	No Trip	Trip	No Trip	Trip	No Trip	Trip	No Trip
Less than High School	88	37	170	98	49	52	123	15
	(47.3%)	(61.7%)	(38.1%)	(51.4%)	(49.5%)	(55.9%)	(43.8%)	(46.9%)
	N=186	N=60	N=446	N=191	N=99	N=93	N=281	N=32
High School Graduate	238	49	556	136	235	64	282	60
	(37.4%)	(51.0%)	(37.8%)	(52.1%)	(35.1%)N	(43.5%)	(39.1%)	(46.5%)
	N=636	N=96	N=1,407	N=261	=669	N=147	N=722	N=129
Voc./Tech Training	23	2	30	7	28	4	23	4
	(37.1%)	(33.3%)	(31.6%)	(58.3%)	(34.1%)	(33.3%)	(34.8%)	(40.0%)
	N=62	N=6	N=95	N=12	N=82	N=12	N=66	N=10
Some College	48	12	236	40	82	12	96	17
	(33.1%)	(63.2%)	(27.7%)	(40.8%)	(26.0%)	(34.3%)	(32.5%)	(43.4%)
	N=145	N=19	N=853	N=98	N=315	N=35	N=295	N=39
Assoc. Degree	18	1	86	10	41	8	30	8
	(29.5%)	(50.0%)	(32.5%)	(33.3%)	(37.3%)	(50.0%)	(33.0%)	(57.1%)
	N=61	N=2	N=264	N=30	N=110	N=16	N=91	N=14
Bachelor Degree	86	6	307	36	126	12	49	11
	(35.7%)	(28.6%)	(29.5%)	(36.4%)	(30.4%)	(66.7%)	(29.7%)	(28.9%)
	N=241	N=21	N=1,041	N=99	N=414	N=18	N=165	N=38
Some Graduate	6	1	35	2	12	0	4	2
	(17.6%)	(50.0%)	(26.1%)	(28.6%)	(27.3%)	(0.0%)	(20.0%)	(66.7%)
	N=34	N=2	N=134	N=7	N=44	N=3	N=20	N=3
Graduate Degree	34	6	245	23	49	7	52	10
	(24.5%)	(54.5%)	(27.1%)	(37.7%)	(29.0%)	(53.8%)	(36.1%)	(50.0%)
	N=139	N=11	N=905	N=61	N=169	N=13	N=144	N=20
Total	541	114	1,665	352	622	159	659	127
	(36.0%)	(52.5%)	(32.0%)N	(48.3%)	(32.7%)	47.2(%)	(36.9%)	(44.6%)
	N=1477	N=217	=5,209	N=729	N=1,902	N=337	N=1,784	N=285

Examining the proportions of proxy respondents within work status categories, shows a consistent pattern across the four surveys for respondents with trips (Table 6). Among these, students had the highest proportions of proxies (ranging from forty five to sixty two percent across the surveys), followed by respondents who work. The proxy proportions of respondents with trips who did not work, were homemakers, or were retired were quite similar to each other, with ranges between twenty five and thirty five percent, in three of the four surveys. In the fourth survey (Lancaster), the proportion of proxy respondents among retired respondents was lower at fifteen percent. Interestingly, the proxy proportion of retired respondents with no trips was much higher than for those with trips, and ranged from forty one to eighty eight percent across the four surveys.

Examining the pattern of proxy responses by income (Table 7) shows the lowest proportion of proxy respondents among respondents in the lowest income group across all four surveys for respondents with trips and those with no trips. However, no consistent pattern in the proportion of proxy respondents by income for higher income groups was found across the four surveys.

Table 8 shows that the proportion of proxy responses increases with the number of people in the household. This pattern was consistent across all four surveys for respondents with trips, and was found in two of the surveys for respondents with no trips. Because members of the same household are the ones called upon to give the proxy report, it is not surprising that there were no proxy respondents in one-person households.

Table 6: Number and Proportion of Proxy Respondents in Each Work Status Group (N) by Trip/No Trip

Work Status	Proxy Respondents in Lancaster		Proxy Respondents in Baltimore		Proxy Respondents in Des Moines		Proxy Respondents in Kentucky	
	With Trips	With No Trips	With Trips	With No Trips	With Trips	With No Trips	With Trips	With No Trips
Working	373 (40.0%) N=931	42 (53.2%) N=79	1,113 (34.5%) N=3,229	84 (41.8%) N=201	433 (35.0%) N=1,236	50 (54.3%) N=92	416 (40.6%) N=1,024	47 (49.0%) N=96
Not Working	12 (25.5%) N=47	3 (50.0%) N=6	67 (26.8%) N=250	22 (18.6%) N=118	30 (33.3%) N=90	12 (41.4%) N=29	31 (34.8%) N=89	7 (36.8%) N=19
Homemaker	35 (25.3%) N=154	20 (46.5%) N=43	92 (25.3%) N=364	36 (50.7%) N=71	28 (24.1%) N=116	15 (27.8%) N=53	45 (23.9%) N=188	16 (45.7%) N=35
Student	13 (61.9%) N=21	3 (100%) N=3	64 (45.1%) N=142	13 29.5% N=44	21 (58.3%) N=36	3 (100%) N=3	27 (58.7%) N=46	3 (75.0%) N=4
Retired/Other	42 (14.7%) N=285	49 (55.1%) N=89	326 (26.7%) N=1,220	209 (87.8%) N=238	110 (25.9%) N=424	83 (50.6%) N=164	140 (32.0%) N=437	55 (41.4%) N=133
Total	541 (36.0%) N=1,504	117 (53.2%) N=220	1,662 (31.9%) N=5,205	364 (54.2%) N=672	622 (32.7%) N=1,902	163 (47.7%) N=342	659 (36.9%) N=1,784	128 (45.0%) N=287

Table 7: Number and Proportion of Proxy Respondents in Each Income Category (N) by Trip/No Trip

Annual Household Income	Lancaster		Baltimore		Des Moines		Kentucky	
	Trip	No trip	Trip	No trip	Trip	No trip	Trip	No trip
Less than $20,000	36 (24.8%) N=145	10 (34.5%) 29	107 (18.6%) N=574	56 (32.4%) 173	38 (24.2%) N=157	41 (45.6%) 90	75 (25.2%) N=298	15 (28.8%) 52
$20,001–$50,000	243 (35.2%) N=690	55 (55.0%) 100	440 (29.5%) N=1,494	123 (56.2%) 219	185 (28.3%) N=653	60 (53.6%) 112	307 (37.9%) N=809	49 (49.0%) 100
$50,001–$70,000	136 (39.3%) N=	14 (50.0%) 28	290 (34.9%) N=832	48 (57.8%) 83	148 (36.4%) N=407	21 (47.7%) 44	87 (35.4%) N=246	19 (59.4%) 32
$70,001–$100,000	78 (40.4%) N=193	15 (68.2%) 22	317 (35.9%) N=883	51 (62.2%) 82	119 (34.0%) N=322	9 (47.4%) 19	87 (44.2%) N=197	21 (48.8%) 43
more than $100,000	48 (36.9%) N=130	8 (88.9%) 9	346 (39.1%) N=886	33 (53.2%) 62	77 (40.5%) N=190	11 (61.1%) 18	49 (44.1%) N=111	10 (43.5%) 23
Total	541 (36.0%) N=1,504	112 (59.6%) 188	1,500 (32.1%) N=4,669	311 (50.2%) 619	567 (32.8%) N=1,729	142 (50.2%) 283	605 (36.4%) N=1,661	114 (41.0%) 278

Table 8: Number and Proportion of Proxy Respondents in Each Household Size Category (N) by Trip/No Trip

People in Household	Proxy Respondents							
	Lancaster		Baltimore		Des Moines		Kentucky	
	Trip	No trip	Trip	No trip	Trip	No trip	Trip	No trip
1	0 (0%) N=162	0 (0%) N=22	0 (0%) N=950	0 (0%) N=145	0 (0%) N=245	0 (0%) N=34	0 (0%) N=186	0 (0%) N=46
2	158 (26.6%) N=593	60 (54.5%) N=110	733 (34.4%) N=2,133	181 (55.0%) N=329	280 (33.7%) N=831	88 (51.5%) N=171	292 (36.5%) N=800	73 (51.0%) N=143
3	113 (43.1%) N=262	26 (60.5%) N=43	374 (41.3%) N=906	77 (77.0%) N=100	126 (40.9%) N=308	37 (52.1%) N=71	167 (45.3%) N=369	24 (64.9%) N=37
4+	204 (48.5%) N=421	31 (68.9%) N=45	558 (45.7%) N=1,220	108 (63.5%) N=170	216 (41.7%) N=518	38 (57.6%) N=66	200 (46.6%) N=429	31 (50.8%) N=61
Total	541 (36.0%) N=1,504	117 (53.2%) N=220	1,665 (32.0%) N=5,209	366 (49.2%) N=744	622 (32.7%) N=1,902	163 (47.7%) N=342	659 (36.9%) N=1,784	128 (44.6%) N=287

The proportion of proxy respondents within household car ownership categories was also examined. Table 9 shows that the proportion of proxy respondents increased as the number of vehicles owned or leased by the household increased. The pattern was consistent for respondents with and without trips across all four surveys.

Table 9: Number and Proportion of Proxy Respondents in Each Household by Vehicle Owned/Leased Category (N) by Trip/No Trip

HH Vehi-cles	Lancaster		Baltimore		Des Moines		Kentucky	
	Trip	No trip	Trip	No trip	Trip	No trip	Trip	No trip
0	6 (27.3%) N=22	6 (27.3%) N=22	0 (--) N=0	61 (35.1%) N=174	0 (--) N=0	3 (21.4%) N=14	0 (--) N=0	2 (13.3%) N=15
1	51 (19.7%) N=259	27 (49.1%) N=55	249 (18.8%) N=1,326	93 (43.9%) N=212	33 (11.4%) N=289	33 (42.9%) N=77	48 (17.3%) N=278	15 (25.9%) N=58
2	283 (38.1%) N=742	46 (54.1%) N=85	771 (35.5%) N=2,174	137 (58.5%) N=234	307 (34.3%) N=896	64 (43.8%) N=146	286 (36.8%) N=778	57 (46.3%) N=123
3+	201 (41.8%) N=481	38 (65.5%) N=58	550 (45.8%) N=1,201	75 (60.5%) N=124	282 (40.2%) N=701	63 (60.0%) N=105	322 (45.8%) N=703	54 (59.3%) N=91
Total	541 (36.0%) N=1,504	117 (53.2%) N=220	1,570 (33.4%) N=4,701	366 (49.2%) N=744	622 (33.0%) N=1,886	163 (47.7) N=342	656 (37.3%) N=1,759	128 (44.6%) N=287

Comparison of Trip Means

The average number of trips for respondents who had reported at least one trip, was calculated for six categories of age and sex, by self or proxy report. Table 10 shows the average number of trips, standard deviation, and number of respondents for each group. Table 11 shows the differences between the mean number of trips of self and proxy respondents in each group and notes the statistical significance of the difference.

Tests of the null hypothesis indicate that the difference between the trip rates for both adult men and adult women, who reported some travel is different from zero, in practical terms that indicates that the reported self-reported, and proxy trip rates are really different from each other. Examining the difference by age and sex, shows that the differences between the trip rates for self and proxy respondents are consistently significant for women age eighteen to fifty four, and range from 0.4 to 1.2 trips/day. Trip rates from proxy responses were not as consistently different from self responses for men in the same age groups (eighteen to fifty four). In the oldest age group (fifty five and over) the differences between self reported and proxy trip rates were more significant for men than for women.

DISCUSSION

This study found that the proportions of proxy responses in household travel surveys that use the same protocol are similar even though they were conducted in different regions and household density areas of the US. The proportion of individuals age eighteen or older responding by proxy was thirty four to thirty eight percent in the four surveys. It should be noted that, trip information from all adults in the household was required for the household interview to be considered complete in these surveys. In surveys with less stringent definitions of a complete household interview, the percentage of proxies would most likely be less. The proportions of individuals who reported no trips on the travel day were very similar at approximately fourteen percent across the four surveys. Again, this is most likely attributed to the same protocol followed in these surveys. Of proxy respondents, sixteen to twenty two percent reported no trips, while this proportion among self-reporting respondents was approximately twelve percent across the surveys. Clearly, a greater portion of proxy respondents reported no trips. This may be because they really did not make any trips. It could also be because they did not fill out the diary completely, and the person making the proxy report was not familiar enough with their trips and activities to provide the information, or the household simply wanted to provide some response for the 'household holdout' and end the survey call-backs. There were no procedures or protocols in the NHTS survey (and therefore in these four add-on surveys) to check on individuals reporting no trips. This suggests that standard procedures for following up on individuals (or at least households) with no reported trips are needed in household travel surveys to determine with more certainty if the record represents no travel or is a case of missing data.

Table 10: Comparison of Trips per Day of Self and Proxy Respondents by Sex and Age

Age	Sex	Lancaster		Baltimore		Des Moines		Kentucky	
		Mean Trips/Day (sd) (N)		Mean Trips/Day (sd) (N)		Mean Trips/Day (sd) (N)		Mean Trips/Day (sd) (N)	
		Self-report	Proxy-report	Self-report	Proxy-report	Self-report	Proxy-report	Self-report	Proxy-report
18-34	Men	4.04 (2.07) (71)	4.30 (2.50) (107)	4.61 (2.43) (295)	3.75 (1.99) (246)	4.14 (2.24) (80)	3.79 (2.23) (89)	4.00 (2.19) (91)	3.68 (1.99) (131)
	Women	5.00 (2.72) (112)	4.19 (2.18) (63)	4.73 (2.57) (455)	3.91 (2.24) (211)	5.03 (2.67) (134)	4.05 (2.31) (64)	5.03 (2.54) (155)	4.32 (2.41) (79)
35-54	Men	4.57 (2.07) (197)	4.16 (2.46) (159)	4.37 (2.37) (615)	3.93 (2.23) (457)	4.79 (2.60) (240)	4.68 (3.03) (181)	4.22 (2.51) (202)	3.78 (2.20) (167)
	Women	5.07 (2.72) (255)	4.58 (2.50) (106)	4.90 (2.63) (930)	4.08 (2.28) (274)	5.64 (3.06) (352)	4.43 (2.42) (113)	4.77 (2.59) (310)	3.81 (2.18) (101)
55+	Men	5.34 (2.82) (194)	4.29 (2.65) (85)	4.72 (2.45) (549)	4.18 (2.35) (273)	4.90 (2.38) (189)	4.28 (2.46) 116	4.61 (2.59) (155)	4.55 (2.56) (128)
	Women	4.96 (2.69) (231)	4.19 (2.18) (81)	4.20 (2.26) (754)	3.98 (2.00) 229	4.59 (2.56) 285	4.20 (2.50) 59	4.24 (2.20) (212)	3.51 (1.82) (59)
All Men Age 18-55+		4.81 (2.71) (462)	4.23 (2.51) (351	4.55 (2.41) (1,459)	3.95 (2.21) (976)	4.73 (2.48) (509)	4.35 (2.71) 386	4.31 (2.48) (448)	3.98 (2.28) (426)
All Women Age 18-55+		5.01 2.74 (598)	4.35 (2.34) (250)	4.62 (2.51) (2,139)	4.00 (2.18) (714)	5.14 (2.85) (771)	4.27 (2.40) (236)	4.66 (2.48) (677)	3.90 (2.19) (239)

Table 11: Mean Trip Differences between Self and Proxy Respondents by Age and Sex

Survey	Sex	Age 18-34	Age 35-54	Age 55+	All Age 18-55+
Lancaster	Men	-0.26	0.41	1.05***	0.58**
	Women	0.81*	0.49*	0.77**	0.66***
Baltimore	Men	0.86***	0.44**	0.54***	0.60***
	Women	0.82***	0.82***	0.22	0.62***
Des Moines	Men	0.35	0.11	0.62*	0.38*
	Women	0.98**	1.21***	0.39	0.87***
Kentucky	Men	0.32	0.44	0.06	0.33
	Women	0.71*	0.96***	0.73***	0.76****

* Significant at .01
** Significant at .001
*** Significant at .0001

The examination of characteristics of proxy respondents indicates that men are more likely to respond by proxy than women. They are also more likely to be: younger, students, less than high school education, coming from a larger household, with three or more vehicles. Although more women than men self reported making no trips on the travel day, among proxy respondents men were more likely than women to have no trips. Among retired respondents the proportion of proxies among those with trips was quite low, while the proportion of proxies among those with no trips was high. Because retired people are usually older (typically age sixty five and older), this may be an age effect. A possible explanation is that the proxy respondents with no trips were less able (due to age related declines) to respond for themselves or travel.

Comparing the average number of trips reported by proxy and self-report shows that overall the difference between them is significant, and that the trip rate reported by proxy is less than the trip rate obtained from self-report. Furthermore, the most consistent significant differences between the proxy and self-report trip rates were among adult women, below age fifty five. This suggests that trip rates estimated from data with proxy responses are most likely biased. Furthermore, it appears that the largest biases may be in the estimates of the travel of young and middle-aged adult women.

From this study, it can be seen that proxy responses in household travel surveys constitute a problem that needs to be addressed by research and standards. Research is needed to understand the reasons for the proxy responses, and how to recognise when they are acceptable and when they are not, and to determine the errors and biases that they introduce. Standards, based on such research, are needed to help minimise the errors and biases that use of proxies brings into transport planning models and practice.

REFERENCES

Bassett, S.S., J. Magaziner and J.R. Hebel (1990). Reliability of proxy response on mental health indices for aged community-dwelling women, *Psychology and Aging*, **5**, (1), 127-132.

Federal Highway Administration (2003). *2001 NHTS Users' Guide*. US Department of Transportation, Washington, DC.

Hill, D.H. (1983). Response Errors in Labor Surveys: Comparison of Self and Proxy Reports in the Survey of Income and Program Participation (SIPP), *Proceedings of the Third Annual Research Conference*, Bureau of the Census, Washington, DC, 229-319.

Maclean, M. and H. Genn (1979). Proxy response in social surveys, *Methodological Issues in Social Surveys*, Humanities Press, Atlantic Highlands, NJ.

Menon, G. and B. Bickert (1995). How well do you know your partner? Strategies for formulating proxy-reports and their effects on convergence to self-reports, *Journal of Marketing Research*, **23**, (1), 75-84.

Moore, J. (1988). Self/proxy Response Status and Survey Response Quality, *Journal of Official Statistics*, **4**, (92), 155-172.

Nelson, L.M., W.T. Longstreath Jr., T.D. Koepsell and G. van Belle (1990). Proxy Respondents in Epidemiological Research, *Epidemiological Reviews*, **12**, 71-85.

Nelson, L.M., W.T. Longstreath Jr., T.D. Koepsell, H. Checkoway and G. van Belle (1994). Completeness and Accuracy of Interview Data from Proxy Respondents: Demographic, Medical, and Life-Style Factors, *Epidemiology*, **5**, (2), 204-217.

Stancliffe, R.J. (2000). Proxy respondents and quality of life, *Evaluation and Program Planning*, **23**, 89-93.

Todorov, A. (2003). Cognitive procedures for correcting proxy-response biases in surveys, Applied *and Cognitive Psychology*, **17**, (2), 215-224.

Wolfgang, G., R. Byrne and S. Spratt (2003). *Analysis of Proxy Data in the Accuracy and Coverage Evaluation*, Census 2000 Report for the Testing Experimentation, and Evaluation Program. US Census Bureau, Washington, DC.

11

SURVEY IMPLEMENTATION

A. *Pat van der Reis, Pretoria, South Africa*
and
Andrew S. Harvey, St Mary's University, Halifax, Nova Scotia, Canada

INTRODUCTION

A serious and promising attempt has been made to propose standards and guidelines for household travel surveys (Stopher *et al.*, 2006). The Survey Implementation workshop was charged with focusing on the proposed implementation standards in order to determine their applicability to various types of household survey in those parts of the world in which the workshop members had expertise (US, Canada, Germany, Israel and South Africa)[21] and considering the extent to which standardisation of implementation procedures is possible worldwide. The basis for the discussions centred around the implementation standards proposed by Stopher *et al.* (2006) and the two resource papers specially prepared for the workshop (Bricka, 2006 and Wargelin and Kostyniuk, 2006). The challenges posed by various implementation practices, their success in collecting quality data, and the need for further research formed the backbone of the discussions.

An initial broad finding was that any statement of required standards of implementation procedures in household travel surveys should include the caveat that some 'standards' may not be applicable worldwide. The group felt that, given cultural differences, guidelines would be more appropriate and perhaps result in more widespread acceptance and application rather than standards. Thus, wherever this chapter refers to 'standards' the

---

[21] Members of the workshop were: Stacey Bricka (USA), Ruth Ditzian Haim (Israel), Andrew Harvey (Canada), Thomas Haupt (Germany), Lidia Kostyniuk (USA), Laurie Wargelin (USA), Pat van der Reis (South Africa), Chester Wilmot (USA).

workshop is really recommending 'guidelines'. For consistency purposes, however, the chapter uses the word 'standard'.

An initial 'standard' requirement should be that survey implementation should be preceded by intimate knowledge of local circumstances in the survey area, as well as of the experiences of earlier researchers in the locality, type of survey being implemented, and that adaptations should be introduced only where clearly necessary. Important issues of particular concern to the workshop included ethics, the scheduling of activities, the use of proxy respondents, including hard-to-reach populations, appropriate ways of contacting respondents, interviewer selection and training, and the need for quality checks.

RECOMMENDED STANDARDS

Ethics

The basic practice standards concerning ethics proposed by Stopher *et al.* (2006) are:

- Anonymity of respondents and confidentiality of information provided should be protected at all times;
- Survey respondents may not be sold anything or asked for money as part of the survey;
- Respondents should be contacted at reasonable times to participate in the survey, and should be allowed to reschedule participation to a different time if that is more convenient for them;
- Survey personnel should be prepared to divulge their names, the identity of research companies they represent, the identity of the agency that commissioned the study, and the nature of the survey being conducted, if requested to do so by the respondent;
- Children under the age of fourteen may not be interviewed without the consent of a parent or responsible adult;
- A respondent's decision to refuse participation in a survey, not to answer specific questions in the survey, or to terminate an interview while in progress, should be respected if that is the respondent's firm decision;
- Respondents may not be surveyed or observed without their knowledge. Methods of data collection such as the use of hidden tape recorders, cameras, one-way mirrors, or invisible identifiers on mail questionnaires, may only be used in a survey if the method has been fully disclosed to the respondent and the respondent agrees to its use.
- A research agency may not release findings prior to the public release of the findings of the organization that commissioned the study, unless approval of the client organization is obtained to do so; and

- A research agency must ensure the reasonable safety of its fieldworkers during the execution of the survey.

Most of these standards were acceptable to the members of the workshop, with the following reservations and suggestions:

- The anonymity and confidentiality requirement is an aspect which may require flexibility and adaptation in certain parts of the world. In some African countries, for instance, respondents have been known to express their displeasure with the fieldworker's assurance of anonymity, making retorts such as 'But I want them to know what I personally think. What is the point of giving my opinion if nobody is going to be told that this is how I feel?'
- As regards the prohibition on asking for money, etc., it was felt that specific mention should be made that any cell-phone costs associated with implementation should not be borne by the respondent.
- Because contacting respondents at reasonable times could greatly increase the time needed for the survey, some flexibility could be introduced, making the point that this does not preclude someone else in the household being contacted, for example, during working hours to provide information on a reasonable time for contacting the respondent.
- The hard-and-fast rule concerning interviews of children under fourteen might need some adaptation, because interviewing children of this age is not regarded as an unacceptable practice in all societies, for example in Israel. Even there, however, it is generally more usual to ensure adult approval.

Other aspects which the workshop felt should be specified under 'ethics' are that:

- No unauthorised person should be able to identify an individual respondent from the data provided;
- Raw data should not be freely available on the Internet; and
- Only selected and fully trained interviewers and survey personnel, registered with an organisation known to adhere to a code of ethical conduct, should be permitted to approach or interview respondents.

Mailing Materials

Proposed basic practice standards are:

- The use of a stamped, return envelope, ideally with instructions on which materials need to be mailed back;
- The use of a large white envelope (4" x 9.5" or larger), with the address printed directly onto the envelope, rather than the use of address labels;

- Print a recognisable return address on the envelope and indicate the contents of the envelope – at least the survey name; and
- Affix postage stamps, especially commemorative stamps, rather than using a franking machine or pre-printed bulk mail.

These basic practice standards were acceptable to the workshop members, although it was felt that more consideration should be given to wording guidelines that would identify ways in which these materials could be expected to improve response rates. It was stressed that, even at this early stage in the survey process, there is a real need to recognise the importance of gaining respondent trust, arousing their interest and establishing a personal relationship through, for example:

- Using an unusual (not only large) size of envelope to make it stand out from other mail;
- Providing an attractive label;
- Indicating that the mail is from an important and respected source; and
- Personalising it as much as possible, perhaps handwriting the address, if practicable.

In the case of countries where face-to-face interviews are more common than mail-back questionnaires or diaries, these standards do not apply. The workshop recommended that standards should also cover the survey materials themselves, such as ensuring an attractive diary cover or show cards that could be used to encourage response. In addition, it has been found of great importance in surveys, for example in South Africa, that a diary or questionnaire should not look bulky and, if both are being used, that they should be combined into one document. Seeing the interviewer turning over many pages (albeit with widely spaced wording in large script) and then producing a second document, has often led to refusals to complete the interview, or at best hasty, ill-considered responses in order to complete the interview as quickly as possible.

Respondent Questions

Proposed basic practice standards are:

- A telephone contact with the sponsoring agency should be provided;
- A toll-free telephone contact within the survey agency (if different from the sponsoring agency) should be provided; and
- Detailed instructions in the form of an informational brochure or fact sheet should be given to the respondent. The information must be presented in an easy to read manner, with appropriate use of graphics where possible.

The workshop noted that respondents in many countries are becoming increasingly suspicious of the genuineness and value of 'yet another survey'. Apart from providing telephone contact numbers (toll-free, if possible) and a brochure or fact sheet through which respondents can satisfy themselves of the legitimacy of the survey, it is important that a standard requirement should be that interviewers for telephone and face-to-face surveys are trained to give a personal explanation of the value of the survey and the reason for selection of the individual. This explanation should sound both plausible and unrehearsed to the respondent (while obviously retaining consistency).

In some countries, such as in Africa and particularly in rural communities, it should be noted that greater acceptance of a survey (and of certain individuals within it being selected for interview) may be achieved by initially approaching a respected member of the community who will, when convinced of the survey's value, readily encourage (or demand!) participation through verbal contact with respondents. Publicity in print media that reach the target market has also been found to encourage survey participation.

Caller ID

The only proposed basic practice standard is:

- Caller ID should be provided by the entity conducting the telephone calls, whether a contracted survey firm, university or government agency, because existing data indicate that providing any ID at all may assist response rates.

The workshop concurred that Caller ID can improve response rates through immediately identifying a legitimate and respected client or survey contractor.

Answering Machines and Repeated Call-back Requests

Proposed basic practice standards are:

- When an answering machine is reached on the initial recruitment/screening call, a message should be left at least once on the call rotation before classifying the number as non-responding. The message should identify the client organization, the nature of the survey and provide a toll-free number for the household to contact should they desire to participate. The message should be short (no more than fifteen seconds) and preferably provided by a 'live' interviewer as opposed to a recorded message.
- When an answering machine is reached on a reminder telephone call, a message should always be left.
- When an answering machine is reached during telephone retrieval of travel information, a message should always be left.

These basic practice standards need to be extended (obviously in a totally different manner) to cover face-to-face interviewing as well, particularly as regards the need to include a basic standard call-back procedure. This is particularly important in those parts of the world where a proper call-back procedure often represents the main difference between professional research organisations of integrity and cheaper fly-by-night ones, and that has a direct impact on response rates..

The need for some flexibility in standards (and for intimate local knowledge of cultural values and mores, in order to identify when this flexibility is necessary) is clearly illustrated in the case of applying these answering machine standards in Israel. Leaving survey messages on answering machines is a definite 'no-no' in Israel. This would never be done and has been found to be most unacceptable to respondents.

The question was raised as to how one would handle the potential respondent bias caused by 'do not call' listings, although it appears that such listings are very rare at present outside the US. Legitimate survey research is, however, exempt from 'do not call' listings in the US, although all respondents are not aware of this.

Incorrect Reporting of Non-Mobility

Proposed basic practice standards are:

- During data collection: A question to verify reported non-mobility should be asked of all persons who report no travel;
- During data coding: An indicator should be included to differentiate between cases where respondents said they did not travel, and those where respondents refused to provide travel data; and
- At the reporting stage: The survey report should include the percentage of non-mobile days.

A proposed advanced practice standard is:

- Questions could be included that gently challenge respondents who report non-mobility by probing for the reasons why no travel was undertaken that day.

It was agreed that these basic and advanced practice standards are particularly relevant in the event of proxy protocols. The conditions under which proxy respondents may be accepted needs to be specified very clearly in the research design, and followed to the letter in the implementation stage of a survey, with appropriate back-checks. The standards pertaining to these requirements have not been lucidly expressed in the 'Proxy reporting' section of Stopher *et al.* (2006).

In their paper, Wargelin *et al.* (2006) concluded from surveys providing travel data in the US through a retrieval telephone interview, that the use of proxy respondents is likely to introduce a definite bias into survey data. A greater proportion of proxies tended to report that the respondent made no trips than was the case for self-reporting. This under-reporting was particularly notable if the respondent reporting the travel data for another member was a woman under fifty five years of age. However, it was also noted that respondents for whom proxies were most frequently obtained tended to be younger, less-educated men from large, low income households. The workshop recommended that:

- Standard procedures should be incorporated for following up even more extensively and urgently on respondents whose data retrieval interview, given by proxy, reported no trips. This should take into account possible 'warning signs' emanating from the sociodemographic characteristics of both the respondent and the proxy.
- Asking the reasons why no travel was undertaken should be a 'basic' rather than an 'advanced' practice standard.
- The listed alternative reasons for no travel should be extended from;
    o Stayed in same place/home all day;
    o Had a medical condition that made travel difficult;
    o Was aged 4 or less;
    o Retired; and
    o Temporarily absent from a job or business.
- To include:
    o Unemployed/unable to find a job, so don't need to travel;
    o Cannot afford transport;
    o Housewife/homemaker; and
    o Work from home.

Reporting Time of Day

Stopher *et al.* (2006) proposed that the basic practice standard for data entry and storage should be undertaken using two fields:

- One for the day number, with the starting day of the diary being Day 1; and
- The other for the time of day, recorded in military time (00:00 – 24:00).

The workshop was in full agreement with this practice standard.

Time of Day to Begin and End Reporting

Proposed basic practice standards are:

- Start and end times for 24-hour travel or activity diaries should be 3.00 am.
- For travel and activity diaries that extend over more than one day, the start and end times should be extended by 24 hours for each additional day.

Stopher *et al.* (2006) note that the rationale behind these practice standards is that start and end times should be selected so that there is little likelihood of beginning and ending the diary in the middle of travel, or in the middle of any other activity other than sleeping. The workshop felt that there was a need for flexibility in the first of these practice standards, because the point of least activity tended to vary in different countries and cultures, and between urban and rural dwellers. The 'low time' was about 5 a.m. in Israel, about 4 a.m. in Canada and closer to 2 a.m. in some parts of Africa. Bricka (2005) reported that starting times varied between 3 and 4 a.m. in the US, but concluded that '...the actual start time is not as important as the need to designate a starting point for the travel period, preferably one at which time most respondents would not be travelling.' It was felt that this should be the basic practice standard rather than one denoting a specific start time.

'MISSING' STANDARDS IDENTIFED BY THE WORKSHOP

The Selection, Training, and 'Tailoring' of Survey Personnel

The selection and training of survey personnel is an important contributor to acceptable response rates and data quality. The workshop felt that basic practice standards for this part of the survey process had been neglected in the proposed standards presented by Stopher *et al.* (2006). The resource paper (Bricka, 2006) was discussed in detail in the workshop, which agreed with Bricka's recommendations that:

- Staff training should take place throughout the life of the project;
- Initial training should encompass the project specifications, the study area, the objective of each questionnaire item and other project specifics;
- Training for telephone contacts (before the recruitment interview, reminder recall and retrieval interview) should take place at least two days prior to the start of each activity;
- A second round of training should be employed to confirm interviewers' proficiency to start the interviewing process; and
- During the fieldwork, training sessions should be held at least once a week to provide data quality feedback, discuss the project's progress and performance, and to solve any problems that may have arisen.

In addition, the workshop regarded the selection of experienced interviewers, or the recruitment and testing of the aptitude of inexperienced interviewers prior to employment, as an aspect that (although obvious to researchers) is not always appreciated by sponsoring organisations.

A discussion on the advisability of 'tailoring' respondent contact with survey personnel, such that only one particular member of the survey staff be assigned to conduct all contact with the respondent (recruiting them, providing reminder calls and undertaking the retrieval interview) led to no clear conclusions in the workshop. No evidence could be provided of the relative advantage or disadvantage of improving rapport through 'tailoring' versus that of staff specialisation and a more structured questioning approach. It was recommended that this was an eminent topic for further research.

Scheduling of the Survey Implementation Process

The workshop agreed that some important standards had been documented by Bricka (2006) and should be included:

- Where advance notification of a survey is given to respondents prior to recruitment, the mail time required for the advance letter to reach the respondent timeously should be tested in advance;
- The timing of the recruitment call cannot be standardised, but should be made:
    - In sufficient time to allow for the subsequent mailing of survey materials; and
    - At the time of highest probability of reaching the respondent.
- Survey packets should be mailed out 'just in time', not too early to risk misplacement, and not too late to risk missing the travel day, preferably one to two days prior to the travel period. Testing the mail lead-times for the geographical areas to be surveyed should be standard in the conduct of any survey.
- A reminder call to the respondent should be made on the day prior to the start of the travel period;
- Retrieval interviews should take place as soon as possible after the travel period, but certainly within a seven-to-ten day freshness window; and
- Processing of survey data should proceed concurrently with data collection, to allow for timely quality checks and geocoding.

Hard-to-Reach Populations

The workshop recognised that there were some circumstances where the standards for contacting and obtaining data from respondents might be difficult to achieve. Leaving such respondents out of a survey would, however, result in sample bias. Hard-to-reach populations included military personnel, rural residents, linguistically isolated respondents, street people and illegal residents.

It was noted that the type of survey which could be conducted might be affected by the particular hard-to-reach group being included in the sample. For instance, in Israel soldiers would not be able to undertake telephone interviews, because they do not have access to telephones. During the week they may have cell-phones, but surveys are not conducted through cell-phones in Israel. The soldiers usually go home for weekends, but interviews are not conducted at weekends either. A further problem is that this group would not be allowed to divulge their travel movements.

IN CONCLUSION

The workshop identified a number of potentially very worthwhile research topics relating to the implementation of travel surveys:

- The development of flexible protocols on interview/interviewer and respondent tailoring;
- The data freshness issue, notably data retrieval and its relationship to the level of detail being collected and the level of recall support (such as a map) provided;
- Developing approaches to combine GPS, multimodal and panel responses over time;
- The effect of call-back time delays in retrieving diaries;
- The implications of cell-phone usage in future surveys; and
- Response comparability across survey methods in multimodal surveys (telephone, postal, personal interview and Internet surveys).

Finally, the workshop recorded its appreciation of the considerable efforts made by Stopher, Wilmot, Stecher and Alsnih in drafting a set of admirable basic practice standards and expressed the hope that, as far as survey implementation was concerned, the workshop had been able to contribute to refining those standards.

REFERENCES

Bricka, S. (2006). Scheduling considerations in household travel surveys. In: *Travel Survey Methods – Quality and Future Directions* (P.R. Stopher and C.C. Stecher, eds), 175-199, Elsevier, Oxford.

Stopher, P.R., C.G. Wilmot, C.C. Stecher and R. Alsnih (2004). Household travel surveys: Proposed standards and guidelines. In: *Travel Survey Methods – Quality and Future Directions* (P.R. Stopher and C.C. Stecher, eds), 19-74, Elsevier, Oxford.

Wargelin, L. and L. Kostyniuk (2006). Self and proxy respondents in household travel surveys. In: *Travel Survey Methods – Quality and Future Directions* (P.R. Stopher and C.C. Stecher, eds), 201-212, Elsevier, Oxford.

Travel Survey Methods: Quality and Future Directions
Peter Stopher and Cheryl Stecher (Editors)

12

THE METROPOLITAN TRAVEL SURVEY ARCHIVE: A CASE STUDY IN ARCHIVING

David Levinson, University of Minnesota, Minneapolis, Minnesota, USA
and
Ewa Zofka, SRF Consulting Group, Minneapolis, Minnesota, USA

INTRODUCTION

While the Cleveland Regional Area Traffic Study in 1927 was the first metropolitan planning attempt sponsored by the US federal government, the lack of comprehensive survey methods and standards at that time precluded the systematic collection of information, such as travel time, origins and destinations, and traffic counts. The first US travel surveys appeared in urban areas after the Federal Aid Highway Act of 1944 permitted the spending of federal funds on urban highways (Weiner, 1997). A new home-interview, origin-destination survey method was developed in which households were asked about the number, purpose, mode choice, and origin and destination of their daily trips. In 1944, the US Bureau of Public Roads printed the *Manual of Procedures for Home Interview Traffic Studies*. (US Department of Commerce, 1944). This new procedure was first implemented in several small to mid-size areas: Lincoln, Nebraska; Little Rock, Arkansas; Kansas City, Missouri; Memphis, Tennessee; New Orleans, Louisiana; Savannah, Georgia; and Tulsa, Oklahoma (Weiner, 1997). Highway engineers and urban planners made use of the new data collected after the 1944 Highway Act extended federally sponsored planning to travel surveys as well as traffic counts, highway capacity studies, pavement condition studies and cost-benefit analysis.

As computer technologies have evolved from mainframe punched cards to reel tapes to minicomputers to personal computers, historic travel survey data are not always readily accessible. Moreover, because of the long time span between surveys (sometimes twenty years), much institutional memory, the computer files, and even documentation is lost between surveys. Among the lost surveys that have been unsuccessfully sought are the 1948 and 1955 Washington, DC Household Travel Surveys and 1970 Twin Cities Travel Behaviour Inventory. Axhausen (2000) identifies the London 1962 transport study data as being lost. The San Francisco Bay Area 1946/47 survey is also reported lost, though later surveys are available, some online (Datamart, 2002). Other researchers have similar tales. Even the extant data are scattered at numerous state departments of transportation (DOT), metropolitan planning organisations (MPO), and local governments. The documentation of results is not necessarily located with the survey tapes, and the methodology may be somewhere else entirely.

While a great deal of effort and research aims to improve the quality of future surveys and analysis, an important and irreplaceable resource, an historic treasure containing records of what people did in the past, is under-utilised and endangered. While this loss has been decried at a number of international conferences, among them TRB (2000), Hensher (2001) and various Transportation Research Board meetings, prior to our study, no organised effort to preserve the data from metropolitan travel surveys in the US had yet been undertaken.

A recent study at the University of California at Berkeley identified some of the available data at the largest metropolitan planning organisations (Porter *et al.*, 1996). However, until now no researcher or centre had systematically set out to acquire, archive, and manage the plethora of surveys from many metropolitan areas. To encourage archiving, Axhausen and Wigan (2003) recommended '1. Increase awareness of the archiving issue (outreach) 2. Begin the survey process with the aim of archiving the data sets in mind. 3. Observe data protection regulations.' Those recommendations are important, but they do not fully address the question of how to deal with past surveys.

The Metropolitan Transportation Council (MTC) of the San Francisco Bay Area (Datamart, 2002) archives travel data for a single metropolitan area. Unfortunately, this agency is unique in making this level of data available freely online. The US Metropolitan Travel Survey Archive extends that approach to multiple areas.

The reasons for having a survey archive are several. Foremost is simply the historical value and scientific understanding that can be obtained by analysing these data. This archive allows the development of a new understanding of how current travel and activity patterns emerged by asking current questions of older data (and developing new questions based on what is learned). Researchers may be able to apply new statistical modelling techniques to older data and learn whether causal factors explaining travel decisions (e.g., frequency of trips, mode or destination choice, time allocation) are stable over time and space. Hypotheses, such as the travel budget hypothesis (e.g., Zahavi, 1974), or the commuting budget hypothesis, that are critical in designing sound transportation policies, can be tested only with long-term data. Second, modellers and practitioners will have additional data on which to validate and calibrate their models, a particularly important requirement as more and more is asked of regional transport planning models, especially in the environmental arena (Garrett and Wachs, 1996). Furthermore, inter-metropolitan comparisons of travel behaviour would assist in adapting the next generation of travel models from one city to another. Third, it will allow the development of new performance measures that can actually be tracked over time, by providing data in much more detail than the invaluable, but geographically broad, Nationwide Personal (Household) Transportation Surveys of 1969, 1977, 1983, 1990, 1995, 2000; or the decennial Census Journey-to-Work surveys that give great information on journey to work, but none on non-work travel.

The need to preserve and protect data so that they remain available for researchers and localities led the project investigators to apply for funding and create the US Metropolitan Travel Survey Archive presented in this chapter. This chapter describes efforts at organising data and developing metadata. A case, applying these approaches to a US Metropolitan Travel Survey Archive is presented. The chapter concludes with some recommendations for archiving data.

METADATA

Metadata allows data to function together. Simply put, metadata is information about information – labelling, cataloguing and descriptive information structured to permit data to be processed. Ryssevik and Musgrave (1999) argue that high quality metadata standards are essential because metadata is the launch pad for any resource discovery, maps complex data, bridges the gap between data producers and consumers, and links data with its resulting reports and scientific studies produced about it. To meet the increasing needs for the proper data formats and encoding standards, the World Wide Web Consortium (W3C) has developed the generic Resource Description Framework (RDF) (W3C 2002). RDF treats metadata more generally, providing a standard way to use Extended Markup Language (XML) to 'represent metadata in the form of statements about properties and relationships of items' (W3C 2002). Resources can be almost any type of file, including of course, travel surveys. RDF delivers a detailed and unified data description vocabulary.

Applying these tools specifically to databases, the Data Documentation Initiative (DDI) for Document Type Definitions (DTD) applies metadata standards used for documenting datasets. DDI was first developed by European and North American data archives, libraries, and official statistics agencies. 'The Data Documentation Initiative (DDI) is an effort to establish an international XML-based standard for the content, presentation, transport, and preservation of documentation for datasets in the social and behavioral sciences' (Data Documentation Initiative, 2004). As this international standardisation effort gathers momentum, it is expected that more and more datasets will be documented using DDI as the primary metadata format. With DDI, searching data archives on the Internet no longer depends on an archivist's skill at capturing the information that is important to researchers. The standard of data description provides sufficient detail sorted in a user-friendly manner.

The implementation of Data Description Initiative standards in travel survey archives, specifically the Metropolitan Travel Survey Archive will enable us to organise survey data into comparable categories. At this point, it is necessary to mention that surveys were conducted by different metropolitan organisations using diverse criteria. The survey archivists' duty is to find the proper data description based on standards. To assist users, it is helpful to convert raw data files into the 'rectangular format' (wherein each record is a row that contains a fixed number of fields) that is recognised by most statistical software (e.g., SAS, SPSS, or Stata). (While this format is useful for statistical software, it separates documentation from the data. Some computer science researchers suggest that, because disk space is no longer scarce, each field of each observation should be fully documented so that the data can be essentially read in plain language, this is the philosophy behind XML). Cross tabulations on-line might be a good source of information for researchers and planners. Axhausen (2003) argues 'On-line tabulation seems an obvious solution to many problems of members of the public, planners, and policy makers: fast and easy access to the data and well produced and valid tables or graphs for the users, central control over the data, quality control of circulating numbers and a reduction in the workload for the planners'.

Because standardisation and reporting of the survey data are highly needed, sophisticated software to manage the data properly is required. NESSTAR (Networked Social Science Tools and Resources), a European social science project providing access to a large amount of data archives over the Internet was initiated by the Norwegian Social Science Data Services, the UK Data Archive, and the Danish Data Archive (Nesstar.org, 2002). A more sophisticated version of NESSTAR is the FASTER (Flexible Access to Statistics Tables and Electronic Resources) project sponsored by the European Commission. The ETHTDA (Eidgenossische Technische Hochschule Travel Data Archive) in Switzerland has been built on the NESSTAR platform. The ETHTDA on-line archive offers all the facilities of the latest NESSTAR server (tabulation, graph creation, regression, etc.) (ETHTDA 2004). The next version of NESSTAR Publisher will allow user-defined interfaces, to enable different groups to view the data in different ways. Researchers plan to define one for travel surveys. The importance of this depends on the number of users anticipated for a particular archive.

Space-Time Research in Australia is conducting another project, ComeIn, promoting metadata standards in data archiving. 'The aim of ComeIn is to develop a general metadata interface that can serve as an integration layer between local metadata repositories and different user tools (resource discovery tools, data dissemination tools, tabulation tools etc.). In order to provide a maximum level of portability across systems and platforms, the ComeIn interface, will, according to the plans be accessible through CORBA, COM, as well as XML' (Norwegian Social Science Data Services, 1999). Other resources for metadata archiving are available in Europe at the Institute for Social and Economics Research affiliated with the University of Essex in the United Kingdom (MTUS - Multinational Time Use Study), which is a similar project to the MTSA.

The Survey Documentation and Analysis software (SDA) developed by the University of California, Berkeley is a set of programs developed and maintained by the Computer-assisted Survey Methods Program to facilitate the documentation, analysis, and distribution of survey data on the World Wide Web (Computer-assisted Survey Methods Program, 2004). SDA software requires data sets to be in a standard statistical format (e.g., SAS, SPSS, Stata) or ASCII (American Standard Code for Information Interchange) together with the full documentation of the files. SDA also offers statistical analysis for the data, such as frequencies and cross-tabulations, comparisons of means (with complex standard errors), correlation matrix, comparisons of correlations, regression (ordinary least squares), logit and probit regression.

Another metadata project is hosted by IPUMS (Integrated Public Use Microdata Series) at the University of Minnesota since 1997. 'Because investigators created survey samples at different times, they employed a wide variety of record layouts, coding schemes, and documentation. This has complicated efforts to use survey data to study change over time. The IPUMS assigns uniform codes across all the samples and brings relevant documentation into a coherent form to facilitate analysis of social and economic change' (Minnesota Population Center, 2004).

Briefly noted are two other metadata specifications. The Virtual Data Centre is currently under development at Harvard-MIT (Virtual Data Center, 2003). For national statistics the Bureau of Transportation Statistics (BTS) of the US Department of Transportation has made a large effort to make data resources publicly available, including Nationwide Personal Transportation Surveys (NPTS) and National Household Travel Survey (NHTS) (Center for Transportation Analysis, 2001).

THE METROPOLITAN TRAVEL SURVEY ARCHIVE PROJECT

The *Metropolitan Travel Survey Archive* is funded by the US Department of Transportation's Bureau of Transportation Statistics and is located at the University of Minnesota at http://www.surveyarchive.org. Figures 1 and 2 are screenshots of the archive in its current state.

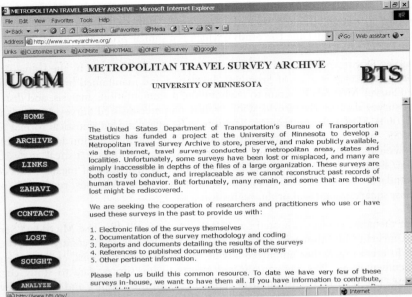

Figure 1: Metropolitan Travel Survey Archive, main page

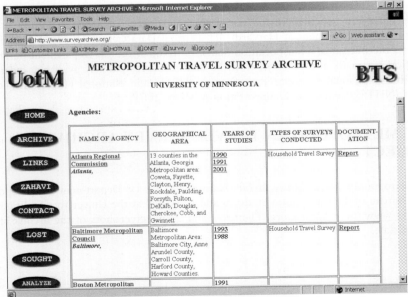

Figure 2: Metropolitan Travel Survey Archive, archive structure page

In the first stage of the project, investigators formally contacted the fifty largest MPOs. Each agency received both formal (letter on letterhead) and informal (email requests to the seemingly responsible staffer) requests. After the first two months many surveys with documentation and reports were collected. However about forty percent of the contacted agencies did not respond. At that point, we started to create a web page on which to put the data that we managed to gather. The following step was to send another set of request letters to these agencies and re-contact people who promised to provide us with the crucial data. By that time, the Metropolitan Travel Survey Archive administered about fifteen travel surveys. Because many reports that had been sent were in a paper version (hard copies) we started, at the same time to digitise documents into a standard downloadable format (pdf) and put it on the Internet. Soon, we announced the project on important transport email lists such as the Travel Model Improvement Program (TMIP), State DOTs' DOT@LISTSERV, and UTSG (University Transportation Studies Group).

Currently, there are over sixty surveys from twenty eight metro areas and states together with documentation and reports available on the project web site (See Table 1). These surveys have been posted in the form they were provided. Each metro area has developed its own survey methodology and data structure, often varying by year, so there are nearly sixty different data formats we are working with. Some differ only in field names, others in the software required to decipher them. Therefore, we have simultaneously undertaken to develop a unified standard to organise our data in a manner that enables database queries to be implemented. To provide researchers and other potential users of this valuable resource with the maximum survey data queries possible and further simple statistical analysis, it is necessary to sort the data properly first.

To achieve uniform data set descriptors, for instance, variables and attribute values/vocabularies, we investigated NESSTAR (Networked Social Science Tools and Resources). NESSTAR combines the functions of a specialised search engine with those of an on-line tabulation tool. The client software, NESSTAR explorer 1.01 (see Figure 3) allows the user to search simultaneously all data sets published by institutions and archives using the NESSTAR system. The selected data sets can be investigated using the metadata provided by the DDI, which is consistently used to describe the data set. Additionally, one can import a data set file to the NESSTAR Publisher, which does the data description. (See Figure 4 and 5 for details).

Another option to achieve the metadata standard is our partnership with the Minnesota Population Center, which publishes online the IPUMS (Integrated Public Use Microdata Series) from Census data at the University of Minnesota. The IPUMS data is being converted to be compatible with the SDA (Survey Documentation and Analysis) format described earlier. The Metropolitan Travel Survey Archive partnership with the Minnesota Population Center provides numerous advantages for the MTSA. First, the new website of the MTSA is now hosted on the Population Center's server and is professionally archived and maintained. Second, part of our data has been prepared with the cooperation of the Population Center to use SDA software. Presently two household travel survey data sets – the Twin Cities 1990 and 2000 Travel Behaviour Inventories – are formatted for and running on the SDA software. Figures 6 to 8 show the described metadata process for the Twin Cities. Specifically, preparing the data for the SDA and metadata standards means obtaining one consistent travel survey database. These travel surveys datasets contain three basic databases: *household*, *person*, and *trip*.

Table 1. Metropolitan Travel Survey Archive Data

Name of Agency	Years of Surveys
Atlanta Regional Commission – Atlanta	1990/1991 2001
Baltimore Metropolitan Council – Baltimore	1993 1988
Boston Metropolitan Planning Organization – Boston	1991
Chicago Area Transportation Study – Chicago	1988-1990
Ohio, Kentucky, Indiana Regional Council of Governments – Cincinnati	1995 1999
Northeast Ohio Areawide Coordinating Agency and Policy Board – Cleveland	1994
North Central Texas Council of Governments – Dallas	1996 1998 1999
Volusia County Metropolitan Planning Organization – Daytona Beach	2002
Denver Regional Council of Governments – Denver	1996-1999
Southeast Michigan Council of Governments – Detroit	1994
Triangle Council of Governments – Durham	1994
Florida Department of Transportation – Fort Lauderdale	1995 1996 1997 2000
Mid-America Regional Council – Kansas City	1992 1993
Central Arkansas Regional Transportation Study – Little Rock	1960-1966 1990 1993 1994
Southern California Association of Governments – Los Angeles	1991
New York Metropolitan Transportation Council – New York	1995 1997-1998
Delaware Valley Regional Planning Commission – Philadelphia	1987-88
Maricopa Association of Governments – Phoenix	2002
Oregon Department of Transportation and Metropolitan Service District – Portland	1994 1996
California Department of Transportation (Caltrans) – Sacramento	1991
East-West Coordinating Council of Governments – Saint Louis	1990
Twin Cities Metropolitan Council – Saint Paul	1970 (no documentation) 1990 2000
Wasatch Front Regional Council – Salt Lake City	1993
San Diego Association of Governments – San Diego	1995
San Francisco Bay Area Transit – San Francisco	1965 1981 1990 1996
Puget Sound Regional Council – Seattle	1989 1990 1992 1993 1994 1996 1997 1999 2000
Metropolitan Washington Council of Governments – Washington	1968 1988 1994
Wilmington Area Planning Council – Wilmington	1964 1988

Source: http://www.surveyarchive.org

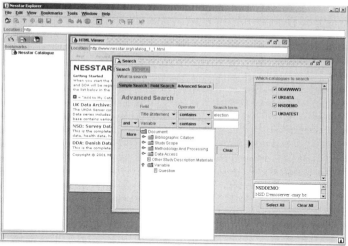

Source: http://www.nesstar.org

Figure 3: Nesstar Explorer 1.01 browser

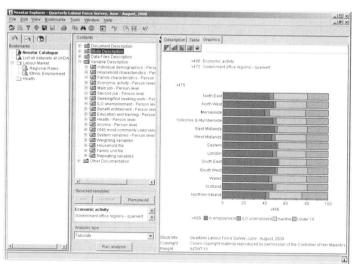

Source: http://www.nesstar.org

Figure 4: Full metadata description in Nesstar

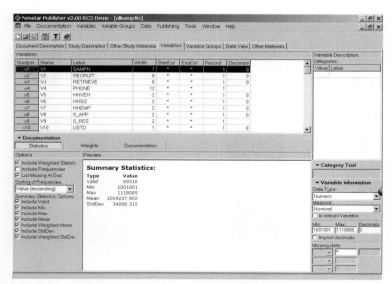

Source: Maricopa Travel Survey elaborated based on the NESSTAR software.

Figure 5: Nesstar Publisher 2.00 version, data documentation and simple statistics

To get one database out of these three, a merging process was performed. The merging procedure was conducted based on the common variables *household ID*, which was present in all three data sets, and *person ID*, which was present in the *person* and *trip* data sets. The resulting data file had one record for each unlinked trip, which included all of the person and household information for the trip maker. Thus there is some redundancy, these data are no longer normalised in the idealised database management way, that is, the same data (e.g., household and person data) are replicated on each trip record. However, because computer storage space is cheap, efficient running time is the objective of the software, so redundant information is preferred to normalised databases. The travel survey data sorted that way and of course stored in the ASCII format is almost ready to be run on the SDA. The last step before the entire Survey Documentation and Analysis procedure can be applied is creating an XML codebook for the metadata (illustrated in Figure 8). The XML codes used for this study introduce the two basic categories in variable description: *string* for categorical variables and *numeric* for other. The metadata script formulated according to the above method provides clear and unified data description for the travel survey datasets. Preparing a survey for SDA takes from one to two days of a skilled data analyst's time, excluding time to clean the data. The data sets of course contain numerous errors and unreasonable responses, many of which cannot be caught without thoroughly working with the data. Some of these can be caught with clear specification of allowable responses.

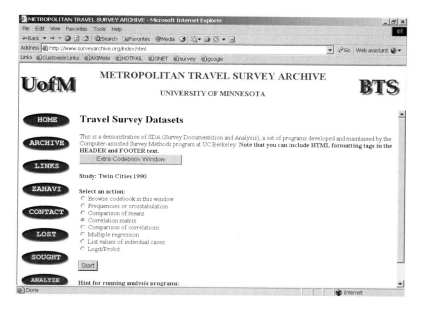

Figure 6. MTSA, Statistical Analysis with SDA for the Twin Cities 1990 TBI

Because of the variety of different formats and methods of description of data that we possess in the archive, it is crucial for travel data archivists to use the professional meta-data software services such as NESSTAR or SDA to make the data efficiently and easily accessed. As mentioned above, it is necessary to convert all data that we have into an ASCII-based 'rectangular format', where the rectangle is the product of the number of rows (observations or records) and columns (fields) as well as creating the XML codes for the data categories description.

The primary aim of the MTSA to store, preserve, and make publicly available US travel survey data has been achieved. Much additional work remains on standardising the data with a common data description file (DDF), enabling simple data base queries from web-based software. At this point the MTSA has achieved proof of concept. Deploying that concept to the hundreds of surveys that have been collected will take significant extra effort.

CONCLUSIONS AND RECOMMENDATIONS

Travel survey archiving is part of the broad data archiving process. Because the travel survey is an important tool of transport planning, it is necessary to collect, store, and make these data publicly available. Travel survey archives, specifically our Metropolitan Travel Survey Archive, are likely to become precious sources of information for transport planners and engineers. That is why global standards for data archiving are needed. Raising the standards for household survey archiving and surveys in general has been discussed at many international conferences; we must now act.

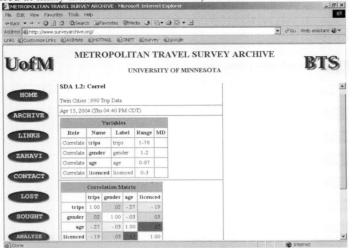

Figure 7: MTSA, Correlation Matrix with SDA for the Twin Cities 1990 TBI

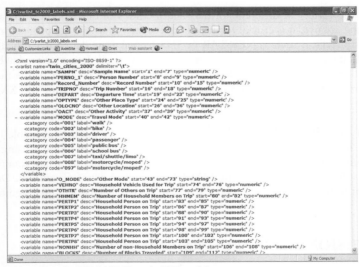

Source: Coded based on the TBI 2000 Household Travel Survey

Figure 8: Metadata XML codes for the Twin Cities 2000 TBI

Standards for data collection proposed by Stopher *et al.* (2003) mainly concentrate on the proper approaches in the designing phase of the survey instrument, specification of the sample size, time of the day in the travel diary reporting, and coding strategies. Standards for describing data should be also considered. Data description for travel surveys is usually associated with metadata and its applications. International standards for data descriptions, such as DDI, provide archive architects with the common variable descriptions used worldwide. That sort of categorising data enables cross-sectional comparisons between travel surveys conducted by different planning organisations not only domestically, but internationally.

A related solution for the archiving problems would be to create an International Travel Survey Archive Project (ITSA). The ITSA project would continue the MTSA idea on an international scale. This project will transform the extant metropolitan travel surveys from a collection of isolated and incompatible data files into an integrated data series on travel behaviour in the US and worldwide (including surveys in both developing and developed countries). The ITSA would comprise travel surveys, supplementary data, reports, and documentation from the oldest extant surveys (currently the oldest survey available in machine-readable form that we are aware of is from 1965) to the present. There are six complementary tasks that need to be considered in the process of creating this archive. First the project will collect machine-readable travel surveys and related data and documentation from metropolitan areas around the world. Second, the project will develop an architecture for harmonising the various data sets. The architecture should include (after Nesstar.org):

- 'Document description', including the bibliographic information;
- 'Study description', which consists of information about citation, principal investigators, who distributed data, keywords about the content, data collection methods, and geographic scope;
- 'File description': the data dictionary or code book;
- 'Variable description' – information about response and analysis units, question text, interviewer instructions, derived variables etc.; and
- 'Other materials' such as questionnaires, coding information, maps, missing values information, URLs, etc.

Then, the surveys will be properly documented and standardised, recoded to a consistent convention, and properly geocoded so that data can be mapped (while ensuring data privacy). Another step is to design and implement a web-based system that will greatly simplify access to information on millions of responses contained in hundreds of data files. The two last steps include some proof-of-concept analysis, demonstrating the interdisciplinary value of using the archive, and implementation – communication with researchers and the public at large.

The comprehensive data series will expand the value of travel survey data by allowing researchers to make consistent comparisons throughout four decades of dramatic change in travel demand. This period saw the construction of the freeways like the interstate highway system and new or expanded rail systems in most major urban areas, the rise of female labour force participation and the two-worker household, changes in willingness to permit children to travel to school unaccompanied, increasing income and wealth, new generations of information technologies, and an overall increase in vehicle ownership to as high as one per licensed driver in some developed countries. Understanding the implications of these trends permits us to study the dynamics of travel behaviour and time use both in the US and elsewhere.

The implementation of all the above-mentioned techniques for data collection, description and archiving, will improve data quality and value for researchers. Clean and well-described survey data in on-line archives constitutes an ongoing information asset for researchers and practitioners. A problem remains that the archive is a project not a process. A more systematic and regular approach for archiving data is required. In some academic disciplines, publication of articles based on surveys requires making the survey publicly available. This provides incentives for researchers to document and make available in public archives surveys they used. Alternatively, since most surveys use federal funds, the federal government could require that surveys (stripped of individual identifying information) be uploaded to a public archive. While we are loath to recommend more regulations, some mechanism beyond an interested researcher calling up every agency one-by-one is necessary to ensure the data survives for posterity.

Continued support is required to maintain these archives, to keep them current with technology, to add surveys, and to format them so that they are compatible and allow easy manipulation by researchers and the public.

REFERENCES

Axhausen K.W. (2000). Presenting and Preserving Travel Data. In: *Transport Surveys: Raising the Standard,* Transportation Research Circular, Number E-C008, Transportation Research Board, Washington, DC, II-F/1-19.
Axhausen, K.W. (2003). Analysis of the MEST and related survey work. In: *Capturing Long Distance Travel* (K.W. Axhausen, J.L. Madre, J.W. Polak and P. Toint, eds), 130-147, Research Science Press, Baldock.
Axhausen, K.W., J.L. Madre, J.W. Polak and P. Toint (2003). Recommendations for a European survey of long-distance travel and associated research. In: *Capturing Long Distance Travel* (K.W. Axhausen, J.L. Madre, J.W. Polak and P. Toint, eds), 298-319, Research Science Press, Baldock.
Axhausen K.W. (2003). Public use of travel surveys: The metadata perspective. In: *Transport Survey Quality and Innovation* (P.R. Stopher and P.M. Jones, eds), 605-628, Pergamon Press, Oxford.
Center for Transportation Analysis (2001). *2001 National Household Travel Survey,* http://nhts.ornl.gov/2001/index.shtml accessed 15 June, 2004.

Computer-Assisted Survey Methods Program (2004). *SDA-Survey Documentation and Analysis*, University of California, Berkeley http://sda.berkeley.edu/ accessed 15 June, 2004.

Datamart (2002). *MTC Datamart Travel Surveys*, http://www.mtc.dst.ca.us/datamart/survey.htm accessed 15 June, 2004.

Data Documentation Initiative (2004). http://www.icpsr.umich.edu/DDI, accessed 15 June, 2004.

Dublin Core (2004). *About the Initiative*, http://dublincore.org/about/ accessed 15 June, 2004.

ETHTDA (2004). *Eidgenossische Technische Hochschule Travel Data Archive*, http://www.ivt.ethz.ch/vpl/publications/ethtda/index_EN accessed 22 March, 2005.

Garrett, M. and Wachs M. (1996). *Transportation Planning on Trial: The Clean Air Act and Travel Forecasting*, Sage Publications.

Hensher, D.A. (editor) (2001). *Travel Behaviour Research: The Leading Edge*, Pergamon, Oxford.

Minnesota Population Center (2004). *IPUMS- Integrated Public Use Microdata Series 'What is the IPUMS'*, University of Minnesota, Minneapolis. http://www.ipums.umn.edu/usa/intro.html accessed 15 June, 2004.

Nesstar.org (2002). Source: http://www.nesstar.org/ accessed 15 June, 2004.

Norwegian Social Science Data Services (1999). *Providing Global Access to Distributed Data Through Metadata Standardizations: The Parallel Stories of Nesstar and the DDI*, http://www.nesstar.org/papers/GlobalAccess.html accessed 15 June, 2004.

Porter, C., Melendy, L. and Deakin, E. (1996). *Land use and travel survey data : a survey of the metropolitan planning organizations of the 35 largest US metropolitan areas*, Berkeley: University of California at Berkeley. Institute of Urban and Regional Development Working paper no. 656.

Ryssevik, J. and S. Musgrave (1999). The Social Science Dream Machine: Resource discovery, analysis and delivery on the Web. Paper given at the IASSIST Conference, Toronto, May. Available at http://www.nesstar.org/papers/iassist_0599.html accessed 15 June, 2004

Stopher P.R., C.G. Wilmot, C.C. Stecher and R. Alsnih (2003). Standards for Household Travel Surveys - Some Proposed Ideas, paper presented to the 10th International Conference on Travel Behaviour Research, Lucerne, August.

US Department of Commerce (1944). *Manual of Procedures for Home Interview Traffic Studies.* US Bureau of Public Roads. Washington, DC.

Virtual Data Centre (2003). *Thedata*, http://thedata.org accessed 15 June, 2004

Weiner, Edward, (1997). *Urban Transportation Planning in the United States: An Historical Overview.* US Department of Transportation. Fifth Edition. (Available on line at http://tmip.fhwa.dot.gov/clearinghouse/docs/utp)

World Wide Web Consortium (2002). *Metadata Activity Statement*, http://www.w3.org/Metadata/Activity.html accessed 15 June, 2004

Zahavi, Y. (1974). *Travel Time Budget and Mobility in Urban Areas.* Federal Highway Administration. Washington DC. US Department of Transportation. May, NTIS PB 234 145.

Travel Survey Methods: Quality and Future Directions
Peter Stopher and Cheryl Stecher (Editors)
© 2006 Published by Elsevier Ltd.

13

PROCESSING, ANALYSIS, AND ARCHIVING OF TRAVEL SURVEY DATA

Gerd Sammer, Institute for Transport Studies, University of Natural Resources and for Applied Life Sciences, Vienna, Austria

INTRODUCTION

Processing, analysis, and archiving of travel survey data seem to be rather routine or boring activities compared to other aspects of travel surveys, such as the design of the survey, sampling, or the design of the survey instrument. However, this part of the process is also very important and influences the quality of the data obtained and its continued accessibility and use in the future. The goal of this chapter is to analyse and identify those activities and procedures that are essential to ensure the data quality in this aspect of survey execution. It suggests quality standards in terms of guidelines, for procedures and content, and discusses how to ensure the execution, the survey procedures, the results, and the original data are adequately documented. A specific focus is given to the consideration of standards for archiving in order to ensure maximum use of the data today and in the future.

No standardised definition of the individual steps and phases of processing, analysis, and archiving for travel surveys exists. The analysis of the relevant literature shows no clear definitions and the terms are often used differently (Richardson *et al.*, 1995; Stopher and Jones, 2003; Sammer, 2000). A basic precondition for quality assurance is the use of a common terminology. In Table 1, we offer a proposed harmonised terminology of the seven main steps (A to G) of the survey procedure, representing a compromise between frequently used terms and a clear and logical structure. Because this chapter deals with steps E to G, the first four steps are not divided into further detail. However, it is evident, that this classification meets all the needs of a subdivision into further steps. The structure of this chapter follows the definitions of Table 1. Not all steps are treated with the same intensity, because this would be beyond the scope of this chapter. Emphasis is placed on those activities that are critical for data quality.

Table 1: Proposed Harmonised and Standardised Terminology

Step	Terminology		
A.	Survey Design		
B.	Sample Design		
C.	Survey Instrument Design		
D,	Survey Implementation (Execution)		
E.	Data Processing	E1.	Database Building
		E2.	Questionnaire Response Editing
		E3.	Coding and Data Entry
		E4.	Data Editing / Cleaning
		E5.	Weighting
		E6.	Expansion
F.	Data Analysis	F1.	Validation
		F2.	Descriptive and Explanatory Data Analysis
		F3.	Data Presentation
G.	Data Documentation and Archiving	G1.	Documentation
		G2.	Archiving

DATA PROCESSING

Data processing seems to be a rather less interesting issue, but is an important part of the survey, which influences the quality of the data produced tremendously. The data processing can be structured into the following six steps: database building, questionnaire response editing, coding and data entry, data editing/cleaning, weighting and expansion.

Database Building

Database building includes the selection of the type of data structure, which is appropriate for the data collected, and the software for the database system. At the beginning the requirements for the database and the software have to be analysed and defined. At this stage, it is helpful to consider also the requirements for archiving and dissemination of the final survey data. Apart from other needs, it is necessary to consider that more complex database systems significantly increase the dissemination price, because database enquiries are not royalty free. In addition, complex database systems have high hardware requirements. Experience shows that relatively simple and robust data base systems have advantages, if a frequent and unproblematic use of the data by different organisations and clients is desirable (DATELINE Consortium, 1999).

There are two types of different data structure used for travel surveys (Richardson *et al.*, 1995):

1. A flat-file data base structure that is used mainly in simple travel surveys with a small sample. This structure provides one record for each responding survey unit, where all information is stored in one record within one data file. This data base structure wastes storage units and is used rather rarely nowadays, even when needed for most of the existing software packages for statistical analysis.
2. Related database structures fulfil the needs of a hierarchical nesting of the data, which occurs often typically in travel surveys: A set of data describes the household characteristics, a subset of data is related to the household members, each household member is linked to a subset of trip data and each trip involves a data set of trip stages. The relational database is mostly used nowadays and fulfils the needs of modern data archiving systems.

The requirements for the quality of the database building include an intensive testing and a detailed documentation. Another issue must be addressed: if the survey design does not use a computer-aided methodology often two separate databases are developed, one for the execution of the survey, which includes all information from the field work, and another that consists of the collected data on travel behaviour. In subsequent scientific analysis, especially for analysing quality and undertaking weighting procedures, information is often needed about the survey procedure, which is not included in the final database. Therefore, it should be a minimum level of quality standard that a version of the final database also includes the information collected during the field-work, or that both databases are linked together in an appropriate way.

Questionnaire Response Editing

A very important activity, to ensure the quality of the collected data, is the editing of the filled-in questionnaires. Before the completed questionnaire of a personal interview survey goes to the coding procedure, the data must be checked for their completeness, consistency, and plausibility. This activity should be natural, but real life differs sometimes. The editing process consists of two stages (Richardson *et al.*, 1995): interviewer and supervisor editing. Both should be done as soon as possible after the interview was carried out. In principle, each interview has to be edited by the interviewer him- or herself. The CATI technique enables this process to be carried out online for completeness, but plausibility checks, which cannot be done automatically, must be done after the interview is carried out. If unclear information is found, the interviewer can contact the respondent again. It is recommended that both responses, the former and the corrected one, should be recorded for error analysis when any corrections were done.

Supervisor editing is necessary for a sub-sample of the interviews collected and is important as a quality check and supervision of the interviewer. It is very important to avoid slackness of the interviewer; therefore, supervisor editing should be a parallel procedure during the duration of the fieldwork with two special intensive phases, one at the beginning and one at the end. A third editing procedure, which is carried out for a small sample by a representative of the client, should be discussed.

Coding and Data Entry

Coding and data entry is one of the steps of the surveying process where a tremendously fast development of methods can be observed. Today, the most frequently used method of coding and data entry is based on interactive computer programs. However, there are some aspects related to coding that influence the quality and especially the compatibility of the data with respect to data analysis, archiving, and comparability of different surveys. Some of these aspects are addressed in the following paragraphs.

Coding Execution

If a computer assists the process of interviewing (e.g., CATI and CAPI), the question arises whether to do all the coding at the same moment the information is collected. On the one hand, the advantage of checking the data consistency on-line is clear; on the other hand, there are some experiences that indicate that the time delay in on-line geo-coding and the interaction needed to obtain a valid location can dominate the interview and may confuse the respondent (Steuart, 1997). In any case, the coding procedure should be executed as soon as possible after the completion of the interview, so that any problem can be resolved while the interview is fresh in the minds of the interviewer and the respondent. There are some other aspects, which should be mentioned to avoid missing quality. Coding should be carried out by a limited number of coders, who are in close contact with one another to discuss questions arising and agree on resolution of those questions immediately. In this way, questions that arise can be resolved and the relevant information disseminated immediately. Of course, coding and data entry is a process that has to be monitored or supervised permanently as a quality control check. The coding information itself (e.g., coder, coding time) has to be recorded as well as the survey data collected. Because interactive computer programs are in use, double coding of each data item seems to be unnecessary. However, there needs to be an examination of the question of whether this practice decreases the quality to an unacceptable extent.

Missing Values and Use of Zero

There is a real need to implement standardisation on how to treat missing values and the use of zero (see also the section on *Missing Data*). Up to the present, considerable variability exists between different surveys, and even within the same survey as to how missing data are recorded. It is very important that missing values are flagged properly so that no confusion is possible especially with using a blank and a zero in a numeric field (Stopher and Jones, 2003). At the 10th International Conference on Travel Behaviour Research in Lucerne, Switzerland, a paper was presented which discusses a proposal for some standardisations to overcome those problems (Stopher *et al.*, 2003):

- No blanks standard: blanks are not legitimate code and all data fields should contain alphanumeric data; zero is used as a form of a nominal variable.
- Missing data standard: missing data must be flagged by a specific code, of which the first digit has to be -9 for missing values independent of the cause. The second digit should be used to code the reason for missing as 'don't know', legitimate skips, or non-applicability of a question etc.
- Correspondence between numeric values and the codes standard: if closed questions are offered in a specific order, the order should be reflected in the codes standard; if any question has the legitimate response zero (e.g., the number of trips of a person or the number of accompanying persons), the code for that response should be the number zero.
- Coding standard for binary variables: in travel surveys a binary variable occurs often as a yes/no response or the gender male/female. To avoid errors it is recommended strongly to code the response 'yes' as 1 and 'no' as 2. For coding the gender use 1 for 'male' and 2 for 'female' while no response is -9.

Standardisation for Flexible Coding of Complex Variables

In most travel surveys, the responses contain variables that involve categories which may vary from survey to survey depending on the specific goals of the surveys. Typical representative variables of that type are income, activity, employment status, education level, means of travel, travel purpose, etc. (Stopher *et al.*, 2003; Stopher *et al.*, 2006). It would be useful to define an international standard for such values, which enhance the comparability of surveys and avoid any ambiguity. Such a coding standardisation would reduce errors because of habitual effects on the one hand and would make comparative analysis easier on the other hand. For example, if the minimum set of standard categories for the travel purpose is 5, it has to be considered how to enable a possible way to extend the number of categories in a compatible way. An idea how this would work is shown in Table 2. The main advantage of this method of *standardised flexible coding* is that an aggregation to the minimum coding categories can be made very easily by just dropping the last digit of the code.

In connection with the 'activity' and 'travel purpose' variables, the categories used in most travel surveys need to be extended, to enable a more appropriate handling for behavioural analysis and modelling. In particular, the 'leisure trip' category comprises about 25 % of all trips, but this categorisation does not meet modelling needs. There is a large variety of leisure activities, such as sporting, cultural, visiting friends, religious activities, etc. (Axhausen, 2003). These different types of leisure activities have varying requirements for modelling exercises. A similar need can be identified (Sammer, 1998) for the characteristics of 'car driver' and 'car passenger', which should be recorded in more detail as 'solo driver', 'driver with accompanying household member' and 'driver with accompanying non household member' (car sharing mode). This specification of categories would meet the requirements of the young research field of behavioural analysis and modelling of measures of mobility management. In this context, the attribute 'people with mobility restrictions' should also be recorded, when this has an impact on general mobility and imposes restrictions on the mobility of accompanying persons.

Table 2: Proposed Standardised Flexible Coding-Scheme for 'Travel Purpose'

Minimum Categories	Minimum Coding	More Detailed Categories	More Detailed Coding
Business	01	- work place related	010
		- non work place related	011
Commuting	02	- home related	021
		- non home related	022
Education	03	- pupil	031
		- student	032
Shopping	04	- food	041
		- non food	042
Leisure	05	- sport activity	051
		- cultural activity	052
		etc.	
Other	06	Other	060
Missing data	-90	- Don't know	- 988
		- Refused	- 999

Geocoding

Today, geocoding belongs to the state-of-the-art for coding origin and destination addresses. However, practical experience shows that there are some as yet unsolved problems, that can lead to missing trip information. Different requirements have to be taken into account for local travel surveys and long-distance travel surveys (Richardson *et al.*, 1995; DATELINE Consortium, 2003a). For local travel surveys, the methods of geocoding that are generally used are: geocoding of full street address, cross street address, landmarks, and geocoding by sampling. The latter can be described as a geocoding imputation method that is used to compensate for incomplete information on locations (see section on *Missing Data*). Even then, it is very important that the geocoding category is also recorded to provide information about the geocoding accuracy.

Local travel surveys require very disaggregated geocoding, of which the most suitable is coding to latitude and longitude. In practice, this results in an achieved proportion of well-coded locations of about eighty percent. In some local travel surveys, the completion of well-coded data can be as high as ninety five percent, when a good data base is available and if respondents are motivated to indicate their addresses accurately. There are two principal solutions to increase this proportion. The first is to go back to the interview stage of the survey and obtain additional information from the respondent. This is the better, but also very expensive way. The second solution is the imputation of the missing addresses, which can be a feasible way, but is not satisfactory for all survey uses.

Geocoding for long distance travel surveys has different requirements, which are similar for out-of-region addresses of a local travel survey. Here the spatial aggregation level needed is not so accurate. In general, coding is required at the level of a traffic analysis zone. Geocoding should be carried out at the most disaggregated level of the collected information from the respondent. Generally this is the city, community or region, where the origin or destination of the region is located. The coded information should include again the latitude and longitude, which represents, in this case, the geographic centre of the city, community, or region. Experiences with the DATELINE project (DATELINE Consortium, 2003a) show a satisfactory proportion of over ninety five percent of well-coded locations.

Data Editing and Cleaning

No standardised term exists for this step of data processing (Table 1). The following terms are used in this context: data editing, data cleaning, and data correction, whilst the term data correction is also used for the weighting procedure. To promote a clear standardised survey technology, it is proposed to introduce data editing and cleaning for this step, which deals with checking the range error, logical consistency, and missing data insofar as errors can be detected during editing and corrected by referring to the original questionnaire, as well as recontacting the interviewer or respondents.

Errors and Their Treatment

It is evident that five main types of bias can occur (Richardson *et al.*, 1995), which need a different treatment to ensure a high quality data set. These types arise from several sources, namely, sample drawing, respondent, interviewer, data coder/typist (Table 3):

- The sample drawing bias which causes a deviation from the principle of random sampling and results in a biased coverage of the population. The treatment of this error is discussed in the section on *Weighting*.
- The range error is mainly a result of typing and recording where the code value is outside of the permissible code for that response. Mostly this error can be eliminated by referring to the original questionnaire, but also double coding of the questionnaires helps to avoid some of these errors.
- Logical consistency errors occur if responses to different questions of one or several persons linked together give inconsistent results, e.g., if the last trip of the day is not to home or if joint trips of the household members do not fit together. To ensure high quality, it is recommended to define survey specific rules on how to deal with identified inconsistencies. A good example for such rules is described in a paper by Arentze *et al.* (1999). This type of error can be corrected in many cases if the questionnaire is checked again. If the inconsistency cannot be

eliminated in this way a new contact with the respondent is very helpful as the experience of the New KONTIV-design has shown, which includes such a procedure (DATELINE Consortium, 2003c; Brög, 2000). This procedure is expensive but very successful.

Table 3: Type, Sample and Treatment of Errors

Source of Error	Type of Identified Errors				
	Sample Drawing Bias	Range	Logical Consistency	Missing Data Unit	Item	Coding Error
Drawing and Coverage of Population	C	-	-	C	-	-
Respondent	B	B	B	C	C	-
Interviewer	B	B	B	B	B	-
Coder, Typist	A	A	A	A	A	A

Classes of Error Treatment:

A: Errors which can be eliminated in most cases by the data editing and cleaning procedure. There seems to be no need to record the code of the corrected values from a quality viewpoint except for the error statistic.

B. Errors which can be eliminated mostly by the data editing and cleaning procedure. The correction procedure should be documented for further investigation and analysis of the original raw data by setting a flag.

C: Errors which have to be treated by the weighting and correction procedure (see the section on *Data Weighting*).

- Missing data (unit and item) can be caused by coders and typists or by the respondent. An error of coders or typists can be eliminated by double coding or checking the questionnaire. The second one is discussed in the section on *Missing Data*.
- The coding error, which consists of a false value, which is not outside of the range of codes permissible for that response, can only be identified by double coding. Double coding requires a great effort, but is the only way to correct this error. If such an error is identified, the correction needs a check of the original questionnaire. A minimum standard requirement should be fixed, so that, in a pilot survey, a sub-sample of the interviews is double coded, to assess the quality of the coders as well as for CATI or mail back surveys. The result of such a pilot survey enables an assessment of the coding quality and may result in a requirement for additional training.

The editing/cleaning procedure needs at least a manageable definition of a useable and complete response. Such a definition fixes which key variables must exist with a defined quality to meet the minimum criteria of completion. It does not seem to be meaningful to define general standards, because the objectives and application of travel surveys are different. In the DATELINE survey, for example, a useable household is defined as one in which the person data meet the following criteria of required person and behavioural data: age, gender, destination of journeys, duration of journeys, purpose of journeys. Some CATI software used for travel surveys eliminate incomplete responses as soon as the full sample has been obtained. This practice leads to a loss of important information for further analysis of several elements of the travel survey. Therefore, it is important that incomplete responses, which are not useable for the sample, be retained and documented as a non-usable return. The definition of a useable response also influences the response rate.

Quality management is based on information. Therefore, the whole editing/cleaning procedure must be documented in a qualitative and quantitative way, defining which data checks were made, and providing a statistical analysis of the frequency of the identified types of errors.

Missing Data

Missing data caused by the respondent need a subtly different treatment. First, we must distinguish between unit nonresponse and item nonresponse (Richardson and Meyburg, 2003). Unit nonresponse occurs where a whole survey unit (a household or a person) fails to respond to the survey. Item nonresponse (Richardson, 2000) is defined as occurring when the respondent has provided responses to most questions, but has failed to answer one or more specific questions (e.g., the trip purpose or the whole trip). It has to be stated that some authors make a distinction between non-reported trips and the item nonresponse (Richardson and Loeis, 1997). Unit nonresponse is discussed in the section on *Data Weighting*. It is appropriate to distinguish between three methods of how to treat the missing information of items:

- Imputation by re-contacting the respondent. One of the most promising procedures to obtain the information for missing data is to re-contact the respondent. This method is part of the new KONTIV design and eliminates the error totally, but requires great effort and is expensive (Brög, 2000). This type of treatment is preferred, compared to the following methods, from the viewpoint of quality.
- Imputation of the missing information by logical consistency checks from other information. Stopher and Jones (2003, p. 30) call this the inference method. To ensure an objective and understandable inference procedure the rules have to be defined for each variable in detail. A very strong quality condition would be that only those imputation actions are accepted that, when done by two independent persons, lead to the same result.
- Imputation of missing data based on associative rules or other procedures (e.g., Monte-Carlo-random based, or neural networks). It is necessary to define a standard of which variables are allowed to be imputed. The question is closely related to the minimum requirements for a useable return of incomplete interviews. This type of imputation should not be allowed for missing items which are part of the defined key variables of a useable household or person data set. One must be aware that any imputation of a key item or variable of the survey (e.g., missing person, trips, destination, trip mode, trip purpose) has the effect of reducing the sample size related to the imputed variable, besides other bias risks. Such a reduced sample size has to be taken into account for calculation of the

sampling errors. The question arises if a limit of the rate of a maximum number of imputations can be or should be defined (Stopher and Jones, 2003, p. 31). In principle such a limitation should not be defined as a general standard, but must be considered for each specific case.

It is important to determine if it is possible and desirable to define minimum standards for imputation methods. An analysis of existing methods, ranging from simple mean imputation to complex hot-deck or neural network imputation, shows large differences in the consequences and quality achievable (Poduri, 2000; Richardson and Loeis, 1997; Wilmot *et al.*, 2003; Han and Polak, 2001). It would not make sense to fix the requirements for a specific method of imputation, but to define a minimum standard of principles not associated with any specific procedure, for example:

- The imputation method should be based on a missing item analysis that takes into account the relation of the missing items to other variables in the current sample, including the result of a validation survey analysis. The imputation should not only ensure that imputation is multiplying data that is not missing, but is also adding data that is missing.
- The number of imputed values should not dominate the number of reported values of the considered variables, being aware that imputation is always a risk and in reality reduces the sample with respect to the type of the imputed variable.
- Key variables of a survey which are a part of the defined 'usable return', as mentioned before, should not be imputed.
- In any case of imputation, the imputation process should be documented totally and the imputed values must be flagged so that the analyst of the data is fully aware which information comes from the respondent and which does not.

Weighting

Data weighting is necessary when the sample is stratified or any other disproportional sampling procedure is used, and if any other bias is expected in the cleaned and corrected data after data editing and cleaning process described above. From a quality viewpoint, the following questions are of interest:

- Under what circumstances is weighting of the data required?
- Which method of weighting is appropriate for the biased data?

Weighting is related to key variables of the data, which have to be defined. For travel surveys the following variables are the main focus: household, person, number of journeys or trips travelled, distances travelled, travel time. The travel-related variables are distinguished through different characteristics, such as purpose and mode. It follows from this that any bias has to be considered in relation to those variables.

Criteria for Weighting

Weighting is necessary where the distribution of the following listed key variables is different between the sample and the population, to achieve congruence between both:

- Household size and car ownership rate in relation to the number of cars;
- Person age, gender and occupation, nationality, etc.; and
- Regional location and the set dates of the survey.

From a quality viewpoint, appropriate weighting is required if statistical tests indicate a significant bias for the following proposed key variables:

- Travel behaviour between respondents and non-respondents characterised by the number of journeys, trips, distance travelled, travel time budget, etc.; and
- Item nonresponse.

The statistical test between the household and person variables requires appropriate secondary independent data sources. For the travel behaviour variables, either a validation survey is needed for non-reported trips, or a nonresponse explorative survey for the unit nonresponse is required, although any other appropriate analysis can be used, e.g., the effect of the number of reminders/contacts on questionnaire response rates ('Response Speed Analysis'). A nonresponse explorative survey has the goal of exploring some key variables of travel behaviour for a subsample of the unit nonresponse. This result can be used to estimate the travel behaviour of nonrespondents. A validation survey of non-reported trips has the goal of surveying a subsample of the respondents again to investigate if all trips are reported.

As an example, the test result for nonresponse bias for the DATELINE survey in Germany is shown in Figure 1 and Table 4. For this test, two different methods are applied: a nonresponse survey and a response speed analysis. The response speed analysis in Figure 1 indicates that respondents who respond earlier are more mobile than persons who respond later in a mail-back survey. The extrapolation of the response speed-function is used to estimate the travel behaviour of nonrespondents. The response speed analysis in Figure 1 indicates a significant bias, whereas the comparison of the average number of long distance journeys of the main survey with the nonresponse exploratory survey shows no significant difference in the average number of journeys per household (Table 4). This result seems to be caused by the very small sample size of the nonresponse survey. One can see that the sample size of the nonresponse exploratory survey should not be too small to obtain significant results.

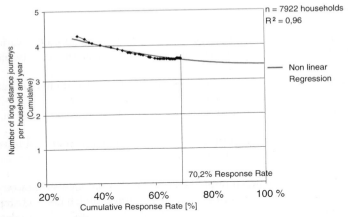

Source: Neumann, 2003, p. 167

Figure 1: Effect of Increasing Response Rate (Response Speed) on the Average Numbers of Long Distance Journeys Caused by Several Reminder Activities, DATELINE Germany

Table 4: Comparison of Long Distance Journeys between Respondents (Main Survey) and Nonrespondents (Nonresponse Exploratory Survey); DATELINE Germany

Source	Sample Size	Number of Journeys/ Household and Year	Standard Deviation	Test Result
Main Survey	7,922	3.60	7.47	$t_0 = 0.29 <$
Nonresponse Exploratory Survey	119	3.40	5.43	$1.65\ (\alpha = 5\%)$

Source: Neumann, 2003, p. 180

Weighting Method

As a general principle, two methods of weighting can be distinguished: factor and unit imputation weighting (Herry, 1995). Whereas factor weighting is used mostly, unit imputation weighting has a minor important standing in practical survey work. Unit imputation weighting follows the idea of eliminating bias in a casual way by enriching the diversity of the distribution of the sample, in contrast with factor weighting which is based on the diversity of the existing distribution of a defined stratification of the sample. From the viewpoint of quality, the unit imputation weighting procedure seems promising and requires further research, in particular for the problem of spatial distributions of origins and destinations.

Weighting Stratification and Sample Size

Factor weighting is the most widely used method, but to ensure high quality in the results, some principles have to be adhered to. Factor weighting is carried out on an hierarchical aggregation level of the survey variables, e.g., household, person, journey, trip stage. On each level, the variables are divided into appropriate multi-dimensional stratification characteristics. For example, on the person level, the multi-dimensional stratifications of age, gender and occupation classes are used. If the population distribution for the multi-dimensional stratification is available from secondary data, it is necessary to test whether the sample size of each class is big enough to ensure an unbiased weighting procedure. As a rule of thumb, the minimum sample size of a stratification should not fall below about thirty cases. This fact has to be considered for the definition of the sample size in relation to the selection of the weighting procedure. To avoid small sample problems, the weighting procedure often is carried out in a stepwise way. This means that the weighting procedure enables only an unbiased boundary distribution of each person characteristic but not of the multi-dimensional distribution of these person characteristics. Such a weighting procedure requires some quality principles:

- The stepwise weighting algorithm should be mathematically consistent (Sammer and Fallast, 1996); and
- It is recommended that an algorithm is used that follows the principle of maximum entropy or minimum information gain (Wilson, 1974; Snickers and Weibull, 1977; Sammer and Zelle, 1982). The goal if this algorithm is to provide an optimal solution for the multi-dimensional matrix of the weighting stratification characteristics by being given a boundary distribution of the weighting characteristics which follows the defined optimum of the maximum entropy condition. As is a matter of course, the weighting procedure must guarantee the original sample size in total by any appropriate standardisation algorithm.

Unit Nonresponse Weighting

Another issue should be addressed. Often the weighting of the unit nonresponse error is carried out by factor weighting of trips. This method ignores the evidence that unit nonresponse is mainly caused by the different willingness of respondents. Therefore the weighting procedure should be performed on the level of persons or households, whether the non-respondent information arises from a nonresponse speed analysis or from a nonresponse explanatory survey. Figure 2 indicates the result of the response speed analysis, namely that the share of households with few long distance journeys increases with a rising response rate for mail back surveys and vice versa. Figure 3 shows the opposite result for a CATI-survey: the share of households with few long distance journeys decreases with a rising response rate.

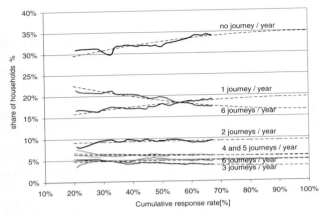

Source: Neumann, 2003, p. 171

Figure 2: Effect of Increasing Response Rate (Response Speed) on Share of Households with Different Long Distance Journeys (≥ 125 km as the Crow Flies), Sample Size = 861 Households, DATELINE Austria

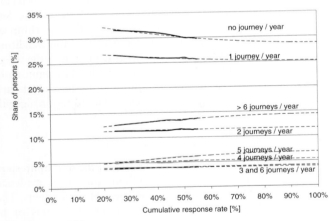

Source: Neumann, 2003, p. 174

Figure 3: Effect of Increasing Response Rate (Response Speed) of CATI-Survey on Share of Persons with Different Long Distance Journeys (≥ 125 km as the Crow Flies), Sample Size = 7,363 Persons, DATELINE France

Weighting Statistics and Documentation

When the weighting procedure is finished, it is important to document the weighting method, including the analysis, so that it is clear how it was carried out. That implies the following:

- Weighting documentation: aggregation weighting level, weighting steps, and stratification algorithm used, target variables of weighting, results of the weighting analysis, critical comment on well solved and less well solved distortions, etc.; and
- Weighting statistics: distribution of weights, effect of the single weighting steps on the target variables and the information on the convergence speed if iterative weighting algorithms are used.

In Figures 4 to 6 some examples of weighting statistics of the DATELINE project are documented, which provide an insight into the quality of weighting and the sample of a travel survey.

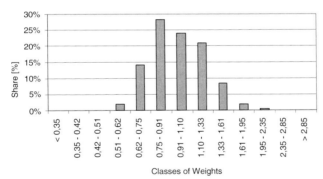

Source: DATELINE, 2003, Weighting and Grossing-up-report, p. 36

Figure 4: Distribution of Weights for Zone NUTS 1 of Austria, DATELINE Austria

Efficiency of Weighting

Data weighting is one of the key steps to achieve high quality data from travel surveys, but, including the necessary analysis, is a resource-consuming effort. Therefore, a balance should be achieved between the increase in the quality of results obtained in each step of the weighting procedure and the effort needed to perform it. This means more emphasis should be put on the cost-benefit ratio of data weighting. An admittedly not representative analysis of reports of travel surveys indicates that for many travel surveys:

- The weighting procedure and its efforts are not well documented; and
- The improvement of the quality of the results of the individual weighting steps is not shown.

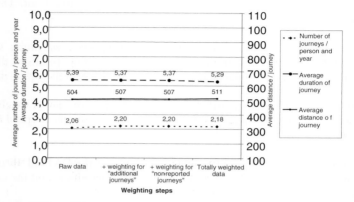

Source: Neumann, 2003, p. 205

Figure 5: Effect of Single Weighting Steps on Average Number of Long Distance Journeys per Person and Year (≥ 125 km as the Crow Flies) and on Mean of Distance and Duration Travelled, DATELINE Austria

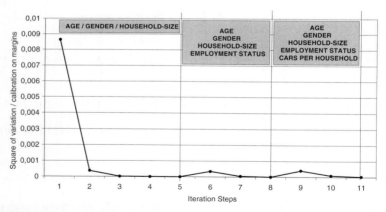

Source: DATELINE 2003, Weighting and Grossing-up-report, p. 38

Figure 6: Convergence Speed (Number of Iteration Steps) of the Simultaneous Weighting Algorithm of DATELINE, Example Finland NUTS 1)

More attention should be paid to the cost-benefit ratio of the weighting procedure, with respect to saving resources.

DATA ANALYSIS

Validation

A validation analysis indicates and verifies the accuracy of the surveyed data and is one of the most important steps of the survey. Before the cleaned, weighted, and expanded dataset is ready for final use, it is recommended to carry out a validation check. The result of such a validation analysis can lead to a loop back to the previous steps of the survey, if it does not fulfil the defined quality level. This validation analysis can be made by two different organisations depending on the function of this validation exercise and the type of quality management:

1. The organisation that is responsible for the survey project, if the validation analysis has the function of a final quality test. This validation check is conventional and should be part of the survey contract if type (2) is not chosen. Some survey studies have included such a validation analysis (DATELINE Consortium, 2003d), but it is not common practice.
2. An independent organisation in the function of a referee or the client itself is responsible for the validation check. An independent referee organisation reviews whether the quality standards are fulfilled. Experience shows that it is very effective if the validation analysis is carried out not only at the end of the survey process, but also an accompanying quality check is implemented to ensure quality at each stage. This can be performed by an independent quality board consisting of independent experts.

In all cases, it is important to define the quality standards at the beginning of the survey and include them in the tender.

The validation check must take into account the specific situation and framework of the travel survey, but some hints can be formulated to achieve high quality:

- Validation survey, recollection of a sub sample (Stopher and Jones, 2003, p.35, Stopher *et al.*, 2003). A validation survey reports the data collection process with a subsample of the data previously collected by interviews. The validation survey is carried out by different interviewers and should use also a different method of data collection. As a rule, the validation survey is focused on some key variables. As a minimum standard, it should include the information that is defined as 'usable terms'. The validation statistic consists of a comparison of the original data and the data collected in the validation survey. The quality of the data is assessed by a comparative statistic, which identifies the discrepancies. Stopher *et al.* (2003) recommend the use of the root-mean-square-error, which provides a dimensionless measure of the average error or deviation of two values of the same variable:

$$\text{RMSE} = \sqrt{\frac{1}{n}\sum_{i}\frac{V_{1,i}-V_{2,i}}{V_{2,i}}} *100[\%]$$

RMSE = root-mean-square-error of variable V (e.g., number of trips)
$V_{1,I}$ = collected value from the main survey
$V_{2,I}$ = collected value from the validation survey
n   = subsample size of the validation survey
i   = index of interviews of the survey

For the interpretation of the results it is necessary to define a limiting RMSE, which is acceptable from the quality viewpoint. Considerations of the appropriate size of the validation survey have to be taken into account.

- Validation survey by passive tracking survey:
New technology enables a complete recording of all person or vehicle movements over the reporting period of a survey. Experiences show (Wermuth *et al.*, 2003, Murakami *et al.*, 2003) that surveys based on GPS or mobile phone are an appropriate instrument to collect data of a subsample of the main survey and to use this information for validating (and correcting) the data. It is recommended that the root-mean-square-error also be used for the presentation of the results of the validation statistics.
- Plausibility check with secondary data (Sammer, 1997):
A plausibility check is the comparison of the result of target variables with appropriate results of independent secondary data sources. The type of plausibility check is dependent on the available data sources, but this should be considered during the preparation phase of the survey. The following possibilities are noted:
  - A check of the total number of trips or journeys that cross a defined cordon, deduced from the travel data and, for example, from independent traffic counts, is an appropriate assessment of the accuracy. In cities with a river, counts on bridges can be made, or other breaks used such as railway lines with few streets that cross. The traffic movements counted at such network sections, differentiated according to modal split, should agree with the registered origin-destination travel behaviour. One should note that differences are not always due to survey errors. Other causes include: differing survey periods, different 'populations' caused by tourist traffic, etc. If one excludes these influences, experience shows that household surveys tend to under-report car and business trips.
  - Comparison of the kilometres travelled for motorised transport deduced from the household survey, with average annual kilometres of the vehicles, determined from an independent car-ownership survey.

The result of the validation analysis is an essential part of the survey documentation. If the result does not fulfil the defined quality standards, then a revision of the weighting/correction step may be appropriate.

Data Presentation

Presentation of data seems to be a very simple issue, using the diverse software on the market. However, from a quality viewpoint, most of the presentations of survey results neglect to inform the user of the results about the statistical accuracy and sampling error (Purvis, 2000). It should be completely normal to provide the confidence interval for a presented key value or, for the comparison of two values, information as to whether their difference is statistically significant or not. However, analysis of existing presentations of travel survey results indicates that information about the accuracy of descriptive statistics is rarely provided. This problem becomes more important when web-based data information systems for travel surveys are publicly available (see the section on *Technology of Metadata and Data Archives on the Market*).

What could be the reasons for such poor reporting? One reason is that valid calculation of confidence intervals and other statistical tests specifically requires taking into account the weighting and correction procedures (Hautzinger, 1997; Sammer, 1997; Brög *et al.*, 1986), and this is not provided for in most of the available software packages.

DOCUMENTATION AND PRESERVATION

Status-quo Analysis

Documentation and preservation of data on and results of transport surveys has become a frequently-discussed topic at international conferences in the past decade, and an increasing number of papers have been produced (Axhausen, 2000, 2001; Axhausen and Wigan, 2003; Pendyala, 2003; Sharp, 2003; Wigan, 2001; Levinson and Zofka, 2006). A survey should not end with the delivery of the data to the primary client if the collected data are also valuable for other clients. While the need and value of high quality documentation and preservation is well recognised in the community of transport researchers, many activities cannot be undertaken if progress is to be made in normal professional practice, especially with respect to the access to transport survey data. The question arises as to the reasons for this unsatisfactory situation. The implementation of institutional websites as a very suitable medium for communication between experts enables good access to information about travel surveys, but, unfortunately, they mostly provide the information in very differing qualities and detail. The full survey data are generally not available. No systematic analysis about this difficult situation has yet been carried out, but some elements are evident:

- The lack of awareness, among public planning agencies and the organisation that carries out a survey, of the importance of such data for the scientific community. The organisations have mostly a commercial and only a limited scientific background, and this does not support in-house initiatives for data preservation.
- The lack of willingness of planning agencies, especially regional ones, to finance the archiving of surveys for further use of the data outside their area of responsibility and interest.
- The absence of an appropriate national organisation in many countries that feels responsible for data preservation. The archiving of data by any international travel organisation could raise legal questions of data protection.
- There are also scientific reasons that should be cited, such as the absence of well understood and adopted patterns, as well as standardisation regarding how to document and archive such survey data in the field of transport.

Summarising the reasons why publicly available documentation of transport data is not the rule, two main classes can be recognised, and these need handling differently:

1. Reasons that may be located in the institutions and their representatives that are engaged in transport surveys. It is very important to raise their awareness of this problem. How can this be initiated in a successful way? It would seem necessary to involve the existing relevant public organizations and scientific networks in starting something like an information campaign to keep this topic on the agenda of relevant conferences and journals.

2. Reasons that are of a scientific nature, such as the absence of clear and easily useable guidelines providing the minimum requirements for standardisation of transport surveys and data archiving. Nevertheless, the methodology of documentation and archiving, and its technology is now well developed (e.g., NESSTAR, web-based data analysis software), even though it has not yet become state-of-the-practice in the field of transport surveys.

Objectives and Requirements on Documentation and Archiving

The objectives and requirements have to be oriented to the involved organisations, persons, and potential users:

- The sponsoring by funding organisations and data owners of such surveys have in general a specific use in mind for the data – primarily for their own purposes. They often do not want to be hindered by documentation, archiving, and maintenance efforts. It is very important that, in the future state-of-the-practice, documentation and archiving becomes a part of the whole survey task and consulting contracts.
- The organisation carrying out the survey must be responsible for the documentation and archiving of the data, because only they have the necessary inside information. However, the following framework conditions must be fulfilled: cost

coverage of the documentation and archiving efforts, clarification where and by which competent organisation the documented data are to be stored and maintained, appropriate and standardised documentation guidelines, and simple (not lavish) implementation procedures for the documentation and archiving.

- Data archives at the national and international level have specific requirements and goals: the data structure of survey data to be archived for optimal inclusion into archiving systems, long-term sponsorship for the archiving costs to enable long-term storage, etc. (Tardy et al., 2000).
- Potential users need easy access to archived data at low cost, with standardised documentation, data characters, data structure and coding to enable comparative analysis of different data sources, etc. The users of data archives fall into two main groups having different needs:
  - o The politically interested users (public planners, policy makers); and
  - o The scientific researchers (professional data user).

Politically orientated users want fast and easy access to results of transport data that are of public interest. They are strongly interested in on-line tabulation systems, that can provide results in a short time. They are also interested in good presentation of the required data results in the form of well understood graphs, tables, and maps. For such cases, it is very important that the results are presented in a way that avoids any misinterpretation that might occur, e.g., coming from statistically non-significant results. Therefore it is very important that any on-line tabulation software tool that is to be used by all comers is provided with a minimum level of statistical validation (e.g., confidence intervals, significance tests). NESSTAR Light Client software provides such tabulation software, but it has the disadvantage that it does not provide the statistical confidence information it should for it to be a common standard (Sammer, 1997). The scientific researchers have different requirements. First, they seek access to metadata information on transport survey data. On-line tabulation is of secondary interest, although it is a valuable tool for pre-analysis. Great interest exists in cross survey comparability of different data resources, and this can be facilitated only by an extensive standardisation of the data structure and coding. The dominant requirement lies in access to the raw data of the surveys.

The outcome of the requirements defined above leads to the conclusion that our present predicament demands the implementation and use of metadata and archives to preserve the collected data and to enable efficient use to be made of it.

Technology of Metadata and Data Archives on the Market

There is no need to reinvent the wheel of metadata and data archives; they are well developed and used in other scientific fields, e.g., the social and behavioural sciences. Besides the data storage itself, metadata are the essential information in a data archive (Axhausen, 2001). Metadata have the following principal function and objectives (Pendyala, 2003):

- Assistance to facilitate the identification, evaluation and retrieval of data sets that are of interest for a specific reason;
- Facility to evaluate the relevance, efficiency, and quality of the identified data sets; and
- Possibility to retrieve the new data of a survey including the documentation and provision of all information that is needed to use the data.

It has mainly been libraries and information system organisations that have developed the formal structure of data description. Specific languages were developed in the past decade, so that numerous metadata standards are now available on the market (Pendyala, 2003; Wigan *et al.*, 2002). It must be emphasised that these DDI standards (the Data Documentation Initiatives – DDI, 2003) are one of the most advanced, flexible, and user-friendly metadata standards. DDI pursues the goal to create an internationally accepted methodology for the content, presentation, transfer, and preservation of metadata about datasets in the field of the behavioural and social sciences, and uses the XML (eXtensible Markup Language), which enables users to make use of the advantages of the web function abilities.

The DDI is used by many national and international data archiving projects. One project must be emphasised because it seems to be very relevant and suitable for transport data and its archiving requirements. NESSTAR (Networked Social Science Tools and Resources – NESSTAR, 2004) is a web-based data analysis software that enables users and publishers of social data to exploit data and information via the web, including on-line tabulation of survey data and other relevant information. NESSTAR offers four different archiving tools:

- NESSTAR Publisher is an advanced data management suite that enables users to convert, enhance and manage data for publication to NESSTAR Server;
- NESSTAR Server allows the data provider to set up an interactive data publishing and dissemination service;
- NESSTAR Explorer produces an integrated data discovery, browsing, and retrieval platform that runs on the user's desktop and interacts with the data on a server; and
- NESSTAR light allows the user to operate most of the services of NESSTAR Explorer but within the confines of a standard web browser. The user can search for, locate, analyse, and download a wide variety of statistical information as well as information relating to the NESSTAR Server and its operation. There is no need for specialised software to be able to view the mobility data stored on the NESSTAR server.

The DDI codebook that is used in NESSTAR still needs a standardised classification for transport surveys that would allow automated processing and ensure completely standardised documentation. In the following section, an improved proposal for the standardised classified documentation is presented for discussion, based on some recent papers (Axhausen and Wigan, 2003; Pendyala, 2003; Richardson *et al.*, 1995; Chalasani *et al.*, 2002) and on the DATELINE-project (DATELINE Consortium, 2003b).

Proposal for a Standardised Classification of Transport Survey Documentation Structure

The following proposal is compatible with the structure of the DDI codebook:

1. *Document description:* Title, abstract, author (of the survey), producers (of documentation), date (of documentation), copyright (of documentation), key words (topic classification), and distributor;
2. *Study description:*
   a. *Overview information:* Title (of the study), objectives, definition of key terms of the survey (journey, trip, trip stage, mode, purpose, activities, etc.), and abbreviations/glossary;
   b. *Administrative details of the survey:* Funding agency/agencies (addresses), producers of the survey and their responsibilities (survey design, data collection, data processing, data analysis), advisory committee, survey/study costs and budget, dates and duration of survey, project management, contact person(s) (addresses), and confidentiality;
   c. *Scope of survey:* Definition of target population, survey units, analysis units, time period covered, and geographical coverage;
   d. *Survey design:* Description of the survey method and concept (reasons for selection, time frame), pilot survey, pretests, validation and nonresponse survey, frequency of data collection (e.g., monthly, quarterly, yearly), and critical feedback considerations concerning experiences with the survey design;
   e. *Sample design:* Sampling units, sampling frame (type, performance in terms of accuracy, completeness, duplication, currency, representativeness) sampling method, sample size (mathematical definition), sampling stratification, data quality and sampling loss, conduct of sampling, problems of sampling, and critical feedback, considerations regarding experiences with and during sampling;
   f. *Survey instrument design:* Question content, format and order, physical nature of the survey instrument, documentation of forms and questionnaire, reasons for the questions selected, and critical feedback analysis and considerations regarding the experiences with the survey instrument;
   g. *Survey implementation and execution:* Survey procedure, interviewer selection, training and supervision, nonresponse treatment, documentation of field-work, protocol of the survey (number of contacts, contact characteristics (date, time, interviewer ID), contact success, proxy reporting, critical reflection of the survey execution, problems of the survey execution, and software used for the survey execution);

h. *Data processing:* Database building, questionnaire editing, coding methods (geocoding), code documentation, data cleaning, correction (imputation), definition of a 'usable return', weighting and expansion procedure, software used in data processing, weighting statistics, critical feedback analysis of the data processing, and problems of data processing; and

i. *Data analysis:* Data quality statistics (with standardised indicators (Stopher *et al.* 2003, Stopher and Jones 2003) e.g., missing values, proxy reporting rate, data cleaning statistics, data validation statistics, sampling error, coverage error, response rate), and a statistical overview of results about the key indicators (rate of non-mobile households and persons, average activity and trip rate per person, average distance travelled per person, modal split of trips, purpose split of trips, etc.);

3. *Data file description:* File name, file structure and dimension, data format, software used to produce the file, unit of variables, number of cases, number of variables, record length;

4. *Variable description:* For each variable in the data set the following information is needed: name and definition of the variable, label, type, code, range of data values, questions in the survey instrument. The variables are ordered hierarchically: household, persons, journey, trip, and trip stage information; and

5. *Other documentation:* References, questionnaires, and other notes.

European Long-distance Mobility Information System (ELMIS)

For the European DATELINE research project, which implemented and carried out a European long-distance travel survey in all former fifteen member states of the European Commission and Switzerland, a European Long-distance Mobility Information System (ELMIS) was developed and implemented. It is a good example of an advanced travel data documentation and archiving system for a rather complex survey. This is partly based on NESSTAR light (DATELINE Consortium, 2003b). It has been available to the public on the web since December 2003 and allows both publisher and user to collect experience with metadata software and archiving systems in practice and, in concrete terms, with NESSTAR. ELMIS is a web-based metadata system over a stand alone MS-Windows application that includes the use of NESSTAR light. The advantages of the system are:

- A large group of users are able to access instantly and make use of the stored information. Any person who has an Internet connection can enter the site and use the application to browse and analyse results.
- Users are able to access the stored data from a less powerful computer and are not obliged to install and manage the application. This avoids, or at least reduces, technical problems left to the user (e.g. installation, environment settings,

storage space, conflicting programmes, etc.). Use of a different operating system or a different hardware configuration is prevented.

- The testing of the application is much easier, as is the detection and solving of technical problems. Interference stemming from the use of another operating system or a different hardware configuration is prevented.
- The future of a web-based system is more certain (stability). A stand-alone application is dependent on developments in the computer industry, which tend to introduce short-term innovations and changes.
- The format of the data supported by NESSTAR is based on the metadata description format (DDI), which follows international standards. This makes the database more interesting to the user community, because it allows for comparisons with other databases for many years to come.

The hierarchy presented in Figure 7 shows the contents and structure of the ELMIS web site, organised by web pages. The contents are organised in three levels of detail, all of which are integrated as main parts of the home page. ELMIS is a web site supported by applications that deliver the DATELINE survey results in a highly interactive way. To allow ELMIS users to browse through the database and perform statistical analyses, the system integrates the NESSTAR server application, which contains a statistical engine. When using ELMIS, the user interacts with the NESSTAR statistical engine through the NESSTAR Light Client (NCL). ELMIS, the client has been adjusted slightly, so that it differs in part from the standard client normally used.

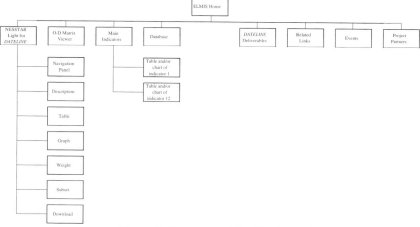

Figure 7: Structure of the ELMIS Web Site

Future Needs in Data Archiving and Documentation

Tremendous progress in archiving and documentation, mainly in the field of social science, and in the development of software tools and archiving technology, has been made. However, a broad range of actions to serve the needs of the travel survey community can be identified, with the aim of raising the quality of documentation and expanding the possibilities and functionality of metadata and archives in connection with the web technology. These needs can be classified into two groups: organisational and institutional needs, and standardisation needs.

Organisational and Institutional Needs

As discussed in the section on *Status-quo Analysis*, it is very important to raise the awareness of the relevant organisations, ministries, agencies, etc. engaged in transport surveys that good documentation, archiving, and preservation of transport data is essential for the development and dissemination of knowledge. At least in the long term, expenses can be reduced for travel surveys if the international transport community would have knowledge of and access to relevant travel data at the national and international level. The formulation of a 'Charter for Transport Metadata' and its dissemination to all relevant organisations dealing with travel surveys would support this goal. The main and important message of such a charter should be the integration of data archiving and documentation in the study contract.

Standardisation Needs for Documentation and Archiving

It is very important to enhance the efforts of standardisation. The opportunities and functionalities of metadata analysis would be enhanced if the level of standardised information about travel surveys were to be improved. On this topic, there is a great need for action within the scientific transport community. Yet, though standardisation is a necessary task, one must recognise that all standardisation should only define a minimum level – one that is achievable with justifiable effort for its development and use. This minimum level should be based on the identification of generically essential elements and characteristics that are common to all surveys and which are accepted by the transport community. Otherwise this exercise is doomed to failure.

- Standardisation of a typology of travel surveys:
  Travel surveys can be classified into a large variety of types; these require different types of document definition. Therefore, archiving needs a hierarchical structure of survey classification that enables those inputting the surveys to assign all types of surveys correctly. Pendyala (2003) made a first proposal that shows how difficult it is to develop a consistent hierarchical structure. Table 5 presents a revised version of that proposal. The following step comprises the development of a typology of the generic and specific characteristics and elements for travel surveys. The list below is intended to serve as a base for developing that typology.
- Development of vocabularies for metadata documentation of transport data (transport thesaurus):

Beside the formal structure of metadata, it will be necessary to develop appropriate vocabularies for the field of transport data. These vocabularies need a broad acceptance among the transport community to provide the full benefit and to make use of the whole functionality possible from such metadata bases. Such a task has to be done in an interdisciplinary and cooperative way. Wigan (2001) suggests that, for example, the relevant committees of IATBR, IATUR, AET and TRB, together with libraries and Social Science Data Archives, should carry out this task. To make a start, one option would be to use the thesaurus of the OECD ITRD Transport document database, the development of which started over thirty years ago.

Table 5: Proposal for a Hierarchical Typology for Standardisation of Document Type Definition of Archiving based on Pendyala (2003)

Travel Survey	Trip Survey	Trip diary
		Long-distance Survey
	Activity Survey	
	Time Use Survey	
Stated Response Survey	Stated Preference	
	Stated Tolerance	
	Stated Adoption	
	Stated Prospect	
Mode/vehicle based Surveys	On-board Transit	
	On-road Travel	
	On-airport	
Passive Tracking Survey	GPS-based	
	Mobile phone based	
	Licence plate based	
Traffic Surveys	Traffic counts	
	Parking Survey	
Qualitative Surveys	Focus Groups	
	Attitudinal Surveys	

- Development of a standardised flexible coding scheme:
  As discussed in the section on *Standardisation for Flexible Coding and Complex Variables*, the development of a standard of a flexible coding scheme for travel surveys would represent a milestone in the development. It should represent the minimum level of documentation that, however, leaves it open to the user to use a further, more detailed coding scheme without losing the minimum level of standardisation. This would open a wide range of possibilities of analysis.
- Enhancement of the metadata standard to accommodate the spatial dimension of data (Pendyala, 2003):
  The spatial dimensions of transport data are evident. It seems that the currently available metadata standards do not take into account the spatial characteristics of travel data as they do the information about time periods covered and time of the data collection. Therefore there is a need to incorporate the spatial dimensions, represented by origin and destination, into the metadata standard format.

CONCLUSIONS

The definition of quality standards and some forms of guidance are also appropriate as a supplement in the steps of data processing, analysis, documentation, and archiving of travel surveys. Analysis of the state of the art indicates that knowledge is well developed, even though some questions need further research. However, this knowledge is distributed among different sources and needs to be put together and standardised in an appropriate way. The definition of a minimum common denominator of standards for data processing and analysis would help to raise the data and output quality. For the definition of quality standards, it is also very important to take into account the cost–benefit ratio between the effort needed to achieve a defined quality of results and the quality level itself. Although this question has been well analysed for surveys in other fields, little such knowledge is evident in the field of transport surveys. The standardisation of elements of travel surveys with regard to documentation and archiving would enable utilisation of all the benefits of the web-based technology of metadata and data archives on the market. However, until that milestone is achieved, a great deal of internationally coordinated work and effort has to be undertaken, requiring a range of institutional, organisational, and funding considerations to initiate successful development. If such quality standards were to become established in all invitations to tender for travel surveys, it would effect a great leap in quality and accessibility of meaningful data for the transport community as a whole.

REFERENCES

Arentze, T., F. Hofmann, N. Kalfs and H. Timmermans (1999). SYLVIA: A System for the Logical Verification and Interference of Activity Diaries, Paper submitted for presentation at the Transportation Research Board Conference, Washington D.C., January.

Axhausen, K.W.(2000). Presenting and Preserving Travel Data. In: *Transport Surveys: Raising the Standards* (P.R. Stopher and P.M. Jones eds), II-F-1 - II-F-19, Transportation Research Circular E-C008, Transportation Research Board, Washington, DC.

Axhausen, K.W. (2003). Aktionsräume und die Suche nach Abwechslung: Aktuelle Ergebnisse von Langzeitbefragungen, Presentation at the Institute for Transport Studies, University for Natural Resources and Applied Life Sciences (Bodenkultur) Vienna, Vienna, Austria, June.

Axhausen, K.W. and M.R. Wigan (2003). The public use of travel surveys: The metadata perspective. In: *Transport Survey Quality and Innovation* (P.R. Stopher and P.M. Jones eds), 605-628, Pergamon Press, Oxford.

Brög, W. (2000). The New KONTIV Design. A Total Survey Design for Surveys on Mobility Behaviour. In *Proceedings of ICES – II*, Second International Conference on Establishment Surveys, Buffalo, New York, June, 353-360.

Brög, W., E. Erl, G. Sammer, O. Schechtner (1986). Gesamtverkehrskonzept Köln, Gutachten zur Verkehrsentwicklung und zum Verkehrsverhalten in Köln und seinem Umland, Methode, Berichtband im Auftrag der Stadt Köln.

Chalasani, V.S., S. Schonfelder and K.W. Axhausen (2002). Archiving Travel Data: The Mobidrive Example, *Arbeitsbericht Verkehrs- und Raumplanung*, 129, Institut für Verkehrsplanung und Transportsysteme (IVT) ETH Transport Data Archive, ETH, Zurich.

DATELINE Consortium (1999). *Description of work of DATELINE*, Technical Annex (Design and Application of a Travel Survey for European Long-Distance Trips, based on an International Network of Expertise), 5th Framework Programme, European Commission –DG TREN.

DATELINE Consortium (2003a). European Coding Book for Long Distance Travel Surveys, *Deliverable D6*, DATELINE (Design and Application of a Travel Survey for European Long-Distance Trips, based on an International Network of Expertise), 5th Framework Programme, European Commission–DG TREN.

DATELINE Consortium (2003b). ELMIS - European Long-Distance Mobility Information System, User Manual, *Deliverable D9*, DATELINE (Design and Application of a Travel Survey for European Long-Distance Trips), based on an International Network of Expertise, 5th Framework Programme, European Commission–DG TREN.

DATELINE Consortium (2003c). Final Report of DATELINE, *Deliverable D6*, DATELINE (Design and Application of a Travel Survey for European Long-Distance Trips, based on an International Network of Expertise), 5th Framework Programme, European Commission–DG TREN.

DATELINE Consortium (2003d). Weighting and Grossing Up Report, DATELINE (Design and Application of a Travel Survey for European Long-Distance Trips, based on an International Network of Expertise), 5th Framework Programme, European Commission–DG TREN.

DDI (2003). *Data Documentation Initiative*. www.icpsr.umich.edu/DDI/index.html Accessed 18 Jan. 2006.

Han, X.L., J.W. Polak (2001). 'Imputation with non-ignorable missing values: a stochastic approach', in K.W. Axhausen, J.L. Madre, J.W. Polak and P.L. Toint (eds), *Capturing Long-Distance Travel,* Research Science Press, Baldock, pp. 1-15.

Hautzinger H. (1997). Design and Analysis of Travel Surveys. In: *Understanding Travel Behaviour in an Era of Change* (P.R. Stopher and M. Lee-Gosselin, eds), 437-468, Elsevier, Oxford.

Herry, M. (1985). Gewichtung der Kontiv 82, *Schriftenreihe der Deutschen Verkehrswissenschaftlichen Gesellschaft e.V.*, Reihe B, B85, Grainau, 164-217.

Levinson, D. and E. Zofka (2006). Processing, Analysing and Archiving Travel Survey Data. In: *Travel Survey Methods – Quality and Future Directions* (P.R. Stopher and C.C. Stecher, eds), 223-238, Elsevier Press, Oxford.

Murakami, M., J. Morris, G. Arce (2003). Using Technology to Improve Transport Survey Quality. In: *Transport Survey Quality and Innovation* (P.R. Stopher and P.M. Jones, eds), 605–621, Pergamon Press, Oxford.

NESSTAR (2004). *NESSTAR 3.0 Highlights*, http://www.nesstar.com Accessed 18 Jan. 2006.

Neumann, A. (2003). *Korrekturverfahren für Stichproben von Verkehrsverhalten-serhebungen der Personenfernverkehrs (Methods of data weighting for samples of long distance travel surveys)*, Dissertation, Institut für Verkehrswesen, Universität für Bodenkultur, Wien.

Pendyala, R.M. (2003). Standards for Archived and Documentation of Travel Survey Data: Challenges and Opportunities, Resource paper, Workshop 1-6, IATBR Conference 'Moving through nets: The physical and social dimensions of travel', 10th International Conference on Travel Behaviour Research, Lucerne, August.

Purvis, C. (2000). Workshop Summary on Data Presentation. In: *Transport Surveys: Raising the Standards* (P.R. Stopher and P.M. Jones, eds), II-F/20-II-F/23, Transportation Research Circular, E-C008, Transportation Research Board, Washington, DC.

Poduri, S.R. (2000). *Sampling Methodologies with Application*, Chapman and Hall/CRC, Boca Raton, London, New York, Washington, 234.

Richardson, A.J. (2000). Workshop Summary of Item Nonresponse in Travel Survey, Causes and Solutions, In: *Transport Surveys: Raising the Standards* (P.R. Stopher and P.M. Jones, eds), Transportation Research Circular, E-C008, Transportation Research Board, National Research Council, Washington, DC, II-F/1-II-F/19.

Richardson, A.J., E.S. Ampt, and A.H. Meyburg (1995). *Survey Methods for Transport Planning*, Eucalyptus Press, University of Melbourne, 492.

Richardson, A.J. and M. Loeis (1997), Estimation of Missing Income in Household Travel Surveys, *Forum Papers, 21st Austral-Asian Transport Research Forum*, 1, 249-266.

Richardson, A.J. and A.H .Meyburg. (2003). Definition of Unit Nonresponse in Travel Survey. In: *Transport Survey Quality and Innovation* (P.R. Stopher and P.M. Jones, eds), 587-604, Pergamon Press, Oxford.

Sammer, G. (1997). Problems and Solutions in Urban Travel Survey. In: *Urban Travel Survey Methods: Measuring the Presence, Simulating the Future* (P. Bonnel, R. Chapleau, M. Lee-Gosselin and C. Raux, eds), 145-159, Les Chemins de la Recherche; Number 42; Programmes Rhône-Alpes.

Sammer, G. (1998). Infrastrukturelle Maßnahmen und Verkehrsmittelaufteilung (Infrastructural Measures and Modal Split), proceedings of the Conference on Innovation in Urban Transport, European Commission, bmvit, Land Steiermark and City of Graz, November, Graz, Austria.

Sammer, G. (2000). Workshop Summary, Workshop on Quality Indicators, Transport Surveys Raising the Standard. In: *Transport Surveys: Raising the Standards* (P.R. Stopher and P.M. Jones, eds), II-E/15-II-E/22, Transportation Research Circular, E-C008, Transportation Research Board, Washington, DC.

Sammer, G. and K. Zelle (1982). A Method for Updating Existing Data Bases of an Origin-Destination Traffic Matrix, *Proceedings of PTRC-Summer Annual Meeting 1982*, Warwick.

Sammer, G. and K. Fallast (1996). A Consistent Simultaneous Data Weighting Process For Traffic Behaviour, *Proceedings of the 4th International Conference on Survey Methods in Transport*, 9-11th September, Oxford.

Sammer, G. and G. Röschel (2001). Mobilitätserhebung der Haushalte in Mödling Austria, 2000, im Rahmen der Erarbeitung des Gesamtverkehrskonzeptes (Household travel survey in Mödling, Austria, 2000, Transport Master Plan), Band Problemanalyse, Stadtgemeinde Mödling, Austria.

Sharp, J. (2003). Data Interrogation and Management. In: *Transport Survey Quality and Innovation* (P.R. Stopher and P.M. Jones, eds), 629-633, Pergamon Press, Oxford.

Snickers, F. and J.W. Weibull (1977). A Minimum Information Principle – Theory and Practice, *Regional Science and Urban Economics*, 7, 137-168.

Steuart, G.N. (1997). Transportation Tomorrow Survey in Toronto: Special Features and DATA Dissemination Program. In: *Urban Travel Survey Methods: Measuring the Presence, Simulating the Future* (P. Bonnel, R. Chapleau, M. Lee-Gosselin and C. Raux, eds), 93-108, Les Chemins de la Recherche, Number 42, Programmes Rhône-Alpes.

Stopher, P.R. and P.M. Jones (2003). Developing Standards of Transport Survey Quality. In: *Transport Survey Quality and Innovation* (P.R. Stopher and P. M. Jones, eds), 1–38, Pergamon, Oxford.

Stopher, P.R., C.G. Wilmot, C.C. Stecher, and R. Alsnih (2003). Standards for Household Travel Surveys – Some Proposed Ideas, Paper presented at the 10th International Conference on Travel Behaviour Research, August, Lucerne, Switzerland.

Stopher, P.R., C.G. Wilmot, C.C. Stecher, and R. Alsnih (2006). Household Travel Surveys: Proposed Standards and Guidelines. In: *Travel Survey Methods – Quality and Future Directions* (P.R. Stopher and C.C. Stecher, eds), 19-74 , Elsevier Press, Oxford.

Tardy, D.R., S.C. Brown, M. Harmon, and R.W. Bradshaw (2000). Engineering and Survey-Exchange (EAS-E), A Standard Engineering Data Format, Technical Draft, by US Joint-Industry Consortium, January.

Wermuth, M. and C. Sommer (2003). Impact of New Technologies in Travel Surveys. In: *Transport Survey Quality and Innovation* (P.R. Stopher and P.M. Jones, eds), 455–482, Pergamon Press, Oxford.

Wigan, M.R. (2001). Enabling and Managing Greater Access to Transport Data through Metadata, *Proceedings of European Transport Conference*,10-12 September, Homerton College, Cambridge, UK.

Wigan, M.R., M.S. Grieco, and J. Hine (2002). Enabling and Managing Greater Access to Transport Data through Metadata, Proceedings of the 81st Annual Transportation Research Board Meeting, Washington DC.

Wilmot, C.G. and S. Shivananjappa (2003). Comparison of Hot-deck and Neural-network Imputation. In: *Transport Survey Quality and Innovation* (P.R. Stopher and P.M. Jones, eds), 543-554, Pergamon Press, Oxford.

Wilson, A.G. (1974). *Entropy in Urban and Regional Modelling*, Pion, London.

Travel Survey Methods: Quality and Future Directions
Peter Stopher and Cheryl Stecher (Editors)
© 2006 Elsevier Ltd. All rights reserved.

14

PROCESSING, ANALYSING, AND ARCHIVING STANDARDS AND GUIDELINES

Orlando Strambi, Escola Politecnica da Universidade Sao Paulo, Sao Paulo, Brazil
and
Rodrigo Garrido, Pontificia Universidad Católica de Chile, Santiago, Chile

INTRODUCTION

The workshop[1] discussed a diverse array of topics related to the stages of processing, analysing, and archiving the results of travel surveys. These topics often get considerably less attention than other aspects of travel surveys, although the usability of the information collected is heavily dependent on the quality of these important steps in survey procedure. Thoughts, ideas, and discussions were motivated by two resource papers presented during the workshop meetings, by Sammer (2006) and Levinson and Zofka (2006). Sammer provided a thorough and detailed proposal of classification, terminology, and issues related to the topics of the workshop, while Levinson focused on the issue of archiving and publishing survey results and documentation on the Internet.

The workshop started from a general recommendation for the conference of producing standards for travel surveys (Stopher *et al.*, 2006). Similar to what happened in some of the other workshops, the participants had to recognise the challenge presented by such a task, considering that travel surveys are generally specific with respect to objectives,

---

[1] Members of the workshop were: Humberto Farias (Brazil), Rodrigo Garrido (Chile), Joost Kolkman (The Netherlands), Matthias Kracht (Germany), David Levinson (USA), Philippe Marchal (France), Gerd Sammer (Austria), Orlando Strambi (Brazil).

resources, timing, methodologies, and spatial characteristics. The discussion in the workshop then moved to a position where a desirable degree of standardisation must be adopted in combination with high quality documentation of the many survey stages. Steps not following general standards or guidelines should be fully documented to preserve the history of the information obtained.

The discussion followed the structure and terminology proposed by Sammer (2006), where the survey stages relating to the workshop were further subdivided into different steps, as shown in Table 1. Stages E, F and G were the focus of the workshop. As expected, the diversity of topics led to discussions at different levels of depth. In some cases, a recommendation was agreed upon, in others, the group identified important pending questions rather than specific answers. The main points raised in the discussions are presented in the following sections. In most cases, they represent a best-practice advice on these stages of conducting travel surveys.

Table 1: Proposal for a Harmonised and Standardised Terminology of the Steps of a Travel Survey Procedure

Step	Terminology		
A.	Survey Design		
B.	Sample Design		
C.	Survey Instrument Design		
D,	Survey Implementation (Execution)		
E.	Data Processing	E1.	Database Building
		E2.	Questionnaire Response Editing
		E3.	Coding and Data Entry
		E4.	Data Editing / Cleaning
		E5.	Weighting
		E6.	Expansion
F.	Data Analysis	F1.	Validation
		F2.	Descriptive and Explanatory Data Analysis
		F3.	Data Presentation
G.	Data Documentation and Archiving	G1.	Documentation
		G2.	Archiving

Source: Sammer (2006)

DATA PROCESSING

Database building

The workshop members pointed to the fact that advance planning and design are essential requirements for a good quality database. They also pointed out that a common database should contain both field work documentation and data collected on travel behaviour. The idea of hierarchical access to different information, by different types of users – from the general public to researchers – has emerged in this and in other instances within the workshop.

Issues of privacy and confidentiality were also raised at this point. It is important to distinguish between the two concepts. Some questions may not be included in a survey due to consideration of individual privacy, or the respondent may refuse to provide information based on privacy concerns. Confidentiality, on the other hand, relates to the commitment of the data holder not to disclose collected information. The success of obtaining sensitive information thus depends on the credibility of the institution or institutions responsible for collecting, archiving, and processing the data. The relevant issue when designing and building a database is, thus, how much confidentiality to offer. There are substantial indications that societies are willing to accept lower levels of personal privacy and confidentiality of information, in exchange for higher levels of security or other conveniences. Confidentiality may be guaranteed by releasing aggregate information only. However, this approach restricts the sort of analysis that can be conducted. An alternative idea, discussed by the workshop, was the introduction of artificial noise in the original data, particularly in spatial attributes. It remains to be seen whether the introduction of noise should be documented and, if so, who has the credibility to keep this information.

Questionnaire Response Editing

Questionnaire editing aims at improving completeness and accuracy of responses. The implied recommendation is for this step to be taken as soon as possible after the data collection, so that, when required, respondents can still be queried about their recorded travel patterns. The workshop also considered the issue of whether editing should be conducted by a third party, in order to improve reliability.

The workshop raised an interesting question: is response editing by recontacting the respondent a sort of imputation of data? Can the information collected at a later stage be considered of similar quality and validity to that obtained during the original survey? This and other matters related to questionnaire editing led the workshop to issue a strong recommendation for the use of a well conceived database version control system, which should keep track of all changes performed. This will allow the analyst using the database to make decisions on how to consider the different types of information. Further, it can allow researchers to investigate the accuracy of edited responses vis-à-vis valid information collected from the respondent.

Coding

Some specific issues related to coding dominated the discussion. First was the representation of missing values. The suggestion was that missing values should be assigned a negative 3 or 4-digit number. Leaving a blank field in the database can lead to different interpretations depending on the software used to manipulate and analyse the data. A related topic was the representation of binary variables as 0/1 or 1/2. A preference for the latter relates to the problems that may arise in some computations using zeros.

A second issue refers to the coding of complex variables. These can be ordered or non-ordered categorical, or continuous variables. Some variables seem more amenable to the use of a hierarchical coding system, such as those used, for instance, in classifying industrial sectors. Activity (or trip purpose) is a clear example of a possible application. While, for some studies, a few categories may suffice, other studies may require a detailed record of different types of activities performed by individuals. A hierarchical system would assign a 1-digit code to major activity classes; adding additional digits would provide for further subdivision into more specific categories. Income was one specific variable deserving attention; a proposal to adopt a common currency standard for coding was advanced by the workshop.

The group also discussed geocoding standards. Acknowledging that, in general, it is not feasible to conduct geocoding of spatial information simultaneously with the collection and coding of other socio-demographic and travel data, the workshop recommended that this be done soon after data collection. The process of geocoding should aim for the finest possible resolution – a one hundred percent precision target. However, it should be recognised that the achievable level of accuracy depends on the quality of existing spatial databases, which vary considerably among regions and countries, the resources available and the objective of the data collection effort. The need to maintain a certain level of confidentiality may be dealt with using the aforementioned approach of introducing artificial noise in the data.

Data Editing

The main topic considered in this regard was the treatment of missing data. The workshop focused on imputation of data, in the cases where this is considered an adequate or a required procedure. Two basic forms of imputation of data were discussed:

- Imputation by recontacting respondents; and
- Imputation by inferring likely values of a variable; this can be done by performing logical consistency checks or by the use of associative rules considering other variables.

Application of each method is case-specific and should always be accompanied by the information that a value has been imputed. While the production of aggregate results can be less affected by a possible bias introduced by imputing values, analysts looking at disaggregate data need to be aware that a specific data value has been imputed.

Special attention was dedicated to the imputation of 'key variables'. Although the definition of what is a key variable may be specific to each survey, variables relating to spatial information were considered to deserve particular care when deciding about imputation criteria.

A final point made by the workshop concerned 'suspect' data, inconsistent with other data describing the individuals or their activity/travel patterns. The recommendation is that suspect data receive the same treatment as missing data.

Weighting

Sample weighting has become a usual procedure in household surveys. The objective of the weighting correction is to adjust the distribution of the expanded sample to reproduce some known population distribution. Weighting is usually applied to the distribution of socioeconomic and demographic characteristics of the population. Conventional statistical expansion of the sample, for the computation of estimates of population values, is based on expansion factors calculated as the inverse of the probability of a specific unit being sampled. While pure random samples have equal factors for all sampled units, stratified samples generally have different expansion factors for each stratum.

Weighting correction is based on a post-stratification of the obtained sample. It considers attributes of the population for which there are good aggregate control estimates, usually Census data. Attributes selected for this post-stratification are those believed to have a strong relationship with travel behaviour. For instance, if men and women have different travel behaviour, and there is a misrepresentation of their proportion in the sample (compared to the population), their distribution should be adjusted to avoid an estimation bias.

Usually multiple attributes are considered for weighting correction, sequentially or simultaneously. The most commonly used attributes are sex, age, household size, and car ownership, the latter when good quality information exists. When a simultaneous multivariable adjustment is considered, more complex mathematical approaches must be adopted to guarantee consistency (Sammer, 2006). The workshop identified a pending question concerning the minimum sample size for classes (or strata) of individuals before a weight can be developed. This may be a problem when many attributes are jointly considered for classification of individuals or households.

The workshop also issued some recommendations concerning the use of weighting:

- First, look at the resulting distributions of weighting factors (but remember that the magnitude of the weights and their relative proportion is still an open question);
- Second, weight for socio-demographics first; if necessary, apply some correction to trips, based on screen counts or other methods. Use trip correction as a last resort only, because, unlike expansion or weighting factors, it does affect the measurement of travel/activity behaviour;

- Third, keep weighting factors separate from expansion factors (and a possible trip correction factor) in the database; and
- Finally, prepare a full documentation on weight development and use.

DATA ANALYSIS

Survey validation was considered a first step in data analysis. Validation prescribes the comparison of estimates of specific variables derived from travel surveys against an independent and, most importantly, reliable data source. In contrast to weighting correction, which is focused on adjusting the distribution of the sample, validation focuses on travel related estimates, such as the number of trips or the distance travelled. It was a consensus among workshop participants that every survey must conduct some form of validation, even when resources are extremely limited.

Validation was contrasted to auditing. The latter was considered a more thorough process, which includes a detailed verification of the procedures adopted in the conduct of the data collection effort, in addition to checking results for consistency with external sources. While validation is usually undertaken by the agency in charge of conducting the survey, the workshop recommends that auditing be executed by a third party institution.

As mentioned before, care must be exercised when comparing screen counts with household survey trips. Rather than a sort of validation, this procedure, when applied, would be considered rather as an adjustment in trip estimates to reproduce observed counts.

A final point concerns the presentation of results. Usually, estimates of totals and averages are presented, with no reference to their confidence and significance levels. It is strongly recommended that information about the statistical significance of results be presented along with the results themselves.

DOCUMENTATION AND ARCHIVING

Although data archiving is not a new process on its own, publishing archived travel survey data through the Internet is a relatively novel idea. Standards and efforts derived mostly from the social sciences are being applied to transportation data. One of the resource papers prepared for the workshop reported on the development of the Metropolitan Travel Survey Archive, a major effort of archiving data from over sixty Origin-Destinations surveys from almost thirty metropolitan areas in the US, collected at different points in time (Levinson and Zofka, 2006). The other resource paper presented the structure of the European Long-distance Mobility Information System (Sammer,

2006). One of the characteristics of these efforts is to use metadata standards and software that provide the user with facilities to conduct their own analysis on-line.

Among the many advantages of systematic archiving, the workshop indicated the following four points as the most relevant:

- *Safety*. It is a major concern when large data collection efforts have been undertaken. This concern is twofold. On the one hand, data losses are not uncommon when the data bank is kept in uncontrolled or spread-out systems. On the other hand, confidentiality of the data must be guaranteed to the public, in the sense that only a reduced number of authorised users will have access to individual data.
- *Accessibility*. After the data collection has taken place, the most relevant goal is to make those data available to the proper users. Systematic archiving should facilitate controlled access to the data.
- *Redundancy*. Transport data collection projects usually involve large amounts of digital memory space and, given the complexity of the information collected in surveys and other data gathering methods, systematic archiving enables the control of data redundancy to the desired level (note that zero redundancy might not be a desired level for some data pieces). Effective redundancy can be achieved by maintaining data banks in an independent outside archive.
- *Possibility of use*. In addition to the accessibility issue, the archiving system facilitates data usability. In fact, the standardisation of the archiving system would allow users in different countries to make use of data kept by authorities/researchers in other latitudes.

The workshop discussion led to a recommended basic archiving architecture:

- *Document description*. Metadata should be one of the main concerns when deciding what to keep along with the main data bank.
- *Study description*. Data in themselves are useless, unless a clear description of the methodology, objectives, and data collection tools is provided to the potential users.
- *File description*. A detailed description of the digital files must be provided.
- *Variable description*. Each one of the single data pieces should be identified along with its units and specific characteristics (e.g., items subjected to imputation must be clearly stated). It is advisable to use existing standards whenever possible (e.g., DDI, DTD, XML).
- *Help*. It is advisable to provide On-Line help to facilitate the usability for a broad array of users.
- *Accessibility hierarchy*. Due to the sensitive character of transport data, a Permission System should be establish to provide/restrict access to the data banks only to specific users. This hierarchy should be known by the respondents beforehand.

- *Version control*. There are many stages in the process of generating usable data from the raw data bank to the final version. These stages may include modifications, validations, imputations. Each stage should be accompanied by a full description of its objectives, methods, tools, and the person responsible for the process. Following the track of stages, an authorised user should be capable of recovering the raw data set from any subsequent version.

The final topic discussed in this workshop was that of harmonisation/consistency. The advantages of harmonisation and consistency are highly dependent on the different agents involved. In fact, governments, modellers, researchers, or the general public have different goals and restrictions and hence the impact of harmonisation and consistency efforts on each one of them are expected to differ. The main advantages are the following:

- *Economies of scale*. Standardisation will achieve cost reductions in software production, questionnaire production, and tendering. It also makes archiving simpler and consequently less costly.
- *Ease of use*. Researchers' and third party's applications can benefit from reading data pieces that follow standard, widely-used protocols. Web-based access would greatly benefit from homogeneity and consistency across archives in different countries.
- *Ease of validation and comparison*. Homogeneous archives facilitate the comparison with other sources by multiple types of users.
- *Quality standard*. Adopting standard protocols in archiving enables the existence of a minimum quality level for surveys and other data collection methods.

REFERENCES

Sammer, G. (2006). Processing, Analysis and Archiving of Travel Survey Data. In: *Travel Survey Methods – Quality and Future Directions* (P.R. Stopher and C.C. Stecher, eds), 239-270, Elsevier Press, Oxford.

Stopher, P.R., C.G. Wilmot, C.C. Stecher, and R. Alsnih. (2006). Household Travel Surveys: Proposed Standards and Guidelines. In: *Travel Survey Methods – Quality and Future Directions* (P.R. Stopher and C.C. Stecher, eds), 19-74, Elsevier Press, Oxford.

Levinson, D. and E. Zofka, (2006). Processing, Analysis and Archiving of Travel Survey Data. In: *Travel Survey Methods – Quality and Future Directions* (P.R. Stopher and C.C. Stecher, eds), 223-238, Elsevier Press, Oxford.

Travel Survey Methods: Quality and Future Directions
Peter Stopher and Cheryl Stecher (Editors)
© 2006 Elsevier Ltd. All rights reserved.

15

QUALITY ASSESSMENT

Peter Bonsall, Institute for Transport Studies, University of Leeds, Leeds, UK

INTRODUCTION

The Brief

The issue of quality and standards was identified as a key theme of the 2001 conference. In their report on that conference, Stopher and Jones (2003a) concluded that more work remained to be done and the issue reappeared as the focus for some of the workshops in the 2004 conference. This chapter is offered as background for this continuing discussion. The conference organisers drew on the conclusions from the previous conference in proposing that the discussions should focus on:

- Developing a definition of data quality;
- Suggesting means by which the achievement of 'quality' might be measured;
- Determining the achievability, or otherwise, of universal measures of quality; and
- Assessing the potential role of benchmarking standards promoted by the International Standards Organisation (ISO) or some similar body.

For the purposes of this chapter, I think it appropriate to start by summarising the debate thus far.

The Problem

In their keynote paper to the 2001 conference, Stopher and Jones (2003b) suggest that, in the absence of agreed standards, many sponsoring agencies are unable to make an informed selection between competing survey contractors or to assess the quality of the delivered product, that many of the contractors do not themselves know if they are doing a good job and, given the lack of standardisation, that the users of survey data often find it impossible to compare results obtained from different surveys. They lament that, given an annual worldwide expenditure on travel surveys exceeding US$50m , '... there is no agreement within the transport profession as to what constitutes a good survey'. They suggest that the absence of appropriate standards is compromising the reliability, usefulness, cost-effectiveness, comparability, clarity, and completeness of travel surveys.

The theme is echoed in other papers from the 2001 conference, but none more so than in that by Axhausen and Wigan (2003) who refer to the problems confronting anyone wishing to conduct meta-analyses. They identify the lack of archiving standards, the variation in definitions, the paucity of good documentation, the idiosyncrasies of some software products, and the widespread adoption of generally sloppy procedures as major causes of the problem.

To the extent that the lack of quality standards leads to data of questionable accuracy, to duplication of effort, and to abortive expenditure, this state of affairs is to be deplored. It would be wasting resources, including public money, professional effort, and respondents' time, and lead to ill-informed policy decisions.

Definitions

Stopher and Jones (2003b) set out the case for the establishment of standards and guidelines for travel surveys and drew a distinction between *standards* and *the measurement of quality*; they saw standards as benchmarks that could be used to define best-practice and provide a means of measuring quality (defined as the achievement of that best practice). They went on to differentiate between standards (minimum acceptable thresholds) and *standardisation* (the adoption of common definitions and procedures that would ensure the achievement of standards and comparability). These are important distinctions to which we will return in a later section of this chapter, where I will make a further distinction between *professional standards* (which relate to the maintenance of proper business practices, adherence to ethical and legal constraints, and the fair and proper treatment of respondents) and *quality standards* (which relate to the use of survey tools and procedures, and procedures that maximise the usefulness and reliability of the data).

Progress?

The need for quality standards in travel surveys has long been recognised. In his presentation at the 1983 conference, Wigan (1985) was characteristically robust in his identification of the problems facing anyone wishing to re-analyse secondary data and in his prescription of solutions. Seven years later, during the 1990 conference, delegates referred to the frustration suffered by researchers and analysts confronted by varying definitions of such straightforward things as road types and vehicle types (Richardson, 1992) and to the problems caused by lack of information on non-responding households (Ampt, 1992).

The 1997 conference had the issue of quality high on its agenda. Papers at that conference addressed issues such as the definition of quality indicators (Kalfs *et al.*, 2000) and the need for higher standards of documentation and archiving (Axhausen, 2000). In their conference summary, Stopher and Jones (2000) highlighted the areas in need of improvement. Reflecting on this during the 2001 conference, Axhausen and Wigan (2003) identified the list of necessary actions that had been implied by the previous discussions, but reported that '... during the past four years, the response to these action points has been rather muted within the transport policy and research community ... the range of activities mentioned has not yet been embraced as part of obvious and normal professional practice'.

The question of quality and standards was a particular theme of the 2001 conference. The first objective of that conference was to 'determine how to measure and assure the quality of transport surveys'. However, Stopher and Jones (2003a) suggested that the submitted papers had demonstrated ' ...the inability of the transport profession to set out a sufficient number of specific standards and guidelines to achieve consistent quality [for] travel surveys in different countries, cultures and contexts'. They went on to conclude that, in the light of what had been agreed during the various workshops, '... there was a general consensus on the need for standards and guidelines' but that '... few recommendations for standards [had] emerged during the conference'. They noted that several workshops had highlighted '... situations where standards may not be able to be set globally' and that '... most workshops concluded that more research was needed before standards or guidelines could be offered'.

A cynical observer might be forgiven for concluding that, despite its avowed focus on quality and standards, the 2001 conference had, like its predecessors, failed to achieve much progress towards the establishment of quality standards and that delegates had merely agreed on a statement of good intentions and an excuse for lack of immediate action. Is it possible that part of the reason for lack of apparent progress is that a significant minority of us are not convinced that the benefits of moves towards quality standards would outweigh the costs?

DIFFERENCES OF OPINION?

Different Needs

Let us begin by considering the different needs of the different parties involved and how each might be affected by the development and promulgation of quality standards.

The clients who commission the surveys would clearly benefit from any improvement in the quality of the product. If the introduction of standards were to increase the reliability of data, or to increase the range of uses to which it could be put, the sponsoring agencies would obviously stand to gain. They would welcome standards that increased the value of their investment or that allowed them to reduce their overall expenditure on surveys. The impact of quality standards on costs and prices is a question to which we will return in a later section.

Practitioners would stand to gain if, by improving standards within the industry, the demonstrable utility of surveys were to increase and the market were thus to grow. More cynically, practitioners would benefit from any increase in business directly attributable to the extra work required to implement the standards – but this would be a short run benefit if the additional costs were to reduce the cost-effectiveness of surveys and so reduce the overall size of the market. The question of the impact of quality standards on costs is again critical.

Most practitioners would hopefully derive increased job satisfaction from any increase in the quality of their product. Firms that see themselves as leaders in terms of quality would presumably welcome the introduction of a system that made their qualities more apparent. However we should be aware that, for some firms, a change in procedures would be an unwelcome intrusion and the introduction of quality audits would be seen as a threat rather than an opportunity.

The attitude of **researchers** in the survey field would probably vary depending on whether they are mainly involved in designing and conducting ad hoc surveys to answer particular research questions, or as analysts seeking to draw conclusions from the results of surveys conducted by others. The survey-designer researcher would welcome guidelines on best practice, but is likely to resist the imposition of standards or definitions that might restrict his or her ability to explore new ways to obtain data and insights into behaviour. The meta-analyst researchers would most certainly welcome the introduction of standards and of standardisation. They would see every advantage in the spread of agreed procedures, standardised definitions, and guaranteed standards.

Among **the general public** there would probably be a welcome for the introduction of any standards and procedures that resulted in fewer surveys, simpler questions, less intrusion and greater rewards for participation. They would probably not welcome any increase in respondent burden. The introduction of best-practice survey methods would tend to reduce the respondent burden, insofar as it would result in more clearly defined and logically ordered questions, clearer instructions, and the abandonment of unrealistically long questionnaires. However, the introduction of standard questions and definitions could *increase* the respondent burden, if the survey designer felt it necessary to use some context-specific definitions *in addition* to the standard ones required to achieve a quality seal of approval. At a more macro level the general public would, if they could perceive it, welcome an increase in the quality of decisions taken by planning authorities but would resent any increase in the cost of making those decisions.

The Impact on Cost

The introduction of quality standards and standardisation should decrease some costs but would probably increase others. The use of standardised procedures and formats should, in the fullness of time, lead to economies of scale in the design of survey instruments, training of staff, analysis of results, archiving, and documentation. It is likely that a market would develop for off-the-peg products and services at lower costs than are possible in a differentiated market. If a rise in survey quality increased the perceived utility of surveys and thus increased the total market for surveys, this could bring further economies of scale and so reinforce the virtuous circle.

On the other hand, increases in cost might result from any the following requirements: to employ more highly qualified staff; to increase the amount of data collected (as might be implied by a requirement to include standard questions and definitions, in addition to those that were specific to the study, or by a requirement to achieve particular sample sizes); to achieve specified response rates; to run additional quality tests on the data; to extend the scope of the documentation; to report on indicators of quality; or to make the results more widely available.

The price paid by clients might also rise or fall depending on whether the imposition of standards were to increase or decrease the number of contractors bidding for the work; if the net effect was to make it easier for new entrants to demonstrate a competency, then competition would tend to depress prices. However, if the introduction of higher standards were to cut the low-cost operators out of the market, prices would rise.

On balance it seems reasonable to conclude that the introduction of quality standards would increase the cost of conducting surveys, but that, by helping to increase the ease with which data can be shared and re-used, and by discouraging wasted expenditure on low-quality surveys, it should lead to a reduction in the cost of useful data. The precise relationship between cost and utility is, of course, difficult to determine and will be context-specific.

THE STATUS QUO

As noted above, there is considerable frustration among some of us that so little progress has apparently been made on the definition and introduction of quality standards for travel surveys. It would be wrong, however, to assume that the industry is bereft of standards or that there is no guidance on best practice. In this section I will review the standards and guidelines that currently exist; starting, at the most basic level, with a discussion of the constraints set by general legislation and moving on to consider standards imposed or recommended by professional bodies and other key players.

Legislation

The conduct of travel surveys, as of any surveys, is increasingly subject to legislation, most notably to legislation on privacy, data storage, freedom of information, and unsolicited communications, but also following legislation on issues as diverse as lotteries (which can limit the use of prize-draw incentives), homeland security (which can restrict 'confidentiality' assurances given to clients and respondents), employment law, and health and safety legislation (each of which can increase the cost of surveys).

Privacy legislation varies from country to country but can restrict the use of certain sample frames, sampling methods and recording media. Data Protection Acts and Freedom of Information Acts in the US, UK, and elsewhere in the European Union, set out rules on the recording of information and storage of data relating to individuals, require organisations to inform individuals if they propose to record or store such data, and grant individuals a right of access to data that identifies them as an individual. The rules on unsolicited communications relate primarily to their use in connection with marketing or advertising but, since some travel surveys might be deemed (by an adventurous plaintiff) to include an element of publicity for a particular mode, a survey company would ignore them at its peril. The UK rules require organisations wishing to cold-call by phone to first check with the Telephone Preference Service to see if the respondent has registered a wish not to be contacted in this way (the Mail preference Service operates in a similar way in respect of unsolicited mail as does a new European Directive – 2002/58/EC – in respect of unsolicited commercial emails). Any company breaching these rules could face serious sanctions.

Professional Standards

A considerable proportion of the transport sector's survey work is conducted by companies who come from the market research tradition. The market research industry has been in existence for over a hundred years and has regulated itself through the introduction of professional bodies and trade associations.

The professional bodies include: the Market Research Society (MRS) founded in the UK in 1896; the American Association for Public Opinion Research (AAPOR) and the World Association for Public Opinion Research (WAPOR) both founded in 1947, the European Society of Opinion and Market Research (ESOMAR) founded in 1948, the (US) Market Research Society (MRA) founded in 1954; the (Canadian) Professional Market Research Society (PMRS) founded in 1960); and three relative newcomers: The Social Research Association (SRA); The Association for Qualitative Research (AQS); and The Association for Survey Computing (ASC). These organisations tend to be territorially specific - although MRS claims membership in 50 countries, ESOMAR now promotes itself as the 'world association of opinion and market research professionals' and AQS and ASC both claim an increasingly international perspective. Website addresses for these bodies are listed in the Appendix to this chapter.

The trade associations also tend to be territorially defined. Examples include the Council of American Survey Research Organisations (CASRO), the (US) Council for Opinion and Market Research (CMOR); the British Market Research Association (BMRA); the German Arbeitskreis Deutscher Markt und Sozialforschungsinstitute (ADM); and the French Syntec Études Marketing et Opinion (Syntec-Etudes). A Europe-wide federation, The European Federation of Associations of Market Research Organisations, (EFAMRO) was formed in 1992 and brings together the national associations of twelve European countries. Website addresses for these bodies are again listed in the Appendix.

The professional bodies and trade associations seek to maintain professional standards through codes of practice that members are required to uphold – with sanctions on those who are in breach, and through publication of guidelines on best practice. The trade associations' codes of practice, such as those produced by ESOMAR (1999) and CASRO (1997, 1998), tend to focus on business ethics. Thus they deal with the respondent's rights (the right to privacy, the right not to be harassed or misled about the length of the interview, the right to terminate an interview without harassment, the right of anonymity, etc.), the client's rights (e.g., ownership of data, and commercial confidentiality), and general good business practice (with respect to business ethics, bribery, advertising, quoting prices, subcontracting work, employing staff, and so on). Many of these issues are covered by legislation (discussed above) and their inclusion in codes of conduct is intended to help member organisations to keep within the law.

The establishment of trade associations and professional bodies was partly a reaction to problems caused by rogue firms whose actions and practices were bringing the industry into disrepute. A similar motivation led to the establishment, in 1978, of the Interviewer Quality Control Scheme (IQCS) with the avowed aim of giving clients the assurance that member organisations would adhere to the highest professional standards (the IQCS website puts this more quaintly; 'the scheme was launched to address the differences in the quality buyers experienced when purchasing fieldwork'). IQCS specifies minimum standards for the training and supervision of field staff and for validating their work. Its standards are enforced through an annual audit of member organisations.

In addition to enforcing mandatory codes of practice, most of the professional bodies and associations also offer more detailed guidelines on best practice. (see for example MRS, 2003; and SRA, 2003). Some of these guidelines are offered as advice while others define the standards that members are expected to adhere to and so become indistinguishable from a professional code of practice. Examples of guidelines offering non-mandatory advice, although they incorporate the relevant parts of the relevant code of practice, include ESOMAR's guidelines on:

- Commissioning Research (ESOMAR, 2002 – this is an interesting example in that it offers advice to customers as well as providers,):
- Conducting Marketing and Opinion Research using the Internet, (ESOMAR, 2003);
- Interviewing Children and Young People;
- Customer Satisfaction Studies; and
- Tape and Video-Recording and Client Observation of Interviews and Group Discussions.

Guidelines that members are required to follow include those published by The Market Research Quality Standards Association (MRQSA). MRQSA was established by the (UK) market research industry in 1995 and BMRA, MRS, SRA AQR and IQCS are all now represented on its board. Its initial objectives were '… to develop quality standards appropriate to suppliers of market research services, and to set up arrangements so that companies could be assessed to the standards objectively by independent third parties'. MRQSA has produced and published quality standards covering generic issues such as quality audits, document control, proposals, quotations, client liaison, and recruitment and training of staff, as well as survey-related issues such as data collection procedures, verification of data collected by unsupervised fieldworkers, data coding, data entry, and verification. These standards have recently been adopted as a British Standard (BS7911) (BSI, 2003) and companies wishing to be certified to this standard are assessed by an MRQSA-approved organisation via an initial appraisal and ongoing surveillance. There is some overlap between BS7911 and the international standard (ISO 9001), which deals more generally with quality procedures and systems, and joint assessments for both standards are recommended. A European Standard, similar in content to BS 7911 has been developed by EFAMRO from the ESOMAR code of practice and it is suggested by MRQSA that they will, together, become the basis of a full ISO standard for surveys in the next few years.

Pressure from Clients

One of the reasons for the success of the ESOMAR code has been the involvement of The International Chambers of Commerce (ICC) in its development. ICC represents the commissioners, as well as providers, of surveys and its endorsement of the code encourages commissioners to demand that providers belong to an organisation that enforces the code. Further pressure on providers to adhere to professional standards comes from specialist lobby groups such as The Association of Users of Research Agencies (AURA). Many clients require their contractors to be members of trade associations such as BMRA and to be certified in respect of standards such as MRQSA/BS7911 or IQCS. They may also expect key personnel to be members of MRS and/or one of the other professional bodies. Some larger clients (e.g., The US Department of Transport and London Underground Ltd) go further in publishing their own guidelines to which contractors are expected to adhere.

The Government Sector

Governments are, of course, major actors in the collection, analysis and presentation of survey data. Not only are they often the main client for such surveys, but they, or their agents, may also be the main organisations involved in the collection and analysis of the data. Several countries maintain national statistical agencies. Examples include: the UK's *Office for National Statistics* (ONS); Germany's *Statitisches Bundesarnt;* Ireland's *Central Statistical Office;* Canada's *Statistics Canada;* and Spain's *Instituto Nacional de Estadística* (INE). Most of these bodies have their own guidelines and procedures to ensure the quality of their output and the efficiency of their procedures (see for example: INE, 1997; Statistics Canada, 1998; ONS, 1997; or ONS, 2002). The maintenance of standards is a prime concern of all these bodies and is often identified in their founding documents. The US government has established an interagency Federal Committee on Statistical Methodology (FCSM) dedicated to improving the quality of federal statistics; its work has focused primarily on data quality and has resulted in the publication of guidelines on issues such as the identification and correction of errors.

A recent review of the procedures and standards of the national statistical agencies of EU countries (Eurostat, 2002) compared the procedures in different member countries, identified problems, and suggested solutions. It is interesting to note that the issues identified in the Eurostat review are very similar to those which have, quite independently, been identified by people working in the field of travel surveys. One of the problems identified was the range of standards achieved in different countries.

The UK's statistical agency can justifiably claim to stand as an example of best practice in the field. Their code of practice (ONS, 2002) sets out the principles and standards that official statisticians are expected to uphold. The code is supported by 12 protocols covering issues such as:

- Professional competencies (covering recruitment, qualifications, and continuing professional development and including the specification of a 'Statistician Competence Framework').
- Presentation, Dissemination, and Pricing (covering issues such as standards of objectivity and clarity, provision of background information on methodologies used, and quality standard achieved).
- Reducing the Respondent Burden (covering issues such as the avoidance of duplication, consistency in definitions, and procedures for monitoring the burden).
- Quality (which covers: indicators of quality; procedures for peer review of methodologies; use of internationally recognised definitions and methodologies, wherever possible; use of scientific principles in questionnaire design, data col-

lection and validation, estimation and analysis; documentation of methods and procedures; quantification of quality and bias; and inclusion of a statement of the degree of compliance with agreed definitions, methods, and practices).

A Survey Methodology Division, within a broader Methodology Group, provides advice to staff and customers of ONS and the statistical divisions of individual ministries. This could include quality assurance for sample designs and methodologies, and information on best practice in survey methodologies. The Division also conducts research on aspects of survey methodology (such as weighting and estimation, sample design, and imputation). A Survey Control Unit is responsible for monitoring the overall volume of government surveys – its aim is '... to promote necessary statistical surveys of the highest quality, prevent bad or unnecessary surveys, and ensure that burdens on data providers is minimised'. Elsewhere in the UK Government structure, specialist groups such as the Transport Statistics Personal Travel Division of the Department for Transport offer specialist guidance on the design and conduct of travel surveys (see DfT, 2004).

The contents of different national statistical agencies' codes of practice differ and reflect their different cultural traditions as much as their experience in the collection of national statistics. Some countries are still at a relatively early stage in the development of a national statistical service, while others have a long established tradition and are concerned with procedural niceties that may be beyond the resources of other countries. Codes of practice also reflect the political context in which they were written – one can for example detect a strong emphasis in the UK code on a desire to minimise the respondent burden (successive UK governments having been accused, particularly by private companies, of repeatedly adding to the burden of 'form filling').

Although most of the procedures and guidelines outlined above relate to a broad range of surveys, government agencies have produced a considerable amount of transport-specific advice and guidance. Bodies such as the US Bureau of Transport Statistics (BTS) and the Transport Statistics Division of UNECE have an obvious interest in the promotion of quality and comparability in transport statistics. UNECE hold a series of international working parties on transport statistics with the aim of producing agreed standards and definitions. One of their recent publications is a glossary of transport statistics terminology (UNECE, 2003).

Training, Conferences and Other Guidance

Many of the professional and governmental bodies referred to earlier see education, training, and the dissemination of best practice as a key part of their role. Their guidelines are often made freely available in the hope that their circulation among practitioners will lead to increases in the quality of work done. A number of the bodies (including CASRO, FCSM, MRA, MRS and BMRA) organise conferences, seminars, or short courses designed to train new entrants to the field in the fundamentals of travel survey methodology, or to bring more experienced practitioners up to date with the latest ideas, techniques, and technologies. Recent conferences organised by FCSM have dealt with issues of some relevance to travel surveys, including:

- Bayes' modelling for small area statistics;
- Approximation methods for covariance matrix estimation estimates used in the analysis of diary and interview data; and
- The reality of metadata: are common data definitions possible?

Some of the professional bodies offer formal training courses or endorse courses organised by others – typically academic institutions or specialist training companies. Several of these courses offer specialist training in techniques of particular relevance to travel surveys – for example a recent web search revealed several courses on stated preference methods and on the use of diaries. Although CASRO runs its own 'University' courses, the most comprehensive courses tend to be those offered by academic institutions. These more comprehensive courses generally lead to qualifications up to and including degree level and cover a range of survey contexts. Several deal with 'social research methods' but none, to my knowledge, are devoted exclusively to travel survey methodology. In addition to formal training of this kind, the dissemination of best practice is promoted through schemes such as the ESRC Survey Link Scheme whereby UK academics and researchers have an opportunity to observe at first hand the data collection phase of large scale surveys such as the National Travel Survey, the International Passenger Survey, and the ONS Omnibus Survey.

Within the travel survey context there is, as we know, an established tradition of specialist conferences – notably the stream of which this is the latest, and of specialist seminars within other conferences – notably the annual conference of the Transportation Research Board and the annual European Transport Conference. The publications from these conferences are, of course, a good source of information on what travel survey procedures or techniques have, or have not, worked well.

For those requiring more comprehensive guidance there is, of course a rich store of textbooks and handbooks offering guidance on best practice relevant to travel surveys. (see for example: Moser and Kalton, 1979; Richardson *et al.*, 1995; TRB, 1986; Neuman, 2000, Bryman, 2001; or chapters in books such as Taylor *et al.*, 2000; Ortúzar, 2000; Ortúzar and Willumsen, 2001). A number of organisations (e.g., The US Department of Transportation – see TMIP, 1996) have prepared guidelines for their own use and some of these have been circulated more widely.

DISCUSSION

So what is the Problem?

It is clear from the previous section that the social survey industry is well served with standards, guidelines, and codes of practice and that there is no shortage of sources of information on good practice or of training in the relevant techniques. What then, is the problem? Why do users of travel data, and some of those prominently involved in the collection of it, think that more action is required?

It is, of course, possible that some of us were not fully aware of the range of standards, codes, and guidelines that already exist. Those who became involved in travel surveys through research into traveller behaviour may perhaps not have recognised the relevance of the standards and procedures within the market research industry or the comprehensiveness of guidelines and advice offered by some of the national statistics agencies. If true, this is unfortunate, because we would have been failing to capitalise on a wealth of knowledge and experience of considerable relevance to our work. The problem is: *how to ensure that our colleagues become aware of this mine of information and advice?*

Some colleagues will argue that the standards and protocols summarised in the previous section are not sufficiently specific to the business of travel surveys and that our specialist view requires its own standards. This takes us back to the distinction between ethical standards, quality standards, standardisation, and the measurement of quality. Few would deny the relevance to travel surveys of the procedural standards promulgated in the market research industry, or national statistics agencies, that relate to the employment and training of staff, the rights of respondents, obligations to clients and end-users, and other ethical issues; but many would argue that travel surveys require more specific standards of quality, some standardisation of definitions and some metric by which to assess their quality.

In respect of the professional/ethical standards, the problem is, perhaps, *how to secure the more widespread adoption of such standards within the travel research community?* In respect of travel-survey-specific quality standards the issues are *what these might be and how they should be encouraged.* In respect of standardisation, the problem is that *we do not yet have any agreement as to what degree of standardisation we should adopt or what the agreed definitions might be.* Similarly, in respect of the measurement of quality, the problem is again that *we have yet to agree whether such measures are required, or precisely what they might cover.*

I will attempt to address each of these issues in turn.

How to Increase the Awareness of Existing Guidelines and Codes of Practice

Many of those involved in providing or commissioning surveys will already be very well aware of at least some of the existing codes and guidelines, because their employers have required it or because they come from the market research tradition. Others, for whom surveys are a large part of their business, will have taken the trouble to explore the literature and websites. The greater problem lies with people who are employed by small organisations who have not really thought about these issues and others, often academic researchers, who have drifted into survey work via their interest in analysing results.

Publicity via papers such as this, at appropriate conferences, may help to spread awareness of the codes and guidelines, but will not reach out to the wider audience for whom survey work is very much a sideline. Some form of outreach is clearly necessary. I suggest that this should include the following elements:

- Circulation of bibliographies, website addresses and so forth to members of research organisations via their newsletters, websites, or bulletin boards (I am thinking here of such organisations as The International Association for Travel Behaviour Research – IATBR, the survey methods committees of the Transportation Research Board and the European Transport Conference, the World Conference on Transport Research Society – WCTRS, the Universities' Transport Studies Group – UTSG, and the Conference of the Australian Institutes of Transport Research – CAITR).
- Lobbying the editors of such journals as *Transportation Research, Transport Reviews,* and *Transport Policy* to accept offers of short articles identifying the value of these codes and guidelines.
- Circulation of bibliographies, website addresses, and so forth to lecturers, programme leaders and professors involved in teaching research methods to students on transport courses.
- Making a point, when acting as reviewers of academic papers, submitted for publication, of asking authors of papers describing the collection of data to state which code they had been following.

As is clear from the preceding section of this chapter, there are numerous examples of guidelines and standards and, rather than publicise all of them, it might be thought wise to concentrate on promoting only those of particular relevance to transport and travel surveys. However, I would hesitate to suggest that any of those I have listed are *not* relevant to transport and travel surveys and would not want to dissuade anyone from following a code that was expected of practitioners in a given country. If, nevertheless, I had to select one code for general use, I would choose the ESOMAR code, because of its widespread acceptance internationally.

How to Secure more Widespread Adherence to Professional and Ethical Standards

To the extent that non-adherence to such standards is a problem in travel survey work, one would like to think that it results from ignorance rather than the deliberate flouting of ethical standards. The actions outlined in the previous section should help to overcome ignorance, but will not themselves put a stop to deliberate bad practice.

One approach would be to unleash customer power by contacting potential commissioners of research, alerting them to the problem (perhaps quoting specific examples of past misdemeanours), and suggesting that they require their survey providers to demonstrate adherence to established ethical and procedural standards. This might be done via letters or short articles addressed to their professional journals, newsletters, or websites. Such an approach would of course be controversial because, if it appears to question the probity of existing surveys, commissioners may become more reluctant to engage in such work in the future or may require contractors to incur additional expense to prove their compliance with the relevant standards. If unprofessional work is causing a problem then this corrective action may be justified, but if not, it would be an unnecessary impediment and expense in the path of travel surveys.

In the context of academic research the 'customer' may be the funding body or research sponsor – in which case the target for emails and letters would be the secretariats and members of peer review panels and, again, one might be concerned that this could make them more reluctant to fund research involving new survey work. However, there are, of course, other 'customers' – the examiners of the eventual theses and the readers of the academic papers. Those of us who act as examiners might like to check the examination ordinances of the universities we serve and, in the unlikely event that they make no reference to ethical standards in the collection of data, might point this out to the relevant authorities. As readers of academic papers, we are all customers, but most readers rely on editors and referees to police the standards; they assume that if a paper describing a survey has been published, then the referees will have satisfied themselves as to the standards of the survey work. However, do they really? I suspect that adherence to basic ethical and procedural standards is assumed, unless there is evidence to the contrary. Is this an area in which we would like to see a tighter rein? Would the benefits outweigh the costs?

The Derivation and Promulgation of Quality Standards.

In their keynote paper for the 2001 conference, Stopher and Jones (2003b) outlined and discussed some quality standards which might usefully be adopted in travel surveys. They addressed the basics of survey procedures, piloting, questionnaire design, implementation, documentation and archiving, and alluded to the particular needs of different types of surveys. Other papers at the same conference pursued specific issues arising in multi-cultural settings (Hirschowitz, 2003; Van der Ries and Lombard, 2003) and in different types of survey (Chapleau, 2003; Pendyala, 2003; Purvis and Ruiz, 2003).

A key message from these papers, as from the whole conference, was that although there may be some basic rules, the range of survey contexts, and the fairly regular emergence of new survey technologies, makes the codification of detailed standards extraordinarily difficult. A more practical approach may be to equip practitioners with insights into the way in which respondents react to different types of queries, to inculcate them with a healthy dose of scepticism as to the possibility of capturing unbiased and objective data, and then rely on their common sense. Thus, we come back to the desirability of education, training, and other, less formal, methods of spreading the message.

What Degree of Standardisation of Definitions is Appropriate?

Widespread acceptance of standard definitions for concepts such as 'access to a car', or for entities such as 'trips', 'households', 'leisure' and 'work', would clearly benefit researchers engaged in meta-analysis or other attempts to compare data from different sources. Standardised definitions would bring comparability, clarity, and reliability and would facilitate analyses that could yield profound insights into traveller behaviour. However, standardisation has negative as well as positive connotations. For some people it implies a straitjacket that will stifle innovation and context-sensitivity. They argue that the appropriate definition, even of basic concepts and entities such as those listed above, is subject to local circumstances and may change over time. For example: the definition of 'access to a car' may need to evolve with the spread of car clubs, or the increased popularity of leasing arrangements, or changes in regulations affecting private use of company cars; the definition of a 'household' will differ from culture to culture and traditional definitions (such as 'people who normally share a main meal') may become outdated with changes in social mores; and the definition of trip purposes can become fraught with the increased possibilities for multi-tasking – indeed the very idea of travel as a discrete activity becomes questionable with the development of mobile communications. The imposition of too rigid a set of definitions would clearly hamper research in travel behaviour. This is seen by many as the heart of the debate; would the benefits of standardisation outweigh the costs?

In fact, of course, few people would seriously suggest that standard definitions could or should be universally imposed. Rather it is suggested that adherence to an agreed set of definitions would be rewarded by awarding an appropriate label or badge of compliance. This badge might be required by national/international statistical agencies, but would otherwise be voluntary. Other things being equal, a research sponsor or lone researcher would hopefully elect to use the agreed definitions, but they would not be compelled to do so. It has been suggested that those who wish to deviate from standard definitions should be required to do so only via additional questions and that they should include the standard definitions as a matter of course. However, although this might sometimes be appropriate, it would generally lead to increased cost, respondent burden, and confusion.

Perhaps the best way forward is to consult widely on an appropriate set of standard definitions and on procedures for periodic review, with a view to then publicising the agreed definitions throughout the industry. The consultation would need to build on and take on board the work of bodies such as UNECE (2003) and would need to include government bodies and user groups. Representatives from the UK would doubtless include ONS, UTSG, and the Transport Statistics User Group, but, given the desirability of achieving international agreement, it would be essential to include equivalent bodies from all the major countries, as well as international organisations such as UNECE and Eurostat. This would be no small task!

Measuring Quality

There are four separate but interconnected issues here:

- Can we agree on what we mean by quality?
- How should we measure quality?
- Who should be responsible for the measurement? and
- How should we promote the provision of the necessary information?

Can we agree on what we mean by quality?

In some areas of survey practice there are commonly accepted measures of quality. Few would dispute that the greater the sample fraction, the higher the response rate, and the greater the representativeness of the original sample, the 'better' will be the result. However, other measures of quality may be less universally accepted and will depend on the context and purpose of the survey. The existence of documentation that makes it possible to identify individual respondents might be welcomed by someone wishing to conduct a repeat survey or link one set of data with another, but would be anathema to someone concerned by the ethical aspects of lack of respondent privacy, or by the influence that lack of anonymity might have on respondents' willingness to give frank opinions.

The fact that a given survey was conducted using traditional best practice for face-to-face interviews and conventional definitions of, say, car ownership, might be comforting to someone wishing to compare the resulting data with that from an equivalent survey conducted ten years previous, but might be of little use to someone whose interest lies in, say, exploring drivers' perceptions of their relationship with their car. Surveyors of attitudes and perceptions may be particularly resistant to rigid definitions of quality; a researcher who has experimented with novel ways of getting respondents to reveal their attitudes, or an innovative way of measuring perceptions, might be particularly aggrieved to find his methodology branded as 'low quality', because it did not follow standard procedures (as an interesting aside, I recall having had considerable difficulty, back in the late 1970's, persuading the UK Survey Control Unit that I should be allowed to ask what would now be described as Stated Preference questions in a survey that I was conducting on their behalf).

It is sometimes suggested that the 'quality' of a survey becomes apparent when its data are analysed and that, other things being equal, the stronger and more significant the model coefficients then the 'better' the survey. I must say that I profoundly disagree with this view! It will clearly be disappointing to the modeller to find no strong relationships within the data, but, if they are not present in the real world, we should not want to find them in the data. It is always possible to construct a survey that will yield what you hope to find, but that does not mean that it is a good survey (Bonsall, 2002)!

I suggest that it would be counterproductive to extend the definition of quality beyond those aspects that can attract near universal support; if there is room to dispute the definition of quality much of its potential benefit will be lost. It may be appropriate to reserve the word 'quality' to describe aspects that are universally accepted and to treat the other items as optional extras that may attract a 'badge of compliance', but would not be used to determine quality. If this approach were adopted, it would then be possible to distinguish between the irreducible minimum standards that should be looked for in all surveys – irrespective of their provenance – and the add-ons whose inclusion would not always be desirable. It would, however, be important to be vigilant in defending the distinction and resisting the inevitable tendency to assume that the add-ons should be included, if they can be afforded. This approach would, again, require a widespread consultation within the industry to identify those aspects that should contribute to a measure of quality and those that should be treated separately.

How should we measure quality?

If we restrict ourselves to measures of quality which command near universal support, the list may be quite short. Some of the indicators identified by Kalfs *et al.* (2000) in their resource paper for the Grainau conference, would certainly be relevant, but others would not. Most people would agree that a core list should include sample size, response rate, and adequate documentation (of sample frame, sampling method, survey method, survey instrument, and analysis methods), but, beyond that, there is likely to be disagreement. As was argued earlier in this chapter, the 'quality' of a survey may result from the informed and skilful application of common sense principles rather than from slavishly following a set of rules. This makes the measurement of quality rather difficult!

One suggestion has been that survey quality should be measured by means of a composite index reflecting the performance of the survey against a number of different criteria. Thus, a survey might be awarded marks for sample size, response rate, use of standard definitions, clarity of questions, and so on, and these marks might then be combined (added or multiplied?) to give an overall index of quality. I have strong reservations about this approach, because it implies that, even if some items are weighted more heavily in the formula, there can be a trade off between, for example, sample size and clarity of questions. I think that a supposedly universal measure of this kind would hide more than it reveals and could mislead the potential user of resulting data into thinking that one survey was better than another whereas, given the use to which the data is to be put, the opposite might be the case.

Another problem with any approach based on scores or marks is that it requires someone (at some cost) to make judgement on some fairly subjective issues. The measurement of adequacy of documentation presupposes that we can agree on what it should include and at what level of detail. My own suggestion would be that the documentation should be sufficient to allow a third party to duplicate the survey exercise in every respect save the date. This clearly requires a much more detailed description of the sample frame, sampling method, and survey instrument than is commonly provided in academic papers and even in some reports to clients. One potential objection to this course of action is that the developers of questionnaires and other survey instruments would resent having to reveal the details of that instrument to potential competitors. I do not think that this objection is tenable; if someone wishes to claim that their data contains useful or interesting information they should be required to reveal precisely how it was collected.

If the adequacy of documentation were to be judged according to whether it was sufficient to allow a third party to duplicate the exercise, this would provide a binary indicator of quality; the documentation would either be deemed adequate or inadequate. Other indicators, such as sample size and response rate, are continuous variables and the definition of adequacy is context-specific (a given sample size or response rate might be deemed excellent in one context but appalling in another). The imposition of a threshold value would be essentially arbitrary. It has been suggested that, as an alternative to sample size, a more useful indicator might be the statistical confidence with which data values can be quoted. This is an interesting idea, but, of course, the variance and hence the confidence intervals would be different for different data items and, as noted above, it might be perverse to award an accolade of quality to a survey on the basis of its failure to reveal any variance in the data! My conclusion is that the sample size, response rate and measured variance in particular data items should be included in the survey documentation and that the adequacy of the documentation should then be the only measure of quality.

Who should be responsible for the measurement?

If the indicators of quality are confined to clear and unambiguous items, such as sample size and response rate, then there is no reason why the organisation that conducted the survey should not be responsible for reporting the values. A self-assessment approach of this kind is recommended by MRQSA.

If the indicators are more subjective then self-reporting is not likely to be very reliable – what survey organisation would award itself less than full marks for clarity of questions or lack of ambiguity of instructions to respondents? If the assessment is to be made by an independent third party, this will inevitably lead to extra costs and a professional framework would need to be constructed to ensure the competence and independence of the assessors. I doubt that the travel research community could afford or service such an overhead.

This, together with the difficulties that would surround any attempt to define a single universally-applicable index of quality and the fact that acceptability thresholds vary with context, lead me to conclude that the final assessment of quality can only be made by the potential users of the data in the light of their particular requirements. This requires an investment in the training of data users, so that they are in a position to judge the suitability of data for a given purpose, and efforts to ensure that the information required to assess quality is made available as a matter of course.

How should we promote the provision of the necessary information?

The most obvious mechanism is to ensure that any codes or guidelines include a requirement on survey practitioners to provide the relevant information for any survey that they undertake. Reputable practitioners should find no difficulty in doing this as a matter of course and commissioners, recognising the value of the information, would soon come to require it.

The mechanism might be rather different in the academic sector, because there is often no obvious client or commissioning body to enforce or require the publication of measures of quality. I suggest that the best route forward is to encourage journal editors and reviewers to require authors to provide access to the full documentation (as defined in above) of the surveys from which they have derived data included in their papers. This would enable the referees, and eventual readers, to judge quality for themselves and would overcome the objection that an author might have to the imposition of insensitive, non-context-specific, standards.

I recognise that this approach would represent quite a departure from the established practice of some journals; authors are often expressly instructed to omit 'unnecessary information' such as copies of survey forms. This instruction is usually given in order to limit the length of papers and may have been understandable when the inclusion of additional material would have necessitated lengthy appendices (although I have always argued for the inclusion of a full description of a survey instrument, including the precise wording of questions, when a paper deals with attitudinal data). In fact, even if editors are reluctant to include full details within the published paper, the advent of the

Internet makes it possible to lodge the relevant material on a website – preferably one owned by the publisher. It is therefore possible to keep the paper itself to a reasonable length while allowing the referee, and eventual reader, the opportunity to see the data in its proper context and to assess the reasonableness of the analyst's interpretation of those data.

In fact I have already asked a number of authors and referees what they think of the suggestion that authors should be required to post full survey details on a website. The suggestion generates an interesting response; some see it as an excellent idea and greet it with enthusiasm while others, with equal conviction, see it as imposing an unnecessary requirement on authors and an unrealistic burden on referees. It seems that a substantial part of the academic community have yet to be convinced that a detailed assessment of data-based analyses demands an understanding of the process by which the data were collected. Perhaps, against this background of opinion, it is hardly surprising that the issue of standards in surveys is so often ignored!

Should we Develop an ISO Standard for Travel Surveys?

I was asked to pay particular regard to the potential role of a new ISO standard for travel surveys; an idea explored by Richardson (2000) for the Grainau conference. ISO standards already exist to define the quality and fitness-for-purpose of products and services (ISO 8402) and to define the process of quality assurance within organisations (ISO 9001), but these do not provide more than a general framework for survey work. However, it appears that an ISO standard for market research, based on BS7911 and the ESOMAR Code, may now be imminent and this will certainly contain much of relevance to travel surveys.

The development of an ISO standard specifically for travel surveys would be a considerable undertaking. It would require a significant investment of time and resources by the travel survey community; a code could not be accepted as an ISO standard unless it had been developed following extensive consultation throughout the industry. I am not convinced that we could agree on enough material of specific relevance to travel surveys to justify a separate ISO standard for our corner of the survey business.

IN CONCLUSION

I have suggested that a reason for the slow progress towards agreement on standards for travel surveys is that there is a genuine concern amongst many of those who are active in the field that the imposition of inappropriate standards would bring additional costs and would be an unwanted impediment to innovation. I have suggested that this concern needs to be addressed very carefully.

I have indicated that, despite slow progress in the travel survey community, the professional bodies in the related field of market research make extensive use of standards and codes of practice and, in theory at least, impose severe sanctions on firms and individuals who fail to meet the required standards. I have described the development of the MRQSA sponsored British Standard (BS7911) and the ESOMAR Code and have indicated that a full ISO standard for market research may be imminent. I have also made reference to the very positive contributions being made by national statistical agencies.

I have suggested that those of us with an interest in improving the standards in travel surveys should adopt and publicise elements of existing codes of practice, but that we should be careful not to go too far in suggesting standard definitions or measures of quality. I have suggested that adherence to standard definitions might be recognised by the award of a badge of compliance, but that compliance with standard definitions should not be assumed to be related to quality. I have concluded that, given the difficulties in measurement and the fact that quality should be defined differently in different contexts, it is not possible or useful to seek to define a universal indicator of survey quality.

I have called for efforts to encourage survey practitioners and authors to provide more details about the methods by which their data were collected. I have suggested that a particular effort should be made to persuade reviewers of academic papers to insist that authors provide full details of their data sources and that, by placing such material on the Internet, some of the traditional objections can be overcome. Finally I have argued that we should not seek to establish a new ISO standard specifically for travel surveys.

REFERENCES

Ampt, E.S. (1992). Summary of Workshop on Weighting of Data. In: *Selected Readings in Transport Survey Methodology* (E.S. Ampt, A.J. Richardson, and A.H. Meyburg, eds), 23-25, Eucalyptus Press, Melbourne.

Axhausen, K.W. (2000). Presenting and Preserving Travel Data. In: *Transport Surveys: Raising the Standards* (P.R. Stopher and P.M. Jones, eds) Transportation Research Circular, EC008, Transportation Research Board, Washington DC, II-F/1-II-F/19.

Axhausen, K.W. and M.R. Wigan (2003). Public Use of Travel Surveys: The metadata perspective. In: *Transport Survey Quality and Innovation* (P.R. Stopher and P.M. Jones, eds), 605-628, Pergamon Press, Oxford.

Bonsall, P.W. (2002). Motivating the respondent: How far should we go? In: *In Perpetual Motion: Travel Behaviour Research Opportunities and Challenges,* (H.S. Mahmassani, ed.), 359-378, Pergamon Press, Oxford.

BSI (2003). *Specification for Organisations Conducting Market Research.* British Standards Publishing Ltd, London.

Bryman, A. (2001). *Social Research Methods.* Oxford University Press, Oxford.

CASRO (1997). *Code of Standards and Ethics for Survey Research.* Council of American Survey Research Organisations. New York.

CASRO (1998). *Survey Research Quality Guidelines.* Council of American Survey Research Organisations. New York.

Chapleau, R. (2003). Measuring the Internal Quality of the Montreal CATI Household Travel Survey. In: *Transport Survey Quality and Innovation* (P.R. Stopher and P.M. Jones, eds), 69-87, Pergamon Press, Oxford.

DfT (2004). *Monitoring Personal Travel for Local Transport Plans,* Note prepared by the Transport Statistics personal Travel Division of the UK Department for Transport, (available at www.clip.gov.uk/documents/Resources/ltpmon.pdf)

ESOMAR (1999). *ICC/ESOMAR International Code of Marketing and Social Research Practice.* International Chamber of Commerce, Paris

ESOMAR (2002). *ESOMAR Guideline on How to Commission Research,* European Society for Opinion and Marketing Research.

ESOMAR (2003). *ESOMAR Guideline on Conducting Marketing and Opinion Research Using the Internet,* European Society for Opinion and Marketing Research.

Eurostat (2002). *Quality in the European Statistical System – The way Forward.* Office for Official Publications of the European Community, Luxembourg.

Hirschowitz, R. (2003). Planning and Managing a Household Survey and a Population Census in a Multicultural and Multilingual Context. In: *Transport Survey Quality and Innovation* (P.R. Stopher and P.M. Jones, eds), 39-47, Pergamon Press, Oxford.

INE (1997). *Manual de Procedimentos da Producao Estatistica,* Instituto Nacional de Estadistica, Madrid.

Kalfs, N., H. Meurs and W. Saris (2000). Quality Indicators. In: *Transport Surveys: Raising the Standards* (P.R. Stopher and P.M. Jones, eds), Transportation Research Circular, EC008, Transportation Research Board, Washington, DC, II-E/I-II-E/14.

Moser, C.A. and G.K. Kalton (1979). *Survey Methods in Social Investigation.* Heinemann Educational Books, London, 2nd Edition.

MRS (2003). *MRS Codes and Guidelines.* The Market Research Society, London.

Neuman, L.W. (2000). *Social Research Methods: Qualitative and Quantitative Approaches,* (4th ed), Allyn and Bacon, London.

ONS (1997). *Statistical Quality Checklist.* Office for National Statistics, London.

ONS (2002). *National Statistics Code of Practice.* Office for National Statistics, London.

Ortúzar, J. de D. (ed.) (2000). *Stated Preference Modelling Techniques.* PTRC Perspectives 4, PTRC, London.

Ortúzar, J. de and Willumsen L.G. (2001), *Modelling Transport,* Wiley, Chichester, 3rd edition.

Pendyala, R.M. (2003). Quality and Innovation in Time Use and Activity Surveys. In: *Transport Survey Quality and Innovation* (P.R. Stopher and P.M. Jones, eds), 181-190, Pergamon Press, Oxford.

Purvis, C.L. and T. Ruiz (2003). Standards and Practice for Multi-day and Multi-period Surveys. In: *Transport Survey Quality and Innovation* (P.R. Stopher and P.M. Jones, eds), 271-282, Pergamon Press, Oxford.

Richardson, A.J. (2000). Guidelines for Quality Assurance in Travel and Activity Surveys, Keynote paper at Conference on Survey Methods in Transport held in 1997 in Grainau, Germany. Available online at http://www.tuti.com.au/Publications/1997/1997IS).pdf

Richardson, A.J. (1992). Summary of Workshop on Safety Surveys. In: *Selected Readings in Transport Survey Methodology* (E.S. Ampt, A.J. Richardson and A.H. Meyburg, eds), 19-22, Eucalyptus Press, Melbourne.

Richardson, A.J., E.S. Ampt and A.H. Meyburg (1995). *Survey Methods for Transport Planning* Eucalyptus Press, Melbourne.

SRA (2003). *Ethical Guidelines.* The Survey Research Association, London.

Statistics Canada (1998). *Statistics Canada Quality Guidelines.* Statistics Canada catalogue 12-539-XIE.

Stopher, P.R. and P.M. Jones (eds), (2000). *Transport Surveys: Raising the Standards,* Transportation Research Circular, EC008, Transportation Research Board, Washington DC.

Stopher, P. R. and P.M. Jones (2003a). Summary and Future Directions. In: *Transport Survey Quality and Innovation* (P.R. Stopher and P.M. Jones, eds), 635-646, Pergamon Press, Oxford.

Stopher P.R. and P.M. Jones (2003b). Developing Standards of Transport Survey Quality. In: *Transport Survey Quality and Innovation* (P.R. Stopher and P.M. Jones, eds), 1-38, Pergamon Press, Oxford.

Taylor, M.A.P., P.W. Bonsall and W. Young (2000). *Understanding Traffic Systems: Data Analysis and Presentation.* Ashgate, Aldershot. 2nd edition.

TMIP (1996). *Travel Survey Manual,* Prepared by Cambridge Systematics, Inc. for the US Department of Transportation and the US Environmental Protection Agency, Washington DC.

TRB (1986). Innovations in Travel Surveys, *Transportation Research Record* 1097, Transportation Research Board, Washington.

UNECE (2003). *Glossary of Transport Statistics.* Report from the working party on Transport Statistics (TRANS/WP.06/2003/6), United Nations Commission for Europe.

Van der Ries, P. and M. Lombard (2003). Multicultural and Multi-language Transport Surveys with Special Reference to the African Experience. In: *Transport Survey Quality and Innovation* (P.R. Stopher and P.M. Jones, eds), 191-208, Pergamon Press, Oxford.

Wigan, M.R. (1985). The Secondary Use of Transport Survey Data. In: *New Survey Methods in Transport* (E.S. Ampt, A.J. Richardson and W. Brög, eds), 131-148, VNU Science Press, Utrecht.

APPENDIX 1: DETAILS FOR TRADE ASSOCIATIONS AND PROFESSIONAL BODIES

Organisation	Date of establishment	Website address
AAPOR	1947	http://www.aapor.org
ADM	1955	http://www.adm-ev.de
AQS	1982	http://www.aqs.org.uk
ASC	1971	http://www.asc.org.uk
AURA	1960s	http://www.aura.org.uk
BMRA	1980	http://www.bmra.org.uk
CASRO	1975	http://www.casro.org
CMOR	1992	http://www.cmor.org
EFAMRO	1992	http://www.efamro.org
ESOMAR	1948	http://www.esomar.org
IQCS	1978	http://www.iqcs.org.uk
MRA	1954	http://www.mra-net.org
MRS	1896	http://www.marketresearch.org.uk
PMRS	1960	http://www.pmrs.aprm.com
SRA	1978	http://www.the-sra.org.uk
Syntec-Etudes		http://www.syntec-etudes.com
WAPOR	1947	http://www.wapor.org

Travel Survey Methods: Quality and Future Directions
Peter Stopher and Cheryl Stecher (Editors)
© 2006 Elsevier Ltd. All rights reserved.

16

POSSIBLE EXPLANATIONS FOR AN INCREASING SHARE OF NO-TRIP RESPONDENTS

Linda Christensen, Danish Transport Research Institute, Lyngby, Denmark

PURPOSE

This chapter reports on some puzzling findings from the Danish National Travel Survey (DNTS). The DNTS was a continuous CATI survey conducted in the period 1992-2003 with 14-16,000 computer-assisted telephone interviews annually.

A continuous travel survey provides important information about changes in travel behaviour. Surprisingly, a decline in transport kilometres was observed in the DNTS in 1998 and an even sharper drop in 2001. The decline was registered for all transport means. Furthermore, the trip rate declined by twelve percent from 1995 to 2001. This trend in overall transport kilometres and trip rates is not found in other traffic observations. For instance, according to traffic counts collected by the Road Directorate, transport kilometres had in fact increased for many years until 2000 when they stabilised for a couple of years (Road Directorate, 2003). The DNTS changes are unlikely to derive from actual behavioural changes and are most probably explained by changes in the data collection methodology.

This chapter focuses on the zero trip rate, because it appears to be the most obvious reason for the unexpected drops in transport kilometres from 1997 to 1998 and afterwards up to 2001. Over the period, the zero trip rate increased by sixty percent, from sixteen to twenty five percent, as shown in Figure 1. In reality, the zero trip rate should change only slightly per year in line with changes in participation in the labour market or as a result of a generation effect as shown by Madre *et al.* (2004).

Figure 1: Monthly Mean of Zero Trip Rate for People Travelling from August 1992 to December 2003 (16–74 Year Age Group)

The objective of this chapter is twofold:

- To show how sensitive continuous surveys can be to small changes in data collection methodology; and
- To find explanations for the observed changes in the DNTS to illustrate the effect of changed methodology.

THE DANISH NATIONAL TRAVEL SURVEY

The DNTS was conducted by Statistics Denmark. Contrary to most other national travel surveys, it was based on a random sample of persons rather than of families. Respondents were selected from the Civil Register of all the inhabitants of Denmark. An introductory letter was sent to respondents in advance to explain the survey. Because only people with listed telephone numbers were called, the letter requested non-listed telephone numbers. Only a few respondents complied with this request.

Respondents to the DNTS were not dedicated to a fixed day. They were sampled for a month, and when an attempt to contact them was successful, they were interviewed about the day prior to the calling day. The calling time was normally from 11 a.m. to 9 p.m. on weekdays and from 9 a.m. to 2 p.m. at weekends.

In order to avoid over-sampling certain weekdays, exactly the same number of respondents had to be interviewed every day. It was sometimes impossible to get enough contacts, e.g., on a summer Sunday. On such occasions, interviews related to this day were resumed on the following day. By the end of the month, it was sometimes impossible to get enough interviews, and interviews related to the last days of the month were undertaken on subsequent days.

Over the years, the data collection methodology changed several times. These changes are expected to influence both the zero trip rate and the trip rate per traveller. From 1997 to 1998 the data collection period was changed from one week each month to the whole month. The monthly number of respondents interviewed was the same before and after the change – except that some interviews were added because the group of respondents was expanded from the age range of sixteen to seventy four to eleven to eighty four.

In the period 1998-2001, the only known change in data collection methodology was inclusion of cell phone numbers in the stock of called numbers, because all telephone numbers from 2000 were listed on a joint list.

POSSIBLE EXPLANATIONS

Effect of Time of Interview

First, the zero trip rate is expected to depend on the day of the reported behaviour. If the distribution of interviews over the week or the year changes, the zero trip rate would change. The calling time of the day might also be important. For instance, sixty percent of respondents were not at home at 11 a.m. on a normal weekday whereas at 6 p.m., the figure was twenty percent. The distribution of calls over the day is unimportant if everyone in the sample is interviewed. However, if some are not interviewed because of insufficient efforts to contact them, people at home much of the time are over-represented. If many calls take place during daytime hours, the bias is greater than for a situation in which evening calls are over-represented.

The random calling method can create a bias in who is contacted, e.g., on weekdays and at weekends. The distribution of respondents over the week is, therefore, dependent on the calling time of day. For instance, if many interviews are conducted during the daytime on weekdays, people not in the labour market are over-represented on weekdays, while respondents in active employment will be more concentrated at the weekend, reporting Friday and Saturday activities. Both biases generate a higher zero trip rate.

Contact Pattern

The change in the number of daily calls and the duration of the interview period from 1997 to 1998 might change the contact pattern and thus result in a different group of respondents with a different zero trip rate. Various methodologies have been used to highlight these changes, and the best variables are presented later in this chapter.

Cell Phone Numbers

According to Figure 2, non-contacts and the share of unlisted telephone numbers changed substantially during the period 1997-2001. The number of people impossible to contact halved from 1997 to 1998, a decrease due to the longer calling period that enabled contact to be established with people returning home from journeys later in the month. However, the figure started to rise again from 2000, and by 2003 non-contact was fifty percent higher than in 1997. De Leeuw & de Heer (2002) reported an international trend with an increase in non-contact of 0.2 percent per year. The increase in the DNTS is much higher.

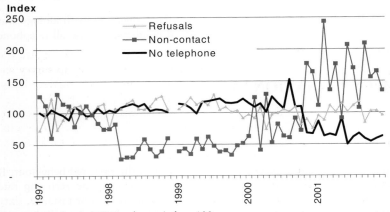

The mean number in 1997 is taken as index=100

Figure 2: Changes in Numbers of Respondents and Non-Respondents (Age Range 16–74)

The percentage of sampled persons without a known telephone number gradually increased from 1997 until the end of 2000 as a result of an increase in the number of mobile telephones and telephone companies. From the end of 2000 when registration of cell phone numbers started, the percentage without a known telephone number dropped to half the level in 1999.

These two developments are clearly interrelated. When cell phone numbers were included and more respondents were called, the number of people who were difficult to contact increased. The explanation seems to be that many cell phones are still registered even though they have been scrapped or switched off. In reality, a large proportion of the extra telephone numbers are merely time consuming and of no use to interviewers.

The emergence of cell phones as an interview medium might also explain some of the increase in the zero trip rate. It is difficult to interview people via cell phone when they are away from home. In these circumstances, the respondent may not be concentrating fully and the interview is short and superficial.

Soft Refusal

An additional explanation for the changing zero trip rate could be the theory of soft refusals. Madre *et al.* (2004) suggested that a disproportionately high percentage of zero trippers is produced by 'soft' refusals and concluded that the expected level of zero trippers in a one-day weekday diary survey should be ten to fifteen percent. In the event of a higher range, they suggest that 'something in the interaction between the survey, the survey protocol, and the fieldwork firm invites the respondents ... to use the soft refusal' and thus avoid reporting their travel activities (Madre *et al.*, 2004, p. 28). The DNTS is carried out as a one-day diary but as part of a whole-week survey. Hence, a higher percentage of zero trippers at the weekend makes a fifteen to twenty percent range of zero trippers realistic. The zero trip rate of twenty five percent in 2001 is accordingly too high.

De Leeuw and de Heer (2002) showed that refusal rates increase in most countries by around 0.3 percent per year but the size of increase differs from survey to survey and from country to country. According to Figure 2, the refusal rate actually increased from 1998 through 1999. However, from the end of 1999 the refusal rate declined again and stabilised at the 1997 level in mid-2000. An explanation for this decline could be extra efforts to get a sufficient number of interviews when non-contact increases. The result of such efforts could be an increase in soft refusals instead. Reluctant respondents who try to avoid an interview by saying 'I never go out' could, for instance, be persuaded to take part by answering 'oh, then I won't need to take much of your time'. The result might be no trips reported.

A higher share of non-contacts in 2001 could be another indication of soft refusals. Chapleau (2003) reported a much higher level of nonresponse from people who were called numerous times. Lynn *et al.* (2002) do not find a higher nonresponse rate if people were called many times without contact being made. Stopher *et al.* (2006) mentioned that a repeated number of appointments before agreeing to participate in an interview is an indicator of a soft refusal. They suggested that respondents who make more than a certain number of appointments should be excluded.

Interviewer Effect

In all kinds of personal interviews, irrespective of whether they are conducted as part of a CAPI survey or, like the DNTS, a CATI survey, interviewers act differently and achieve different results according to, e.g., unit nonresponse and item nonresponse (many references to interviewer effects can be found in Groves *et al.*, 2002). This can result in a decreasing trip rate or even an increasing zero trip rate. Battellino and Peachman (2003) point to the problem with some kind of boredom or tiredness after conducting many interviews. They offer recommendations for addressing this problem.

Interviewer experience might also result in better results. Both Chapleau (2003) and Pahkinen and Pastinen (2001) reported lower refusal rates with experience. On the other hand, persistent attempts to reduce potential refusals by persuading respondents to participate could result in a higher percentage of soft refusals.

Because the interviewers' salary depended on the number of interviews achieved, interviewers had a financial incentive to reduce interview time. An easy way to reduce interview time is to be less eager to record a maximum number of trips, which results in a reduced trip rate. This could also explain the high zero trip rate recorded by some interviewers.

Interviewers did not interview on the same days, which naturally influenced their zero trip rates, because interview time of day and week is very important for the resulting zero trip rate. Therefore the interaction between interviewer and time of interview had to be included in the analyses.

Information about age and gender is available to the interviewer when he decides to call a respondent. Thus, the interviewer may tend to call people aged over sixty during daytime hours on weekdays and younger people in the evenings and at the weekend. Therefore the interaction between interviewer, time of interview, and age of the respondent had to be included in the analyses.

METHODOLOGY AND RESULTS

The data analysis was carried out as a logistic regression on a disaggregated dataset with each respondent as an observation. The dataset is based on an interview-log file supplemented by information on the number of trips reported by the respondents. Eighty-one thousand observations are available from 1997 to 2001. The analysis used a binary logit model to compute the probability of the zero trip rate being zero.

The purpose of the methodology applied was to identify variables or groups of variables that may explain differences between years. The influence of a variable can change either because the combination of the values of a variable changes, e.g., if the share of interviews reporting Sunday activity increases, or because the influence of a variable on the zero trip rate changes, e.g., if some of the interviewers are less eager to get all information about trips made by the respondent.

Year dummies were included in the regression as independent variables to describe changes in behaviour year by year. The year dummy was also included in interaction with the significant variables. A significant change in this interaction in some years indicates that the influence of the variable with which the year dummy interacts has changed in the given years.

The independent variables describing the data collection methodology should normally be supplemented by socio-economic variables to control for bias. The analysis presented in this chapter only takes age and gender into account. This approach has been selected in order to highlight the influence of the data collection methodology on results.

Two analyses were carried out, one for the period 1998-2001 for the age range 11-84 and one for 1997-1998 for the age range 16-74.

Overall Results

The result of the logistic regression from the period 1998-2001 is presented in Table 1. Only the significant variables are listed. Some of the presented effects are not significant, but are included because their second-order interactions are significant.

Table 1: The Chi-Square Statistics of the Logistic Regression for the Period 1998 to 2001

Source	DF	Chi Square	Pr>Chi Square
Year 2001	1	10.9737	0.0009
Age	1	97.8600	<.0001
Age^2	1	325.2386	<.0001
Time of call and interview day	7	133.8521	<.0001
Age * Time	7	19.9703	0.0056
Age^2 * Time	7	19.1101	0.0078
Month	3	59.6437	<.0001
Interviewer	8	107.3402	<.0001
Interviewer experience	6	18.8651	0.0044
Interviewer * experience	30	58.3029	0.0015
Year 2001 * Interviewer	6	13.4271	0.0367
Interviewer * Time	23	52.3245	0.0005
Contact pattern	3	123.3585	<.0001
After end of month	1	11.6610	0.0006
Number of non-contacts	7	28.3647	0.0002
Number of appointments	3	13.9770	0.0029
Mobile telephones	1	5.0994	0.0239

The result of the regression from the 1998-2001 period is that the year dummy of 2001 is significant, but none of the other year dummies are. This means the model does not fully explain changes over the year. 2001 still shows an inexplicable increase in zero trip rate. The logistic regression from the period 1997-1998 includes most of the same variables but fewer interactions thanks to the smaller number of interviews - 28.000. The year dummy is insignificant and the changes are fully explained.

Effect of Time of Interview

As expected, Table 2 shows that the zero trip rate depends on the day of reported behaviour. The zero trip rate is higher at weekends than on weekdays and higher on Sundays than on Saturdays.

The zero trip rate also depends on the time of day the call was conducted. According to Table 2, the zero trip rate on Saturdays for respondents interviewed after 11 a.m. on Sundays is fairly high related to contacting earlier on Sundays or on Mondays. Because more than two-thirds of the Sunday respondents are contacted after 11 a.m., the reported zero trip rate on Saturdays seems to be biased. A Sunday evening interview period might change the zero trip rate, with respondents reporting more travelling activities on Saturdays.

Table 2: Estimated Zero Trip Rates 1998-2001 Depending on Calling Time and the Day to which the Interview Relates

Calling time	Interview relates to	Zero trip rate
Day	Weekday	19 %
Evening	Weekday	14 %
Saturday	Weekday	12 %
Sunday morning	Saturday	17 %
Sunday after 11	Saturday	20 %
Monday	Saturday	16 %
Monday	Sunday	29 %
Holiday	Sunday / Public holiday	32 %

The intention was to keep the distribution of the interviews over the day and week the same. However from 1998, far fewer interviewers were active each day than previously, which made it more difficult to allocate the right number of interviewers to each period of the day. This resulted in more respondents with high zero trip rates being interviewed during weekday daytime hours and fewer interviewed in the evenings. Even so, changes in calling time contribute only little to the increase in the zero trip rate in both periods.

Age and Gender

Age is significant in both the first and second order, whereas gender is not. The zero trip rate increases significantly with the age of the respondent. The difference between the elderly and the young is slightly smaller at weekends than during the rest of the week (Figure 3).

Because the composition of the age groups did not change much from 1997 to 1998, the large difference in zero trip rate between age groups cannot explain any change in the zero trip rate. However, in interaction with calling time, age contributes to the increase in the zero trip rate from 1997 to 1998. About half of the increase is explained by change in calling time and the impact this has on the age distribution over days of the week. The influence on the zero trip rate from 1998 to 2001 is only marginal.

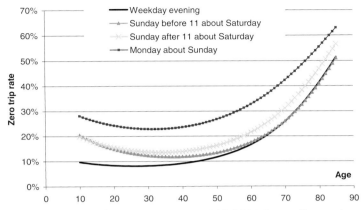

Figure 3: Estimated Zero Trip Rate in 1998-2001 Depending on Age and Calling Time

Contact Pattern

A variable indicating the time span between the successful call and a prior call is significant in the regression model. As shown in Figure 4, a person contacted the day after a day on which he was called without contact has a slightly lower probability of reporting no trips on the previous day. This is a natural outcome because the behaviour on the day to which the interview refers is dependent on the day of the earlier call. If the respondent is contacted later on the first calling day, he is also less likely to be a zero tripper. This is typical for a person on the job market who can only be contacted in the evening. He is rarely a zero tripper. On the other hand, the zero trip rate for a respondent contacted at the first call does not differ significantly from that for a respondent contacted more than one day after a prior call.

To conclude, if a person is not contacted on the first calling day, the timing of the next call is not important provided it is not the following day. If contact is not established at the first call on a certain day, it is important to call the person again later on the same day to try to get contact. If this contact pattern is followed, it does not matter that the respondents are not sampled on a fixed day. However, the survey did not follow this rule. In 1997 respondents were more often contacted the day after an earlier call than later on, resulting in a slightly lower zero trip rate in 1997. Furthermore, they were more frequently called several times each day, which slightly reduced the zero trip rate. This difference explains only a small part of the change in the zero trip rate from 1997 to 1998 and none from 1998 to 2001.

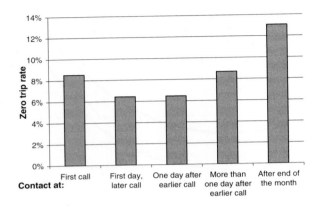

Figure 4: Estimated Zero Trip Rate in 1998-2001 Depending on the Time Span between the Successful Call and a Prior Call and on Calling after End of the Month

Soft Refusal

The most surprising result from the analyses of the contact pattern is a fifty percent higher zero trip rate for respondents contacted one or more days after the end of the month (Figure 4). These respondents had been called several times earlier without an interview being achieved and would be expected to have a very low zero trip rate. Two explanations are possible: one is the possibility of a soft refusal and the other is that respondents have forgotten some trips, primarily the short ones. The zero trip rate for respondents reporting an activity more than one day ago, but not at the end of the month, is not significantly different from that for everyone else. This indicates that the discrepancy is not caused by difficulty remembering trips.

In 1997, a higher share of respondents was contacted after the end of the month than in the following years. The longer period with fewer calls per day makes it easier to complete interviewing within the period. The effect from calls after the end of the month cancels out the effect from more calls only one day after a prior call. This means that changes in contact pattern do not explain the increasing zero trip rate from 1997 to 1998, nor after 1998. The monthly mean share of refusals is not significant. The analysis therefore does not support the possibility of a change from refusal to soft refusal.

The number of calls with non-contact and the number of appointments before making contact are both significant. As expected, the zero trip rate decreases if more than one call is necessary to get contact, but only up to a certain number (Figure 5). If the respondent is contacted more than four times without contact, the zero trip rate is higher. The rate reaches a maximum of twenty five percent above the level without any non-contact calls if six non-contact calls are necessary. The zero trip rate decreases slightly again if the number is even higher, perhaps because some people have been away from home for a longer period and have now returned to their normal activities at home. If more than four appointments are made, the estimated level of the zero trip rate is one third higher than without earlier appointments.

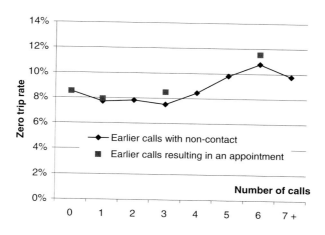

Figure 5: Estimated Zero Trip Rate in 1998-2001 Depending on the Number of Calls Resulting in Appointments or Non-Contact Before the Successful Call

Both variables show that it is problematic to continue attempting to make contact after many calls. The risk of a soft refusal interview increases. We agree with Stopher *et al.* (2006) that attempts to establish contact must stop after four appointments. An interview after many non-contacts is not a good solution either. Because persistence to call might result in contact with respondents who have been away on long distance travel, many non-contact calls are more acceptable.

We assess the overall effect on the zero trip rate from soft refusal to be about 0.3 percent following contact after many fruitless appointments and non-contact calls, and contact made on calling after the end of the month. This is little in relation to the large change in zero trip rate.

Cell Phones

Interviews conducted on a cell phone generate a significantly higher zero trip rate than those conducted on a landline telephone (fifteen percent higher). Because the cell phone calls in 2001 were few, this factor only explains 0.1 percent of the increase in the zero trip rate from 1998 to 2001. The impact of cell phone interviews might increase in the future.

Interviewer Effect

Some DNTS interviewers reported significantly different behaviour from the other in-terviewers in terms of both zero tripping and trip rate. The effect was handled by intro-ducing a dummy for each of these interviewers or from two of them together. The rest of the interviewers were divided into three groups: a large middle group, used as a ref-erence group, a group reporting a slightly higher zero trip rate, and a group reporting a slightly lower percentage of zero trippers. Each of these groups was included in the re-gression with a dummy for the group as a whole.

The interviewer effect was very significant. Experience affected performance, too. Some interviewers reported an increasing zero trip rate as they conducted more interviews. However, for most of the interviewers, experience did not affect the results after the initial learning period. In other words, it appears that some of the interviewers became more passive, not attempting to encourage respondents to remember their trips.

In the period from 1998 to 2001, the variables with the greatest influence on the mean zero trip rate are the dummies for the interviewers. The estimated zero trip rate in-creased from 10.5 percent to 15.7 percent for the reference respondent at the reference calling time due to differences in interviewer performance from 1998 to 2001. When the interviewer effect is corrected for calling time, the influence from the interviewer is reduced. The explanation for the changes from 1998 to 2001 is almost entirely related to the interviewers.

The number of interviews by interviewers who perform poorly increased over the years. In 1998, the reference group of interviewers and the two groups recording a slightly higher or lower zero trip rate accounted for eighty eight percent of all interviews. In 2001 these groups accounted for only sixty nine percent of the interviews.

The effect of the interviewer in isolation was a small increase in the zero trip rate from 1997 to 1998 but the combined effect of interviewer and time increases the difference. To conclude, changed interviewer performance and calling time of the interviewers ac-count for half of the change in zero trip rate from 1997 to 1998.

In February 2002, Statistics Denmark held an instruction meeting for all interviewers at which they were confronted with the declining trip rate and instructed to exercise more care in registering all trips. According to Figure 1, the trip rate increased from March to a level on a par with 1997-1998.

CONCLUSIONS AND RECOMMENDATIONS

With the background of the analyses in this chapter, it is possible to draw some more general conclusions and make some recommendations for other continuous travel surveys. The analysis of the possible explanations for the substantial increase in the zero trip rate shows that the main reason is related to interviewer performance. An increasing number of interviews were conducted by a few interviewers with much higher zero trip rates than the rest. The importance of keeping a continuous check on interview quality and results – percentage of zero tripping, trip rate and kilometres per trip – in relation both to a general trend and to interviewer performance cannot be emphasised strongly enough. This is a particular problem in continuous surveys that are vulnerable to changes in trends due to changed procedures or performance.

Changes in the distribution of calling time over the week will, of course, change the zero trip rate. More unexpected is that changes in calling time on the calling day can influence which age groups are contacted on the actual day resulting in a changed zero trip rate.

The analysis seems to support the soft refusal theory, but resulting only in a small change in zero trip rate. Many calls with non-contacts and many fruitless appointments is one of the reasons. Persistence to get extra interviews at the end of an interview period is another.

The analysis shows that a change from establishing contact exclusively through a landline telephone to including mobile telephones also changes the results. It is far more difficult to contact people with cell phone numbers because they are often switched off or scrapped. This is time consuming and expensive. Furthermore, cell phone contacts increase the resulting zero trip rate because the cell phone is good for short calls, but not suitable for calls requiring a great deal of thought. Problems with fewer listed telephone numbers and an increasing number of cell phones will increase in the future.

The DNTS is based on the principle of interviewing about the day prior to the day of contact. It differs in this respect from most other national surveys. The analyses show that the many examples of biased results and variations in the calling day can be related to this method. Interviews about a specific day and intensive calls the following day provide the best results. However, if contact is not successful on this day, the next call can be conducted on a later day but not the day after. It is often necessary to make an appointment for a new call. If this is the case, the day of the appointment has to be selected randomly and not on the first day the respondent is at home.

REFERENCES

Battellino, H. and J. Peachman (2003). The Joys and Tribulations of a Continuous Survey. In: *Transport Survey Quality and Innovation* (P.R. Stopher and P.M. Jones, eds), 49-68, Pergamon Press, Oxford.
Chapleau, R. (2003). Measuring the International Quality of a CATI Travel Household Survey. In: *Transport Survey Quality and Innovation* (P.R. Stopher and P.M. Jones, eds), 69-87, Pergamon Press, Oxford.

de Leeuw, E. and W. de Heer (2002). Trends in Household Survey Nonresponse: A Longitudinal and International Comparison. In: *Survey Nonresponse* (M. Groves, D.A. Dillman, J.L. Eltinge and R.J.A. Little, eds), 41-54, Wiley Series in Probability and Statistics, New York.

Groves, M., D.A. Dillman, J.L. Eltinge and R.J.A. Little (2002). *Survey Nonresponse,* Wiley Series in Probability and Statistics, New York.

Lynn, P., P. Clarke, J. Martin and P. Sturgis (2002). The Effects of Extended Interviewer Efforts on Nonresponse Bias. In: *Survey Nonresponse* (M. Groves, D.A. Dillman, J.L. Eltinge and R.J.A. Little, eds), 135-147, Wiley Series in Probability and Statistics, New York.

Madre, J.-L., K.W. Axhausen and W. Brög (2004). Immobility in travel diary surveys: an overview. Arbeitsberichte Verkehr- und Raumplanung, 207, Institut für Verkehrsplanung und Transportsysteme (IVT), ETH Zürich, Zürich.

Pahkinen, E. and V. Pastinen (2001), Monitoring the Quality of Passenger Travel Surveys of Long Duration, paper presented at the Conference on Survey Quality and Innovations, South Africa, August.

Road Directorate (2003): www.vd.dk or webapp.vd.dk/interstat/frontpage.asp

Stopher, P. R., C.G. Wilmot, C.C. Stecher and R. Alsnih (2006). Household Travel Surveys: Proposed Standards and Guidelines. In: *Travel Survey Methods – Quality and Future Directions* (P.R. Stopher and C.C. Stecher, eds), 19-74, Elsevier Press, Oxford.

Travel Survey Methods: Quality and Future Directions
Peter Stopher and Cheryl Stecher (Editors)

17

QUALITY ASSESSMENT

Barbara Noble, Department for Transport, London, UK
and
Simon Holroyd, National Centre for Social Research, London, UK

WORKSHOP AIMS

Assessing the quality of data is important because doing so enables users to assign credibility to data. However, it is not clear how to define quality nor how to measure it. Hence this workshop[1] set out to:

- Develop a definition of data quality;
- Suggest means by which data quality can be measured; and
- Suggest how the results of such assessments should be interpreted in terms of what they reveal about data quality.

In doing so the workshop bore in mind the diversity of travel survey methods used throughout the world and how this affects the assessment of data quality and whether universal measures of data quality are achievable or not. The workshop also considered whether the International Standards Organisation (ISO) can usefully play a role in measuring, and ultimately in establishing and maintaining, travel survey data quality. In addition, the workshop considered detailed suggestions made in Stopher *et al.* (2006).

---

[1] Members of the workshop were: Patrick Bonnel (France), Peter Bonsall (UK), Linda Christensen (Denmark), Camilo Correal (Mexico), Epaminondas Duarte, Jr. (Brazil), Antoine Haroun (Canada), Simon Holroyd (UK), Susan Liss (US), Barbara Noble (UK), and Jens Rumenapp (Germany).

DEFINITION OF DATA QUALITY

The discussion was focused around the resource paper (Bonsall, 2006). The workshop acknowledged that there is no agreement within the international transport profession as to what constitutes a good travel survey. In his paper, Bonsall (2006) argues that this is a serious problem because it compromises the reliability, usefulness, cost-effectiveness, comparability, clarity, and completeness of travel surveys. He discusses at length the reasons why consensus has not been reached and identifies factors that have driven common definitions and standards in other parts of the survey industry.

Fitness for Purpose

Rather than re-enter this discussion and produce a definition which would be as likely to be challenged as previous definitions have been, the workshop took the pragmatic step of defining data quality as 'fitness for purpose' by which the workshop meant that data should possess the characteristics required by its user for the purpose to which the user intends to put it. When talking of 'users', the workshop had in mind such people as clients, contractors, respondents, colleagues and editors.

Documentation

Of course, the author of a research paper cannot know in advance all the uses to which others will want to put their data. The workshop's response to this was to encourage authors of all research papers to provide extensive documentation of their research methodology, so that users can scrutinise it and make their own decision about whether or not the findings of the study fulfil the criteria demanded by the use to which they want to put the data.

MEASURING DATA QUALITY

The workshop agreed that, when determining the fitness for purpose of a study and its findings, users should consider the following four issues (prioritised, starting with the most important):

1. Validation and comparison against relevant independent data;
2. Representativeness of the sample;
3. Procedural issues; and
4. Headline indicators.

Validation and Comparison Against Other Relevant Data

Although novel research findings are exciting, a finding which is out of line with those of previous studies is more likely to be the product of the research design than a radical change in travel behaviour.

Example of Validation by Considering Trends

For example, Christensen (2006) examined an unexpected drop in 1998 in the number of transport kilometres and trips per person reported by the Danish National Transport Survey. After a considerable amount of analysis, Christensen concluded that the main reason for the drop was not a change in travel behaviour, but a change in the survey methodology that collected information about this behaviour.

Example of Validation by Considering Different Sources

Madre also presented a paper (Armoogum *et al.*, 2004) comparing time spent travelling from the French and Belgian National Travel Surveys with Time Use surveys for these countries (see Appendix for Abstract). In particular, this paper notes that the Time Use surveys recorded lower proportions of people (compared with the travel diary surveys) reporting that they did not make any trips on the survey days. This 'immobility' rate may be seen in some cases as a 'soft refusal', because travel survey respondents realise that the survey burden is much reduced if they do not report any trips.

Survey Parameters for Use as Indicators of Quality

Indicators that the workshop recommended should be compared with data from other surveys were:

- Trip rate (trips per person per day);
- Immobility rate (the percentage of respondents who did not make a trip);
- Trends in data from the same survey;
- Time budget (the time spent travelling per day); and
- Trip kilometres (the total distance travelled).

Of course, not all data, which bear comparison with those collected from other sources, are reliable but the workshop agreed that data which are out of line with those of other surveys should be questioned.

Representativeness of the Sample

Depending on the purpose to which the user would like to put the findings of a given travel survey, the workshop agreed that the representativeness of the sample over time and space should be considered. By 'representativeness over time' the group meant that the period about which data are collected should be similar to the period of time in which the user is interested. For example, a user interested in general travel behaviour would want data from all seven days of the week, not just weekends, because travel behaviour at weekends is markedly different to that during the week. Such a user might also want to ensure the data were collected from all months of the year because some months, such as those which include the holiday season, involve travel behaviour which is untypical of that displayed during the rest of the year.

By 'representativeness over space' the group meant that all geographical areas where the travel behaviour of interest might be displayed should be sampled in a fashion that maps directly onto the geographical area in which the user is most interested. Hence, the user interested in rural travel patterns in northern France would want to know that the data were collected from a rural area with similar characteristics to those present in the north of France. It should be straightforward for survey documentation to include sufficient detail on timing, geography, and sample design to enable users to check that the survey is fit to be used for their particular purpose.

Representing the Population from which the Sample is Drawn

The workshop also agreed that the sample should be representative in terms of the characteristics of the people from whom data are collected. This means that the user should be able to find out whether the people from whom data were collected are similar to those in whom the user is interested in terms of characteristics such as their:

- Demography;
- Car ownership;
- Incomes;
- Education levels; and
- Any other characteristics relevant to the user's objectives.

These characteristics need to be checked against reliable sources, such as a population census, or statistics derived from population registers or major population surveys. Again, such comparisons should be included in the survey documentation.

Procedural Issues

As Christensen's paper illustrated, changes in survey procedures can have a major impact on the nature of the survey findings. In the case of the DNTS, Christensen (2006) attributes much of an observed drop in the number of transport kilometres and trips per person to a move away from a one-week data collection period to a period spread across a whole month. Such details and changes must be well documented. Piloting major change is essential and, in some cases, parallel running of two methodologies may be needed to understand changes in survey results.

The workshop identified a variety of survey procedures which should be documented fully for users to be able to judge the quality, or fitness for purpose of the survey. These included the potential effects of :

- The proportion of proxy interviews that are allowed;
- The extent of the burden the survey places on respondents (such as the time taken per interview);
- If pretest and pilot studies were conducted;
- Training and motivating interviewers by the research organisation; and
- How respondents' motivation to participate has been addressed, for example through the use of incentive payments or through interviewers' approaches to convincing them to take part.

Data Handling

The workshop was also keen that researchers should make it clear to users how they went about cleaning and preparing the data collected. This would include descriptions of how the data were coded and how missing values were imputed. Ideally, imputed data should be flagged. It would also include any weighting procedures that were applied and the basis on which these weighting procedures were defined.

Headline Indicators

The criteria described above were identified by the workshop because they can give a direct indication of whether a survey's findings can be applied to a particular situation a user may have in mind. However, the group also identified a list of indicators that reveal something of the context within which the survey was conducted and thereby indicate the extent to which one can have confidence in its findings.

The first of these was the response rate for the survey. This is one of the most commonly-examined indicators of survey quality, but the workshop argued that, when viewed in isolation, it does not reveal enough to make judgements about fitness for purpose possible. The group agreed that more important than the overall response rate are:

- The extent to which the achieved sample is representative of the population in which the user is interested (see the section on Data Representativeness, above); and
- Whether data have been collected from a sufficiently large number of people to bring the standard error down to a level that is acceptable for the user's objectives.

This does not mean that response rate is unimportant, simply that it should be viewed in the context of the actual data collected. So that a user can establish the implications of a reported response rate, the researcher needs to give details of how the response rate has been defined. For example, the researcher should state whether or not partial datasets have been allowed and, if so, how complete a dataset had to be, to be included. In addition to the response rate definition, the workshop agreed that it would be valuable for researchers to show a breakdown of how the response rate was calculated. This would include such details as the total number of cases falling under each of the following headings:

- Co-operating fully;
- Co-operating partially;
- Non-contact;
- Other unproductive;
- Unknown eligibility; and
- Ineligible/deadwood.

Stopher *et al.* (2006) recommend using the American Association of Public Opinion Research (AAPOR) formula for the calculation of response rates, and gives a detailed description. This is likely to be suitable in many cases, but bearing in mind the need to consider international diversity, commissioners of travel surveys should also consider using an existing standardised formula used in their own country for social surveys. Of course, the user would also need to know the sample size and the sampling fraction, i.e., the ratio of the sample to the population.

Other information considered by the workshop for inclusion in survey documentation included the client or sponsor of the research; the organisation which conducted it; and the amount of money spent on the research. These were considered useful pieces of information because of what they reveal about how the survey might have been conducted.

Finally, other essential information includes:

- A copy of the questionnaire;
- The coding manual; and
- A list of definitions.

HOW SHOULD QUALITY BE IMPROVED IN PRACTICE?

Workshop participants agreed on the need to spread the word, particularly to encourage excellent documentation. Each of clients, contractors and interviewers need education and support in order to achieve high quality travel surveys. One early win might be to convince journal editors that good documentation of the details of surveys reported should be an essential requirement for the acceptance of work for publication. Workshop and conference participants should make every effort to encourage good practice in their own surveys, and more widely in their own countries, by example, by education of students, and by education of the wider transport research community through articles, seminars, and conferences.

REFERENCES

Armoogum, J., K.W. Axhausen, J.-P. Hubert and J.-L. Madre (2004). Immobility and Mobility Seen Through Trip Based versus Time Use Surveys, paper presented to the 7th International Conference on Travel Survey Methods, Costa Rica, August.
Bonsall, P. (2006). Quality Assessment. In: *Travel Survey Methods – Quality and Future Directions* (P.R. Stopher and C.C. Stecher, eds), 279-302, Elsevier Press, Oxford.
Christensen, L. (2006). Possible Explanations for an Increasing Share of No-Trip Respondents. In: *Travel Survey Methods – Quality and Future Directions* (P.R. Stopher and C.C. Stecher, eds), 303-316, Elsevier Press, Oxford.
Stopher, P.R., C.G. Wilmot, C.C. Stecher, and R. Alsnih. (2006). Household Travel Surveys: Proposed Standards and Guidelines. In *Travel Survey Methods – Quality and Future Directions* (P.R. Stopher and C.C. Stecher, eds), 19-74, Elsevier Press, Oxford.

APPENDIX 1 – ABSTRACT OF OFFERED PAPER

Immobility and Mobility Seen Through Trip Based versus Time Use Surveys

Jimmy Armoogum and Jean-Loup Madre, Department of Economics and Sociology of Transports (DEST), National Institute of Research on Transports and Safety (INRETS), France; Kay W. Axhausen, Institute for Transport Planning and Systems (IVT), Swiss Federal Institute of Technology (ETH) Zurich, Switzerland; Jean-Paul Hubert, Facultés Universitaires Notre Dame de la Paix Namur, Belgium

Mobility surveys are not the only data source giving insights on trip making, especially on immobility for which an overestimation can sometimes be suspected because of 'soft refusals'. Different approaches can be adopted to describe mobility:

- In trip based surveys, information on movements is collected (time and location of departure and arrival, purpose, mode, etc.) with sometimes a question on 'reasons for staying at home' if no trip is recorded on the surveyed day; and
- In time use surveys (TUS), activities (not only trip purposes) are registered throughout the day on a precoded grid with ten-minute time brackets.

Transport surveys are very costly and therefore they are few and far between nowadays. For instance, in France, the last NPTS was in 1993-94 and the next one is planned to be in 2007, which means a gap of 14 years. At the end of the 1990s, EUROSTAT had conducted an harmonised time use survey in all European Countries. One can ask how are these two types of surveys comparable and is it possible to gather trips in time use surveys?

These survey sources give different points of view on the same phenomena: trip making. The main issues to be discussed concern both data quality and data analysis. The study is based on national surveys conducted in Belgium and in France.

18

HANDLING INDIVIDUAL SPECIFIC AVAILABILITY OF ALTERNATIVES IN STATED CHOICE EXPERIMENTS

John M. Rose and David A. Hensher, The University of Sydney, Australia

INTRODUCTION

The growing evidence on the ability of stated choice (SC) experiments to represent decisions made in real markets (Burke *et al.*, 1992; Carson *et al.*, 1994) has made them a popular data paradigm in the elicitation of behavioural responses of individuals, households, and organisations over diverse choice situations and contexts. SC experiments allow for the parameterisation of the marginal utilities of attributes of alternatives in a choice experiment (Louviere and Hensher, 1983; Louviere and Woodworth, 1983) as well as an estimation of the impact on the marginal utilities, given the presence and absence of competing alternatives (Anderson and Wiley, 1992; Batsell and Louviere, 1991; Lazari and Anderson, 1994). Yet despite the realism inherent in the methodology, SC experiments produce asymptotically efficient parameter estimates only through the pooling of choice observations obtained over multiple respondents (Huber and Zwerina, 1996), unless the number of person-specific observations is very large. A typical SC experiment might involve respondents being asked to undertake a number of choice tasks involving the choice from amongst a number of labelled or unlabelled alternatives defined on a number of attribute dimensions, each in turn described by pre-specified levels drawn from some underlying experimental design. The number of choice tasks undertaken will be up to the total number of choice sets drawn from the experimental design. Consequently, an archetypal SC experiment might require choice data collected from 200 respondents, each of whom were observed to have made eight choices each, thus producing a total of 1,600 choice observations.

Realism in SC experiments arises from the fact that respondents are asked to undertake similar actions to those they would in real markets (i.e., respondents are asked to make 'choices' between a finite, but universal, set of available alternatives, just as in real markets). However, for any individual respondent, realism may be lost if the alternatives, attributes, and/or attribute levels used to describe the alternatives do not realistically portray that respondent's experiences or, in terms of 'new' or 'innovative' alternatives, are deemed not to be credible. With regard to the attributes and attribute levels used within a SC experiment, significant prior preparation on behalf of the analyst may reduce the possible inclusion of irrelevant or improbable product descriptors within the choice sets shown to respondents (Hensher *et al.*, 2005). In addition, for quantitative variables, pivoting the attribute levels of the SC task from a respondent's current or recent experience is likely to produce attribute levels within the experiment that are consistent with those experiences and, hence, produce a more credible or realistic survey task for the respondent (Hensher and Greene, 2003). The selection of what alternatives to include within an SC experiment, however, is not so straightforward.

A significant proportion of products and services offered in real markets exhibit uneven degrees of distribution coverage (Lazari and Anderson, 1994). Such unevenness in availability may be either geographical, temporal or both. For example, train services may not be available to certain suburbs due to a lack of existing infrastructure or a train strike on a specific day might temporarily remove the train alternative from an individual's choice set. Such constraints on availability are likely to be population wide (or at least impact upon a large proportion of the population) and, as such, have an even impact over the entire study population. In SC experiments, such impacts may easily be handled through the removal of the affected alternatives from choice sets shown to respondents (removal may be from all choice sets within the experiment or subsets of choice sets to test availability effects in the presence or absence of an alternative). Other factors, however, may result in the non-availability of an alternative at the individual level. For example, for a specific journey, an individual may not have access to a car because a partner is using the vehicle, or alternatively, the household may not be able to afford a car in the first place.

The problem of non-availability of alternatives at the individual level poses problems in the construction of SC studies due to the possibility that the alternatives available across the population will not be evenly distributed. The presence or absence of an alternative in the choice sets offered to an individual should reflect the specific context or situation faced, or likely to be faced, by that individual, in order to maximise the realism of the experiment for that individual. Thus, depending on the specific circumstance of the study, what may be required is the tailoring of SC experiments and experimental designs to reflect the choice context that is likely to be faced by each individual sampled respondent. This, however, challenges current design practice with regard to labelled SC experiments, in which it is common to construct a single experimental design and apply this single design to all sampled respondents, irrespective of the true choice situation faced by each individual respondent.

Several researchers have addressed the issue of the presence or absence of alternatives in SC designs. Batsell and Polking (1985) and Raghovarao and Wiley (1986) each propose models to estimate availability effects of alternatives. Anderson and Wiley (1992) provide theory for the generation of SC experiments for the estimation of availability effects for models inclusive of brand effect only and provide an extensive catalogue of SC experiments capable of the estimation of such effects. Anderson *et al.* (1992) studied availability effects by randomly assigning respondents to available modes in a mode choice task and concluded that the inclusion of availability effects may result in considerable improvement in the predictive ability of SC experiments. Lazari and Anderson (1994) develop the theory further by allowing for the generation of experimental designs capable of estimating both availability and attribute cross effects and also provide a generous catalogue of designs. The methods proposed by the above authors have tended to address two types of availability problems; (i) all alternatives vary in their availability and (ii) some alternatives vary whilst others are fixed in presence across all choice sets. However, each approach addresses population wide problems of availability. They do not address issues of availability at the individual respondent level. That is, the presence or absence of an alternative within a choice set is predetermined by the underlying experimental design rather than being driven by the choice situation faced by each specific individual respondent. Thus, research efforts to date have been limited to examining the impact non-availability of an alternative has upon choice behaviour of populations (see Louviere *et al.*, 2000), rather than reflecting individual or household level constraints that may exist disproportionately across the population.

In this chapter, we construct SC experiments in which the alternatives present within the choice sets are respondent specific, and hence, reflect individual differences in the choice contexts that are likely to exist within real markets. We discuss the construction of respondent specific availability designs for orthogonal fractional factorial designs and go on to demonstrate through the use of an empirical example, how SC experiments, generated using the principles discussed in the theoretical section of the chapter, may be employed in practice.

The chapter is organised as follows. In the next section, we discuss the construction of individual specific availability designs using orthogonal fractional factorial experimental designs. The third section provides an empirical example of the strategies outlined in the second section. The fourth section concludes with a discussion of the material covered within the chapter.

HANDLING INDIVIDUAL SPECIFIC AVAILABILITY OF ALTERNATIVES

Consider a simple experiment involving three alternatives, each described by two attribute dimensions each of four levels. Assuming the estimation of alternative specific linear main effects only, the smallest SC experiment will require seven degrees of freedom (the theoretical minimum number of choice sets is equal to the number of attribute related parameters to be estimated from the design, plus one. In this case, six degrees of freedom are required for each of the six attributes (A-F), plus an additional degree of freedom; see, for example, Hensher *et al.*, 2005 or Rose and Bliemer, 2004). The smallest balanced orthogonal fractional factorial main effects only design has eight choice sets. An orthogonal two level blocking column is also generated, such that each respondent will view only four of the eight choice sets. An example design is shown in Table 1. The design in Table 1 utilises what are known as orthogonal codes, where each value shown represents a different level of the attributes of the design (represented as columns in the table). The values used in the design are such that the sum total of all the levels shown for each attribute is zero (e.g., -3 -1 +1 +3 = 0). This coding structure is used, because it provides certain properties that allow for the examination of interaction effects when considering orthogonal designs (see Hensher *et al.*, 2005). The correlation matrix for this design is shown in Table 2

Table 1: $4^{(3 \times 2)}$ Fractional Factorial Design with Eight Runs

Choice set	Alternative 1		Alternative 2		Alternative 3		Block
	A	B	C	D	E	F	
1	1 [24]	-1	1	-3	3	-3	-1
2	3	-3	-1	1	-3	1	-1
3	-1	3	3	-1	-1	3	-1
4	-3	1	-3	3	1	-1	-1
5	3	1	1	3	3	1	1
6	-1	-1	-3	-3	1	3	1
7	-3	-3	3	1	-1	-1	1
8	1	3	-1	-1	-3	-3	1

Table 2: Correlation Matrix for the Design Shown in Table 1

		Alternative 1		Alternative 2		Alternative 3		Block
		A	B	C	D	E	F	
Alternative 1	A	1.0						
	B	0.0	1.0					
Alternative 2	C	0.0	0.0	1.0				
	D	0.0	0.0	0.0	1.0			
Alternative 3	E	0.0	0.0	0.0	0.0	1.0		
	F	0.0	0.0	0.0	0.0	0.0	1.0	
Block		0.0	0.0	0.0	0.0	0.0	0.0	1.0

---

[24] The values used in Table 1 (i.e., -3, -1, 1, 3) are used only to be consistent with those used within the experimental design literature. As far as the authors are aware, these values are used solely for historical, and not mathematical reasons (see Hensher *et al.*, 2005 or Louviere, 1988).

The problem of respondent specific availability of an alternative only occurs if a blocking column is used to assign respondents to subsets of treatment combinations of an experimental design. The removal of columns of an orthogonal design will not induce correlations; the removal of rows will. Hence, removal of an alternative, analogous to removing columns of a design, will not impact upon the orthogonality of the design, if the all treatment combinations from the full design are utilised, even with the pooling of data obtained from multiple respondents. Correlations will be induced, however, if there exist unequal replications of treatment combinations within the data, or alternatively, if rows of a design are not equally represented, even if the treatment combinations themselves are. To demonstrate, consider a situation in which a respondent, assigned to the first block of the design shown in Table 1, is faced with a choice situation where alternative three is not considered a feasible alternative, and hence, is removed from all choice sets shown to that respondent. For the second respondent, assigned to block two, all alternatives including the third alternative represent realistic options. This situation is represented in Table 3. The missing cells of the design result in a loss of orthogonality, as demonstrated in the correlation matrix shown in Table 4.

Table 3: $4^{(3 \times 2)}$ Fractional Factorial Design with Eight Runs and Missing Cells

Choice set	Alternative 1		Alternative 2		Alternative 3		Block
	A	*B*	*C*	*D*	*E*	*F*	
1	1	-1	1	-3			-1
2	3	-3	-1	1			-1
3	-1	3	3	-1			-1
4	-3	1	-3	3			-1
5	3	1	1	3	3	1	1
6	-1	-1	-3	-3	1	3	1
7	-3	-3	3	1	-1	-1	1
8	1	3	-1	-1	-3	-3	1

Table 4: Correlation Matrix for the Design Shown in Table 3

		Alternative 1		Alternative 2		Alternative 3		Block
		A	*B*	*C*	*D*	*E*	*F*	
Alternative 1	A	1.0						
	B	0.0	1.0					
Alternative 2	C	0.0	0.0	1.0				
	D	0.0	0.0	0.0	1.0			
Alternative 3	E	0.4	-0.2	0.0	0.4	1.0		
	F	0.0	-0.4	-0.4	-0.2	0.8	1.0	
Block		0.0	0.0	0.0	0.0			1.0

The removal of rows from segments of an orthogonal experimental design will generally result in a loss of orthogonality for that design. The level of loss of orthogonality will depend upon the design itself as well as which row segments are removed. Independent of the level of loss, however, given that the key criterion in the design of orthogonal fractional factorial experimental designs is orthogonality, any loss of orthogonality may be a source of concern for SC analysts (see Watson *et al.*, 2000 for a discussion on the efficiency properties of orthogonal designs on SC experiments; alternatively, see Bliemer and Rose (2005) for an argument as to why such concerns are perhaps unwarranted).

Assuming the desire to maintain both orthogonality in SC data sets and realism in the choice task at the individual level, we propose the generation of sub-designs, drawn from a single master design, each of which provide for the presence of only those alternatives within the choice sets shown, as deemed feasible by individual sampled respondents. For example, let us assume that the design shown in Table 1 represents our master design. Three sub-designs are possible. These are shown as Tables 5 through 7 and include all possible scenarios (along with the design shown in Table 1) that individual respondents might face in terms of the availability of alternatives. That is, a respondent might have available to them only (i) alternatives one and two, (ii) alternatives one and three, or (iii) alternatives two and three. The master design, which includes all three alternatives (Table 1), represents the case where a respondent could feasibly choose from all three possible alternatives.

Table 5: Sub-Design for Alternatives 1 and 2 only

Choice set	Alternative 1		Alternative 2		Block
	A	B	C	D	
1	1	-1	1	-3	-1
2	3	-3	-1	1	-1
3	-1	3	3	-1	-1
4	-3	1	-3	3	-1
5	3	1	1	3	1
6	-1	-1	-3	-3	1
7	-3	-3	3	1	1
8	1	3	-1	-1	1

Table 6: Sub-Design for Alternatives 1 and 3 only

Choice set	Alternative 1		Alternative 3		Block
	A	B	E	F	
1	1	-1	3	-3	-1
2	3	-3	-3	1	-1
3	-1	3	-1	3	-1
4	-3	1	1	-1	-1
5	3	1	3	1	1
6	-1	-1	1	3	1
7	-3	-3	-1	-1	1
8	1	3	-3	-3	1

Table 7: Sub-Designs for Alternatives 2 and 3 only

Choice set	Alternative 2		Alternative 3		Block
	C	D	E	F	
1	1	-3	3	-3	-1
2	-1	1	-3	1	-1
3	3	-1	-1	3	-1
4	-3	3	1	-1	-1
5	1	3	3	1	1
6	-3	-3	1	3	1
7	3	1	-1	-1	1
8	-1	-1	-3	-3	1

Once the master and sub-designs have been generated, the feasible set of alternatives are determined for each respondent and, once known, respondents are allocated to blocks from the appropriate design. For paper and pencil surveys, lead-in-questions may be employed to determine which alternatives to include in the choice task and show cards used to provide the response stimulus. For CAPI and web based surveys, similar questions may be asked before the choice task takes place. However, smart programming may be used to assign respondents to blocks of the appropriate design in a manner that not only ensures realism in the choice task, but also equal replication of blocks across the entire data set.

To demonstrate, consider an SC study involving only four respondents. Questions prior to the presentation of the SC task reveal that respondents one and two consider all three possible alternatives to be feasible alternatives, whilst respondents three and four do not consider alternative three to be a viable alternative in the choice context suggested within the experiment. Using the master design shown in Table 1 and the sub-designs shown in Tables 5 through 7, respondents one and two are assigned to the two blocks of the master design and respondents three and four, to the two blocks of the third sub-design (Table 7). The pooled data for the designs would look as shown in Table 8 below. The correlation matrix for the pooled design data is given in Table 9.

The assignment of respondents to designs showing only realistic alternatives at the respondent level provides for more realistic SC experiments. In this section, we have demonstrated how those undertaking SC studies may maintain realism in the choice tasks undertaken by individual sampled respondents, whilst preserving orthogonality if the underlying experimental design generated is an orthogonal fractional factorial design. In the next section of the chapter, we demonstrate an empirical example using design principles as outlined above.

Table 8: Pooling Designs with Different Availability Coverage

Choice set	Respondent	Alternative 1		Alternative 2		Alternative 3		Block
		A	B	C	D	E	F	
1	1	1	-1	1	-3	3	-3	-1
2	1	3	-3	-1	1	-3	1	-1
3	1	-1	3	3	-1	-1	3	-1
4	1	-3	1	-3	3	1	-1	-1
5	2	3	1	1	3	3	1	1
6	2	-1	-1	-3	-3	1	3	1
7	2	-3	-3	3	1	-1	-1	1
8	2	1	3	-1	-1	-3	-3	1
1	3	1	-1	1	-3			-1
2	3	3	-3	-1	1			-1
3	3	-1	3	3	-1			-1
4	3	-3	1	-3	3			-1
5	4	3	1	1	3			1
6	4	-1	-1	-3	-3			1
7	4	-3	-3	3	1			1
8	4	1	3	-1	-1			1

Table 9: Correlation Matrix for the Pooled Design Shown in Table 6

		Alternative 1		Alternative 2		Alternative 3		Block
		A	B	C	D	E	F	
Alternative 1	A	1.0						
	B	0.0	1.0					
Alternative 2	C	0.0	0.0	1.0				
	D	0.0	0.0	0.0	1.0			
Alternative 3	E	0.0	0.0	0.0	0.0	1.0		
	F	0.0	0.0	0.0	0.0	0.0	1.0	
Block		0.0	0.0	0.0	0.0	0.0	0.0	1.0

AN EMPIRICAL EXAMPLE

Experimental Set-up and Data Collection

In 2003, the Institute of Transport Studies (ITS) (University of Sydney), on behalf of the New South Wales (NSW) state government, undertook a patronage demand study as part of an evaluation of possible investment options in public transport infrastructure in the north-west sector of metropolitan Sydney[25]. The principal aim of the study was to

---

[25] The north-west sector is approximately twenty five kilometres from the Sydney central business district (CBD). It is the fastest growing sector of Sydney in terms of residential population and traffic build up. It is also one of the

establish the preferences of residents within the study area for private and public transport modes for commuting and non-commuting trip purposes. Once known, the study called for the preferences to be used to forecast patronage levels for various currently non-existing transport modes, specifically possible new heavy rail, light rail or busway modes. Independent of the 'new' mode type, the proposed infrastructure is expected to be built along the same corridor (Figure 1).

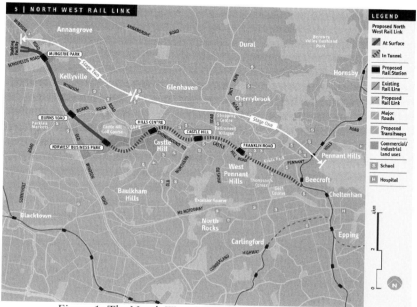

Figure 1: The North-West Sector and Proposed New Rail Link

To capture information on the preferences of residents, a SC experiment was generated and administered using CAPI technology. Sampled residents were invited to review a number of alternative main and access modes (both consisting of public and private transport options) in terms of levels of service and costs within the context of a recent trip and to choose the main mode and access mode that they would use if faced with the same trip circumstance in the future. Each sampled respondent completed ten choice tasks under alternative scenarios of attribute levels, and in each instance, chose the preferred main and access modes. The experiment was complicated by the fact that alternatives available to any individual respondent undertaking a hypothetical trip depended not only on the alternatives that the respondent had available at the time of the 'reference' trip, but also upon the destination of the trip. If the trip undertaken was intraregional, then the existing busway (M2) and heavy rail modes could not be considered viable alternatives, because neither mode travels within the bounds of the study

---

wealthiest areas with high car ownership and usage and a very poor public transport service with the exception of a busway system along the M2 toll road into the CBD of Sydney.

area. If, on the other hand, the reference trip was interregional (e.g., to the CBD), then respondents could feasibly travel to the nearest busway or heavy rail train station (outside of the origin region) and continue their trip using these modes. Further, not all respondents have access to a private vehicle for the reference trip, either due to a lack of ownership or to the vehicle being unavailable at the time when the trip was made. Given that the objective of the study was to derive an estimate of the patronage demand, the lack of availability of privately owned vehicles (either through random circumstance or non ownership) should be accounted for in the SC experiment. Failure to account for the non-availability of the private vehicle alternative would likely result in biased patronage demand forecasts, both in terms of the main mode chosen and the mode chosen to access the main mode.

The master experimental design for the mode SC study required a total of forty seven attributes (forty six in four levels and one in six levels for the blocks) and had sixty runs; that is, there are six blocks of ten choice sets each. The design was constructed using a procedure that simultaneously optimised the minimisation of the D-error of the design as well as the correlations (for a discussion of D-error, see for example, Huber and Zwerina, 1996). The final design had correlations no greater than ± 0.06. The design generated allowed for the estimation of all main mode and access mode alternative specific main effects. Within each block, the order of the choice sets has been randomised to control for order effect biases. The experiment consisted of different task configurations designed to reflect the alternatives realistically available to a respondent, given the reference trip circumstance reported by the respondent earlier in the CAPI interview: The configurations consisted of (i) with/without car, (ii) inter/intra regional trips, (iii) new light rail versus new heavy rail, new light rail versus new busway and new heavy rail versus new busway. These configurations were included to provide more realism in the scenarios shown to individual respondents. To maintain efficiency and minimise correlations within the data set, a maximum number of complete designs have to be filled within each configuration. Using the CAPI program, if the first respondent has a car available for an intra-regional trip with new light rail and heavy rail alternatives present, she is assigned to block one for that configuration. If the second respondent is in the exact same configuration, she is assigned to the second block otherwise she is assigned to block one of the appropriate design configuration. Once a configuration has all blocks completed, the process starts at block one again.

The trip attributes associated with each mode are summarised in Table 10. These were identified from extensive reviews of the literature and through input from a technical advisory committee chaired by the NSW Ministry of Transport.[26]

For currently existing modes, the attribute levels were pivoted off the attribute levels captured from respondents for the reference trip (Figure 2). Respondents were asked to complete information regarding the reference trip, not only for the mode used for the

---

[26] A peer reviewer, Dr Neil Douglas was also engaged by the Ministry of Transport to provide advice on the study.

reference trip, but also for the other modes they had available for that trip. Whilst asking respondents to provide information for non-chosen alternatives may potentially provide widely incorrect attribute levels, choices made by individuals are made based on their perceptions of the attribute levels of the available alternatives and not the reality of the attribute levels of those same alternatives. As such, it was felt that asking respondents what they thought the levels were for the non-chosen alternatives was preferable to imposing those levels on the experiment, based on some heuristic given knowledge of the attribute levels for the actual chosen alternative.

Table 10: Trip Attributes in the Stated Choice Design

For Existing Public Transport Modes		For New Public Transport Modes		For the Existing Car Mode
Fare (one-way)		Fare (one-way)		Running Cost
In-vehicle travel time		In-vehicle travel time		In-vehicle Travel time
Waiting time		Waiting time		Toll Cost (One way)
Access Mode:	Walk time	Transfer waiting time		Daily Parking Cost
	Car time	Access Mode:	Walk time	Egress time
	Bus time		Car time	
	Bus fare		Bus time	
Egress time			Bus Fare	
		Egress time		

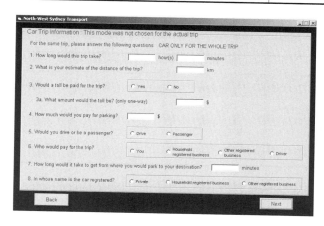

Figure 2: Example Screen to Establish Current Car Mode Trip Profile

The design attributes used in the SC experiment, each had four levels. These were chosen as the following variations around the 'reference' trip base levels obtained from the respondent prior to undertaking the choice task: -25 percent, 0 percent, +25 percent, +50 percent. The times and costs associated with currently non-existent public transport modes were established from other sources. The levels shown in Table 11 were provided by the Ministry of Transport as their best estimates of the *most likely* fare and service levels. To establish the likely access location to the new modes, respondents were also asked to view the map (Figure 1) and choose a particular station[27] (shown in Figure 3), which is used in the software to derive the access and line-haul travel times and fares. Example SC screens are shown in Figures 4 (interregional trip with car) and 5 (intraregional trip with car).

Figure 3: Example Screen to Establish New Public Mode Station and Access Profile

Table 11: Base Times and Costs for New Public Transport Modes

	Dollars \$	Busway (mins)	Heavy rail (mins)	Light Rail (mins)
Mungerie Park	1.8	33	22	33
Burns Road	1	27	18	27
Norwest Business Park	1	22.5	15	22.5
Hills Centre	1	18	12	18
Castle Hill	0.2	13.5	9	13.5
Franklin Road Beecroft	0.2	7.5	5	7.5

A total of 453 respondents (223 commuters and 230 non-commuters) completed the survey. Respondents were selected according to a stratified random sampling frame within a pre-defined study area. The catchment area for the study was divided into geographical blocks. These blocks were randomly selected, after which streets were randomly sampled, and after which random households were selected. Within each household selected, individuals were screened for eligibility. This was all subject to a quota of

[27] The map was shown so that respondents would be able to locate the proposed stations in relation to their residential address. This is essential so that we can gather the least unreliable measure of access times to the stations/bus stops. The attribute levels of the access times (the *getting to main mode* attributes) will be 'switched or pivoted off' these reported levels. Without these, the attribute levels for the access modes cannot be determined and that part of the model cannot be estimated.

sixty two to sixty four individuals per existing mode, given the usual budget constraints imposed on project-based studies.

All surveys were conducted at a residential address on weekends and weekdays. A screener questionnaire was used to ensure that respondents were at least eighteen years of age (as a result of ethical considerations) and lived at the household. Respondents also were the person present in the household who had had the most recent birthday. The requirements for an in-scope trip were that the trip was made in the previous week and that the trip was at least fifteen minutes in length (to ensure that respondents could at least meaningfully consider taking a public transport alternative). Trips also had to be such that they were made roughly along the proposed north-west corridor; and car trips were excluded where the car was used as part of travel during work hours. Interviewers made two callbacks if the eligible respondent was not at home or unavailable at the time to be interviewed.

Once an eligible respondent was located, the respondent then chose a trip, indicating to where the trip was made and what the purpose was. The interviewer checked that the trip was roughly east-west in line with the proposed corridor. A preliminary question determined whether the car alternative would appear as part of the stated choice experiment as a *main* mode. Subsequent CAPI screens gathered information as to whether the respondent has a car available as an *access* mode. The average survey response time was thirty four minutes, including preliminary screening questions and respondents were not offered any incentive to participate.

Table 12 shows the coding employed in data entry for the socio-demographic questions. The number of hours worked, household size, and number of children present within the household were treated as continuous variables. All remaining variables were collected as categorical variables.

Table 12: Coding used for Socio-demographic Variables

Variable	Coding
Age	Coded in middle of range - 24, 30, 40, 50, 60, 70
Employment	1=Full time 2=Part time(<30hrs) 3=Casual 4=Not at all in last 6mths
Hours worked per week	As reported
Annual Personal Income	Coded in natural units (using top of range): 0, 10, 15, 20, 30, 40, 50, 60, 80, 100, 120
Household size	As reported
No. of children in HH	As reported
Gender	1=male, 0=female
Main mode	1=Bus, 2=train, 3=M2Busway, 4=car

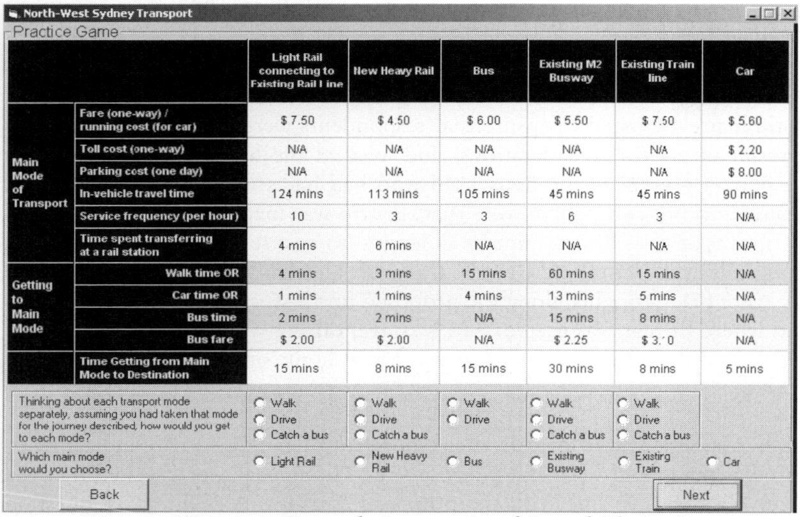

North-West Sydney Transport

Practice Game

		Light Rail connecting to Existing Rail Line	New Heavy Rail	Bus	Existing M2 Busway	Existing Train line	Car
Main Mode of Transport	Fare (one-way) / running cost (for car)	$ 7.50	$ 4.50	$ 6.00	$ 5.50	$ 7.50	$ 5.60
	Toll cost (one-way)	N/A	N/A	N/A	N/A	N/A	$ 2.20
	Parking cost (one day)	N/A	N/A	N/A	N/A	N/A	$ 8.00
	In-vehicle travel time	124 mins	113 mins	105 mins	45 mins	45 mins	90 mins
	Service frequency (per hour)	10	3	3	6	3	N/A
	Time spent transferring at a rail station	4 mins	6 mins	N/A	N/A	N/A	N/A
Getting to Main Mode	Walk time OR	4 mins	3 mins	15 mins	60 mins	15 mins	N/A
	Car time OR	1 mins	1 mins	4 mins	13 mins	5 mins	N/A
	Bus time	2 mins	2 mins	N/A	15 mins	8 mins	N/A
	Bus fare	$ 2.00	$ 2.00	N/A	$ 2.25	$ 3.[illegible]0	N/A
	Time Getting from Main Mode to Destination	15 mins	8 mins	15 mins	30 mins	8 mins	5 mins
Thinking about each transport mode separately, assuming you had taken that mode for the journey described, how would you get to each mode?		Walk / Drive / Catch a bus	Walk / Drive / Catch a bus	Walk / Drive	Walk / Drive / Catch a bus	Walk / Drive / Catch a bus	
Which main mode would you choose?		Light Rail	New Heavy Rail	Bus	Existing Busway	Existing Train	Car

Back | Next

Figure 4: Example Inter-regional Stated Choice Screen

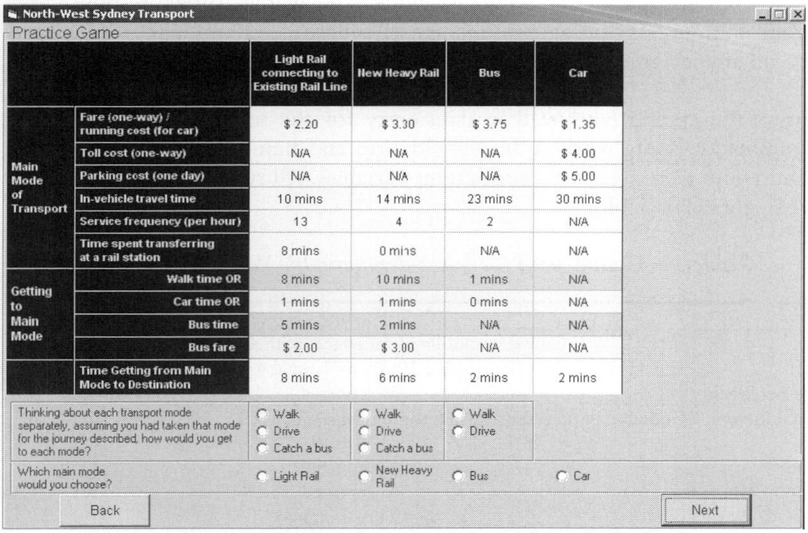

North-West Sydney Transport

Practice Game

		Light Rail connecting to Existing Rail Line	New Heavy Rail	Bus	Car
Main Mode of Transport	Fare (one-way) / running cost (for car)	$ 2.20	$ 3.30	$ 3.75	$ 1.35
	Toll cost (one-way)	N/A	N/A	N/A	$ 4.00
	Parking cost (one day)	N/A	N/A	N/A	$ 5.00
	In-vehicle travel time	10 mins	14 mins	23 mins	30 mins
	Service frequency (per hour)	13	4	2	N/A
	Time spent transferring at a rail station	8 mins	0 mins	N/A	N/A
Getting to Main Mode	Walk time OR	8 mins	10 mins	1 mins	N/A
	Car time OR	1 mins	1 mins	0 mins	N/A
	Bus time	5 mins	2 mins	N/A	N/A
	Bus fare	$ 2.00	$ 3.00	N/A	N/A
	Time Getting from Main Mode to Destination	8 mins	6 mins	2 mins	2 mins
Thinking about each transport mode separately, assuming you had taken that mode for the journey described, how would you get to each mode?		Walk / Drive / Catch a bus	Walk / Drive / Catch a bus	Walk / Drive	
Which main mode would you choose?		Light Rail	New Heavy Rail	Bus	Car

Back | Next

Figure 5: Example Intra-regional Stated Choice Screen

Table 13 shows the descriptive statistics for the work segment. The mean age is 43.1 years with an average annual gross personal income of $64,100. The proportion of male to females is equally split.

Table 13: Descriptive Statistics for Work Segment

Statistic	N	Mean	Std. Deviation	Minimum	Maximum
Age	223	43.1	12.5	24	70
Hours worked per week	223	37.6	14.6	0	70
Annual Personal Income ($000's)	223	64.1	41.8	0	140
Household size	223	3.78	2.30	1	8
No. of children in household	223	1.05	1.09	0	4
Gender (male =1)	223	50.4	-	0	1

Of the 223 respondents interviewed as part of the work sample, 199 had access to a motor vehicle for the surveyed trip. This represents 89.24 percent of the sample. Table 14 shows the descriptive statistics for the Non-Work sample. This sample differs significantly to that of the Work sample, with 36.7 percent of the sample being male and the mean age of 46.5 years. The average household size is 3.3 and the annual gross personal income is $28,500. 83.04 percent of the non-work segment had a car available for the surveyed trip.

Table 14: Descriptive Statistics for Non-Work Segment

Statistic	N	Mean	Std. Deviation	Minimum	Maximum
Age	230	46.5	7.97	0	70
Hours worked per week	230	15.60	18.98	0	80
Annual Personal Income ($000's)	230	28.5	28.59	0	140
Household size	230	3.30	1.46	1	8
No. of children in household	230	0.73	1.04	0	4
Gender (male =1)	230	36.7	0.48	0	1

The percentage of those sampled for Non-Work trips with regards to motor vehicle availability was marginally less than that of the Work sample. In the Non-Work sample, as shown in Table 15, 83.04 percent did have a car available for the surveyed trip.

Table 15: Percentage of Non-Work Segment Who Had a Motor Vehicle Available for the Trip

Car available	Frequency	Percent
Yes	191	83.04
No	39	16.96
Total	230	100

The trip purpose frequencies for the Non-Work sample are described in Table 16. The majority of the Non-Work trips consisted of social/recreational trips.

Independent of trip segment, each alternative within the SC experiment represents a combination of main mode and access mode possibilities. Thus, for example, alternative one represents the new light rail alternative accessed via walking, whilst alternative two represents the new light rail alternative accessed via private vehicle (either driven by the respondent or by some other party). Depending on the trip specific context, each respondent faced between eight and fifteen alternatives per choice set; eight for trips within the study region with no main mode car alternative – two new modes with three access modes each (walk, drive or bus), plus an existing bus mode with two access modes (walk and drive) – and fifteen alternatives for a trip outside of the study catchment area with all modes available – two new modes with three access modes each, the existing bus service (with two access modes), existing M2 busway and train services (with three access modes each), and a privately owned vehicle.

Table 16: Frequencies of Trip Purposes for Non-Work Segment

Trip Purpose	Frequency
Shopping	31
Visiting friends/relatives	27
Education	49
Social/recreational	81
Personal business	32
Other	10
Total	230

The data reported herein have been edited and cleaned extensively for outliers, caused by either a respondent providing a questionable attribute level in the base data that is used to construct the levels in the stated choice experiment, or an interviewer entering a value incorrectly (we suspect that where this occurred, it was a decimal place problem, e.g., 63 instead of 6.3).

Model Results

Table 17 shows the model results for both the commuting and non-commuting segments of the data. For each segment, two models are presented; a multinomial logit model (MNL) and a mixed logit model (ML). In estimating the commuter models, an exogenous weighting variable – personal income – has been used. No exogenous weighting has been applied to the non commuting models. For the commuting segment, both the MNL model and the ML model are statistically significant with pseudo R^2s of 0.34 and 0.343 respectively. The likelihood ratio test of differences between the two models (for five degrees of freedom difference – five additional spread parameters) at the 95 percent confidence level (i.e., -2LL = 25.688 against $\chi_5^2 = 11.07$) suggests that we can reject the null hypothesis of no difference, and conclude that the ML model is preferred to the MNL model on this criterion.

For the non-commuting segment, the MNL and ML models are also statistically significant with pseudo R^2s of 0.339 and 0.346 respectively. As with the commuting segment, the likelihood ratio test of differences between the two models (with five degrees of freedom) suggests that the ML model is preferred over the MNL model (i.e., -2LL = 86.138 against $\chi_5^2 = 11.07$).

Table 17: Commuting and Non-Commuting Model Results

Attribute	Alternative	Commuting Trips				Non-commuting Trips			
		Multinomial Logit		Mixed Logit		Multinomial Logit		Mixed Logit	
		Coeff.	t-ratio	Coeff.	t-ratio	Coeff.	t-ratio	Coeff.	t-ratio
Constant	New LR Walk	3.722	8.403	3.589	6.829	3.718	11.545	3.362	8.582
Constant	New LR Drive	0.657	1.634	0.409	0.839	-0.363	-1.226	-0.764	-2.067
Constant	New LR Bus	0.532	1.572	0.248	0.570	0.214	0.810	-0.227	-0.657
Constant	Train Walk	2.130	5.442	1.901	3.953	3.172	11.032	2.740	7.519
Constant	Train Drive	-0.415	-1.166	-0.761	-1.685	-1.063	-3.858	-1.592	-4.470
Constant	Train Bus	0.098	0.301	-0.263	-0.615	0.235	0.926	-0.307	-0.903
Constant	New Busway Walk	0.219	0.277	0.054	0.064	1.818	4.943	1.575	3.648
Constant	New Busway Drive	-0.434	-1.030	-0.667	-1.319	-1.567	-4.098	-1.916	-4.293
Constant	New Busway Bus	-0.006	-0.016	-0.249	-0.543	-1.226	-3.432	-1.587	-3.734
Constant	Bus Walk	2.363	6.763	2.181	4.869	1.735	6.691	1.360	3.987
Constant	Bus Drive	0.452	1.279	0.164	0.364	-0.464	-1.755	-0.931	-2.677
Constant	M2 Busway Walk	1.902	5.400	1.706	3.773	1.859	6.919	1.473	4.180
Constant	M2 Busway Drive	-0.686	-1.782	-0.982	-2.053	-1.721	-5.700	-2.180	-5.750
Constant	M2 Busway Bus	-0.215	-0.618	-0.527	-1.172	-0.372	-1.419	-0.841	-2.408
				Random Parameters (means)				Random Parameters (means)	
Fare	All Public Transport	-0.176	-10.431	-0.233	-9.958	-0.270	-18.941	-0.379	-16.782
Running cost + toll cost	Car	-0.120	-3.714	-0.163	-3.173	-0.218	-7.665	-0.277	-5.456
Parking cost	Car	-0.020	-2.162	-0.041	-2.751	-0.026	-2.959	-0.112	-2.836
Main mode in-vehicle time	All Public Transport	-0.054	-22.065	-0.066	-18.212	-0.034	-19.987	-0.042	-18.029
Main mode in-vehicle time	Car	-0.031	-7.171	-0.054	-5.538	-0.040	-8.387	-0.070	-6.149
				Random Parameters (spread parameters)				Random Parameters (spread parameters)	
Fare	All Public Transport			0.233	9.958			0.379	16.782
Running cost + toll cost	Car			0.163	3.173			0.277	5.456
Parking cost	Car			0.041	2.751			0.112	2.836
Main mode in-vehicle time	All Public Transport			0.066	18.212			0.042	18.029
Main mode in-vehicle time	Car			0.054	5.538			0.070	6.149
Fixed attribute parameters									
Access time, wait time and transfer time, walk	All Public Transport	-0.124	-14.142	-0.130	-14.259	-0.122	-20.812	-0.127	-21.008
Access time, wait time and transfer time, bus	All Public Transport	-0.011	-2.853	-0.013	-3.257	-0.017	-5.394	-0.021	-6.216
Access time, wait time and transfer time, drive	All Public Transport	-0.050	-5.111	-0.055	-5.412	-0.011	-1.835	-0.017	-2.639
Egress Time	All Public Transport	-0.017	-3.046	-0.020	-3.219	-0.058	-13.446	-0.061	-12.961
Egress Time	Car	-0.055	-3.247	-0.070	-2.945	-0.082	-5.522	-0.091	-3.992
Fixed socio-demographic parameters									
Gender Walking	All Public Transport	1.903	8.079	2.389	7.771	-0.715	-3.709	-0.838	-3.259
Gender Bus	All Public Transport	1.298	5.967	1.793	6.129	-0.596	-3.170	-0.735	-2.897
Gender Drive	All Public Transport	1.312	5.593	1.816	5.936	-0.595	-3.013	-0.744	-2.850
Personal Income	Bus, Busway	-0.007	-3.812	-0.007	-3.686				
Fixed contextual parameters									
Inside catchment area trip	All rail	1.062	6.489	1.187	6.609	0.797	6.323	0.828	6.003
Model Diagnostics									
LL(0)		-4113.144		-4113.144		-6647.855		-6647.855	
LL(β)		-2712.149		-2699.305		-4387.659		-4344.590	
Chi-square		2801.989		2827.678		4520.392		4606.530	
D.F.		28		33		27		32	
Pseudo-R²		0.340		0.343		0.339		0.346	
No. obs		2230		2230		2300		2300	

For both ML models, we have specified the marginal utilities of five attributes to be estimated as random parameters. They are a generic public transport fare parameter, a generic public transport main mode travel time parameter, a car cost parameter (estimated from a variable formed by aggregating the running cost and toll attributes), a car in-vehicle travel time parameter, and a car parking cost parameter. To ensure that all individual-specific parameter estimates will be of the same sign, the random parameter estimates have each been drawn from constrained triangular distributions (see for example, Hensher and Greene, 2003, Hensher *et al.*, 2005). For the commuting segment, the mean and spread parameters of the random parameter estimates are all highly significant with asymptotic *t*-statistics ranging from (in absolute values) 2.751 (parking cost) to 18.212 (main mode public transport in-vehicle time). The random parameter estimates for the non-commuting segment show similar levels of significance, ranging from 2.836 (parking cost) to 19.987 (main mode public transport in-vehicle time). As such, there exists significant preference heterogeneity for the marginal utilities held for the fare and travel times of the main mode public transport modes as well as for the cost and travel times of those who had access to a car for the specific trip context of the experiment.

In the SC experiment, the access time, wait time and transfer time (between new modes and the existing rail line) were treated as separate attributes within the public transport alternatives. The best model was achieved, however, by aggregating these attributes to form a single 'access, wait and transfer time' variable for each of the public transport modes (e.g., if respondents saw five minutes access time, four minutes wait time and six minutes transfer time, these were combined into a single new variable with a value of fifteen minutes). Parameter estimates for the composite non-main-mode-in-vehicle time variable has been specified as generic across main modes, but alternative specific across access modes. That is, separate access walk, bus and drive parameters are obtained for this composite time variable, independent of the main mode being accessed. Whilst all three parameter estimates are statistically significant and of the expected sign, across both trip segments, the magnitude for the walk access is significantly higher than other access mode parameters, suggesting a larger disutility for walking to a main mode than for accessing the main mode either using a bus or a car, independent of whether the trip is for commuting or non-commuting purposes. With regard to egress times, all four models provide evidence for greater levels of disutility being associated with increases in egress times for car trips than for public transport trips.

In addition to the modal trip attributes, for the commuting segment, we have included two socioeconomic effects (gross personal income and gender) and one trip context effect (whether the trip remains within the catchment area or not). For the non-commuting trip segment, income was found to be statistically insignificant and hence was removed from the model. For both trip segments, the dummy coded gender variable (male = 1) has been specified as alternative specific across the three access modes but generic across the main public transport modes. For commuting trips, males are less time sensitive towards longer access times, but this is reversed for non-commuting trips where females are less time sensitive to increases in access trip times. The gross personal income variable has been entered into the existing bus and M2 busway utility functions with the resulting parameters being negative for all commuter segment models. This suggests that those individuals with higher personal incomes possess lower preferences for these two main mode alternatives than do lower income individuals.

A single trip context variable has been included in the utility functions associated with the rail alternatives (i.e., new rail, light rail and existing rail) of all four models. Coded one for inter-regional trips and zero for intra-regional trips, the positive parameter estimates for both the commuting and non-commuting segments suggest that higher levels of utility are obtained from use of rail when the trips are inter-regional as opposed to intra-regional.

Behavioural values of travel time savings (VTTS) for the various trip time aspects are summarised in Table 18. For the ML model, the VTTS have been derived using the conditional parameter estimates (Hensher *et al.*, 2005). All of the VTTS have a distribution in the positive range. The VTTS for public transport main mode in-vehicle times are lower than those for car main mode in-vehicle times for all models except the commuting MNL model. Confirming our earlier finding that respondents have a stronger preference against accessing main mode public transport alternatives by walking, the VTTS for walking are consistently ten times greater than the VTTS for use of bus access modes and approximately double the VTTS for car access modes for commuting trips, and approximately ten times the VTTS for both car and bus access modes for non-commuting trips. The VTTS for egress times for car main modes are higher, independent of trip purpose, than the VTTS for public transport egress times. Of interest, however, the VTTS for car main mode egress times are higher for commuting trips, but the VTTS for public transport modes are higher for non-commuting trips. With this one exception, the VTTS for commuting trips are larger than those for non-commuting trips.

Table 18: Commuting and Non-commuting Values of Travel Time Savings

Attribute	Alternative	Commuting trips			Non-commuting trips		
		MNL	ML		MNL	ML	
			Mean	St. Dev.		Mean	St. Dev.
Main mode in-vehicle time	Public Transport	$18.35	$16.85	$2.47	$7.57	$6.71	$1.06
Main mode in-vehicle time	Car	$15.49	$19.70	$1.41	$11.07	$15.20	$0.88
Access time, wait time and transfer time, **walk**	All Public Transport	$42.13	$33.55	$3.29	$27.07	$27.67	$1.99
Access time, wait time and transfer time, **bus**	All Public Transport	$3.81	$3.48	$0.34	$3.80	$3.34	$0.49
Access time, wait time and transfer time, **drive**	All Public Transport	$17.10	$14.13	$1.39	$2.56	$2.78	$0.41
Egress Time	All Public Transport	$5.80	$5.10	$0.50	$7.57	$9.78	$1.45
Egress Time	Car	$27.32	$25.66	$1.39	$22.52	$19.93	$1.45

DISCUSSION AND CONCLUSION

In this chapter, we have shown how to construct SC experiments that account for individual differences in the availability of alternatives, without loss of orthogonality. The strategies we outline require in-depth probing of respondents prior to the SC experiment commencing. The alternatives shown in the SC experiment are then tailored to the individual given the specific decision context and situation which exists or is likely to exist in the future. The empirical example we have used demonstrates that respondents are capable of completing complex choice tasks in a meaningful manner when the choice tasks presented are realistically framed, and hence, cognitively meaningful to the individual.

It is important to note that the techniques outlined herein are applicable only to a specific subset of SC studies. Studies involving unlabeled alternatives (usually within mode experiments) do not lend themselves to the methods we describe within this chapter. It is also important that the researcher consider the purpose of the experiment before consideration as to the use of these methods is given. If for example, the research objective is to study possible future scenarios, then it is foreseeable that currently 'unavailable' alternatives should be given to respondents given that such alternatives may be available to them in the future. As one reviewer noted, often one wishes to examine the issue of behavioural change as a function of choice set dynamics, or the researcher maybe interested solely in preferences. Hence, some studies may require that currently unavailable alternatives be made available within all choice set tasks, independent of the current choice context faced by individual respondents.

The empirical example outlined demonstrates that the strategies we outline do not impair the ability of respondents to understand or perform the choice task presented. Nevertheless, the empirical study reported does not allow for a comparison of the impact of not allowing for individual specific availability of alternatives to current practice where all alternatives are presented, independent of individual choice contexts. Future research should, therefore, consider examination of such a comparison. In particular, research might focus on the issue of cognitive burden given the presence of currently unavailable alternatives. Further research may also concentrate on the realistic portrayal of other design aspects such as the attributes and/or attribute levels as well as the response format used to gather data.

The empirical example outlined demonstrates the need for further evaluation of task complexity in SC experiments. Recent research has tended to focus on the impact of design dimensionality upon the cognitive burden of respondents. As we have demonstrated here, it is possible that such research efforts may be somewhat misdirected. For some, the SC experiment we have employed would be considered too burdensome for respondents to undertake meaningfully, however, 453 respondents did so without incentive and the empirical evidence is very plausible. Although further research is required, we postulate that when confronted with a realistic SC experiment, respondents are capable of meaningful participation independent of the design dimensionality. That is, we suspect that for SC experiments, what counts is the believability of the choice task and the relevancy of the alternatives, attributes, and attribute levels shown to the respondents.

REFERENCES

Anderson, D.A. and J.B. Wiley (1992). Efficient Choice Set Designs for Estimating Cross-Effects Models, *Journal of Marketing Research*, 3 (October), 357-370.

Batsell, R.R. and J.J. Louviere (1991). Experimental analysis of choice, *Marketing Letters*, 2, 199-214.

Batsell, R.R. and J.C. Polking (1985). A New Class of Market Share Models, *Marketing Science*, 4, 177-198.

Ben-Akiva, M. and S.R. Lerman (1985). *Discrete Choice Analysis: Theory and Application to Travel Demand*, MIT Press, Cambridge.

Bliemer, M.C.J. and J.M. Rose (2005). *Efficient Designs for Alternative Specific Choice Experiments*, Working Paper, University of Sydney, February.

Burke, R.R., B.A. Harlam, B.E. Kahn and L.M. Lodish (1992). Comparing Dynamic Consumer Choice in Real and Computer-Simulated Environments, *Journal of Consumer Research*, 19 (June), 71–82.

Carson, R., J.J. Louviere, D. Anderson, P. Arabie, D. Bunch, D.A. Hensher, R. Johnson, W. Kuhfeld, D. Steinberg, J. Swait, H. Timmermans and J. Wiley (1994). Experimental Analysis of Choice, *Marketing Letters*, 5 (October), 351-367.

Hensher, D.A. and W.H. Greene (2003). The Mixed Logit Model: The State of Practice, *Transportation*, 30 (2), May 133-176.

Hensher, D.A., W.H. Greene and J.M. Rose (2004). *Deriving WTP estimates from observation-specific parameters using classical inference methods*, Working Paper, University of Sydney, April.

Hensher, D.A., J.M. Rose, and W.H. Greene (2005). *Applied Choice Analysis: A Primer*, Cambridge University Press, Cambridge.

Huber, J. and K. Zwerina (1996). The Importance of Utility Balance and Efficient Choice Designs, *Journal of Marketing Research*, 33 (August), 307-317.

Lazari, A.G. and D.A. Anderson (1994). Designs of Discrete Choice Experiments for Estimating Both Attribute and Availability Cross Effects, *Journal of Marketing Research*, 31 (August), 375-383.

Louviere, J.J. (1988). *Analyzing Decision Making: Metric Conjoint Analysis (Quantitative Applications in the Social Sciences)*, SAGE Publications.

Louviere, J.J. and D.A. Hensher (1983). Using Discrete Choice Models with Experimental Design Data to Forecast Consumer Demand for a Unique Cultural Event, *Journal of Consumer Research*, 10 (December), 348-361.

Louviere, J.J. and D.A. Hensher and J.D. Swait (2000). *Stated Choice Methods: Analysis and Application*, Cambridge University Press, Cambridge.

Louviere, J.J. and G. Woodworth (1983). Design and analysis of simulated consumer choice or allocation experiments: an approach based on aggregate data, *Journal of Marketing Research*, **20**, 350-367.

Raghovarao, D. and J.B. Wiley (1986). Testing Competing Effects Among Soft Drink Brands. In: *Statistical Design: Theory and Practice: Proceedings of a Conference in Honour of Walter T. Federer* (C.E. McCulloch, S.J. Shwager, G. Gasella and S.R. Searle, eds), 161-176, Ithaca, NY, Cornell University.

Rose, J.M. and M.C.J. Bliemer (2004). *The Design of Stated Choice Experiments: The State of Practice and Future Challenges*, Working Paper, University of Sydney, April.

Watson, S.M., J.P. Toner, T. Fowkes and M. Wardman (2000). Efficiency Properties of Orthogonal Stated Preference Designs. In: *Stated Preference Modelling Techniques* (J. de D. Ortúzar, ed.), 91-101, PTRC Education and Research Services Ltd, London.

Travel Survey Methods: Quality and Future Directions
Peter Stopher and Cheryl Stecher (Editors)
© 2006 Elsevier Ltd. All rights reserved.

19

STATED PREFERENCE SURVEYS: AN ASSESSMENT

Peter M. Jones, Centre for Transport Studies, UCL, London, UK
and
Mark Bradley, Consultant, Santa Barbara, California, USA

INTRODUCTION

Stated preference (SP) techniques have been applied in the field of transport studies for more than twenty years, and in marketing for more than thirty years. Both fields of study were represented by participants in the workshop, who were drawn from five continents[28]; this provided the opportunity to compare and contrast experiences from different contexts. The workshop reviewed the whole process of SP design and application, and considered whether it would be appropriate to propose standards for the use of SP in transport studies. In the main, it concluded that the types of application are so diverse that there is quite limited scope for setting standards – what would be inappropriate in one context might be the best approach in another – and that principles and guidelines would be more appropriate, supplemented by examples of good practice. Areas of consensus and disagreement were identified, as well as areas requiring further research.

---

[28] Workshop members were: Gustavo Baez (USA), Mark Bradley (USA), Jennifer Dill (USA), Peter Jones (UK), Marina Lombard (South Africa), Juan de Dios Ortuzar (Chile), Kaethe Podgorski (USA), John Rose (Australia), Pedro Szasz (Brazil), Harry Timmermans (Netherlands).

ELEMENTS OF AN SP SURVEY: STATE OF PRACTICE

Figure 1 provides a representation of the various elements that underlie an SP survey and analysis. Together with the workshop resource paper (Rose and Hensher, 2006) and three presented workshop papers (Podgorski *et al*, 2004; van der Reis *et al*, 2004; van der Waerden *et al*, 2004), this provided a framework for identifying issues to be addressed during the workshop discussions.

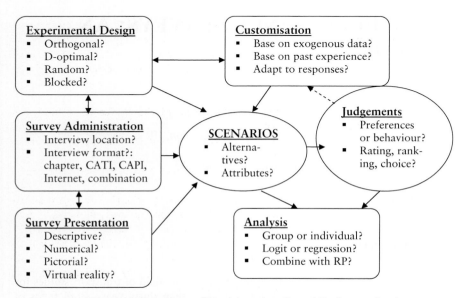

Figure 1: Elements and Decisions in a Stated Preference Study

The Respondent's Perspective

The interview location can vary from one SP application to another. Where face-to-face interviews are involved, respondents are most typically interviewed at home or in their workplace, and are asked about a recent trip that then forms the context around which the exercise is based. In the case of a study of public transport trips, the interviews may be carried out in the course of the journey (e.g., on-train interviews).

The interview format is a key decision that has crucial implications for how the survey can be designed and presented to respondents. Where mailback or telephone interview procedures are used, respondents may be intercepted during the course of a relevant journey (i.e., choice-based sampling), or contacted at home using an appropriate telephone number or mailing address sampling frame. In many countries, a combination of methods is now often used when personal, face-to-face interviews are not feasible:

- Recruitment via intercept or random telephone survey;
- Customisation based on recruitment information;
- Mailing of the customised questionnaire; and
- CATI retrieval of responses via the telephone (often giving respondents the option of completing the same questionnaire over the Internet instead).

From the perspective of the respondent, the core of the SP survey involves being presented with a number of scenarios, or tasks, each one representing a possible situation that they might encounter when planning or undertaking a trip. Each scenario consists of a description in the form of three elements, which can be varied between scenarios in a controlled manner by the analyst:

- The alternatives or options that are the object of the choice (e.g., modes of travel, destinations, departure times);
- The attributes that describe the characteristics of that feature (e.g., travel times or costs); and
- The levels or values of each of the attributes in this particular option.

The combinations of alternatives, attributes and levels are specified according to an experimental design, and there are many types of designs, ranging from statistically optimised or orthogonal designs to completely random selections. Designs – particularly the attribute levels – can either be standardised across respondents, or they can be customised to reflect the circumstances experienced by each individual (e.g., taking into account reported current walk time to bus stop, or non-availability of a private car), so that the options are seen as realistic by each respondent.

A degree of customisation can be achieved by pre-preparing a series of designs and selecting the appropriate one, based on exogenous segmentation data (e.g., for those making long or short trips); but full customisation requires the use of computer software, either in the interview itself (if face-to-face), or as a part of the procedure for preparing mail-out questionnaires. Telephone surveys now routinely use computers (CATI), so customisation can easily be built into the program.

There are various ways in which this information might be presented to respondents, depending in particular on the nature of the attribute. Most commonly, quantitative variables are described numerically with an appropriate label (e.g., 'twenty minutes'), and qualitative variables in words (e.g., 'rough road surface'). However, some SP studies have used pictorial forms to convey the nature of each option (e.g., using a sketch or photograph), and exceptionally sound has also been used.

The key response task that the respondent is asked to carry out is to make judgements about the attractiveness of the alternatives, either with a view to establishing a preference for one option over another, or likely choice behaviour if confronted with these options while carrying out some activity (e.g., travelling from home to work).

There are generally three ways in which respondents might be asked to express such judgements:

- By rating options, one at a time, on a scale (e.g., from 1 to 100);
- By ranking a set of options; or
- By choosing between two or more options.

In the latter case, this might represent a straight choice from a set of alternatives (equivalent to selecting the highest ranked option); or, where options are presented two at a time, respondents can be asked to express a strength of preference (or likelihood of adopting) one option over the other (e.g., Definitely A, Probably A, …).

In cases where respondents are asked to choose between two possible behaviours (e.g., Option A = Car and Option B = Bus), then the realism of the responses can also be increased by including an 'opt-out' response (e.g., would not travel – if these were the only options available). Respondents are usually asked to make a series of judgements by performing successive tasks (e.g., ten pairwise choice situations), and in some applications they may be asked to take part in several such series of tasks.

The format in which the survey is delivered can influence the scope for using different presentational forms for each option and also the ways in which respondents are asked to make judgements. Telephone interviewing (CATI) is most restrictive in this respect, in that all information has to be conveyed verbally, unless material is sent by post or handed to the respondent prior to the interview (e.g., as part of an intercept survey). In this case, it is subject to similar advantages and limitations as any 'pen and paper' approach (NB: it is potentially less restrictive than a mailback survey, because the interviewer can add an explanation as to the nature of the task – albeit remotely via the telephone).

Computer-based SP surveys are now very common in some areas of application and in some parts of the world, either in a face-to-face survey or via the web. They provide maximum flexibility in terms of customisation and adaptation (see below), and provide scope for using multi-media forms of presentation (animated pictures, sound, virtual reality, etc.). However, the computer screen can be rather restrictive in some situations: making it much more difficult to ask respondents to rank options than handing them the information on cards, for example, and limiting the amount of information that can be conveyed on one screen. For this reason, SP surveys involving options with large numbers of attributes are usually presented on sheets of paper or on cards.

Important to the success of the SP survey is the way in which the exercise is introduced and explained to respondents. Here the framing of the context of the exercise is of particular importance. This includes both the reasons respondents are given for the purpose of the survey, and the context in which they are asked to make their judgements (e.g., 'imagine you were going shopping tomorrow and had the following options …).

The Analyst's Perspective

The analyst has to pay careful attention to all the above aspects, in the context of knowing:

- The primary purpose of the SP survey (e.g., to obtain values of travel time, by given population segments, or to forecast the likely patronage of a proposed light rail scheme);
- The method(s) to be used for data analysis and model estimation; and
- Any budget constraints (e.g., limited funding ruling out face-to-face interviewing).

There are many links between the analysis techniques that are used and the ways in which the SP task is presented to respondents. The former may limit the number of attribute levels that can be handled during estimation, for example, and the latter may dictate the type of analytical method that can be used (e.g., ranking data implies using an 'exploded' multinomial logit model). A particular challenge for the analyst is to obtain data that meets all his/her requirements without over-burdening the respondent, or asking them to undertake a task that seems unrealistic.

Often, in order to implement the experimental design that is developed for the SP survey (which ensures that the combinations of features, attributes and levels that are presented to respondents are statistically efficient for the purpose in hand), it may be necessary to break the exercise down into component parts. In particular:

- Where designs require a large number of repeated judgements to be made, the design may be 'blocked', so that any one respondent is only asked to complete a subset of all the responses that are required for efficient statistical estimation; and
- Where there are a large number of attributes, the design may be sub-divided into several exercises, each using only a controlled subset of the full attribute set, but usually with one attribute common across the exercises (typically cost). Note that this approach is more suitable in studies where the focus is on measuring the relative valuation of attribute levels, rather than predicting choice behaviour in real situations. In the latter case, it is generally considered more realistic to include all relevant attributes in a single exercise.

Customisation of features, attributes and levels can increase the realism of the task from the viewpoint of the respondent, but, in some cases, this can reduce the efficiency of the estimation – although this varies according to the form of estimation that is used.

Some studies have used a procedure known as adaptive conjoint analysis, in which the levels of the attributes presented to respondents in subsequent tasks are influenced by the judgements that they have already expressed – in an effort to 'home in' on their trade-off levels. When using this approach, however, the analyst must be very careful to analyse the data in a manner that accounts for the adaptation used – otherwise the resulting estimates may be biased due to endogenous correlations introduced into the design.

One major limitation of SP surveys arises where the results are to be used to predict behaviour. The evidence has consistently shown that well designed SP surveys can produce reliable coefficient estimates, that indicate the relative importance of each attribute in making judgements, but that these results need to be scaled in order to make accurate estimates of future collective behaviour.

This requires the use of RP (revealed preference) data, usually collected from respondents as part of the same survey (e.g., by asking about existing behaviour for the topic covered by the SP survey and the available alternatives that were rejected). However, where this is not available, it could be obtained from independent RP surveys, or else limited to other information on aggregate market shares or elasticities.

WORKSHOP CONCLUSIONS

Workshop participants identified a number of general principles that should underlie any application of SP, as well as several more specific analytical guidelines. They also found several areas of disagreement, either due to conflicting evidence, or due to the appropriateness of adopting different procedures in different application areas.

Recommended Principles for SP Applications

It takes a great deal of skill, effort, understanding of the choice context, and an understanding of respondents' perceptions, to design a good SP study:

1. Start the SP design process by considering the study objectives and the nature of the target respondents: ensure that the methods used fit the requirements of the study, rather than selecting a method (experimental design, estimation procedure, etc.) and 'forcing' the SP exercise into a predetermined format. Do not copy an existing design and assume that it is transferable. Each study has unique features that need to be recognised and incorporated into the design. If carefully designed, it appears that SP techniques can be used in different cultural contexts, among population groups varying widely in literacy levels (see Van der Reis *et al*, 2004).

2.   Be prepared to put a substantial amount of the study effort into understanding the viewpoint and requirements of the particular target groups, the ways in which they approach decision-making and the terminology they use to describe attributes. Use focus groups and other qualitative techniques (incorporating photographs and other stimulus materials, as appropriate), and thoroughly pilot the application before full-scale implementation. Cultures may vary, for example, in the ways in which time is perceived and measured, and groups may vary in their awareness of small time differences.

3.   Maximise the realism of the SP exercise, to ensure that respondents 'take the exercise seriously' and give considered judgements. This includes:
      a. Anchoring the exercise around actual trips/situations as much as possible;
      b. Reminding respondents of real constraints that they face;
      c. Introducing the exercise by providing adequate detail and a balanced description of the task and its components;
      d. Customising the choice sets – only include realistic alternatives;
      e. Customising the attribute levels – ensure that they are realistic compared to current levels; BUT
      f. Generally avoid customising the set of attributes (to avoid estimation problems).

4.   Recognise that a balance needs to be struck in the experimental design between complete realism and efficiency. Where factors are not included in the experimental design that might influence choices, then indicate explicitly to respondents that these are being held constant across the options being presented.

5.   Provide a thorough, balanced explanation of what is being required of respondents:
      a. Explain the choice task and describe the attributes.
      b. Drawings may be helpful in describing attribute levels, but photographs are prone to be misleading, because they may contain unintended visual cues; stimuli need to present in a controlled manner.

6.   Much effort needs to be put into interviewer selection and training, because poorly trained interviewers can have a significant effect on the results of SP face-to-face or telephone interviews. The workshop paper by Van der Reis *et al.* (2004) reports that, in one study, most of the poorly completed interviews were administered by just ten percent of the interviewers.

Analytical Guidelines for SP Studies

1.   The conventional assumption that orthogonal designs should be used to minimise correlations and – by implication – maximise statistical efficiency is over-rated for many kinds of SP tasks. There are other types of designs, such as D-Optimal designs, that may be more appropriate for discrete choice models (see Rose and Hensher, 2006). Correlated designs can be created to

optimise the estimation of specific relationships between variables, such as the 'value of time'.

2.   Where many comparisons between options are needed for model estimation, due to the inclusion in the design of a large number of attributes and levels, then use appropriate blocking of designs to minimise respondent burden by apportioning large designs across the sample. Task simplification can also be aided by developing a series of linked exercises, each displaying options containing only a portion of the total attribute set (although this is more appropriate for valuation studies than for choice forecasting studies).

3.   To avoid any biases due to the order of presentation of attributes and options, as well as to counter any possible errors due to respondent fatigue effects, randomise the order of presentation of options, attributes, and choice tasks across the sample, where possible.

4.   While customisation can help to improve realism, do NOT customise either the set of attributes shown to each respondent, nor the levels based on respondents' preferences (e.g., by using adaptive conjoint). To do so will lose the controlled nature of the experiment and make estimation difficult and unreliable. Adaptation is only advisable if the analyst is well aware of the estimation problems and has a strategy to avoid them.

5.   Good computer software is needed to assist in generating experimental designs, particularly when attribute levels and choice tasks are being customised. However, this needs to be coupled with an understanding of how to use the software, and its limitations, assumptions, etc.

6.   It is important to account for within-respondent correlation when carrying out the analysis: do NOT treat each task response from the same individual as an independent observation, particularly when there are large numbers of responses from each individual. Methods of accounting for within-respondent correlation include the jackknife technique and, more recently, mixed-logit estimation.

Some Areas of Disagreement

Workshop members differed in their judgements about appropriate guidelines on a number of issues. These are noted below, together with the reasons for these differences, where these could be identified.

1.   There was no agreement on a single 'best' means of asking respondents to exercise judgements among options. The use of rating scales, for judging single options one at a time, may be suitable for eliciting preferences, but not predicting behaviour. In the latter case, pairwise choices with a measure of strength of certainty of choice are most efficient. Where multiple trade-offs are involved (requiring examination of more than two alternatives at the

same time), then a single choice, or a ranking may provide appropriate forms of respondent judgement.

2. What is the largest/most complex reasonable SP task for a respondent? Here views varied considerably, according to the context:

   a. About six choice alternatives per scenario were considered the maximum in transport studies, while in marketing studies ten or more choice options may be presented at once. It seemed more appropriate to include larger numbers when, for example, considering all the main brands in a well defined market – when not to do so would then distort the results of the SP exercise. These issues have been further explored in a recent paper by Caussade *et al.* (2005).

   b. Transport analysts tend to limit the number of attributes per option (within one exercise) to around five or six, and rarely more than ten. In other areas, twenty or more attributes may regularly be presented at one time – though usually through the media of pen-and-paper rather than a computer screen.

   c. Number of choice scenarios per exercise. Again, transport analysts tend to err on the side of caution, by typically limiting the number of replications to around ten. In other areas, thirty two choice tasks per respondent may be more typical, with some studies having asked respondents to undertake well in excess of sixty choice tasks or sets of judgements.

3. How should 'warm up' responses be treated? Views differed as to whether they should be dropped (and hence be generated outside the main experimental design), on the grounds that they represent a learning phase and are unreliable; or whether they should be included in the main design and in the analysis. Transport analysts were more likely to include them in the analysis.

4. What constitutes an 'illogical' response, and should it be dropped from the analysis? Several related issues arise here: can 'illogical' responses be identified easily, particularly in more complex SP designs and in experiments with non-generic alternatives (e.g., mode choice)? Where they can, are respondents being illogical, or taking into account factors relevant to them that are not explicitly included in the experimental design? In the case of lexicographic responses, in particular, it is difficult to be certain whether this results from the respondent not taking into account all the attributes in their selection of options, or whether the range of levels on key attributes is too narrow for trading to occur.

5. What is the appropriate supporting role for RP data? Here views varied considerably among participants, from regarding RP as being suitable just for establishing market shares (in order to facilitate the calculation of endogenous constants) through to its full use in joint estimation with SP data. The appropriate extent of use of RP data seems to depend on the quality of the data, and on the degree to which the RP responses have been constrained by local supply/market conditions (e.g., where there is one dominant retail centre, then RP data would reveal very little about consumer preferences).

RECOMMENDATIONS FOR FURTHER RESEARCH

The workshop discussions identified a number of areas where either existing knowledge is insufficient to draw clear conclusions, or the issue does not appear to have been addressed by the research community at all. Seven research priorities were identified.

1. Determining Criteria for Success and Validity

The crucial question in any SP survey is whether the data that have been collected and analysed are a valid representation of the preferences and behaviour of the target population. In part, the factors that determine this are the same as in any population survey, being affected by the sampling frame, sampling procedures, patterns of nonresponse, etc. However, in the case of SP, there are additional concerns relating to the realism of the responses.

Currently, this is dealt with at both the data checking and model estimation stages. The data are screened, and – in the case of a customised SP exercise – respondents may be excluded if they have provided estimates of attribute levels that are well outside a realistic range, or if they exhibit illogical judgements. Some analysts identify lexicographic responses, and estimate models with and without these respondents. Further cases may be removed during the model estimation process. It is also possible to assess internal validity, by withholding some judgement data and forecasting these choices from the remaining data. However, internal validity and a good model fit may not be sufficient to have confidence that the estimates are replicating actual preferences and choices. Further work is required to develop standard procedures for judging success and the validity of findings. This is likely to involve more extensive external validity checks, including a comparison of SP-based forecasts with 'revealed' behaviour, after implementation of the new feature that generated the need for the SP survey. Clearly, a number of such 'estimated' versus 'reported' validation checks must be carried out in order to be able to generalise the results.

2. Information Provision and Survey Framing

We know very little about the influence that the information, we provide to respondents before we ask them to complete the SP tasks, has on the judgements that they make – although many authors have warned of the possibility of 'policy response bias'. The workshop paper by Podgorski *et al* (2004) shows how the provision of additional background information can influence respondent support for different pricing policies – although, in this case, to a relatively limited extent.

There is scope for (unintended) influence at three points in the interview:

- The way in which the survey is introduced to respondents (i.e., the purpose of the survey, the client, etc.);
- The context in which each respondent is asked to complete the tasks (e.g., 'imagine you were making your regular commuter trip...'); and
- The background information about each attribute (in addition to that shown as part of each option). For example, if journey reliability is presented in a graphical manner, then the meaning of the representation may need to be explained to respondents before the options are presented.

Here it necessary to strike a balance, between:

- Overloading respondents versus not giving them enough information to ensure that they carry out the tasks as intended; and
- Encouraging them to think freely enough to accept the possibility of using a new alternative that includes non-existing features (e.g., a busway), without them becoming so unconstrained as to ignore the restrictions under which they carry out their day-to-day travel and activities.

Further research is needed to address these issues. As yet, we do not even know whether they are a potential source of minor or major bias.

3. The Influence of Presentation Formats

Very little is known about the influence of the form of presentation of information on each of the options on the judgements made by respondents. Previous research has indicated a possible order effect (e.g., more attention paid to attributes at the head of a list), and this has resulted in the recommendation made by the workshop to rotate the attribute order. However, there are many other aspects of presentation that might also be having a subtle and unintended influence on responses.

Two related aspects were addressed by the workshop:

- The amount of detail provided about each attribute (in particular, when describing the levels of each attribute); and
- The form of presentation of that information (words, numbers, graphics, pictures, sounds, etc.).

The workshop paper by van der Waerden *et al* (2004) suggested that more detailed verbal attribute descriptions affect the judgements made by respondents, and this requires further investigation.

During the nineties, alongside the growing use of computer assisted interviewing, various studies started exploring the scope for using colour in the presentation of options, leading on to the use of photographs and other pictorial stimuli. In the experience of workshop participants, the tendency to use colour and photographs has diminished, due to the concern that this might be introducing unintended stimuli into the SP exercises. In one study, using photographs to display features of old and refurbished railway stations, respondents were found to be influenced strongly by the weather conditions at the time the different pictures were taken. However, as multi-media interview capability becomes more widely available, it is inevitable that pressure will increase to provide respondents with richer depictions of the modal alternatives, etc. Research is, thus, urgently required to provide guidelines as to how to use this capability in an enriching rather than a distorting manner.

4. The influence of Interview Media and Survey Location

Interviewer administered SP interviews are carried out in a variety of locations, from homes to workplaces, or railway carriages to shopping areas; they usually employ 'pen and paper' or computer-based interviewing techniques. Telephone surveys are invariably carried out with respondents in their home (unless mobile phone numbers are used), while mail-back surveys are sent to respondents' homes, but might be physically completed anywhere (e.g., in the course of an air journey). Internet surveys might be accessed anywhere in the world, either while in a particular location, or on the move.

Relatively little research has been carried out into the influence of the interview media on the pattern of responses. The potential influence of the media on presentation format has been identified as a research question above. Here we consider more the related questions of the location where the respondent completes the task, and how this relates to the timing of the journey (or other activity) used as the choice context.

Interviewer and non-interviewer administered surveys have their strengths and weaknesses. The presence of an interviewer may influence the judgements made by a respondent and distort their pattern of responses (interviewer number may be a significant variable in an SP analysis), and put respondents under time pressure; on the other hand, the interviewer can explain what is required and guide the respondent through the stages of the exercise.

What is even less well understood is the potential influence of timing of the SP exercise in relation to the activity which provides the choice context. Specifically, there is no evidence to show whether carrying out an SP exercise in the course of the target activity (e.g., while shopping, while travelling on a train) has any effect on the results compared to carrying out the same SP exercise some time after the target activity/trip has been completed. This issue is of considerable importance, because, in multi-modal studies, it is common to use a mix of interview locations – but varying type of location systematically according to the travel mode currently being used for the target trip.

5. The Treatment of Complex Choices

Most SP studies, at least in the field of transport, focus the choice context on a single event (e.g., 'your last trip to X to shop'), and on a single choice, such as time of day, or mode of travel. Often, in reality, the decisions people make relate to a whole series of similar events and may involve multiple choices. This is recognised, to a limited degree, in studies involving commuter travel, where cost information for different modal options may be presented on a monthly or annual, as well as a daily basis, to increase the realism of responses. Another example is provided by congestion pricing SP experiments that consider changing departure times for both the outbound and return legs of a commuting tour, while also including the options to change mode instead of departure times.

What is currently very poorly handled in SP are:

- Decisions to vary the frequency of making a given trip, depending on the options on offer;
- Varying the mix of use of modes on different occasions (e.g., driving to work once a week, taking the bus the other days) – especially where this mix might alter in response to certain options; and
- Making complex choices (e.g., going to destination X by car versus going to destination Y by train).

There are important research issues here, affecting the context and framing of the SP exercise, the experimental design, option presentation, and model estimation.

6. Temporal Dimensions to SP Choices

Two broad issues arise here. The first concerns the temporal stability of the preferences that are expressed, and the second the time frame over which the choices expressed in an SP survey are likely to be realised in practice.

The value of SP and other related research would be greatly diminished if the preferences exhibited by respondents in such surveys were very transitory and ephemeral – unless this reflected random variation around a stable, aggregate population profile. It would be very valuable in SP research to learn more about the stability of preferences and the factors which may contribute to changing preferences. Here SP panel data would be required.

We might expect preferences to alter in response to changes in personal circumstances (e.g., change in family lifecycle stage, or a substantial change in personal income), but exogenous factors might also exert a strong influence, such as changing social attitudes to the use of public transport, or the willingness of people to pay directly for the use of roads. The influence of marketing, in particular, is recognised to be an important factor in the rate and extent of take-up of new products (e.g., a light rail system), and this also relates directly to the second aspect requiring additional research.

One question which nobody in the workshop was able to answer was 'how quickly might we expect the predictions made from an SP-based model to be realised in practice?' (i.e., the 'ramp-up' period). Although every effort is made to maximise the realism of the context and content of an SP exercise, conceptually it differs crucially from reality in two important respects:

- Respondents are provided with 'perfect information' or, at least, all the information that the analyst believes is necessary for the respondent to make an informed choice; and
- Respondents are asked to act as if they were making the choice at that moment in time.

In reality, respondents do not have perfect information – at least not instantly, without undergoing a search process – and they do not re-evaluate their decisions on every occasion that they undertake the target trip/activity, particularly where the activity is routine in nature. This suggests that SP forecasts will tend to reflect the maximum likely market penetration. What is uncertain is how long it would take in reality to reach this optimum level – if, indeed, it is ever reached – once a new service is provided. This is likely to depend on a variety of factors, including whether respondents are confronted directly by the new or changed feature (e.g., higher toll charge) or whether it is an 'optional' feature that they may not directly encounter (e.g., new modal alternative), and, in the latter case, on the quality and effectiveness of the marketing of the new service. This is a seriously under-researched area of great importance, where researchers will need to draw on other literatures, including diffusion theory, prospect theory and learning theory.

7. An International Cross-Discipline Review of Evidence

The workshop discussions were greatly enriched by bringing together members who had a broad range of SP experience across a diverse range of fields (transport, housing, retailing, etc.), and in both a developed and developing country context. In some cases, it was evident that different practices had evolved in the different subject areas and geographic regions. This might be due in part to different contextual conditions (e.g., the infrequent but major and discrete nature of housing choices versus the less significant decisions on trip re-routing), but, in other cases, it seemed more to reflect different prevailing professional opinions – thus providing opportunities to compare and contrast experiences.

Uncharacteristically, the workshop participants admitted that we do not yet know everything about the best ways to apply SP techniques. As a result, the workshop strongly recommends that a broad review of SP experiences across different regions and disciplines be undertaken, in order to draw on this wide range of knowledge and help develop guidelines for future SP studies in the transport sector.

REFERENCES

Caussade, S., J. Ortúzar, L.I. Rizzi and D.A. Hensher (2005). Assessing the influence of design dimensions on stated choice experiment estimates, *Transportation Research B*, **29** (7), 621-640.

Podgorski, K.V., K.M. Kockelman and S. Kalmanje (2004). Survey work for assessing new policies: identifying public response to and preferences for variations on toll roads and congestion pricing. Paper presented at the 7th International Conference on Travel Survey Methods, Costa Rica, August.

Rose, J.M. and D.A. Hensher (2006). Handling individual specific availability of alternatives in stated choice experiments. In: *Travel Survey Methods: Quality and Future Directions* (P.R. Stopher and C.C. Stecher, eds),337-358, Elsevier, Oxford.

Van der Reis, P., M. Lombard and I. Kriel (2004). A qualitative analysis of factors contributing to inconsistent responses in stated preference surveys. Paper presented at the 7th International Conference on Travel Survey Methods, Costa Rica, August.

Van der Waerden, P., A. Borgers and H. Timmermans (2004). The effects of attribute level definition on stated choice behaviour. Paper presented at the 7th International Conference on Travel Survey Methods, Costa Rica, August.

20

PANEL SURVEYS

Dirk Zumkeller, University of Karlsruhe, Karlsruhe, Germany
Jean-Loup Madre, National Institute of Research on Transports and Safety (INRETS), Arcueil, France
Bastian Chlond, University of Karlsruhe, Karlsruhe, Germany
and
Jimmy Armoogum, National Institute of Research on Transports and Safety (INRETS), Arcueil, France

INTRODUCTION

In recent years, travel demand throughout the world has been heavily influenced by a variety of external factors and processes. These include economic growth or stagnation, growing or declining incomes, demographic changes such as the aging of the population in numerous western societies, the impacts on working structures caused by the globalisation of the economy, and even changes to the political landscape such as the upheaval in Eastern Europe and the growing strength of the European Union.

In view of these developments, numerous endogenous interventions in the transport system (e.g., telematics, public transport improvements, high speed rail-systems) have been conducted or at least planned. It can be assumed that future behavioural changes are influenced not only by these interventions, but also by exogenous factors such as types of housing, changes in working patterns, and increasing leisure time. The impacts of all these developments become clearer if one tries to understand them as behavioural changes resulting from changes of temporal, monetary, and organisational budgets and regimes as well as the personal status on the individual level.

In the past, data collection for infrastructure planning was oriented to traffic modelling and focussed on peak hours for an 'average' weekday. However, now the main interest is shifting from designing infrastructure to a better understanding of individual behaviour, to try to influence behaviour in a way that improves the use of our infrastructure.

Moreover, it can be argued that a solution to environmental issues is a change in travel behaviour towards a more sustainable mobility. If one wants to understand how people behave in different situational contexts, data are necessary which measure the same people in different situations. Indeed, the variability in behaviour, the flexibility of a person to react and the identification of constraints and regimes is only detectable from a longitudinal perspective. However, the usual cross-section or snapshot-oriented surveys of the behaviour of one day give only poor descriptions of ongoing changes and hardly allow us to distinguish real changes in behaviour from external evolutions caused by specific trends (for instance, low growth rate and high unemployment in Continental Europe during most of the nineties).

Thus, data sources are necessary that enable the researcher to understand which processes are ongoing and how changes are happening. This, in turn, magnifies the need for a temporal dimension in our data. However, when doing so, we have to be careful about the two following problems:

1.   The rhythms of mobility during consecutive days and changes occurring between successive periods (with an appropriate time unit to be defined) are apparently different problems; and
2.   Panels measure combined changes, which are caused by both external factors and endogenous interventions.

This chapter comprises an overview about the characteristics and advantages but also methodological problems of panel surveys (second section), while, in the third section, examples of existing panel surveys about travel behaviour are introduced. Because the chapter is intended to give an overview about the current state of panel surveys, the fourth section, which shows some different approaches for making use of panel data, is intended only to show the variety of approaches. The chapter ends with open questions that can be understood as suggestions for further research.

DEFINITIONS, CHARACTERISTICS, ADVANTAGES AND DISADVANTAGES

Characteristics of Panel Surveys from a Theoretical Point of View

How to Measure Change in Behaviour?

Traditionally, transport data collection has focused on the production of net accounting statistics. However, for the proper assessment of change this is problematic, because changes occur in various directions, but in most instances the changes do not totally counterbalance each other. For example in Grenoble, the proportion of new inhabitants is paradoxically higher in central cities than in outer suburbs. However, the proportion of households leaving central cities to settle in the suburbs is higher than that of those leaving the outer suburbs, which explains urban sprawl (Bussière and Madre, 2002). In-movers to one area are not the same as people who have moved out of the same area, and their behaviour is not sensitive to the same factors (prices, regulations, etc.). Thus, in order to understand the development over time and its determining factors, it is insufficient to look at the net changes; instead the behaviour of different individuals at different points in time must be considered. Three main ways can be used to capture changing behaviour:

- By asking persons or firms how they would change their behaviour in the future. These 'prospective methods' are Interactive Interviews (II), Stated Preference (SP), Stated Response (SR), etc.
- By observing these changes in the past for a long enough period; these 'longitudinal methods' are based not only on panel surveys, repeated surveys, or mobility biographies, but also on data from official statistics.
- In principle, it is possible to ask people at one point in time retrospectively to get intrapersonal information about time spans of the past (e.g., 'mobility biographies'). Such data enable the researcher to use the analytical advantages of panel data, but the information can be biased by respondent error (selectivity phenomena, transfiguration of the past, and simply forgetting). Therefore, it is important to distinguish between 'panel surveys' and 'panel data'. Because the emphasis of this chapter is on the surveys rather than on the data, the retrospective approaches have been excluded from the scope.

For a better understanding of the conditions of change, one cross-section (snapshot) is not enough; only repeated observations or 'moving pictures of trajectories' (i.e., generic panel surveys) are adequate tools. The collection of such data is very costly (e.g., on the North Europe High Speed Train) and presents difficulties over the longer period; in addition, their analysis is not straightforward (e.g., a clear assessment of what is due to transport supply and to the socio-economic context).

Definitions and Conceptual Characteristics

In empirical social research a survey is designated as a panel when the same survey units are contacted at different times, measuring the same characteristics. This makes it possible to capture changes as a function of time or underlying factors. We start with some definitions and classifications, that are illustrated in Figure 1:

- **Repeated Cross Sections.** Repeated surveys within a population at different points in time with different individuals (completely independent samples) are a series of cross-section surveys not panels. They can be used for temporal analyses, but the amount of information available is rather restricted, because only the net changes between any points in time can be analysed. Repeated cross-section data are sometimes treated as panel data, in so called 'pseudo' panels. This is based on the idea that certain cohorts (defined by the year of birth) are followed over time and are re-identifiable. This relies on the assumption that they aged with comparable biographies, attitudes and experiences. However, it must be stressed that the intrapersonal aspect is getting lost and this only works if the interpersonal variation within a certain age group is rather low. Against the backdrop of the individualisation of lifestyles this approach is not satisfactory.

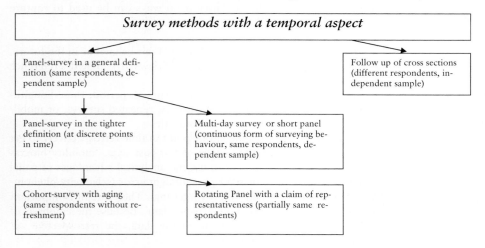

Figure 1: Survey Methods with a Temporal Aspect

Given that we are talking about two dimensions in temporal terms (multi-day and multi-period data) we have to distinguish between the following designs:

- **The Multi-day Survey ('Short Panel').** The continuous form of observation is often defined as a short panel. Examples are the measurement of behaviour over one week, a month, or even longer (see MOBIDRIVE (Axhausen *et al.*, 2000, or the Uppsala Panel in the eighties (Hanson and Huff, 1988). These approaches are used for longitudinal surveys, i.e., multi-day data of one week.
- **The Panel Survey (in a Closer Definition).** The observation at different discrete points in time of the same items is defined as a panel survey in its special form or tighter definition. It is distinguishable from repeated cross section surveys, which follow the same design, but use independent samples.

Another aspect is related to the question of whether the sample has to remain representative of the population over time or is allowed to age naturally with the survey:

- A cohort-study is an observation of exactly the same survey objects over time (that is the normal form in medicine or pharmaceutics). The sample is aging with the survey. A special form is a before-and-after-study with the same objects with the intended inclusion of an event or a measure affecting respondent behaviour.
- A rotating panel aims to maintain representativeness by the refreshment of those objects being lost. These 'new' objects have to be chosen in such a way that the sample can represent the (changing) total for a certain time span such as a year.

Advantages of Panel Surveys Compared to Cross-sectional Surveys

To identify the analytical advantages of multi-day and multi-period data, it makes sense to compare their characteristics against the cross-sectional/snapshot and panel surveys, respectively (see Kitamura 1990).

Cross-sectional Surveys

- There is no notion available about the regularity or irregularity of individual behaviour, because the frequency distribution of activities or trips over time is unknown.
- Infrequent activities, for example, long distance trips, are not captured adequately and are underestimated, because they normally form a considerable part of multi-day activities.
- It is not possible to distinguish between intrapersonal and interpersonal variability (e.g., the classic example of transit use: Does a percentage of ten percent of all trips to work by transit mean that all persons are using transit one out of ten days, or that ten percent of all persons use transit every day?) In the first case the observed variability/modal variance is intrapersonal only, while in the latter case the variance has to be interpreted to be interpersonal only. By comparing the results of two cross-sections it is impossible to identify behavioural changes on an individual level.
- For the case of repeated cross-sectional surveys, only net changes between any cross-sections are identifiable and quantifiable in the sense of the marginal values or changes in the marginal distributions. We have to assume the reversibility of effects. For example, persons who acquire a car will behave like persons who already owned a car, and vice-versa. This can lead to misinterpretations in causal analyses, and lead to incorrect assumptions regarding effectiveness of policy measures.

Panel Surveys

These problems and methodological weaknesses of snapshot/cross-sectional surveys are avoidable. The distinction must be made between panel surveys in their tighter definition and the so-called short panels of multi-day data. The benefits of panels (defined more tightly as multi-period surveys) include:

- They are better for causal analysis, because the temporal sequence of causes and effects is known (assuming that panel waves are frequent enough to catch the changes).
- They are better for measuring the effects of changes in external factors, e.g., is the purchase/disposal of a car the reason for or the consequence of changed mobility requirements. For a moving household, we can observe the pre- and post-move equilibria (e.g., in terms of car ownership and use). Thus in principle, panels allow for causal analyses, because the temporal sequence of causes and effects is known (assuming that the panel waves are frequent enough to catch such a sequence).
- As mentioned above, repeated cross sectional surveys only allow comparison of aggregate values or marginal distributions (net changes). Using panel surveys, it is possible to measure the gross changes within the transition matrix. For example, Table 1 shows the number of households that changed numbers of vehicles between 1994 and 2002 in the German Mobility Panel.
- The identification of gross changes and their potential compensation allows much more information on the dynamics of changes, that also can be modelled using Markov Chains, for example. Thus, by means of panel data, it is possible to analyse these gross changes as well as compensatory effects. These have, in the past, (without the more process oriented panel data) often been wrongly interpreted as stability and have resulted in a specific cross-sectional view of the process of transport development.
- Using the temporal and intrapersonal aspects the building of models about the dynamics of change is becoming more promising: The potential to improve demand forecasts is obvious.
- Once a panel is established, it can be used rapidly to identify unexpected changes, e.g., the massive petrol price increases in 2001 in Germany.
- A more general basic panel can be used as a control group when comparing to special panels established for 'before and after' studies, related to measures such as teleworking, or a reduction of car trips by areas with low access to private cars. With the help of a 'special' measure-specific panel with the same design as used for the general panel it can serve as a control to monitor external changes[29].

The benefits of short panels, in the sense of multi-day panels (e.g., with a one-week survey period in each wave), include:

- A one-week survey period is well suited for obtaining the desired findings: the week represents a culturally accepted unit of time in which most of the day-to-

[29] See for example the project 'Living with Reduced Car-Ownership)', (Chlond *et al.*, 2000).

day variation is included (such as frequency of work days, leisure activities, shopping activities), of which most are usually repeated in that weekly rhythm[30].

Table 1: Changes in Household Car Ownership Between 1994 and 2000

Cars Before \ Cars After	0	1	2	3	4+	Marginal distribution (before)
0	294	22	1	-	-	317
1	9	1,590	93	7	-	1,699
2	-	79	569	23	1	672
3	-	4	24	61	4	93
4+	-	1	1	3	8	12
Marginal distribution (after)	303	1,696	688	94	13	2,794

Source : German mobility panel, cumulated transitions between 1994 – 2002, (Dargay *et al.*, 2003)

- Information about the travel and activity behaviour of a week provides insight into the frequency of activities, modal use, etc. Additionally, we obtain information about the regularity and repetition of behaviour, when weeks are repeated after one or two years.
- Multi-day journeys (which comprise a large part of long-distance mobility) are represented better within a multi-day survey (e.g., long-distance weekly commuting, which, in developed societies, is becoming more and more relevant, can be identified).
- The total observed variation in a sample can be divided into interpersonal and intrapersonal parts. Looking at behaviour over one week, it becomes clear what is typical of an individual's behaviour and how it differs from others, while, in snapshots, the systematic differences between persons are hidden. Figure 2 illustrates how classifying a population into groups of modal behaviour (groups of multimodality) is time dependent – the number of persons using different modes over time – increases and converges with an increasing duration of report.
- Information on the intrapersonal multiplicity of behaviour of individuals can be obtained by the use of short panels. Thus it is possible to estimate the degrees of freedom as well as possible alternatives available to individuals in their day-to-day decisions. This comes against the background that the impacts of future telematic approaches can be better predicted in terms of how they can help people organise their lives such as:
  - o In which way an adaptation of behaviour can take place (temporally, activity sequence);
  - o Are there observable attitudes such as the commitment to a certain mode (mono-modality), or an enlarged choice set (multimodality)?

---

[30] The results of the Uppsala Panel (Hanson and Huff, 1988) or the MOBIDRIVE-Panel (Axhausen *et al.*,, 2000) are of central importance for research and development of the idea of longitudinal data surveying and analysis. For reasons of practical application, we want to concentrate here on shorter multi-day data such as a period of one week.

o How much of the behaviour or the activities is ruled by routines or habits (repetition within the observed time period)?
o How often disturbances can be observed in the sense of deviations from a rule?
o Which persons are more or less flexible in terms of their adaptability to distortions of their organisational framework (e.g., the husband is involved in an accident)?

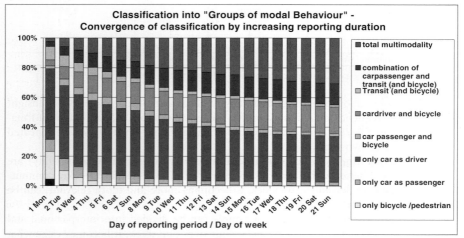

Source: Data of the German Mobility Panel

Figure 2: Illustration of the Convergence of the Classification with an Increasing Duration of Report (max. 3 weeks)

General benefits of panels, from a methodological viewpoint, include:

• Panel surveys permit greater statistical reliability for a given sample size than cross-sectional surveys; and
• Measuring or answering errors that arise in a definite and systematic form can be identified in longitudinal surveys (e.g., the forgotten trip back home can be identified by comparison with other days, or other forgotten trip items can be completed with the knowledge of the trip characteristics of other days, and fatigue effects can be identified at least in the aggregate).

The timing of waves is also an important issue for panel surveys. Kitamura *et al.*, (2003) have shown that, for a stochastic discrete behavioural process, the estimates are more accurate when the period between two waves is shortened. The authors say that maximum accuracy is achieved with a continuous survey. However, from an empirical perspective it would be difficult to manage a continuous panel because of the respondent burden.

Empirical Problems of Panel Surveys

Despite the analytic advantage of panels identified in the preceding section, some special problems must be acknowledged and discussed. The main problem with panel surveys is the nonresponse bias created by sample attrition between waves, and fatigue within waves (see Hensher, 1987 and Chlond and Kuhnimhof, 2003). Most of the time, the correction of this bias is made using weighting procedures.

Random Sampling Versus Stratified Sampling

As respondent burden is usually higher than for snapshots or cross-sections, it is necessary to have reliable participants. This raises questions about how strict 'random' sampling might increase the nonresponse problem. The implications are that recruitment for a panel has to be done with great care, based on a multi-stage recruitment covering a random sample, to identify a set of persons willing to participate and a sub-sample of those finally participating. This clearly results in a certain selectivity of the process, which is discussed later.

Attrition, Mortality and Fatigue Effects

Normally in panels a decline in the willingness to report can be observed. This is understandable because, at the beginning, the participants are curious about the topic of the survey. As a logical consequence of the repetition their motivation declines. This decline we define as attrition. However, as this decline has several dimensions, we have to distinguish between the attrition between panel waves (people do not want to report again, this effect we call 'panel mortality') and the attrition within waves (which often has been defined as 'panel fatigue') as a result of which people start to report with less accuracy in multi-day surveys.

Mortality (Attrition between Waves). As a consequence of respondent burden, many participants drop out between waves. Normally only a share of participants can be persuaded to participate again in another year. This share will be higher, the more care has been invested in motivating the participants, keeping in touch with them during periods when no survey is conducted, and informing them about the results. Figure 3 shows the attrition process between waves relating to the original sample size: it makes clear that a certain degree of mortality is almost a natural law. Mortality analyses in the German MOP showed that high attrition occurs when any changes in the household which can be interpreted as a 'social stigma' (e.g., divorce, becoming jobless) occur. Therefore, certain events, which presumably are of importance for a detailed picture of mobility, cannot be covered on a level proportional to the whole population.

Higher attrition can be expected with higher respondent burden or extended time without contacts. Attrition can never become zero, because certain individuals move out of the scope of the survey, because of 'mortality' in its original meaning, or because they will migrate, which is of major interest for monitoring spatial developments and associated changes of mobility behaviour.

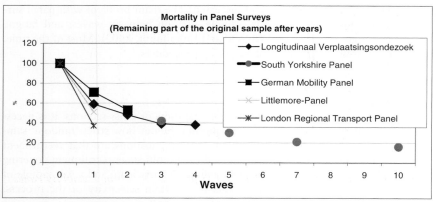

Sources: German Mobility Panel, Littlemore Panel, London Regional Panel, South Yorkshire Panel and Longitudinal Verplaatsingsondezoek

Figure 3: Mortality in Panel Surveys about Travel Behaviour

As a consequence the following aspects need attention:

- The gap between two waves should not become too large (otherwise the re-participation of former participants declines).
- There is a need to stay in touch with the participants (e.g., by informing them about results, Christmas greetings, birthday cards, etc.), even in times where no survey is planned, to maintain current addresses.
- The participants must know about their burden in advance. A solution can be to limit the number of waves for participants.
- Due to respondent burden, it is important not to overburden a panel survey with too many aspects.

Fatigue (Attrition Within a Wave). This effect mainly concerns multi-day surveys. Because participants have to report all the trips/activities of a period, the willingness to report at all will decline (they stop reporting from one day to the next – a kind of item nonresponse), and some will try to ease their workload by underreporting (e.g., by transforming complex trip- or activity-chains into only one trip), see Figure 4.

Because the mobility at the weekend is normally lower than during working days, there is some danger of such effects being hidden. A simple solution is to start with equally distributed 'start-days' in order to distinguish between day-of-the-week-effects and fatigue effects. It should be emphasised that although we cannot identify exactly those who were underreporting, on an aggregate level, we can estimate the errors.

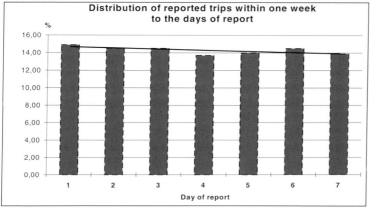

Figure 4: Attrition of the Number of Reported Trips from the German Mobility Panel

Thus, the rate of decline of different mobility indicators can be considered as a measurement to assess the rate of completeness of the reporting and it is possible to weight and expand the data of the later days with a weight resulting from the rate of decline on an aggregate level (Kitamura and Bovy 1987; Kunert 1992). The following glance at different mobility indicators reveals interesting interrelationships.

1. The decline of reported immobility mainly results from finishing reporting at a certain point in time during the week (people give up reporting).
2. The decline of the reported trips mainly results from 1, but also from the fact that short trips are consciously combined and omitted. Because the decline of the reported mobility rate explains about seventy five percent of the decline of the reported trips, the first effect is certainly dominant.
3. The decline of the reported distance should normally completely be explained by the decline of the reported trip-making, because combining trips has no significant effect on the overall distance reported, except in the case when short trips are entirely omitted.
4. The decline of the reported duration can be explained – apart from leaving off short trips with slow modes –in the same way as the decline of the reported distance.

These aspects show how the multi-period data allow for the interpretation of the results and how the completeness of data can be affected by methodological artefacts[31]. The results show, additionally, that a refusal to report can wrongly be confused with no trip-making. However with panel data for one week it is possible to get a more realistic impression about the share of trip-makers (Axhausen *et al.*, 2003).

---

[31] For the MOP a correction by weighting (for the cross-sectional results for a certain year) is only required, if the attrition rate for each year is significant. In most years, the decline is so small that such a correction is not needed.

Altogether, the attrition rates and their significance can serve as a measurement of the quality of reporting. When considered as a comprehensive effect, it becomes clear that the attrition rate provides a reliable measurement of the overall data quality in terms of reliability and completeness. If we take the example of the Puget Sound Transportation Panel, which is not based on a rotating refreshment sample, but is mainly based on a systematic self-selection over the years, the sample is not representative of the population (which is changing over time) and, therefore, special weighting procedures are needed (see Ma and Goulias, 1997a).

Selectivity Phenomena

It becomes likely that a multi-stage recruitment process and the repetition of data collection in a panel creates selectivity related to the characteristics of participating households. Thus, the idea of being able to create a representative sample of a population over time is endangered.

Selectivity has to be analysed with care. Good practice is to compare the participants not only in terms of their socioeconomic and demographic characteristics, but also with the results of cross-sectional surveys, where respondent burden is less. For the MOP, a selectivity study has been performed by asking potential participants at the very first contact about their mobility. The results (Chlond and Kuhnimhof, 2003) have been positive so far, showing that the 'repeaters' cannot be distinguished from the drop-outs in terms of their mobility (no underrepresentation of people with high or low mobility), but only in socioeconomic terms (younger and older persons are less likely to participate than the thirty five to sixty age group). This can be handled easily with appropriate weighting, provided secondary statistics with the relevant characteristics exist.

One benefit of a rotating panel is to reduce selectivity bias over the lifetime of the panel; the 'survival' of participants within the panel should be restricted resulting in a rotating panel. Because the ratio between new participants and repeaters will be stable, there is less risk of selecting only participants with certain characteristics. Furthermore the refreshment process can be used to control, and thus avoid, selectivity over time.

Panel Conditioning

People may adapt their behaviour to the topic of the survey. This is a problem in surveys in which attitudes or opinions are asked. It can be assumed that this is not critical for surveys about transport behaviour and activities, perhaps with the exception of surveys with a focus on attitudes towards certain modes. It may be a topic of debate if we observe a change in revealed behaviour as a result of a changed reporting behaviour. However, this is an attrition effect, mentioned above. On the other hand, we may expect people to increase their trips, because they are being asked to report activity or mobility.

Panel Aging

A cohort panel can be limiting because the sample is aging, by design. If the objective of the panel is to represent a total population, e.g., of a region or country, a rotating panel with planned refreshment can be a better design.

Strategies and necessary considerations for refreshment. A simple replacement of drop-outs by households with the same socioeconomic or demographic characteristics would be a solution, but it would be better to distinguish between 'new units' (e.g., young individuals who have just left the household of their parents) and 'rotating units' who replace drop-outs. Symmetrically among drop-outs, it is important to distinguish between 'disappeared units' (e.g., resulting from death) and new refusers. Although difficult, it would allow for the distinction of changes that are due to the renewal of the population and those that are due to changing behaviour for the actual population. By constraining the number of waves per participant, the special problems associated with a panel (attrition, conditioning, distortions in connection with increasing respondent burden) can potentially be reduced. The appropriate number of waves certainly depends on the topic, amount of questions, and work-load of the survey.

If the number of waves, the mortality rates per wave, and the total sample size is known (or at least can be estimated), it is possible to establish a constant proportion of new participants and repeaters. These stable proportions have several advantages:

- Attrition effects can be weighted in the same way independently of the year;
- There are no methodological artefacts by different cohorts in terms of size and constitution, because the recruitment procedure can be performed in a standardised process; and
- Different cohorts[32] will have the same proportions in all waves.

Sample Sizes and Weighting Procedures

Normally, we are confronted with small sample sizes, panel attrition, and panel selectivity. Thus weighting of panel data is a challenging task and several possibilities have to be discussed. Because drop-outs have specific characteristics, the idea of a self weighting panel is promising. Those with the same characteristics as the drop-outs are treated by giving them a higher weight. The problem is that we do not know whether we use the correct weighting variables. Does the drop-out correspond to the weighting variable or not? (e.g., Horowitz, 1997; Pendyala and Kitamura, 1997).

---

[32] Cohort can have a different meaning in combination with multi-period surveys: 1. A cohort comprises individuals born during the same period. 2. A cohort consists of the set of persons who participate in the same waves. Here the second meaning should be understood.

Normally certain 'interesting' transitions are rare incidents (e.g., giving up car-ownership, moving, etc.), and, in relation to the limited sample sizes, statistical analyses are rather restricted. In addition, as mentioned above, the transitions will be biased by selectivity phenomena. Therefore, the approach of summing up or merging the transitions of several years makes sense. This results in one transition matrix between the periods n and $n+t$, the weighting procedure can follow the distribution at the period n, which has to be chosen in the middle of all merged periods. However, this approach is only acceptable if we have stable conditions of the total over several years.

Cost of Panel Surveys – Economic Considerations

Panel surveys are sometimes considered as more costly than traditional cross sectional surveys, because their initial start-up costs are usually higher. The cost for setting up a panel is clearly higher than for cross sections, because the set–up has to be done with more care and planning. Keeping the sample representative requires much effort and experience about response behaviour. If there is too much time between waves of a panel, and the overall population is shifting rapidly, the benefits of a panel may be lost, and repeated cross-sections may be more appropriate.

A decision to use a panel has to be taken in the long run. The data will be relevant and useful only after a couple of years (and not at once) – with the exception of using the data to monitor demand. If an authority is able to make a commitment for several years of data collection, and is interested in causal analysis, it should vote for the establishment of a panel. An authority requiring information with high variance for one moment in time may prefer a large cross-sectional survey.

When the recruitment of (reliable) participants becomes more and more difficult and thus expensive, the relative cost of recruitment becomes more relevant compared to other elements of the survey. For participants who respond more than once the relative cost of recruitment declines. Professional market research firms have already learned this and have established their 'access panels' with willing-to-answer people.

Additionally, panel surveys may have high quality data with lower costs for cleaning data. The repeaters are the more motivated participants compared to those who only report once. Moreover the information collected on different occasions is useful to check the data and to correct (item) nonresponse. This means that the efforts to clean the data are less and raw data cleaning is more efficient. This has to be calculated against the attrition of panels and the selectivity phenomenon. As a panel continues, the additional marginal cost for each wave will be relatively small. Also, one has to calculate these smaller additional marginal costs in addition to the analytical benefits.

After ten years, the German MOP reveals some interesting results: the recruitment of a cohort with 350 to 400 households with about 1.95 reporting persons per household for a week and attrition rates of about 0.3 to 0.25, results in about 900 households and 1,800 to 1,900 person-weeks with about twenty five trips per person per week. With rough marginal cost for surveying of €140,000 to €150,000, one reported trip costs €3 to €3.50, one person costs €80 per wave, and one household about €160. Compared with the German NTS of 2002 (MiD Mobility in Germany, 2002) with an average cost per household of €70 and only one day of reporting, the cost per reported trip is about €10 (but it has to be mentioned that the information collected per trip is more detailed in the latter case). Considering the unit of surveyed number of trips or person-days, a longitudinal approach is the more cost effective. Another issue is the sample size: establishing a panel instead of two independent samples results in a smaller sample size for the panel study, since the between-sample variance is eliminated.

Comparison in Terms of Accuracy Between a Panel with Two Waves and Two Cross-Sectional Surveys

As mentioned above panel surveys permit greater statistical reliability for a given sample size than cross-section surveys or in other words we can achieve the same statistical reliability with a smaller sample depending on the level of variance. For the example of the Urban Mobility Plan for the Metropolitan Area of Paris, it was shown (Armoogum, 2002) that the statistical reliability is higher (a smaller confidence interval) for a panel compared to two independent cross sectional samples, where both surveys used the same sample size. For the example of two waves surveys at two points between 2001 and 2005 the modal split of public transport (indicator P_2) is the variable.

Let: $VAR(P_2^{2001})$ be the variance of the indicator P_2 for the year 2001
 $VAR(P_2^{2005})$ be the variance of the indicator P_2 for the year 2005

The Variance of $(P_2^{2005} - P_2^{2001})$ is then equal to (see Armoogum, 2002):

$$VAR\left(P_2^{2005} - P_2^{2001}\right) = VAR\left(P_2^{2005}\right) + VAR\left(P_2^{2001}\right) - 2*\rho\sqrt{VAR\left(P_2^{2005}\right)*VAR\left(P_2^{2001}\right)}$$

where ρ is the correlation between P_2 for the years 2001 and 2005.

Normally we do not know the value of the coefficient of correlation (ρ). If we have any information about ρ from other surveys we can derive different functions of the width of the ninety five percent confidence interval for a panel-sample with two waves on the one side and two independent samples on the other. Based on assumptions for ρ, four different functions of the width of the ninety five percent confidence intervals can be derived. Figure 5 illustrates the effect: assuming a realistic indicator of the share of public transport (by any other information) of about 3.4 percent, we can show the confidence intervals for different coefficients of correlation and sample sizes:

- The coefficient of correlation $\rho=1.00$ for a sample of 500 individuals;
- The coefficient of correlation $\rho=0.75$ for a sample of 2500 individuals;

- The coefficient of correlation ρ=0.50 for a sample of 5000 individuals;
- Two independent samples for a sample of 10,000 individuals.

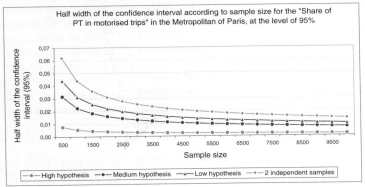

Figure 5: Half Width of the Confidence Interval According to the Sample Size

This example shows that the panel approach reduces the survey cost for the Urban Mobility Plan for the MAP by fifty percent (assuming that the coefficient of correlation is ρ=0.75) compared with using two independent samples.

EXISTING EXAMPLES OF PANEL SURVEYS

Panels about Mobility and Transport

The German Mobility Panel

After massive growth rates of mobility demand in the eighties, the upheaval in East Germany in 1989 and the German reunification in 1990, the German ministry of transport found it necessary to monitor the passenger transport demand and to generate a data-source which could give more insight into the processes of change to be expected and to be forecast. For these purposes the German MOP has been set up and designed as a multi-purpose instrument:

- For the monitoring of mobility demand to represent the (changing) total over time (→ a new refreshment of the sample per year was required);
- For the observation of the intrapersonal variance of mobility patterns (→ longitudinal survey of activities and trips for one week); and
- For the analyses of changes of mobility demand (→ yearly repetition as a panel).

Thus the survey had to be designed as a hybrid covering these competing aims and respecting respondent burden as well as the financial situation. The survey includes the characteristics of households and persons and a one week diary (time of start and end of a trip, purpose, mode, distance). The survey takes place each year between the second half of September and mid-November, a season reflecting behaviour not being distorted by holidays or extreme weather conditions. A sample across all seasons was considered, but rejected due to the small sample size.

The stratified random household sampling used the three variables: household size, household type (describing the socioeconomic status), and a spatial factor. Each year about 350 to 400 'fresh' households are recruited to (hopefully) stay for a total of three years within the panel, leading to an approach of a three year rotating panel. Within these cohorts, a mortality of about twenty five to thirty percent of the households has been the average. With the cohort size of about 350 'fresh' households per year, each transition from one year to the next comprises about 450 households which are 're-peaters'. This results in a total sample size of about 750 to 800 households per year. During the set up phase (1994 – 1999), the survey was performed only in the old federal states (former 'old' Federal Republic). From 1999, the survey has been extended to the 'new' states in the former German Democratic Republic. This (late) extension has been the result of the lack of IT-infrastructure for surveying in former East Germany (e.g., lack of private phones in the beginning).

The competing objectives of the MOP, as mentioned above, led to the following compromise: the claim of representativeness could be achieved by the rotation of the panel and the drop out of participants. Because of using a one-week diary, an attempt to reduce burden was made by limiting the reporting of activities and trips such that only residence address is captured in sufficient detail to be geocoded. Data-quality and completeness are claimed to be high. Plausibility checks of reported behaviour are performed in different stages of the survey and data processing. The sample sizes and sample development between 1994 and 2002, reflecting the cohort approach, are shown in Figure 6.

Amongst others, the following analyses have been done so far, reflecting the different application possibilities:

- Observation of travel demand as repeated cross-sections (this observation belongs to the permanent tasks within the commissioning by the German Ministry of Transport (e.g., Zumkeller *et al.*, 1999; Zumkeller *et al.*, 2001);
- Variation of mobility behaviour between years (Kloas *et al.*, 2000);
- Aspects of mobility within one week (frequencies of activities and modal use);
- Variability and flexibility within one week (Zumkeller *et al.*, 1999);
- Analysis by statistical-econometric models (Hautzinger, 2000);
- Analyses of neural networks for explaining modal choice (Heidemann *et al.*, 1999);

- Comparison of transport behaviour in West and East Germany (Zumkeller *et al.*, 2002);
- Influence of increase in gas taxation on mobility demand;
- Interdependencies between household members;
- Identification and description of multi-modal persons (Kuhnimhof *et al.*, 2006);
- Dependency from cars: car related or car-independent lifestyles; and
- Identification of multimodal person-groups.

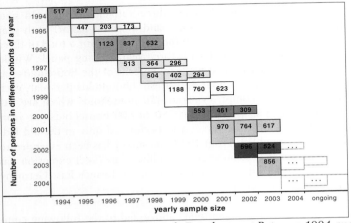

Figure 6: Sample Sizes and Sample Development Between 1994 and 2003/2004 (Ongoing) of the German Mobility Panel

A special selectivity study has been performed, to determine which selectivity phenomena exist within the MOP. In brief, the result was the following: most of the selectivity phenomena are related to socioeconomic characteristics of households or persons and are not mobility related. Thus, the results of the survey can be corrected by weighting procedures based on appropriate secondary statistics.

Puget Sound Transportation Panel (PSTP)

The transport panel with up to now the greatest longevity is the Puget Sound Transportation Panel (PSTP) in the Seattle Region in the US (Murakami and Watterson, 1989; Murakami and Ulberg, 1997). It was designed as a general purpose urban household panel mainly focused on transport, but also created as a tracking device for the dynamics of employment, work characteristics, household composition, vehicle availability, travel behaviour, attitudes and values, trip-making behaviour, and the travel decision making process. It started in 1989 and has, up to now in the regions where it is still alive, already achieved nine waves. It has not been set up regularly (there is a gap of two years between two waves, also the season of surveying has not always been the same). Thus, certain patterns and figures are not strictly comparable. Nevertheless, this example does show the feasibility of a panel over a time span of more than a decade with the same participants. There is a permanent refreshment, which keeps the sample size at about 1,500 to 2,000 households per wave.

The data available for analysis include household and person information as well as a detailed record from a two-day travel diary (to limit the effects of fatigue), which certainly raises some questions about the limited amount of variance covered on the day to day basis. Thus, it can be regarded as a multi-period, but not a multi-day panel. Since 1997, the original objectives were enriched by the introduction of questions on traveller information system use, telecommunications, and computer ownership and use. Furthermore a shift from a trip based to an activity based approach has been introduced. Both changes – or rather enrichments – clearly raise questions about comparability. However, for a sample with known characteristics the addition of such further questions makes sense, because there is much comparable information for other survey items available. The PSTP data have been used so far for different analyses (Goulias and Ma, 1996) as follows, which show the universality of the survey approach:

- Perceptions of travel modes and revealed behaviour (Ulberg, 1991);
- Application of different weighting approaches based on attrition and drop-out probabilities (Pendyala *et al.*,1993);
- Analyses of stability of activity and travel patterns (Mannering *et al.*, 1994);
- Analyses of multiple selections using a probit modelling approach (Chung and Goulias, 1995);
- Classification of activity and travel patterns by clustering approaches;
- Activity multi-level models, analyses of long term dynamic aspects of travel behaviour (Ma and Goulias, 1997b);
- Application of latent class analysis methods to demonstrate the multiplicity of potential paths of change (Goulias, 1999);
- Identification of lifestyle-clusters (Krizek, 2003);
- Identification of interdependencies between household members/interactions between persons (Goulias *et al.*, 2003); and
- Time allocation to activities and travel, improved modelling for mode choice (Pendyala 2003).

LVO - Longitudinaal Verplaatsingsonderzoek

This survey of a sample of households all over the Netherlands is important because the number of waves (ten) as well as the sample size (between 1,687 and 1,928 households per normal[33] wave) characterises it as the largest transport panel up to now (BGC, 1991; Baanders and Slootman, 1982). It started in March 1984 and ended in autumn 1989.

---

[33] The mortality between waves was compensated by refreshment, but as the end of the panel was foreseeable, no further refreshment took place from March 1988 onwards.

This survey had no orientation upon a certain purpose or objective; it has been used as a universal instrument for data supply and analysis. By reasons of its scientific potential, it has been well documented. Many experiences, mainly concerning the survey design, have been published and could subsequently be used for other panels, such as the German MOP. It has been designed as a multi-purpose panel and is both multi-period (the participants have been asked to report every half year) and multi-day (to fill in a trip diary for a whole week). Besides the trip diary (in six-month intervals for one week each) with the detailed reporting of origins and destinations, people had to answer many questions in a personal interview that also included retrospective questions, as well as questions about long distance travel. As a result of such immense respondent burden, the willingness to participate has been reported as low; also, the willingness to report more than one wave showed mortality rates up to forty seven percent (between two waves). The sampling did not represent the population but over-sampled interesting household groups, such as customers of public transport, and persons for whom a reduced willingness had to be expected.

The following analyses have been done amongst others, which used the panel character of the data and the collected information:

- Analyses of mobility determining factors (Kitamura and van der Hoorn, 1987);
- Analysis of transit users in the flow of time/description of changes in mobility as a result of changes in mobility determining factors (Goodwin, 1989);
- Improved modelling for mode choice (Golob and Meurs, 1987);
- Decision modelling for modal orientations as a result of travel time budgets (Golob, 1990); and
- Influence of car-ownership on traffic generation (Kitamura, 1989).

The experiences with the LVO (Meurs and van Wissen, 1989) led to recommendations which are of importance for the set-up and long-lasting viability of a panel. These recommendations emphasise the necessity to reduce respondent burden or at least not to overcharge both the survey and thus the participants.

The 'Parc-Auto-Sofres' in France

Sofres, a French market research institute uses half of the Metascope data base (i.e., about 20,000 French[34] households panelised since 2002). Every month 2.5 percent of the sample is renewed, which means each year about 3,000 new households are added. The panellists receive no money as incentive to respond to the surveys, but each year have a gift and participate in a lottery. To help panellists to participate in the surveys, there is a free phone number and a monthly information letter. The sample of 10,000

---

[34] It concerns households living in France, earlier only households whose head had the French nationality.

households from 'Parc-Auto-Sofres' is contacted in December or January. The questionnaire is designed by INRETS and Sofres and financed by ADEME (the French Agency for Environment and Energy Management), the French Car Manufacturers Committee, the French Federation of Insurance, and the Department of Road Safety of the Ministry of Transport. The aim is to follow the evolution of car ownership and car use. Each panellist completes a self-administered questionnaire describing all private cars and light trucks available in their household. The essence of the questionnaire remains the same for each annual wave. It contains:

- A socioeconomic and demographic description of the household and of one randomly chosen individual, driver or not;
- Car ownership; and
- Description of (a maximum of) three cars in the household with their technical characteristics (age, type of vehicle, and type of fuel) and car use (total and annual mileage, for commuting and other main purposes of use, estimated fuel consumption per one hundred kilometres, etc.).

Each year, we have a sample of respondents of about 6,500 to 7,000 households, which is weighted according to five criteria to make the sample representative of the whole of France. The database 'Parc', organised, maintained and exploited at INRETS since 1984, gathers all the annual waves of this survey together. It allows us to follow the dynamic evolution of car ownership and car use by both instantaneous global indicators (such as total fleet size, averages of mileage, and consumption) and longitudinal analyses, using disaggregated pairing of the observations present in consecutive annual waves of the panel data. Each household is supposed to stay in the panel for three or four years, but we have identified 1,750 households who have responded almost continuously for at least ten years. Because the questionnaire is more time-consuming for households with cars, households without cars, or those that became carless a long time ago, are easier to recruit and retain and are, thus, over-represented in the panel. For example, twenty two percent of households are non-motorised according to the 1994 wave, but this increases to almost twenty five percent in the sample of the households who gave full interviews from 1994 to 1998.

Socioeconomic Panels

The role of the socioeconomic panels can be seen as complementary to the transport panels: with comparably large samples they can be used to weight the results of the more specific surveys of transport and mobility, and additional information is given (for example moving houses) that is necessary for forecasting travel demand. With respect to survey methods the socioeconomic panels show the potential for keeping panel samples alive and up to date. As a typical representative, the German SOEP is presented in more detail.

The German Socioeconomic Panel (SOEP)

The SOEP (Hanefeld, 1987) is a wide-ranging representative longitudinal study of private households. It provides information on all household members, consisting of Germans living in the Old and New German States, foreigners, and recent immigrants to Germany. The Panel was started in 1984. In 2001, there were more than 12,000 households, and more than 22,000 persons sampled. Some of the many topics include household composition, occupational biographies, employment, earnings, health, and satisfaction indicators. The SOEP data give researchers the opportunity to observe and to analyse political and social transformations. The data supply information about objective as well as subjective living conditions, the process of change in various areas of life, and the links between these areas and the changes themselves. The panel data are produced by personal interviews, and this personal support and care of the participants explains the very low mortality rates as well as the good data-quality. A special idea of the SOEP is the self-generation of participating households. If a person leaves a participating household in order to set up a new one, or to become a member of another household, this 'new' household becomes automatically a sample member. Thus, the sample can be kept up to date. Analyses with relevance to transport behaviour and travel demand have focussed on migration (e.g., housing patterns and mobility, residential mobility). The main emphasis of the data application lies in dynamics of income, social welfare, and employment. Up to the Spring of 2004, the data base of literature includes nearly 2,400 publications which made use of the SOEP data.

There are some questions about transport and mobility such as moving house, commuting (distances, durations and frequencies), and car-ownership. These questions are asked regularly. Others, such as the car availability at the level of persons, driving license, usual use of modes for certain activities, have not been asked regularly, but can be regarded as 'hinges' to other surveys such as the new KONTIV (Mobilitaet in Deutschland), which also has been designed by the DIW (German Institute of Economic Research). This example shows that panels can be kept alive by means of an appropriate support and supervision of the respondents. Comparable examples with large sample sizes are the Panel Survey of Income Dynamics (PSID) in the United States or the European Community Household Panel (ECHP).

ANALYSES AND MODELLING

There are different types of analyses which range from the monitoring of cross-sectional results to the tabulation of changes, formalised analysis using clustering, or econometric methods. Much has been written about the value of panel surveys in the book *Panels for Transportation Planning* (Golob et al., 1997). In this section, we give some examples drawn from our experience, using recent methodologies developed in panel econometrics. First, we show the advantages of individual data over a long period through examples using different modelling approaches (duration models, Markov-chains, random parametric logit). Even when only semi-aggregated data (e.g., of age cohorts at different points in time) are available, we show that panel econometrics present many advantages for forecasting purposes.

Using Individual Data

Examples of Descriptive Analysis

When analysing changes of behaviour with respect to an 'event' (e.g., replacing a car) and looking for behavioural changes being the impact of that event, the behaviour is too much affected during the period t when this event happens (e.g., the annual mileage is not clearly attributed to the new or to the old car). Thus, it is better to compare the 'levelled' behaviour in $t-1$ and $t+1$, which means that the periodicity of the survey has to be much shorter than the periodicity of the event. For instance, in France, over different periods (purchases from 1985 to 1990, in 1991 and in 1992, and finally in 1993) our longitudinal investigations in the panel data base, matching up the vehicles over three successive annual waves of 'Parc Auto', have shown the following results (Hivert, 1996).

The replacement of a petrol car by a diesel car concerns motorists who already had a high annual mileage with their petrol cars (15,000 to 16,000 km/year versus less than 12,000 km/year in the total petrol fleet) and is, moreover, accompanied by a substantial increase of annual mileage (variation about + 3,000 to + 4,000 km, observed in the year following the replacement). In the first and longest period (1985/1990), we have shown that this increase occurs without a significant decrease in the mileage of other available cars in the household. The opposite replacement (return to petrol) concerns 'average diesel car users' (19 to 20,000 km/year) and appears to be accompanied by an important decrease in annual mileage (4,000 to 5,000 km, observed in the year following the replacement). The sample size for this 'old diesel car user' transition, however, is associated with little significance.

Another example is the international comparison of decreasing car ownership (Dargay *et al.*, 2003). About seven percent of British, five percent of French and four percent of German households reduce car ownership between any two years; but a slightly larger proportion increases car ownership. The majority of car ownership decreases are only partial. Decreases of car ownership to zero occurs in only 1.7 percent of British, 1 percent of French and 0.2 percent of German households. In Germany the 'norm' appears to be to own at least one car. British households show the greatest volatility in car ownership; this result, that we have already encountered in different contexts – e.g., car ownership elasticity to income growth (Dargay *et al.*, 2000) – is explainable by the different cost burden of keeping a car. The likelihood of reducing car ownership increases with the number of cars in the household, according to the volatility of household structures. Thus, slow overall increase in car-ownership (net changes) conceals rather large changes for individual households, which can be seen as an indication of the potential for influencing behavioural change. For further understanding of changes, clustering approaches have been used for 'new diesel car users' (Hivert, 1999) or households changing their residence.

Hazard-Based Duration Models: Vehicle Transactions

Hazard-based duration models have been applied in the transportation field to represent people's behaviour along a time dimension, such as activity duration (e.g., Ettema *et al.*, 1995; Bhat, 1996a; Bhat, 1996b; Kitamura *et al.*, 1997; Kitamura and Fujii, 1998) and departure time choice (Bhat and Steed, 2002). Some studies have applied competing risks models, which account for the presence of several possible types of events at the end of the duration (such as the holding of a vehicle). The choice between new and used vehicles, or the type of transaction was included in some studies of vehicle transaction (Gilbert, 1992; Hensher, 1998; Yamamoto *et al.*, 1999).

The effects of the accelerated vehicle retirement programs and inspection programs have been examined by several studies (Hsu and Sperling, 1994; Dill, 2001; Adda and Cooper, 2000). Most of these focus on the efficiency of the measures in reducing emissions, and the household vehicle transaction behaviours are represented by rather simple models. The estimation of the household vehicle transaction behaviour can be based on comparisons between aggregate statistics (e.g., development of the average yearly mileage of all panel participants) with and without the implementation or modification of the measures. However, typical two-wave panel data, either aggregate or disaggregate (i.e., individual) data, cannot be utilised to distinguish the effects of the policy measure from those of the economy, because they do not possess information to estimate separate parameters of the respective effects. The policy measure changes between the two points in time, but so does the economy, producing perfect correlation between the two. Omitting the latter in the model estimation would result in a coefficient estimate of the policy measure that represents the effects of the economy as well. If time series for a longer period are available, the two factors can be separated. But still, the time series which can be understood as 'aggregate panel data' may prevent a rigorous understanding of individual behaviour, because the aggregate models cannot fully capture the individuals' vehicle transaction behaviours. That is why it is an important issue to maintain panel surveys over long time periods (e.g., the 1,750 households who have responded almost continuously for at least ten years in Parc-Auto-Sofres) (Yamamoto *et al.*, 2004). Additionally, control groups can help to separate the effects of the policy measures from more general processes as the economic development.

Modelling Processes with Panel Data (Markovian Processes)

It can be shown that estimates and models on both cross-sectional and longitudinal data have different results, thus enabling us to make use of the characteristics of panel data.

Forecast by Simple Extrapolation. Often it is assumed that the yearly rates of change estimated from the past will be also valid within the future (simple extrapolation). Even when many different cross-sectional observations are to be analysed, the fit of the data and curves, respectively, will be a matter of subjectivity and without a knowledge about the transitions between different system states there is the need of very general assumptions about the rules which govern the process. Even when assuming a logistic curve, it is not known in which phase of growth the process is, but the assumptions which are a necessary prerequisite are of central importance for the form of the curve and the forecast results.

Forecasts Using Panel Data with Transition Probabilities and Markov-Chains. The forecasts can be massively improved, if the transition probabilities between two points in time are known. Making use of longitudinal intrapersonal information, i.e., panel data, enables us to observe the rates of change on an individual level over time. Thus probabilities for any person to shift at one point in time to the next, e.g., in the level of car ownership, can be calculated and aggregated to transition probabilities.

The transitions between any points in time can be described as a stochastic process. By means of the panel data we are enabled to produce a transition matrix that gives information on the probability that a person will remain in the next period in the former state or will shift to another. The probabilities are independent of the states of earlier periods. Such stochastic processes (discrete points in time, independent transition probabilities) are so called Markov chains. If the transition probabilities remain the same between two points in time they are called homogenous Markov chains. Persons will change from an age class into the next age class. Under these assumptions one obtains a homogeneous Markov chain with a transition matrix, thereby enabling us to produce forecasts for any future point in time, given that the transition probabilities over time are valid.

Compared with a prognosis by simple extrapolation, one will get mainly for elderly people higher rates of car-ownership. This makes sense looking at the inertia within the process of motorisation. Because a car, once available, will be kept also in the future, also elderly people will as a majority keep their cars. This example illustrates the situation we can observe in most west European societies. While in the past a lot of elderly people did not own cars, because never before in their lives had they owned one, in the nearer future with the effect of the higher motorised cohorts the car-availability will rise massively and become similar to those rates we can observe for the younger age classes today (Zumkeller *et al.*, 2001). By the use of panel data, such developments can be observed and modelled. The only problem remains the assumption of transition probabilities. However, this example shows that using panel data generates much more possibilities to produce plausible and understandable forecasts, which are not directly derivable by cross-sectional data.

Use of Multi-day Data to Describe and Explain Behaviour. For more than a quarter of a century travel modelling has been activity based. If we have only single-day data, we have to assume that every person will behave the same on the next day as the observed day (assumption of uniformity). Although this may be partially true for certain activities (e.g., work), it is rather unlikely for other activities such as shopping (one has to go shopping once the refrigerator becomes empty) and unless one is a soccer professional one will not go for training on a daily basis. We, therefore, expect longer cycles of participation for certain activities, or we might expect considerable variation in patterns of activity participation, durations and sequencing. The same applies to mode choice. For a person who uses the car on a certain day, we cannot be one hundred percent certain they will use the car on other days, because the situational context may be completely different.

The earliest in analysing and interpreting multi-day data were Hanson and Huff (1986, 1988), as well as Pas and Koppelman (Pas 1987; Pas and Koppelman 1987). They found a considerable day-to-day variability. In order to cope with the variability, Kunert (1992) divided the total variability observed and showed that the intrapersonal part of variation is even higher (roughly sixty percent) for trips.

The next research stream went into the direction of analysing the variability in order to simulate behaviour. The basics are the sequence alignment method (e.g., Lipps, 2002; Chlond *et al.*, 2001) to analyse and model intrapersonal behaviour. As a result the skeleton of behaviour and the variations based on that skeleton could be separated in order to quantify the 'potential room for manoeuvre'.

Another research stream is the analysis of frequencies as the examination of the participation of individuals in certain activity days across multiple days (e.g., to estimate the duration between successive activity participations). The period between certain activities is measured in days; the methodology used for analysing and modelling is a hazard-based duration model structure (probability of participation in a certain activity depends on the time period already elapsed since the previous activity of this certain type). This type of research is always necessary to show which activities are more or less 'adjustable' (due to policy measures or interventions), and at which time the participation in such an activity becomes sufficiently pressing that the rate of flexible reaction will decrease. The main work has been done so far by Bhat (2001), Bhat *et al.* (2002). The main emphasis lies on shopping. Thus, more research on activity scheduling is needed and multi-day data and process data will be necessary ingredients.

Concerning survey methods, random parameter logit models were estimated to test for fatigue effects, for serial correlations between days, and the usual sociodemographic and day of week effects. No serial correlations could be identified (autoregressive term, lag 1), nor significant fatigue effects, and the sociodemographic variables showed the usual patterns (Axhausen *et al.*, 2003).

Forecasting from Partially Aggregated Data (Aggregation from Person Groups)

Even when no panel survey is available to describe individual personal behaviour, the benefits of using panel data are numerous. They provide more information than either cross-section or time-series data, thus allowing more complex behavioural model specifications, while providing more reliable parameter estimates. Panels permit the investigation of the dynamics of adjustment, which is impossible with cross-sectional data, while maintaining individual variation, which is lost in aggregate time-series data. Finally, the use of panels allows controlling for individual and temporal heterogeneity, which would otherwise lead to biased estimates.

Are Elasticities Identical for all Individuals in the Panel?

Most commonly in panel data analysis, either a fixed or random effect model is used to account for heterogeneity. In the former case, the heterogeneity between cross-sectional units and/or time periods is specified by individual and/or time specific intercept terms, while in the latter, the heterogeneity is captured by individual and/or time specific error components. Both of these specifications assume that the coefficients of the explanatory variables included in the model are the same for all cross-sectional units and over time. This may not be a valid assumption. In a traditional regression model, it is statistically impossible to allow for both individual and time-varying coefficients, because it would require the estimation of more coefficients than available observations. Even the possibility of estimating either individual or time-varying coefficients is limited, because it would require either a long time period compared to the number of cross-sectional units, or vice versa. In order to circumvent this problem, instead of treating the regression coefficients as fixed variables, they can be viewed as random variables with a probability distribution. This 'random-coefficients' approach greatly reduces the number of parameters to be estimated, while still allowing the coefficients to differ amongst cross-sectional units and/or over time. A Bayesian method can be used, in which the parameter estimates are a weighted average of pooled regression and individual time-series regression, so that each individual regression is 'shrunk' to tend to the pooled regression estimates. The use of these shrinkage estimators allows the estimated coefficients to vary across individuals, while not sacrificing the efficiency of the estimates. We have applied this method to compare price, income and service elasticities for public transport in England (forty six counties) and in France (sixty two cities), by using a common set of variables and similar time periods (Bresson *et al.*, 2003; Dargay *et al.*, 2004).

Panel Data versus Time-Series: The Example of Road Traffic

Panel data analysis addresses at least two different issues: it increases considerably the volume of data on which traffic forecasts are based and it allows taking into account an "individual' dimension in a richer way than by using time series analysis. The choice of this 'individual' dimension depends on the availability of partially aggregated time series and on the explanatory power of this factor concerning travel behaviour. On both of these points of view, the geographic dimension – regional for a nationwide analysis (Pirotte *et al.,* 1997), national for international comparisons (Johanson *et al.,* 1997) – seems appropriate.

By comparison with longitudinal analysis (conducted separately for twenty one regions) and with adjustment on aggregated time series (total for France), we have shown that the pooled data analysis according to the regional dimension gives more accurate medium run forecasts (for 1993 based on time series 1975 to 1990).

Concerning the volume of data, a large number of individual observations cannot totally replace a too short time period for observations. This period has to match with the forecasting period. Moreover, this period should contain different economic phases; it would be very dangerous to base long term forecasting on data collected only during a slow growth period (for instance the early nineties in continental Europe) or during a boom (see forecasts for after 1973 based on even rather long after-war time series).

By pooling data, we reduce the forecast bias and variance components. On the other hand, we increase the covariance component that expresses the random errors. Even if heterogeneity is taken into account only by fixed effects and not by individual elasticities, the pooled model is better adapted for forecasting regional car traffic than the time series approach. Therefore, if there is no misspecification, panel data econometrics are the best way to take into account heterogeneity among regions. There is still ongoing work on time-dependent utility models. Moreover, more could be said about the right data analysis and augmentation with secondary data to build new forecasting systems or about modelling time-dependent processes and dynamic population sampling (Kitamura *et al.,* 2003).

OPEN QUESTIONS AND CLOSING REMARKS

The general concept of this workshop is to further develop our knowledge about activity orientated panel surveys by discussing potentials and risks in the light of an increasing number of these surveys being conducted. To pre-empt this discussion, we raise a sequence of issues to be discussed, which clearly are by no means complete and are open to modification.

The Need to Design a Balanced Compromise

When decisions have to be made about a long term commitment, a potential panel has to cope with manifold challenges. This applies to the question of in-home and out-of-home activities, because the transitions between both are becoming less and less distinct, and the incorporation of contacts via different telecommunication services. Furthermore, a clearer understanding about the behavioural skeleton and the associated flexibility and variance built around it, would be helpful. Finally, all that information should be available for longer time periods.

However, all these challenges are in conflict with the quite pragmatic question: how can we realise such a survey with respect to the limitations of respondent burden, and temporal and financial budgets? Having said this, the following questions need clarification:

- Will it be possible to reduce respondent burden by simplifying the questioning process? This includes issues of the sequence of questions (how can we take advantage of the process of repetition?), the number of questions, the potential support by future telecommunication services, etc.
- Is the approach of a basic panel (being restricted to the necessary minimum) and additional 'specific panels' promising?
- Is data merging, i.e., the combination of data sets with different individuals, a promising approach (provided a major proportion of the common variables of participants was agreed upon before starting the 'specific panels')? We understand the 'data merging approach' as the generation of an artificial – i.e., simulated – sample with characteristics coming from different surveys.
- What are the potentials and risks of cohort-samples (without refreshment) compared to rotating samples (with refreshment)?

Most research is based on small samples. Trials in the Netherlands (LVO), the US (PSTP), and Germany (MOP, MOBIDRIVE) show, in principle, how far we can go, but also where the risks are hidden.

The Privacy Issue

Panel surveys are by definition prone to privacy issues. A lot of information is collected and stored with addresses about individual behaviours and attitudes. A re-identification of individuals is, therefore, easier compared to the less complex information normally available from cross-sectional surveys. Of course there will be cultural differences related to the question of privacy and the associated resistance, but nevertheless the following questions have to be raised:

- Is income level perceived to increase the reluctance to answer under different cultural conditions?
- Does the inclusion of in-home activities go too far, or can it be incorporated in an acceptable way?
- Is a long term retrospective inclusion of 'privacy issues' a solution?

The Non Response Problem

It has been quoted and it can be shown that the conditions to control the selectivity of panel surveys are much better than for cross-sectional surveys. However, a necessary prerequisite certainly is a careful investigation of the recruitment process. This appears feasible, because the long term character of a panel makes it relevant to allocate some resources to a special selectivity study during the set-up phase, to clarify the following questions:

- Is the process of mortality selective, and if yes, to what extent?
- Random sampling versus stratified sampling: what are the advantages and disadvantages?
- Can the level of bias be controlled to the extent that the resulting error of the raw data is low enough to permit correction by a weighting process?
- What level of error of the raw data is acceptable?

Technical Solutions

We can ease the respondent burden by automatic Global Positioning System (GPS) or Global System for Mobile Communications (GSM) orientated survey methods (at least for the transport part of the survey) and, perhaps, we can ease the burden of the non-transport part by Palm-Tops or hand held computers. This may increase the participation rate, but may have higher risks related to selectivity effects. Furthermore, the privacy and data protection issue may be affected as well, leading to the following questions:

- Does the incorporation of technology increase bias because of differences in familiarity with these technologies?
- How can technology improve destination location reporting/recording?
- How far can we go in asking destinations for geocoding?
- Can cellular phones be used effectively in panel surveys?

What Are the Limits of Panels?

Although the benefits of a panel approach have been highlighted, the problem of differentiating exogenous and endogenous factors on changes in travel behaviour remains. When a behavioural change occurs between any two episodes, we do not know which causes (external or endogenous) did result in which effects (or behavioural changes) and to what extent. Things are even worse. In a very narrow sense, a behavioural change is the difference between two episodes of behaviour and the time span between these episodes can be an hour, a day, a month, a year, or more. Thus – again in a narrow sense – we have to state that each single episode happened in a different context, or situation. Therefore, we have to conclude that the difference we measure is a combined difference that is dependent on the amount of similarity of both situational contexts.

As a consequence, a separation of external and endogenous parts of the measured changes is only possible by the introduction of additional information. We, therefore, have to discuss, which type of information may be useful to solve this problem. *In situ* surveys, such as stated preference (SP), stated response (SR) or interactive interviews (II) may serve as a platform for that discussion.

Closing Remarks

We have shown that panel surveys have a lot of advantages from a theoretical point of view. On the other hand, panels have some disadvantages which are mainly of practical importance. With respect to the present situation of the transport market, we are confronted with many exogenous processes that have probable behavioural impacts, on the one hand, and will result in effects on travel demand. Additionally, we see a growing heterogeneity within societies and, therefore, a real data need for the variety of people's behaviour and its developments. Therefore, the need for panels is higher than ever.

From the viewpoint of the 'surveying', we are confronted with the situation that telephone marketing and mailboxes (both electronic and conventional), crammed with advertisements, spoil the possibilities for surveys with scientific issues: people are becoming resistant to any further bothering by market researchers. We now have improved technical possibilities to ease respondent burden, to enable us to collect real longitudinal information for a period of weeks, months, or even more and to ease geocoding. However, this raises privacy issues. Summing up these conflicting considerations, the questions as formulated above will be the ones we have to answer within the next years.

Let us see what the future will bring.

REFERENCES

Adda, J. and R. Cooper (2000). Balladurette and Juppette: a discrete analysis of scrapping subsidies, *Journal of Political Economy*, **108** (4), 778-806.

Armoogum, J. (2002). Mesure de la précision pour suivre la dynamique de la demande de déplacements et le suivi des plans de déplacements urbains, *Report for the PREDIT (French Research Framework Program)*, 11 pages.

Axhausen, K.W., M.O. Gascon and J.-L. Madre (2003). Immobility: A microdata analysis. Paper presented at the 10th IATBR Conference, Lucerne, 23 pages.

Axhausen, K.W., A. Zimmermann, S. Schönfelder, G. Rindsfüser and T. Haupt (2000). *Observing the rhythms of daily life: a six-week travel diary*. Arbeitsberichte Verkehrs- und Raumplanung, 25, Institut für Verkehrsplanung und Transporttechnik, ETH, Zürich.

Baanders, B. and K. Slootman (1982). A panel for longitudinal research into travel behaviour. In: *Recent Advances in Travel Demand Analysis* (S. Carpenter and P.M. Jones, eds), 450-464, Gower, Aldershot.

BGC – Bureau Goudappel Coffeng, Projektbureau IVVS (1991). *Het Longitudinaal Verplaatsingsonderzoek - Kenmerken en Gebruik*, Deventer.

Bhat, C.R. (1996a). A hazard-based duration model of shopping activity with nonparametric baseline specification and nonparametric control for unobserved heterogeneity, *Transportation Research B*, **30**, 189-208.

Bhat, C.R. (1996b). A generalized multiple durations proportional hazard model with an application to activity behaviour during the evening work-to-home commute, *Transportation Research B*, **30** (6), 465-480.

Bhat, C.R. (2001). Duration modelling. In: *Handbook of Transport Modelling* (D.A. Hensher and K.J. Button, eds), 91-111, Pergamon Press, Oxford.

Bhat, C.R. and J.L. Steed (2002). A continuous-time model of departure time choice for urban shopping trips, *Transportation Research B*, **36**, 207-224.

Bresson, J. Dargay, J.-L. Madre and A. Pirotte (2003). The main determinants of the demand for public transport : a comparative analysis of England and France using shrinkage estimators, *Transportation Research A*, **37** (7), 605-627.

Bussière Y. and J.-L. Madre (2002). Démographie et transport : villes du nord et villes du sud, *l'Harmattan editor*, 477 pages.

Chlond, B and. Kuhnimhof, T. (2003). Selectivity and Nonresponse in the German Mobility Panel: Selectivity Impacts on Data Quality due to Nonresponse in Multi-Stage Survey Recruitment Processes, paper presented at the 'Workshop on Item Nonresponse and Data Quality in Large Social Surveys', Basel, 18 pages, www.mobilitaetspanel.de/downloads , Accessed November 2005.

Chlond, B., O. Lipps and D. Zumkeller (2001). Konstanz/Variabilität des Verkehrsverhaltens bei gleichen Personen, Endbericht BMV FE 70.595/1998, Karlsruhe 2001 (Stability and variability of travel behaviour for identical persons. Research Report for the German Ministry of Transport, 147 pages, www.mobilitaetspanel.de/downloads Accessed November 2005.

Chlond, B., V. Wassmuth and D. Zumkeller (2000). *Autoarmes Wohnen und Arbeiten (Living and Working with reduced car-ownership)*, Schlussbericht im Auftrag des Bundesministers für Verkehr, Bau und Wohnungswesen (BMVBW), Forschungsauftrag BMVWB 77 395/96, November.

Chung, J.-H. and K.G. Goulias (1995). Sample Selection Bias with Multiple Selection Rules: Application with Residential Relocation, Attrition and Activity Participation in the Puget Sound Transportation Panel, *Transportation Research Record No. 1493,*128 -135.

Dargay, J., J.-L. Madre and A. Berri (2000). Car ownership dynamics seen through the follow-up of cohorts: comparison of France and the United Kingdom, *Transportation Research Record No.1733*, 31-38.

Dargay, J., M. Hanly, B. Chlond, L. Hivert and J.-L. Madre (2003). Demotorisation Seen through Panel Surveys: A Comparison of France, Britain and Germany, paper presented at the 10th IATBR Conference, Lucerne, August, 37 pages. www.cts.ucl.ac.uk/tsu/ Accessed November 2005.

Dargay J., A. Pirotte, J.-L. Madre and G. Bresson (2004). Economic and Structural Determinants of the Demand for Public Transport: An Analysis of a Panel of French Urban Areas Using Shrinkage Estimators, *Transportation Research A*, **38**, 269-285.

Dill, J. (2001). Design and Administration of Accelerated Vehicle Retirement Programs in North America and Abroad, *Transportation Research Record No.1750*, 32-39.

Duncan, G.J., T.F. Juster and J.N. Morgan (1987). The Role of Panel Studies in Research of Economic Behaviour, *Transportation Research A*, **21**, 249-263.

Ettema, D., A. Borgers and H. Timmermans (1995). Competing Risk Hazard Model of Activity Choice, Timing, Sequencing, and Duration, *Transportation Research Record No. 1493*, 101-109.

Gilbert, C.C.S. (1992). A duration model of automobile ownership, *Transportation Research B*, **26**, 97-114.

Golob, T.F. (1990). The Dynamics of Household Travel Time Expenditures and Car Ownership Decisions, *Transportation Research A*, **24**, 443-463.

Golob, T.F. and H. Meurs (1987). A structural model of temporal change in multi-modal-travel demand, *Transportation Research A*, **21**, 391-400.

Golob, T.F., R. Kitamura and L. Long (Eds) (1997). *Panels for Transportation Planning – Methods and Applications*, Kluwer Academic Press, Norwell, MA.

Goodwin, P.B. (1989). Family Changes and Public Transport Use 1984 – 1987, *Transportation*, **16**, 121–154.

Goulias, K. and J. Ma (1996). *Analysis of Longitudinal Data from the Puget Sound Transportation Panel. Task C: Past Uses of PSTP Databases*, US Department of Transportation, Federal Highway Administration, Washington, DC.

Goulias, K.G. (1999). Longitudinal Analysis of Activity and Travel Pattern Dynamics Using Generalised Mixed Markov Latent Class Models, *Transportation Research B,* **33**, 535-557.

Goulias, K.G, N. Kilgren and T. Kim (2003). A Decade of Longitudinal Travel Behaviour Observation in the Puget Sound Region: Sample Composition, Summary Statistics, and a Selection of First Order Findings. Paper presented at the 10th IATBR Conference, Lucerne. www.ivt.baum.ethz.ch/allgemein/pdf/goulias.pdf Accessed November 2005.

Hanefeld, U. (1987). *Das Sozio-ökonomische Panel - Grundlagen und Konzeption*, Frankfurt.

Hanson, S. and J.O. Huff (1986). Classification Issues in the Analysis of Complex Travel Behaviour, *Transportation*, **13**, 271-293.

Hanson, S. and J. Huff (1988). Systematic Variability in Repetitious Travel, *Transportation*, **15**, 111-135.

Hautzinger, H. (2000). Auswertung des Mobilitätspanels mittels statistisch-ökonometrischer Panelmodelle, Vortrag anlässlich des DVWG-Workshops Dynamische und statische Elemente des Verkehrsverhaltens – Das Deutsche Mobilitätspanel in Karlsruhe, to be published in *Schriftenreihe B*, DVWG (Ed.), Bergisch-Gladbach.

Heidemann, D., M. Bäumer, H. Hautzinger, G. Haag and B. v. Stackelberg (1999). *Erprobung und Evaluierung von Modellen der Statistik und der Künstlichen Intelligenz als Instrumente zur Analyse des Mobilitätspanels*, Schlussbericht, im Auftrag des BMV, Heilbronn/Stuttgart.

Hensher, D. (1987). Issues in the Pre-Analysis of Panel Data, *Transportation Research A*, **21**, 265-285.

Hensher, D. (1998). The Timing of Change for Automobile Transactions: Competing Risk Multispell Specification. In: *Travel Behaviour Research: Updating the State of Play* (J. de D. Ortúzar, D.A. Hensher and S. Jara-Diaz, eds),487-506, Elsevier, Oxford.

Hivert, L. (1996). Le comportement des nouveaux diésélistes, *Rapport final de Convention INRETS/MIES*, 117 pages.

Hivert, L. (1999). Dieselisation and the 'new dieselists' behaviour: recent developments in the french car fleet, European Energy Conference 'Technological progress and the energy challenges', session 13 'Transport and CO2 policies' , Paris.

Horowitz, J.L. (1997). Accounting for Response Bias. In: *Panels for Transportation Planning – Methods and Applications* (T.F. Golob, R. Kitamura and L. Long, eds), 207-210, Kluwer Academic Press, Norwell, MA.

Hsu, S.-L. and D. Sperling (1994). Uncertain Air Quality Impacts of Automobile Retirement Programs, *Transportation Research Record No. 1444*, 90-98.

Johansson O. and L. Schipper (1997). Measuring the Long-Run Fuel Demand of Cars, Separate Estimates of Vehicle Stock, Mean Fuel Intensity, and Mean Driving Distance, *Journal of Transport Economics and Policy*, 31 (2), 277-292.

Kitamura, R. (1989). A Causal Analysis of Car-Ownership and Transit Use, *Transportation*, 16, 155-173.

Kitamura, R. (1990). Panel Analysis in Transportation Planning: An Overview, *Transportation Research A*, 24, 401-415.

Kitamura, R. and S. Fujii (1998). Two Computational Process Models of Activity-Travel Behaviour. In: *Theoretical Foundations of Travel Choice Modeling* (T. Garling, T. Laitila and K. Westin, eds), 251-279, Pergamon Press, Oxford.

Kitamura, R., C. Chen and R. Pendyala (1997). Generation of Synthetic Daily Activity-Travel Patterns, *Transportation Research Record No. 1607*, 154-162.

Kitamura, R. and P.H.L. Bovy (1987). Analysis of Attrition Biases and Trip Reporting Errors for Panel Data, *Transportation Research A*, 21, 287-302.

Kitamura, R. and T. van der Hoorn (1987). Regularity and Irreversibility of Weekly Travel Behaviour, *Transportation*, 14, 227-251.

Kitamura, R., T. Yamamoto and S. Fujii (2003). The Effectiveness of Panels in Detecting Changes in Discrete Travel Behavior, *Transportation Research B*, 37, 191-206.

Kloas, J., H. Kuhfeld and U. Kunert (2000).Konstanz bzw. Variabilität des Verkehrsverhaltens bei gleichen Personen, Analyse des Mobilitätspanels 1994 bis 1998, im Auftrag des BMV, Berlin.

Kuhnimhof, T., B. Chlond and S. von der Ruhren (2006). The Users of Transport Modes and Multimodal Travel Behaviour – Steps Towards Understanding Travelers' Options and Choices, Paper prepared for presentation at the 85th Annual Meeting of the Transportation Research Board 2006, 12pages.

Kunert, U. (1992). Individuelles Verkehrsverhalten im Wochenverlauf, *DIW Beiträge zur Strukturforschung 130*, Berlin.

Lipps, O. (2002). Individual Activity Pattern Variation and Reactions to Planning Measures, Paper presented at the FOVUS 2002 conference, *FOVUS 2002 proceedings*, Stuttgart.

Ma, J. and K.G. Goulias (1997a). Systematic self-selection and sample weight creation in panel surveys: The Puget Sound transportation panel case, *Transportation Research A*, **31** (5), 365-375.

Ma, J. and K.G. Goulias (1997b). An Analysis of Activity and Travel Patterns in the Puget Sound Transportation Panel. In: *Activity-Based Approaches to Travel Analysis* (D.F. Ettema and H.J.P. Timmermanns, eds), 189-207, Pergamon Press, Oxford.

Mannering, F., E. Murakami and S.-G. Kim (1994). Temporal Stability of Traveler's Activity Choices and Home-Stay Duration: Some Empirical Evidence, *Transportation*, **21**, 371-392.

Meurs, H. and L. van Wissen (1989). The Dutch Mobility Panel: Experiences and Evaluation, *Transportation*, **16**, 99-119.

Murakami, E. and W.T. Watterson (1989). Developing a Household Travel Panel Survey for the Puget Sound Region, *Transportation Research Record No. 1285*, 40-46.

Murakami, E. and C. Ulberg (1997). The Puget Sound Transportation Panel. In: *Panels for Transportation Planning, Methods and Applications* (T.F. Golob, R. Kitamura and L. Long, eds), 159-192, Kluwer Academic Press, Norwell, MA.

Pas, E.I. (1987). Intrapersonal Variability and Model Goodness-Of-Fit, *Transportation Research A*, **21**, 431-438.

Pas, E.I. and F.S. Koppelman (1987). An Examination of the Determinants of Day-to-Day Variability in Individuals' Urban Travel Demand, *Transportation*, **14**, 3-20.

Pendyala, R. M. (2003). Time Use and Travel Behavior in Space and Time. In: *Transportation Systems Planning: Methods and Applications* (K. G. Goulias, ed.),2-1 – 2-37, CRC Press, Boca Raton, FL.

Pendyala, R.M., K.G. Goulias, R. Kitamura and E. Murakami (1993). Developments of Weights for a Choice Based Panel Survey Sample with Attrition, *Transportation Research A*, **27**, 477- 492.

Pendyala, R.M. and R. Kitamura (1997). Weighting Methods for Attrition in Choice Based Panels. In: *Panels for transportation planning – Methods and applications* (T.F. Golob, R. Kitamura and L. Long, eds), 233-257, Kluwer Academic Press, Norwell, MA.

Pirotte A., G. Bresson and J.L. Madre (1997). Comparison of Forecast Performances of Car Traffic: Time Series Analysis Versus Panel Data Econometrics, Paper presented at the 8th IATBR Conference, Austin, Texas.

Ulberg, C. (1991). Perception of Travel Modes and Measured Travel Behaviour: Findings from the Puget Sound Transportation Panel, Paper presented at the 6th International Conference on Travel Behaviour, Quebec.

Yamamoto, T., J.-L. Madre and R. Kitamura (2004). An Analysis of the Effects of French Vehicle Inspection Program and Grant for Scrappage on Household Vehicle Transaction, *Transportation Research B*, **38**, 905-926.

Zumkeller, D., B. Chlond and O. Lipps (1999). Das Mobilitäts-Panel (MOP) – Konzept und Realisierung einer bundesweiten Längsschnittbetrachtung, *Schriftenreihe der Deutschen Verkehrswissenschaftlichen Gesellschaft*, Heft B 217, 33-72.

Zumkeller, D., B. Chlond and W. Manz (2001). *Panelauswertung 1999/2000 – Schlussbericht*, Forschungsauftrag BMV FE 70.608/2000 im Auftrag des Bundesministers für Verkehr, Bau- und Wohnungswesen, Institut für Verkehrswesen der Universität Karlsruhe. www.mobilitaetspanel.de/downloads Accessed November 2005.

Zumkeller, D., B. Chlond and O. Lipps (2002). *Der Anpassungsprozess von Ost an West – schnell aber nicht homogen*, Internationales Verkehrswesen, November, 523-528.

Travel Survey Methods: Quality and Future Directions
Peter Stopher and Cheryl Stecher (Editors)

21

MOVING PANEL SURVEYS FROM CONCEPT TO IMPLEMENTATION

Elaine Murakami, Federal Highway Administration, Washington, DC, USA
Stephen Greaves, University of Sydney, NSW, Australia
and
Tomás Ruiz, Technical University of Valencia, Valencia, Spain

INTRODUCTION

The measurement, understanding and, ultimately, prediction of travel behaviour change in response to sociodemographic changes, external economic and political factors, and specific interventions in the transport system are of paramount concern to policy makers in the new millennium. This chapter focuses on longitudinal methods, specifically those involving the use of panel surveys. This discussion reviews the use of panels, different types of panels, panel design and other methodological considerations, and weighting of panel data, with a view towards providing recommendations and needed research to take panels from concept to implementation. It is based on the discussions of a workshop[35] at the 7th International Conference on Travel Survey Methods.

Panel surveys can be defined as surveys of the same respondents at two or more discrete points in time – this is distinguishable from repeated cross-sectional surveys, in which completely different individuals are sampled. While there are many examples of panel surveys in social science, marketing, and health-related research, the use of transport panels is still relatively rare. Most that have been developed have been to address typical before-and-after questions, usually involving two waves. Only three long-term

---

[35] Workshop members were: Stephen Greaves (Australia), Martin Lee-Gosselin (Canada), Elaine Murakami (USA), Ram Pendyala (USA), Matthew Roorda (Canada), Tomas Ruiz (Spain), Klaas van Zyl (South Africa), and Dirk Zumkeller (Germany).

transport panels have been used, and of those, only two are currently active: the German Mobility Panel (MOP, www.moilitaetspanel.de) and the US Puget Sound Transportation Panel (PSTP).

As documented in Zumkeller *et al.* (2006), much is already known about the rationale for using panels, relative advantages and disadvantages over repeated cross-sectional surveys, specific design issues, usage of the data, and economic considerations. In addition, there have been several significant research efforts using panel data in a variety of analytical and modelling applications. However, despite all these advances in knowledge, the reality is that the use of panels in travel-behaviour research is still relatively rare. While several well-known reasons are behind this, arguably the most fundamental problem has been that, as a profession, we have not been able to provide sufficient evidence on why panels are better suited to answering the policy questions of today, to convince funding agencies to fund such an undertaking.

PANEL DESIGNS

Within the general definition of a panel survey are several sub-classifications that reflect different purposes and involve different methodologies:

1. *Panel without refreshment – Cohort Survival Surveys*: The same group of respondents is tracked over time, thereby maintaining the natural ageing of the sample. This design is often used in epidemiological studies where the objective is to monitor a group of participants over an extended time period.

2. *Panel without refreshment – Before-and-After Surveys*: While there may be some overlap with the previous definition, the key issue here is to survey the same group of respondents before and after some intervention or event, to assess to what extent any change of behaviour is due to the intervention. This is (arguably) the most widely-used form of transport panel. It is now also becoming increasingly common to conduct more than one after survey to assess the critical issue of the sustainability of any behaviour change.

3. *Panel with refreshment*: As panel members leave the survey due to natural causes, out-migration, or refusal to continue, they are refreshed with members of similar sociodemographic characteristics (e.g., the PSTP).

4. *Rotational panel*: Respondents are deliberately only kept in for a specified amount of time, such as three waves in the case of the MOP. The purpose is to maintain a representative sample by regular refreshment.

5. *Split panel*: Involves a simultaneous cross sectional and panel at every wave of measurement, which, while cited to be the preferred approach (Kish, 1985), is clearly likely to be prohibitively expensive.

6. *Special Access Panels*: Used primarily by market researchers to form a panel and then conduct different surveys on that sample.

In addition to these well-known distinctions, three further classifications are proposed:

7.   *Multi-Instrument Panels:* Based on the principles of special access panels, designed to try to understand the process of activity scheduling and travel both in the short and long-term (Roorda and Miller, 2004).

8.   *Pseudo panels*: The use of pseudo panels was introduced by Deaton (1985) for the analysis of consumer demand systems. Pseudo panels are formed by grouping households or individuals into cohorts on the basis of shared characteristics, and constructing the cohort variables as the average values for the households/individuals included. The cohorts are then traced over time forming a panel. In grouping individual households into cohorts, we lose information about the variation among households within each group, so that estimates obtained on the basis of group means will generally be less efficient than estimates based on the individual data. In addition, since the cohorts are followed over time, the characteristics chosen in forming the cohorts should be time-invariant. Pseudo-panel data have been used to study income elasticities for transport expenditure (Berri *et al.*, 1998), car ownership dynamics (Dargay *et al.*, 2000), and household travel demand (Dargay, 2003).

9.   *'Opportunistic' panel surveys.* To re-contact and re-interview a survey sample not originally designed to be followed over time. High attrition should be expected.

WHY PANELS?

The advantages of panel surveys are well-known and have been described extensively in the literature. The following is a summary of their most important features.

Dynamic Change

Panel surveys are the only method of tracking change *dynamically* at an individual level (Kitamura, 1990a). When panels are designed with a duration of several years, they are capable of capturing long term effects on travel behaviour, especially changes to residence, workplace location, vehicle ownership, and household composition. They are able to find population sub-groups of particular interest, e.g., people who have changed residence location.

Sample Size

Panels are able to provide greater statistical reliability for a given sample size than cross-sectional surveys, when the difference between two measures is analysed (Moser and Kalton, 1979). Zumkeller *et al.* (2006) show how the survey cost can be reduced when a two-wave panel is considered versus taking two independent samples for measuring the change of the modal share of public transport among motorized trips. Stopher and

Greaves (2004) demonstrate the sample size required to measure a change in VKT using a panel to be on the order of one quarter of that required if two independent cross-sectional samples were used to maintain the same level of statistical reliability.

Exogenous and Endogenous Change

A critical issue in policy development is to be able to separate out the impacts of an ex-ogenous change (e.g., change in family circumstances, rise in petrol prices) from an in-tervention in the transport system (e.g., increasing transit service). Panels are more con-ducive to the formation of control and target groupings, which are seen by some as the only definitive means to assess to what extent the change is due to the intervention. Ki-tamura (1990a) indicated that repeated surveys to the same respondents make it possi-ble to control unobserved explicative factors. Thus, the identification of the cause-effect relationships is easier.

Cost

As noted in the resource paper, while initially panels are a higher resource undertaking, over the long-run they may prove cheaper than a cross-sectional survey of an equivalent number of respondents. For instance, Lawton and Pas (1996) indicated that panel sur-veys versus repeated cross–sectional surveys can save about fifty percent of total costs from the second wave of data collection.

Modeling Results

Dynamic models achieve better prediction results because longitudinal and panel data contain more information per unit of analysis than non-periodic data (Kitamura, 1990a). The French study using panel data on implications of diesel versus petrol con-sumption and prices and annual VKT (Zumkeller *et al.*, 2006) is an excellent example.

KNOWN CHALLENGES WITH THE PANEL APPROACH

While the benefits of using a panel are well-extolled, the barriers to implementation must be clearly understood and lowered for usage for this technique to become more widespread.

The Importance of Recruitment

Recruitment into a panel survey is likely to be lower than a one-time cross-sectional, because the respondent burden is higher. It is important (ethics) to disclose to potential respondents the expected burden of full participation. For example, Roorda and Miller

(2004) achieved only a sixteen percent response rate in an in-depth panel with three waves. Similarly, at the start of the Puget Sound Transportation Panel, recruitment to the panel was fifty six percent, compared to a one-time cross sectional survey of sixty two percent (Murakami and Ulberg, 1997).

In the German Mobility Panel (MOP), the guideline of the recruitment process was not to get as many respondents as possible into the survey but to recruit reliable respondents who would participate in the entire three year survey. After a complex multistage recruitment process, only a small share of initially contacted persons takes part in the MOP. The related nonresponse problem has been controlled by a special investigation of the selectivity of the recruitment process, which resulted in a specific stratification of the sampling process. Thus the drop-outs of the previous year affect the size of the strata of the following year (Kuhnimhof and Chlond, 2003).

Minimising Attrition

Attrition, or the dropping out of panel participants in later waves of the survey (Kitamura, 1990b) always occurs. Besides the reduction of the effective size of the panel sample, attrition can bias any results from the analysis of the survivors, if it is non-random. Therefore, reducing attrition is a matter of great concern in the design of any panel survey.

If a survey is not designed as a panel, and the respondents are approached later for a follow-up survey, high attrition should be expected. In the Spanish test reported by Ruiz (2004), 62.1 percent attrition occurred in the second survey wave. Attrition of about fifty percent was found in the second wave of the South Yorkshire Panel Survey (Goodwin, 1986). Both surveys were initiated as cross-sectional studies. Thus, it is highly recommended to inform potential respondents about the special characteristics of a panel survey. This could result in a reduction in the initial response rate, as explained before, but will improve the participation from the second survey wave.

Attrition should be anticipated. Evidence from European and US panels shows that similar populations are likely to drop out. These include: younger adults who are more likely to change residence, lower income households, and older persons who feel that transport issues are less important to them and lack interest in continuing. It is probably a good idea to over-sample these populations at the beginning, and also to make sure their higher attrition rates are addressed in panel refreshment. In the MOP, a full pre-test was conducted so they would have a good estimate of attrition when they implemented their full panel (Zumkeller *et al.*, 2006).

In general, econometric approaches for correcting attrition bias involve estimating the probability of dropping-out. The results can be used to construct an adjustment term that can be included as a regressor in the outcome equation to correct for the selected nature of the resulting sample (Heckman, 1979).

In the PSTP, Ma and Goulias (1997) found that survey participation was selective at different stages of data collection. When comparing the characteristics of PSTP panel members to Census data, panel participants vary both at the original recruitment and after attrition over multiple waves. They develop a probabilistic method for weights accounting for selectivity over these different stages.

Golob *et al.*, (1997) used an ordered-response probit model to describe attrition during the three-wave panel survey to evaluate the San Diego I-15 carpool lanes project. A weight was formulated for each respondent and for each wave as the reciprocal of the probability that a respondent would participate in that wave.

In addition to minimising respondent attrition, interviewer attrition can be a concern as well. In the Automobile Demand Project, Hensher (1986) found the fact that the respondent knew the interviewer had a positive effect on retaining participants in the study. The interviewers were informed that their collaboration in the entire panel survey was very important. They were sent a thank you letter, an annual lottery ticket and a Christmas greeting card to encourage their collaboration. However, only ten out of nineteen interviewers continued in the second survey wave. Six new interviewers were recruited for the second wave and only one out of sixteen abandoned the survey in the third wave. Similar to the panellist attrition, interviewers' abandonment is higher in the second panel wave than in subsequent waves . Van Wissen and Meurs (1989) and Morton-Williams (1993) point out the importance of achieving a stable relationship between interviewers and panellists in reducing attrition rates. For instance, in the DNMP, when the same interviewers collected the data given by the panellists, the attrition rate was lower than fifteen percent.

Designing Maintenance Strategies

It is important to have a maintenance program in place at the beginning of any panel. It will help in reducing attrition and increasing the quality of the data. The initial contact with the panellists should be used to collect as much relevant information as possible and to later correct for any attrition biases (Kitamura, 1990b). To optimise the response at subsequent waves, the interviewer in the first wave should record all information that may be of help in locating the respondent's address and in calling at an appropriate time (Morton-Williams, 1993). For example, one should ask for a contact address of a respondent's close friend or relative (Hensher, 1987) and/or ask for email address and/or workplace telephone numbers (Roorda and Miller, 2004).

Frequent communication with panel members (e.g., sending out greeting cards) appears to be an effective method of household or individual location and, therefore, attrition reduction (Kitamura, 1990b; Tourangeau *et al.*, 1997). This may include active telephone assistance (Miller and Crowley, 1989), Christmas cards (MOP – Zumkeller *et al.*, 2006), holiday cards (Zumkeller *et al.*, 2006; PSTP – Murakami and Watterson,

1990), information bulletins (Quebec – McCray *et al.*, 2002; PSTP – Murakami and Watterson, 1990; MOP – Zumkeller *et al.*, 2006; NFO – Infratest, 2001).

Given that the researcher has information about Wave N-1, in subsequent waves the researcher can reduce burden by providing respondents with information from the last time and asking for confirmation of previous information and/or any major changes in household circumstances (Trivellato, 1999; Purvis and Ruiz, 2003). For example, a vehicle availability listing can easily be reviewed. This also serves as a quality check for the Wave N-1 data.

Incentives

The extra demands placed on respondents in panel surveys, particularly when these extend over several waves, suggests that the use of incentives must be considered. In the Toronto Panel Survey, two incentives were used (Miller and Crowley, 1989): a lottery ticket to encourage participation in the initial interview given in advance at the transit stop, and financial incentives to encourage continued participation in the panel survey. This involved entering all active panel members in a weekly cash lottery. Six winners were selected from this group each week and sent checks for the amounts won. One $50 check and five $10 checks were awarded each week. However, incentives in the PSTP appeared to be more effective in increasing first wave response rates than in reducing attrition (Murakami and Ulberg, 1997). Households that received no financial compensation in Wave 1 had a higher retention rate in Wave 2 (83.7 percent stayers in Wave 2) than households in the other incentive categories (about 80 percent stayers in Wave 2). More research is needed on the effects of the use of incentives in transport panel surveys.

Duration of Monitoring

The multi-day design has several advantages. First, it is well-known that the inherent day-to-day variability in travel implies that the duration of the monitoring period must logically be extended beyond one day. (This also reduces the sample sizes required to maintain the same level of statistical reliability, because it reduces the intra-sample variance (Stopher and Greaves, 2004)). Second, data error due to underreporting can be corrected by having data during a longer survey time available. Thus, the observation of at least a whole week allows for more comprehensive data and for intrapersonal variation. However, the trade-off between increasing respondent burden and potential trip reporting fatigue, as well as attrition, must be considered in the survey design.

The PSTP uses a two-day diary, while the MOP uses a one-week diary. It may even be necessary to extend this further as results from a six-week travel survey known as MOBIDRIVE have shown (Axhausen *et al.*, 2000 cited in Zumkeller *et al.*, 2006). A longer period of analysis provides the opportunity of studying travel associated not only with daily routine activities but also with spontaneous, planned, or pre-planned activities as defined by Doherty (2003):

1.   Routine activities (going to work, dropping off/picking up a child at day care, daily coffee/tea stops);
2.   'Planned' activities. Activities that require a conscious effort – taking care of an ill person, going to the beach with a friend; and
3.   Spontaneous activities.

Frequency of Monitoring

The frequency of monitoring seemingly depends on balancing respondent burden against the nature of the event being analysed and the period of time over which we want to monitor behaviour. In the PSTP, and the MOP, the frequency of monitoring is every year, reflecting the particular purposes of those surveys. For behavioural change surveys in response to a particular intervention, we probably want to know something about change immediately after the intervention and then at regular points in the future to ensure the sustainability of such change.

MOVING PANELS FROM CONCEPT TO PRACTICE

Broadly speaking, panel surveys are being utilised typically in the transport field for the following three objectives:

1.   Monitoring Travel Behaviour: Dutch National Mobility Panel (DNMP), German Mobility Panel (MOP), Puget Sound Transportation Panel (PSTP);
2.   Monitoring Travel Behaviour in response to discrete events (Before and After Studies, Travel Demand Management or other policy; and
3.   New use of the panel approach for understanding process decisions (McCray *et al.*, 2003, Roorda and Miller, 2004)

There are few general purpose government-sponsored panels in transport. Zumkeller *et al.* (2006) provides an excellent resource in documenting the German Mobility Panel, established in 1994 and the French Parc-Sofres panel, established in 1976 (Zumkeller *et al.*, 2006). The classical references are the Dutch National Mobility Panel, running from 1984 to 1989 (Van Wissen and Meurs, 1989) and the Puget Sound Transportation Panel, from 1989 up to now (Murakami and Ulberg, 1997, Goulias *et al.*, 2003).

On the other hand, panels have been applied in practice more frequently for before and after studies. These include projects for evaluating both changes in infrastructure and policies (Stokes, 1988; Baanders *et al.*, 1989; Giuliano and Golob, 1990; Pendyala *et al.*, 1991; Loos *et al.*, 1992; Bradley, 1997; Golob *et al.*, 1997; CRT Madrid, 1997; Admundsen *et al.*, 1999; Keuleers *et al.*, 2002).

However, it is recommended to collect panel data for three or more time periods (Bradley, 1997). Data analysis is limited if the number of time points observed is small. This is particularly true for predicting elasticities beyond a single period. More within-person observations are necessary to include additional time lags and to separate more accurately the influences of state-dependence and person-dependence differences.

Nowadays there are a number of opportunities for applying panel survey techniques in the transport field. Both the private and the public sector can benefit from the advantages of panel surveys. In the recent years, at national and international levels several agreements like the Kyoto Protocol (UNFCCC, 1997) have been adopted to stabilise greenhouse gas concentrations in the atmosphere. One way of limiting emissions is trying to change people's travel behaviour, in particular, to reduce automobile usage by recommending people shifting to bus, walk, or bicycle for specific trips. Once someone intervenes, there is a need to monitor if any change has occurred. A non-partisan monitor is preferred.

Hensher (1997) pointed out the importance of collecting event information using panel surveys for estimating the time stream of revenue associated with private investments. The time it takes for different proportions of potential users to switch is important in establishing a reliable base of future patronage. Event data provide richer information about the process of change than does the observation of the state. Event data can account for not only sequence but timing and duration, which are also important in establishing causal ordering.

Public administrations also have interest in knowing the impacts of transit investments. For example, the Federal Transit Administration in the United States is requiring the completion of a before and after study for all projects seeking a full funding grant agreement. This study has two purposes: (1) to expand insights into the costs and impacts of major transit investments; and (2) to improve the technical methods and procedures used in the planning and development of those investments (FTA, 2000).

Both private and public institutions should be aware of the importance of getting enough funding for a multi-wave panel survey at the beginning. Otherwise the probability of success decreases rapidly. For instance, the MOP panel was 'sold' as needed at the point of German reunification (Zumkeller *et al.*, 2006). The PSTP was originally funded with a two-year grant from the US Department of Energy. The project continued since then with funding from the Puget Sound Regional Council (Murakami and Ulberg, 1997; Goulias *et al.*, 2003). On the other hand, the San Francisco Bay Area Household Panel, which was envisioned to start in 1990, failed to be implemented due to lack of funding (Purvis, 1997).

RESEARCH IDEAS

Below are ideas for research that should be pursued.

1. There is a need to document benefits of panel surveys:
   a. Panel versus Cross-sectional data. One way to demonstrate the benefits of a panel approach is to compare using panel data to cross-sectional data, and specifically to test models developed with the different kinds of survey data. As Kish recommends (per Paaswell, 1997), combining panel and cross-sectional data may offer the best results for describing population changes and forecasting travel behaviour. The Puget Sound Regional Council (the MPO in Seattle) may be a source of these data.
   b. A synthesis project covering in depth the current state of practice with transport panel surveys. In addition, this project should provide comparative evidence on issues such as panel designs, sample size, attrition rates (between waves, within waves), correlations of key parameters both within (if multi-day designs are used) and between waves, costs compared to repeated cross-sections.
2. More training is needed on applying statistical methods to transport panel data. This exists in other fields; we do not have to reinvent the wheel!
3. There is a need to learn more about some qualitative research techniques like biographic (also known as life history) studies and apply them to transport panel studies. These are a group of strategies that generate, analyse, and present the data of an individual's experiences unfolding over time (Goulias, 2003).
4. Compare adding retrospective questions to a one-time survey to panel data. Some types of questions that might work in a retrospective survey include: employment status, work location, residential location, vehicle ownership, and main mode for commute trip. These would be compared to results from a panel study to see if rates of change are similar.
5. Using general purpose market research panels for transport surveys. Many market research groups have empanelled members as regular survey respondents. While there have been criticisms that these respondents may be particularly biased, others believe that they may provide a good representation of the general population, especially as characteristics can be controlled (age, sex, income, education).
6. Determining the spacing between waves for a general purpose travel behaviour panel. The German Mobility Panel uses a one-week data collection period for 'daily travel'. A subsample is surveyed between the yearly waves about car usage and fuel consumption, thus making a half yearly contact interval. Additionally, a linked 'extra sample' with retrospective and prospective interviews for long distance travel of one year per person was repeated for three years. Is a one-year interval appropriate for capturing daily travel?

7.   Focus groups on 'conditioning' effects and travelling, or reporting of travelling. This response error has been extensively studied in general panel surveys (see Kasprzyk *et al.*, 1989), but only tested in one travel panel survey. In the DNMP, the average of non-reported weekly trips increased from 2.27 per household in the first wave to 8.35 per household in the seventh wave (Meurs *et al.*, 1989).

8.   Use of panels to observe process rather than (or in addition to) outcomes. As mentioned before, this can be achieved not only collecting observed data, but also asking respondents when an event occurred.

9.   Include questions about attitudes, perceptions and choices in panel survey questionnaires. Only the PSTP have collected this type of data which have been analysed by Sunkanapalli *et al.* (2000). These data are important components in the travel behaviour decision process. Attitudinal data cannot be collected using retrospective questions (Duncan *et al.*, 1987). Therefore, panel data are required to design attitudinal dynamic models.

10. Include questions about the reasons why respondents stay in the panel. This information could be very useful in testing and correcting attrition bias.

REFERENCES

Amundsen, A.H., R. Elvik and L. Fridstrøm (1999). Effects of the 'Speak Out!' Campaign on the Number of Killed or Injured Road Users in the County of Sogn Og Fjordane, Norway. *Series: TØI report 425/1999. Institute of Transport Economics.* (in Norwegian).

Baanders, A., R.H. De Boer and E.P. Kroes (1989). Impact of a New Railway Line on Travel Patterns: The Flevo Line in The Netherlands. *PTRC 17th Summer Annual Meeting.* Proceedings of Seminar, Brighton.

Berri, A., Gardes, F., Madre, J-L and Starzec, C. (1998). Income Elasticities for Transport Expenditures in Canada, France, Poland and the USA: An Analysis on Pseudo-Panels of Expenditure Surveys. Paper presented at the 8th *World Conference on Transport Research*, Antwerp, Belgium.

Bradley, M. (1997). A Practical Comparison of Modelling Approaches for Panel Data. In: *Panels for Transportation Planning: Methods and Application* (T.F. Golob, R. Kitamura and L. Long, eds), 281-304, Kluwer Academic Publishers, Norwell, MA.

CRT Madrid(1998). *Estudio sobre la Variación de Hábitos de Modo de Transportes en el Corredor de la N – VI.* Unpublished report, Consorcio Regional de Transportes de Madrid. (in Spanish), 80 pages.

Dargay, J.M. (2003). Household Car Travel in the UK: a Pseudo-panel Analysis. CD-ROM Proceedings of the 82nd *Annual Meeting of the Transportation Research Board*, Washington, DC.

Dargay, J., Madre, J-L and Berri, A. (2000). Car Ownership Dynamics as seen Through the Follow up of Cohorts: A Comparison of France and the UK. *Transportation Research Record No. 1733*, 31-38.

Deaton, A. (1985). Panel Data from Time-Series of Cross-Section, *Journal of Econometrics*, **30**, 109-126.

Doherty, S.T. (2003). Should We Abandon Activity Type Analysis? Paper presented at the 10*th* *International Conference on Travel Behaviour Research*, Lucerne, August.

Duncan, G.J., F.T. Juster and J.N. Morgan (1987). The Role of Panel Studies in Research on Economic Behaviour. *Transportation Research A*, **21** (4/5), 249-263.

Federal Transit Administration (2000). *Final Rule on Major Capital Investment Projects.* http://www.fta.dot.gov/library/policy/ns/bandaqanda.htm.

Golob, T.F., R. Kitamura and J. Supernak (1997). A Panel-Based Evaluation of the San Diego I-15 Carpool Lanes Project. In: *Panels for Transportation Planning: Methods and Application* (T.F. Golob, R. Kitamura and L. Long, eds), 97-128, Kluwer Academic Publishers, Norwell, MA.

Goodwin, P.B. (1986). A Panel Analysis of Changes in Car Ownership and Bus Use. *Traffic Engineering and Control*, **27** (10), 519-525.

Goulias, K.G. (2003). On the Role of Qualitative Methods in Travel Surveys. In: *Transport Survey Quality and Innovation* (P.R. Stopher and P.M. Jones, eds), 319-330, Elsevier, Oxford.

Goulias, K.G., N. Kilgren and T. Kim (2003). A Decade of Longitudinal Travel Behaviour Observation in the Puget Sound Region: Sample Composition, Summary Statistics, and a Selection of First Order Findings. Paper presented at 10*th* *International Conference on Travel Behaviour Research*, Lucerne, Switzerland, August 2003.

Giuliano, G. and T.F. Golob (1990). Using longitudinal methods for analysis of a short-term demonstration project, *Transportation*, **17**, 1-28.

Heckman, J. (1979). Sample Selection Bias as a Specification Error, *Econometrica*, **47**, 153-161.

Hensher, D.A. (1986). Longitudinal surveys in transport: an assessment. In: *New Survey Methods in Transport* (E.S. Ampt, W. Brög and A.J. Richardson, eds), 77-98, VNU Science Press, Utrecht.

Hensher, D.(1987), Issues in the Pre-Analysis of Panel Data, *Transportation Research A*, **21**, 265-285.

Hensher, D.A. (1997). The Timing of Change: Discrete and Continuous Time Panels in Transportation. In: *Panels for Transportation Planning: Methods and Application* (T.F. Golob, R. Kitamura and L. Long, eds), 305-319, Kluwer Academic Publishers, Norwell, MA.

Kasprzyk, D., G. Duncan, G. Kalton and M.P. Singh (eds) (1989). *Panel Surveys*. John Wiley & Sons, New York.

Keuleers, B., G. Wets, H. Timmermans, T. Arentze and K. Vanhoof (2002). Stationary and Time-Varying Patterns in Activity Diary Panel Data: Explorative Analysis with Association Rules, *Transportation Research Record No. 1807*, 9-15.

Kish, L. (1985). Timing of Surveys for Public Policy, *Australian Journal of Statistics*, **28** (1), 1-12.

Kitamura, R. (1990a). Panel Analysis in Transportation Planning: An Overview, *Transportation Research A*, **24** (6), 401-415.

Kitamura, R. (1990b). Longitudinal Surveys. In: *Selected Readings in Transport Survey Methodology* (E.S. Ampt, A.J. Richardson and A.H. Meyburg, eds), 9-11, Eucalyptus Press, Melbourne.

Kuhnimhof, T. and Chlond, B. (2003). Selectivity and Nonresponse in the German Mobility Panel: Selectivity Impacts on Data Quality due to Nonresponse in Multi-Stage Survey Recruitment Processes, Paper presented at the Workshop on Item Nonresponse and Data Quality in Large Social Surveys. Basel.

Lawton, T.K. & Pas, E.I. (1996). Resource Paper, Survey Methodologies Workshop. In: *Proceedings, Conference on Household Travel Surveys: New Concepts and Research Needs*. Conference Proceedings No. 10, Transportation Research Board, Washington, DC, 134-169.

Loos, A., E. Kroes and T. van der Hoorn (1992). The Household Panel Survey in the M10 Amsterdam Beltway Study, paper presented to the First US Conference on Panels for Transportation Planning, October 25-27, Lake Arrowhead, California.

Ma, J. and K. G. Goulias (1997). Systematic Self-selection and Sample Weight Creation in Panel Surveys: The Puget Sound Transportation Panel Case, *Transportation Research A*, **31** (5), 365-377.

McCray, T., M. Lee-Gosselin, C. Leclerc and F. Joud (2002). The Design of a Panel Survey on the Organization of Spatio-Temporal Behaviour in the Quebec City Region, paper presented to the International Colloquium SSHRC-MCRI & NCE-GEOIDE *The Behavioural Foundations of Integrated Land-Use and Transportation Models: Assumptions and New Conceptual Frameworks*, Quebec, 16-19 June.

McCray, T.M., Lee-Gosselin, M.E.H. & Kwan, M.-P. (2003), Netting action and activity space/time: are our methods keeping pace with evolving behaviour patterns? Paper presented at the 10th International Conference on Travel Behaviour Research, Lucerne, August.

Meurs, H., L. van Wissen and J. Wisser (1989). Measurement Biases in Panel Data, *Transportation*, **16**, 175-194.

Miller, E.J. and D.F. Crowley (1989). Panel Survey Approach to Measuring Transit Route Service Elasticity of Demand, *Transportation Research Record No. 1209*, 26-31.

MOP (www.mobilitaetspanel.de): Information about the German Mobility Panel and the possibility to download a variety of conference papers and reports

Morton-Williams, J. (1993). *Interviewer Approaches*. SCPR, Social and Community Planning Research, Dartmouth Publishing Co., Aldershot, 231 pp.

Moser, C.A. and G. Kalton (1979). *Survey Methods in Social Investigation*, 2nd. Ed., Heinemann Educational Books, London, 550 pages.

Murakami, E. and W. T. Watterson. (1990). Developing a Household Travel Survey for the Puget Sound Region, *Transportation Research Record No. 1285*, 40-48.

Murakami, E. and C. Ulberg (1997). The Puget Sound Transportation Panel. In: *Panels for Transportation Planning: Methods and Application* (T.F. Golob, R. Kitamura and L. Long, eds), 159-192, Kluwer Academic Publishers, Norwell, MA.

NFO-Infratest (2001): *Haushaltspanel zum Verkehrsverhalten, Endbericht zum Paneljahr 2000/2001*. NFO Infratest Verkehrsforschung im Auftrag des

Bundesministeriums für Verkehr, Bau- und Wohnungswesen, Endbericht zu Projekt 70.570/1998 (available at: www.mobilitaetspanel.de).

Paaswell, R.E. (1997). Why Panels for Transportation Planning? In: *Panels for Transportation Planning: Methods and Application* (T.F. Golob, R. Kitamura and L. Long, eds), 21, Kluwer Academic Publishers, Norwell, MA.

Pendyala, R.M., K.G. Goulias and R. Kitamura (1991). Impact of Telecommuting on Spatial and Temporal Patterns of Household Travel, *Transportation*, 18, 383-409.

Purvis, C.L. (1997). Planning for Panel Surveys in the San Francisco Bay Area, In: *Panels for Transportation Planning: Methods and Application* (T.F. Golob, R. Kitamura and L. Long, eds), 193-206, Kluwer Academic Publishers, Norwell, MA.

Purvis, C.L. and T. Ruiz (2003). Standards and Practice for Multi-Day and Multi-Period Surveys. In: *Transport Survey Quality and Innovation* (P.R. Stopher and P.M. Jones, eds), 271-282, Elsevier, Oxford.

Roorda, M.J. and E.J. Miller (2004). Toronto Activity Panel Survey. A Multi-Instrument Panel Survey, Paper presented at the 7th *International Conference on Travel Survey Methods*. Costa Rica, August 1-6.

Ruiz, T. (2004). Attrition in Transport Panels: A Survey, Paper presented at the 7th *International Conference on Travel Survey Methods*. Costa Rica, August 1-6.

Stopher, P.R. and Greaves, S.P. (2004) 'Sample Size Requirements for Measuring a Change in Behaviour', paper presented at the 27th Australian Transport Research Forum (ATRF), Adelaide, Australia, September 2004.

Sunkanapalli, S., R.M. Pendyala, and R.M. Kuppam (2000). Dynamic analysis of traveler attitudes and perceptions using panel data, *Transportation Research Record No. 1718*, 52-60.

Tourangeau, R., Zimowski, M. y Ghadialy, R. (1997). *An Introduction to Panel Surveys in Transportation Studies*, Federal Highway Administration, Chicago, IL, 55 pp.

Trivellato, U. (1999). Issues in the Design and Analysis of Panel Studies: a Cursory Review, *Quality and Quantity*, 33, 339-352.

UNFCCC (1997). *The Kyoto Protocol*. http://unfccc.int/resource/convkp.html.

Van Wissen, L.J.G. and Meurs, H.J. (1989). The Dutch Mobility Panel: Experiences and Evaluation, *Transportation*, 16, 99-119.

Zumkeller, D., Madre, J-L., Chlond, B. and Armoogum, J. (2006). Panel Surveys. In: *Travel Survey Methods – Quality and Future Directions* (P.R. Stopher and C.C. Stecher, eds), 375-412, Elsevier, Oxford.

Travel Survey Methods: Quality and Future Directions
Peter Stopher and Cheryl Stecher (Editors)
© 2006 Published by Elsevier Ltd.

22

ENERGY CONSUMPTION ESTIMATION WITH A SHIPPER AND TRANSPORT CHAIN SURVEY

Christophe Rizet, INRETS, Arcueil, France
Jimmy Armoogum, INRETS, Arcueil, France
and
Philippe Marchal, INRETS, Arcueil, France

ENERGY CONSUMPTION AND SHIPPER SURVEYS

Over one quarter of greenhouse gas emissions in France comes from the transport sector and this share is growing: there is no sign of saturation of transport energy use. Therefore, climate change mitigation requires profound changes in world transport, either in the form of energy efficiency improvements or by changing transport demand. We are beginning to understand the determinants of demand, as expressed in vehicle-kilometres, for passenger travel (vehicle ownership, age, location) and the consequence these determinants have on energy consumption, pollution, and greenhouse gas emissions. These determinants are much less well known for freight, while effective intervention with a view to reducing the impact of road and air freight requires in-depth knowledge about the factors that influence firms in their logistical choices. This lack of knowledge is due to several factors: the theoretical complexity of the problem, the insufficiencies of resources that have been made available for freight compared with passenger transport, and the inadequacy of the existing data. With regard to data, the shipper surveys that INRETS has developed seem to us to have considerable, as yet unexploited, potential.

This chapter explains the methodology used to cope with the estimation of energy consumption in the new 2004 survey: the analysis made on previous surveys data to test this possibility and the different improvements made to the survey methodology to adapt the questionnaire, to improve the distance calculation and the checking of transport chain coherence and to optimise the sampling.

French Shipper Surveys

Since the first survey in 1988, French Shipper surveys have been designed to analyse the determinants of freight transport demand. They incorporate two major components: the tracing of a selection of shipments from their departure from the plant up to their arrival to the consignee, and the description of the shippers' organisational features influencing its transport choices. In this chapter, we describe how the new 2004 shipper survey has been adapted to enable the analysis of energy consumed in freight transport and to relate it to the determinants of freight transport demand.

To analyse freight transport demand, particularly in the case of complex transport chains, INRETS has developed a monitoring system, which is known as the shipper surveys. This was successfully used for the first time in France in 1988. The main objectives are to:

- Obtain knowledge about freight transport chains from end to end in terms of mode or vehicle interconnections, and also the way in which the chains are organised; and
- Provide an understanding of the logistical determinants of the shippers, on the basis of, in particular, the nature of the activity, the size, and the logistical choices of the shipper, and also with a view to conducting modelling.

A new objective in the 2004 Shipper and Operator Survey (Enquête Envois CHargeurs Opérateurs – ECHO) is to quantify energy consumed in freight transport, at a very disaggregate level. Similar to other transport data, energy data cannot be measured directly in the field, but needs to be estimated with the aid of a mathematical model (Garrido, 2003). When energy is known, pollutant emissions can be computed with a specific emission factor for each type of pollutant and vehicle.

Data Collection in the Survey

In the French shipper surveys, data are collected at three levels (Rizet *et al.*, 2003):

- At the shipper company level: after a few questions about the volume and structure of the company's ingoing and outgoing transport flows and its own fleet of vehicles, a face-to-face interview on the economic characteristics of the firm is administered to the logistics manager of the company, with regard to its production, distribution and storage practices, its relationships with its customers and suppliers, and the management and communications systems it uses. This description of the firm's industrial and logistical organisation is supplemented by a transport section that deals with the firm's relationships with carriers, terms of access to the various types of infrastructure, and how responsibility for transport is shared between the firm and its partners.

- At the consignment level: at the end of the company questionnaire, the last twenty consignments are listed, three of which are selected randomly and then followed until they reach their final consignee. The consignment questionnaires, which are filled in either with the logistics manager, or the dispatching manager, deal with the economic relationship between the shipper and the customer and the terms of business between the two, in particular regarding deadlines. The physical and economic characteristics of the consignment are described, as is the division of responsibilities with regard to transport organisation and the contractual allocation of transport costs and associated services. The initial data required to reconstruct transport chains is also collected at this level, with the identification of the consignee and the operators to whom the firm has entrusted the consignment. The different participants identified here are interviewed in their turn by telephone, not face-to-face.

- At the participant and journey link level: fairly short questionnaires (because they are administered by telephone) relate to the economic characteristics of these participants (activity, status, size, location), the information systems and transport application software used, and the use of rail-road combined transport. They also give a picture of the participant's role with regard to the consignment, its links with the shipper, the consignee or the principal, and the services provided. The participants have, themselves, contacted other participants who are identified so they can be questioned in their turn, so the description of the transport chain will be complete up to the final consignee. The transport leg questionnaires are filled in by the participants who have performed transport. These questionnaires break down the transport operation into as many legs as there are modes, vehicles, or stops required to process the freight (logistical services such as product finishing, labelling, packaging, consolidation, etc.). The information collected can be used to identify intermediate points of passage and the services that are provided there (in particular grouping with other goods in the same vehicle), to reconstruct the distances and various journey and transit times and to find out the weight of the entire load carried by the vehicle.

The transport chains are, therefore, reconstructed by passing from one participant to the next, on the basis of the task each has performed. This monitoring has been conducted either up to the French frontier (in the 1988 survey) or throughout Western Europe (in a test survey conducted in 1999, as well as in the 2004 survey) and includes an interview with the consignees in Western European countries. For consignments that travel beyond this limit, only the participants who operated in Europe are questioned, with journeys being reconstructed until the first transfer point after the frontier has been crossed. The data needed for energy analysis principally concerns the 'leg' and 'journey' levels, the latter being considered as a succession of legs or transport chains. Energy consumption is expressed in grams of oil equivalent (goe) and sometimes related to tonne-kilometres of the shipment (goe/tkm) in order to compare the energy efficiency of different shipments or shipment types. To adapt the survey to this objective of quantifying freight transport energy consumption and the influence of logistical practices on energy consumption, we used two small samples from 1999 surveys.

ESTIMATION OF ENERGY CONSUMPTION

Using two 1999 small samples, we estimated energy consumed per shipment and evaluated the potential of shipper surveys for analysing freight transport energy consumption in relation to the logistical decisions made by companies. The main objective was to propose improvements to the questionnaires and to quantify energy consumption at a very disaggregate level in the new 2004 shipper survey (Rizet and Keïta, 2002). Using the former survey data (before specific adaptation), energy consumed per shipment has been estimated as follows: consumption has been modelled by type of vehicle; with these models, the energy consumed by the vehicle is estimated per leg on the basis of the distance covered. A proportion of the fuel consumed is then assigned to the consignment, based on the percentage of the total load it represents and, finally, the energy consumption of all the legs in the transport chain are summed for the consignment.

Road Transport

For road vehicles, on the basis of published work, we identified a specific per vehicle consumption for the different types of vehicle distinguished in the survey. We concentrated on the influence of the load, the only variable known in the previous survey, so we used the results from Roumégoux (1995), which are summarised in Table 1. Finally, using the 'on road' data, we estimated fuel consumption, in litres/100 kilometres, as:

$$\text{Consumption} = 0.892 \text{ total weight} + 10.0$$

Table 1: Unitary Fuel Consumption and Mean Speeds for Different Types of Vehicle and Road Depending on the Load

Vehicle and Weight (Empty/Full Load)	Load	On Road		On Motorway	
		Speed (km/h)	Consumption (litres/100)	Speed (km/h)	Consumption (litres/100)
Van (1.8 t.)	Empty	76.5	9.1	123.7	16.4
Van (3.5 t.)	Full load	74.2	10.8	117.7	17.0
Lorry (12.0 t.)	Empty	68.9	23.4	88.4	25.7
Lorry (19.0 t.)	Full load	66.8	28.2	84.7	29.5
Articulated (13.5 t.)	Empty	69.2	25.1	88.0	27.0
Articulated (40.0 t.)	Full load	62.2	43.6	75.6	42.1

Source: Roumégoux, 1995

In the test using the 1999 data, we considered an average deadhead run coefficient for each type of vehicle, as estimated from the national road freight transport survey

(Transports Routiers de Marchandises – TRM) conducted by the French Ministry of Transport. The estimated energy consumption in litres has been converted to goe with the density of diesel fuel taken at 0.84 kg per litre. One improvement in the 2004 survey is that empty running will be asked for each leg, instead of using a national coefficient.

Other Modes

For non-road modes, in the previous surveys, it was not possible to apply this method, because neither the type of vehicle nor the weight of the total load was known. For this test, we simply applied a national per tonne-kilometre average consumption for each mode, using French figures estimated on an average national basis. For air transport, the energy consumption estimated is that of a Boeing B737, the most-used plane in Europe, which has been estimated on the basis of the MEET Project's Work (Kalivoda and Kudrna, 1997). The following relationship has been used between the consumption (in tonnes of kerosene), the payload (in tonnes) and the distance covered:

$$\text{Consumption (per tonne of payload)} = 0.0002*\text{distance} + 0.024$$

It should be noted that this consumption would be lower with an Airbus A310 or A320; what we have here, therefore, is an upper bound. To calculate per leg consumption, we used an average loading rate of fifty percent in tonnage, a deadhead run rate of fifteen percent and took the density of kerosene as 0.8 kg/litre. This gives average energy efficiency for air freight transport of nearly 500 goe/tkm. For other modes we used data provided by the ADEME (the French Agency for Energy), as shown in Table 2.

Table 2: Energy Consumption for Non-Road Modes

Mode	Consumption Rate (goe/tonne-kilometre)
Full train	8.3
Combined transport	11.7
Wagon	16.2
Sea transport	4.6
Pushed barge	8.5
Self-powered barge	12.6

Source: Based on ADEME data, taking 1 kWh=222 goe as the primary energy equivalence (at production).

The main improvement in the 2004 survey is to give the elements to compute energy consumption per leg for non-road modes, as well as for road legs, instead of using national average figures; the new questionnaire includes questions on the type of vehicle and the weight of the total load carried during the journey.

The Variability of Consumption per Transport Chain

For observed road legs in the 1999 surveys, the estimated consumption for a shipment, in goe, has been divided by the number of tonne-kilometres travelled to get a unitary consumption, in goe/tkm. These unitary consumption figures of road legs vary greatly, from 20 to more than 100,000 goe/tkm. Three factors are important to explain this variation of consumption per consignment and per leg:

- The consumption is calculated on the basis of the total weight of the vehicle estimated on the basis of its capacity: consumption varies between 45.7 litres/100 kilometres for a 25 tonne payload vehicle, that is to say 1.82 litres per payload tonne/100 kilometres and 11.3 litres/100 kilometres for a small 1.5 tonne payload lorry, that is to say 7.53 litres per payload tonne; the ratio of consumption per payload tonne varies between 1 and 4.1.
- The computed per consignment fuel consumption also takes account of a deadhead run coefficient which, for the 1999 surveys, is roughly estimated on the basis of the payload category and the type of transport operation: this varies from twenty percent for small hire and reward lorries to fifty six percent for large own account vehicles, i.e., a ratio of 1 to 1.3.
- In particular, the consumption that is assigned to a consignment takes account of the loading rate of the vehicle (which is the reciprocal of the vehicle capacity utilisation coefficient, that is the ratio between the weight of a load and the payload) which can vary between 1 (when the weight of the load is equal to the capacity) to 25 tonnes/5 kilograms (a vehicle with the maximum capacity with the smallest load) i.e., a ratio of 1 to 5,000.

The minimum road transport unitary consumption is then 20 goe/tkm, for a vehicle carrying 25 tonnes (maximum authorised load) in hire and reward operation and the maximum is more than 100,000 goe/tkm, for the same vehicle carrying 5 kilograms in own account operation. It is clearly the weight of the load which is mainly responsible for the dispersion of unitary consumption.

For modes other than road transport, the consumption has been estimated directly by applying a unitary consumption figure to the kilometre tonnage of the consignment on the leg: there is therefore no dispersion. Average values can be computed either for each transport mode or for each type of transport chain, summing the energy consumption for different legs. For non-road transport chains, end legs make a relatively minor contribution to consumption: the average values for transport chains are still about 30 goe/tkm for exclusively road chains and the values for the other chains are similar to those used for the principal mode: around 500 goe/tkm for air chains, thirteen for river transport, eight to sixteen for rail (depending on the percentage of full trains), ten to twelve for rail-road combined transport, and five for sea transport.

The variability of unitary consumption for road transport legs is the most surprising result of this analysis; one consequence, for other modes, is that our highly simplified data fail to show this variability, and are, therefore, inappropriate to analyse this reality. Another consequence is that the computation of average consumption for a type of consignment is very imprecise; this variability leads to a lack of accuracy when we measure average energy consumption, for example when comparing different subgroups to test some hypothesis.

The Low Accuracy of Average Energy Consumption

Different hypotheses were tested to analyse the influence of logistical choices on energy consumption. One of these tests was on Just-in-Time (JIT): we classified shipments in three groups according to the delivery time requested by the customer. Then we compared the characteristics of these three groups of shipments (Rizet and Keïta, 2002). As shown in Table 3, the first result is that the average weight of consignments is lower when the delivery time is short. In the table, below average unitary consumption seems to follow the same trend: they are lower for the least urgent consignments because these can use rail and sea transport. However, the confidence intervals, linked to the accuracy of the estimators of average consumption, are so low that it is not possible to reach a definite conclusion on this point.

Of course this problem of confidence interval should be improved by the size of the sample in the 2004 survey (thirty times more important than in each of the 1999 surveys). Nevertheless the problem remains serious and several improvements were introduced in the new survey to upgrade the accuracy of our estimate.

Table 3: Unitary Consumption According to the Requested Maximum Delivery Time

Delivery Time	Observations	Survey 1 Unitary Consumption		Observations	Survey 2 Unitary Consumption	
		Average	Confidence interval		Average	Confidence interval
1 week max.	199	43	0 - 1108	81	50	0 – 1424
2 to 3 weeks	64	19	0 - 1842	82	68	0 – 2263
> 3 weeks	31	8.8	0 - 5060	113	25	0 – 3072
Total	294	10	0 - 992	276	26	0 – 1510

GEOCODING AND THE DISTANCES

The new survey is based on a CAPI that integrates a pre-geocoded list of worldwide origin and destination place names. The aspects related to geocoding and distances estimation are considered here in three stages: first, in the preparation process before the realization of the survey, a worldwide list of pre-geocoded places has been integrated in the CAPI; second, during the implementation, a tool enables the cartographic checking of the multimodal transport chains collected; and, finally, in the processing of the collected data, distances are computed.

Setting up a List of Pre-Geocoded Places in the CAPI

Unlike our previous surveys, the new shipper survey has been designed with computer-assisted methods (CAPI and CATI). The initial question concerning location data collection was how to 'feed' this software. In the case of France, an existing consistent database has been integrated into the CAPI, for those steps where precise place names or transport terminals used are asked. Taking into account the coverage of the survey and the rate of international shipments to be surveyed, a method has been designed to obtain equivalent lists for foreign countries.

During the test period of the survey, a draft database, partially extracted from the NIMA database, from the National Geospatial-Intelligence Agency (NGA) was used. The main problem with this draft database was the presence of double values in the full name. We had for example three 'Frankfurts' in Germany, but the interviewer was unable to detect which one in the list was the 'main Frankfurt', which one was the 'small' city near Nuremberg, or the 'small' city near Berlin. Considering the number of place names in the NIMA database (approximately five million names), it was impossible to imagine a manual elimination of these double names for the whole database. An automated process was developed, using another worldwide database containing a limited number of cities, but with population estimates.

This process was based on the detection, for each NIMA place, of the nearest important city, taking into account a population threshold adapted for each country. The distance between the double value and this important city was also added into the new generated name. With this method, the three identical 'Frankfurts' in the initial database became:

1.   Frankfurt /45/Nurnberg;
2.   Frankfurt /82/Berlin; and
3.   Frankfurt /0/Frankfurt.

The figures between the slashes indicate the straight-line distance, in kilometres. This format was chosen based on the specification of the CAPI, particularly the limitation in the number of characters. Additionally, and to adapt to the coverage of the survey, which supposes the interview of transport companies abroad, these important cities are indicated in French, but also in the local language or in English. When, for a given country, a place is not detected in the list used in the CAPI, the interviewer inputs this name totally by hand, and additionally asks for the name of the nearest important city; this relatively rare occurrence will be the subject of specific processing to obtain a consistent set of geocoded places.

The CAPI thus set up, with an incremental searching with auto-completion in the list of places, will first limit the data entry duration for the interviewer and, therefore, the global duration of the interview, and indirectly the global quality of the data collected. It will also reduce significantly the risks of misspelled names.

Validation of the Multimodal Transport Chains

The first work consists in achieving consistency between the places resulting directly from the lists of the CAPI, with those input by hand. With this intention, various algorithms of similarity tests between strings are applied: each non-geocoded place is compared for a given country to all of the places present in the CAPI list, and the results are sorted according to their 'similarity rate'. This semi-automatic process makes it possible to correct possible spelling mistakes quickly. The additional information on the nearest important city allows a decision between the possible double values obtained. When this method does not make it possible to identify a place with certainty, the observation collected for this leg is temporarily unused, until a complementary validation process from the interviewers.

On the basis of the complete set of geocoded observations, several checks are performed. The usual first step consists of checking the correct sequence of the various places used in the successive legs of the same shipment. Immediate work with geocoded places also makes it possible to control for a given mode sequence collected, consistency between the means of transport used, and the real possibilities offered, taking into account the geography of the areas or countries concerned, and the knowledge of the infrastructure and services. A simple geometrical checking then makes it possible to detect the shipments containing incorrectly answered places used: the sum of the straight-line distances of the various legs is reported to the 'direct' straight-line distance between the origin of the first leg of the shipment, and the destination of its last leg. When this ratio of distances is higher than two, a manual check is performed, to understand which part of the shipment could be indicated incorrectly.

The chains considered as 'non-suspect' at the end of this process are visually checked on a map quickly, using the shipment cartographic control tool designed for this purpose. Given that the processing duration of these controls is relatively low, after reception of the intermediate files of the survey, it is possible to ask the interviewer to call back the corresponding company, to correct the data and limit the number of unusable shipments.

Distances and Alternative Transport Chains

In the previous shipper surveys, the distances for road transport were estimated on the basis of a straight line, applying a global correction factor, without taking into account the geographical characteristics of the countries and regions, or the development of the motorway network. In the analysis of the 1999 survey, energy consumption was related to tonne-kilometres on the basis of the distance covered by the consignment on transport networks. We have also related them to kilometre tonnages on the basis of straight-line distances (per/tkmSL) in order to assess the impact of the circuitous route followed by consignments either because of the networks, or because they need to transit through a terminal in order to be grouped together, which generally involves an additional distance between the consignment's origin and final destination. By comparing the unitary consumption for these two types of distance (straight line and network distance), we can measure the 'excess consumption' caused by the lengthening of distances because, of the form of the networks or because of passing through a transhipment point. In the case of road chains, this unitary excess consumption amounts to twenty nine percent; for own transport operations, we have confirmed that excess consumption is greater in the case of chains with multiple legs (forty four and fifty four percent respectively for the NPDC and Mystic Surveys) than for chains with a single leg (twenty one and twenty six percent).

In the 2004 survey, when all the chains reconstituted by the end of the previous processing are considered as valid, the 'real' distances on the modal networks are then estimated for each leg. This 'routing' aspect is based on the use of network databases. The networks are detailed enough for road, rail and waterborne estimations inside Europe. In the case of intercontinental shipments, a great circle distance calculation tool is used for marine and air legs. One of the main advantages of working with precise origin-destination shipments is the possibility of testing alternative transport policies, especially those aimed at road traffic limitations. This approach will allow estimating the effect on energy consumption for the same set of origin-destination links, by generating alternative transport chains, evaluated with a modal share model.

OPTIMISING THE SAMPLE

When estimating energy consumed for a type of transport, two types of inaccuracy may arise: sampling inaccuracy, i.e., errors caused by the fact that we observe only a sample and not the whole population, and non-sampling errors which are mainly due to measurement errors and to nonresponse (Armoogum, 2002). The estimation of energy consumption per shipment depends on the mode of transport, the type and age of vehicle, the tonnage of the shipment, the tonnage of the load (weight of all the shipments in the vehicle), the distance travelled, etc. Some of these variables are very difficult or impossible to collect.

In the light of the high cost of this survey and of the available budget, the 2004 sample will be around 3,230 firms with 9,700 shipments. To have a sufficient number of observations on the different modes, this sample is designed to obtain about one third of non-truck shipments (with a random sample we should have only five percent of non-truck shipments); more precisely, we want at least eight percent railway shipments (i.e., nearly 800 railways shipments), eight percent maritime shipments; eight percent air shipments, four percent (400) combined rail-road shipments, and two percent (200) river shipments; furthermore, we want twenty five percent of international shipments and, because of the Nord Pas-de Calais region's contribution in the funding of the survey, we want 900 firms from this region.

The sampling protocol is the same as for the European Mystic survey (see Rizet *et al.*, 2003), where a two step sample was used: a first sample among the firms and then, per firm, three shipments are randomly chosen among the last twenty shipments and tracked up to the final customer. In order to reach our sampling objectives we stratified the population of firms using the exhaustive SIRET file of French firms, with a higher sampling rate among strata that have a higher proportion of firms using non-road modes; then, in the choice of the three shipments of a firm, we gave a higher probability to 'non-road' shipments.

Sampling the Firms

To stratify the firms, we defined the profiles of non-road user and exporting companies, using three variables of the SIRET file: the activity of the firms, its location, and the number of employees. We used a logit model that we applied to the 1988 shipper survey data, in order to find out the profiles of firms which are using the 'rare' modes or which are exporting – the firms we want to over-sample (Armoogum and Madre, 2003). The results, in terms of activities, number of employees and location are shown in Table 4. In 1988, the selection methodology of shipment consisted in taking the last three shipments. 'Rare' mode users are those firms where at least one of the shipments is made by the 'rare' mode that we consider. As the number of waterways shipments was very low we did not consider this mode (there were only four shipments with this mode in 1988).

Table 4: Dimensions that Explain the Use of 'Rare' Modes (at the level of one percent)

Firms that used the following modes:	Activity	Number of Employees	Firm's localisation
Rail	Yes	No	No
Maritimes	Yes	No	No
Air	Yes	Yes	No
Combination rail-road	Yes	No	No
International	Yes	Yes	No
From Nord-Pas-de-Calais region	No	No	Yes

Source: INRETS calculations from 1988 Shipper Survey.

With a logit model, we find that the activity of the firm allows us to capture (in the sample) non-exclusive road shipment firms and also firms that export. The use of the firm's location will favour the inclusion in the sample of firms from the Nord-Pas-de-Calais region and also 'waterway' shipments. On the other hand, the number of employees doesn't bring any information for non-truck shipment, except for air shipment.

So, if we want non-truck users we have to use the firm's activity and if we want nine percent of firms from the Nord-Pas-de-Calais region we have to treat the location variable. In the exhaustive SIRET database of French plants, 700 activities are detailed and different groups of activities are coded. Starting from the sixty 'divisions', we constructed thirty nine groups of activities in order to keep the continuity and the homogeneity of the production process (Guilbault *et al.*, 2002). The analysis of non-truck clients' profiles, in terms of detailed activities and location, has been completed with data from SNCF (the French railway company), with the Customs file (for maritime and international shipments), and the file from VNF (the French waterways company). All this information allowed us to build subgroups of activities and location with a higher probability of using non-road shipments. We have then seventy nine subgroups.

The budget of the 2004 survey allows a sample size of about 3,230 firms (the sampling rate is about four percent). Optimising the sampling schemes is an important issue, especially in the core of firms, because of its heterogeneity. For example, if we take a uniform random sample of 3,230 firms without any optimisation, the total number of shipments is known within a confidence interval of ±60 percent at the level of ninety five percent confidence and we should expect about ninety five percent of truck shipments in the sample.

If we take a sample of 3,230 firms, stratified on the activity, the accuracy of the estimates is (at the ninety five percent level):

- With an optimisation on the tonnage:
    - The total number of shipments is known within ±60 percent and total tonnage within ±25 percent;
- With an optimisation on the number of shipments:
    - The total number of shipments is known within ±20 percent and total tonnage within ±70 percent.

If we take a sample of 3,230 firms, stratified on the number of employees of the firms, the accuracy of the estimates are (at the ninety five percent level):

- With an optimisation on the tonnage:
    - The total number of shipments is known within ±10 percent and total tonnage within ±14 percent;
- With an optimisation on the number of shipment:
    - The total number of shipments is known within ±8 percent and total tonnage within ±18 percent.

The optimum accuracy in terms of tonnage is achieved when we have the distribution given in Table 5 for the number of employees. Thus, the five groups of numbers of employees are introduced as a stratification criterion to improve the precision of the estimators.

Table 5: Stratification for an Optimum Accuracy in Terms of Tonnage

Groups by Number of Employees	Number of Firms in the Population	Number of Firms in the Sample
6-19 employees	35,572	385
20-49 employees	26,317	579
50-499 employees	15,319	1,717
500-999 employees	622	352
1000 employees or more	197	197
Population	78,027	3,230

Sources: INRETS from SIRET of Insee (2002) and Chargeur (1988).

Finally, to reach our objectives we have to use the seventy nine modal subgroups in combination with the five groups of numbers of employees; therefore, we stratify the population into 395 (79 × 5) sub-subgroups. Due to the fact that not all combination of modal subgroups and groups of numbers of employees exist in the file, we finally get 300 strata. The allocation of the 300 samples (one sample in each stratum) is guided by the calibration on the marginals of the activity and the marginals of the numbers of employees; this methodology should lead us to achieve the objective (one third of non-truck shipments) and to have a maximum of accuracy in our estimates Besnard, 2002).

Sampling the Shipments

In each surveyed firm, at the end of the interview, the CAPI captures the last twenty shipments, their mode of transport and destination. Then, within these last twenty shipments, the CAPI selects three shipments that will be surveyed and tracked up to their final customer. In order to increase the sample of non-road modes, these three shipments are selected with an unequal probability, road shipment having the lowest probability to be selected. These probabilities are computed in order to adapt the sample to our objectives both in term of modes and destinations and stored in a file. At any time during the data collection, these probabilities can be modified to achieve the objectives of sample size for non-road and international shipments.

CONCLUSION

The shipper surveys developed by INRETS, enables to estimate the energy consumed in the transport of each shipment and to relate it to the logistical characteristics of the shipper and shipment. Using 1999 data, we could quantify energy consumed per road shipment, compare the energy consumption for consignments with different logistical characteristics, and so analyse the influence of the logistical choices of the firms on energy consumed in freight transport. This analysis proved that the processing of energy consumption at a very disaggregate level is possible for road transport and it suggested some improvements to the questionnaire, to adapt the new survey to the quantification of energy. Apart from these new questions, two major modifications were introduced in the survey, to improve the accuracy of our estimates.

We integrated a pre-geocoded list of worldwide origin and destination place names in the CAPI that will increase significantly the quality of origins, destinations, and distances and, therefore, energy consumption estimates. This system is also designed to enable a quick visual validation of the multimodal transport chains obtained during the survey implementation, allowing call-backs to the operators in case of erroneous information.

In the new survey, the sampling has been optimised and this optimisation follows the two levels of the sampling procedure: a first optimisation on the choice of firms and the second on the choice of shipments. This optimisation greatly increases the accuracy of estimates.

REFERENCES

Armoogum, J. (2002). *Correction de la non-réponse et de quelques erreurs de mesure dans une enquête par sondage: application à l'Enquête Transports et Communication 1993-94*, INRETS Report Number 239.

Armoogum, J. and J.-L. Madre (2003). Sample Selection. In: *Capturing Long-Distance Travel* (K.W. Axhausen, J.-L. Madre, J. Polak and P. Toint, eds), 205-222, Research Science Press, Baldock.

Besnard, F. (2002). *Optimisation du plan de sondage pour une enquête sur les transports de marchandises*, Rapport de stage INRETS-IUT de Vannes.

Garrido, R.A. (2003). Insights on Freight and Commercial Vehicle Data Needs. In: *Transport Survey Quality and Innovation* (P.R. Stopher and P.M. Jones, eds), 413-426, Pergamon Press, Oxford.

Guilbault, M., J. Armoogum and C. Rizet (2002). *Enquête ECHO - Rapport méthodologique d'étape*, INRETS - METL, 45 pp. + annexes

Kalivoda, M.T. and M. Kudrna (1997). *Methodologies for Estimating Emissions from Air Traffic*, MEET European Project, task 3.1, deliverable 18, 60 pp. + annexes.

Rizet, C., M. Guilbault, J. C. van Meijeren and M. Houée (2003). Tracking along the Transport Chain via the Shipper Survey. In: *Transport Study Quality and Innovation* (P.R. Stopher and P.M. Jones, eds), 427-441, Pergamon Press, Oxford.

Rizet, C. and B. Keïta (2002). *The Logistical Choices of Companies and Energy Consumption*, INRETS - ADEME report, 91 pp.

Roumégoux, J.P. (1995). Calcul des émissions de polluants des véhicules utilitaires, *The Science of Total Environment*, 169, 205-211.

Travel Survey Methods: Quality and Future Directions
Peter Stopher and Cheryl Stecher (Editors)

23

GOODS AND BUSINESS TRAFFIC IN GERMANY

Manfred Wermuth, Technical University at Braunschweig, Braunschweig, Germany
Christian Neef, Technical University at Braunschweig, Braunschweig, Germany
and
Imke Steinmeyer, Technical University of Berlin, Berlin, Germany

DEFINITION OF GOODS AND BUSINESS TRAFFIC

Commercial Traffic in Germany

As in other countries, much less research has gone into goods traffic and business passenger traffic than into private passenger traffic, even though commercial traffic is gaining significance especially in the industrialised world. The intention of this chapter is to present surveys that were conceived with the aim of compensating for the lack of research in this sector in Germany.

Household surveys are the most valuable source for acquiring data on passenger traffic, because they supply the required information for all distances travelled by people within a defined period of time, including the means of transport they use and the purpose of each trip. Similar surveys performed for goods traffic would, by analogy, have to consider the distances travelled, loading processes, and possibly also the processing of the goods handled, i.e., processes that are of eminent relevance for logistics. Although it is a highly complex task to ensure that the complete goods handling chain is covered, in theory, it could be solved at the consignor's end, i.e., households or business units. A major problem in this context is the question as to where to draw a dividing line within the population of all forwarding units, from which a representative sample can then be taken. However, because in the course of handling processes, goods are also transported by people, who normally use vehicles, goods traffic surveys can, at least for part of the handling process, also be conducted by interviewing people, e.g., drivers in households, business units, etc., or common carrier drivers.

In Germany, highly efficient mandatory traffic statistics have been compiled and are updated on a regular basis by different federal offices. One of these is the Federal Office for Motor Traffic (FOMT) with its central vehicle register, showing the essential details for any vehicle registered in Germany. The traffic performance of large goods vehicles (lorries and tractor trailers) of a payload of more than 3.5 tonnes is, in addition, established on an annual basis in the form of a representative sample of five per million (about 212,000 vehicles), covering a period of three days (so-called semi-weeks). These road haulage statistics are also mandatory, which means that there is an obligation to supply the required data under the federal traffic statistics act.

A recent research project (Wermuth *et al.*, 1998) has, however, shown that traffic statistics, and, more precisely, goods and business passenger traffic statistics, are incomplete, because they do not adequately cover such smaller vehicles as motorcycles, passenger cars, and lorries with a payload of up to 3.5 tonnes. Another research project (Brög and Winter, 1990) has shown that only about one third to one half of all trips forming part of business passenger traffic are reported in connection with written household surveys. This means that a major portion of business passenger traffic is not even considered in connection with passenger traffic statistics. Commercial traffic – which is understood to include both goods and business passenger traffic – should be the focus of specific surveys, because, especially for trips using passenger cars and small lorries (delivery vans), it is often not possible to draw a clear line between goods and passenger traffic.

Commercial Traffic and its Structure

In the past, a number of attempts have been made to structure commercial traffic and to delimit its sub-categories. Frequently used definitions are listed in Wermuth *et al.* (1998) and Steinmeyer (2004), however a generally accepted definition is as yet not available. This can be explained by the fact that, unlike private traffic, this sector has not been studied in depth. In addition, it is often necessary to arrive at a pragmatic definition of terms that relate to the purpose of the survey. A general distinction that can be made in the traffic sector is the one between private and commercial traffic. Commercial traffic in turn falls into the two main categories of:

- Goods traffic, i.e., trips made primarily with the aim of transporting goods; and
- Business passenger traffic, i.e., trips primarily made for a business or official purpose, including or not including goods transport. This category also covers trips made for purposes of passenger transport, e.g., a bus driver's trips for a public transport company.

It is not always possible to decide clearly whether, according to its primary purpose, a trip forms part of goods or business passenger traffic. This applies, for instance, to trips made to maintain the operability of a vehicle (e.g., trips to the garage or the petrol station). This is why a third category may be included:

- 'Other commercial traffic', i.e., trips made for a combination of purposes or a different purpose.

Sub-categories of goods traffic, including the required empty and return trips, are:

- Commercial goods traffic, i.e., goods transported between places of production and consumption; and
- Works traffic, i.e., a company's own goods transported on their own account.

Business passenger traffic, including the required empty and return trips, includes the sub-categories of:

- Service traffic, i.e., a combination of goods and passenger traffic, in which not only the person rendering a service, but also tools, spare parts or other goods are carried;
- Business and service traffic, i.e., trips made for a business purpose; and
- Passenger traffic, i.e., trips made for the purpose of transporting other people (e.g., trips made by bus drivers, taxi drivers, etc.).

Trips made as part of business passenger traffic, or what was called 'other commercial traffic' above, obviously also involve the transport of goods, materials, machinery, equipment, and the like. Any empty and return trips, such as those back to the company premises or the parking space fall under the same category as that of the preceding trip.

Figure 1 provides a general idea of the functional structure of motor vehicle traffic. The different traffic sectors are defined with a view to the (primary) purpose of a trip made. A detailed classification for private traffic using motor cars has been omitted, for the purposes of this research.

Methods Used for Commercial Traffic Surveys

Typical problems of commercial traffic surveys are the heterogeneity of the actors and the recordable units (business units, vehicles, and persons), as well as the complex structure of movements and trips (shuttle trips for official and business purposes versus multi-destination trips, in particular as part of goods and service traffic). This, together with the different structures involved (sectors of industry, distribution of places of work, demographic and settlement structures, available infrastructure, and the like), forms the background against which business traffic surveys have to be developed with a view to specific information needs and the investigated regions.

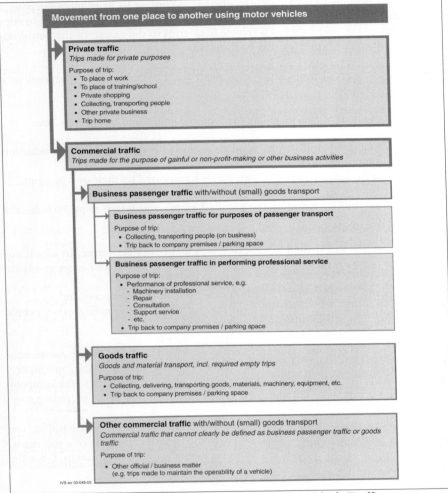

Figure 1: Functional Structure of Motor Vehicle Traffic

As for the way in which a study is designed, a distinction has to be made between non-recurring and repeat surveys. Cross-sectional surveys consider a defined number of statistical units at one specific point in time, while longitudinal surveys are repeated at annual intervals, which, in the case of a panel, also relate to the same business units, in order to highlight developments or constants.

Before dealing with the two principles of commercial traffic surveys in detail, a general assessment is made of the survey methods used in this sector. These include:

- Household surveys that expressly consider trips made for official/business purposes in travel diaries;
- Interviews with the owners of vehicles registered for private and/or commercial use, the central vehicle register of the FOMT serving as a basis;
- Interviews conducted in enterprises or business units, with the aim of recording all business-related trips and movements of their employees;
- Analysis of transport documents;
- Analysis of travel expense reports;
- Roadside traffic counts; and
- Short interviews at points of access to business units, industrial estates, for specific cross sections, or in the form of cordon surveys.

Table 1 provides an overview of the advantages and disadvantages of the survey methods listed above.

The commercial-traffic-specific details that traffic counts supply relate mainly to truck traffic, which means goods traffic, because it is difficult to differentiate between different vehicle size groups merely from visual appraisal. Hence, this method does not show the percentage of passenger cars that are used for commercial traffic purposes. Neither do such counts supply any information on trip purpose (goods transport, service rendered, empty trip, etc.), destinations, utilisation factors, and the like. This method is an appropriate instrument primarily when used for verifying computed network use, or to furnish information of a more general nature on the relationship among different types of vehicles.

Short roadside interviews indicate the percentage by which certain traffic purposes are represented in commercial traffic on road cross-sections. It should be noted that such interviews imply time restrictions, which only allows a limited number of aspects or questions to be covered. They are also difficult to organise, they rely on the support of local authorities, and require police presence. This kind of interviewing can be used for comprehensive assessment of how traffic volumes are produced or of individual participation. If target groups are approached in a well-designed manner, this method allows different aspects to be covered.

Household interviews produce the problems mentioned, i.e., a very wide sample has to be defined in order to get a meaningful response. A second problem is that business passenger traffic cannot be covered fully in this way. Interviews with car owners and employees in industry, however, supply clearly defined insights, and can be conducted in a number of ways.

Table 2 lists the advantages and disadvantages of different data collection methods. The figure shows that each method has its specific advantages and disadvantages, so that the question as to which method should be used has to be determined with a view to the purposes for which surveys are conducted. Such aspects as the financial and human resources involved, as well as the time required have to be weighed carefully. Irrespective of any specific advantages and disadvantages, combinations of a number of methods should always be considered.

Table 1: Methods Used for Business Traffic Surveys and Their Advantages and Disadvantages

Data Collection Using	Advantage	Disadvantage
Household Interviews	▪ All persons moving for a professional purpose can be covered. ▪ All purposes for which trips are made and all means of transport can be considered. ▪ The population can be determined, and sampling can be made, with a relatively high degree of accuracy.	▪ There are normally no links to places of work or any other commercial parameters. ▪ A relatively large number of persons contacted has no relevance for the survey (cost factor!). ▪ Vehicle use, trips chain, etc. difficult to assess with the required detail. ▪ Trips made for official or business purposes are often not stated. ▪ Often limited to certain regions or local districts.
Interviews with Car Owners	▪ Population (car ownership) can be defined at a high degree of precision and relevance, using the central vehicle register of the FOMT. ▪ Country-wide data acquisition. ▪ Clear regional distinction possible. ▪ Car owners are contacted personally. ▪ Questionnaires can be sent out for specific aspects and in the required numbers. ▪ Activities, destinations, etc. for any business traffic purpose can be covered.	▪ Address of car owner is not necessarily identical with the location of a vehicle and the area in which it is used. ▪ Restriction to motor-vehicle based business traffic. ▪ When using the central vehicle register only national concept possible; national/non-national concept necessitates exchange with neighbouring countries.
Interviews in Enterprises or Business Units	▪ A two-stage process (1 – general business survey; 2 – vehicle travel diary survey) allows both general business data and travel-related data to be considered. ▪ Such a first step reduces the number of addresses and provides for sample stratification on the basis of the replies received. ▪ Activities, destinations, etc. for any business traffic purpose can be covered. ▪ All means of transport used for the trips can be covered.	▪ Difficult to assess the population. ▪ No data set known that would cover all companies, business units, or places of work, and that provides for a clear distinction. ▪ Substantial input of organisational work and time to set up an address data bank and find out telephone numbers. ▪ Business traffic with vehicles of private owners cannot be covered. ▪ Limited to certain regions or local districts.
Roadside Interviews	▪ All types of traffic, purposes and vehicle categories can be covered. ▪ Micro census linked with data available from counts or long-term census points supplies detailed insights into business traffic.	▪ Substantial organisational input, since local authorities have to be integrated. ▪ Limited duration of interviews, i.e., only some essential key questions can be asked. ▪ Data expansion may be difficult.
Traffic Counts	▪ Count data can be used for comparison between road network data and extrapolated results. ▪ Fairly efficient method providing rough characteristics.	▪ Data on personal behaviour as a road user and vehicle use cannot be recorded. ▪ Only supplies data for cross sections; no source-target relationships. ▪ Vehicles cannot be associated with business traffic or purposes of trips beyond any doubt.

Table 2: Types of Survey Methods and Their Advantages and Disadvantages for Business Traffic Surveys

Data Collection Using	Advantage	Disadvantage
Mail Out/Mail Back	▪ Respondents have more time to think about the questions and their answers. ▪ Respondents are not influenced by personality and conduct of interviewer. ▪ Questionnaires can be taken along for on-trip recording of distances travelled. ▪ Less cost-intensive than personal or telephone interviews. ▪ Two-stage approach allows the number of documents sent out to be controlled.	▪ Questionnaire must be simple and self-explanatory. ▪ There is no way of telling whether the questionnaire was completed by the target person himself/herself. ▪ Hardly any room for explanations and motivation, e.g. in case of communication problems. ▪ More organisational requirements if sample recovery is difficult to control. ▪ Low recovery rate, if no additional measures are taken. ▪ High postage costs.
Personal Interviewing	▪ Direct contact with interview partners. ▪ Possibility to respond to questions, possibly a higher recovery rate. ▪ Travel diaries can be handed out in the required numbers. ▪ Postage to be paid only for the travel diaries returned.	▪ High costs involved for interviewers. ▪ Considerable organisational requirements for the interview. ▪ Pre-interview phone calls necessary to make appointments and be sure that the respondent will be available for an interview. ▪ Respondents may be influenced by personality and conduct of interviewer. ▪ Interviewers require adequate training.
Telephone Interviewing	▪ Low material costs, since no detailed documents have to be prepared. ▪ A data entry form in the PC allows answers to be entered during the interview. ▪ Plausibility checks in parallel with data acquisition. ▪ Interviewers can be monitored. ▪ Travel diaries may be sent out in the required numbers.	▪ Non-availability of useful selection criteria (more people decide not to have their private telephone numbers listed, subscribers to mobile phone service normally not shown in directory). ▪ Interviewers require adequate training. ▪ Conversation has to be limited in time and thus in the number of aspects covered. ▪ Respondents may be influenced by personality and conduct of interviewer. ▪ It may be necessary to send out survey material, as certain questions cannot be answered 'off the cuff'.
Internet Interviewing	▪ Easier to handle than classical interviewing methods (automatic filtering, irrelevant questions, omitted, etc.). ▪ Costs involved are low. ▪ Results available without much delay.	▪ Unlike telephone, email and Internet are not generally available (representative sample selection!). ▪ Certain technical skills required to complete Internet questionnaires. ▪ Interviewing costs have to be borne by respondents.
Traffic Count Using Mobile Phones	▪ Easy access to respondents. ▪ Exact data available on place and time (automatic transmission and plausibility check). ▪ Easy handling for respondents. ▪ Interactive questionnaire possible. ▪ Long-term surveys without any loss in quality (low level of input requirements). ▪ Immediate availability of traffic data (immediate processing in EDP systems).	▪ High recruiting requirements. ▪ Time consuming development of voice files for voice-operated questionnaires (interactive voice response system). ▪ Network providers must be prepared to make locating data available.

NATIONWIDE SURVEY 'MOTOR VEHICLE TRAFFIC IN GERMANY 2002' (KID 2002)

Objective and Survey Design

Objective of the Nationwide Survey

Capital expenditure programmes on a federal and regional level, and the development of traffic management concepts are two examples where the Federal Ministry of Transport, Building, and Housing (BMVBW) has to rely on a sound motor traffic data base. To compensate for information gaps, the ministry commissioned a project group with the preparation and implementation of a nationwide motor traffic survey to focus on commercial traffic and motor vehicles up to a payload of 3.5 t. Partners to the project were the Institute of Transportation and Urban Engineering IVS, Technical University Braunschweig, (Univ.-Prof. Dr. M. Wermuth, project management); the FOMT KBA; the Institute of Applied Transport and Tourism Research IVT e.V.; WVI Prof. Dr. Wermuth Verkehrsforschung und Infrastrukturplanung GmbH, dealing with transport research and infrastructure planning; and Project Research Management Consultants Transport and Traffic P.U.T.V.

Because vehicles of both commercial and private owners are used for goods traffic and business passenger traffic, the survey had to consider all types of vehicles. The methodological approach and the general concept to be used in the survey were prepared under a pilot research project (Wermuth *et al.*, 2001). The main survey was conducted under the research project 'Motor Vehicle Traffic in Germany 2002' ('Kraftfahrzeugverkehr in Deutschland 2002' (KiD 2002)) (Wermuth *et al.*, 2003).

The aim of the research was to develop a concept for, and conduct, a nationwide survey based on motor vehicle commercial traffic; to produce empirical parameters on that basis, in particular on traffic volume and traffic performance; and to develop recommendations for future surveys with a particular view to commercial traffic. One of the primary objectives of the research was to create a data base of current relevance to commercial traffic.

Survey Design

The underlying concept of this survey is to consider the vehicle day both as an item under investigation and as a survey item, and to use the central vehicle register of the FOMT as a sampling source. This nationwide traffic survey is thus based on the concept of domestic registration.

The daily routine of vehicle usage cannot be surveyed for either all vehicles nor for individual vehicles on all days. This is why a sampling procedure is employed, which means that vehicle usage is surveyed only for a random sample of vehicle days, i.e., for a random choice of vehicles and an equally random choice of day (date of survey or reporting day). The parent population of this survey is thus the total number of all vehicle days from which a random sample was drawn.

The central vehicle register of the FOMT, as a basis for the selection, provides almost ideal conditions for the selection of a representative sample. Because the register of all motor vehicles registered in Germany is updated on a daily basis, the selected basis is in full agreement with the parent population basis, and is thus fully known in terms of both volume and structure. At the same time this basis offers advantages in terms of the theory of sampling, as it renders sample plan phasing superfluous, which would adversely affect the accuracy of the results, and which is, for instance, necessary for household surveys. This is because each element of the parent population is included in the sampling basis and is clearly identifiable. In addition the central vehicle register supplies a number of vehicle and owner features that have an effect on vehicle usage and that can be utilised for effective parent population stratification, and thus contribute to the accuracy of the results.

The survey is conceived as a mail out/mail back survey for a defined reference date. The questionnaire has the form of a diary that does not only contain the set of questions, but also supplies the respondent with the necessary information on the procedure and data protection, as well as assistance for how to complete the questionnaire.

Vehicles of commercial owners account for a major portion of commercial traffic, but those of private owners are also used for official/commercial purposes. This means a complete and extensive analysis of commercial traffic has to consider all types of vehicles and all groups of owners. For reasons of research efficiency, it was decided that the survey should concentrate on vehicle groups frequently used for commercial traffic purposes and for which little information is available as to their contribution to this transport sector, rather than on vehicle groups that are already represented in other surveys. Against this background, the nationwide KiD 2002 survey was given a structure that falls into one main and three additional surveys as shown in Figure 2.

In the main survey, which is at the centre of KiD 2002, the following types of vehicles were subjected to closer analysis:

- Motorcycles of commercial owners;
- Passenger cars of commercial owners;
- Lorries of commercial owners (up to, and including, a payload of 3.5 tonnes); and
- Lorries of private owners (up to, and including, a payload of 3.5 tonnes).

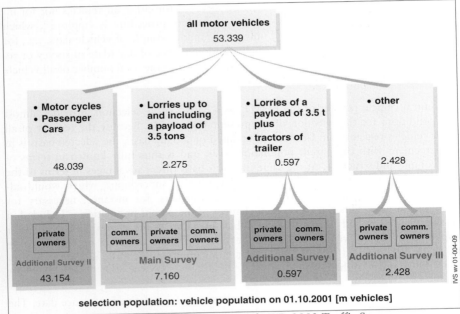

Figure2: System of the Nationwide KiD 2002 Traffic Survey

Additional Survey I is to link up to the official road haulage statistics, and covers lorries of a payload of 3.5 tonnes plus and tractor-trailers. A link with the traffic survey 'Mobility in Germany' ('Mobilität in Deutschland') (MiD 2002), which used the KONTIV design and was conducted simultaneously as a household survey, was produced by Additional Survey II. This second element covers the vehicle groups of privately-owned motorcycles and passenger cars. Additional Survey III covers all other vehicles and supplies information on traffic using motorbuses used outside regular service, other tractors, emergency and protection vehicles, motor homes, and all other officially registered vehicles. These four sub-surveys together produce a complete picture of road-based commercial traffic. On the basis of this structural system chosen for KiD 2002, a vehicle-based, an owner-based, a spatial, and a temporal stratification are made for representative sampling.

Survey Preparation

Pilot Test for Method Verification

The feasibility of the survey method, the aspects to be covered by the survey, and the preparation, implementation and evaluation procedures for such a nationwide traffic survey were verified as part of a KiD 2002 methods analysis (Wermuth *et al.*, 2001), using a pilot test with a total of 1,980 vehicles. For the pilot test, three versions of a questionnaire were developed, which differed in layout and survey handling. The groups included in this pilot test were passenger cars of commercial owners, lorries of up to and including 3.5 tonnes payload of commercial owners, and lorries of up to and including 3.5 tonnes payload of private owners.

The response rate and the quality of the answers exceeded the expectations by far and thus confirmed that the methodological concept and the number of questions asked were appropriate. As a general conclusion of the favourable results produced in the pilot study, it was recommended, that the concept should be implemented in terms of both its contents and organisational structure, with due consideration having being given to the experience gathered in the pilot test and to the improvements proposed for concept optimisation.

Survey Documents

The survey documents sent out to the owners of the selected vehicles included the following:

- Cover letter;
- Endorsement letter of the trade associations;
- Questionnaire with questions on vehicle and owner;
- Travel diary (for trips on reference day);
- Data protection declaration;
- Notes on how to complete the questionnaire and on participation in the survey; and
- Prepaid reply envelope.

The cover letter, the questionnaire for vehicle and owner, the travel diary, the data protection declaration, as well as the notes together form a twelve-page brochure. The questionnaire falls into two main sets of questions.

A first general set of questions asks for vehicle- and owner-specific data that are not available from the central vehicle register, or, if so, not with the required detail. This concerns questions on:

- Location of the vehicle;
- Use as a leased or rented vehicle;
- Sector of industry of the owner or the main user;
- Company size, showing number of employees, or household size;
- Vehicle fleet size of owner; and
- Vehicles taken off the road.

For the travel diary, the users had to enter the following data for the first eleven trips on the reference date:

- Address and type of origin;
- Start time;
- Purpose of trip;
- Type of load;
- Gross weight of load;
- Type of goods carried;
- Number of passengers;
- Use of a trailer/semi-trailer;
- Address and kind of destination;
- Time of trip end; and
- Trip distance.

To reduce the time requirements for the respondents in case of intensively used vehicles, while at the same time also covering the type of structure of additional trips or parts of trips, a reduced set of questions was asked for trip numbers twelve to eighteen. For any additional trips on the reference date, only the number of trips beyond the recorded eighteen trips, as well as their total distance, had to be entered.

Attached to the survey material was a letter from the central trade associations of the German industry, in which they emphasised the significance and benefits of this nationwide traffic survey and asked the car owners receiving the material to participate in the survey.

Stratification Concept for the Main Survey

To ensure that reliable vehicle use data are obtained for all groups of vehicles, all parts of the country and all periods of the year, sample stratification was used. The parent population was stratified in terms of functional (vehicle and owner characteristics), geographical (district of registration, owner base), and temporal (weekday, season) characteristics, that are known to have an influence on the way vehicles are used and that are available for the parent population from the central vehicle register. The functional stratification characteristics actually used were the type of vehicle, owner group, type of drive system, sector of industry of the owner, vehicle age, and the piston displacement (in the order shown).

The industry sector of the vehicle owner is a major stratification characteristic. The German classification of industries issued by the Federal Bureau of Statistics (WZ 93) comprises seventeen chapters. Since 1 July, 2001, the FOMT has been using this systematic classification for its central vehicle register as a means of coding data about the profession or trade of self-employed vehicle owners. Because this classification, which has also been adopted for KiD 2002, is compatible with the classification used by the European Union for industry sectors (NACE Rev. 1), and also with the classification developed by the United Nations Organisation for that purpose (ISIC Rev. 3), the classification standards can be compared on an international level.

Geographic stratification was done on the basis of the systematic approach of the Federal Office for Building and Regional Planning (BBR), in which administrative districts and towns not belonging to a federal state are classified as separate categories, depending on settlement homogeneity (BBR, 2000). For the KiD 2002 survey, the nine types of administrative districts were used to form four suitable geographic units.

On the basis of these stratification criteria and their distinctive features, the strata were determined according to the homogeneity of the annual vehicle mileage obtained from the earlier 1990/1993 mileage survey. For this purpose, the total vehicle population for the KiD 2002 survey was subdivided into 145 strata, so that the main survey comprised ninety nine strata (Figure 3), Additional Survey I comprised twelve strata, Additional Survey II comprised twenty nine strata, and Additional Survey III comprised five strata. The selected sample of each vehicle group was distributed proportionally over the different strata, such that it reflected the parent population distribution (vehicle population in the central vehicle register). To ensure that stratum-based evaluation results were statistically significant, a minimum number of interviews was required for each stratum (240 vehicles per stratum in the main survey and 260 vehicles per stratum in the additional surveys).

The surveys were conducted over a period of one year between November 2001 and October 2002. During this period, four samples were taken. The main survey covered eight survey phases and the additional surveys four surveying phases. Each phase lasted exactly one week for the primary run and one week for the reminders, with seven reference days each. The sixteen survey weeks or 112 survey days thus covered about one third of the year and, because the survey weeks were almost uniformly distributed over the entire year, seasonal factors and school holidays, which may have an effect on the kind of vehicle usage, were accounted for adequately. The selected sample was also uniformly distributed over the groups of weekdays Monday, Tuesday to Thursday, Friday, Saturday and Sunday, and vehicles of the weekday group Tuesday to Thursday were, in turn, uniformly distributed over the individual weekdays.

Implementation

Implementation Procedure

With each of the four sampling procedures, the selected samples were drawn randomly from the central vehicle register of the FOMT for two successive phases of the main survey and always for one phase of the three additional surveys. This was done in compliance with the stratification and sample plan specifications. To avoid duplicate sampling, vehicles already selected were marked. However, vehicle owners under whose names more than one vehicle was registered could be contacted repeatedly for the survey, but always for another vehicle.

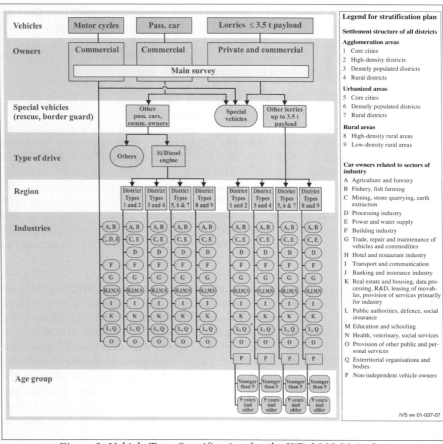

Figure 3: Vehicle Type Stratification for the KiD 2002 Main Survey

Mailing was timed such that each vehicle owner received the survey about one week in advance of the reference date assigned to him. He was asked to complete the general set of questions in the questionnaire during this week and to make sure that the survey documents were passed on to the driver using the vehicle on the reference date. This one-week margin was essential, especially for cases in which the vehicle base and the address of the owner were not the same, so that transmission of the material to the driver might require some extra time.

In case the questionnaire was not returned to the FOMT within a period of two weeks after the defined reference date, and in case the Office had not received a reply indicating refusal to cooperate, reminders were sent out. This meant that, for each nonresponse in the primary run, the survey documents were compiled and sent out a second time with a new reference date. The handling time for this reminder was the same as that for the primary run. Completed questionnaires were passed on for data entry, and all other questionnaires were destroyed as required under the data protection regulations. Figure 4 shows the survey design described above.

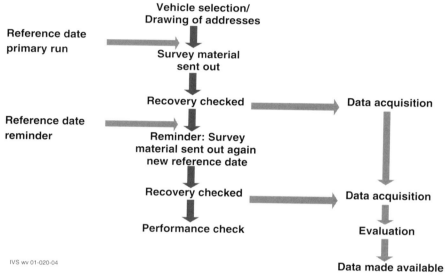

Figure 4: Survey Design

Measures Accompanying Project

To improve respondent acceptance and to make sure that the expected response rates were achieved, a number of measures were taken to accompany the project. The main target groups for these measures were the vehicle owners who had received the questionnaire, and also the drivers of the selected vehicles, who were offered additional information on the survey and, more importantly, assistance in completing the questionnaire. In addition, anybody else seeking information could make use of this source of information. Apart from the covering letter of the trade associations mentioned above, the following measures were offered during the survey period:

- A hot-line and information service was set up;
- An Internet homepage was created under KiD 2002 (http://www.verkehrsbefragung.de);

- Owners of a large vehicle fleet could rely on personal assistance; and
- The survey was presented in the trade press, on seminars, in statistics workshops, and for vehicle owners with very large transport fleets.

Survey Organisation

For quantification of the response rate, the following characteristics of the individual sample sizes are of relevance. The size of the selected sample typically decreases from one stage to the next until the net sample remains.

Selected Sample
The selected sample refers to the vehicle volume selected from the central vehicle register. Under the federal survey, a total of 87,098 vehicles were selected for participation in the main survey, 3,517 vehicles for Additional Survey I; 8,298 vehicles for Additional Survey II; and 1,816 vehicles for Additional Survey III.

Gross Sample
The gross sample was produced after the selected sample had been corrected to consider the so-called 'false losses' (e.g., 'error in the central vehicle register', 'mail undeliverable', etc.), most of which are due to constant changes in the register data when vehicles are entered in, or deleted from, the register, or when they are reregistered. These losses do not affect the quality of the data, because the vehicles concerned were no longer registered, or the owner addresses did not exist any longer on the relevant reference date, so that they did not form part of the sample any more. For the main survey, the gross sample included 79,079 vehicles; for Additional Survey I 3,260 vehicles; for Additional Survey II 7,644 vehicles; and for Additional Survey III 1,662 vehicles.

Response Sample
The response sample was produced after the gross sample had been corrected to account for 'real losses', i.e., those refusing to participate and non-respondents. The response sample thus relates to the number of questionnaires returned, without considering the quality of entries in the questionnaires. For the main survey, the response sample covered 44,841 vehicles; for Additional Survey I 2,575 vehicles; for Additional Survey II 4,355 vehicles; and for Additional Survey III 1,182 vehicles.

Net Sample
The response sample includes a certain number of questionnaires that are not fit for use. When reducing the response sample by these 'unfit' questionnaires, one finally arrives at the net sample, i.e., the total number of cases that can be used. For the main survey, the net sample volume covered 43,861 vehicles; for Additional Survey I 2,537 vehicles; for Additional Survey II 4,249 vehicles; and for Additional Survey III 1,131 vehicles. The usable recovery is finally obtained as the quotient between the net sample and the gross sample.

The recovery rates achieved with the different sub-surveys of KiD 2002 were about ten percent above the results expected from the methods analysis. All survey phases thus showed the following recovery rates:

- Main survey 55.5 percent (motor cycles and passenger cars of commercial owners, lorries up to, and including, 3.5 tonnes payload);
- Additional Survey I 77.8 percent (lorries of 3.5 tonnes payload plus semi-trailer motor vehicles);
- Additional Survey II 55.6 percent (privately owned motorcycles and passenger cars);
- Additional Survey III 68.1 percent (other vehicles with official registration number); and thus
- Federal survey 56.5 percent (all vehicles).

From the above, it follows that the total number of cases that could be used for the federal survey is higher by 4,914 (approx. 10 percent) than was expected from the methods analysis. Another 25,019 net cases of the regional surveys mentioned could be added to the total of 51,778 net cases in the federal survey, so that a total of 76,797 cases could be utilised for evaluation.

Evaluation

Data Acquisition and Preparation

Data acquisition started with visual inspection of the returned questionnaires, i.e., before the first data were entered. As required under the data protection regulations, only the data from completed questionnaires were used. To ensure that these data were of a high quality, great significance was attached not only to correct transmission of the data supplied in the questionnaires, but also to the plausibility of these data. The plausibility check comprised two stages, with the first stage implemented in the entry program such that only admissible characteristics and attributes were accepted. The second stage of the plausibility check followed after data entry had been completed, which means that the complete daily report for a vehicle was analysed in respect of contents and logical relationship between the details furnished. Any data records found to be implausible were classified as cases that could not be utilised and were rejected.

Another major element of the second stage of the plausibility check was a comparison between postcodes and addresses reported in the questionnaires. For this purpose, addresses shown as vehicle base, as well as addresses of owner, point of origin and destination, were translated as accurately as possible into geo-coordinates, due regard always being given to the relevant data protection regulations. A GIS was then used to project these coordinates to a digital map and check them for correct correspondence of post code area and coded address. This geocoding not only increases the quality of the data, but also allows the data collected on vehicle use to be shown in a geographic correlation and at almost any optional geographic aggregation level. The quality achieved with geographic address coding is illustrated in Figure 5.

Nonresponse Analysis, Weighting and Extrapolation

The real nonresponse losses may distort results, if there is a relationship between the willingness of the owners to respond and whether or not their vehicle is used. The readiness of respondents to answer questions depends on certain structural characteristics of the vehicle owner and the vehicle. For private owners it is found to be forty eight percent and is, thus, slightly lower than the rate established for commercial owners. In the latter group, the response rate varies for different industry sectors. The type of vehicle and the settlement structure (town/country) also correlate with the response rate. The differences in the response rate produce minor distortions with regard to these characteristics, but these can be corrected by certain 'structural adjustments' (post-stratification) when the data are extrapolated, for which purpose the data supplied by the central vehicle register are used again. To find out whether the willingness to respond may also be determined by characteristics of vehicle use, so that undesired 'primary' nonresponse effects could be expected to occur, a subsequent telephone survey was conducted for nonresponse cases randomly selected from the main survey (nonresponse sample).

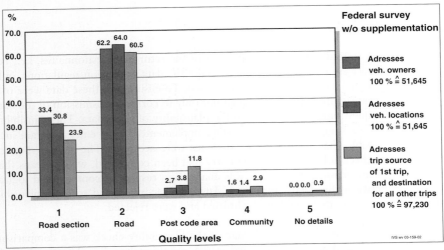

Figure 5: Quality of Address Geocoding for the National Survey

A comparison of the characteristics of vehicle use between respondents and non-respondents in the main survey showed that the refusal to respond – in terms of 'unit nonresponse' – evidently also had to do with vehicle use and not only with structural characteristics of the owner and the vehicle, for which a subsequent structural adjustment as part of the extrapolation is adequate. This primary nonresponse effect concerns the characteristic of traffic participation ('Vehicle used on reference day yes/no'): the nonresponse analysis revealed that vehicle owners whose vehicle was not used on the reference day showed a higher willingness to participate in KiD 2002 than owners of a vehicle used on that day. The KiD 2002 distortion, which results from unit nonresponse and favours the immobile vehicles, can be corrected in the extrapolation by introducing a weighting factor. Item nonresponse analyses had a pragmatic orientation and meant that follow-up measures were taken if structural characteristics of vehicle and owner were missing or remained vague.

KiD 2002 Basic Evaluation

Also part of the research was a basic evaluation. This evaluation remained limited to the characteristics that permit an explanatory description to be given for business traffic and thus serve as a basis for more detailed in-depth analysis. Like publications with road haulage statistics, the results in the basic tables are characterised by a quality standard, which is defined by the quality criteria 'number of vehicles in the net sample' and 'simple relative standard error'.

The results obtained from the basic evaluation confirm the significant role of commercial traffic as one element of road traffic. Of all motor vehicles officially registered in Germany, including motorcycles and privately-owned passenger cars, 64.6 percent (Mon.-Fri.) and 56.7 percent (Mon.-Sun.) are mobile per day. On Mondays to Fridays, 24.1 percent of these mobile vehicles are used at least once per day for official/business purposes and on Mondays to Sundays, 20.7 percent are used. From the vehicle groups considered in the KiD 2002 main survey, 70.7 percent for Monday to Friday, and 64.7 percent for Monday to Sunday of the mobile motorcycles and passenger cars of commercial owners, and 89.7 percent (Monday to Friday) and 88.0 percent (Monday to Sunday) of the mobile lorries, with a payload of up to and including 3.5 tonnes, are used at least once per day for official/business purposes.

The number of trips made by all motor vehicles registered in Germany is 37,958 million per year, 6,331 million of which are made by the vehicle groups of the main survey alone, i.e., by small vehicles in commercial use. All these trips taken together add up to 715.9 billion vehicle kilometres per year – 557.8 billion vehicle kilometres (77.9 percent) on workdays Monday to Friday, and 158.1 billion vehicle kilometres (22.1 percent) on Saturdays, Sundays, and public holidays. When considering the total vehicle traffic produced by all motor vehicles registered in Germany, commercial traffic accounts for:

- 26.5 percent (Monday to Friday) and 23.1 percent (Monday to Sunday), based on number of trips; and

- 33.7 percent (Monday to Friday) and 28.4 percent (Monday to Sunday), based on annual road performance.

When considering the types of vehicles included in the main survey – as the major element of the KiD 2002 survey – commercial traffic contributes to the annual road performance of the different types of vehicles with the following percentage figures:

- 69.6 percent (Monday to Friday) and 63.8 percent (Monday to Sunday) for passenger cars and motor cycles of commercial owners; and
- 87.9 percent (Monday to Friday) and 85.8 percent (Monday to Sunday) for lorries up to and including 3.5 tonnes payload.

However, the passenger cars and motorcycles of private owners (as an absolute figure and as a sum total of all vehicles of this group) account for a substantial portion of the road performance that can be classified as commercial traffic. At about 63.8 billion vehicle kilometres, this performance is almost identical with that of passenger cars and motorcycles of commercial owners (about 64.6 billion vehicle kilometres).

It is normal to distinguish between goods traffic and business passenger traffic within commercial traffic. For purposes of the KiD 2002 survey, reported trips were classified according to their purpose. However, there was another type of trip which had an official/business purpose, but its (primary) cause was not to transport goods or passengers, or to render a professional service. These other official/business trips were normally made to maintain the operability of vehicles, and were classified as 'other commercial traffic'. All remaining traffic was referred to as 'private traffic'.

When analysing the annual road performance (Monday to Sunday) with respect to the different traffic sectors, it is found that, for all motor vehicles registered in Germany, goods traffic accounts for 10.0 percent, business passenger traffic for 14.2 percent, other commercial traffic for 4.2 percent. and private traffic for 71.6 percent of the total annual road performance. The classification of the annual road performance of the different vehicle groups according to types of traffic is shown in Figure 6.

Apart from illustrating 'global' characteristics of motor vehicle traffic, and, in particular, of commercial traffic, the data recorded can also be used to determine additional characteristics of how motor vehicles registered in Germany are used. Vehicle-related and trip-related characteristics that were considered to be essential for such considerations are listed in Table 3 for weekdays, Monday to Friday.

Recommendations

Wermuth *et al.* (2003) make a number of recommendations for the design and implementation of future motor traffic surveys, based on the experience gained from the surveys described in this chapter. One of the central recommendations is that the general design of this survey, as well as the concrete structure of its different elements, should be adopted for vehicle traffic surveys and, in particular, for surveys conducted for commercial traffic using motor vehicles. A key role is for these surveys assigned to the central vehicle register of the FOMT to be a source for the selection of representative samples in the German context.

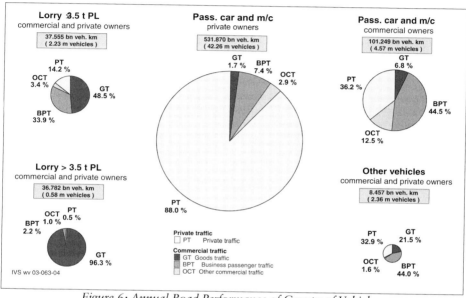

Figure 6: Annual Road Performance of Groups of Vehicles

In addition to the more general recommendations made for the organisation of surveys and the specific recommendations on the aspects to be covered by the survey programme, attention is drawn to nonresponse analyses which are regarded to be indispensable, because they allow possible distortions to be avoided, i.e., deviations between the (evaluation) results and the real distribution of characteristics in the parent population. Any distortions noted may then be corrected by weighting factors used for the individual data records and/or by structural adjustments in the extrapolation (stratification after sampling).

Address data are recommended to be geocoded, due regard being given to data protection regulations. In this way, GISs can be used for evaluation. Data users can then define the correlation between the data collected and geographical data in whatever way they choose. Geocoding can, in addition, be used to subject address data to extensive plausibility checks, both with respect to individual data and within the context of the programme reported for one specific day.

Table 3: Selected Characteristics for Weekdays, Monday to Friday

KiD 2002 sub-survey		AS II	MS	MS	AS I	AS III
Groups of vehicles		Pass. car & m/c private owners	Pass. car & m/c comm. owners	Lorries ≤ 3.5t PL	Lorries > 3.5t PL & tractors of trailer	Other motor vehicles
Weekdays		Mon-Fri	Mon-Fri	Mon-Fri	Mon-Fri	Mon-Fri
Vehicle-related characteristics – traffic volume						
Percentage mobile vehicles	[%]	65.5	69.7	69.8	74.7	17.8
Veh. trips per mobile veh.	[trip/veh*d]	3.4	4.3	5.6	5.5	4.3
Veh. Trips per mobile veh., BT	[trip/veh*d]	0.4	2.8	5.0	5.5	3.6
Percentage load trips, BT	[%]	22.5	21.9	72.7	78.4	36.0
Traffic involvement per mobile veh	[min/veh*d]	74.7	118.9	115.8	374.1	104.5
Vehicle-rated characteristics – road performance						
Veh. Road performance per mobile veh [veh km/veh*d]		57.2	108.0	87.5	321.4	59.9
Veh. Road performance per mobile veh, BT[veh km/veh]		8.5	75.2	77.0	320.0	43.5
Goods transport performance per mobile veh, BT [tkm/veh*d]		4.3	3.4	43.9	3,108.3	196.5
Trip-related characteristics						
Mean distance per trip, BT	[km]	18.4	25.9	14.7	55.0	11.2
Mean distance per trip, PT	[km]	16.1	22.3	19.1	/	21.0
Mean duration per trip, BT	[min]	31.0	33.1	28.1	83.8	26.4
Mean duration per trip, PT	[min]	21.4	26.0	25.8	/	27.9
Mean volume goods transported per load trip	[kg]	97.3	114.1	483.8	8,978.4	3,486.9

One of the conclusions to be drawn is the need for data updates. It is recommended that KiD surveys be conducted on a continuous basis, using small-sized samples to be sure that federal traffic planning can rely on a current and sound data base. Should periodic updates be preferred, it is recommended that these be made at five-year intervals.

Outlook

The KiD 2002 transport survey, conducted at the federal level, greatly improves the information available for German traffic statistics. This applies, in particular, to commercial traffic using small vehicles. The large number of characteristics collected with the questionnaires, as well as the data attached to the data records from the central vehicle register of the FOMT, can be used for the computation of a wide range of specific features. When combined, the vehicle details available from the central vehicle register and the details of vehicle usage obtained from the surveys can be analysed in many different ways to reflect the use of motor vehicles, in general, and for purposes of commercial traffic, in particular.

The insights gained and data collected with the KiD 2002 survey will make it possible, for the first time, for vehicle-based commercial traffic to be accounted for in future traffic concepts and planning programmes in a way that reflects adequately their significance to society and industry, in both volume and structure. Transport policy, as well as transport planners and economists, will thus have an instrument at their disposal that allows them to adapt their objectives and activities more closely to requirements.

The data collection methods employed in the KiD 2002 survey have proved to be successful and efficient for both nationwide and regional surveys conducted to collect data on motor vehicle traffic and, more specifically, on their role as part of commercial traffic. Unlike household surveys and business surveys, the KiD method is, in the opinion of the authors, the only method available to date that allows motor vehicle-based commercial traffic to be covered in all its aspects, including commercial traffic using vehicles of private owners. In principle, it is possible to translate the method to other vehicle-based surveys, using other geographic and/or temporal criteria or relating to other aspects (types of vehicles, sectors of industry, survey programme, etc.).

Once the data are available for scientific purposes, they may trigger a process in the commercial traffic sector that can be compared to traffic research developments experienced after establishing the KONTIV samples for passenger transport. In particular, transport modelling will benefit from the data base now available with in-depth traffic research activities. One central aspect of such activities will be the development of existing or new commercial traffic models.

REFERENCES

Brög, W. and G. Winter (1990). *Untersuchungen zum Problem der „non-reported-trips" zum Personen-Wirtschaftsverkehr bei Haushaltsbefragungen*, Schriftenreihe Forschung Straßenbau und Straßenverkehrstechnik, Heft 593, Bonn, 1990.

BBR (2000), *Raumordnungsbericht 2000*, Bundesamt für Bauwesen und Raumordnung Bonn.

Steinmeyer, I. (2004). Kenndaten der Verkehrsentstehung im Personenwirtschaftsverkehr – Analyse der voranschreitenden Ausdifferenzierung der Mobilitätsmuster in der Dienstleistungsgesellschaft. In: *Harburger Berichte zur Verkehrsplanung und Logistik* (E. Kutter and L. Sjöstedt, eds), Bd. 3, Huss-Verlag, München.

Wermuth, M., H.-H. Binnenbruck, S. Machledt-Michael, S. Rommerskirchen, H. Sonntag and R. Wirth (1998). *Bestandsaufnahme notwendiger und verfügbarer Daten zum Wirtschaftsverkehr als Grundlage pragmatischer Datenergänzungen*, Schlussbericht zum Forschungsprojekt FE 01.145 G96C im Auftrag des Bundesministeriums für Verkehr, Braunschweig.

Wermuth, M., F. Amme, H.-H. Binnenbruck, R. Hamacher, E. Hansjosten, H. Hautzinger, D. Heidemann, H. Löhner, H. Lönneker, M. Michael, C. Neef, P. Ohrem, R. Wirth and S. Wulff (2001). *Kontinuierliche Befragung des Wirtschaftsverkehrs in unterschiedlichen Siedlungsräumen – Phase 1, Methodenstudie/ Vorbereitung der Befragung*, Schlussbericht zum Forschungsprojekt FE 70.632/2000 im Auftrag des Bundesministeriums für Verkehr, Bau- und Wohnungswesen, Braunschweig.

Wermuth, M., R. Wirth, C. Neef, H. Löhner, J. Hilmer, H. Hautzinger, D. Heidemann †, W. Stock, J. Schmidt, K. Mayer, M. Michael, F. Amme, P. Ohrem, E.

Hansjosten and H.-H. Binnenbruck (2003). *Kontinuierliche Befragung des Wirtschaftsverkehrs in unterschiedlichen Siedlungsräumen - Phase 2, Hauptstudie*, Schlussbericht zum Forschungsprojekt 70.0682/2001 im Auftrag des Bundesministeriums für Verkehr, Bau- und Wohnungswesen, Braunschweig.

Wermuth, M.; H. Hautzinger, Ch. Neef and W. Stock (2003). *Erhebung zum Kraftfahrzeugverkehr in Deutschland KiD 2002 – Erhebungsmethode und Ergebnisse*, in Tagungsunterlagen zu 19. Verkehrswissenschaftliche Tage Dresden, 22.09.-23.09.2003, TU Dresden, Dresden.

Wermuth, M. and Ch. Neef (2003). Die bundesweite Verkehrserhebung Kraftfahrzeugverkehr in Deutschland (KiD 2002), in VDI-Gesellschaft Fahrzeug- und Verkehrstechnik (Hrsg.): *VDI-Berichte Nr. 1799 Gesamtverkehrsforum 2003*, pp. 163, VDI Verlag GmbH, Düsseldorf.

Travel Survey Methods: Quality and Future Directions
Peter Stopher and Cheryl Stecher (Editors)
© 2006 Published by Elsevier Ltd.

24

ISSUES RELATED TO FREIGHT TRANSPORT DATA COLLECTION

Arnim H. Meyburg, Cornell University, Ithaca, New York, USA
and
Rodrigo Garrido, Pontificia Universidad Católica de Chile, Santiago, Chile

INTRODUCTION AND BACKGROUND[36]

Freight movements are the result of economic activities among spatially separated production, processing and consumption sites. The specifics of these movements are the result of decisions made by a variety of actors/agents, such as shippers, carriers, distributors, freight forwarders, receivers, consumers, etc.

Individual agents may be unaware of (or not care about) actions of the others further up or down the supply chain, hence freight (shipment) movement information can be fragmented and incomplete. For example, a shipper may not care what carriers transport its shipments along what path and in what kind of conveyance, as long as the shipment reaches the ultimate destination at the expected time and at the contracted shipping charge. Yet, all of these elements of the freight movement process affect what the travelling public observes and encounters and what infrastructure needs to exist for both the private and the public sectors.

---

[36] This chapter is based on workshop discussions among the following: Oscar Ivan Aristizabal (Mexico), Rodrigo Garrido (Chile), David Kurth (USA), David Levinson (USA), Arnim Meyburg (USA), Christophe Rizet (France), Imke Steinmeyer (Germany), Pedro Szasz (Brazil), and Manfred Wermuth (Germany).

UNDERSTANDING BEHAVIOUR OF AGENTS INVOLVED AND LOGISTICS ISSUES

Clearly, transport planners and analysts will want to understand the motivation behind freight transport decisions and expectations embodied in the shipper, carrier, forwarder, receiver, consumer, i.e., all agents involved in the process. Immediately, logistical questions arise when trying to observe, measure, understand and analyse freight movements. Dependent on what element of the process is investigated or what agent in the logistical supply chain is involved, the questions of sampling frame, or more generally sample design, arise. Different geographic reference frames come into play in this context. In addition, information/data necessary to understand, analyse and/or model long-term economic changes and their effect on freight movements play an important role in understanding of freight movements. Clearly, only longitudinal data will be able to detect these changes. Again, the question arises at what geographic scale the data collection should take place and who among the different agents involved should be part of the data gathering. Also, it is not clear as to how specific data have to be with respect to the different elements of the supply chain.

Freight transport planners and analysts require an understanding of how firms operate, especially how they make their locational, logistical and transport/shipment decisions. Unfortunately, much of that information is not easily accessible to public-sector analysts and planners, due to proprietary confidentiality concerns of the private sector.

Of course, if agents in both sectors become convinced that access to this information, properly encoded to ensure confidentiality, is mutually beneficial for the long-term health of the firms and most importantly, the well-informed planning process and investment decision-making in the public sector, access to such data will be feasible. Firms need to appreciate that poor information is likely to lead to poor investment decisions in transport infrastructure and operations.

DEFINITION OF FREIGHT MOVEMENTS

Definitional ambiguities and inconsistencies are major roadblocks to freight transport data collection and to the ability to gain a comprehensive view of freight transport in a study area. Observing local freight movement without the regional or national context would be futile when trying to understand the underlying reasons for these movements.

A good example of definitional issues in freight transport is the comprehensive study of commercial transport conducted by Wermuth *et al.* (2006). The study surveyed all commercial movements because, in a strict sense, all transport other than trip-making by individuals involves commercial transactions of some kind. Hence, this commercial trip definition includes conventional freight, as well as any trips that provide service, such as trips by service vehicles, express delivery and taxis. The motivation behind this study was to include a large segment of trip making that typically is captured neither by conventional freight transport surveys nor by conventional passenger surveys. This German study team was in the enviable position of having had access to a perfect sample frame through the Federal Department of Motor Vehicles and governmental authority to strongly encourage responses.

The significant finding was that 33.7 percent of the annual vehicle mileage driven in Germany is attributable to commercial vehicles, a percentage that far exceeds what was expected based on previous studies. Clearly, this finding will affect any policy or investment decisions concerning commercial vehicle traffic in the future. This may pertain to infrastructure investments, vehicle taxation, tolls, route restrictions, special lane designations, parking, loading and unloading priorities, special permits, etc. In short, a whole range of operational, infrastructure, and financial decisions can be made on the basis of a well-defined and executed commercial vehicle study.

Many previous studies of freight movements across the globe suffer from the fact that they typically investigate only a relatively small segment of commercial vehicle traffic. They each tend to have their own particular specific definition of freight vehicles, and somewhat limited view of the supply chain relationships and transport connections. An understanding of the trip elements is crucial to the overall planning of the supply-chain characteristics. It represents the only way for managers and planners and policy decision makers to understand where and how improvements can be made, where problems are likely to arise, and what investment decisions need to be made.

From these particular characteristics of the freight movement process can be derived a number of overriding and/or underlying issues that affect the understanding of the process, the associated data needs and any efficiency improvements that may be desirable. The overriding issues that characterise freight movements are the diversity of carriers, shippers, forwarders, receivers, customers, and vehicles. All are involved or feed into the freight movement decision process. While many survey methodology issues are analogous to those on passenger travel survey methodology, clearly some aspects are particular to freight and add complexity to the data gathering process.

The availability of good-quality sample frames drives the quality of the sample, and ultimately the data. Access to suitable sample frames vary vastly by country, and within countries by survey and study objectives in relation to issues of proprietary data.

COMMODITY- VERSUS VEHICLE-BASED SURVEYS

Knowledge about both commodity flows and vehicle flows is necessary. Clearly, the study objectives will determine which type of information is necessary to answer the questions at hand. In general, it is clear that commodity-based surveys will disclose much more useful and comprehensive information about the flow of commodities, because they will disclose the characteristics of the shipments (size, weight, possibly value, etc.), as well as their true origins and destinations.

Hence, commodity-based surveys are much more useful for understanding the freight movement process and the characteristics of the supply chain for specific commodities and/or industry sectors. Of course, in the end, for decisions concerning infrastructure investment in the public sector and operational decisions in the private sector, it will become important to understand what specific commodity flows translate into what specific commercial vehicle moments and patterns.

A NATIONAL FREIGHT DATA PROGRAM

Many of the concerns and issues raised in the preceding sections could be addressed through the development of a unified freight data programme at the national level, possibly even at the international level. A special committee of freight data experts was convened by the US National Research Council (TRB) in 2002/03 to develop a framework for the creation of such a program (TRB, 2003).

This program would serve as a quasi census for freight. It would constitute a base framework to develop standards, definitions and core elements of the program. Major elements would be surveys of shippers, carriers, distributors, and receivers, supplemented by data obtained by freight informatics (i.e., ITS and traffic monitoring data).

The guidelines and standards provided by such a freight data program would allow up- and downward integration and compatibility. This would make the data applicable at different geographical scales (local, regional, national). Such a program could then, relatively easily, be supplemented by additional data collection for specific purposes or for different geographic reference frames. It would apply uniform terminology, definitions, data gathering techniques across surveys, and advocate using the same in supplementary surveys.

SELECTED RESEARCH ISSUES FOR FREIGHT DATA COLLECTION

Based on the preceding discussion, a number of research issues can be identified and recommendations can be made, as to what focus future research into freight data collection methods and practices should have:

- Understand the decision processes of shippers, carriers, forwarders, customers, etc.

- Understand the fundamental issues in freight and how to derive a methodology for freight survey design. Freight means many different things to different people.
- Understand group decision processes, i.e., decision-making by the group of decision makers involved in shipment movements.
- Investigate the feasibility of a clearinghouse for public and private information (including use of non-invasive data collection).
- Investigate different approaches to obtain an understanding of freight flows.
- Develop guidelines for best survey practices that are transferable and recommended. Inflexible standards seem to be inappropriate, given the diversity of survey scenarios present in the freight sector.
- Facilitate exchange of best freight survey practices.
- The future will likely bring the more widespread use of non-invasive data collection technologies (transponders, tracking). However, it is important to note that these techniques may not automatically render data for all analysis purposes. The identification of these limitations is important.
- Striving for the unambiguous specification of the study purpose will help generate data collection efforts that will produce the required data. As is the case on the passenger side, survey purpose and objectives play the overriding role in determining what approach and technique to apply in a freight movement survey, what sample frame to choose, and what survey method to apply.
- Adopt the concept of a National Freight Data Programme.
- Investigate the practical ability to implement the national freight data framework proposed in TRB Special Report 267 (TRB, 2003). While the framework is probably the most comprehensive effort to date of looking at the big picture for freight data collection, significant work needs to be performed to get from the concept of this framework to practical uses.
- Form an international group/committee focused on freight forecasting models and data.

REFERENCES

TRB (2003). A Concept for a National Freight Data Program, *Transportation Research Board Special Report 276*, Transportation Research Board, National Research Council, Washington, DC.

Wermuth, M., Neef, C., and Steinmeyer, I. (2006). Goods and Business Traffic in Germany. In: *Travel Survey Methods – Quality and Future Directions* (P.R. Stopher and C.C. Stecher, eds), 427-450, Elsevier, Oxford.

Travel Survey Methods: Quality and Future Directions
Peter Stopher and Cheryl Stecher (Editors)

25

IN SEARCH OF THE VALUE OF TIME: FROM SOUTH AFRICA TO INDIA

N. J. W. Van Zyl, Stewart Scott International Pty (Ltd), Pretoria, South Africa
and
M. Raza, MDP Consultants, New Delhi, India

INTRODUCTION

The route choice behaviour of potential toll route users and their perceived values of time (VOTs), which determine their choice of route, are critical in modelling the toll income stream of a proposed toll road. This is also fundamental in assessing the financial risks of the financiers of the toll road investment. Internationally the most acceptable approach is to use individual choice or discrete choice models calibrated on the potential users' actual route choice behaviour (revealed preference – RP) as well their intended behaviour (stated preference – SP). The VOT is subsequently used in network transport models such as EMME/2 and SATURN so that these models reflect the correct distribution of trips amongst alternative routes for each Origin-Destination pair of the trip matrix. VOTs are therefore critical parameters in the trip assignment process and it is important that VOTs are estimated accurately.

This chapter describes three value of time studies that were conducted for the purpose of two toll road studies in South Africa and one in India. These studies were the most significant in contributing towards research knowledge in South Africa.:

- Scheme development of N4 Platinum toll road conducted by the Bakwena Platinum Corridor Concessionaire (BPCC). This study is referred to as the *Platinum Study*, and was conducted in 2000 (Stewart Scott, 2000).
- Scheme development of Gauteng freeway network as toll routes conducted by the Gauteng Super Highways Consortium (GSHC). The study is referred to as the *Gauteng Study*, which was conducted in 2001 (Stewart Scott, 2001).

- National Highway Corridor Public Private Partnership (PPP) Project conducted by DHV for the National Highways Authority of India (NHAI). This study is referred to as the *India Study,* which was conducted in 2002 (Stewart Scott, 2002).

Travel surveys, and especially SP surveys, in developing countries such as South Africa and India face major challenges. It is hoped that sharing this knowledge with the international community will assist in the transfer of knowledge that will improve the application of SP techniques in these countries.

This chapter emphasises the survey and modelling methodology, factors impacting on route choice behaviour, and interesting trends observed from the results. Various survey techniques to elicit information from road users on their actual (RP) and intended (SP) route choice behaviour are discussed, as well as the important considerations in the design of the survey and the SP experiment. Finally, recommendations are made with regard to further research to be conducted on survey techniques and VOT studies, especially to improve their application in developing countries.

It should be noted that the two South African toll road studies reported here were done for private concessionaires, which restricted the publication of sensitive information. The Platinum toll road was awarded in the mean time, but the Gauteng Freeway toll initiative is not yet concluded. Less detailed results on the Gauteng study are, therefore, reported, with the focus more on survey techniques.

BACKGROUND

Estimation of VOTs From Discrete Choice Models

Discrete choice models, or individual choice models, are very popular worldwide to simulate the choice behaviour of transport users for policy testing and travel forecasting purposes. Traditionally, most of these models were developed for mode choice studies. With the international trend to finance new high order roads by means of tolling, route choice studies have become more popular. Discrete choice models are specifically used to estimate VOTs of road users, because the models capture accurately the underlying choice behaviour of the specific target market of the planned toll road. The models also allow the impact of any factor influencing the VOTs to be estimated, such as the trip purpose, income, road standard, etc.

The VOT is estimated as follows from the formulation of the logit discrete choice model. Consider the simple route choice situation between a toll road and its alternative, or parallel, non-tolled road. The utility that the road user derives from each route can be formulated in terms of toll fee and travel time:

$$U_{toll} = c * C_t + t * T_t + M_t \qquad (1)$$

$$U_{alt} = c * C_a + t * T_a \qquad (2)$$

where:

U_{toll} and U_{alt}	=	utilities of the toll road and alternative road, respectively;
C_t and T_t	=	user cost and the travel time on the toll route, respectively;
C_a and T_a	=	cost and time on the alternative route;
c and t	=	cost and time coefficients which are estimated on survey data of road users' perceived travel times and costs by means of special logit model calibration programs; and
M_t	=	constant, attached to the utility of the toll road, that captures any factor not related to the variables in the model – cost and time in this case – that may relate to safety and convenience of using the toll road relative to that of the alternative road.

In general terms, the value of time is defined as the rate of change of utility relative to the rate of change in travel time, divided by the rate of change of utility relative to the rate of change in the cost. For a linear utility function such as equations 1 and 2, the VOT is simply the ratio of the time coefficient to the cost coefficient:

$$VOT = t / c \qquad (3)$$

If time was measured in minutes and cost in cents, the VOT is given in cents per minute.

Any variable in the utility function can be expressed in terms of monetary values by taking the ratio of the coefficient of that variable to the cost coefficient. By taking the ratio of the toll road constant (M_t) to the cost coefficient, one gets the value of the safety and convenience that road users attach to the toll road. This is often referred to as the motorway bonus in international literature. By making the utility functions more complex one can derive more information from the model. For example, by breaking up the cost variable into running cost and toll fee cost, one can estimate the VOTs related to running cost and toll fee. The surveyed data can also be segmented by trip purpose and/or income level to estimate the VOTs for different trip purposes and income levels.

Louviere *et al.* (2000) derived a VOT function by introducing quadratic and multiplication cost and time terms in the utility function. In this way they could estimate how the VOT would vary by the level of the toll fee and the travel time. They developed an empirical valuation function to test the influence of different toll and travel time regimes on travellers' route choices. The study showed an inverse relationship between VOT and trip length, i.e., for a given toll, travellers are willing to pay less money for a unit saving in travel time for longer trips than for shorter trips.

Various market research techniques can also be used to obtain information from targeted road users. Revealed preference surveys obtain road users' current route preferences, costs and times, for existing toll route corridors. Stated preference surveys present potential toll road users with hypothetical choices between the proposed toll road and the alternative road and request their stated choices between the routes.

SP models normally perform better than RP models, because RP data often lack variation and suffer from empirical correlations and interactions that hide the underlying choice behaviour. However, SP models suffer from various biases in responses, such as a strategic/policy bias, in which respondents try to influence the experiment to favour a certain strategy/policy, or make errors between intended and real life choices.

Bhat and Castelar (2002) formulated and applied a unified mixed-logit (ML) framework for the joint analysis of RP and SP data that accommodates four behavioural considerations:

- Inter-alternative error structure i.e., extending RP-SP methods to accommodate flexible competitive patterns by relaxing the assumption of Identical and Independent Distribution (IID) of the error terms assumed by the multinomial logit (MNL) model;
- Scale difference between the RP and SP data generating processes;
- Unobserved heterogeneity effects i.e., unobserved differences between decision-makers; and
- State-dependence effects referring to the influence of actual (revealed) choices on the stated choices of the individual.

The model was applied to examine the travel behaviour of the users of the San Francisco Bay Bridge. A RP survey, using a forty eight hour travel diary, served as a reference to the SP survey. Six alternatives and five variables were included in the model testing process. Cross-sectional and panel data were used. The ML model estimation was achieved using quasi-random Monte Carlo simulation techniques. It was concluded that it is advantageous to combine RP and SP data to overcome the inherent problems of each. Addressing the four behavioural factors and the interactions between them is important to simulate travel behaviour accurately and also to determine realistic VOTs.

Review of International Experience on Toll Route Choice Modelling

To learn from overseas experience a literature search was conducted on SP surveys for route choice and toll road modelling. At the time of the South African studies, limited information was found, because most SP studies dealt with mode choice. Useful information extracted from overseas literature is summarised below:

- The following are important factors influencing road users route choice in the urban environment: (Abdel-Aty *et al.*, 1995):
    - Travel time;
    - Road Type;
    - Congestion;
    - Occurrence of stops and traffic signals; and
    - Uncertainty/unreliability of travel time.
- The heterogeneous nature of routes, with varying characteristics along the length of the route, makes route choice modelling more complicated than urban mode choice modelling (Bovy and Bradley, 1985).
- VOTs may vary by trip purpose, income group, mode, occupation group, personal circumstances, amount of leisure time available, and travel conditions (Bradley and Gunn, 1990).
- Market research amongst users of the SR91 toll road in California during 1996/97 indicated that many commuters overestimate their actual time savings, e.g., twenty minutes perceived versus thirteen minutes actual (Cal Poly State University, 2000).
- A major research study conducted by the Institute of Transport Studies at Leeds University (UK) makes available the net outcome of a very large amount of British empirical evidence regarding the impact of a large number of travel attributes on VOTs (Wardman, 1990). The relevant key findings of the study are:
    - Not only do the money values vary across different circumstances, but there can also be considerable variation in the valuations expressed in units of in-vehicle time;
    - Business values are, as expected, the highest, followed by commuting values that, in turn, tend to be higher than leisure values;
    - The effect of distance on the money values was in most cases positive and very similar although not particularly strong. This is in addition to higher values for inter-urban trips of thirty miles or more.
    - There is a reasonable degree of correspondence between RP and SP values of in-vehicle time. However, this correspondence is progressively weakened for out-of-vehicle time, headway and interchange. Indeed, the divergence between the RP and SP values for headway and interchange is a cause for some concern.
    - It appears that the money value of an attribute varies with the monetary unit used. Valuations expressed in units of toll fee are the lowest whilst those expressed solely in terms of car running costs are highest.

Historic Review of South African VOT Studies

At the time of the bidding phase of the N4 Platinum toll road scheme, it was found that there was no recognised database in South Africa in respect of the values of time for traffic and transport studies. However, there were different sources of information, that permitted a value judgment to be made. These sources of information were:

1.   Values of time as ascertained by the Central Economic Advisory Service in the late 1980s were based on income rates. These values are normally used in economic evaluation studies, but are not sufficiently accurate to explain route choice behaviour of road users in a particular road network context.

2.   Revealed Preference survey work conducted for the N3 toll road that concluded that the attraction to this toll road is best defined in terms of a cumulative monetary value (i.e., inclusive of time, safety, comfort and convenience costs) for light (Class 1) vehicles of R80.00 per hour (1997 Rand value).

3.   Stated Preference survey work conducted on the N4 Maputo Corridor, between Maputo in Mozambique and Witbank in Mpumalanga, which concluded relatively low values of time, but in conjunction with high motorway bonuses (i.e., to account for safety, comfort and convenience factors and a preference for higher standard routes).

The BPCC subsequently recommended that the South African National Roads Agency (SANRAL) develop a values of time database for South Africa, because this would greatly assist in the various future toll road studies. When appointed as Preferred Bidder, the BPCC and its traffic auditors decided to conduct comprehensive RP and SP studies in order to refine the VOTs for use in the final traffic model. This initiated a number of SP and RP value of time studies in South Africa.

Application of VOTs to Traffic Forecasting Models

The VOTs for various market segments are typically applied in network traffic models to estimate the traffic volumes on the proposed toll road and the surrounding road network, using models such as EMME/2 and SATURN. The models use deterministic or stochastic network equilibrium assignment techniques to determine traffic volumes under various levels of congested conditions. Monetary cost variables are converted into equivalent travel time by applying the value of time from RP and SP surveys to cost variables. A generalised time function is, therefore, used instead of a generalised cost one. Other factors such as travel time reliability, safety, comfort, and convenience are also converted to equivalent travel time using the coefficients of calibrated discrete choice models. Typically these non-time/cost factors act as a net positive factor for the toll road relative to alternative routes and they are combined into a single constant, called a 'toll road bonus'. International traffic auditors of the traffic models that are developed for toll road concessions have very strict accuracy criteria. Typical requirements are:

- VOTs must be estimated from SP surveys for various relevant market segments of road users.
- A base year traffic model must be estimated, distinguishing between different market segments, to simulate the current observed traffic volumes, travel times, and road network conditions. The average VOT for each segment is applied to

the traffic model and would typically distinguish between three to four trip purposes for light vehicles, as well as heavy vehicles, and also between the morning and afternoon peak periods, and the off-peak period. This would result in twelve to fifteen separate models, which is a time consuming and expensive exercise.

- The traffic model is subsequently validated against independent traffic counts not used in the estimation. The model must be able to simulate the observed traffic volumes and travel times within a certain small error margin.

The Platinum traffic model was developed in terms of international best practice and was also thoroughly audited by an external international traffic auditor. This process was also applied to the Gauteng model.

The inherent differences between discrete choice models and aggregate network assignment models pose certain problems when applying logit models to network models. For example, applying the logit model in a network assignment routine using a straightforward deterministic equilibrium assignment does not converge under congested network conditions. To overcome these problems an estimation procedure in the network model, EMME/2 or SATURN, was developed that proved to be very successful. First, the stochastic user assignment (SUE) is used in the network model. The logit discrete model is also stochastic, which gives some basis for similarity between the two models. The principle of the SUE assignment model is that the cost as defined by the model is the 'correct' average cost, but that there is a distribution about the average as perceived by individuals. The perceived cost is therefore simulated by selecting a cost at random from the perceived distribution of costs on each link. Certain parameters in the assignment model are subsequently adjusted until the toll diversion function of the network model (percent use of toll road versus the alternative route as a function of the toll fee) fits the toll diversion curve, obtained from the SP model. Florian (2004) developed an algorithm in EMME/2 that applies a logit route choice model in a multi-class assignment and that converges. This algorithm has been used in various toll road applications and proved successful. Its application in South Africa would certainly be worthwhile to pursue in subsequent toll road studies.

Dynamic microsimulation models applied to small congested sub-areas are becoming increasingly popular (Florian, 2004). These models simulate the driving behaviour of individual vehicles, and route choice is governed by discrete choice models. A more recent development is dynamic quasi microsimulation models targeted at the tactical level for larger sub-regions. These microsimulation network assignment models, therefore, allow direct application of behavioural discrete choice models, eliminating the incompatibility problems experienced with strategic network assignment models.

Experience of SP Surveys in Developing Countries

The numerous and acute problems experienced in surveys among a population with a large proportion of less-literate people in developing countries are well reported by van der Reis and Lombard, (2001), Del Mistro and Arentze (2002), and van Zyl *et al.* (2001). These problems are particularly problematic in SP surveys, which require high-quality data on the travel behaviour and preferences of a sample of transport users. The problems relate to sampling procedures, respondent selection bias, questionnaire design relating to language, culture and numeracy, and interviewing procedures. The concern that survey methods used in developed countries might not always be transferable to developing countries, motivated a research project in South Africa to test various hypotheses regarding the performance of SP mode choice models among less-literate commuters. (Del Mistro and Arentze, 2002). The following conclusions were drawn from the research:

- SP data can be collected from less-literate respondents provided that the choice tasks are not too complex. The relatively low level of model fit (adjusted Rho-square value of 0.18) and the high number of invalid responses identified in the qualitative interviews, indicated that SP can be problematic in this context.
- A high degree of care needs to be taken during interviews to ensure that respondents give reliable responses based on the presented hypothetical situations rather than on a desire to be polite, appear intelligent, or use values from their own experience.
- The possibility that mode choices are based on non-compensatory rules need to be investigated further.
- The reasons for the apparent discrepancies between the statistical analyses and qualitative research also need to be investigated further.

In view of the above experience in South Africa and the requirement to provide only average VOTs by market segment for traffic forecasting models, the following guidelines were used generally:

- Keep SP surveys to simple binary choices between the proposed toll route and the non-tolled alternative route;
- Use only face-face personal interviews;
- Limit the number of variables to three or four, and limit the number of choices per respondent; and
- Conduct recruitment and interviews at filling stations, the roadside, or toll plazas, adjacent to the targeted route, because it is difficult to locate potential respondents afterwards at home or at work. This results in only a limited time period being available for interviews, which also requires short and simple SP designs.

Another characteristic of South Africa and India, which is often typical of developing countries, is the limited travel choices of road users. Public transport is very poor and restricted and offers limited choice to car users. Route choice is also limited and alternative routes are often congested and in a poor condition. Hence, sensitivity tests of the impact of VOTs indicated that the toll route attraction is not very sensitive to VOTs.

RP AND SP SURVEY METHODS

Overview of Toll Road Studies

A brief overview of the three selected toll road projects for the purpose of this chapter are given here in order to put the surveys into perspective.

N1/N4 Platinum Toll Road

Figures 1 and 2 show locality maps of the Platinum toll route and the freeways in Gauteng province, respectively. The N1/N4 Platinum Toll Route project consists of some 100 kilometres of the existing national road N1 between Pretoria and Warmbaths, running north-south, and some 380 kilometres of the existing national road N4 from Pretoria to the Botswana border, running east-west. The N1 North links Gauteng province with Zimbabwe to the north, while the N4 West links Gauteng to Botswana to the west. The N4 Platinum route forms part of the coast-to-coast Maputo-Walvisbay Spatial Development Initiative linking Mozambique, South Africa, and Namibia. This was one of a number of Build Operate Transfer (BOT) Toll Road Concessions that the SANRAL had put out to tender on a concession basis. The project involved the upgrading of the existing road, construction of toll plazas at various strategic locations, including provision of Electronic Toll Collection (ETC) gates at toll plazas. The toll route has recently been completed, except for one bypass near Rustenburg, a major town along the route.

Parts of the route are urban freeways in the vicinity of Pretoria, one of the three metropolitan areas in Gauteng province, while the other routes are intercity rural roads. The urban/rural nature of the toll routes made the traffic model very complex, and the route choice surveys had to distinguish between urban and rural traffic.

The BPCC was appointed by SANRAL as scheme developer, and the BPCC subsequently won the bid to implement the project. A SATURN traffic model was built of the toll routes and parallel main roads, as well as part of the urban network in Pretoria. The traffic model was used to determine the toll traffic attraction, yearly toll income over the next thirty years, and impact of the toll route on the main road network. Accurate values of time were critical for the correct estimation of the toll attraction and toll income stream estimation for the financiers of the BPCC.

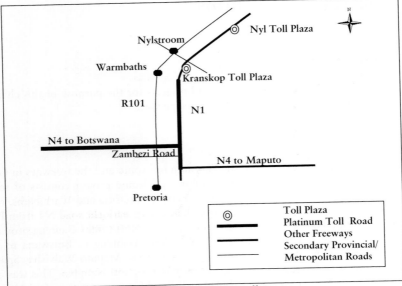

Figure 1: Platinum Toll Route

Gauteng Toll Freeway Network

The primary corridor forming part of the freeway network of Gauteng province is the two freeways linking greater Johannesburg and greater Pretoria, which is the busiest intercity corridor in Africa with current traffic volumes on the order of 200,000 vehicles per day (see Figure 2). SANRAL, together with the Gauteng Department of Public Transport, Roads and Works, conducted a feasibility study to develop the freeway network in Gauteng as an integrated toll route network. The high traffic volumes, acute congestion, and complexity of the network demanded best practice solutions for the technical, financial and environmental challenges faced by the project.

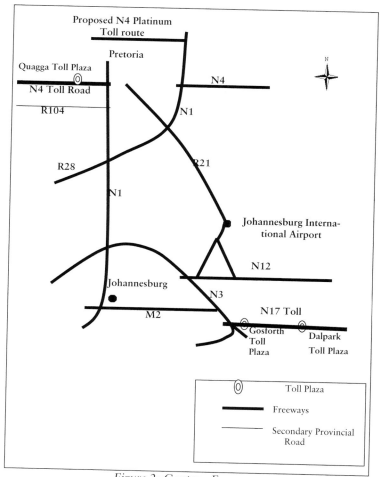

Figure 2: Gauteng Freeways

The GSHC was formed and appointed by SANRAL to develop the scheme as a potential PPP project. The main toll road strategy was to upgrade freeways to four lanes in each direction, with two outer lanes acting as toll express lanes, while the inner two lanes are un-tolled. A SATURN traffic model was built of all the main roads in Gauteng to test the impact of tolling the freeways and to estimate the toll income streams for the next thirty years. Numerous network scenarios were tested, consisting of the upgrading of existing freeways and construction of new freeways. The results of the traffic model were also used in a financial model to determine the project financial feasibility. A microsimulation model was developed for critical sections of the network to test the performance of urban toll plazas, using ETC methods, and the toll express lane concept.

To test the toll express lane concept, accurate values of time for various market segments were required as the level of traffic congestion and travel time savings between the parallel un-tolled and tolled lanes were the determining factors for road users' choice to use the tolled lanes or not. Various congestion-pricing strategies were also tested including higher toll fees during peak periods than during off-peak times.

India PPP Corridor

Figure 3 shows the PPP Corridor in India. The corridor is situated in the state of Gujarat, linking Porbandar in the south to Radhanpur in the north. The length of the National Highway along the corridor is 507 kilometres. The corridor forms part of the Golden Quadrilateral road network, which the NHAI is in the process of developing as part of a thirty year programme. Commercially viable sections of the network will be funded through tolling under PPP contracts. The main purpose of the study to determine VOTs was to evaluate funding models for the Porbandar- Radhanpur corridor, including funding from tolling.

RP versus SP Surveys

Earlier value of time studies in South Africa indicated RP values of time to be much higher, in a more realistic range, than SP values. This is in contrast to experience overseas, where RP and SP surveys often indicated very similar values. This was a major concern, because SP models provided better model fits compared to RP models, but SP models suffer from various biases, such as negative emotions towards tolling, especially in urban areas, and differences between stated and actual preferences. Although international traffic auditors required only SP studies, the bidding Consortia preferred to conduct RP surveys as well to validate SP values of time. The studies reported here all made use of both RP and SP surveys.

Apart from the normal problems associated with RP surveys and models, another problem was to find an existing toll route with a viable parallel main road close to the proposed toll route. Both in South Africa and India, toll roads are not that extensive and the RP surveys did not cover the target market of the SP surveys, which were conducted amongst the potential toll road users. This provided another source of unknown error.

In the case of the Platinum study, the RP and SP studies were conducted independently by two study teams and their market research companies. However, the background questions were made compatible to compare the sample profiles. The RP surveys conducted for the Platinum study were also relevant to the Gauteng study, which subsequently only required additional SP surveys.

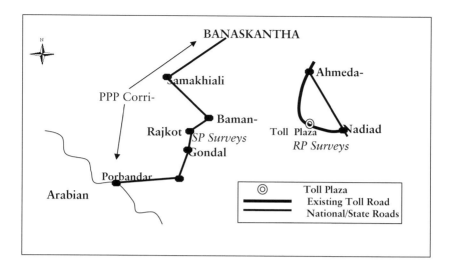

Figure 3: India Proposed Toll Route

In India, the RP and SP surveys were conducted by different companies, both managed by the same consultant team. The RP surveys were done by a traffic survey company and the SP surveys by a market research company. The South African consulting firm also managed the surveys in conjunction with a local transport engineering consulting firm, which was crucial for the success of the surveys.

Survey Methods

The early SP studies in South Africa all made use of pen and paper interview methods, which was also the case in the Platinum study. One market research company in South Africa introduced CAPI using lap top computers, and transferring data via the Internet on a daily basis during surveys. CAPI was, therefore, used for the first time in a route choice survey during the Gauteng study, with great success.

CAPI provided major benefits, by allowing real time validation of responses, direct computerisation of data, and presenting the SP levels as percentage deviations from respondents' current personal travel characteristics. The greater variation in the data, obtained in this way, improved the performance of the models. SP levels could also be adjusted during the survey – fieldworkers downloaded revised questionnaires by dialling in via modem to headquarters when up-loading the survey data after the day's work. This opportunity was used during the Gauteng study, when daily monitoring of responses indicated that too many respondents did not change their choice between the toll route and the alternative route. The later study in India used pen and paper, because CAPI was not available among the local market research companies. Being unfamiliar with local conditions and, because this was a first for all the teams involved in the study, it was considered important to keep methods and designs as simple as possible.

Past experience with SP studies in South Africa indicated that face-to-face interviews are crucial to ensure good results. Further, among low-income groups, telephone ownership and postal services are limited, which ruled out telephone and postal surveys. Postal surveys also suffer from low response rates and require higher literacy of the respondent. All the studies therefore employed face-to-face interviews.

Recruitment Techniques

To ensure that only potential toll road users were interviewed for the SP studies, roadside interviews were conducted at filling stations on existing roads that were proposed to be tolled. For the RP surveys, roadside interviews were conducted at existing toll plazas, while road users on the alternative routes were intercepted by traffic police for interviewing, or were intercepted at filling stations on the route. The draw-back of roadside interviews is the limited time available to interview road users, which makes it not an ideal interview environment for SP surveys.

In the case of the Gauteng surveys, freeway users were recruited at so called ultra-cities (filling stations adjacent to the freeway with their own interchange) and interviewed at a convenient location afterwards. It proved to be difficult to make appointments with willing respondents at suitable times and locations, especially business people, so that various incentives had to be used to make successful appointments. Incentives included gift vouchers or a light meal at a restaurant where the interview could be conducted. In India the interviews were conducted at roadside cafes, or dhabas, which were conveniently located at short intervals. Recruitment went much faster than in South Africa, even amongst business people.

Heavy vehicle users posed a different problem, because drivers do not always make their own route choices, but rather their managers. For these cases, the managers were phoned in the South Africa studies. In India, a sample of drivers was interviewed, as well as a sample of managers of freight transport companies owning large fleets.

Market Segmentation

Market segmentation was critical, because trip purpose and income generally indicate significantly different values of time. The following typical segmentation was used, with minor differences depending on the local context:

- Light vehicles – low and high income for the following trip purposes:
  o   Business;
  o   Commuter;

          ○ Social / other;
- Heavy vehicles:
  - ○ 2 axles;
  - ○ 3- 4 axes; and
  - ○ 5 and more axles.

Stratified random sampling was adopted to achieve minimum samples based on location, trip purpose, and vehicle class, with random selection of respondents within each stratum. Market segmentation posed a challenge in India, because of the many socio-economic and cultural/religious groups, as well as many vehicle classes. Vehicles such as two- and three- wheelers, and three-wheel trucks occur in significant numbers. Light vehicles such as jeeps are often rented with a driver, in which case, the client was interviewed and not the driver. In India, we also attempted to distinguish different categories of freight to test the impact of different types of freight on the VOT. The Gauteng survey focused on commuters and business light vehicle trips, because these were the most critical for the estimation of the toll express lane attraction rates. These users were also most likely to experience unacceptable congestion in view of work requirements.

Survey Locations and Sample Sizes

A guideline of between seventy five and one hundred interviews per market segment were used for the SP surveys, suggested by international experience (Ortúzar and Willumsen, 2000). Survey locations and sample sizes are described briefly below.

Platinum Study

In the RP survey, 869 respondents were interviewed on existing toll roads and their alternative routes in Gauteng province and the province north of Gauteng, consisting of drivers of 619 light vehicles, 97 commercial LDV's and 153 heavy vehicles. The RP sample on the existing N1 toll road in the vicinity of Warmbaths and Nylstroom to the north of Pretoria covered the Kranskop and Nyl toll plazas and the R101 alternative route. The sample on the existing N17 toll freeway in the East Rand (region east of Johannesburg) covered the Gosforth and Dalpark toll plazas and alternative metropolitan routes. The RP sample on the existing N4 toll route to the west of Pretoria covered the Quagga toll plaza and R104 alternative route, (see Figure 1).

For the SP study, 500 light vehicle users and 100 heavy vehicle users were interviewed on the N1 just to the north of Pretoria at the Petroport filling station adjacent to the freeway, and on Zambesi drive in Pretoria North, an urban main road running parallel to the proposed N4 West route. A stratified sample of fifty in each of twelve market segments were used. The twelve market segments distinguished short and long distance trips, three light vehicle trip purposes for short trips (business, commuter, and other), two light vehicle trip purposes for long trips (business and other), heavy vehicles (short and long trips), and low and high-income light vehicle users.

Gauteng Study

The SP survey targeted light vehicles only, including a sample of 150 commuters and 150 business users. A minimum sample size for low- and high-income users was also targeted. The most viable and efficient method was to intercept people at the ultra-city filling stations adjacent to the N1 freeway between Johannesburg and Pretoria, and the Engen filling stations adjacent to the R21, between Pretoria and the Johannesburg International Airport, (see Figure 2). No special RP surveys were conducted, because comprehensive RP surveys conducted at the rather limited number of existing toll roads in Gauteng province were available from the Platinum surveys.

India Study

The existing toll road corridor between Nadiad and Ahmedabad to the east of the proposed PPP toll road was the closest location for the RP survey. (See Figure 3.) Roadside interviews were conducted at Randhavanj on the toll route and at Barsola on the parallel non-tolled route. The SP surveys were done to the south and north of Rajkot, covering the Porbandar-Gondal link and Bamanbore-Samakhiali-Banaskantha link along the total PPP corridor. The roadside interviews were supplemented by large freight operator interviews in these locations, i.e., Ahmedabad, Rajkot, and Junagadh.

During a ten-day period, 1,375 SP interviews were conducted, whilst 2,504 RP interviews were conducted during a six-day period. Minimum sample sizes were targeted by vehicle class (light private, light commercial, and heavy vehicles), trip distance category (short and long), and trip purpose (commuter, business, holiday, and other).

DESIGN OF SP EXPERIMENTS

Choice Contexts

Careful consideration was given to the choice context in the SP experiments, to present realistic route choice scenarios to respondents, yet keeping it simple to obtain reliable choices. Both the Platinum and the India projects involved upgrading a road to be tolled, or building a new road, and the availability of one viable alternative route. This context was described simply as choosing between a high standard toll road and a lower standard alternative road with the toll road offering a saving in travel time, less traffic congestion, better and well-maintained road surface, and improved safety and security.

Road users were, in general, familiar with the concept of toll roads and bridges and they could relate to the experimental context. However, the toll express lane concept in the Gauteng study was unfamiliar to respondents, and raised many questions during the

Focus Group discussion and the pilot survey. It was decided subsequently to simplify the presentation of the toll express lanes by presenting it as two parallel freeways of the same standard, the one being tolled and the other one un-tolled. The tolled freeway was presented as having much less congestion, offered shorter travel times, and only allowed light vehicles to use it. In this way the choice context was still realistic, but it avoided possible confusion about the toll express lanes.

In the Platinum study respondents were asked to rate their preference for the tolled route and existing road on a five-point scale i.e., strongly prefer freeway, prefer freeway, no preference, prefer ordinary road, strongly prefer ordinary road. In the Gauteng and India studies, respondents were asked to indicate their choice for either the tolled freeway or the existing road.

Inertia to Change

A typical phenomenon, 'inertia to change', was encountered, similar to that found during mode choice SP studies in South Africa (van Zyl *et al.*, 2000; Del Mistro and Arentze, 2002). This is a major problem in SP surveys in South Africa and relates to the 'state-dependence' factor analysed by Bhat and Castelar (2002) using Panel surveys. However, it goes beyond an 'influence of actual choices on the SP choices'. It is manifest in a very strong preference for the existing mode or route, leading to a high proportion of respondents choosing only the existing alternative, even if the new alternative is made very attractive. Some semi-literate respondents also have difficulties in understanding the SP game context and make choices based only on their current experience of the offered alternatives. This problem is compounded by the sensitivity of road users in South Africa to the tolling of commuter routes due to budget constraints to pay for a road on a daily basis. Another factor is the high levels of road user taxes (fuel, vehicle license, municipal rates, and taxes) that are used for other government priorities and not applied to improve roads and public transport systems. Within limits this problem can be accepted as normal behaviour, and the challenge is to formulate a design that allows for trade-offs and testing respondents' boundary values of time.

The problem of 'inertia to change' and how to deal with it was much debated during the Platinum and Gauteng studies. One solution is to present respondents with time and cost trade-offs in other non-emotional contexts. However, value of time is very context specific and one would not know what the error would be caused by the difference in context. Offering trade-offs just between fuel costs and travel time savings in a route choice situation is a closely related context, but experience indicated that values of time based on fuel costs may be valued differently; some studies found that the VOT based on fuel cost was higher than that of toll fees. In general, to overcome this problem, great care had to be taken to choose the appropriate SP levels, describing the choice context and controlled variables with fixed levels, train fieldworkers properly and thoroughly explain the SP game to respondents.

Inertia to change was especially a problem in the Gauteng study amongst commuters, due to their sensitivities of tolling the freeways in Gauteng. The India and Platinum study did not experience this problem. Both these studies involved intercity toll roads, although some commuter traffic in the Platinum study was also targeted.

SP Variables and Levels

Because the main purpose of the SP studies was to determine the VOT, the toll fee, fuel cost, and travel time variables were the most important to include in the experiments. The roadside interviews also did not allow time for lengthy interviews, and the number of variables had to be limited. The complexity of the Gauteng study, involving freeways in an urbanised area, required additional variables to be tested, such as the reliability of predicting travel time, and hence departing earlier to allow for unexpected congestion. To determine the most significant factors impacting route choice along the Johannesburg-Pretoria corridor and to test road users' understanding of the toll express lane concept, focus group discussions were conducted prior to the SP surveys. A spreadsheet was used to determine boundary arrays to define the SP levels such that the boundary values of time with respect to toll fees and fuel costs covered a wide range within plausible limits. All questionnaire designs were pilot tested to ensure that respondents understood the experiment, did not get fatigued, and would switch their choices between the toll and alternative route options. Table 1 gives the main SP design parameters of the three studies.

Platinum Study

As indicated in Table 1, four variables were included with three to four levels each i.e., travel time on the toll freeway and the existing 'ordinary road', toll fee, and the extra fuel cost on the freeway. The freeway was presented as a route that may involve a longer distance to access in order to enjoy the saving of travel time. This allowed the VOT to be estimated separately for toll fees and fuel cost. Twenty five SP tests were too many to present to each respondent and therefore tests were randomly divided into three blocks. Each block of eight to nine choices was offered to respondents on a random basis. A zero toll fee was included in the SP levels of the tolled freeway, which allowed a toll dummy variable to be included in the utility function to capture any strategic or emotive response to tolling. In view of the pen and paper method used, four separate questionnaire designs were developed for light and heavy vehicles, and short and long distance trips, using 75 kilometres as a cut-off point.

Gauteng Study

Apart from the usual travel time and toll fee variables, it was also felt important to include two additional travel characteristics that were important for the strategic and microsimulation models in an urbanised, highly congested environment. Earlier departure for commuters on the existing freeway relative to the toll freeway as a result of congestion, and the number of incidents per month (commuter and business) were also presented as SP variables. Incidents are occurring frequently on the N1 and R21 freeways, almost on a daily basis resulting in long delays.

Table 1: SP Design Parameters for Light Vehicles (Selection of Experiments)

Study	Variables	Range	Levels per Variable	Choices per Respondent
Platinum Short trips (<75 km)	Travel time on toll freeway	10 to 20 mins	3	3 blocks, with 8 to 9 choices per block
	Travel time on alternative route	20 to 30 mins	3	
	Toll fee	R0 to R25	4	
	Extra fuel cost on freeway	R0 to R15	4	
Gauteng Commuters Experiment 2	Departure time	Fixed at normal departure time	1	9 choices
Gauteng Business trips	Departure time	Fixed at preferred departure time	1	
	Total travel time existing highway	As now (reported time)	1	
	Total travel time Toll expressway	As now x 0.7 to x 0.9	3	
	No of incidents per month, existing highway	0.2 x trips per month to 0.5 x trips per month	3	
	No of incidents, toll expressway	1 per month	1	
	Toll fee	R1 to R6	3	
	Total travel time existing highway	As now (reported time)	1	9 choices
	Total travel time Toll expressway	As now x 0.7 to x 0.9	3	
	No of incidents, existing highway	0.2 x trips per month to 0.5 x trips per month	3	
	No of incidents, toll expressway	1 per month		
	Toll fee	R1 to R15	3	
India Short trips (< 100 km)	Total travel time saving of toll route versus current time	10 to 25 mins	3	16 choices
	Toll fee	Rs 3 to Rs 15	4	
	Fuel cost saving of toll route versus current cost	Rs 0 to Rs 8	3	

Four SP variables with three levels each were, therefore, tested amongst commuters and business users. These were total travel time, departure time (only for commuters), number of incidents per month, and toll fee. Two experiments were offered to commuters, each with three variables. In the first, departure time was tested with the number of incidents at fixed levels. In the second, the number of incidents was tested, with departure time at fixed levels. Travel time and toll fee were included in all the experiments. Each experiment yielded nine choices per respondent to obtain a main effects orthogonal design. The use of CAPI allowed SP levels of the new toll freeway to be estimated during interviews based on each respondent's reported travel time and departure time for his or her current trip. SP levels, in ratios, were programmed into the CAPI questionnaire, and the program generated the actual levels on the laptop in a table for each choice situation. Respondents who were 'captive' to their existing, un-tolled, situation were prompted to confirm that they understood the SP game and to confirm their choices. They were asked subsequently for reasons for choosing only their existing route.

Following the pilot test, some vital changes were made to the choice context and the SP levels to ensure better trade-offs between variables and switching of choices between the existing route and tolled freeway. SP results were monitored on a daily basis and after a few days of surveys, it was necessary to make a few further adjustments to SP levels. The new design was made available on the network server of the market research company and fieldworkers downloaded the new questionnaire when they uploaded their responses for the day. The use of CAPI and the Internet allowing changes during the survey proved to be very beneficial and successful. However, it required more preparation time beforehand to program and test the CAPI questionnaires.

India Study

In view of previous experience, the unfamiliar environment, and the need to focus on travel time and cost variables in order to determine values of time, it was decided to adopt a very simplified design. As indicated in Table 1 three variables with three to four levels each were selected, i.e., travel time saving of toll route relative to alternative route, toll fee on toll route, and fuel cost saving of toll route relative to alternative route. Formulating variables in terms of travel time and fuel cost saving reduced the number of variables, although this prevented distinguishing route-specific coefficients for these variables. An orthogonal design, yielding sixteen choices per respondent, was selected. Initial concerns that sixteen levels were too many, were allayed during the pilot tests and the sixteen choice design was also used for the main survey.

In view of the fact that a pen and paper method was used, four designs had to be formulated to cover short and long distance trips, with a 100 km cut-off point, and for light and heavy vehicles. Extra attention was given to fieldworker training, pilot testing, daily monitoring of results, and feedback to fieldworkers to resolve problems.

COMPARISON OF VALUES OF TIME BETWEEN STUDIES

Performance of Route Choice Models

Although a wide range of tests of the designs and questionnaires were performed, as well as checking and validation of responses during the surveys, the ultimate quality of the surveys were judged by the performance of the route choice models. Conventional multinomial logit estimation procedures were performed, and values of time were only determined from significant models and from cost and time variables that were significant and that indicated the correct signs.

Similar to international experience, SP models performed much better than RP models. Travel times and costs were often not well reported, which required extensive validation to be performed. Records with outliers were subsequently excluded. The large RP samples allowed the data bases to be reduced without yielding too low samples.

Results of Platinum Study

The Platinum models performed well and key variables were significant. VOTs were determined for each of the identified market segments. VOTs were distinguished between short and long-distance trips, but, due to the complexities of applying these differences in the traffic forecasting model, trip weighted average VOTs were determined across trip distance categories. Table 2 compares the VOTs from the SP and RP surveys for various trip purposes and vehicle classes. The following patterns in the VOTs are apparent:

- The VOTs seem to be in the correct order and the differences between the user segments seem intuitively correct.
- For light vehicles, business trips display the highest VOTs followed by commuters, and Other trips indicating the lowest VOTs. This is similar to international experience.

Table 2: Summary of VOTs by User Segment for N4 Platinum Toll Model

User Segment		High-income VOT (R per hr)		Low-income VOT (R per hr)	
		RP	SP	RP	SP
Light Vehicles					
	Commuters	58	57	34	48
	Business	90	95	90	61
	Other	48	45	32	43
Heavy vehicles					
	2 axles	87	79		
	3-4 axles	116	127		
	5 x axles	126	127		

- Low-income users have lower VOTs than high-income users.
- For heavy vehicles, the larger vehicle classes that pay higher toll fees, display higher VOTs.
- The VOT of commuters is much higher than their average income rate i.e., eighty one per cent higher.
  - The RP and SP VOTs are very similar with a few minor exceptions. The different target populations of the RP and SP surveys could explain these differences. The similar results produced by two independent study teams following different survey approaches generated a lot of confidence in the values of time for the toll income modelling purposes.
- Motorway bonuses indicating the value of safety and convenience offered by toll roads were valued at approximately R14 per hour for light vehicles. Heavy vehi-

cle drivers did not display a significant motorway bonus indicating that they do not value the apparent non-commercial value of freeways in terms of comfort, safety, and convenience.

Results of Gauteng Study

The Gauteng models did not perform very well possibly due to the sensitivities surrounding tolling of urban freeways. Rho-square values on the order of 0.16 were found. In most cases, the coefficients were very significant at a ninety five percent confidence level and higher. The key time and toll fee coefficients for commuters were significant at more than ninety nine percent.

In view of the SP problems experienced regarding road users' sensitivities to tolling, SP data were combined with RP data to obtain more reliable values of time. RP survey data were, therefore, extracted from the Bakwena database for this purpose. RP data for the N17 toll freeway (Springs to Johannesburg) were used as this is the most urbanised existing toll route in Gauteng. The conventional nested RP and SP logit modelling approach was used.
The following results were obtained:

- The differences in the VOT between different trip purposes displayed similar patterns to that of the Platinum study, although the actual VOTs were lower than those of the Platinum study.
- Departure time and number of incidents were significant at more than ninety five percent, providing no evidence to reject the hypothesis that these factors impact on route choice. Earlier departure times, due to traffic congestion on the existing freeway, are perceived negatively by commuters. Commuters would therefore be willing to pay to be able to depart at normal hours.
- The number of incidents on the existing freeway, resulting in long delays and unpredictable arrival times, was significant for both commuters and business users. This factor is also much more important to business users than commuters.
- Income, or proxy for income such as car ownership, was found to be significant, and low-income users displayed lower VOTs than high-income users.
- SP values of time were lower than the RP values, which correlates with the results reported by Bhat and Castelar (2002) for the San Francisco Bay Bridge, also an urban environment. This is in contrast to the results of the Platinum study, where good RP and SP similarities were found, which refers mainly to a rural environment. It seems that these results are caused by typical RP problems that tend to overestimate VOTs, and SP tolling biases that tend to underestimate VOTs. The research by Bhat and Castelar will be worthwhile to pursue in developing countries as well.

Comparison of India and South African results

The SP models in India performed better than those in South Africa. Very good model fits to the data were obtained with Rho-square values ranging between 0.26 and 0.47 for light vehicles, and ranging between 0.34 and 0.57 for heavy vehicles.

No sensitivities to tolling were encountered in India. However, the RP data of the India study did not allow any models to be estimated, because of high correlations between travel times and costs of the tolled and alternative routes, amongst others. Instead, boundary values of time were estimated from the RP data, based on the ratio of the toll fee to travel time saved.

Tables 3 and 4 give the VOTs obtained from the SP and RP surveys respectively. The following conclusions were drawn:

- Values of time related to toll fees and those related to fuel costs were fairly similar in India. Other studies indicated that road users are more willing to pay in terms of fuel cost rather than toll fees, and therefore values of time in terms of toll fees are generally lower than those for fuel costs. This pattern was observed in the case of some user segments.

Table 3: India Values of Time for Light Vehicles (Rupees per hour)

User Segment	Based on Toll Fee SP	Based on Fuel Cost SP	Boundary RP
All	18	18	56
Commuter	14	13	58
Business	19	18	58
Holiday	12	17	50
Other	15	17	50
Low Income (< Rs 20 000)	18		
Medium to High Income (> Rs 20 000)	18		
Low to Medium Income (< Rs 50 000)	17		
High Income (> Rs 50 000)	20		
Short Trips (< 100 minutes)	7		
Long Trips (> 100 minutes)	17		

Table 4: India Values of Time for Heavy Vehicles (Rupees per hour)

User Segment	Toll Fee SP	Fuel Cost SP	Boundary RP
All	19	19	113
Two-axle	21	20	106
Three-axle	12	12	124
Three + Multi-axle	8	8	159
Low Value (< Rs 50 000)	18		
High Value (> Rs 50 000)	31		
Bulk Commodities	18		
Perishable/Processed Commodities	21		
Short Trips (< 100 minutes)	18		
Long Trips (> 100 minutes)	21		

- In general there was not much variation in VOTs of different trip purposes. The VOT of business trips was somewhat higher than for other trip purposes. This trend was similar to the South African studies. The VOT of holiday trips was the lowest, with that of commuter and other trips being the same and somewhat higher than that of holiday trips. This pattern differs from other studies, which indicates higher VOTs for commuter trips than for social/recreational trips.
- As expected, higher income users indicated a higher VOT compared to lower income users, although this difference is not as large as found in South Africa.
- The highest difference between user segments was found between short and long travel time trips, with the VOT of long trips more than double that of short trips. Short trips were probably made more frequently and time savings were less, and therefore users were likely to be less willing to pay a toll for short trips. On face value this trend is opposite to that found by Louviere and Hensher (2000) for Sydney urban trips using a non-linear utility function, which indicated that for a given toll fee, the VOT decreases with trip distance. However, the contexts of the two studies are totally different. The differences in VOT between short and long distance trips in India refers to trips shorter and longer than 100 km, which includes the difference between commuter and business/holiday trips. The Sydney results refer to urban trips ranging from five to ten minutes total trip times. To make a valid comparison, the India data set should be analysed in the same way as the Sydney one, estimating a non-linear utility function for each trip purpose.
- The goodness of fit of the RP models in India was very poor and RP values of time could not be estimated. Instead average RP boundary VOTs were determined, which were found to be double the average SP VOT. When comparing the RP and SP VOTs, one must also consider that the surveys were done in different locations and different techniques were used.

In contrast to the SA studies, the VOTs in India were much lower than average income rates, just opposite to the results indicated by the South Africa studies.

The following results were obtained for heavy vehicles:

- The overall average VOT of heavy vehicles in India was roughly similar to that of light vehicles, although the maximum VOT of different heavy vehicle classes was much higher than the maximum VOT of different light vehicle segments. In the South Africa studies, heavy vehicles indicated a much higher VOT than light vehicles across all market segments. The lower than expected VOT of heavy vehicles supported the responses on the importance rating of route choice factors by respondents, which indicated costs to be much more important than travel time.
- The VOT of larger vehicle classes (three and multiple axles) was lower than that of smaller vehicles (two axles). This pattern was opposite to that found in the South Africa studies, and might have been due to measurement errors.

- The highest difference in VOT between user segments was indicated among low and high value loads. This pattern was also evident among time-sensitive /high-value commodities (perishable and manufactured goods) compared to low-value/non-time-sensitive goods (bulk commodities). The interest on the average value of loads offered a benchmark VOT for heavy vehicles, because capital locked in transit is unproductive and the owner would value this at the cost of borrowing money. Assuming interest of sixteen percent per annum, the average financing cost per hour was much lower than the VOTs of heavy vehicles. Other factors that place a premium on travel time savings, such as customer service and delivery of food products in a fresh state, were therefore more important than financing cost.
- Long trips indicated a higher VOT than shorter trips, which was similar to the trend shown by light vehicles, but not to the same extent.
- Similar to the South Africa studies, the motorway bonus factor of toll roads in India was found to be significant for both light and heavy vehicles. This result supported the attitudinal responses on important factors, e.g., road safety, driver comfort, and safety from crime. This finding differs from the Platinum study with respect to heavy vehicles that indicated a zero motorway bonus.

The motorway bonus was between sixteen and seventeen percent of the average value of time, only slightly lower than for the South Africa studies.

CONCLUSIONS AND RECOMMENDATIONS

This chapter has reviewed the procedures, methods, and results of determining VOTs from RP and SP surveys for the purposes of toll road feasibility studies. The focus is on the challenges faced in the context of developing countries, such as South Africa and India. The two SP studies in South Africa and one in India produced well-performing models and values of time for different market segments, with interesting similarities and differences. A reliable set of values of time for various trip purposes and user segments were established from the Platinum and Gauteng studies that can serve as a useful benchmark for future studies in South Africa. For a first study, good results were achieved in India, although more research is needed to establish a reliable benchmark of values of time for different market segments. Although the main patterns of VOTs for different market segments were found to be very similar to those of international experience, direct comparison with more sophisticated research conducted internationally could not be made because of the different contexts and methods used.

Various survey techniques were employed, and although some worked better than others, they can all be used with fruitful results. The following conclusions are drawn:

- VOTs governing the route choice behaviour of road users were found to be much different than the average income per working hour for light vehicles, or financing costs of freight locked in transit, that is normally used in economic evaluation studies. For the purpose of toll road feasibility studies, it is, therefore, important that VOTs are estimated for each toll road context using SP and RP survey techniques.

- The SP experimental context must be kept simple but realistic, using binary choices as far as possible.
- RP surveys should be conducted as well and combined with the SP data. RP surveys need to be as close as possible to the target market and the socio-economic profile of the target market. The research by Bhat and Castellar seems worthwhile to pursue in developing countries. Identifying an RP choice context, trading off time and cost by the target SP market, seems important for the application of their techniques.
- Focus groups should be used for new concepts unfamiliar to road users.
- Where possible, use of CAPI should be made to relate SP levels to each respondents existing situation, to achieve greater variance in the data, and to perform better quality control.
- In view of possible problems such as 'inertia to change' sample sizes should preferably be more than 100 per market segment.
- Although roadside interviews are the most practical and cost-effective, roadside recruitment and interviews at home or work provide a more ideal SP environment.
- Testing of boundary arrays is important to ensure a range of cost versus time trade-offs.
- Ideally the number of choice scenarios per respondent should be limited to eight or nine. If more choices are required, they should be tested thoroughly, or a block design should be used.
- At least three levels of each variable should be used, and preferably more.
- The availability of dynamic microsimulation models of traffic and formulation of strategic traffic model algorithms allowing direct application of discrete route choice models to traffic models, will hopefully improve the quality of traffic models and their ability to simulate travel behaviour.
- The application of variable VOTs as a function of toll fee and trip distance to network traffic models needs to be evaluated. The capability to apply discrete choice models directly to network traffic models seems to make this possible.

Various factors that significantly impact on the value of time were quantified:

- Market segments, in terms of passenger versus goods, trip purpose, and vehicle class;
- Income and socioeconomic status of light vehicles drivers;
- The level of congestion experienced and number of incidents causing delays;
- Urban versus rural toll roads, also related to the frequency of trips;
- Departure time;
- Length of the trip; and
- Factors relating to the standard of the road, safety, and convenience.

It is recommended that further research be conducted on the following aspects:

- Including more variables impacting on route choice as a result of tolling, in addition to time and cost, as well as interaction with other choices such as ride-sharing, mode choice, and even changing location of residence and workplace.
- Solutions to the problems experienced with SP biases relating to the sensitivities towards urban toll routes in South Africa need to be investigated. The research by Bhat and Castellar seems to offer a potential solution, but it needs to be evaluated in a developing country context.
- Evaluating alternative methods to obtain more reliable RP route choice data from road users. It is expected that face-to-face interviews, in an unhurried environment, would give better results. The use of aids to assist the respondent, such as maps indicating route distances and travel times, should also be evaluated.
- Direct comparison of RP and SP values of time by applying both methods on the same sample of road users in the context of an existing toll road. Again, the research by Bhat and Castellar needs to be evaluated in a developing country context.
- The potential of the new generation network traffic models allowing direct application of discrete choice models developed from SP surveys needs to be exploited, including the application of variable VOT functions.
- It is recommended that the national roads agencies in South Africa and India continue to support comprehensive SP and RP studies for all future toll road studies in order to build up a comprehensive data and knowledge base.
- The completion of the N4 Platinum toll route provides an unique opportunity to conduct after surveys and test both RP and SP models on the same target market.
- It is appreciated that the technique used to estimate values of time was based on the assumption that road users display compensatory utility maximisation route choices. This assumption should be tested to determine whether non-compensatory models yield better results. However, this will require a similar toll traffic modelling approach as well.

REFERENCES

Abdel-Aty, M.A., R. Kitamura and P.P. Jovanis (1995). Investigating Effect of Travel Time Variability on Route Choice Using Repeated Measurement Stated Preference Data, *Transportation Research Record No. 1493*, 39-45.

Bhat, C.R. and S. Castelar (2002). A Unified Mixed Logit Framework For Modeling Revealed and Stated Preferences: Formulation and Application to Congestion Pricing Analysis in the San Francisco Bay Area, *Transportation Research B*, **36**, 593-616.

Bovy, H.L. and M.A. Bradley (1985). Route Choice Analyzed with Stated Preference Approaches, *Transportation Research Record No. 1037*, 11-20.

Bradley, M.A. and H.F. Gunn (1990). Stated Preference Analysis of Values of Travel Time in the Netherlands, *Transportation Research Record No. 1285*, 78-88.

Cal Poly State University (2000). *Continuation Study to Evaluate the Impacts of the SR91 Value-Priced Express Lanes*, Final Report to State of California Department of Transportation, San Luis Obispo, 102 pp.

Del Mistro, R. and T. Arentze (2002). Applicability of Stated Preference for Mode Choice Studies Among Less Literate Commuters, *Journal of the South African Institution of Civil Engineers*, **44** (4), 16-24.

Florian, M. (2004). Network equilibrium models for analysing toll highways, Paper presented to the South African EMME/2 Conference, Pretoria, INRO.

Louviere, J.J. and D.A. Hensher (2000). Combining Sources of Preference Data, Resource Paper for IATBR 2000 9th International Association for Travel Behaviour Research Conference, Gold Coast, Queensland, Australia, 2-7 July.

Louviere, J.J., D.A. Hensher and J. Swait, DS. (2000). *Stated Choice Methods. Analysis and Application*, Cambridge University Press, Cambridge.

PWV Consortium (2000). *Gautrans Toll Strategy. Toll Modelling Results*, Report to Gautrans, 134 pp.

Stewart Scott (2000). *N4 Platinum Toll Road Contract. Revealed Preference Study for the Traffic Modelling Project*, Report to the Bakwena Platinum Corridor Consortium, 134 pp.

Stewart Scott (2001). *Value of Time from Revealed and Stated Preference Study*, Working Document No. 4 submitted to Gauteng SuperHighways Consortium, 17 pp.

Stewart Scott (2002). *DHV National Highway Corridor, Public Private Partnership Project for the National Highways Authority of India: Stated Preference Study to Determine Values of Time*, 20 pp.

Van Der Reis, A.P. and M.C. Lombard (2001). Multi-Cultural and Multi-Language Surveys, with Special Reference to the African Experience. In: *Transport Survey Quality and Innovation* (P.R. Stopher and P.M. Jones, eds), 191-208, Pergamon Press, Oxford.

Van Zyl, N.J.W., M.C. Lombard and T. Lamprecht (2001). The Success of Stated Preference Techniques in Evaluating Travel Options for Less Literate Transport Users in a Developing Country with Specific Reference to South Africa, paper presented to the International Conference on Transport Survey Quality and Innovation, Kruger National Park, South Africa.

Wardman, M. (1990). *A Review of British Evidence on the Valuations of Time and Service Quality*, University of Leeds Working Paper 525, Leeds, 62 pp.

26

INVESTMENT-GRADE SURVEYS

Johanna Zmud, NuStats, Austin, Texas, USA

INTRODUCTION

This workshop[37] examined the challenges and opportunities that investment-grade studies bring to travel survey design, implementation, and analysis. Investment-grade studies provide traffic and revenue forecasts, which are characterised by the level of their accuracy, reliability, and credibility, for toll facilities and new transport services. An investment grade study is the last evaluation to be conducted for a toll facility project before going to the bond market, to raise capital for the construction and implementation of the project. Toll authorities issuing bonds can (and have) suffered significant economic damage if the traffic and revenue estimated does not materialise. This summary of critical issues relating to investment-grade surveys is based primarily on the contents of the workshop resource and offered papers and the discussion among the workshop participants.

INTRODUCTION TO THE ISSUE

Throughout the world in both developed and developing counties, there has been increased interest in toll road planning and construction as governments explore alternative methods of financing transport infrastructure and as tolling has become an attractive option for managing traffic demand on increasingly congested highways. Highway

---

[37] Workshop Participants: Gustavo Baez (USA), Laverne Dimitrov (South Africa), Thomas Haupt (Germany), Marcela Munizaga (Chile), Gerd Sammer (Austria), Klaas Van Zyl (South Africa), Johanna Zmud (USA).

infrastructure traditionally has been funded through general government budgets and dedicated taxes and fees rather than tolls. However, scarce traditional funding sources have led to increasing interest in toll roads as an alternative way of meeting highway needs. Several factors will continue to feed the global interest in toll facilities, including a worldwide trend toward commercialisation and privatisation of state-owned facilities; the success of toll road facilities in raising capital; and advances in tolling technology, making tolling more efficient and convenient.

Toll projects typically rely on capital markets for their funds and, as such, they bring highway service into the market economy. The economics of toll road projects vary widely depending on their function, physical characteristics, and traffic profile. The predictability of market demand is a particularly sensitive variable for toll facility economics, and this issue is the intersection point between toll facility economics and travel surveys.

MARKET DEMAND

Market demand for toll roads is measured in terms of actual or expected traffic levels, predictability of expected traffic, and willingness of users to pay tolls. Determining the elasticity of demand for toll facilities typically involves analysis of trip purpose, driver income, congestion levels, travel time savings, the availability of alternative travel routes, among other factors. Each factor is used as an input in the travel demand forecast model. The output of such models is critical in demonstrating a revenue stream of sufficient magnitude and predictability to obtain financing. The travel demand forecasting process involves the creation of travel demand or 'trip tables' that identify the demand for mobility between different origin and destination pairs and then an assignment model that distributes those trips on to the travel network by mode based on the location, capacity, and travel characteristics of its different components. Toll models are typically quite complex multimodal models; most important, as with all models, a toll model is only as good as the data going into it.

INVESTMENT-GRADE SURVEYS

To be successful, toll facilities must generate revenues sufficient to cover debt service and other project costs. Historical data have indicated varying success of toll facilities in covering their debt service. Some analysts have attributed poor economic performance to overly optimistic traffic and revenue estimates.

The concept of investment-grade surveys has been introduced into the travel surveys lexicon to account for the high importance placed on requirements for accuracy, reliability, and credibility of survey data that will be used to garner an investment-grade rating on a toll facility project's debt. It is critical for transport agencies, investors, and bond rating agencies to have reliable means of assessing toll road demand and revenue. Recently, bond rating agencies have become more conservative in their ratings process and are looking more closely at the data and methodologies upon which the forecasts are based. Unfortunately, there are few, if any 'standards' for the criteria that define a traffic and revenue study as 'investment-grade'.

CRITICAL ISSUES RAISED AT WORKSHOP

Because the challenges and opportunities inherent in designing, implementing, and analysing investment-grade surveys are relatively new dilemmas faced by travel survey researchers, the workshop participants focused on the key issues that need to be considered and require further research. After much discussion, it was resolved that the key issues could be organised into nine categories as identified below.

1.   Value of Time

The decision of whether or not to use a toll facility is based largely on the value of time (VOT). The literature related to the value of travel time is extensive, and there are many 'rules of thumb' that have evolved from this literature. However, true understanding of the factors influencing value of time and the variations in its estimation still require further research. In addition, value of time estimates are primarily derived from data captured through stated preference (or response) surveys, which are themselves an area rich in the need for further study. The issues related to deriving and applying value of time estimates are as follows:

- SP (VOT) should be based on RP behaviour and distribution (not mean);
- RP (VOT) may be used as a back up;
- Market segmentation is critical – socioeconomic segments and travel segments (time of day / direction);
- Other options (mode choice) should be tested;
- Congestion effects must be accounted for;
- Impact of electronic toll collection is unknown;
- Need to know if VOT changes over time (e.g., with income); and
- Need to know the effect of marginal utilities of time versus cost.

2.   Route Choice

Reliable estimates of toll facility traffic and revenue cannot be done in a vacuum, outside of issues in modelling the route selection process. Perceived travel times and a combination of other factors determine the final route choice, which in turn influence the decision to use a toll facility. Issues raised in connection with route choice were:

- Inclusion of variables impacting route choice;

- Inclusion of non-time/cost factors (e.g., subjective: safety, continuity, fear, reliability);
- What is the effect of route information system; and
- What influence does electronic toll collection have?

3.   Social Impacts of Tolling

Just as any roads, toll roads can have significant social impacts in the manner and location of their construction and operation. These can be both positive and negative. The workshop participants felt it was important to consider such social impacts when estimating traffic or revenue. Specific topics that were raised included:

- High cost of road construction versus affordability of tolls to road users;
- Trade-off of public transport or highway infrastructure expansion;
- Need for total cost/benefit analysis in the evaluation (sound investment?) as opposed to a purely financial benefit (does it make money?); and
- Need to have a parallel free road

4.   Criteria of Financiers (Bond Market)

Credit rating agencies play a key role in evaluating the risks associated with toll facility investments. While the agencies have been making attempts to make the rating process more transparent in recent years, their methodologies are largely an 'unknown.' Key issues relating to investment-grade surveys are:

- Importance of base year versus long-term revenue;
- Definition of 'accuracy' of the revenue forecasts;
- Requirements: data types and survey methods;
- Traffic counts to occupancy, variance over time of day, seasons, Average Annual Daily Traffic (AADT);
- Speed delay, travel time measures; and
- Need sufficient funds to finance proper (rigorous) traffic and revenue studies.

5.   Relationship between Finance and Quality

In the economic evaluation of the road scheme, it is vital that an accurate estimate of travel on the road is produced. Yet, even when a new road is built and is not tolled, the estimation of traffic and revenue is not a simple matter, because of the complexities of interaction between different parts of the network, estimating values of time, etc. However, with the additional complexity of tolls, forecasting is more complex still. However, how comprehensive does the forecast need to be and how far ranging must the sensitivity tests be to consider the robustness of the proposed financial arrangements?

There are then inherent trade-offs that must be considered between financing and quality. The workshop began to identify the factors that determine such trade-offs, including:

- Who is the client (government, concessionaire, private sector, bond market)?
- Sharing of risks (private/ government).

6.   Heavy Vehicles

Heavy trucks take their toll on a region's environment and road network. Truck traffic contributes to air pollution and, insofar as increased truck traffic has to be accommodated by highway construction, to the loss of open space. Truck traffic is also an important contributor to wear and tear and congestion on the road network. Therefore, it is important to capture the heavy truck market demand for toll facilities, as well as their value of time and/or pricing elasticities. Issues specific to heavy vehicles were:

- Sensitivity to tolling;
- Who makes the decision to pay the toll (driver, manager);
- Are bigger companies more sophisticated in route choices;
- How much control does company has over driver route choice;
- Heavy vehicles do most of damage to road surface; therefore, must they pay more?
- Consider heavy-vehicle only tolls; and
- Does truck traffic discourage passenger vehicles on toll facility?

7.   Market Segmentation

Market segmentation schemes employed in establishing the investment-grade survey populations need to accommodate the various factors that have been shown to impact values of time significantly. Survey designers may need to consider 'new' market segments. Considerations relating to market segmentation include:

- Capture non-time and non-cost data influences;
- Capture current social-economic / demographic data;
- Use secondary data if current and good quality; and
- Do not borrow VOTs.

8.   Modelling Issues

To be successful, toll facilities must generate revenues sufficient to cover debt service and other project costs. Project economics are determined by a number of factors, including the toll facility's function, physical characteristics, and market demand. The predictability of market demand is a particularly complex variable for toll facility economics because of the difficult of forecasting traffic and revenues on previously un-tolled highways. Experience with this has been quite variable. Improving the travel demand modelling process for toll facilities is a critical issue. In addition, the data required as inputs to the models are significant for travel survey researches. Modelling issues raised by workshop participants included:

- How to incorporate subjective data (SP models can assist);
- Formalising the distribution of VOT and other parameters;
- Specifying the output level of confidence (how to validate models and determine confidence levels);
- Determining guidelines for appropriate assignment models;
- Need for improved models (dynamic stochastic, microsimulation, process data); and
- Sensitivity analysis of base year, long-term forecasts (Monte Carlo simulation, demographic projections, traffic).

9.   Quality Guidelines

'Quality' as it applies to investment-grade surveys is an evolving concept, because criteria for what constitutes an investment-grade survey is still ill-defined. Workshop participants thought it was the right time to begin to formulate guidelines and checklists on many issues that need to be considered in the pursuit of quality objectives in the execution of surveys to collect data as inputs to travel demand models for toll facilities. The focus of the guidelines would be on how to assure quality through effective and appropriate design of an investment-grade survey from inception through to data evaluation, dissemination, and documentation. It was expected that such quality guidelines would be useful to those engaged in the planning and design of surveys and other statistical projects, as well as to those who evaluate and analyse the outputs of these projects. Issues relating to quality guidelines include:

- State of the art survey methods and data quality (standards via NCHRP 8-37);
- Results must be reproducible;
- Methods and models must be transparent;
- Good documentation is required;
- To achieve confidence levels of output (toll revenue forecast) need to set confidence levels for input;
- Assess trade-offs in base year (short term) and long-term forecast accuracy;
- A peer review independent auditor is needed; and
- Sufficient funds are needed for survey work.

27

PROCESS DATA FOR UNDERSTANDING AND MODELLING TRAVEL BEHAVIOUR

Mark Bradley, Santa Barbara, California, USA

INTRODUCTION

In making 'the case for qualitative methods in transportation research', Weston (2004) points out that 'qualitative and quantitative research methods are not two approaches to answering the same question, they are two approaches to two different *types* of questions'. In general terms, quantitative research is best for answering the 'who', 'what', 'where', 'when' and 'how' questions, while qualitative research is best for answering the 'why' questions, while also providing a deeper understanding of the other questions. For example, in addition to asking *how* a person travelled to their destination for a given trip, one could ask *why* the person chose to travel in that manner, as well as *how* the person came to that decision. The latter question implies a longer time horizon – how did the person's decision process unfold over time in order to make a particular choice.

While qualitative research methods are certainly needed and valuable, it may not be constructive to define them always in contrast to quantitative methods. Perhaps there are hybrid approaches that combine the strengths of both approaches to address questions that neither approach by itself can answer. The remainder of this chapter is devoted to sketching out such a hybrid approach for the collection of process data. Because process data is a new term that is not widely used in transport research, it needs to be given a working definition. In this chapter, process data refers to a combination of quantitative and qualitative information, collected systematically to reveal individual travel choice processes over time. Such data can be used both to expand the scope of knowledge for making policy decisions and to expand the scope of models of household travel behaviour. Given that the definition above can be interpreted quite broadly, it is perhaps best to define process data through the use of examples and contrasts.

WHY COLLECT PROCESS DATA?

Travel demand modelling often seems to be stuck in a loop. The type of data available limits our models, while the data collection is generally designed to meet the specifications of other recent surveys and models. At least that is the situation for the major regional household surveys that are collected as the basis for most of the travel demand models in the United States. Even though the recent forecasting systems may include sophisticated activity-based microsimulation models, those advanced models are typically based on the same type of trip diary data that have been collected for decades. Although the survey instruments, retrieval methods, and geographical precision of the data have been greatly improved, the *type* of data collected has not changed substantially – it is still usually restricted to quantitative or simple categorical data on choice outcomes, so-called revealed preference (RP) data.

The situation for stated preference (SP) data, based on choice outcomes in hypothetical situations, is much the same. While the use of hypothetical choice situations opens the door to a wide range of possibilities in terms of the type of data collected, these possibilities have largely remained unexplored (although some interesting exceptions are discussed in the third section). Over the years, SP data collection techniques have been tailored to provide data that mimic RP data as closely as possible in assuming that RP data is the best benchmark of external validity. As a result, while SP data share many of the strengths of RP data, they tend to share many of the limitations as well.

Much of the qualitative research done in transportation research is carried out in order to improve the design of quantitative survey instruments. Examples are preliminary focus groups or personal interviews to test the wording of concepts and questions and to test whether 'all' important factors have been included in the main survey design. However, designers of large-scale surveys typically try to avoid the types of issues that must be answered with open-ended questions or that require much probing by the interviewer or reflection by the respondent. As a result, the only qualitative information is provided by the preliminary survey itself, and the focus of such surveys tends to be limited to the point that they rarely provide new insights about the dynamic processes underlying the choice behaviour of interest. With very small sample sizes, any interesting new information is typically in the form of anecdotal evidence and difficult to generalise to a wider population. On the other hand, there have been many examples of qualitative research in transport research that do not suffer from these limitations, and there is certainly scope for many more (Weston 2004).

If most of the RP, SP and qualitative data that we collect are designed to fit into the same cross-sectional quantitative modelling framework, why is this a problem? From a modeller's perspective, it is a problem because even our best econometric choice models explain only a fraction of the variation that is found in actual choice behaviour. There are many types of additional information that could be used to improve the explanatory power of the models. Sources of unexplained variation are usually assumed to relate either to the characteristics of particular individuals or to the characteristics of particular historical choice contexts. This reflects somewhat the age-old dichotomy of 'nature versus nurture'. In modelling terms, 'nature' is reflected by concepts such as heterogeneity, individual-specific taste variation, variety seeking, and risk aversion. Relevant types of data are those on attitudes, perceptions and personality traits. The 'nurture' side is reflected in concepts like state dependence, path dependence, habit, and inertia. Relevant data include those on past choice histories, important events and transitions, habits, and constraints. Both common sense and available evidence indicate that both individual-specific and context-specific differences are important, and that all of these types of data can be useful in explaining choice behaviour.

As is typical in travel demand modelling, we have tended to resort to complex econometric techniques to avoid having to use 'soft' data on unobservable phenomena such as attitudes, information, and perception. An example is the use of complex model specifications, such as mixed-logit and generalised extreme value (GEV) models, to estimate distributions of individual-specific differences (e.g., taste variation) across the population. These new methods are promising ways of offering better predictive validity, but it is difficult to relate the additional statistical evidence to other variables and thus translate the findings into language that policy-makers – and even many modellers – can understand. The collection of additional process data would complement these new estimation techniques by offering new covariates to help explain the differences that are identified across the population.

Another example is the collection of longitudinal panel survey data in order to estimate dynamic choice models that can sort out the effects of heterogeneity (individual-specific effects) from those of state dependence (history-specific effects). Despite the avid interest of researchers in panel surveys and dynamic models, their use in travel demand research does not appear to be increasing. Some possible reasons are the cost of data collection, the complexity of weighting the data to account for various survey biases, and the difficulty of estimating statistically correct dynamic models. Another possible reason is that the data collected at each point of the survey tend to be limited to the same type of quantitative data that is collected in most purely cross-sectional surveys, resulting in the same lack of explanatory power as mentioned above for advanced cross-sectional models. The models can provide statistical evidence on the magnitude of certain dynamic phenomena, but are limited in their ability to explain the phenomena in terms of concepts directly related to the underlying dynamic choice process, such as information acquisition, attitude formation, and cognitive perception biases. Collection of data related to such processes would provide additional variables to make dynamic models more informative.

Given the potential advantages, why are we so reluctant to use process-related variables in our models? Even if the explanatory power of the models would be greatly improved, it is generally assumed that the improved models would not be useful for long-range forecasting, because we cannot predict distributions of all of the input variables in future populations. The need for long-term forecasts tends to limit our models to a few basic population variables such as household size, employment, income, and age, for which we can obtain or generate some long-term forecasts. This paradigm has effectively prevented the introduction of any additional variables related to attitudes, perceptions, information, constraints, habits, or past histories, all of which could be very useful in guiding policies. Because we assume that we would not be able to use such variables in our regional forecasting models, we have not been adamant about collecting the data that would be necessary. If this logic could be reversed, we would first collect the data and prove its usefulness in the modelling process, and then adapt our forecasting procedures in order to accommodate it – ideally by using different types of models for different policy purposes rather than relying on a single long-range forecasting model for everything. As the following examples show, many in academia are already leading the way in collecting and using new types of data to model choice behaviour. A greater interest in and contribution to that work in the wider policy and modelling communities would be of benefit to everyone[38].

A REVIEW OF PROTOTYPES AND EXAMPLES

In this section, the focus is on research approaches that meet all or most of the following criteria:

- Use a structured, systematic survey process;
- Collect both quantitative and qualitative information;
- Collect data on both decision outcomes and processes;
- Collect data on both objective and subjective choice factors; and
- Become more feasible and/or attractive with recent advances in survey technologies.

'Intelligent Travel and Activity Diaries'

One of the first approaches with these characteristics to be used in travel demand research was the 'situational' survey approach, reported by Brög and Erl (1980) and by Goulias *et al.* (1998). This approach begins with a description of actual behaviour, similar to traditional household travel surveys, but then uses the reported behaviour as a basis for asking more in-depth, interactive questions that elicit perceptions and other subjective factors. Many applications of this technique have suggested that individual-specific subjective factors are much more important in driving choice processes than is generally realised. On the basis of such findings, Brög has developed the 'individualised marketing' approach, described in John and Brög (2001).

---

[38] For a more in-depth discussion of many of the issues raised above, refer to the chapter from the Workshop on Modellers' Needs from the 5th Conference on Travel Survey Methods (Arentze *et al.*, 2000).

Some of the pioneering research into the dynamic processes behind household travel behaviour was carried out at the Transport Studies Unit at Oxford in the 1970s and 80s (Jones *et al.*, 1983). One particular outcome of that research was The Household Activity and Travel Simulator (HATS) (Jones, 1979). This innovative survey method uses data from a typical travel and activity diary survey, and lays it out on a schematic colour-coded board showing each household member's trips and activities on a timeline. Important constraints can also be shown schematically. The household members are then asked how they would adjust their activity schedules as a result of specific changes such as shifts in work hours, parking charges, retail hours, transit services, road pricing, etc. With the advent of portable laptop computers for household interviews, a computerised version of this method (ATAQ) was created and tested in Adelaide, Australia (Jones *et al.*, 1987).

A key feature of the HATS approach is that, like the best customised SP research, it uses a hypothetical framework structured around observed choices. Any stated changes can be recorded in this same framework, making the resulting data amenable to quantitative analysis. In contrast to most SP research, however, the survey structure is open-ended enough to allow for collection of a variety of additional data on the process that respondents go through while deciding on changes to their activity patterns, including which alternatives are considered and then rejected. Unfortunately, all of the surveys done with this approach have been quite small-scale and exploratory in nature, so that its wider potential in providing new types of data for modelling has never been fully tested. It has, however, inspired a number of related survey approaches, including the CATS survey method which is focused more specifically on the allocation and use of cars within households (Lee-Gosselin, 1990).

As personal computers have become lighter and less expensive, it has become possible to put hardware in respondents' homes and have them complete computerised versions of travel and activity diaries, as opposed to completing diaries by hand. One example of this approach is the SMASH method from Eindhoven University (Ettema *et al.*, 1995), one of the data sources used to create the ALBATROSS activity-based model system. Another example is the CHASE method (Doherty and Miller, 2000). In these methods, the respondent can fill in planned activities before the diary days, and then adjust those plans over time. When the respondent eventually fills in the actual schedule for the diary day, some of the travel and activities will have been pre-planned and done according to plan, some will have been pre-planned but adjusted at the last moment, while others will not have been pre-planned at all. The computer algorithm is clever enough to identify each type of situation and ask appropriate questions regarding the decision process that led to the schedule adjustment, new trip/activity or cancelled trip/activity. From this type of data, Doherty (2003) was able to show that our typical classification of activities by purpose is often not adequate to predict which activities will be given priority in the activity scheduling process. On the basis of such analyses, we may be able to identify a few key questions regarding timing and location flexibility that should be added to the telephone retrieval stage of activity diary surveys.

'Information Acceleration'

Another important example is the *Information Acceleration* (IA) approach, developed at the MIT Sloan School of Management. Compared to most SP-type approaches, this method moves more fully from a *hypothetical* choice environment to a *simulated* choice environment. The emphasis is on the information search process in contexts when people are faced with new and unfamiliar choice alternatives. In order to investigate the purchase decision process for electric vehicles (Urban *et al.*, 1996a), respondents were allowed to request various types of information about the vehicles, including mock-ups of television commercials, newspaper and magazine reviews, word-of-mouth opinions, and dealer sales pitches. A test ride in a driving simulator was also available. By systematically varying the content of each of these simulated information sources, the importance of each piece of information in determining the simulated purchase could be measured. The information search process itself could also be recorded and analysed, a possibility lacking in stated preference experiments, where the information given to each respondent is pre-determined.

Another interesting application of IA was carried out by Walker (1994) to look at the influence of automated traveller information systems (ATIS) on route choice and departure time decisions. Information about highway congestion levels and travel times was available to respondents in the form of mock-ups of real-time telephone messages and in-vehicle messages. General information about the ATIS system and how to use it was available as mock-ups of newspaper articles, printed brochures, and word-of-mouth. Perceptions and intended decisions were measured both before and after the information search process. Then, the respondent entered a travel simulator, in which he or she experienced the 'actual' simulated congestion and travel times resulting from the decision. In contrast to infrequent decisions such as vehicle purchases, traveller information systems can be used on a repeated basis. So, in the ATIS context, it was possible to apply the IA approach in an iterative framework and study the learning process by measuring post-travel changes in perceptions and attitudes, as well as their influence on the next round of information search and decision-making.

The IA approach requires a large investment of time from both the survey designers and the respondents. Due to its expense and its usefulness in the context of new product development, the method has been used mostly for corporate market research, where most of the results have been kept proprietary. Nevertheless, Urban *et al.* (1996b) were able to provide an overview of various applications, as well as the results of tests of the validity of the quantitative results. This is one of the few survey techniques that has been able to provide qualitative insights about dynamic search and decision processes, while also providing useful quantitative forecasting models. As computer and Internet technology for creating simulated choice environments becomes easier to use, the feasibility and affordability of this type of survey method should continue to improve.

'Intensive Market Monitoring'

Another area of growing interest is in studies that look specifically at the effect of mar‐
keting policies to influence travel behaviour. As opposed to 'hard' policies to change in‐
frastructure or service levels, these studies concentrate on 'soft' policies that use infor‐
mation and marketing techniques to influence peoples' awareness and perceptions of
the existing options. Jones and Sloman (2003) describe a pair of European Commission
(EC) projects to look at such policies. The INPHORMM project uses a conceptualisa‐
tion of behavioural change based on a process of 'five As': (1) *awareness* of a problem,
(2) *acceptance* of a need for change, (3) a change in *attitudes* toward choice alternatives,
(4) *action* to initiate a change, and (5) *assimilation* of this new behaviour into everyday
life. A follow-on project, TAPESTRY, extends the framework to look more at longer-
term dynamics. The last three 'As' are divided into separate elements highlighting the
dynamic components: (a) change in attitudes becomes change in perceptions and (re‐
)evaluation of the options, (b) action to initiate a change becomes making a new deci‐
sion and then trying out the new decision in terms of experimental behaviour, and (c)
assimilation of the new behaviour becomes longer term adoption of habitual behaviour,
as well as feeding back as learning to influence awareness, acceptance, and attitudes.

After developing a useful conceptual framework, the EC studies depended on various
site-specific monitoring studies and opinion and attitude surveys to gauge the effects of
specific policy measures. When attempting to translate these results solely to the UK
context, Jones and Sloman raise some crucial issues regarding the results: Are they
transferable across regions? Are the policies synergistic or redundant when applied in
combination? The authors conclude that, to answer such questions, 'our conceptual
models of travel behaviour need to be expanded to recognise more fully these various
subjective elements of travel decision making', and that 'one of the key limitations from
a research perspective is lack of data. … In particular, stated preference exercises need
to be more sophisticated, in at least two respects: in the treatment of information defi‐
ciency and uncertainty, …, and in their recognition of respondent's interest in, or will‐
ingness to consider, a change in behaviour'. The IA approach and the
HATS/ATAQ/CATS approach described above are extensions of SP survey methods in
these directions, while the SMASH/CHASE family of approaches forms the basis of a
similar extension of RP survey methods.

Of course, whenever possible it is desirable to use an actual choice environment rather
than a simulated one. An example of such a study is described by Sheehan (1999). In
this study, a 'quasi-longitudinal survey was administered over a four month period to
assess dynamics in an individual's learning and valuing response to the CarLink car
sharing innovation over time'. Different educational media were distributed to respon‐
dents at three points in time, with an identical questionnaire on perceptions and atti‐
tudes completed at recruitment and after each of the three educational media, followed
by final focus groups and a stated intentions questionnaire regarding use of the car shar‐
ing system. The same questionnaires were administered to a control group, who did not
receive the educational media. In this study, the analysis was limited to straightforward
binary hypothesis testing and descriptive analyses. The study framework, however,

could easily be extended to include predictive modelling of both the stated intention to use the car share system and the actual (RP) decision whether or not to use the system, as influenced by receiving various combinations of the information sources. In other words, such experimental policy introductions provide an ideal opportunity to carry out a 'real world' version of the Information Acceleration market simulation method.

Others

While the focus above is on a few specific lines of research, a wide variety of additional studies have been done that have yielded types of data that would also be very useful in a more comprehensive process data framework. These include:

- Studies of choice set consideration and formation (Fiorenzo-Catalano *et al.*, 2003);
- Mode choice segmentation methods based on attitudinal statements (Outwater *et al.*, 2003);
- Relationships between vehicle choice, attitudes, and personality traits (Collantes and Mokhtarian, 2002); and
- Direct and innovative questioning on the desirability of travel (Handy *et al.*, 2003).

Clifton and Handy (2001) provide additional examples and ideas for the use of qualitative methods.

SOME ISSUES TO CONSIDER

Some might think it optimistic to assume that any single modelling approach could accommodate all of the various types of process data mentioned in the preceding section, along with all of the more conventional variables found in existing models. From a modeller's perspective, however, a model is just a method of using (and sometimes generating) theories and statistics to reproduce measurements and observations. In other words, if we can measure or record it, we can model it. From this perspective, the crucial question is to what extent is it possible to obtain accurate and realistic data on process variables from surveys? In the next section, we step back and look at this question in a more critical light.

Realism and Validity

In SP research, there has been a long-running debate about the external validity of choice data derived from hypothetical contexts. There have been dozens of papers in marketing research and transport research investigating the statistical properties of various SP survey components, but such studies are generally tests of internal validity.

True tests of external validity are less common, and there are no conclusive results to report – see Louviere *et al.* (2000) for the most comprehensive discussion of the research. One of the critical determinants of the validity of SP data is the level of clarity and realism with which the survey can be customised, worded, and presented to the respondent. These issues have been discussed less often in the literature, partly because these aspects of design are as much an art as a science. Some discussion can be found, however, in Bradley (1988), Lee-Gosselin (1996), and Faivre d'Arcier (2000).

A technique such as Information Acceleration (IA) that simulates the choice environment in more detail than most SP surveys will seem more realistic to the respondents. Thus, the validity of the data should be improved. On the other hand, the survey requires more thought from the respondent and increases the respondent burden. On balance, it seems that as long as the simulated choice environment is realistic and detailed enough to allow the respondent to follow what feels like a natural, unforced choice process, the resulting simulated choices will also be realistic. In fact, IA is one type of hypothetical survey where providing more information will only make the respondents' job easier because each respondent only looks at the information that he or she wishes to.

Instrument Effects on Process

It is probably unrealistic to hope to create a completely objective, realistic survey method to collect detailed process data. Even in methods like CHASE (Doherty and Miller, 2000), where all the responses correspond to actual trips and activities, it is inevitable that the attention that the survey focuses on certain aspects of behaviour will influence the actual behaviour to some extent. The more integrated the survey is with the behaviour, as it unfolds through time, the more likely this influence is to occur. On the other hand, if the survey is not integrated with the choice process through time, then it will either be completely hypothetical (before the actual choice), or else be completely *post hoc*, at which point the respondents' perceptions, awareness and attitudes may already have been influenced by the choices carried out.

The last issue raises an interesting question: Are *post hoc* surveys, based on recollection of actual choices, likely to give us a more accurate picture of decision processes than are pre-choice surveys based on hypothetical situations? Because most of our existing travel surveys indeed rely on post-choice recollection, this is a crucial question, and one that is impossible to answer without empirical evidence. Ideally, we could avoid the question altogether by administering the survey in periods before, during <u>and</u> after the choices, as is done in CHASE and is simulated in many IA applications, but that may not be realistic for many surveys.

Because process data may deal with quite subtle and complex aspects of behaviour, to what extent can these aspects be revealed in simulated environments? From the viewpoint of traditional cognitive psychology, people learn through actual experience, so only 'real world' experiments are likely to be valid. From the viewpoint of social learning theory (Bandura, 1977), however, people also learn and act through example and through imagination. In a sense, people already make many decisions based on hypothetical outcomes that they imagine may occur. Once the person actually tries an alternative, the actual outcomes will influence the imagined ones for later choices. There is always an interplay going on between inner experience and outer reality.

Social marketing theory (Andreasen, 1995) provides similar insights about the evolution of experience and perceptions, also observing that many people adopt new types of behaviour slowly over time in order to avoid anxiety that might be caused by too sudden a disruption. It may be difficult to capture such a slow adaptation process in a simulated choice environment that is collapsed in time. This fact would argue toward administering repeated shorter simulations over more 'natural' time intervals. Mahmassani and Herman (1990) were the first to use such an approach in transport, conducting day-to-day interactive simulations of commuters' departure time decisions. In most cases, such an approach would greatly increase survey costs and attrition rates, except perhaps in cases where a respondent panel already exists. The possibility of administering simulated choice environments over the Internet would make repeated surveys over time much more feasible. With fast Internet connects, respondents can view videos, hear audio clips, run travel simulators – nearly everything that was done in the Information Acceleration surveys of ten years ago could now be done on-line.

Objective versus Subjective Perspectives

Another philosophical question that arises is whether or not people are capable of telling us about the true underlying reasons for their behaviour. In travel behaviour research, we use insights from various branches of applied psychology, including behavioural psychology, cognitive psychology, and environmental psychology (Garling, *et al.*, 2002). One area of psychology that is rarely considered is depth psychology, based on the well-known research and theories of Freud, Lacan, Jung, and others. A basic tenet of depth psychology is that much of the motivation ('drive') underlying our behaviour is unconscious, especially to ourselves. If this is so, respondents cannot always tell us accurately why they make certain choices, unless perhaps they first undergo many hours of psychoanalysis. This viewpoint would argue for a survey approach that concentrates on asking about perceptions, attitudes, experiences, etc., but lets the statistical analyst sort out how and why these factors influence the behavioural process rather than taking respondents' explanation of their behaviour for granted.

It is interesting that a similar debate also occurs in other areas of sociology. In the sociology of religion, for example, this is referred to as the 'insider/outsider' problem (McCutcheon, 1999). Some sociologists and anthropologists, often called 'reductionists', believe that religious behaviour can only be studied from the outside through observation, because those that adhere to a religion are too caught up in it to reflect on it objectively. At the other extreme are those, sometimes called 'romantics', who believe that *only* those who are 'inside' of a religion can make accurate observations about it. Most researchers fall somewhere between those two extreme viewpoints, and one would expect the same to be true regarding researchers of travel behaviour. Anyone who travels is an 'insider' to some extent, although different people face vastly different travel situations. It may be enough that researchers avoid placing too much weight on either their own explanation or the respondents' explanation of behavioural processes, and try to design surveys so that both can be explored.

Goulias (2001) lays out a similar dichotomy in comparing 'positivist' to 'non-positivist' epistemologies underlying different qualitative data collection approaches. Like most of our theories and models, data collection in travel behaviour research is mainly based on the positivist view, assuming the existence of an objective and unique reality that can be understood completely through analysis. Although we must keep one foot within this paradigm to produce useful quantitative tools, we will also need to step partially outside it if we want to achieve a more complete understanding of the subtlety and variety of travel behaviour. Such an interplay describes a more flexible research paradigm that allows for interactions between inductive and deductive streams of research, as explained and envisioned by Kurani and Lee-Gosselin (1997). From the various streams of qualitative research approaches, one that seems much in line with this philosophy is Grounded Theory (Corbin and Strauss, 1998). This approach stresses the interaction between data and analyses at varying levels of objectivity, while maintaining an emphasis on methodological rigour and standards for evaluating and validating the results. Very recently, Northcutt and McCoy (2004) have combined ideas from Grounded Theory with ideas from Systems Theory in order to recommend a hybrid interactive survey approach.

Research into unconscious motivations for purchase decisions has proven very successful in several product areas. This type of market research tends to remain proprietary, but there is some journalistic reportage available. Bradsher (2000) reports in-depth research done for Chrysler to distinguish SUV buyers from minivan buyers. Although the two groups were nearly identical along sociodemographic dimensions, the psychological profiles of the two groups tend to be quite different along dimensions such as fear of crime, social attachments and aspirations, and attitudes towards family and wealth. The questions used go beyond typical attitudinal questions in order to look also at emotional and instinctual influences, most of which respondents are not able to verbalise on their own without imaginative types of response stimuli. Much of the research into auto decisions has been influenced by Rapaille, who has worked for Chrysler, Ford and General Motors. His work and views are further described by Hitt (2000), who writes: "Most researchers would conduct focus groups; they would ask questions and record responses. That would be a mistake, for the responses, Rapaille believes, would reflect back simply what people think they should say: taste, quality, price. Such straightforward questions are aimed at the cortex, the seat of the intellect. Rapaille directs his queries to what he calls the 'reptilian' part of the brain, often using methods similar to dream analysis. Using such methods, he found that many peoples' earliest associations with SUVs are military jeeps and trucks, thus providing an armoured vehicle against violence and crime in the streets."

Another researcher who believes that questionnaires and focus groups rarely dig deep enough to uncover the motivations for consumer decisions is Zaltman (2003) of Harvard Business School. In Zaltman's view, 'consumers' deepest thoughts, the ones that account for their behaviour in the marketplace, are unconscious. Not only that, those thoughts are primarily visual as well (Eakin, 2003). Imaginative use of visual stimuli can be valuable in uncovering behavioural aspects that cannot be evoked using verbal questions and prompts.

Several academic researchers are now going one step further and wiring respondents brains, performing MRIs of brain activity while the respondent is making decisions in simulated environments. Camerer of CalTech reports findings that emotions play a much larger role in supposedly rational decision-making than most people expected. 'A lot of traditional economists would say that feelings are the tip of the iceberg, and that rational thought is what lies below, determining your choice. Neuroscience would say that the huge part of the iceberg is the feelings' (D'Antoni, 2004). It seems that researchers tend to fall into one of these views or the other, and rarely have collected both types of data together – rational decision tradeoffs as well as underlying feelings and associations for complex dynamic decision processes – so that their relative contributions to decision-making can be judged on a level playing field. Perhaps that is a challenge that we can help to overcome as researchers in the area of travel decision processes.

CONCLUSIONS AND RECOMMENDATIONS

This chapter makes a case for more widespread collection and use of process data to support transportation policy, both directly and indirectly, through travel demand modelling. Travel surveys generally collect information on the outcomes of decision processes. Trip/activity diary surveys, for example, tell us about the locations people decide to visit, the things they decide to do there, and the modes they decide to use to get there. The surveys tell us little or nothing about how the people came to those decisions. The other types of information that might be useful, depending on the decision context, include:

- What other alternatives did a person consider?
- What other alternatives were possible?
- Was the decision planned in advance or made on the spur of the moment?
    o If planned in advance, how far in advance, and did the plans change over time?
- Was the decision dependent on other decisions that were made?
- Which decision factors were most important?
- What information did the person have regarding those factors?
    o How and when did the person acquire that information?
    o What other information would have been useful?

- o Why did the person not have that information?
- o How would the person go about getting that information?
- Had the person made the particular decision before?
  - o If so, did the person tend to make the same choice each time or did it vary?
  - o If it varied, why would the person choose differently at different times?
- Was the decision made jointly with other(s)?
  - o If so, how did the different people enter into the decision?
  - o Is so, was there a negotiation or a trade-off of priorities?
- Did other people (employers, etc.) indirectly influence the decision?
  - o If so, what was their influence?
- How did past experiences influence expectations regarding the decision?
- Were there any recent major changes that influenced the decision?
- Were there any expected future changes that influenced the decision?
- What roles did variability, uncertainty, and risk play?
- Did the person have any strong attitudes about the choice alternatives?
  - o If so, when and how did those attitudes develop?
- Does the person have any strong unconscious feelings or associations regarding the alternatives?

This long list is only a partial one, and the reader can probably think of other questions that would be relevant in particular decision contexts.

Figure 1 shows, at the left, the key types of data and modelling assumptions used in methods based on choice outcomes. At the right are shown the additional types of data and assumptions that can be tested using survey and modelling methods based on both outcomes and processes. Note that these methods can still include any or all aspects of traditional models – there is no intention to reinvent the wheel. What makes process-based methods more 'rounded' is their ability to simultaneously include or test other non-traditional aspects.

Table 1 contrasts the 'process data' survey approaches envisioned in this chapter with typical revealed preference and stated preference survey approaches, in terms of the basic philosophy, the burden on various study participants, and the ways in which different types of data items are or could be elicited. It is probably inevitable that collection of process data will require more expertise and time and effort on the part of everyone – survey designers, interviewers, respondents, data processors, and data analysts. On the other hand, we would expect these types of data about underlying decision processes to be quite transferable across regions, so it would be feasible and advantageous for several regions and/or researchers to pool resources in collecting the data. Thus, while the sample size from any one location may be smaller than what we are accustomed to, the total sample would be adequate for very detailed modelling.

Process data should not be viewed only as a substitute for the revealed preference and stated preference data we typically collect. In fact, it can be a complement to help us interpret the data on observed (or hypothetical) behaviour. Just as revealed preference information is often collected in stated preference surveys, process data may be collected in revealed preference and stated preference surveys. The current relationship between SP and RP data collection provides a useful illustration: sometimes RP data are collected as an initial basis for customization in an SP survey, and sometimes SP data are collected as a follow-up survey for a subsample of an RP survey, but the two types of data are often collected and analysed in a coordinated manner.

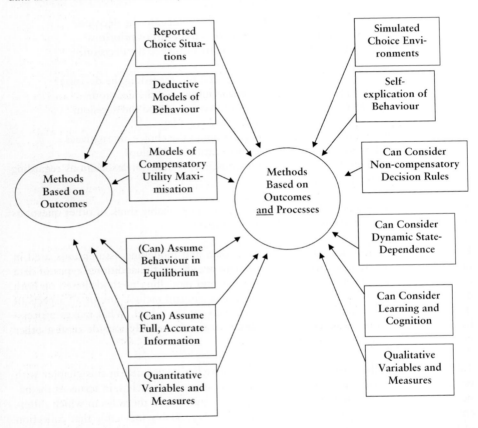

Figure 1: Schematic Comparison of Outcome-Based and Process-Based Methods

Table 1: Contrast of Data Collection Approaches

Approach to Different Types of Data Items	'Typical' Revealed Preference Data	'Typical' Stated Preference Data	Envisioned Process Data
The 'philosophy'	'Tell us what you did last Thursday, and we'll figure out why. We'll assume it was mainly because of X,Y and Z, because those are the only variables we have measurements of.'	'Tell us what you would have done last Thursday if these were your options, and we'll figure out why. We'll assume it was mainly because of X,Y and Z, because those are the only variables we showed you.'	'Tell us what you did last Thursday, and how and why. Tell us what you would have done last Thursday if things were different, and how and why. We'll assume as little as possible before-hand (except that you are capable of answering detailed questions about your own behaviour).'
Burden on survey designers	Moderate. Surveys have become standardised to a large degree.	Higher. Requires knowledge of experimental design, experience with asking hypothetical questions.	Highest. Must allow for a wide variety of types of responses, but still keep the survey structured enough for data to be useful.
Burden on interviewers	Moderate. Response capture is typically automated.	Higher. Respondents may need some guidance with hypothetical questions.	Highest. Questions tend to require more probing, branching, etc. Interviewer is typically more a 'part of the process'.
Burden on respondents	Moderate. Questions are fairly simple and factual, although there may be very many of them.	Higher. Hypothetical questions may be unfamiliar and require trade-off of several factors.	Highest. Respondent is asked for more self-reflection and is less constrained in the type of response.
Burden on data processors	High. A great deal of data cleaning and addition of geographical detail is typical.	Lower. Data is usually fairly self-contained and pre-determined by the experiment.	Probably High. Depends on the amount of structure in the questions and the amount of open-ended information that needs to be interpreted/coded.
Burden on analysts	High. Must investigate a wide range of possible variables, and often cope with poor quality data.	Lower. The analysis is to a large extent pre-determined by the survey design.	Highest. Analysis requires both innovation and synthesis to deal with unfamiliar types of data
The relevant choice (dependent variable)	Reported using a structured format	Elicited using a structured format	Elicited using a structured format, but with more open-ended possibilities.
Assumed choice mechanism	Trade-off among attributes using utility maximisation	Trade-off among attributes using utility maximisation	Not assumed, but elicited using detailed questions.
The set of relevant choice alternatives	Inferred, based on networks, auto ownership, age, etc.	Pre-defined, sometimes customised based on elicited information.	Elicited, probing to either 'build up' or 'pare down' the consideration set.
The values of choice attributes (independent variables)	Inferred, based on networks, zonal data, reported demographics, etc.	Pre-defined, sometimes customised based on elicited information.	Perceptions elicited, not assuming perfect information. Questions may deal with information acquisition.
Effects of difficult-to-quantify variables (variability, safety, comfort, reliability, etc)	Rarely considered due to lack of measurements.	Sometimes included in hypothetical contexts, but often difficult to portray understandably to respondents.	Both perceptions and effects can be elicited. Visual stimuli and more open-ended survey formats may prove particularly useful.

Approach to Different Types of Data Items	'Typical' Revealed Preference Data	'Typical' Stated Preference Data	Envisioned Process Data
Additional situation constraints	Usually not considered.	Often asked about in order to set context, but not used directly	Can be probed in detail, either in a structured or open-ended format.
Effects of past experiences and choices.	Occasionally measured using structured longitudinal or retrospective data	Often asked about in order to set context, but not used directly	Can be probed in detail, going back from the present or forward from the past.
Effects of future expectations.	Very rarely considered.	Very rarely considered.	Can be considered.
Effects of attitudes, personality, politics, etc.	Sometimes measured using structured psycho-metric methods.	Sometimes measured using structured psycho-metric methods	In addition to more structured methods, can probe into related issues such as formation of attitudes. Can also probe into less conscious motivations and feelings.

RECOMMENDATIONS

1. **Collect Process Data to Both Test and Develop New Theories and Model Structures.** The sophistication of the newest model theories, structures and estimation methods is going beyond what existing empirical data can either explain or validate. One example is microsimulation models of household activity and travel, either rule-based or utility maximisation-based. When modelling many simultaneous choice dimensions, there are many possible ways the decisions could be sequenced. For example, what are the causal relationships between departure time scheduling, trip chain complexity, and mode choice? Data on choice outcomes alone does not appear sufficient to provide much guidance on such questions.

2. **Collect Process Data to Aid in Development of Dynamic Choice Models.** Collection of longitudinal data has been a valuable step in developing dynamic models, however development has not progressed as rapidly as we might have hoped. Process data would be a particularly useful complement in this regard.

3. **Collect Process Data to Enhance the Explanatory Power of New Model Estimation Techniques.** Advances in computing power and programming have made advanced estimation methods such as mixed logit and GEV models widely available. However, the additional statistical results from such models are often difficult to translate into behavioural terms. Because these results typically relate to heterogeneity and latent factors behind decisions, process data on those same types of factors would be valuable.

4. **Collect Process Data in Coordination with Introductions of New Policies or Services.** The type of questions and issues most relevant for process data fit very well into the framework of before and after studies designed around changes in the real world travel environment. In addition to providing the

most useful type of data for model estimation and validation, process data provide immediate data for identifying how well the policy is working and, just as importantly, why that is the case.

5.   **Look for Ideas from Other Research Fields.** Few research fields in the social sciences have as strong a quantitative bias as the study of travel behaviour. While this has yielded some strengths relative to other fields, it also means that other fields may be able to provide more useful examples in the area of process data. Some areas to keep an eye on are experimental psychology, sociology, human geography, marketing science, research into energy usage, research into health and lifestyle, research into housing decisions, and research into education and learning. It would also be very useful to import programming expertise from the gaming software community.

6.   **Exploit the Internet and Mobile Survey Technology of the (Near) Future.** As we are envisioning a new stream in data collection, it will be valuable to think about what can be done as the Internet becomes more ubiquitous and powerful as a survey medium. Internet-based surveys can include video and other visual stimuli, can allow respondents to search many types of databases, can provide access to on-line mapping and GIS for location coding, can incorporate learning algorithms to administer intelligent personalised questionnaires, and can administer interactive gaming and simulation with multiple respondents (i.e., multiple household members). Voice prompting is already possible, and technologies for voice data capture and recognition are improving rapidly.

Hand-held computers, GPS technology, and wireless technology are improving just as fast or faster than Internet technology. Most of the features that will be possible for Internet surveys in the home and office will also be possible to complete in vehicles or while walking or using public transport. (Bio-monitoring of stress and exertion levels would also be possible if such data were useful.) Zhou and Golledge (2004) describe a prototype application of an activity diary survey administered via hand-held computer.

ACKNOWLEDGEMENTS

Thanks go to Kostas Goulias, Keith Lawton, and Maren Outwater for providing comments and suggestions for this chapter.

REFERENCES

Andreasen, A.R. (1995). *Marketing Social Change: Changing Behaviour to Promote Health, Social Development and the Environment*, Jossey-Bass, San Francisco.
Arentze, T., H. Timmermans, F. Hofman and N. Kalfs (2000). Data Needs, Data Collection and Data Quality Requirements of Activity-Based Transport Demand Models. In: *Transport Surveys: Raising the Standard* (P.R. Stopher and P.M.

Jones, eds), II-J/1-30, Transportation Research Circular, Number E-C008, Transportation Research Board, Washington, DC.

Bandura, A. (1977). *Social Learning Theory.* Englewood Cliffs, NJ, Prentice Hall.

Bradley, M.A. (1988). Realism and Adaptation in Designing Hypothetical Travel Choice Contexts, *J. of Transport Economics and Policy,* 22 (1), 121-137.

Bradsher, K. (2000). Was Freud a Minivan or SUV Kind of Guy?. *New York Times.* July 17.

Brög, W. and E. Erl. (1980). Interactive Measurement Methods: Theoretical Bases and Practical Applications. *Transportation Research Record No. 765,* 1-6.

Clifton, K. and S. Handy. (2001). Qualitative Methods in Travel Behaviour Research. In: *Transport Survey Quality and Innovation* (P.R. Stopher and P.M. Jones, eds), 283-302, Pergamon Press, Oxford.

Collantes, G. and P.L. Mokhtarian (2002). How Much Do I Travel?: Modeling Subjective Assessments of Personal Mobility. Transportation Research Board 2002 Annual Meeting CD-ROM.

Corbin, J. and A. Strauss (1998). *Basics of Qualitative Research: Techniques and Procedures for Developing Grounded Theory,* Sage Publishing, Thousand Oaks.

D'Antonio, M. (2004). How We Think: Brain Researchers are Using MRIs to Predict Our Decisions Before They Are Made, *Los Angeles Times Sunday Magazine.* May 2.

Doherty, S.T. (2003). Should We Abandon Activity Type Analysis? paper presented to the 10th International Conference on Travel Behaviour Research, Lucerne. http://www.ivt.baum.ethz.ch/allgemein/iatbr2003.html.

Doherty, S.T. and E.J. Miller (2000). A Computerised Household Activity Scheduling Survey, *Transportation,* 27 (1), 75-97.

Eakin, E. (2002). Penetrating the Mind by Metaphor. *New York Times: Art and Ideas.* February 23.

Ettema, D., A. Borgers and H. Timmermans (1995). SMASH (Simulation Model of Activity Scheduling Heuristics): Empirical Test and Simulation Issues, Paper presented at the Conference on Activity Based Approaches: Activity Scheduling and the Analysis of Activity Patterns, Eindhoven, The Netherlands, May.

Faivre d'Arcier B. (2000). Hypothetical Situations : The Attempt To Find New Behavioural Hypotheses. In: *Transport Surveys: Raising the Standard* (P.R. Stopher and P.M. Jones, eds), II-L 1-18, Transportation Research Circular, Number E-C008, Transportation Research Board, Washington, DC.

Fiorenzo-Catalano, S., S. Hoogendoorn-Lanser and R. van Nes (2003). Choice Set Composition Modeling in Multimodal Travelling, paper presented to the 10th International Conference on Travel Behaviour Research, Lucerne, http://www.ivt.baum.ethz.ch/allgemein/iatbr2003.html.

Garling, T., A. Garling and P. Loukopoulos (2002). Forecasting Psychological Consequences of Car Use Reduction: A Challenge to an Environmental Psychology of Transportation, *Applied Psychology: An International Review,* 51 (1), 90-106.

Goulias, K.G., W. Brög and E. Erl. (1998). Perceptions in Mode Use Choice Using the Situational Approach: A Trip by Trip Multivariate Analysis for Public Transportation. Transportation Research Board 1998 Annual Meeting. Preprint 981355. Washington, DC.

Goulias, K.G. (2001). On the Role of Qualitative Methods in Travel Surveys. In: *Transport Survey Quality and Innovation* (P.R. Stopher and P.M. Jones, eds), 319-330, Pergamon, Oxford.

Handy, S., L. Weston and P. Mokhtarian (2003). Driving by Choice or Necessity? paper presented to the 10th International Conference on Travel Behaviour Research, Lucerne, http://www.ivt.baum.ethz.ch/allgemein/iatbr2003.html.

Hitt, J. (2000). Does the Smell of Coffee Brewing Remind You of Your Mother? *New York Times Sunday Magazine*, May 7.

John, G. and W. Brög. (2001). Individualised Marketing – the Perth Success Story, Paper Presented at the Conference on Marketing Public Transport, Auckland, NZ. http://www.dpi.wa.gov.au/travelsmart/pdfs/pubtransnz.pdf .

Jones, P.M. (1979). HATS: A Technique for Investigating Household Decisions, *Environment and Planning A,* 11 (1), 59-70.

Jones, P.M., M.C. Dix, M.I. Clarke and I.G. Heggie (1983). *Understanding Travel Behaviour,* Gower Publishing, Aldershot.

Jones, P.M., M. Bradley and E. Ampt (1987). Forecasting Household Response to Policy Measures Using Computerised Activity-Based Stated Preference Techniques. *Proceedings of The 1987 Conference on Travel Behaviour,* Aix-en-Provence.

Jones, P. M. and L. Sloman (2003). Encouraging Behavioural Change Through Marketing and Management: What Can Be Achieved? Paper presented to the 10th International Conference on Travel Behaviour Research, Lucerne, http://www.ivt.baum.ethz.ch/allgemein/iatbr2003.html.

Kurani, K. and M. Lee-Gosselin. (1997). Synthesis of Past Activity Analysis Applications. Proceedings of the TMIP Activity-Based Forecasting Conference. New Orleans, LA. http://tmip.fhwa.dot.gov/clearinghouse/docs/abtf/kurani.pdf .

Lee-Gosselin, M. (1990). The Dynamics of Car Use Patterns Under Different Scenarios: A Gaming Approach. In: *Developments in Dynamic and Activity-Based Approaches to Travel Analysis* (P.M. Jones, ed.), 251-271, Gower Press, Aldershot.

Lee-Gosselin, M. (1996). Scope and Potential of Interactive Stated Response Data Collection Methods, In: *Conference on Household Travel Surveys: New Concepts and Research Needs. Transportation Research Board Conference Proceedings 10.* National Academy Press, Washington, DC, 115-133.

Louviere, J.J., D.A. Hensher and J.D. Swait (2000). *Stated Choice Methods: Analysis and Application.* Cambridge University Press, Cambridge.

Mahmassani, H.S. and R. Herman. (1990). Interactive Experiments for the Study of Tripmaker Behaviour Dynamics in Congested Commuting Systems, In: *Developments in Dynamic and Activity-Based Approaches to Travel Analysis* (P.M. Jones, ed.), 272-298, Gower Press, Aldershot.

McCutcheon, R.T. (ed) (1999). *The Insider/Outsider Problem in the Study of Religion: A Reader,* Cassel, London.

Northcutt, N. and D. McCoy (2004). *Interactive Qualitative Analysis : A Systems Method for Qualitative Research,* Sage Publications, Thousand Oaks.

Outwater, M., S. Castleberry, Y. Shiftan, M. Ben-Akiva, Y. Shuang Zhou and A. Kuppam (2003). Use of Structural Equations Modeling for an Attitudinal Market

Segmentation Approach to Mode Choice and Ridership Forecasting, Paper presented to the 10th International Conference on Travel Behaviour Research, Lucerne http://www.ivt.baum.ethz.ch/allgemein/iatbr2003.html .

Shaheen, S. (1999). *Dynamics in Behavioral Adaptation to a Transportation Innovation: A Case Study of CarLink—A Smart Carsharing System.* UCD-ITS-RR-99-16. Davis, California. October, 232 pp.

Urban, G.L., B.D. Weinberg and J.R. Hauser (1996a). Premarket Forecasting of Really New Products, *Journal of Marketing*, **60** (1), 47-60.

Urban, G.L., J.R. Hauser, W.J. Qualls, B.D. Weinberg, J.D. Bohlmann and R.A. Chicos (1996b). *Validation and Lessons from the Field: Applications of Information Acceleration,* MIT Sloan School of Management. WP # 3882.

Walker, J.L. (1994). *Modeling traveler response to traveler information systems: Laboratory simulation of information searches using multimedia technology,* M.S. Thesis, Dept. of Civil and Environmental Engineering, MIT, Cambridge, MA.

Weston, L.L. (2004). The Case for Qualitative Methods in Transportation Research. Transportation Research Board 2004 Annual Meeting CD-ROM.

Zaltman, G. (2003). *How Customers Think: Essential Insights into the Mind of the Market,* Harvard Business School Pub., Cambridge, MA.

Zhou, J. and R. Golledge. (2004). Real-time Tracking of Activity Scheduling/Schedule Execution Within Unified Data Collection Framework. Transportation Research Board 2004 Annual Meeting CD-ROM.

28

COLLECTION AND ANALYSIS OF BEHAVIOURAL PROCESS DATA: CHALLENGES AND OPPORTUNITIES

Ram Pendyala, University of South Florida, Tampa, Florida, USA
and
Stacey Bricka, NuStats, Austin, Texas, USA

INTRODUCTION[39]

For the past several decades, the analysis of revealed and stated preference travel survey data sets has undoubtedly shed much light on human activity and travel patterns in a wide variety of contexts. These data sets have consistently provided high quality information about 'outcomes', i.e., the actual behaviour that is, or is likely to be, exhibited under a set of conditions. While such data are valuable in describing and modelling travel demand characteristics and patterns, they does not provide information about the underlying decision processes and mechanisms that drive and lead to the travel outcomes measured in travel surveys. Recent developments in activity-based approaches to travel demand analysis, the design of sophisticated data collection tools, and qualitative data analysis techniques have motivated behavioural researchers to move towards collecting data about behavioural planning processes that are typically characterised by trade-offs, negotiations, substitutions, constraints, perceptions, and agent interactions. Methods such as those developed by Doherty and Miller (2000), where individuals are

---

[39] The authors are grateful to the following individuals for their valuable input in the preparation of this chapter: Peter Bonsall (UK), Mark Bradley (USA), Tom Cohen (UK), Peter Jones (UK), Marina Lombard (South Africa), Nancy McGuckin (USA), Barbara Noble (UK), Matthew Roorda (Canada), Felipe Targa (USA), and Pat van der Reis (South Africa). Their valuable insights and great sense of humour helped shape many a discussion that found their way into this chapter.

asked to record information about their decision processes, have proven successful in collecting information about human activity-travel scheduling and execution processes. Process data essentially help identify the factors that influence a decision process, describe the process itself, and finally inform the researcher on the specification of the model system or systems that best represent the decision processes underlying a behavioural phenomenon.

The collection and analysis of process data adds an unique and valuable dimension to the field of travel behaviour, which is fundamentally concerned with explaining complex and dynamic *processes* underlying activity and travel patterns. Traditional travel survey data sets provide information on the actual activity-travel patterns and choices of individuals; behavioural researchers have generally attempted to infer decision processes from such data (Bradley, 2006). While such data are certainly of great value to describing and modelling behavioural outcomes, they are not able to provide information on the fundamental 'how' and 'why' questions that form the basis of behavioural decisions. In other words, outcomes-based data sets provide information on 'what' people do, while process-based data sets provide fundamental information on 'how' and 'why' people do what they do. Process data provide a framework for the explicit recognition and incorporation of the time dimension because any 'process', by definition, can occur only over a period of time. Thus, process data can prove valuable to the study of behavioural dynamics that is critical to the development of the next generation of travel demand forecasting model systems.

Recent developments in qualitative research methods have motivated further the collection and analysis of behavioural process data (Goulias, 2003). Clifton and Handy (2003) note that process data and qualitative research methods can play an important role in defining choice sets, identifying factors, such as values and perceptions, that affect choices, establishing connections between long- and short-term choices, exploring unique travel needs and constraints, and understanding interactions among agents. Their list clearly points to the key benefits that travel behaviour researchers can derive from the collection and analysis of process data. In short, qualitative and process data provide explicit information on how different types of interactions, social dynamics, and constraints affect decision-making processes in an activity-travel behaviour context. Qualitative surveys, that explore decision-making behaviour in a variety of contexts, are seeing increasing application as they help refine travel behaviour hypotheses and quantitative data collection efforts (Mehndiratta *et al.*, 2003). These surveys ask people expressly to explain 'how' they perceive activities, space, and time, 'how' and 'why' they arrive at various decisions and choices, and 'how' and 'why' various constraints and interactions affect their activity-travel behaviour Qualitative surveys, often conducted through in-depth interview techniques, probe deeper into behavioural processes that form the basis of activity-travel interactions and dynamics in time and space.

Process data may be collected in several different contexts. In addition to the traditional passenger travel context, one may need to probe behavioural processes underlying freight travel decision-making, business and residential location decision-making, and institutional decision-making. This chapter focuses exclusively on process data for passenger travel behaviour analysis. However, it is likely that many of the challenges, issues, and opportunities, discussed in this chapter in the context of passenger travel, apply to freight travel, business location, and institutional decisions as well.

The remainder of this chapter is organised as follows. The next section offers a framework for defining process data and its relationship to more quantitative outcomes data. The third section provides the motivation for process data collection and identifies advantages associated with collecting and using process data. The fourth section offers a discussion on the methods for and challenges and issues associated with the collection of process data. The fifth and sixth sections respectively address the research needs and funding opportunities in the process data collection arena. Finally, concluding remarks are offered in the seventh section.

DEFINING PROCESS DATA

Before defining process data, one needs to define the term 'process'. A process generally refers to a sequence of events, information acquisition steps, and/or decisions that eventually lead to an outcome. Any process is characterised by information acquisition and utilisation; there are three levels of information absorption that should be considered in any process data collection effort:

1. *Active*: Active information absorption occurs when an individual seeks out the information, obtains the information, and utilises the information for making a decision. For example, if an individual obtains a bus schedule, consults the schedule, and then decides to wait at the bus stop, then active information absorption has taken place.
2. *Passive*: Passive information absorption occurs when an individual does not actively seek out the information, but simply receives the information without any special effort. For example, if a friend provided information about a transportation service, then the individual receiving the information absorbs it passively and decides how and when to use that information.
3. *Subliminal*: Subliminal information absorption occurs through cultural values, social norms, and individual and collective experiences that occur over time. No explicit information transmission takes place in the process, but the individual is receiving subconscious messages that affect behaviour.

Thus, process data intend to describe the sequences, procedures, and ways in which people make decisions by focusing on how people collect, absorb, assimilate, interpret, and use information to make decisions. In short, process data intend to reveal the cognitive process underlying decision-making behaviour. Any definition for process data must be able to encompass the range of dimensions identified here.

Based on the discussion above, one can construct a framework that defines and positions process data relative to more traditional outcomes data. Figure 1 shows the framework. The top one-third of the large box is the information-acquisition part of the framework. Various stimuli and sources provide the individual information that can be used for making decisions. The middle one-third of the large box is the decision-making part of the framework. In this section, an individual combines the information acquired with his or her own experiences, cultural values, perceptions, situations, constraints, and interactions to make decisions. These decisions, in turn, lead to certain outcomes, actions, or lack thereof. These actions (or lack thereof) constitute the third (bottom part) of the framework. Essentially, process data encompass this entire framework and provide information on the entire mechanism that is embodied by the framework. On the other hand, outcomes data only capture information about actual actions, i.e., the bottom part of the framework. Thus, in this definitional framework, outcomes data are contained within the overall process data framework. Note that the boxes referring to constraints, situations, and interactions on the left hand side and values, experiences, and personality on the right hand side overlap into the top information acquisition section of the framework. This is because people's values, experiences, constraints, and so on may be influenced by information and stimuli and/or may constitute information sources by themselves.

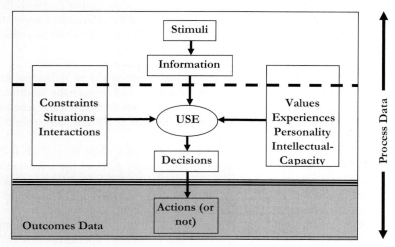

Figure 1: Framework for Defining Process Data

The framework in Figure 1 can be used to define process data. Process data may be defined broadly as qualitative and quantitative information that contributes to an understanding of how and why an individual or group acquires information on activity-travel options, filters the information through personal characteristics and traits (such as values and experience), and constraints (such as cost and time) and makes decisions leading to activity-travel actions (outcomes).

MOTIVATION FOR PROCESS DATA COLLECTION AND ANALYSIS

This section provides a discussion of the reasons for collecting and analysing process data. The collection of process data is fundamentally motivated by our imperfect understanding of how people make decisions. The advantages offered by, and potential applications of, process data are identified with a view to establishing the basis for collecting such data in transport studies.

Key Questions Answered by Process Data

Process data collection is motivated by the nature of the questions that are being asked and need to be answered. In other words, one can determine whether process data need to be collected by first establishing the key questions that need to be answered. In general, process data collection is warranted when the researcher is interested in understanding how and why a certain activity or travel decision is made by one or more individuals. Traditional outcomes-based data provide poor or insufficient explanation of the reasons underlying activity and travel decisions.

Some of the key contributions that process data can make to shedding light on behavioural decisions include, but are not limited to, the following:

1. Process data can help document *path-dependent evolutionary processes* underlying behaviour. Because process data include information on the sequence of events, steps, or decisions that took place along the way to an action, the time-dependent process can be unravelled.
2. Process data can help explain *why people are different*. Often, outcomes data reveal that two or more individuals exhibited the same behaviour, yet are different when they respond to a stimulus. Process data can explain how and why people are different by examining the process by which people arrive at decisions. In other words, process data can help explain the irrationality and randomness of behaviour like never before.
3. Process data can help *identify the measures, strategies, or policies* needed to bring about a change in behaviour. Transport planning decisions often rely on expectations about people changing their behaviour in response to a policy. Process data can help define the magnitude of the stimulus required to bring about a change, because they examine how and why people make decisions in response to external stimuli, experiences, values, and information.
4. There is much interest in understanding the underlying processes that lead to *non-travel decisions*. Some individuals either do not or cannot travel. Out-

comes data simply reveal that the individuals did not engage in travel in a certain period, but shed no light on why they did not travel and how they arrived at such a decision. Process data can help inform studies aimed at exploring social exclusion and equity.

Thus, process data are capable of shedding light on behaviours or decision mechanisms that are often least understood, but for which an understanding is most desired. Here are some of the behavioural questions that fall into this category:

1. How are habits formed and what contributes to behavioural inertia (say, in the context of commute mode choice)? What does it take to break habit and overcome behavioural inertia?
2. How do travellers respond to unexpected congestion? What aspects of the activity-travel pattern get altered, in what order, and in what way?
3. How are longer term residential and work location decisions made and how do they relate to the medium and short term vehicle ownership, mode choice, and activity timing, duration, and location decisions?
4. What are the nature of agent-based interactions and constraints, both within and outside the household, and how do they influence activity-travel decisions?
5. What is the behaviour underlying route choice decisions? How and when do route choice decisions get affected in the presence of traveller information about incidents, congestion, route diversion, events, and so on?
6. How do travellers develop expectations about service quality, travel time reliability, and other performance measures that affect decisions? How are personal and third-party experiences factored into the development of expectations?
7. Are there different types of travellers based on personality traits, decision-making processes, cultural values and perceptions, and attitudes? If so, what is the typology of travellers based on these behavioural dimensions and how is that related to the conventional socio-demographic market segmentation often used in studies utilizing outcomes data?

The above lists illustrate the key contributions that can be made and behavioural questions that can be answered by process data.

Advantages of Process Data

While the previous section highlighted the broad contributions and behavioural questions addressed by process data, this section focuses on the more specific advantages associated with collecting and using process data. It is important to identify the specific advantages of process data, so that planning agencies who fund data collection efforts would consider including a process data collection component in an overall travel survey. The advantages offered by process data are that they:

- Can help *inform the design of traditional structured travel surveys.* There may be instances when the exact questions or options that need to be included in a traditional structured travel survey are not known. Then, process data collected through a more in-depth open-ended interview can be used to identify the specific questions, question wording, response categories, and policy options that need to be included in the traditional survey.

- Can help *inform the structure and specification of travel demand forecasting models*, thus increasing the level of confidence associated with travel forecasts. If travel demand forecasting models are specified to reflect actual decision processes better, then it follows that forecasts from such models constitute superior predictions of human behaviour over time.

- Can be used to identify the driving forces *underlying variations observed in outcomes data.* The extent of variance in behaviour explained by traditional socio-economic and other exogenous variables is very small. Process data may be the only way to explain what has so far remained unexplained.

- And models that are developed based on such data might be *more transferable* than traditional travel data and models, because process data describe the most fundamental decision-making mechanism underlying travel choices and decisions. Just as disaggregate travel data and disaggregate travel models are considered more transferable than aggregate data and models, process data and process models would be more transferable than disaggregate data and models. Whether this is true in reality is a research question yet to be addressed.

- Help *identify explanatory factors, constraints, and interactions* that are virtually impossible to measure and identify through traditional travel data collection efforts. Thus, process data provide information that is otherwise missed in travel surveys.

- Can be used to obtain information on the *level or unit of travel analysis* in the context of different decisions. Activity-travel decisions may be made at a multitude of levels including person, household, business, trip, tour, chain, day, week, month, season, year, and so on. The true dimensions at which travel decisions are made can be identified through process data.

- Are often collected through more open-ended and qualitative surveys. Therefore, respondents have the ability to provide descriptive answers that are typically not obtained in traditional surveys. Process data collection can result in the *identification of new integrated (packages of) policy options* that may not have been considered otherwise.

- Can help *reveal unintended consequences of policies and actions* – information that would be very hard to collect in traditional travel surveys. Transport and land use policies are usually implemented with the expectation that they will bring about certain changes or benefits. However, there may be unintended consequences that were not considered at the time of policy formulation and implementation that process data may reveal.

- Can help _reveal the travel impacts of non-transport policies_ (say, land use and telecommunications policies) and vice versa, because policies in one sector of the economy may have impacts in another sector. Process data attempt to capture the entire range of experiences, values, and decisions that people are likely to make under different conditions, hence revealing such impacts.

Potential Applications of Process Data

The advantages associated with process data can be beneficial in numerous transport planning and policy making applications. A few application contexts where process data can make an unique contribution are described in this section.

First and foremost, process data can be applied in the context of specifying the structure and form of activity-based microsimulation models of travel behaviour aimed at producing forecasts of travel demand. Activity-based microsimulation systems often involve a series of submodels that are chained together sequentially. This sequence assumes implicitly that behavioural decisions are made by individuals in a certain order or structure. Process data can be used to inform, modify, enhance, and refine the basic structure of the model system, the sequence in which the submodels are chained, and the specification and form of the models themselves. It is this potential application that has activity-based modellers interested in collecting and analysing process data.

A second noteworthy application area is that of traveller response to intelligent transport systems (ITS). ITS applications comprise a wide array of technologies and systems that can be deployed to assist travellers, alter travel behaviour, and improve efficiency. The impacts of ITS technologies can be predicted accurately only if transport professionals know how and why people respond to information and adopt or embrace technology. While people tend to embrace and rely on certain technologies, they also tend to shun others. ITS technology deployment is also a very expensive undertaking; understanding how and why people utilise ITS and the information they provide can greatly benefit ITS deployment efforts.

A third application area that one might consider is transport safety. Government organisations often use information campaigns and public advertisements to encourage people to use the transport system safely. Campaigns to discourage mobile phone use while driving, encourage seat belt use, encourage helmet use by cyclists, discourage mid-block street crossing, and encourage proper vehicle maintenance are examples of public safety notices that are commonly used. People receive this information, process it, combine and filter the information with their own experiences, values, and perceptions, and then make decisions leading to actions. This sequence of events and behaviour can only be understood and described by collecting process data. In other words, the success or failure of safety and other public information campaigns rests on the ability of the analyst to collect and analyse process data.

The above constitute a representative sample of application areas covering a wide range of fields, i.e., travel modelling, traffic operations (ITS), and transport safety. Thus, it can be seen that process data potentially can be used in a wide variety of application contexts and the transport profession as a whole can benefit immensely from the collection and use of these data.

COLLECTING PROCESS DATA

Process data tend to be collected through more in-depth and open-ended interviews, that purport to gather detailed responses about how and why people behaved and acted in a certain way and the sequence of decisions (and factors affecting them) that contributed to the observed behaviour or action. Due to the in-depth and intensive nature of the survey data collection effort, process data collection efforts tend to use small samples in comparison to traditional structured travel surveys that are usually administered to relatively large samples for obtaining quantitative statistics of desired precision and confidence levels.

Figure 2 shows how one might be able to view the survey continuum between a detailed process data collection effort and completely structured traditional travel survey. At the top of the rhombus, one is collecting detailed process data through an in-depth and open-ended interview format from a small sample. At the bottom of the rhombus, one is undertaking a large sample, structured data collection effort with a view to drawing inferences about the population under study that can be generalised.

The remainder of this section is devoted to describing appropriate survey methods and elements, potential pitfalls, and issues and challenges associated with collecting process data.

Survey Methods, Design Elements, and Techniques

The survey design and methodology is largely dictated by the objective of the study and the expected use of the process data that will be collected. It is very important to define clearly the objective and purpose of the survey and the behavioural or planning questions that need to be answered using the data. Without a clear objective statement, it will be very difficult to design an appropriate survey and collect the needed data.

It is also important to note that information about behavioural processes can be collected in traditional travel surveys that focus on outcomes. The potential for collecting information about or inferring behavioural processes from traditional surveys should not be dismissed. In fact, travel behaviour researchers have relied on outcomes-based data sets to draw inferences regarding behavioural decision-making processes for several decades. The opportunity now presents itself to go further in the quest to understand behaviour by collecting process data explicitly through carefully designed surveys and experiments. However, this should not rule out the possibility of including several process questions (i.e., more open-ended questions that ask an individual how and why he or she arrived at a certain decision or choice) in a traditional travel survey. Including even a few process questions in a traditional survey can go a long way in shedding light on human behaviour without imposing an undue burden on the respondent.

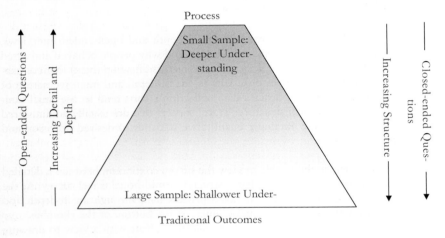

Figure 2: The Data Collection Continuum

When asking questions about behavioural processes, it would be ideal if the questions and survey can be designed such that people describe their decision and planning process without being asked explicitly to do so. It is possible that asking process questions explicitly might lead the respondent to become so aware of his or her decision-making mechanism that he or she will consider altering it in the course of the survey, particularly if he or she deems the mechanism to be suboptimal. Thus, in designing a process survey, consideration should be given to designing a series of questions that provide information about the decision process without explicitly asking the respondent to describe the process *per se*.

Surveys that purport to collect process data tend to be more open-ended and in-depth interviews where respondents are asked to provide detailed explanations and responses to questions about how and why they made certain decisions and choices. Thus, process surveys can benefit from qualitative research methods, including focus groups and in-person face-to-face interviews. Moreover, process surveys could make use of technology: web- and computer-based survey instruments that lead respondents through a series of questions and steps that elicit behavioural process information (Doherty and Miller, 2000). In these surveys, respondents are provided computerised survey instruments in which they enter and save information over a certain period of time, so that their decisions, and the process that contributed to the decisions, can be recorded.

Consideration should also be given to the design and application of multistage surveys, where detailed data from a small sample process survey is used to inform the design of a larger sample traditional structured travel survey. The detailed information from the process survey can be reduced, so as to develop a focused series of more specific and structured questions and policy options to be included in the large sample structured traditional outcomes survey. Such a hybrid survey design would provide information about both behavioural processes and outcomes.

While there are several qualitative and technology-based methods that can be brought to bear for collecting process data, there are many unanswered questions and research issues associated with process survey design and administration. These are addressed later in the chapter. However, there are several key aspects that define process data that may be useful in formulating process surveys. For example, process data are supposed to describe processes that occur over time. This means that process surveys should collect data that describe the state of an individual at multiple time points and the evolutionary path taken by the individual in transitioning from one state to the next. Therefore, an analyst interested in collecting process data would be well served by asking retrospective and prospective questions, using open-ended questions that capture descriptions of evolutionary paths, and adopting longitudinal survey designs.

Potential Pitfalls

In the context of process surveys, careful consideration should be given to the format, design, and administration of the survey instrument, to avoid collecting misleading and erroneous data. Here are some of the potential pitfalls of which a process survey designer should be wary:

- A process survey design, by nature, may *lead or influence respondents* to answer questions in a certain way. Process surveys require respondents to engage in greater articulation and higher levels of thought and introspection. This may lead to respondents becoming more aware of their own decision processes (which were more subconscious previously), reinforcing or loosening their prejudices, and adapting their responses accordingly. However, it should be noted that this aspect of process surveys may also constitute a significant merit. In fact, the entire manner in which a survey participant adapts and responds to a process survey may shed considerable light on his or her behavioural processes.
- *Cognitive dissonance* may occur, where a respondent deliberately provides misleading responses when answering a process survey, which may occur due to increased awareness of the respondent because of participating in the survey.
- Respondents may impose *self-censorship* where they disclose information in a selective manner. The bits and pieces that are missing (or censored) will then have

to be deduced by the survey researcher. This may lead to erroneous conclusions regarding the true behavioural process followed by the respondent.

- In the desire to streamline the survey design and administration procedure, there may be a *tendency to impart structure* to the survey instrument. In some instances, a certain amount of structure may be necessary to avoid undue complexity and keep the respondents on the topic of interest. However, care should be taken to avoid imparting structure to the survey instrument to the point where respondents are too constrained to offer detailed process data.

- As mentioned earlier, process data recognise the time dimension associated with evolutionary processes and decisions explicitly. However, what is the *time horizon or duration of evolutionary behaviour* for which data need to be collected in a process survey? How much data about historical and anticipated behaviour need to be collected to understand the evolutionary process? The appropriate time horizon can be determined largely from the phenomenon under study; however, even when this phenomenon is well-defined, the time horizon may not be so well defined. For example, in determining frequency of shopping trips, is it appropriate to obtain data on decision processes underlying shopping trip-making for one day, three days, one week, one month, one season, or one year?

- Quite often, the tendency of travel behaviour researchers and modellers is to search for the single behavioural relationship or process that leads to observed outcomes. However, it is possible that there is a *suite of behavioural processes* followed by people and households under different conditions. Intra-person and inter-person variations in behavioural processes need to be recognised in survey instrument design. Individuals may adopt a certain behavioural process in a fleeting manner and then proceed to adopt another process (in the suite) when faced with different conditions.

- Any survey of behavioural processes should explore the *role of cultural differences* in decision-making behaviour, particularly in an international context. Sometimes, differences in behavioural processes and outcomes are due to cultural norms and values and not to conscious cognitive processes.

- Due to their intensive nature, process surveys are likely to be *more expensive* on a per unit basis. Thus, careful consideration should be given to total information content in the survey design, i.e., the product of information per unit and the number of units from which information is obtained. For a fixed budget, there is likely to be a clear trade-off between the level of detail collected from each behavioural unit and the sample size.

- The *appropriate unit of analysis* must be determined. Some behavioural processes are individual-specific, while others may be more household or group-specific. Depending on the nature of the phenomenon under investigation, an appropriate unit of analysis must be chosen for the survey.

Finally, due to the evolutionary and time-dependent nature of process data, one might suppose that panel surveys offer the ideal mechanism for collecting data about behavioural processes. However, this is not necessarily true. While panel surveys offer rich information about the state of a behavioural unit at multiple points in time, they do not necessarily offer any information about the evolutionary process that was followed in transitioning from one state to the next. In fact, it is perfectly feasible to collect process data from a traditional cross-sectional survey, as long as questions eliciting information about evolutionary processes are designed and administered to survey participants.

This point is illustrated by looking at the two pictures shown in Figure 3. In the first picture (top), all of the women are seated and the men are standing. In the second picture (bottom), taken a few moments later, all of the men are seated and the women are standing. The same individuals are observed at two time points and therefore these pictures constitute a panel. While these panel observations show the state of the individuals at two points in time, they provide no information about the process by which these individuals transitioned from one state to the next. To obtain information about the evolutionary process that occurred, one would have had to observe the individuals explicitly during the transition, or ask one or more of the individuals to describe the transition. The pictures suggest a very orderly pattern of behaviour, when in fact, the transition may have been completely chaotic.

Figure 3: A Pair of Panel Observations of a Group of Individuals

Issues and Challenges

As with any area of research that is in its infancy, the design and administration of behavioural process surveys is fraught with issues and challenges. Because these issues and challenges are described in greater detail in the next section, only a brief outline is provided in this section in the interest of brevity.

The degree of structure that can be imparted to a process survey decreases as the level of knowledge about the behavioural process under investigation decreases. If a process is not well understood and very little is known about it, then the survey is inevitably going to be loosely defined, open-ended, and more qualitative in nature. These types of surveys are best administered through in-depth face-to-face interviewing techniques as opposed to phone- or mail-based techniques. In-depth face-to-face interviews are expensive and logistically more difficult to design and administer. In addition, collecting process data is challenging because of the following aspects:

- Behavioural processes are not well defined and tend to be *random in nature* – possibly more random than outcomes. Measuring such a random phenomenon is inherently difficult.
- In process surveys, the researcher is attempting to capture *subliminal and subconscious* messages, processing mechanisms, and decisions. As such, it may be difficult for the respondent to articulate and describe them or for the researcher to elicit them.
- People may consider their behavioural and decision making processes to be *private* in nature. They may be sensitive to sharing such information freely.
- The *time duration* for which the behavioural process needs to be probed is not well defined, even for well defined activity and travel characteristics.
- The sheer *complexity* of the behavioural and cognitive decision-making process makes it difficult to comprehend, describe, and elicit.
- Due to the intensive nature of the survey, *respondent burden* and effort is high. Respondents may find the surveys complex, lengthy, and unduly intrusive. Responses may be censored, modified, or adapted according to the survey, thus leading to erroneous data.
- It is likely that individuals with certain traits are more likely to participate willingly in these types of surveys than others. This may lead to *sample bias*. The results cannot then be easily generalised.
- Interviewers must be well-trained and highly qualified to administer these surveys. They must be careful not to lead or influence the respondent, unduly pry the respondent, or overburden and bias the respondent. *Interviewer burden*, training requirements, and selection criteria are, therefore, more demanding.

The above illustrate the challenges and issues faced by researchers and professionals interested in understanding behavioural processes.

RESEARCH NEEDS

Research must be undertaken and process data must be collected to address the challenges and issues identified in the previous section. The study and understanding of behavioural and cognitive processes is multidisciplinary, because there are facets of psychology, sociology, cognitive science, anthropology, geography, and so on that define these processes. It is imperative that the transport research profession build multidisciplinary teams that are capable of blending theories and methods across an array of disciplines for collecting, analysing, and interpreting process data (Targa and Clifton, 2004). It would be extremely useful to compile a multidisciplinary synthesis of behavioural decision theories, cognitive processes, and psychological motivations that shed light on human actions and choices. The synthesis should document representative samples of process data collection efforts in various fields of inquiry to learn about experiences in the field. This synthesis can lead to defining a typology of traveller types, where the typology is defined by personality traits, experiences, values, and decision processes as opposed to traditional socioeconomic market segmentation variables.

Further, the multidisciplinary synthesis can help in designing a study whose results could be used to characterise people by nature in a broader context, without necessarily limiting the typology to the travel behaviour arena. This could be accomplished by designing a survey where individuals are asked to make decisions in a controlled and simple experimental context. By observing people in the context of this experimental study, a broader typology of human behaviour can be derived. This characterisation of human nature would help in defining a behavioural typology that would apply to a wide array of application contexts in the transport arena.

Research should be conducted to illustrate and demonstrate the effectiveness of behavioural process data collection in a real situation. Transport interventions occur on a regular basis as capacity is increased or decreased, new services are introduced, old services are discontinued, pricing strategies are changed, etc. Before and after studies aimed at understanding behaviour changes in response to the intervention could include a process data collection component. The data collected can be analysed, interpreted, and communicated to demonstrate the insight and practical utility of these surveys.

Even if a special purpose process survey cannot be conducted in conjunction with a real project, questions that elicit process data could be added to traditional data collection instruments. These questions would constitute 'how' and 'why' type questions where people are being asked to explain the reasons for and process followed in arriving at a decision or action. The answers to these questions should be used to inform model specification, enhance behavioural interpretation, and communicate results to policymakers. Questions could also focus on eliciting data about constraints and flexibility.

The question of transferability of process data cannot be ignored. One of the potential merits of collecting and using process data to specify models is that the data, and the models so specified, are more easily transferable across contexts because they represent the most fundamental aspect of decision-making. Controlled experiments conducted in different contexts can help shed light on the transferability of process data and models. Also, the issue of transferability needs to be addressed at different levels of behavioural units of analysis, i.e., transferability needs to be studied across people, space, and time.

The major research needs lie in the design and testing of methods for collecting process data. It would be beneficial to conduct a carefully designed experiment where alternative methods for collecting process data can be applied, tested, and compared with respect to their effectiveness and efficiency. Three types of experiments should be considered – a real world transport system change, a controlled demonstration experiment conducted in the field, and a controlled experiment of a simulated situation (with and without stimuli) conducted in the laboratory. In each of these experiments, three types of data collection efforts can be tested – in-depth personal interview, a periodic longitudinal survey (panel), and a more traditional computer or web-based survey with retrospective questions that collects historical information (Haroun and Miller, 2004). In addition, the survey can be administered on an individual basis or through focus groups. Comparisons of the data and results from such a battery of experiments can help answer the following questions:

- What is the most effective method for administering process surveys, both from a respondent and an interviewer perspective?
- What is the degree of structure that should be imparted to the questions? How open-ended and closed-ended should the questions be? Similarly, how open-ended and closed-ended should the response options be? The experiments can help test alternative question structures.
- How can the information from a process survey be reduced and focused into a smaller set of questions and issues to be included in a larger sample survey?
- What is the impact of administering the survey in a group setting as opposed to on an individual basis? When is it appropriate to administer a process survey in a focus group format as opposed to a one-to-one format?
- What is the impact of different survey methods and question designs on respondent burden, conditioning, and bias?
- What is the impact of different survey methods and question designs on interviewer burden, training, and bias?
- How can respondent conditioning be minimised where it is not desired, or used effectively where it is desired?

The research needs identified in this section are critical to advancing and applying process data in transport planning and modelling.

FUNDING OPPORTUNITIES

Funding for process data collection needs to be examined from two different perspectives. First, funding is required to undertake fundamental research into the design and administration of process surveys. Fundamental research is needed to understand how best to collect, analyse, and interpret the data, and communicate the results. Second, funding is needed to collect process data in the field in the course of ongoing projects in the real world context. Agencies must be made aware of the opportunity to collect process data in conjunction with an ongoing project and asked to provide the supplementary funds needed to collect, analyse, and interpret the data.

There are many potential areas of application for process data. Hence, the potential set of agencies and entities willing or interested to fund process data collection can be very large. With respect to collecting process data in conjunction with ongoing projects, agencies dealing with a host of transport issues and questions should be approached to add a process data collection effort. Either an additional survey can be conducted as part of the study, or questions can be added to an existing survey to obtain additional information about the behavioural process driving the phenomenon under study. Potential application areas include smart growth, housing and urban development, safety campaigns and studies, ITS deployment, toll and pricing strategies, transit use, and environmental issues.

Private industry, including auto manufacturers, information providers, and advertising agencies, may be interested in funding process data collection efforts. They are interested in understanding how people process information, adapt to changes in system characteristics, and make decisions. The telecommunications industry is another entity that may be interested in collecting and analysing process data, because it is concerned with how people view and adopt different types of technology and web-based services. Any study examining the process underlying the adoption of technology and telecommunications could also explore how technology affects travel decisions and choices.

Major institutions, such as the World Bank, Asian Development Bank, and Inter-American Development Bank, have transport projects underway in many different countries of the world. These institutions should be asked to include a process survey in conjunction with their ongoing or planned projects. By collecting data in a variety of geographical, cultural, and transport contexts, the transferability of process data can be studied on a global scale. The role of cultural values in explaining international differences can be determined.

Various government organisations and foundations deal with issues where behavioural processes are extremely relevant. The US Department of Homeland Security, and various other emergency management agencies, are interested in behavioural processes that drive people's evacuation decisions when faced with a threat. The Center for Disease Control and the National Institute of Health, along with the Robert Woods Johnson

Foundation, are interested in how people process and perceive the time-space continuum and engage in active lifestyles from a public health perspective.

In this context, the question remains as to how funding for process data collection may be obtained from these entities in the context of their ongoing activities and projects. The ideal way to make this happen would be to piggyback small process data collection efforts on ongoing and existing projects at zero or minimal additional cost to the agency or entity. The data collected should be compiled, analysed, interpreted, communicated, and utilised effectively to demonstrate proof of concept. The information must be presented so that decision makers and agency personnel see clearly the insights and benefits offered by the data. The agency personnel need to understand how the information from a process survey can be turned into structured relations that shed light on why a certain phenomenon is observed. It behoves the research community to demonstrate clearly the way in which such data can make a real difference in how models are specified, inferences are drawn, impacts are measured, and potential actions are considered for implementation. By providing a clear proof of concept, agencies can be made to understand the need for funding these types of data collection efforts on a routine basis as part of their ongoing project activities.

In the previous section, a series of fundamental research needs in the area of process data collection and survey design were identified. It is unlikely that transport agencies would be able and willing to fund fundamental research on this topic. Fundamental research that examines transferability of process data, compares alternative survey and experimental designs, assesses respondent conditioning and burden, and demonstrates utility of process data in a variety of application contexts is required. Such research will help advance the state-of-the-art and state-of-the-practice in activity-based microsimulation modelling and multimodal transport policy analysis from a behavioural perspective. The Transit Cooperative Research Program (TCRP) Synthesis program of the Transportation Research Board in the US may provide an avenue for compiling a multidisciplinary synthesis of knowledge on this topic. The US Department of Transportation may be able to fund research on controlled comparisons of survey designs and models (specified, developed, and estimated with and without process data) through its Travel Model Improvement Program. The National Science Foundation (NSF) and other research foundations may be another set of entities that would support fundamental research in this topic area. For example, the collection and analysis of behavioural process data is very relevant to the recent NSF solicitations on Human and Social Dynamics. These are the types of opportunities that could benefit travel behaviour researchers interested in collecting and analysing process data.

CONCLUSION

This chapter provides an overview of the challenges and opportunities associated with collecting, using, and analysing process data for behavioural research. The recent surge in activity-based model development has clearly motivated the collection of behavioural process data as researchers attempt to incorporate increasing degrees of behavioural realism in the model structure and specification. The chapter provides an overview of survey methods and design considerations and the numerous issues and challenges associated with collecting process data. Finally, the chapter outlined a series of research needs and potential funding opportunities for conducting fundamental research on this topic and for actually collecting the data in a real project situation.

The newness of this field precludes the development of standards for collecting process data. Much more needs to be learned about the collection and use of process data before standards can be developed. However, it is clear that much needs to be done in this arena and behavioural researchers should strive to incorporate process data collection and analysis where appropriate. Quite often, traditional travel surveys include process data questions that attempt to understand values, attitudes, perceptions, and reasons underlying a decision or choice. However, the profession has not sufficiently utilised and communicated this information to demonstrate the applicability of such data in transport policy analysis and decision-making. If one were to attempt to develop a standard, then it would be that more process data needs to be collected as part of traditional travel surveys. A few process data questions should be added to every travel survey to understand behavioural decisions better, and the process data so collected must be used and communicated effectively.

REFERENCES

Bradley, M. (2006). Process Data for Understanding and Modelling Travel Behaviour, In: *Travel Survey Methods – Quality and Future Directions* (P.R. Stopher and C.C. Stecher, eds), 491-510, Elsevier, Oxford.

Clifton, K.J. and S.L. Handy (2003). Qualitative Methods in Travel Behaviour Research. In: *Transport Survey Quality and Innovation* (P.R. Stopher and P.M. Jones, eds), 283-302, Elsevier, Oxford.

Doherty, S.T. and E.J. Miller (2000). A Computerized Household Activity Scheduling Survey, *Transportation*, 27 (1), 75-97.

Goulias, K.G. (2003). On the Role of Qualitative Methods in Travel Surveys. In: *Transport Survey Quality and Innovation* (P.R. Stopher and P.M. Jones, eds), 319-330, Elsevier, Oxford.

Haroun, A. and E.J. Miller (2004). Retrospective Surveys in Support of Dynamic Model-Building, Paper presented at the Seventh International Conference on Travel Survey Methods, Costa Rica, August.

Mehndiratta, S.R., R. Picado and C. Venter (2003). A qualitative survey technique to explore decision-making behaviour in new contexts. In: *Transport Survey Quality and Innovation* (P.R. Stopher and P.M. Jones, eds), 303-318, Elsevier, Oxford.

Targa, F. and K.J. Clifton (2004). Integrating Social and Psychological Processes into the Land Use-Travel Behaviour Research Agenda: Theories, Concepts and Empirical Study Design, Paper presented at the Seventh International Conference on Travel Survey Methods, Costa Rica, August.

29

APPLICATIONS OF NEW TECHNOLOGIES IN TRAVEL SURVEYS

Jean Wolf, GeoStats, Atlanta, Georgia, USA

TRAVEL SURVEY TECHNOLOGY INVENTORY

Within the past several decades, the first significant technological enhancement in travel survey methodology was the use of computers to collect diary-type survey data in an electronic format. This technology could support complex branching patterns, automated error checking, and sample management. The primary methodologies used for electronic data collection have been computer-assisted telephone interviews (CATI), computer-assisted personal interviews (CAPI), and computer-assisted self-interviews (CASI). CATI has typically been implemented on PCs; CAPI on laptops, PCs, and handheld devices; and CASI via the Internet.

The next major technological enhancement for the collection of travel survey data has been the use of passive location data collection technologies, including Global Positioning System (GPS) data loggers that can collect second-by-second location, position, and speed data. A comprehensive description of GPS and its ability to provide location information for household travel surveys can be found in the Handbook of Transport Geography and Spatial System (Wolf, 2004; Stopher, 2004). The first passive GPS study conducted as part of a major household travel survey occurred in Austin in 1997 (Casas and Arce, 1999; Pearson, 2001). Since then, numerous other vehicle-based GPS studies have been conducted in the US. In these studies, participants are provided with the GPS loggers for the duration of the study and participation in the GPS component is completely voluntary.

Other passive location tracking capable technologies, including personal cell phones and Radio Frequency Identification (RFID) tags/readers used in electronic toll systems, are also capable of providing travel details, although both of these have seen limited travel survey application to date, most likely due to privacy issues in obtaining personal cellular location data from wireless data services and the infrastructure requirements necessary for a regional RFID tag and reader system. In addition, more and more automobile manufacturers are including GPS-based navigation and safety (i.e., OnStar) systems in their vehicles, but again, these systems are designed to assist the driver, not to provide complete tracking details to an unknown public agency.

One variation to passive data collection (or measurement) technologies is active/ interactive technologies which include both passive GPS data collection and a computerised user interface to initiate the collection of GPS data and/or to collect additional details about each trip and destination. This methodology for collecting travel data has been around since 1996, when the US Federal Highway Administration (FHWA) conducted the first GPS pilot study (Wagner, 1997) with a vehicle-based system that included a personal digital assistant (PDA) coupled with a GPS receiver. Other subsequent studies have further explored the use of PDAs and GPS (Draijer *et al.*, 2000; Frank *et al.*, 2004). Many PDAs on the market today support GPS attachments or plug-ins. In addition, Garmin International, a large manufacturer of GPS equipment, recently released the iQue, which is the first fully integrated PDA and GPS device to reach the market.

Both passive and active GPS logging technologies can be designed for vehicle-based logging or for person-based logging, which enables capture of all modes of travel. In-vehicle systems are generally better performers, given the fixed mount position (usually roof, windshield, or trunk mount) and the vehicle power source. Key issues facing person-based loggers (or wearable loggers) include the portable power source and capacity, the form factor (including size, weight, and wearability), and GPS antenna visibility to the sky (required to obtain GPS satellite signals).

Standard GPS positioning accuracy has proven to be in the five to ten metre range, with differential GPS techniques capable of providing accuracy in the two to five metre range for moving vehicles or people. In the GPS world, positional accuracy can be defined as the absolute difference (in metres) between the GPS-calculated location and the true location. The precision of GPS positioning refers to the variability of a specific measured location across time. These two attributes have a significant impact on the ability to identify the travel paths and destinations of study participants confidently based solely on the GPS data and accurate spatial datasets.

Other augmentations are available to fill in locations where GPS signals are not easily captured, such as in urban canyons or underground. These augmentations include dead reckoning (DR) sensors and Assisted GPS (A-GPS). Dead reckoning uses a continuous source of speed (e.g., from an odometer or accelerometer) and heading (from sensors such as magnetic compasses and gyros) to fill in missing GPS points. A-GPS uses a wireless network, with its own GPS receivers, to predict the GPS signal that a given handset will receive and to relay that information to the handset; this technology may also provide sufficient indoor location.

Finally, there are several methods for transferring the GPS and related data from devices deployed in travel surveys. For short duration studies – one week or less – it is usually sufficient to download the collected data when the devices are retrieved from study participants. However, for longer-term studies, it is desirable to have remote transfer capabilities, which can be provided through a cellular (or digital wireless) connection or through an in-home modem-based solution. The ongoing convergence of cell phone, PDA, and GPS technologies make the feasibility of long-term travel surveys attainable in the near future.

The next section covers what has become the 'traditional' use of GPS in household travel surveys. Following this, emerging uses of GPS are presented, followed by a brief review of similar technology trends.

'TRADITIONAL' GPS STUDIES

It has long been suspected that people tend to underreport their travel in diary-based surveys (more so in diary-only surveys, but to a lesser extent using CATI retrieval methods). Quantifying this level of underreporting has been a desire of transportation planners everywhere who use these trip rates in their travel demand models. GPS offers a completely passive method for capturing all trips made, and by deploying passive GPS loggers in tandem with CATI-based household travel surveys, it has proven possible to collect both reported and measured travel from study participants without increasing respondent burden. By instrumenting a subsample of households with in-vehicle GPS loggers, GPS studies conducted to date have performed comparisons of reported and measured vehicle trips. These comparisons have resulted in the identification of unreported trips, whose characteristics, along with the characteristics of the reporting household and persons, have been analysed to identify the correlates of underreporting. Using these correlates, customised trip rate correction factors can be developed and applied to the appropriate households in the larger sample.

In 1996, the US FHWA sponsored a research study in Lexington, Kentucky focused on the use of GPS and PDAs to collect travel survey data (Murakami and Wagner, 1999). The first regional travel survey to use only GPS loggers (with no PDA) was conducted in Austin, Texas in 1997. In this study, 117 households were instrumented with GPS data loggers and reported their travel via CATI retrieval. A total of 186 vehicles were instrumented. Although this study proved that the approach was feasible, analysis of the GPS data proved challenging, because the data were collected while Selective Availability (the intentional degradation of GPS signal accuracy) was active (Casas and Arce, 1999; Pearson, 2001).

After the Austin GPS study, the next wave of GPS studies began in the US in 2001, following the 2000 census. Table 1 below shows the vehicle-based GPS studies conducted in the past three years, along with the GPS study descriptions.

Table 1: Traditional GPS Studies Conducted To Date

Study name	Date of study	Unit of analysis	# Travel days	Total days in study	# Deployed (households)
California Statewide HTS	Feb - Oct 2001	Vehicle	1 day	79	517
SCAG (Los Angeles) HTS*	Sep – Dec 2001 Jan – Mar 2002	Vehicle	1 day	NA	820
Pittsburgh HTS	Sep - Dec 2001	Vehicle	1 day	38	74
Ohio Statewide HTS*	2001 - 2002	Vehicle	1 day	NA	NA
Laredo (Texas) HTS	Mar - May 2002	Vehicle	1 day	45	187
St. Louis HTS	Sep - Nov 2002	Vehicle	1 day	44	313
Tyler / Longview (Texas) HTS	Sep - Nov 2003	Vehicle	1 day	61	367
Kansas City HTS	Feb - Apr 2004	Vehicle	1 day	62	294

* These studies were conducted by Battelle; information was obtained from NuStats and Battelle (2004) and Pierce *et al.* (2003). All other studies were performed by GeoStats. The full analysis of the California Statewide Travel Survey GPS Study is covered in Wolf *et al.* (2003), and Zmud and Wolf (2003).

Table 2 shows the deployment, completion, and percent missed trips statistics found in these passive, in-vehicle studies. In addition, the percent missed trips is a study average and is based on total GPS trip counts compared to total CATI trip counts for the same vehicles. These have not been adjusted for missing GPS trips, which would cause the rates to be higher. Finally, **these rates are not to be used for the entire sample**; regression analyses are required to determine the appropriate correction factors based on the significant correlates for underreporting. Analyses and results of the California Statewide GPS Study and the Ohio Statewide GPS Study are available in papers by Wolf *et al.* (2003), Zmud and Wolf (2003), and Pierce *et al.* (2003).

Table 2: Deployment, Completion, and Missing Trip Statistics

Study Name	# Deployed (households)	# Deployed (all vehicles)	GPS Completes (Per/Veh)	GPS & CATI Completes (all vehs)	% Missed Trips (overall)
California Statewide HTS	517	920	NA	292	23%
SCAG (Los Angeles) HTS*	820	1217	631	293	35%
Pittsburgh HTS	74	149	101	46	31%
Ohio Statewide HTS*	NA	NA	NA	NA	NA
Laredo (Texas) HTS	187	348	234	87	81%
St. Louis HTS	313	666	428	150	11%
Tyler / Longview (Texas) HTS	367	646	350	197	NA
Kansas City HTS	294	548	462	228	11%

These GPS studies and their corresponding methodologies have been evolving with each study performed. Given the newness of GPS in travel surveys, each study reveals new insights about appropriate methodologies and what needs to be improved in subsequent studies. As such, the methodology for generating trip rate correction factors is considered experimental.

WEARABLE GPS STUDIES

As mentioned earlier, all 'traditional' GPS studies have taken a vehicle-based approach, primarily because 1) the vehicle's power system can be used to power the GPS loggers; 2) GPS signal reception is better if the antenna is mounted on a vehicle roof or windshield as compared to being worn somewhere on the body; and 3) once installed, all vehicle trips are sure to be captured, as compared to a wearable device that may be forgotten by the participant when travelling. In addition, a vehicle-based approach has been acceptable to modellers who are focused on vehicle trips, especially in the vehicle-dependent USA. However, it has been recognised that if wearable GPS loggers were available that met project needs, these would be the preferred tool for personal mobility data collection. Research trends for wearable GPS logging devices have split into two distinct paths – those that include a user interface (typically a PDA) and those that are completely passive.

PDA/GPS Applications

Early research on the use of wearable GPS logging devices for travel survey data collection included a PDA component for collecting additional travel details. The first study of this type occurred in the Netherlands in 1997, with a custom-built PDA, a GPS receiver and antenna, and a DGPS antenna (Draijer *et al.*, 2000). This study deployed the wearable equipment package to 151 participants to compare GPS performance across different travel modes and to assess GPS system usage by survey respondents. Although the researchers concluded that it was possible to use GPS to monitor trips with various modes of travel, the equipment package (which weighed approximately two kilograms) was considered heavy by study participants and was consequently reported to be left behind on a significant number of walk, cycling, and public transport trips.

The next study to use a wearable PDA/GPS combination was the SMARTRAQ Non-Motorized Travel/Physical Activity Study, which was a subcomponent of the Atlanta Regional Household Travel Survey. The primary purpose of the GPS-based physical activity study was the development and testing of a person-based methodology to collect the spatial and temporal aspects of urban travel objectively, especially non-motorised travel. Of the 8,069 households participating in the regional travel survey between spring 2001 and spring 2002, 542 participants received an electronic travel diary implemented on a Palm PDA that included a GPS component. The total weight of this wearable package was approximately 1 kilogram. Results of this study were recently presented (Frank *et al.*, 2004) and will be released this spring in a project report for the Georgia Department of Transportation.

One variation of a PDA/GPS tool for collecting travel survey data can be found in the ongoing evolution of CHASE (Computerised Household Activity Scheduling Elicitor), a computerised tool for capturing the activity scheduling process of study participants (Doherty, 2002). Early versions of CHASE were implemented on laptop PCs, without a geographic component. As CHASE evolved, it was enhanced to support some GIS

(Kreitz and Doherty, 2002) and even GPS capabilities (Doherty *et al.*, 2001). Most recently, it appears the implementation of the CHASE approach will be broken down into discrete segments that include an initial, limited amount of preplanning/scheduling, followed by passive GPS data collection, and then finishing with additional prompting for scheduling decisions that were not detected (Doherty and Papinski, 2004). Plans for implementation of this latest approach include the use of a PDA/ cellular phone connected to a BlueTooth GPS, combined with a hand-held web-based survey interface to be tested in the autumn of 2004.

Passive GPS Applications

In 2002, the London Department for Transport sponsored a research study investigating the use of GPS in travel surveys (Steer Davies Gleave and GeoStats, 2003), with a specific focus on evaluating how GPS could enhance the London Area Transport Survey (LATS). Wearable GPS data loggers (the Wearable GeoLogger™ by GeoStats) were selected for this study, which consisted of a three-day data collection effort for 154 study participants. For the first two days of data collection, participants were asked to carry the loggers with them throughout the day. On the third day, they were asked to carry the loggers and to fill out a simple trip log. When the equipment was collected on the fourth day, a short recall survey was conducted using the trip log as a basis.

This study found that even in London's demanding environment with many trips made by bus, train, and underground subway, GPS loggers performed effectively in collecting data across all modes of travel. When the person travelled out of view of the GPS satellites, the data collected could still identify where the signal was lost and where it was regained, thus confirming an underground trip segment occurred. Of all possible days for data collection, eighty two percent of the days yielded usable GPS data. The remaining eighteen percent were not usable primarily due to either a lack of use (i.e., the participant did not carry it) or misuse (there were some communication problems regarding the proper way to carry or wear the device). This study also found that London participants were receptive to the technology, and although a few comments were made about the size and weight of the GeoLoggers, concerns about security and privacy were less than expected.

CELLULAR POSITIONING STUDIES

In a paper by Wermuth *et al.* (2003, studies involving two GSM-based travel activity collection systems (TeleTravel System and personal Handy-phone System) were presented. The TeleTravel System was implemented in Germany on a commercial mobile phone that included an electronic questionnaire to collect trip details and utilised GSM (a mobile radio network) for both periodic data transmission as well as location identification to within one hundred metres on average. The Personal Handy-phone System was developed and tested in Japan; it consisted of a mobile communications system that provided position accuracy levels within sixty metres on average. This system was tested in tandem with a simple activity diary survey.

Since these studies, there has not been much research in the use of cellular-based positioning as a sole means of collecting travel survey data – most likely due to the lower accuracy levels available compared to GPS accuracy levels (five to seven metres, typically) as well as the ongoing delay of full E911 implementation in the US (which has driven the enhancement of cell phones to provide location within one hundred metres for emergency calls). It is much more likely that as cellular phones with GPS chips become more commonplace, Assisted GPS (AGPS), which provides additional information to the GPS receiver from outside sources using wireless data transfer, will prove to be the best cellular solution for providing accurate location outdoors with a much greater coverage area than GPS alone – and that indoor traces will also be available. However, there are several key issues with the use of this technology for collecting travel behaviour; these include privacy concerns about collecting data without traveller consent and the challenge of working with a variety of cellular network standards and providers (especially in the US). Of course, the benefits of this promising cellular/GPS solution, including both enhanced location determination and remote data transfer that enables long-term data collection efforts, should lead to more studies leveraging this technology in the near future.

EMERGING GPS STUDIES

It is likely that the use of GPS in travel surveys to audit reported travel behaviour is merely the first step in accepting the technology for collection of highly accurate travel data. Now that this acceptance seems to have arrived, recent trends indicate that someday GPS may be used to replace some or all components of traditional travel survey data collection methods. Of course, the costs of GPS studies are still much higher than traditional methods. However, there have been discussions lately within the travel behaviour survey community that smaller sample sizes with longer survey periods for each participant may provide greater value than large-scale 24-hour surveys (Murakami *et al.*, 2003). In addition, the generation and use of synthetic datasets may also offer a method to augment smaller GPS studies. There are two emerging areas for GPS in travel surveys: 1) GPS-based prompted recall and 2) GPS-only data collection.

GPS-based Prompted Recall

In GPS-based Prompted Recall studies, households are recruited into the travel survey through traditional means (e.g., an advanced mailing followed by a telephone recruitment call). During this recruitment call, basic household sociodemographic data, travel modes, and habitual destination address information (e.g., home, work, school, daycare, grocery shopping) for each person in the household are collected. GPS loggers are then provided for all household vehicles or household members (over a given age) for the duration of the assigned travel period. The GPS data are then processed, leveraging the recruitment call information, and presented back to the respondents for confirmation and/or correction of derived trip details and the completion of other traditional elements that cannot be derived from GPS data, such as number of travel companions and destination activities.

The implementation of prompted (or assisted) recall can occur through a combination of methodologies and technologies, including mail out/mail back letters with trip tables and maps, CATI personnel using a computer application that presents prompted recall details and collects responses, and computer assisted self interviews (CASI) implemented via the Internet, personal digital assistants (PDAs) with GPS, or GPS-enabled PDA cell phones. Evaluation of GPS-based prompted recall techniques for travel survey data collection was first reported by Louisiana State University (Bachu *et al.*, 2001). Since then, other projects have tested GPS-based prompted recall methods as well. Currently, GPS-based prompted recall is being used in the Kansas City Household Travel Survey to collect details on unreported trips, and the 2004 Sydney Household Travel Survey plans to provide GPS devices to 100 to 150 households and to collect additional trip details via prompted recall. If the methodology and technology supports periodic GPS data processing throughout the data collection period (such as what can be supported through wireless data transfer and/or CASI solutions), it is very feasible to have participants in the study for long periods of time with the prompted recall occurring throughout the data collection period.

GPS-only Data Collection

GPS-only data collection consists of passive GPS data collection (in-vehicle or wearable) with full trip detail derivation/imputation occurring during data processing. This methodology requires no further contact with the study participants, which could greatly reduce costs as well as participant burden. In addition, the entirely passive nature of this method makes long-term data collection periods practical.

Significant research has occurred over the past four years to develop algorithms that automate the identification of trip details once considered difficult, if not impossible, to determine from GPS data, including trip purpose and travel mode (Wolf, 2000; Wolf *et al.*, 2001; de Jong and Mensonides, 2003; Wolf *et al.*, 2004; Chung and Shalaby, 2004a, Chung and Shalaby, 2004b). Initially, algorithm development was slow as researchers worked through the feasibility of deriving various trip variables. More recent algorithm development has been driven by projects that have accumulated GPS data for hundreds of participants for an extended period of time, resulting in trip counts in the 50,000 to 500,000 range. When dealing with historical datasets of this size and duration, it is simply infeasible to go back to the participants to ask for missing details. The next section presents several of these studies in more detail.

DATA COLLECTED IN OTHER STUDIES

The implementation of GPS technology in other transport-related studies is generating incredibly large datasets of high-resolution GPS details collected from personal automobiles in travel survey study areas. Safety and road pricing studies have been the leading applications for long-term GPS data collection. Here are a few recent examples:

- **Sweden Speed Adaptation Study**. The recent Swedish Intelligent Speed Adaptation (ISA) study was concerned with the traffic safety effects of in-car speed information systems (Hultkrantz and Lindberg, 2003). The three systems, a different one installed in each city (Borlänge, Lund and Lidköping), informed the driver in real-time about violating the posted speed limits by a blinking light, by a sound, by increasing the resistance of the accelerator, or by combinations of these. In each case, an in-vehicle unit measured the location and speed of the vehicle by GPS, looked up the posted speed limit from a suitably enriched network database, and informed the driver of speed violations when they occurred. These vehicles were observed for up to two years, and in the Borlänge component, the speed and location data of each vehicle were transmitted at regular intervals to a central server and stored for later analysis. Researchers at the Swiss Federal Institute of Technology in Zurich and Lausanne, along with GeoStats, have been processing and analysing this dataset for trip-making details, including trip end identification, trip purpose imputation, and route choice behaviours (Wolf *et al.*, 2004; Frejinger, 2004).
- **Copenhagen Road Pricing Experiment**. Four hundred vehicles were instrumented with GPS-based devices for eight to ten week control and experimental periods in this AKTA road pricing experiment conducted in Copenhagen. Pricing schemes included zonal and cordon based rates, which varied by peak and non-peak hours; these prices were displayed back to the participants in real-time as an accumulated cost for each trip as it was underway. The GPS data were collected and analysed to determine the behavioural impacts of the different pricing schemes, (Nielsen and Jovicic, 2003). The research team recognises the richness of the dataset with respect to opportunities for evaluating route choice, trip patterns, and speed. Research efforts currently are focused on estimating route choice under the various tolling models.
- **Commute Atlanta**. In 2001, Georgia Tech was awarded a FHWA Value Pricing Pilot Program project grant for a study to evaluate the impact of mileage-based insurance rates on commuter behaviour. In the past year, more than 250 households in the Atlanta region have been recruited into this study. Event data recorders (EDR) have been installed in the household vehicles; these EDRs collect second-by-second GPS data and speed, and transmit these data on a daily basis. Researchers at Georgia Tech have begun the exploration of these data to improve understandings about travel behaviour (Li *et al.*, 2004).

There are also numerous other applications for GPS-instrumented vehicles, including fleet tracking and vehicle theft prevention and/or recovery. Perhaps one of the more interesting non-transport applications for GPS-instrumented vehicles was a city-wide art project conducted in Amsterdam; Amsterdam RealTime attempted to visualise the mental maps of city residents by examining their travel behaviour (www.waag.org/realtime /Amsterdam). This two-month project invited all city residents to carry a PDA/cell phone connected to a GPS receiver and antenna. GPS data were transmitted in real-time to a central location where the data were projected into the exhibition space.

If these datasets are made available, travel behaviour researchers and modellers will have enough data to keep themselves busy for years. Of course, there will always be some data elements missing, so it is desirable for secondary users of such datasets to be involved in the study design. The tradeoff for this involvement is typically more requirements, higher costs, and longer implementation schedules. Privacy issues may also arise. Cost sharing and data sharing agreements are beneficial for establishing relationships between primary and secondary user groups.

In a recent publication on assessing road user charges (Forkenbrock and Kuhl, 2002), Forkenbrock acknowledges the numerous benefits for transport planning if road user fee systems gathered additional information to support technical travel demand analyses. Given that the implementation of a system that enables the assessment of road user charges is the primary objective, and that there are significant privacy issues with the collection of the additional elements required by planners (such as trip origin and destination locations, as well as travel routes), Forkenbrock recommends that only user charge data should be collected in the initial implementations.

CONCLUSIONS

It is clear that GPS technologies have much to offer in the passive collection (or measurement) of detailed travel behaviour data. When enhanced with cellular positioning (such as in A-GPS) and transmission capabilities, GPS logging devices are a powerful tool for collecting multiday and multiperiod survey data with little or no respondent burden. At the last Transport Survey Quality Conference at Kruger Park, Murakami *et al.* (2003) reported on the benefits, barriers to use, data issues, and utility of technologies for travel surveys. Since then, the expanding use and exploration of technology applications, specifically GPS-based technologies, in travel surveys have furthered the understanding of the issues as well as resolutions. For example, the high costs of GPS studies are driven by equipment and deployment costs. These can be reduced significantly by using smaller sample sizes over longer time periods. The use of wireless or modem-based data transfer methods will also enable participation for extended periods of time.

Although it seems unlikely that GPS methods will replace traditional methods any time soon, it seems equally likely that applications of GPS will progress from the traditional use as an auditing tool for reported behaviours to a supplement (e.g., prompted recall) or replacement (e.g., GPS-only) for traditional diary and CATI survey methods – at least on a small scale. In addition, the proliferation and adoption of consumer devices with GPS, cellular, and/or PDA capabilities offers the opportunity to leverage existing hardware already in the hands of study participants for collecting detailed travel behaviour information. The availability of massive vehicle-based GPS datasets collected for other purposes facilitates algorithm development, testing, and implementation for all types of GPS-based travel surveys. As these data processing and imputation routines are proven to be accurate, this reuse or repurpose of data may, in itself, lead to very cost-effective solutions for generating (vehicle) travel behaviour datasets without ever deploying a single GPS device for a travel survey.

Of course, travel behaviour researchers are interested in all modes of travel, and therefore, wearable GPS devices are desirable over vehicle-based solutions. There is much promise in this area, because consumer-driven services such as child, elderly, and parolee tracking are bringing technology improvements that include reductions in size, power demand, and price in wearable devices. Other form factor improvements have focused on the wearability of these devices, and can be seen in products such as GPS watches and Bluetooth (wireless) GPS receivers. These improvements should help to address concerns about participants either forgetting to carry or deciding not to carry wearable loggers. For a more interactive solution, the integration of GPS with PDAs and PDA/cell phones offers the ability to collect additional trip details either in real-time or immediately after travel occurs; size, performance, and power demand are all areas of continuing technology improvement for these devices.

To provide an incentive for travel survey study participation beyond offers of cash or gifts, the latest efforts have focused on making participation easier or more convenient, such as what can be offered in Internet-based solutions. GPS technology is passive by nature, which does make participation easier than traditional methods. Other ideas to increase response rates include making participation more like a game, which can be implemented through a combination of GPS and user interface (Internet, PDA, PC) tools, perhaps the basis of which could be GPS-based prompted recall. Another interesting game-like approach has been tested by researchers in The Netherlands, who are exploring the use of virtual reality systems as a means of collecting travel data (Tan and Timmermans, 2004).

Other technologies not covered in this chapter deserve acknowledgement for their potential roles in collecting or generating travel survey data; these include Internet surveys and PDA/laptop/Tablet PC technologies for use in face-to-face or self-administered surveys as well as simulation-based data generation methods (Stopher *et al.*, 2001). As travel survey researchers move forward in their quest to collect more and better data, it seems obvious that there will not be one solution, but rather a combination of high, low, and no technology solutions that can be implemented singularly or in tandem (i.e., mixed mode surveys) to collect accurate and representative datasets. It is also clear that GPS and cellular technologies belong in this toolset.

REFERENCES

Bachu, P., R. Dudala, and S. Kothuri (2001). Prompted Recall in Global Positioning Survey: Proof of Concept Study, *Transportation Research Record No. 1768*, 106-113.

Casas, J. and C. Arce (1999). Trip Reporting in Household Travel Diaries: A Comparison to GPS-Collected Data, Paper presented at the 78th Annual Meeting of the Transportation Research Board, Washington, DC, January.

Chung, E. and A. Shalaby (2004a). Development of a Trip Reconstruction Tool to Identify Traveled Links and Used Modes for GPS-based Personal Travel Surveys, Paper presented at the 83rd Annual Meeting of the Transportation Research Board, Washington, DC, January.

Chung, E. T. Y., and A. Shalaby (2004b). An Integrated GPS-GIS System for Personal Travel Surveys, Poster presented at the GEOIDE Annual Conference, Quebec, May.

de Jong, R. and W. Mensonides (2003). *Wearable GPS device as a data collection method for travel research*, ITS working Paper 03-02, Institute of Transport Studies, Sydney.

Doherty, S. T., N. Noël, M. Lee-Gosselin, C. Sirois and M. Ueno (2001). Moving Beyond Observed Outcomes: Integrating Global Positioning Systems and Interactive Computer-Based Travel Behaviour Surveys, *Transportation Research Circular No. E-C026*, March 2001, Transportation Research Board, National Research Council. Washington, DC, 449-466.

Doherty, S. T. (2002). Interactive Methods for Activity Scheduling Processes. In: *Transportation Systems Planning: Methods and Applications* (K. Goulias, ed.), 7-1 – 7-25, CRC Press, New York.

Doherty, S. T. and D. Papinski (2004). Is it Possible to Automatically Trace Activity Scheduling Decisions? Paper presented at the *Conference on Progress in Activity-Based Analysis*, Vaeshartelt Castle, Maastricht, The Netherlands, May.

Draijer, G., N. Kalfs, and J. Perdok (2000). GPS as Data Collection Method for Travel Research, *Transportation Research Record No. 1719*, 147-153.

Forkenbrock, D. and J. Kuhl (2002). *A New Approach to Assessing Road User Charges*, Public Policy Center, University of Iowa.

Frank, L., J. Wolf, J. Chapman, T. Schmid (2004). Measuring How We Move Through Space: Capturing Non-Motorized Travel and Physical Activity Through the Application of GPS Technology in Atlanta, paper presented at the Active Living Research Annual Conference, San Diego, January.

Frejinger, E. (2004). *Route Choice Modelling with GPS Data*, Diplomarbeit, Department Mathematik, EPF, Lausanne, March.

Hultkrantz, L. and G. Lindberg (2003). Intelligent Economic Speed Adaptation, Paper presented at the 10th International Conference on Travel Behaviour Research, Lucerne, August.

Kreitz, M., and S.T. Doherty (2002). Collection of Spatial Behavioral Data and their Use in Activity Scheduling Models, *Transportation Research Record No. 1804*, 126-133.

Li, H., R. Guensler, J. Ogle, and J. Wang (2004). Using GPS Data to Understand the Day-to-Day Dynamics of the Morning Commute Behaviour, paper presented at the 83rd Annual Meeting of the Transportation Research Board, Washington DC, January.

Murakami, E. and D.P. Wagner (1999). Can using GPS improve trip reporting? *Transportation Research C*, 7 (2-3), 149-165.

Murakami, E., J. Morris, and C. Arce (2003). Using Technology to Improve Transport Survey Quality. In: *Transport Survey Quality and Innovation* (P.R. Stopher and P.M. Jones, eds), 499-506, Pergamon, Oxford.

Nielsen, O. and G. Jovicic (2003). The AKTA Road Pricing Experiment in Copenhagen, Paper presented at the 10th International Conference on Travel Behaviour Research, Lucerne, August.

NuStats and Battelle (2004). *Year 200 Post-Census Regional Travel Survey: GPS Study Final Report*, Submitted to the Southern California Association of Governments.

Pearson, D. (2001). Global Positioning System (GPS) and Travel Surveys: Results from the 1997 Austin Household Survey, paper presented at the 8th Conference on the Application of Transportation Planning Methods, Corpus Christi, Texas, April.

Pierce, B., J. Casas, and G. Giamo (2003). Estimating Trip Rate Under-Reporting: Preliminary Results from the Ohio Household Travel Survey, paper presented at the 82nd Annual Meeting of the Transportation Research Board, Washington, DC, January.

Steer Davies Gleave and GeoStats (2003). *The Use of GPS to Improve Travel Data, Study Report*. Prepared for the DTLR New Horizons Programme, Submitted to the London Department for Transport.

Stopher, P.R., S.P.Greaves, S. Kothuri and P. Bullock (2001). Simulating household travel survey data: application to two urban areas, Paper presented to the 23rd Conference of Australian Institutes of Transport Research, Monahs University, December.

Stopher, P.R. (2004), GPS, Location, and Household Travel. In: *Handbook on Transport Geography and Spatial Systems* (D. Hensher, K. Button, K. Haynes, and P. Stopher, eds), 433-449, Elsevier, Oxford.

Tan, A. and H. Timmermans (2004). Paper-and-Pencil Retrospective Activity-Travel Diary versus Virtual Reality Re-enactment Sessions to Collect Activity-Travel Pattern Data: A Validation Study, Paper presented at the 83rd Annual Meeting of the Transportation Research Board, Washington, DC, January.

Wagner, D.P. (1997). *Report: Lexington Area Travel Data Collection Test; GPS for Personal Travel Surveys*, Final Report for OHIM, OTA, and FHWA.

Wermuth M., C. Sommer and M. Kreitz (2003). Impact of New Technologies in Travel Surveys. In: *Transport Survey Quality and Innovation* (P.R. Stopher and P.M. Jones, eds), 455-482, Pergamon Press, Oxford.

Wolf, J. (2000). *Using GPS Data Loggers to Replace Travel Diaries in the Collection of Travel Data*, Dissertation, Georgia Institute of Technology, School of Civil and Environmental Engineering, Atlanta, Georgia.

Wolf, J., R. Guensler, and W. Bachman (2001). Elimination of the Travel Diary: An Experiment to Derive Trip Purpose from GPS Travel Data, *Transportation Research Record No. 1768*, 125-134.

Wolf, J., M. Loechl, M. Thompson and C. Arce (2003). Trip Rate Analysis in GPS-Enhanced Personal Travel Surveys. In: *Transport Survey Quality and Innovation* (P.R. Stopher and P.M. Jones, eds), 485-498, Pergamon Press, Oxford.

Wolf, J. (2004). Defining GPS and GPS Capabilities. In: *Handbook on Transport Geography and Spatial Systems* (D. Hensher, K. Button, K. Haynes, and P. Stopher, eds), 411-431, Elsevier, Oxford.

Wolf, J., S. Schönfelder, U. Samaga, M. Oliveira and K.W. Axhausen (2004). 80 weeks of GPS Traces: Approaches to Enriching Trip Information, *Transportation Research Record No. 1870*, 46-54.

Zmud, J. and J. Wolf (2003), Identifying the Correlates of Trip Misreporting - Results from the California Statewide Household Travel Survey GPS Study, Paper presented at the 10th International Conference on Travel Behaviour Research, Lucerne, August.

Peter Stopher and Cheryl Stecher (Editors)

30

USING COMBINED GPS AND GSM TRACKING INFORMATION FOR INTERACTIVE ELECTRONIC QUESTIONNAIRES

Matthias Kracht, German Aerospace Centre (DLR), Berlin, Germany

INTRODUCTION

Most data on individual travel behaviour has been collected with traditional approaches of interviews or paper and pencil questionnaires. Only in the past decade have an increasing number of GPS based transport research projects been carried out. This is because the use of tracking technologies promises a higher level of data quality and the equipment is becoming affordable and usable.

The demand for more precise and reliable spatial data is partly derived from the paradigm shift from macroscopic to microscopic data analysis and modelling. In addition to simple origin and destination coordinates, more complex data about the whole route are needed. Two tracking technologies provide this information. GPS technology provides very accurate data, but is not always available due to technical restrictions like open view to satellites, which is especially crucial when participants use public transport. The Global System for Mobile Communications (GSM) is virtually always available, but it is not as accurate spatially. As a result, tracking technologies can improve the spatial information of the whole trip only under certain conditions. Because of technical constraints like power supply or weight, most of the early research projects focused on vehicle-based transport, mainly by private car. Recent feasibility tests on tracking in public transport produced poor results that led to systematic problems in environments with a large share of public transport.

Another reason for spending so much effort in developing new data acquisition technologies is human inability to report geographic information as precisely and reliably as is needed for transport research. It has been reported, that people cannot provide this kind of data by themselves. In a feasibility study in Germany, information collected by a CATI has been used to geocode self-reported trips. The results showed that about fifty percent of the origins and/or destinations could not be matched to a street section, and seventy to eighty percent could not be matched to an address (INFAS, 2001). However, even with 100 percent usable data, geographical route information is too complex to be included in classic questionnaires for now and most probably in the future. Facing these problems researchers are looking for alternatives to conventional CATI or PAPI. Parallel to the development of new tracking technologies, the introduction of CASI implemented on mobile electronic devices allows new approaches in transport research. This technology provides the opportunity to react on missing tracking data and to fill these gaps by adapted answer requests.

Tracking technologies cannot provide reliable data in every situation. Tracking accuracy and reliability are limited by technical constraints. However, even inaccurate tracking data, combined with electronic questionnaires, can provide useful information to support user response. This chapter describes how the parallel use of mobile electronic questionnaires and GPS/GSM tracking technologies can be used either to collect missing data or to correct inaccurate tracking data.

NEW TECHNOLOGIES IN TRANSPORT RESEARCH

Two major technologies have had a large influence on travel survey design and implementation in transport research during the past ten years. First, these are the tracking technologies of GPS and, more recently, GSM. Second are electronic questionnaires offline and online, as well as stationary and portable computer-based surveys. Wermuth *et al.* (2003) gave a comprehensive outline of the impact of new technologies. In this chapter, we discuss some additional work that is related to proposed alternative concepts for travel survey data collection. Tracking vehicles and individuals with GPS and GSM technology can be divided into two main approaches. The first is passive tracking without direct user response during the trip. The second approach is active tracking where user response is used to add additional information simultaneously to the recorded GPS/ GSM tracks. Active tracking with user response became particularly practical, because mobile equipment like personal digital assistants (PDAs) provided the necessary performance and user friendliness.

Tracking with GPS Technology

The first study using GPS technology for transport research was passive tracking along with traditional reported travel data in Austin in 1998 (Casas and Arce, 1999). This study focused mainly on the comparison of traditional (PAPI, CATI) and GPS based surveying. This study was followed by a number of other studies mainly focusing on vehicle based and in particular on car based transport (e.g. Wolf *et al.*, 2003; Zmud and Wolf, 2003). This restriction on vehicle based surveys is due to the fact that early GPS equipment was limited by the power supply provided in vehicles. At the same time, the equipment was also heavy and bulky. Bachu *et al.* (2001) used passive GPS data collection to carry out a Proof-of-Concept Study. They used printed maps showing the reported travel path to support prompted recall after the respondents finished the GPS survey. Stopher *et al.* (2004) conducted recently a prompted recall survey presenting maps of the reported trips via the Internet to respondents. Other research focused on the full trajectory of the trip (or multiple trips) as recorded by a GPS logger. Yalamanchili *et al.* (1999) used this characteristic of GPS data to analyse trip-chaining behaviour. Wolf *et al.* derived both trip rates (Wolf *et al.*, 2001) and trip purposes (Wolf *et al.*, 2003) from GPS data in combination with land use data.

Many of the current active GPS studies use some kind of user interface like a PDA attached to the GPS device to collect further information about the trip in real time or close to the trip event. One of the earliest surveys using this technology was the Lexington study carried out by the Battelle Memorial Institute in 1996 (Battelle Memorial Institute, 1997; Murakami and Wagner, 1999).

The first GPS pilot project focussing on the examination of all travel modes was done by the Dutch Transport Research Center (AVV) in 1997. They used active GPS equipment that could be carried outside a car, but which was still heavy (2 kilograms weight). Looking at the quality of the results, the pilot study demonstrated that it is possible to monitor individuals in different travel modes. However, comparing the different modes, there is a big difference regarding the tracking availability. Car users were tracked for ninety percent of their trips, while tram and train passengers were tracked only for fifty percent of their trips. The results of this research project also show a resistance to use the GPS equipment during walks, bicycle rides, and public transport, as well as for some travel purposes such as shopping or visits. This might have been caused by the size and weight of the equipment (Draijer *et al.*, 2000).

In a pilot study in Sydney, Hawkins and Stopher (2004) compared the rejection of face-to-face interviews and GPS tracking. They showed some significant differences between the two methods. The three main concerns of the participants about GPS tracking were user burden in general, already participating in the face-to-face interview, and privacy concerns. De Jong and Mensonides (2003). carried out a feasibility study tracking travel in public transport, in this case on different commuter trains in Sydney. These data show similar results in terms of tracking quality in public transport, especially in trains. Good tracking results were detected only in trains with overhead windows or on seats directly by the windows.

A study with wearable GPS devices done by Steer Davies Gleave and GeoStats (2003) under complex conditions in London produced promising results. The study applied

GPS tracking and CATI to compare the data quality of both approaches. It was shown that GPS tracking could already provide important information for correction factors, and the authors proposed that GPS tracking could take over CATI to a large extent within the next four years. One ambitious goal, using GPS technology, is the elimination of the travel diary, as Wolf *et al.*(2001) expressed it. Ideally, not only the track of each trip, but also the travel mode and even the trip purpose, should be detected automatically just by analysing the tracking data. Looking at the results of Draijer and de Jong, further improvement is necessary to reach this goal.

Tracking with GSM Technology

In transport research, the literature reveals only very few reports on GSM as an alternative for tracking. Besides projects dealing with location based services mainly focusing on commercial aspects, only a few projects are reported that applied GSM tracking technology for transport research purposes. Hato and Asakura used GSM tracking technology to collect time-space activity data (Hato and Asakura, 2001; Asakura and Hato, 2001). They used a passive approach to collect the time-space activities of ten individuals for a two-week period in 1998. In addition, the participants were asked to fill out a simple paper and pencil form for both weeks. The tracking accuracy ranges from 18 to 225 metres. The best accuracy was found in dense urban areas.

The TeleTravel System (TTS) project was carried out, using a similar approach, in 2000 in Germany (Wermuth *et al.*, 2001). This project combined GSM tracking technology and an electronic travel diary to determine the travel behaviour of the respondents. In this project the GSM tracking technology has been shown to produce an accuracy of about 50 to 100 meters with the highest precision in urban or densely populated areas.

Rutten et al. (2004) proved the GSM tracking in a test field in Noord Braband, Netherlands for a period of twelve month in 2003. The main goal of the study was to determine travel times and speeds for the road network. With respect to this goal they reported good quality of the tracking data on rural and interurban roads. The results in dense inner city areas need to be improved.

All of the surveys, discussed above, demonstrated the general applicability of GSM tracking technology for traffic research. However, it has been reported in a number of tests that the highest accuracy level of GSM tracking is approximately fifty metres in dense areas, which will limit the analysis of travel behaviour to some extent.

A new standard is promising a better coverage level for GSM tracking in the US: the Enhanced 911 (E911) mandate of the US Federal Communications Commission. The mandate requires service providers to give the location information of wireless 911 callers to public emergency-service agencies within an accuracy of one hundred metres sixty seven percent of the time and 300 metres ninety five percent of the time. 'The

FCC established a four-year rollout schedule ..., beginning October 1, 2001 and to be completed by December 31, 2005'. (FCC, 2005). A major disadvantage for GSM tracking compared to GPS tracking are the costs per tracking point. The standard charge of fleet management companies in Europe range from about twenty to fifty Euro Cents (e.g., FleetOnline, 2005).

Complex Questionnaires on Mobile Electronic Devices

To apply the active tracking approach, there needs to be a man-machine-interface to communicate with the respondent. For this purpose, many of the recent active tracking surveys used electronic questionnaires on PDAs to meet these requirements. Starting with easy to use adaptations of paper and pencil questionnaires on standard cellular phones up to complex activity-based diaries on PDAs, the use of mobile electronic questionnaires has gained increasing interest and use in transport research.

Doherty and Miller (2000) developed an activity based electronic questionnaire (CHASE) on stationary computers and transferred this tool to PDAs. An activity-based approach with extended activity planning functionality (Ex-ACT) is also applied in a German study carried out by Rindsfüser *et al.* (2003). Recently they have done a feasibility study with the aim to include GPS tracking in their research approach.

Sommer developed a very easy to use approach to collect basic trip data on standard cellular phones (Sommer, 2002). A cellular phone SIM card has been developed which can be used to collect the basic trip information like mode, purpose and time on every cellular phone. The German Aerospace Centre (DLR) applied a similar procedure with reduced complexity, based on standard WAP and java technology which is currently in a field test.

A new approach to communicate with respondents is interactive voice systems (IVR). This has been done in two ways. Zhou and Golledge (2004) used a voice system installed on PDAs with the capability to connect to a server via a (short range) wireless network. This voice system serves mainly as an alternative man-machine-interface. Sommer and Wermuth (2004) extended their SIM card approach and applied an interactive voice system to get trip information like mode and purpose.

Bringing It Together

Accuracy and availability of spatial information provided by GPS and GSM technology, as discussed in the literature, is summarised in Table 1. Due to the technological restrictions and advantages of both technologies, it is quite clear that GSM tracking can complement GPS tracking in many situations. However, up to now there are no known reports in the literature where both tracking technologies have been used together for transport research. Even with parallel use of both tracking technologies, there might be some situations where user response is necessary to generate reliable results.

Table 1: Accuracy and Availability of Spatial Information

Technology	Information Accuracy			Information Availability		
	Origin	Route	Destination	Origin	Route	Destination
GPS	+++	+++	+++	++	++	++
GSM	++	++	++	+++	+++	+++
Questionnaire	+	-	+	+	-	+

+++ = good, ++ = sufficient, + = poor, - = no data

None of the CASI tools, discussed above, integrate the actual tracking data into their questionnaires in real time. This might be due to the large amount of data that needs to be processed or stored on the PDA. Using GSM technology for tracking provides also the opportunity to transfer data in real time and, thus, the use of remote computer power for calculation and data storage. With this technology, real time integration of tracking results parallel to user response becomes an opportunity.

The following section describes recent results with parallel GPS/GSM tracking. Based on the results, several approaches for GSM tracking improvements are proposed. The way in which real time integration of tracking results into electronic questionnaires can reduce the complexity of questionnaires and thus user burden is also described.

TRACKING WITH GPS/GSM TECHNOLOGY IN PRACTICE

As described above, most of the GPS tracking projects in the past focused on vehicle-based transport mainly by private car, due to the constraints of GPS technology, such as power consumption, weight, reception in public transport vehicles, etc. When tracking individuals in all transport modes, the participants were asked to wear the equipment in a special manner. Most of the projects used a GPS antenna placed on the shoulder strap of a bag. The bag was used to store a passive data logger, power supply, and sometimes a portable computer when active user response was required. One can imagine that this equipment has an impact on the respondent's behaviour and on the willingness to participate in such a survey (Draijer *et al.*, 2000).

The aim of the field test is to track individuals in a controlled situation in public transport. Berlin has a large share of public transport trips (twenty two percent), so that use in public transport is critical for Berlin. Thus, the design of the equipment should be as handy as possible to minimise the influence on the respondent's behaviour. To meet this requirement, we have chosen two devices (GSM, GPS) which can be carried easily. Size and weight of the devices are similar to a standard PDA or cellular phone. The equipment used in the test drive has the specifications shown in Table 2.

Given that eighty percent of the inhabitants in the study area own a cellular phone, we assume that carrying similar devices of comparable size and weight does not bother people too much. The devices do not need to be connected to a separate power supply and thus can be carried independently in different pockets. We also assume that not all people would like to carry a GPS on top of the shoulder. For this reason, we tested some other positions, to find out whether they would provide reliable GPS tracking data, especially when these data can be complemented with GSM tracking data. Two major goals were pursued:

1. Develop tracking equipment that will reduce the user burden in terms of carrying comfort as much as possible and, at the same time, provide accurate and reliable tracking data of an acceptable quality.
   a. Test the GPS tracking capabilities of the equipment in different positions on the body to determine the best compromise of tracking capability and convenience for the respondent; and
   b. Test the GSM tracking availability parallel to the GPS tracking.
2. Develop routines for an electronic diary that will use the tracking data for an adapted, situation-based user response. Real time adaptation of tracking results can be used to reduce the complexity of questionnaires and, thus, user burden.
   a. Develop a combined GPS/GSM tracking concept; and
   b. Develop user interfaces that will use tracking information for adapted user response to increase the accuracy/availability and close the gaps left by GPS/GSM tracking.

Table 2: Equipment Used in the Test Drive

Characteristic	*Cellular Phone/ PDA*	*GPS Device*
Data Storage Capacity	128 MB RAM + variable SD-card memory	Data logger functionality with 8MB (expandable)
Operating System	Windows CE	N/A
GPRS Functionality	Yes	No
Independent Run Time	~15 hours continuously	~10 hours continuously
Weight	190 grams	100 grams
Size	130 x 70 x 20 mm.	110 x 53 x 24 mm.
Bluetooth Port	Yes	Yes

Simultaneous Tracking with GPS/GSM Technology

The following example shows how the use of both tracking technologies simultaneously can increase the data availability and accuracy. These examples are results of a series of test drives during the years 2002/2003. The study site was Berlin.

Tracking accuracy and reliability is highly dependent on the position in which the survey participants carry the GPS device (de Jong and Mensonides, 2003). This analysis is based on a test drive with eight participants at the same time period (approximately 14:00 to 16:00) of a single day. The eight participants were divided into four groups (marked group 1 to 4 on the right hand side of Figure 1) who took different, predefined routes by commuter train (S-Bahn) in Berlin. Each participant carried four GPS devices on predefined positions of the body (one at each shoulder (S), two at the belt (B) or in pockets (P) of the coat close to the belt). At the same time, one participant of each group carried a cellular phone in the backpack, which has been tracked during the test drive (Kracht and Ruppe, 2004).

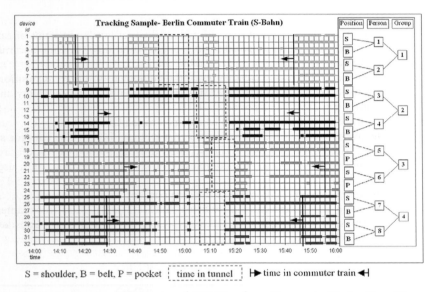

S = shoulder, B = belt, P = pocket ┆ time in tunnel ┆ ▶ time in commuter train ◀

Figure 1: Presence or Absence of GPS Signals on Commuter Trains Over Time

The data from the two GPS receivers were analysed with respect to data availability during the trips as well as data accuracy. Figure 1 depicts the recording of signals during each journey and for all GPS devices. Each device is plotted as a single horizontal line. A gap in the line describes missing tracking data. Devices 13 and 19 were configured incorrectly and thus did not provide usable data. The figure shows that only nine out of thirty six GPS devices (6, 9, 10, 17, 18, 22, 26, 29, and 30) provide constant tracking results with less than ten minute gaps at a time – except tunnel times (box with dashed line). All these devices were placed on the shoulder of the participants. This was expected due to the characteristics of GPS technology and the chosen test environment. However, there are also some GPS devices not carried on the shoulder that show fair results (20, 23, 24, 31, and 32). Especially those devices carried in the pockets of a coat, basically at the same position as those on the belt, but not covered by heavy clothing, showed good results.

The GPS tracking on each of the four routes (group 1 to 4) show some similar patterns, as plotted in Figure 1. The presence and absence of GPS signals on different routes show a characteristic 'pattern' for each route, e.g., the pattern of presence and absence of GPS signal before and after the tunnels. The pair of GPS devices placed on the shoulder or on the belt (pocket) of each respondent show similar results on most routes. When the signal on a test drive is not available at one of the paired devices the other device shows generally similar results. These 'patterns' might be caused by external conditions, such as the built environment close to the rail tracks or train stations.

Analysis over time shows that the shoulder position, in contrast to the belt, is more crucial than the left or right hand position on the body. The GPS devices on the shoulder provide the best results, followed by the devices in the pocket. The devices on the belt show the poorest results on all routes and persons. The position in the pocket might be a place where tracking requirements and user burden result in a good compromise. Due to the short test drive, this needs to be proved in further tests. The GSM devices of all four groups showed constant connection to a base station over the complete travel time (not shown in Figure 1). Assuming that the tracking accuracy of this technology in areas with dense population can reach about one hundred metres and less, as has been reported, this will close the gaps left by the GPS tracking.

Figure 2 shows an example of how GSM tracking can fill the spatial gaps when a GPS signal is missing. The map shows the tracks of GPS devices 22 and 24 (see also Figure 1). In addition, the sites of the GSM base transceiver stations, that are connected to the GSM device during the same drive, are plotted to indicate the proximity and, thus, the potential tracking accuracy to the real track. The test drive starts in the south-east corner of the map, turns right (north) onto the ring structure and comes back to the starting point.

As Figure 1 already indicates, the GPS device 22 provides good tracking data. This is confirmed by the spatial pattern of Figure 2. There are only a few gaps left at the northern part of the test drive. On the other hand, device 24 shows very poor GPS tracking results. Only the first part of the test drive (in the southeast part, done by walking to the train station) provides good GPS results. The largest part of the trip, taken by commuter train, is documented only by very few GPS tracking points. However, even with the view tracking points of device 24, the change between two commuter trains has been tracked (see dots in the very north and west of the map).

The GSM track outlined by the plotted GSM transceiver stations on the map (round and square symbols) show that, in an urban area like Berlin, the distance of GSM transceiver stations to the real track is relatively small. In this test drive, the GSM transceiver stations represent the location of the station itself, but not a calculation of the respondent's actual location. Both GPS tracks can be complemented by GSM tracking to fill the gaps. The GPS tracking of device 22 is nearly complete and the GSM tracking has to fill only a few gaps in the north. On the other hand, the GPS tracking points of device 24 can serve as reference points to adjust the more inaccurate GSM tracking. The square symbols represent a GSM base transceiver station in a tunnel and indicate that the respondent used a train tunnel that is equipped with GSM functionality. This is the case for most of the rail and subway network in Berlin as well as in other large cities.

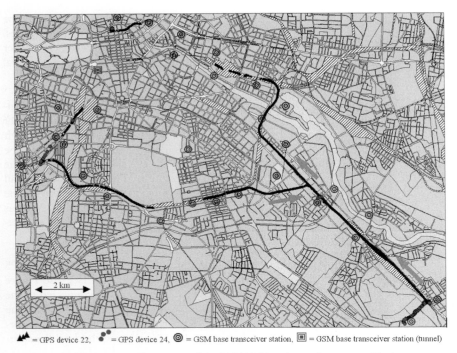

▲▲ = GPS device 22,   •°•° = GPS device 24, ◎ = GSM base transceiver station, ▣ = GSM base transceiver station (tunnel)

Figure 2: Spatial Pattern of GPS/GSM Signals on Commuter Trains

The analysis of the GPS tracking data leads to the conclusion that tracking individuals in commuter trains does not provide reliable data in all situations. It has been shown that GSM tracking can close the gaps left by GPS tracking in some environments. It is expected that the development of the GPS/GSM database, as it is described in the following section will further improve the GSM tracking capability and accuracy.

ALTERNATIVE CONCEPTS FOR TRAVEL SURVEY DATA COLLECTION

Data collection and analysis, based on passive tracking approaches, rely heavily on good data quality. For example, the determination of traffic mode based on speed measurements derived from GPS tracking data will only work with very accurate data. As discussed and shown above, tracking data are often not in the appropriate condition to allow this kind of analysis. In this case, other approaches, such as historic tracking data bases and active tracking with adapted user response, are useful to ensure data quality and reliability.

GSM Tracking with an Historic GPS/GSM Tracking Data Base

A GSM network consists of serving cell areas structured by cell borders (A) (see Figure 3). In addition to the cell borders there are field strength borders (B) within each cell which divides the cell into concentric zones around each GSM station. The determination of the actual position will be done by measuring the field strength of each base transceiver station in sight of the cellular phone. A second approach is the Time Difference of Arrival (TDA) of the signal of each base transceiver station. The intersection of all measurements will be the actual position of the phone. Figure 3 shows an ideal situation not influenced by the "real world" like landscape, buildings and other factors affecting the signal spreading and thus the shape of a cell border. Neglecting those environmental effects GSM tracking would provide distorted results. Thus the knowledge of the "real world" cell borders and field strength borders would increase the GSM tracking quality.

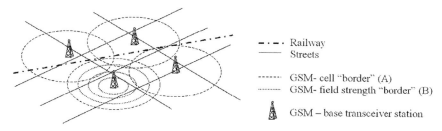

Figure 3: Schematic Figure of GSM Tracking (Ideal Tracking Conditions)

Once the approach of parallel GPS/GSM tracking (as described above) has been used for a longer period, a historic GPS/GSM tracking data base can be established. This data base will consist of the GSM transceiver station ID, the transceiver station location and the GSM field strength and/or TDA at every logged GPS position. This information reflects the cell borders and field strength borders influenced by 'real world' conditions like landscape and built environment. GSM tracking with this 'real world' cell borders might be much more realistic than measuring the theoretical position assuming there would be a homogenous space with no interferences.

GSM tracking based on the described historic GPS/GSM tracking database concept could be done on different accuracy levels, as follows:

1.   The (average) border of each GSM serving cell will indicate the area in which the participant stays. Tracking the moving participant over a time period will provide a sequence of all cells and thus a trajectory.
2.   As outlined in Figure 3 the field strength or TDA can increase the tracking accuracy. The signal strength within each serving cell can be understood as a virtual border subdividing each serving cell. These smaller areas will increase the tracking accuracy.

This data base will provide the opportunity to track only with GSM technology with better accuracy. This could be necessary when the GPS signal is temporarily not available or GPS equipment is not available and a less precise accuracy level can be accepted.

It is well known that the spatial spreading of field strength is influenced by a number of effects like building shadows, weather, and mirror effects. Because some of these effects are not stable over time, the GSM tracking approach, described here, is – compared to the accuracy of GPS tracking – still only an approximation of the real position. However, even when the accuracy of GSM tracking might be sometimes inaccurate, the tracking results can be used for adapted data collection.

Data Collection with Adapted User Response

Based on the parallel use of GPS and/or GSM tracking, the knowledge of the respondent's location can be used for adapted user response and, thus, reduce user burden. Portable electronic devices equipped with GPS/GSM can be used to interview the respondents in real time on site. The knowledge of the location will be used to reduce the amount and the complexity of questions asked. Questions about origin, route, destination, or transport mode will be asked only if tracking data are unclear and need to be specified. With respect to the tracking data availability, the interaction intensity with the respondent will vary as shown in Figure 4.

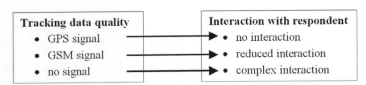

Figure 4: Influence of Tracking Quality on Respondent Interaction Needs

All of these tracking technologies can be used for adapted data collection. Each tracking accuracy level can be used to adjust questions asked in an electronic questionnaire to an appropriate level. This can be done by reducing the written context menu (Figure 5) or by providing adequate graphical support like maps (Figure 6). The use of adapted data collection becomes necessary when the accuracy level or the reliability of the tracking information is to low. This will happen when, for example, too few GPS satellites are in view; the GSM serving cell area is to large; or the time gap between the last known tracking point and the actual time is too large.

A GPS signal with good quality will provide all information needed to determine the track and sometimes even the mode of the trip. Thus, in this case, interaction with the respondent is not necessary. Tracking with the GSM signal might require some interaction with the respondent, assuming that the tracking data need to be more precise than provided by the GSM technology. The interaction with the respondent can be reduced as described in the following paragraph.

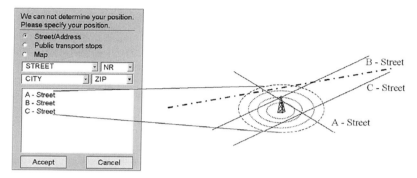

Figure 5: Respondent Interaction with Reduced Menu Content

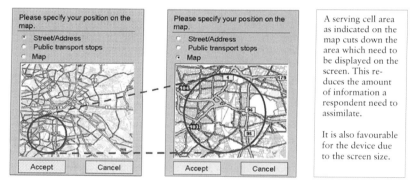

Figure 6: Respondent Interaction with Map Support

An inexact knowledge of the location given by GSM tracking can be used to present a reduced menu content. This can be done when asking for origin/destination information like street name. Having a rough knowledge of the location of a respondent, all streets within a certain vicinity (e.g., a GSM serving cell, see Figure 3: A-Street) can be selected and presented on the screen (see Figure 5) and thus reduce the interaction with the user. The same procedure can be applied for other spatial information like public transport stations or zip codes.

Sometimes respondents feel more comfortable when their response is assisted by maps (Figure 6). Even with incomplete or inaccurate tracking data the origin or destination of a trip can be specified by presenting the estimated area on a map and asking the respondent for specification. The knowledge of the actual GSM cell ID for example can be used to present this area on a map at the mobile device. The same approach can be used when the information about a route is incomplete, or the accuracy level is less precise than required. In this case, the estimated route can be presented on a map and the user asked to confirm or adjust the route, as is done in the prompted recall approach (Bachu *et al.*, 2001; Stopher *et al.*, 2004). These concepts for adapted data collection are currently under development. First tests with map supported data collection in real time or on site, based on GSM tracking, have shown good results (Ruppe, 2004).

CONCLUSION

Obtaining transport data of good quality is one of the major demands in transport research. One attempt to increase data quality and, thus, data accuracy and availability is using new technologies. Much research has been done on GPS/GSM tracking technology and electronic questionnaires in transport research. This chapter has focused on parallel GPS/GSM tracking and adapted data collection with electronic questionnaires on mobile electronic devices. It has been shown that parallel GPS/GSM tracking is a good opportunity to complete incomplete GPS tracking data (e.g., Figure 2). The proposed GSM tracking approach based on a GPS/GSM database might only work in cities or dense areas because of a sufficient density of GSM base transceiver stations and the size of the data base. Further tests will prove whether the proposed concept will be suitable on a larger scale and under everyday conditions as intended.

Asking people to wear technical equipment over a long time can always cause nonresponse or drop out effects that will influence the research results. These effects are even stronger if the equipment is heavy or bulky. Using GSM tracking technology in combination with adapted user response as described (e.g., Figures 5 and 6) might enable researchers to provide more user friendly equipment. The loss of tracking data accuracy might be compensated by information collected with adapted user response. However, the influence of higher user burden due to active user response in comparison to passive tracking data with no user response needs to be examined in future research.

The application of the proposed approaches depends on the research goal in mind. Both tracking technologies provide data at different accuracy levels. At the same time it is assumed that GPS equipment becomes as handy and user friendly as GSM equipment. Researchers have to decide what accuracy level is applicable according to their research requirements. New technological developments will provide further opportunities for transport research. The Universal Mobile Telecommunications System (UMTS) technology promises better tracking capabilities than GSM. Additional satellite tracking services like GALILEO might increase the tracking availability. There is also strong evidence that GPS and GSM technology will merge into a single device in the future. However, GSM tracking is still a very new approach in transportation research. The test showed promising results but there are still many open questions to be answered.

REFERENCES

Asakura, Y. and E. Hato (2001). Analysis of travel behaviour using positioning function of mobile communication devices. In: *Travel Behaviour Research: The Leading Edge* (D.A. Hensher, ed.), 885-899, Pergamon, Oxford.

Bachu, P. K., T. Dudala and S.M. Kothuri (2001). Prompted Recall in a GPS Survey: A Proof-of-Concept Study, *Transportation Research Board, 80th Annual Meeting*, Paper No. 01-2510, 18 pp., Washington, DC.

Battelle Memorial Institute (1997). *Global Positioning Systems for Personal Travel Surveys: Lexington Area Travel Data Collection Test, FINAL REPORT.* A report to Office of Highway Information Management (HPM-40), Office of Technology Application (HTA-1), Federal Highway Administration, US Department of Transportation Washington, DC, 92 pp.

Casas, J. and C. H. Arce (1999). Trip reporting in Household Travel Diaries: A Comparison to GPS-Collected Data, *Transportation Research Board, 78th Annual Meeting*, CD-ROM, Washington, DC.

de Jong, R. and W. Mensonides (2003). *Wearable GPS Device as a Data Collection Method for Travel Research*, Working Paper ITS-WP-03-02, Institute of Transport Studies, University of Sydney, Sydney, 23 pp.

Doherty, S. and E. J. Miller (2000). A Computerized Household Activity Scheduling Survey, *Transportation*, 27 (1), 75-97.

Draijer, G., Kalfs, N., and J. Perdok (2000). GPS as a data collection method for travel research: The use of GPS for the data collection for all modes of travel, *Transportation Research Board, 79th Annual Meeting*, Paper No. 00-1176, 15 pp., Washington, DC.

FCC (Federal Communications Commission) (2005). *Enhanced 911 - Wireless Services*, http://www.fcc.gov/911/enhanced/ , accessed on 17 July 2005.

FleetOnline (2005). Mobile Phone and GPS tracking with FleetOnline™!!!, http://www.fleetonline.net/fol/du/ge , accessed on 17 July 2005.

Hato, E. and Y. Asakura (2001). New Approaches for Collecting Time-space Activity Data using Mobile Communications System, *Transportation Research Board, 80th Annual Meeting*, Paper No. 01-00671, 25 pages, Washington DC.

Hawkins, R. and P. Stopher (2004). *Collecting Data with GPS: Those who reject, and those who receive*, Working Paper ITS-WP-04-21, Institute of Transport Studies, University of Sydney, Sydney, 15 pp.

INFAS (Institut für angewandte Sozialwissenschaft GmbH) (2001). *Geokodierung von Quelle und Ziel von Wegen als Grundlage zur Ermittlung von Fahrleistungsdaten*, Schlussbericht, Machbarkeitsstudie zur Fahrleistungserhebung im Auftrag der Bundesanstalt für Straßenwesen (BASt), FE 82.189/2001, Bonn, Germany.

Kracht, M. and S. Ruppe (2004). *Parallele Ortung mit GPS und GSM Technik*, Deutsches Zentrum für Luft und Raumfahrt – DLR, Institut für Verkehrsforschung - IVF, Berlin, Technischer Bericht (forthcoming), Germany.

Murakami, E. and D. P. Wagner (1999). Can using global position system (GPS) improve trip reporting?, *Transportation Research C*, 7, 149-165.

Rindsfüser, G., H. Mühlhans, S.T. Doherty and K. J. Beckmann (2003). Tracing the planning and execution of activities and their attributes – Design and application of a hand-held scheduling process survey, paper presented to the 10th International Conference on Travel Behaviour Research, Lucerne, Switzerland.

Ruppe, S. (2004). *Konzeption und Entwicklung einer interaktiven Positionsabfrage zur Verbesserung der endgerätebezogenen GSM-Ortung*, TFH Wildau/ DLR Berlin.

Rutten, B., M. van der Vlist, and P. de Wolff (2004). GSM as the source for traffic information, *ETC 2004 – European Transport Conference*, Strassbourg, 13 pp.

Sommer, C. (2002). *Erfassung des Verkehrsverhaltens mittels Mobilfunktechnik: Konzept, Validität und Akzeptanz eines neuen Erhebungsverfahrens*, Institut für Verkehr und Stadtbauwesen, Technische Universität Braunschweig, 463 pages, Aachen, Germany.

Sommer, C. and M. Wermuth (2004). 'Mobile Anwendungen auf Basis von GSM-Ortung und IVR-Systemen', *IMA 2004 – Informationssysteme für mobile Anwendungen*, 292-308.

Steer Davies Gleave, GeoStats (2003). *The use of GPS to improve travel data, Use of GPS in Travel Surveys*, Study Report, DTLR New Horizons Programme, London.

Stopher, P., A. Collins and P. Bullock (2004). *GPS Surveys and the Internet*, Working Paper ITS-WP-04-18, Institute of Transport Studies, University of Sydney, Sydney, 15 pp.

Wermuth, M., M. Garben, J. Janecke, H.-H. Evers, R. Wirth and C. Sommer (2001). *TTS TeleTravel System, Telematiksystem zur automatischen Erfassung des Verkehrsverhaltens*, Abschlussbericht für das Bundesministerium für Bildung und Forschung, bmb+f, Förderkennzeichen 19 M 9807A 0, Bonn, 177 pp.

Wermuth, M., C. Sommer and M. Kreitz (2003). Impact of New Technologies in Travel Surveys. In: *Transport Survey Quality and Innovations* (P.R. Stopher and P.M. Jones, eds), 455-482, Elsevier, Oxford.

Wolf, J., R. Guensler and W. Bachmann (2001). Elimination of the travel diary: An experiment to derive trip purpose from GPS travel data, *Transportation Research Board, 80th Annual Meeting*, Paper No. 01-3255, 22 pp., Washington, DC.

Wolf, J., M. Loechl, M. Thompson and C. H. Arce (2003). Trip Rate Analysis in GPS-Enhanced Personal Travel Surveys. In: *Transport Survey Quality and Innovations* (P.R. Stopher and P.M. Jones, eds), 483-498, Elsevier, Oxford.

Yalamanchili, L., R. M. Pendyala, N. Prabaharan and P. Chakravarthy (1999). Analysis of global positioning system-based data collection methods for capturing multi-stop trip-chaining behaviour, *Transportation Research Record No. 1660*, 58-65.

Zhou, J. and R. Golledge (2004). Real-time Tracking of Activity Scheduling/ Schedule Execution Within Unified Data Collection Framework, *Transportation Research Board, 82nd Annual Meeting*, Conference CD-ROM, 25 pp., Washington, DC.

Zmud, J. and J. Wolf (2003). Identifying the Correlates of Trip Misreporting: Results from the California Statewide Household Travel Survey GPS Study. Paper presented at 10th International Conference on Travel Behaviour Research, Lucerne.

Travel Survey Methods: Quality and Future Directions
Peter Stopher and Cheryl Stecher (Editors)

31

NON-WEB TECHNOLOGIES

Martin E.H. Lee-Gosselin, Université Laval, Quebec, Quebec, Canada
and
Andrew S. Harvey, St. Mary's University, Halifax, Nova Scotia, Canada

PARTICIPATION AND SCOPE

This workshop comprised thirteen participants from nine countries, of whom eight had developed and/or undertaken surveys supported by non-web technologies[40]. As summarised in Table 1, we considered a fairly long list of such technologies. However, we agreed to focus mostly on survey applications of 'LADs' – Location/time Aware Devices – such as Global Positioning Systems (GPS) and mobile telephone technologies. In addition, we covered, to some extent, technologies that are used to support or supplement LADs, such as dead reckoning systems, accelerometers, and electronic systems for vehicle identification and toll collection. We would have liked to include computing developments, especially mobile computing, more broadly in our discussions, but within the time available we chose to limit ourselves to those that can be linked to LAD data, such as electronic schedulers on Personal Digital Assistants (PDAs) or virtual reality displays. We recognised that computer-supported survey methods such as Computer-Aided Self-administered Interviews (CASI) were close in concept to Web-based methods and would probably be covered by another workshop. On the other hand, we did include in our scope the use of the Web and the Internet for data transmission and for obtaining feedback from participants in LAD-supported surveys.

---

[40] Participants were: Camillo Coreal (Mexico), Jennifer Dill (USA), Epaminondas Duarte, Jr. (Brazil), Andrew Harvey (Canada), Simon Holroyd (UK), Matthias Kracht (Germany), Martin Lee-Gosselin (Canada), Philippe Marchal (France), Elaine Murakami (USA), Rami Noah (Israel), Mira Paskota (Serbia), Dorothy Salathiel (UK), Jean Wolf (USA).

Table 1: Types of Non-web Technologies Initially Considered by the Workshop

Technology	Description
Location/time-aware devices (LADs)	Loggers with GPS; GSM phones with PDA; RFID transponders; RDS/broadcast FM triangulation systems
Supplementary mobile technologies	Gyroscopes/dead reckoning/INS/micro-accelerometers; very local data transfer, e.g. by Bluetooth, Infrared
Ground data	GIS layers; aerial photos, etc
Representation and respondent interfaces	GIS displays; scheduling aids; virtual reality, etc.
Traffic/user monitoring	Electronic toll collection systems; licence plate tracking systems
Mobile and networked computing	(To support post-processing and prompted recall, but not CATI, CAPI, CASI, Web surveys, etc.), including data exchange, e.g. by GSM-GPRS, WiFi or Blackberry

PAPERS: AN INITIAL DISCUSSION OF THE STATUS AND APPLICATION OF THE RELEVANT TECHNOLOGIES

In addition to the Resource Paper (Wolf, 2006), the workshop benefited from a contributed paper by Kracht (2006), who had undertaken experiments to compare the performance of GPS and GSM tracking of personal travel by a variety of modes under the conditions of a large German city (Berlin), which like many European conurbations has a dense digital cellular telephone network. The paper revealed very variable signal outage problems when respondents used public transport, and provided useful insights into the issue of antenna placement. While it also showed some promise for using a combination of GPS and GSM to resolve ambiguity, it was pointed out that this depends on having a reasonably good GSM resolution – often one hundred metres or better in Germany, according to the work of Wermuth (2001). Such a resolution is unlikely to be available in lower density urban environments with large GSM cells, such as in much of North America, and therefore other supplementary technologies will be required there, such as inertial dead reckoning systems or triangulation on FM transmitters or, if their expansion continues, nodes in WiFi networks.

In a recapitulation of some main points from her Resource Paper (Wolf, 2006), Wolf helped the workshop reflect further on the current status of LAD technologies. She noted that there are still significant limitations on person-based loggers compared to what survey researchers would see as the ideal, lightweight user-friendly hardware-software package. Although several groups are working on it and progress is being made, there is much left to do before the combination of on-device and post processing software meets the needs of activity, time-use, and travel surveys. While batteries have improved greatly, internal batteries such as those used by mobile phones cannot yet support continuous GPS processing for more than six to eight hours, well below what would be required for a device that is always on, without opportunistic recharging during waking hours. Nevertheless, external battery packs similar in size and weight to those used by video cameras are now proving viable power sources for multi-day applications. A key related issue is the training that respondents require to deploy LAD loggers correctly: three workshop participants had been involved in a pilot multi-day application in the UK, and noted that deployment was sometimes degraded towards the end of the observation period. One way to increase quality control and reduce the complexity of instructions is to automate the transfer of data, typically using the GPRS protocol over GSM digital phone networks: until recently, the costs of transmitting the fairly large data files generated by LAD loggers were a barrier for researchers and applied agencies.

Following the discussion of these two papers, the workshop felt the need to put the uses of these technologies into a framework for technology-aided travel surveys, rather than treat each of them in isolation.

CLARIFICATION OF USE, DESIGN, AND MANAGEMENT OF NON-WEB TECHNOLOGIES

The workshop's shared understanding of how current technologies fit into a travel survey design sequence can be summarised as shown in Figure 1. Although not discussed in detail by the workshop, it was clear that the technologies have important implications for *initial stages of total survey design*, notably sample design and recruitment, and the potential biases associated with these.

Of special importance is the training of respondents (1 in Figure 1). Although the tendency is to automate, to the maximum extent possible, the activation and de-activation of tracking devices, and the transfer of data (notably by periodic wireless transmissions), some equipment in use requires respondents to perform these steps. If the data transfer involves home computing equipment, extra effort may be required to reduce selection bias. Even if a tracking device is fully automatic, respondent training is still critical for two reasons: to meet ethics standards, respondents must know how to manually deactivate the device if they wish not be tracked, and how to reactivate it afterwards; and with currently available technology, antenna placement requires fairly detailed instructions that vary by travel mode.

There are currently a number of different technical designs for the actual data collection (2) and data transfer (3). Mobile packages for tracking people tend to be either special survey devices that are returned to the laboratory for data retrieval, or adaptations of 'smart phones' using GPRS, store-and-forward transmission. Packages involving data transfer by special docks with landline modems, or via home computers, were discussed, but as yet seemed rare. Although some person trackers incorporate additional inputs (such as physical activity measures), complementary LAD technologies (for example gyroscopes or accelerometers) have been almost entirely confined to vehicle-based packages. Vehicle packages, to the extent that they are used for periods of weeks or months, increasingly use wireless data transfer. All packages can involve real-time input from respondents.

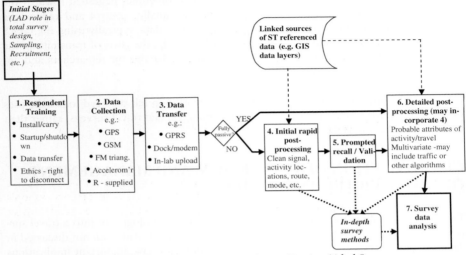

Figure 1: Stages of Location/time Aware Device Aided Surveys

The workshop needed to sort out the way that the large quantities of microdata are cleaned and processed. There is a need for initial post-processing that involves at least the treatment of aberrant or illogical data, and the separation of activity locations from travel delays. After this, post-processing algorithms resolve many ambiguities to identify the route, and sometimes the probable attributes of both activities and travel, including the most likely mode. The algorithms vary from commercially available matching to sophisticated applications written specifically for travel surveys: for example, one participant cited the adaptation of recent dynamic traffic assignment algorithms to improve the prediction of travel mode in complex central city areas. Post-processing is an iterative process, and may involve two steps or one. On one hand, if the design uses prompted recall, the front end of post-processing is performed rapidly (4) to present a skeleton activity/travel schedule to the respondent by some means such as a web page, a transmission to a smart phone or a telephone interview (5). The validated/completed schedule is then fed to the detailed post-processing stage (6). On the other hand, if the mobile package is intended to be fully *passive*, that is requiring no interaction at all with the respondent except for training, installation, and de-installation, (4) is incorporated into the detailed post-processing (6).

The workshop was aware of the beginnings of the exploitation, in post-processing, of *linked sources of spatio-temporally referenced data*, notably GIS data layers giving: road and transit network attributes; the characteristics of stations and activity centres such as shopping centres; or land-use. In principle, such data can enter into either or both stages of post-processing, (4) and (6).

Outputs from post-processing are, of course, used at the analysis stage (7), but (4), (5) and (6) may also be used as input to *in-depth survey methods*, such as Stated Response. Indeed, interviews undertaken for prompted recall (5) could be extended as part of an in-depth survey, perhaps incorporating other technological aids such as GIS imaging or virtual reality. Finally, survey data analysis (7) may benefit from similar technologies to explore and display results.

WHAT HAS AND HAS NOT CHANGED SINCE THE 2001 CONFERENCE

Non-web technologies became a concentration of this conference series with the 2001 Kruger conference in South Africa. The stages shown in Figure 1 reflect the workshop's view of thinking about survey design three years later. We noted that the major changes since 2001 were:

- More technologies, and more multiple, linked technologies;
- In high-income countries, the increasing penetration of mobile data exchange (e.g., WiFi) and accompanying reductions in data transmission costs; and
- Increasing internationalisation of standards for LAD systems (e.g., GPS-Galileo).

However, the shift to *person-based* LAD-supported surveys was incomplete. On the positive side, there were great improvements in the miniaturisation, functionality and performance of (mass market) components, such as GPS, smart phones, and wireless data transfer. Data transfer telemetry (mainly GPRS/mobile phone) became almost affordable. In Canada for example, unlimited data transition from one mobile phone was, at the time of the workshop, Cdn$50 per month: with the rapid growth in the demand for bandwidth transmission of photos and videos from mobile phones, these costs can be expected to fall. Data storage problems have largely been solved with the proliferation of memory cards developed for digital photography. On the negative side, as noted in Wolf (2006), internal batteries were still below the sixteen hour continuous duty cycle threshold, and it is was clear that robust survey staff procedures and training need more work. Perhaps more difficult to solve was the need for much more integrated, intelligent post-processing to automate the detection of travel mode and activity/purpose, using space-time profiles from the survey itself and the linked external data discussed in the preceding section: the workshop consensus was that we were probably more than a year away from such integration.

FURTHER DISCUSSION OF LAD TECHNOLOGIES

The main charge of the B series workshops was to identify and to prioritise survey research issues, and to suggest relevant sources of funding for highest ranked issues. In preparation for this, the workshop next set itself the task of looking at the advantages and disadvantages of the various technologies that fell within the scope that we had adopted. A list of the main discussion points with respect to advantages and disadvantages is shown in Table 2. Note that, in a few cases, the advantages and disadvantages are linked, but the table should mostly be read as two independent lists of what came up. They reflect the state of these technologies in survey applications as of mid-2004.

Table 2: Discussion Points on Advantages and Disadvantages of LAD Technologies

Advantages	Disadvantages
Growing potential to track indoors	Problems indoors and off transportation networks
Extending observation periods	Power needs for person-based
Tracking location and route	Physical burden on respondent
Spatial and temporal accuracy	High cost of equipment
Completeness (trips)	Rapid obsolescence
'Real time' availability	Privacy concerns
Level of detail, with or without user input	Require user collaboration input (burden)
Global applicability	Heavy data post processing
Spatial coverage	Limits on data storage
Linking to other data	Data archiving
Multi-modal capabilities	Fixed infrastructure required
Wide range of methods of representation/feedback	Working with service provider (e.g. telcoms) can be difficult
Freight applicability	

Few of the points in Table 2 were new, but the workshop attempted to link the advantages and disadvantages to the current state of particular technologies. This part of the discussion had two, related major foci. The first concerned which combination of person-based mobile equipment and post-processing was most likely to lead to the correct estimation of activity types and periods: most of these occur at locations off the road and transit networks, notably inside buildings, that generate signal outages. It was arguable whether the spread of wireless computer links such as WiFi would improve location/time awareness on a wide enough basis for it not be necessary to contemplate using complementary technologies to help interpret outages of one technology alone, for example GPS-GSM and GPS-gyroscope combinations. The second focus concerned the adequacy and universality of fixed infrastructures that survey researchers might wish to count upon.

PRIORITY RESEARCH ISSUES

Throughout the workshop, we noted survey methodological research needs. At the end, we asked each participant to identify their two highest priorities. Collectively, the highest ranked were:

- Generic piloting of comprehensive LAD-aided data collection strategies, including: sample size and timing issues (given the possibility of long observation periods), mixed survey modes, etc.;
- Evaluations of prompted recall methods for long and short observation periods;
- Comparisons of the benefits and problems of LAD-aided versus other travel surveys – not just trip rate, but the utility and quality of numerous types of data; and
- Development and testing of post-processing techniques, with or without GIS data layers, fast and slow.

Also considered were:

- Detailed studies of observer effects (on reporting and behaviour), device acceptability, etc.;
- Graphical and other representation for feedback to respondents, linked to both linguistic and computer literacies;
- Long distance travel applications; and
- Strategies for keeping respondent anonymity in the highly disaggregated spatio-temporal data, and privacy solutions.

In addition, we were asked to reflect on ways of funding such methodological research. On the technological side, the participants expected that funding would be most likely as a by-product of research on Intelligent Transport Systems/Transport Telematics or pricing/tolling systems. However, the European Commission's research programmes could be interested in the wake of the recent agreement to harmonise Galileo and GPS systems. Health agencies might also be motivated to join forces with transport agencies to improve methods of monitoring physical activity in connection with travel: this was a reminder to look beyond travel surveys to related behaviours, such as time use, for which there is a strong demand for data.

CONCLUDING OBSERVATIONS

To conclude, we asked ourselves what other messages would be useful to the broader travel survey research community at this time. The first was a warning: the highly detailed data obtained by non-web technologies raise archiving, access, and privacy issues that need sensible translation to those legislating and setting rules. The example was given of the vehicle monitoring data from Commute Atlanta (US): the raw data must, by law, be destroyed six months after the end of the project. The precedents we set now for the forms of data that can be conserved, accessed, and analysed may determine their usefulness for years to come. Second, faced with a rapid obsolescence of some of these technologies, we must insure that the basics of data collection systems talk to each other (interoperability). Finally, the workshop gave numerous examples of the current thirst for realistic advice about these technologies on the part of those who are implementing travel surveys. As travel behaviour is rather unimportant compared to all the main drivers of research and development of the relevant technologies, the open sharing of our experience with them becomes all the more critical.

REFERENCES

Kracht, M. (2006). Using Combined GPS and GSM Tracking Information for Interactive Electronic Questionnaires. In: *Travel Survey Methods – Quality and Future Directions* (P.R. Stopher and C.C. Stecher, eds), 545-560, Elsevier, Oxford.

Wermuth, M., M. Garben, J. Janecke, H.-H. Evers, R. Wirth and C. Sommer (2001). *TTS TeleTravel System, Telematiksystem zur automatischen Erfassung des Verkehrsverhaltens*, Abschlussbericht für das Bundesministerium für Bildung und Forschung, bmb+f, Förderkennzeichen 19 M 9807A 0, Bonn, 177 pp.

Wolf, J. (2006). Applications of New Technologies in Travel Surveys. In: *Travel Survey Methods – Quality and Future Directions* (P.R. Stopher and C.C. Stecher, eds), 545-560, Elsevier, Oxford.

ACKNOWLEDGMENTS

We would like to acknowledge the financial support of the project *"An integrated GPS-GIS system for collecting spatio-temporal microdata on personal travel in urban areas"* of the Canadian Network of Centres of Excellence in Geomatics, GEOIDE, in the preparation of this chapter.

32

CHARACTERISTICS OF WEB BASED SURVEYS AND APPLICATIONS IN TRAVEL RESEARCH

Rahaf Alsnih, Institute of Transport and Logistics Studies, University of Sydney, Sydney, Australia

INTRODUCTION

Over the past decade, when conducting surveys by telephone, an increasing number of calls had to be made to achieve contact (Zmud, 2003; Dillman, 1998). However, a high number of calls remained unresolved. This is a result of households adopting new technology such as answering machines, caller id, increased cell phone use (some households only have cell phones and not a land line and it is costly to obtain these numbers if wanting to contact these households by telephone), and multiple phone line households. In addition, thirty percent of households in the US have unlisted telephone numbers (Dillman, 1998). These factors make it much harder for the researcher to contact the household successfully, resulting in greater survey costs (Zmud, 2003; Groves and Couper, 1998; Dillman, 1998; Cook *et al.*, 2000).

Due to increased difficulties in contacting prospective respondents, thus contributing to low response rates for both mail and telephone surveys, and advances in technology, new survey modes have emerged that are relatively cheap to administer. For example, e-mail surveys require the same level of effort to respond as telephone surveys (Dillman, 1998). There is no need for reply paid envelopes; e-mail and web surveys decrease respondent burden, in relation to self-administered surveys (Dillman, 1998).

However, some problematic issues have been identified in relation to Web-based surveys. The most important of these are sample design and representativeness, data quality, anonymity and information security, technological incompatibilities and disruptions. This chapter looks at the evolution of survey methodologies in social science and transport research. Design issues in relation to Web based surveys are discussed along with the advantages and disadvantages of this type of survey. Experiences of the author will shed some light on important design features of Web based surveys, in a transport context. Furthermore, special issues in terms of travel surveys are discussed.

SURVEY METHODOLOGY AND RESPONSE RATES

Social science survey methodology has evolved to adapt to new technology and the benefits that arise from using this technology. Figure 1 shows the evolution of data collection methods. Survey methodologies have changed because of changes in societal organisation and culture, available technology, increased survey costs and decreasing response rates leading to increased survey error (Dillman, 1998). The adoption of new data collection modes is viewed as a way to combat decreasing response rates.

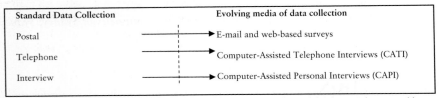

Source: Adapted from Illieva *et al.*, 2002, WARC, © 2005 Copyright and database rights owned by WARC.

Figure 1: Evolution of Data Collection Methods

Travel surveys have long had the problem of poor response rates and increasing unit costs. The complex nature of data required often leads to the development of a rather complicated survey instrument. This, in addition to the survey environment, contributes to the high incidence of nonresponse. The nonresponse issue for travel surveys has resulted in biased data sets because characteristics of non-respondents are different to characteristics of respondents (Richardson, 2000; De Heer and Moritz, 2000). For example, characteristics of non-respondents to travel surveys, found in numerous studies, are very low and very high income; high and low mileage drivers; young single males and females; zero vehicle use; people residing in metropolitan areas, and households with children (De Heer and Moritz, 2000; Richardson, 2000; Kam and Morris, 1999). Thus, nonresponse bias must be minimised to obtain an accurate picture of people's travel behaviour. Given this and other problems encountered in travel and social science research, researchers have embraced the idea of Web-based surveys for the following reasons:

1. Low distribution and retrieval costs;
2. Automated data entry;

3. The ability to include visual aids and animation to assist in the respondent's recollection of travel over the assigned travel days;
4. Quick response times;
5. Automated skip patterns and randomisation of questions (particularly important in stated choice experiments); and
6. The ability to obtain information about response behaviour (Gunn, 2002; Illieva *et al.*, 2002; Lazar *et al.*, 1999; Bosnjak and Tuten, 2001; Couper, 2000; Schonlau *et al.*, 2001; Thompson *et al.*, 2003; Stopher *et al.*, 2004).

Despite the benefits of Web based surveys, the application of these in the present survey environment results in coverage error, because not everyone has access to the Internet (Dillman and Bowker, 1999). This results in relatively low response rates to Web based surveys, especially for surveys of the general population. In addition, it is usually acknowledged that people with e-mail communication facilities exceed those with Internet connections. Table 1 demonstrates the low response rates of e-mail surveys compared to mail surveys: average response rates for eleven studies that used both mail and e-mail data collection methods were 46.16 percent and 38.72 percent respectively. Given that these studies were not of the general population, response rates were not especially high. Thus, we expect response rates to Web based surveys to be even lower.

Table 1: Response Time and Response Rate: E-mail Versus Mail

Authors	Technique	Response Time (days)	Response Rate (%)
Ranchhold and Zhou (2001)	E-mail	N/A	6
	Mail		20
Bachman et al. (1996)	E-mail	4.68	52.5
	Mail	11.18	65.6
Weible and Wallace (1998)	E-mail	6.1	29.8
	Mail	12.9	35.7
Schaefer and Dillman (1998)	E-mail	9.16	58
	Mail	14.39	57.5
Tse et al. (1995)	E-mail	8.09	6
	Mail	9.79	27
Mehta and Sivadas (1995)	E-mail	2-3	54.3
	Mail	21	56.5
Wygant and Lindorf (1999)	E-mail	2	50
	Mail	9.16	32
Parker (1992)	E-mail	N/A	68
	Mail		38
Schuldt and Totten (1994)	E-mail	N/A	19.3
	Mail		56.5
Tse (1998)	E-mail	2.58	7
	Mail	8.49	52
Kiesler and Sproull (1986)	E-mail	9.6	75
	Mail	10.8	67
Average response time and rate	E-mail	5.59	38.72
	Mail	12.21	46.16

Source: Illieva *et al.*, 2002, WARC, © 2005 Copyright and database rights owned by WARC.

Further, it appears that the response rates shown in Table 1 are based on the number of completed surveys (retrieval stage only). Transport surveys are usually two stage surveys: a recruitment stage and a retrieval stage. Thus, for comparison, the retrieval response rate for a recent study conducted by the Institute of Transport and Logistics Studies (ITLS) was 54.5 percent. This is much higher than the average response rates for the mail and e-mail studies shown in Table 1. Importantly however, the methodology behind the Web based survey conducted by ITLS was different to the methodologies of the studies listed in Table 1. The study undertaken by ITLS involved telephone recruitment and this enabled an e-mail message to be sent to recruited respondents, providing the URL and password required to access the survey. The studies listed in Table 1 did not use this methodology, or the same type of survey. However, it is unlikely that a difference in measurement, arising from the different data collection modes alone, resulted in the relatively large difference in response rates. Topic salience is more likely to be the major factor affecting response rates given that respondents to the ITLS study were households recently affected by bushfires and these households were asked to take part in a bushfire evacuation study. Thus, different survey methodologies, different survey types, as well as the survey topic and the survey environment, affect response rates (Ettema *et al*, 1996; Melevin *et al.*, 1998; Schneider and Johnson, 1994).

TYPES OF WEB BASED SURVEYS

There are essentially two types of Web based questionnaires:

1. Open to any visitor – There is no control over who visits or completes the survey, except that the sample is only of Internet users. A hidden Internet survey is a subcategory of this type of Internet survey and is better known as a pop-up survey. Visitors to a web site are randomly selected to participate in the survey. A hidden window pops up alerting people to the survey and asks whether viewers would like to participate. Obviously, this type of Internet survey is only viewed by people visiting the web site (Bradley, 1999; Gunn, 2002; Couper, 2000); and
2. Closed – Respondents are invited to visit the website and complete the survey, which is usually password protected. Respondents may be recruited through the telephone, or e-mail, and provided with the URL and password, through an e-mail or letter. This survey type is most likely to be used in a two or more stage survey. The first stage is the recruitment stage and this may be through mail, CATI or e-mail.

In terms of e-mail surveys, there are only two types:

1. Simple e-mail message with questions; and
2. E-mail message that acts like a cover letter, and includes the survey attachment.

An e-mail message with an embedded URL is not an e-mail survey, described as such by Bradley (1999). The respondent is requested to participate through an e-mail message and asked to access the survey through the included URL. Essentially, this is e-mail recruitment for a Web based survey.

With Web based surveys, the assumption is that the respondent has Internet access and is confident in the use of this technology. However, in the US in 2002, Internet penetration was only 65 percent of households (Resource Systems Group Inc., 2002). This has important implications for Web based surveys in relation to sample representativeness, especially if the survey is of the general population. For example, in a study by Myles and Tibert (1998), it was found that the Internet sample was not representative of the population in relation to an election outcome, even after weighting. In addition, if respondents are recruited through e-mail, problems may arise because people may change their Internet Service Provider, and in turn, change their e-mail address and their mailboxes may also become full, which prevents any messages from being read. This usually results in more non-deliverables when compared to traditional mail-out surveys (Cobanolgu *et al.*, 2001), and is a reason why e-mail surveys are not as popular as Web based surveys.

Sampling and Representativeness

Probability based sampling is when the sample is selected by chance, and population members have a known and non zero chance of being selected. Most common types of probability based sampling include simple random, systematic, stratified, and cluster (Couper, 2000; Schonlau *et al.*, 2001). For Internet surveys, a sampling frame for Internet users and subscribers is not readily available and this means that it is difficult to determine the probability of the sample selected for the Internet survey.

In relation to closed Web based surveys, respondents are recruited from other sources and invited to the website (Bradley, 1999). This may reduce coverage error, somewhat compared to the other Web based survey types, because people are recruited from sources other than e-mail lists and visitors to websites. However, only people with access to the Internet are able to respond to the survey. Thus, various forms of bias and error arise in the resulting data set from Web based surveys, such as:

1. Coverage bias – This is a function of the proportion of the target population that is not covered by the frame. Many people still do not have access to the Internet.
2. Nonresponse bias – Demographic characteristics of Internet users are different from those of non-users. For example, online surveys overrepresent males, college graduates, and the young (Couper, 2000; Resource Systems Group Inc., 2002; Woong Yun and Trumbo, 2000; Bradley, 1999; Thompson *et al.*, 2003). Males were more likely to respond to Web based surveys whereas females were more likely to respond to telephone surveys (Dillman *et al.*, 2001). This is different to coverage bias, because people who may have access to the Internet may prefer not to respond over the Internet. In addition, those without access to the Internet would not be considered eligible to participate in an Internet survey, thus would not be defined as non-respondents.

3. Measurement error – This could arise from the effects of different browsers; respondents see different structures of the survey according to the capability of their Internet browser (Couper, 2000; Dillman and Bowker, 1999; Thompson *et al.*, 2003).

4. Sampling error – The result of surveying a sample of the population rather than the entire population. This is a major concern for Web based surveys of the general population because the sample obtained is not representative of the population due to coverage and nonresponse bias.

Overall, travel surveys conducted solely over the Internet are likely to suffer from non-response and coverage bias, in particular. Given that the Internet is a relatively new survey mode, investigation is required to understand respondent and non-respondent behaviour better, and the characteristics of non-respondents (defined as those eligible to participate in the survey but terminate part way through the survey) to enable better design and execution of Internet travel surveys.

As previously mentioned, not everyone has access to the Internet, and of those who do, it is not known how competent these individuals are in relation to Web navigation. The following section lists the different types of computer user and describes the issues that accompany this.

RESPONDENT AND EQUIPMENT CAPABILITIES

Computers with Internet connection have different capabilities (Bradley, 1999). This affects how respondents access and view the Web based survey. This is shown in Table 2.

Table 2 shows that developments in technology have outpaced user ability, further emphasising the need to understand computer user familiarity with the Internet. In addition, the thirteen different types of computer user identified, with respect to Web based surveys, have not been addressed adequately, or acknowledged by some survey practitioners. Yet, understanding the types of computer user would result in better survey design and better application of survey methodology. For example, coverage bias results because not everyone has access to the Internet, and of those who do, the capability of users varies greatly (Bradley, 1999). In addition, some people's experience in computer use may be so limited that they are unable to complete the survey. This type of computer user may be more likely to fall into a particular demographic, thus adding to non-response bias. Obviously, more research is required to obtain the current status in relation to user capability. Also, an understanding of the concept of confidence in Internet use is necessary to facilitate the development of more appropriate Web based survey instruments.

Table 2: Types of Computer User

Type	User Ability		Equipment Capability	
	e-mail	Use Browser	Use for e-mail	Use for Browsing
1	Yes	Yes	Yes	Yes
2	Yes	Yes	Yes	No
3	Yes	Yes	No	Yes
4	Yes	Yes	No	No
5	Yes	No	Yes	Yes
6	Yes	No	Yes	No
7	Yes	No	No	Yes
8	No	Yes	Yes	Yes
9	No	Yes	Yes	No
10	No	Yes	No	Yes
11	No	No	Yes	Yes
12	No	No	Yes	No
13	No	No	No	Yes

Source: Bradley, 1999, WARC, © 2005 Copyright and database rights owned by WARC.

QUALITY AND VALIDITY OF WEB BASED SURVEYS

It is important for survey research to obtain data of good quality; poor quality data usually stems from bad survey design and inappropriate use of survey modes. Data quality is a combination of low unit and item nonresponse, honest responses, completeness of responses in relation to open ended questions, and the absence of data entry errors – this last should not be an issue for Web based surveys due to the automation of data entry (Shonlau *et al.*, 2001). Usually, data quality is measured by the percentage of item and unit nonresponses in the final data set. Interestingly, researchers readily accept that face-to-face and CAPI yield data of better quality due to relatively high response rates. However, these interview methods are also more likely to produce socially desirable responses and this does not necessarily equate to better quality data (Dillman, 1998).

One study, wherein the sample was experienced in Internet use, claimed that Web responses contained fewer random and systematic errors than telephone surveys (Gunn, 2002). According to a study conducted by Cobanoglu *et al.* (2001), it was found that the data of highest quality were from Web-based surveys; however, the target population was a sample confident in Internet use and Internet users have been identified as having higher levels of socioeconomic status than non-Internet users (Dillman *et al.*, 2001; Resource Systems Group Inc., 2002; Alvarez and VanBeselaere, 2003; Arentze *et al.*, 2004). Miller *et al.* (2002) found in their study that Web-based surveys did not compromise data quality nor was a measurement difference observed in relation to pen and pencil surveys with respect to test reliability of the key statistics. However, more research is needed to confirm these findings in relation to studies of travel behaviour.

Interestingly, some researchers question the sincerity of Internet responses (Illieva *et al.*, 2002). Possibly, this is because many Web based surveys are designed so that respondents are not allowed to leave questions unanswered. This is one of the reasons why the

Web based survey mode is gaining popularity: lower item nonresponse rates and a perception that the data collected is of good quality. However, it is not known whether respondents enter true or false responses to questions they would prefer not to answer.

A major concern with online surveys, especially general population surveys, relates to the validity of data due to the sampling frame. The issue of representativeness arises, as well as that some people are more computer literate than others, which may contribute to measurement errors and nonresponse bias. In addition, a complex online survey will add to computer literacy problems and increase the rate of unit and item nonresponse.

However, despite these concerns, the benefit of online travel surveys is that they may capture a group of traditional non-respondents to conventional travel surveys: the larger households and households of higher socio-economic status. For example, the results of two studies using the Internet for data collection, showed that respondents to Web based travel surveys were predominantly larger households and households of higher socioeconomic status, compared to the households that responded to telephone interviews, or through the mail (Resource Systems Group Inc., 2002; Arentze *et al.*, 2004). Households responding over the Internet recorded higher trip rates than households that responded through the mail (Resource Systems Group Inc., 2002). Larger household size should naturally equate to more trips and the number of adults in the household has a positive relationship with number of trips made; hence, the results observed (Resource Systems Group Inc, 2002; De Heer and Moritz, 2000; Richardson, 2000; Kam and Morris, 1999).

In addition, it may be that busy people, traditionally non-contactable households, find the Internet option more appealing because they are not bound to sit and respond at a certain time, which occurs during a CATI or personal interview. They are also not required to send anything back physically: something which they do not have time to do. Busy people, also, are usually not at home; hence, the non-contact status when the survey is being undertaken.

However, it cannot be stated that Web based travel surveys, as the single survey mode used, result in a better measurement of trip rates because higher trip rates can be calculated. The instrument may be useful to capture trip rates of larger households and households of higher socioeconomic status, because these households prefer to respond using the Internet, but other demographic groups are not captured by this survey mode. Web based travel surveys, as single mode surveys, should only be conducted if all of the target population have access to the Internet. (Dillman *et al.*, 1998). Also of importance is how to assess computer literacy amongst people with access to the Internet (Dillman *et al.*, 1998). Households may have access to the Internet, yet certain members asked to participate in the survey may not be experienced in Web navigation (Lazar and Preece, 1999). Survey practitioners often overlook this.

STRENGTHS AND WEAKNESSES

Single Mode and Multimode

In the past, travel surveys were often single mode mail surveys. This was because technology was not available to support other survey collection methods. Further enhancements to Computer Assisted Telephone Interviewing (CATI) techniques, first implemented in the 1960s, led to the wide use of CATI during the 1980s and 1990s for most national surveys in the US (Dillman, 1998). However, the usefulness of both mail and CATI recruitment and data retrieval methods decreased dramatically over the past few years. This is due to public annoyance with research surveys in general, a likely outcome of the over surveying associated with marketing, and increased difficulties in contacting households personally, or through the telephone, due to more call screening devices, multiple phone lines, increasing use of mobile phones and increased security around housing, especially residential estates.

Despite this, however, some people still prefer to respond through mail and telephone surveys. For example, a Nonresponse Study conducted in the US, by ITLS in conjunction with NuStats, offered non-respondents to a travel survey the choice of four data retrieval methods: mail, Internet, telephone and personal interview. The initial respondents chose to respond through the mail (77.8 percent). This was not surprising given the low socioeconomic status of the areas investigated. Internet usage, and hence Web based surveys, are linked to households of higher socioeconomic status; the mail survey option is often linked to households of lower socioeconomic status (Dillman *et al.*, 2001; Resource Systems Group Inc, 2002; Alvarez and VanBeselaere, 2003; Arentze *et al.*, 2004). In addition, the survey modes were applied in a hierarchical manner. The mail option was offered first; for the households that did not respond through mail or the Internet, CATI was then offered, etc. However, the Internet option was offered at the same time the mail option was, and respondents preferred the mail option.

From these results, and findings in the literature, it is advised that Web based travel surveys be part of a mixed mode travel survey (Couper, 2000; Gunn, 2002; Schonlau *et al.*, 2001; Schaefer and Dillman, 1998). This will overcome representation problems associated with Web based travel surveys in the present survey environment, and in turn, improve response rates (Illieva *et al.*, 2002; Schonlau *et al.*, 2001; Lazar and Preece, 1999). In addition, mixed mode surveys allow for the introduction of Web based surveys to households not accustomed to this technology; people may become more aware of the uses of the Internet, and in the future, they may readily embrace Internet surveys by gaining an understanding about the Internet prior to being asked to participate in future Internet surveys (Cobanoglu *et al.*, 2001).

Some arguments against the use of multimode surveys arise from concerns about social desirability, acquiescence (especially in relation to face to face interviews), primacy and recency effects, and question order effects (Dillman, 1998; Woong Yun and Trumbo, 2000). However, differences between modes can be insignificant if a simple survey design is adopted (Cobanoglu *et al.*, 2001). Responses to Web based surveys are expected to resemble responses to mail surveys, because both survey modes are self administered survey modes (Dillman *et al.*, 2001). In addition, whether a particular survey mode results in data of better quality, ultimately depends on the survey design, survey methodology, and the research topic under investigation. The likelihood of problems associated with the use of multi-modal surveys can be reduced if a simple and coherent survey structure is adopted for all survey modes to be employed.

ADVANTAGES OF INTERNET SURVEYS

Web based surveys are popular because:
1. They are easier to execute – it is simple to send e-mail reminders to recruited respondents, and multiple mail outs to respondents are not required;
2. Faster response time – enables reminders to be sent sooner rather than later and this should positively affect response rates;
3. Automation of data entry saves times and other resources, as well as the likelihood of correct data entry; automation of data entry allows for a dynamic error checking ability; and
4. This medium is much cheaper especially if large samples are required (Illieva *et al.*, 2002; Schonlau *et al.*, 2001; Lazar and Preece, 1999; Couper *et al.*, 2001; Thompson *et al.*, 2003; Gunn, 20002).

In addition, complex skip patterns in Web based surveys are not seen by respondents, improving their cognitive ability and increasing the likelihood of good quality data (Gunn, 2002). However, given the current survey environment, measurement error may prevail if mail and Internet survey modes are only used in a mixed mode survey: if there are complex skip patterns, then the mail mode is likely to suffer from high levels of item and unit nonresponse. This may be exacerbated if most of the respondents to the mail survey are of lower socioeconomic status. This problem may be overcome if a simple survey design is employed.

Surveys incorporating SP experiments benefit greatly from the Internet mode, because the Web based survey allows for the automatic randomisation of choice sets that each respondent sees. This is very important and reduces the burden associated with the randomisation of choice sets in pen and paper surveys, which require numerous versions of the same survey to be printed to incorporate all the randomisation of choice set possibilities. This consumes a lot of precious resources, adding to survey costs.

Another advantage of Web based surveys to the survey practitioner is getting a better understanding of respondent behaviour. Web based surveys can supply metadata in addition to the responses given to the survey questions: a reconstruction of the response process (Bosnjak and Tuten, 2001). However, in order to obtain the complete log for each individual, each question needs to be displayed separately, and each page of the questionnaire must be downloaded separately from the server and not reside in the Web browser's cache (Bosnjak and Tuten, 2001). This area requires further investigation, especially in relation to Web based travel surveys.

From the respondent's perspective, an advantage of electronic surveys over traditional survey modes is that they can be completed at the respondent's discretion, and can be visually pleasing and easy to complete (Cook *et al.*, 2000). One aspect of respondent burden is reduced, because respondents are not required to physically return anything. This may be especially appealing to busy people who do not have spare time to do this and would actually perceive this as a chore. For example, two reasons stated by respondents, familiar with the Internet, for completing a travel survey over the Internet, were convenience and that the Internet was a faster method and a less time consuming way to respond (Resource Systems Group Inc, 2002).

DISADVANTAGES

Coverage bias is a major disadvantage of Web based surveys (Cook *et al.*, 2000; Dillman and Bowker, 1998). Interestingly, however, one paper claimed that Web based surveys provide access to a wide audience (Illieva *et al.*, 2002). This may be so if the survey is not of the general population and if the majority of the target population is known to have access to the Internet. Also stated in this paper was that researchers have less control over who accesses the survey than for mail surveys (Illieva *et al.*, 2002). This is not necessarily so; the method of recruitment employed, and the type of Web based survey used are the determining factors. For example, if respondents are contacted through e-mail and the URL is embedded in this message, then researchers have control over who enters the survey.

Technological problems are also a major disadvantage associated with Web based surveys (Thompson *et al.*, 2003; Couper, 2000). Server disruptions can occur without the researcher's knowledge. This leads to a loss of online survey time and results in many avoidable survey terminations. In addition, technological problems can be exacerbated if complex survey designs are employed: surveys may appear differently in different browsers. The different appearance of the survey may distract from the respondent's cognitive ability. This may increase the likelihood of measurement error, because people with different levels of computer literacy may answer questions differently. Also, technological problems may compound measurement error if more than one survey mode is used. This is so because, if a combination of self administered survey modes and interview aided survey modes are used for the same survey, a complex survey design will most likely lead to incorrect and missing information coming from the self administered survey modes.

Complex Web based surveys, coupled with technological limitations (e.g., old personal computers, incompatible browsers, etc.) can make it impossible for the respondent to download the survey. In addition, it may take so much time to download the survey that the respondent closes the survey before the download is complete (Dillman and Bowker, 1999; Gunn, 2002). The likely outcome is a biased sample because of the high number of Internet survey terminations (non-respondents). In addition, Web based surveys with complex skip patterns need to be tested vigorously to ensure that skip patterns are behaving as required and that data entry is occurring correctly (Schonlau *et al.*, 2001).

Table 3 depicts some of the advantages and disadvantages of Web based surveys in relation to mail surveys. Costs of the return of the survey borne on the respondent are usually minimal; however, this is a function of size of the survey file(s) and the Internet connection. For example, an individual may be connected to the Internet with a high speed connection, but Internet usage is capped at monthly intervals. If download of the survey consumes the monthly download limit imposed by the Internet Service Provider, then the respondent will incur a cost as a result of completing the survey. This is an important issue for travel surveys containing maps and other visual aids. If the respondent is connected to the Internet with a dial-up connection, asking respondents to complete travel surveys containing maps and animations will be even more problematic: download times will be excessive and result in many survey terminations.

Table 3: Comparison of Mail and Internet Surveys

Characteristic	Mail	Web
Coverage	High	Low
Speed	Low	High
Return Cost	Preaddressed/pre-stamped envelope	no cost to the respondent
Incentives	Cash or other incentives can be included	coupons may be included*
Wrong addresses	Low	High
Labour needed	High	Low
Expertise to construct	Low	High
Variable cost/survey	about $1.00	Minimal

* *Cash incentives (the most effective) may be offered to participants during the recruitment phase if mail or CATI recruitment is employed (pre-incentive).*

Source: Adapted from Cobanolgu *et al.*, 2001, WARC, © 2005 Copyright and database rights owned by WARC.

In addition, in other parts of the world, some people pay for access to the Internet by the minute. If these respondents cannot perceive a direct benefit from participating in the travel survey over the Internet, they are unlikely to do so because of the cost involved, especially if the survey will take a long time to complete. Table 4 shows examples of costs associated with mail and Web based surveys.

Table 4 shows that the fixed costs for Web based surveys are much higher than for mail surveys due to the level of expertise and time required to develop these surveys

(Schonlau *et al.*, 2001). If a small sample is required, Web based surveys are likely to be more expensive than traditional survey modes due to high fixed costs associated with programming the survey. To some extent this fixed cost can be reduced by using templates of previous Web based surveys or highly reusable software. For example, ITLS uses a system where the survey components can be specified from an XML file. This means that a Web based survey can be constructed by a person with moderate technical competence in a reasonably short period of time. Any additional capabilities that need to be programmed into the system can be reused in future surveys; they do not need to be programmed again. Additionally, reusable software is more reliable and so requires less testing, which further reduces fixed costs. Therefore, a high fixed cost for the first Web based survey led to significantly lower subsequent fixed costs. Also, variable costs are negligible for Web based surveys compared to the variable costs for mail surveys. In the end, total costs for Web based surveys are much less than for mail surveys.

Table 4: Summary of Costs

Method	Fixed Cost	Unit Cost	Quantity	Variable Cost	Total Cost
Mail	$67.50	$1.93	100	$193.00	$260.50
Web	$107.50	*$0.00	100	$0.00	$107.50

* Assuming that the survey files are not sizable

Source: Adapted from Cobanolgu *et al.*, 2001, WARC, © 2005 Copyright and database rights owned by WARC.

From the perspective of respondents, a major disadvantage of Web based surveys relates to anonymity and data security, even though personalisation of contact was sometimes favoured by respondents (Woong Yun and Trumbo, 2000; Thompson *et al.*, 2003; Illieva *et al.*, 2002). This is also a concern of survey practitioners, because data recorded should not be tampered with or seen by external sources. Placing the survey on a secure server with adequate firewall protection should alleviate security problems.

Another disadvantage of Internet surveys is the lack of knowledge regarding the characteristics of non-respondents to Internet surveys. Without this knowledge, survey practitioners will not be able to counteract the issues which concern non-respondents. However, this problem should be eradicated in the future.

Design Considerations

In the early days of Web based surveys, design traditionally focused more on programming than survey methodology. Nowadays, navigation and flow are realised as important elements in the design of Web based surveys, because of the visual stimulus and the fact that respondents have control over the comprehension of questions read. Design is also important for face to face and CATI interviews. However, the interviewer can help the respondent through the questions, whereas for mail and Web based surveys, interviewers are not available. Therefore, good survey design is crucial.

There are a myriad of ways to develop and structure Web based surveys using colour, fonts and styles, etc. However, fancy Web based surveys usually require a longer time to download and may accentuate browser incompatibilities (Gunn, 2002; Dillman *et al.*, 1998). Plain Web based surveys give a better response rate than those with a fancy design and structure (Dillman *et al.*, 1998). A fancy design may distract the respondent from the survey task: cognitive research has found that surveys with complex skip patterns confuse the respondent if questions are not numbered appropriately because respondents believe they are to answer every question (Couper *et al.*, 2001; Gunn, 2002). In addition, in a multimodal survey, the mail survey cannot have a complex skip pattern. This contributes to the increased likelihood of measurement error.

Longer questionnaires are associated with lower response rates and take longer to download; people get annoyed with this and close before the download is complete (Gunn, 2002). The results of a nonresponse study conducted by ITLS, showed that shorter surveys, requiring less time to complete (under twenty minutes), were preferred by respondents. It is important to keep the questionnaire brief and concise, and to break the survey into sections, if required. For example, a Web based survey, devised to understand household evacuation behaviour during an urban bushfire emergency, was divided into three sections. The first asked about household demographics. Whilst not typical, given that no income related questions were asked (most often the questions causing households to terminate or refuse), demographic questions were asked first to ease respondents into the survey. The second section related to the respondents' most recent bushfire experience, and the third section was the SP experiment.

Before beginning to design the survey, the researcher must be aware of the research environment at the time that the survey is to be conducted, the population to be surveyed (this should be well planned and described in the research methodology stage), and technological limitations associated with Web based surveys (Schonlau *et al.*, 2001). According to Dillman *et al.* (1998), there are three criteria associated with good Web based survey design:

1. Design should consider technological and user limitations;
2. Logic of how computers operate and how people expect surveys to operate must be considered; and
3. Web based surveys should be designed to enable their incorporation in a mixed mode survey.

With this in mind, the successful implementation of Web based surveys involves three crucial steps:

1. Design the survey on paper – This is essential if the survey is to be used as part of a mixed mode survey; other survey modes will be adapted from the pen and paper survey. This will help minimise measurement error. Both Web based surveys mentioned, undertaken by ITLS, were designed on paper first.

2. The survey methodology should be pre-determined.
3. The survey should be carefully transformed from its pen and paper status to the Web. The survey must be error proof, and should be accessible from all browsers to reduce respondent burden and download time (Lazar and Preece, 1999). This reinforces the need to adopt a simple survey design.

Other factors that also need to be taken into account before the survey is designed relate to the use of panel surveys and incentives. However, the effects of conditioning, in relation to Web based panel surveys, are not known (Couper, 2000), nor are the effects of monetary incentives on nonresponse rates to Internet surveys. These areas require investigation. Addressing theses issues will help in the development of a good survey instrument and this is most useful when adopting a mixed mode survey strategy.

DESIGN PRINCIPLES

The following are design principles specifically for Web-based surveys. These principles may also be applied to the design of other mode type surveys, with slight modification. First, an introduction to a Web based survey should be welcoming, motivational, convey the ease of responding, and instruct the respondent how to proceed (Dillman, *et al.*, 1998; Lazar and Preece, 1999). Figures 2 and 3 show the introduction and welcoming screens of the Bushfire Survey, conducted by ITLS.

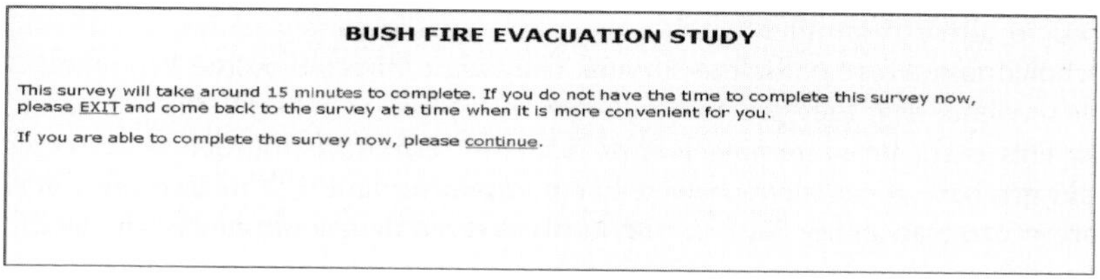

BUSH FIRE EVACUATION STUDY

This survey will take around 15 minutes to complete. If you do not have the time to complete this survey now, please EXIT and come back to the survey at a time when it is more convenient for you.

If you are able to complete the survey now, please continue.

Figure 2: Introduction Screen for the Bushfire Study

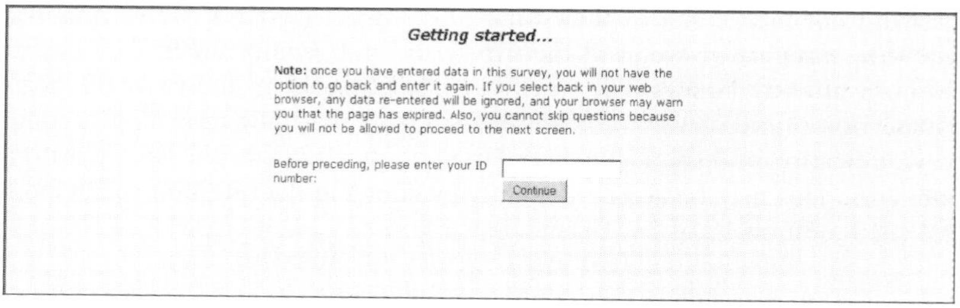

Getting started...

Note: once you have entered data in this survey, you will not have the option to go back and enter it again. If you select back in your web browser, any data re-entered will be ignored, and your browser may warn you that the page has expired. Also, you cannot skip questions because you will not be allowed to proceed to the next screen.

Before preceding, please enter your ID number:

Continue

Figure 3: Welcome Screen to the Bushfire Survey

A key feature was that respondents were informed of the time required to do the survey before they actually began the survey. This enabled the respondent to close the survey if they did not have the time to complete it at that moment. This helped ease respondent frustration and reduce avoidable terminations, thus reducing the rate of nonresponse.

Instructions to navigate through the survey should be clear and shown throughout. They should be placed before the following question or section is shown and, depending on the topic, the survey, and the target population, respondents may not have to answer every question to progress through the survey. This may be achieved through the use of scroll down screen surveys (Dillman *et al.*, 1998). However, allowing respondents to view all the questions may lead to respondents believing that the survey will take them longer than specified, which may result in avoidable terminations. In addition, when scroll down surveys are used, it cannot be determined if a respondent opens the survey and decides not to complete it, or whether the respondent has completed all the survey but forgot to send it (Couper *et al.*, 2001; Bosnjak and Tuten, 2001).

If question order and logical progression are features of the survey, then every question will have to be answered; therefore, scroll down screen surveys cannot be used. Question length and wording become even more important because the respondent's level of comprehension must be maintained to enable high quality data to be obtained, given the increased level of respondent burden.

Two recent Web based surveys, designed by the ITLS, were not scroll down screen surveys because both incorporated a SP experiment. Given that respondents could not scroll down to view the entire survey, for flow and logical reasons, the survey was programmed to allow respondents, who chose to exit the survey before completing the stated choice task, to re-enter the survey. They were directed to the beginning of the scenario sequence that they previously did not complete, to rekindle the logical thought process. This extra programming helped decrease respondent burden because respondents did not have to re-enter previously entered information. This also reinforced the password protection ability because previously entered data could not be changed.

Data entry boxes should be used sparingly to reduce respondent burden. For example, respondents who completed the bushfire survey actually enjoyed participating because the survey did not take much of their time to complete (around twelve minutes), the questions were straightforward, and the survey did not require much data entry at all (minimum use of entry boxes). The word "Finally", should be shown at the beginning of the last section of the survey to inform respondents that they have almost completed the survey. Indicating to respondents how far along they are into the survey is preferred by respondents. This may be achieved simply by showing the question the respondents are up to, e.g., question 12 of 26 (Gunn, 2002).

Importantly, before the study is undertaken, a pilot test should be conducted to assess the survey's appearance, flow, design, and respondents' comprehension of the questions asked. This will enable any revision of the survey instrument, if required, to be made before commencement of the main survey.

Recruitment and Repeated Contacts for Web Based Surveys

Interaction with the respondent can be classified into three distinct phases: contact, response, and follow-up. Each of these phases may be conducted using a different medium: telephone, mail, Web, or face to face (Schonlau *et al.*, 2001). For initial contact, this should not be by e-mail, because it is not known how often people check or if people access their e-mail regularly (Bradley, 1999). For surveys of the general population, this will add to the coverage bias problem encountered by Web based surveys in the present survey environment. In addition, it may be best to use a number of recruitment modes to achieve a higher contact rate.

Past research has indicated that increasing the number of contacts will result in higher response rates. It was found that the number of contacts increased response rates regardless of the survey mode(s) used (Dillman and Bowker, 1999). Pre-notification letters (as for traditional mail out and telephone surveys), simple survey design, personalised cover letters, and follow up reminders have been shown to increase response rates to Internet surveys (Cook *et al.*, 2000). A pre-notification letter should be sent out before the main data collection period begins. These letters legitimise the study in the minds of respondents, given that the research agency undertaking the study is clearly shown, and respondents are provided with a number to contact to voice any concerns or questions. In addition, confidentiality assurances must also be stated in pre-notification letters and this further enhances the study's legitimacy from the perspective of the respondent. For example, pre-notification of an online survey resulted in a faster response time (Cook *et al.*, 2000). This usually relates to higher response rates and data of better quality (Richardson, 2000). Response time to Web based surveys can also be controlled by the researcher to a certain degree, by informing respondents that the survey will remain online for a limited time (Illieva *et al.*, 2002). ITLS adopted this approach for two of its recent Web based travel surveys.

If respondents have been recruited through a telephone interview and it has been determined that the respondents have Internet access and are contactable at the e-mail address provided, an e-mail contact with an embedded URL adds the personal approach and this improves response (Dillman, 1978; Dillman, 2000). For example, respondents to the bushfire survey were recruited using the telephone and e-mail addresses were obtained during this conversation allowing for the URL and password of the survey to be sent to the respondents through e-mail. Given that no incentives were offered, and that respondents could only respond over the Internet, the response rate was relatively high. It may have been even higher had technical problems with the server, on which the survey was located, not arisen. This prevented a number of respondents from accessing the survey and, because of their frustration and lack of knowledge about the actual problem, these respondents did not re-attempt to access the survey.

This emphasises the importance of the use of multimodal surveys in general population surveys, especially when one of the modes offered is the Internet, despite that the above example was not a study of the general population. In addition, it is important to give people the option to choose how to respond. Respondents appreciate this and therefore, data obtained are likely to be of better quality.

REVIEW OF RECENT INTERNET TRAVEL SURVEY APPLICATIONS

Over the past few years, a few Web based travel surveys were developed. Extensive documentation for many of these applications is not readily available. However, this section describes recent Internet travel surveys briefly, as well as the associated strengths and weaknesses of these surveys.

Web based travel diaries were developed by the Resource Systems Group, Inc. primarily to test the concept of respondent-interactive geocoding as well as the likelihood that the highly affluent, highly educated, and mobile would respond over the Internet, given the difficulty to contact this group using traditional CATI recruitment (Resource Systems Group, Inc, 1999). To enable interactive geocoding, a specific GIS package, MapObjects®, was used. Maps were displayed graphically and respondents were asked to enter the specific location information. Given that the target population for this survey was the highly educated, it was not expected that respondents would have difficulty with reading the maps. However, this is likely to be a problem if this survey were to be used as a single mode, general population survey, because not everyone is able to read and understand maps.

Overall, the actual design of the survey looked cumbersome. This gives the impression that more effort than that needed was required to complete the survey. Respondent burden was considered an issue: design of a survey is very important especially when the target population is a group with limited spare time. Importantly, it was acknowledged that the Web based survey option should be offered as part of a multi-modal survey approach given that Internet users are not representative of the population (Resource Systems Group Inc., 1999).

An Internet household activity survey, called the Internet Computerised Household Activity Scheduling Survey (iCHASE), was developed soon after the computerised version of the CHASE survey (CHASE) was developed (Doherty and Miller, 2000; Lee *et al.*, 1999). Before respondents were asked to complete the CHASE survey, an up-front interview was conducted with the household to obtain the household activity schedule. This information was entered into the database so that it could be used in the week long CHASE survey. The CHASE survey was a burdensome exercise: average time taken for respondents to complete each day's entries was sixteen minutes. This equated to an average of 112 minutes per respondent to complete the entire survey.

The iCHASE survey was based on the CHASE survey. However, revision of the survey task was not conducted because the authors did not regard the CHASE survey as a burdensome exercise for the respondents (Doherty and Miller, 2000). This is surprising given that most people, who are likely to participate in travel surveys over the Internet, are very busy people who are not likely to complete long surveys. Unfortunately, results of a pilot of the iCHASE survey are not known.

Another Web based travel survey application was developed to obtain traveller responses to Advanced Traveller Information Systems (ATIS) (Kraan *et al.*, 2000). Respondents were recruited through e-mail; therefore, the sample was biased because Internet users are not representative of the general population. The authors acknowledged that the Internet mode is good for specific studies but that it should be used with other data collection modes for studies of the general population, given the sample bias issue (Kraan *et al.*, 2000). However, an important point raised is that it is not known how CATI responses differ from Internet responses in terms of data quality. This requires investigation, especially given that the CATI survey is a very common survey mode used, especially in the United States.

A Web based Origin Destination Travel Survey was developed by Abdel-Aty (2003). This study involved mail-out and roadside distribution of the survey instrument, but offered mail back and Internet retrieval options to respondents. Like other Web based travel surveys, it was stated that the Web based survey was easy to navigate for those familiar with the Internet (Abdel-Aty, 2003). In addition, the sample obtained was biased – more males, the more affluent, and those with higher levels of tertiary education responded. In the concluding comments, the author stated that the Internet could be used as a supplementary data collection mode. This is a familiar recommendation given Internet penetration and use.

A completely different Web based travel survey is the Prompted Recall Survey. The ITLS has been using GPS devices as a means to provide more accurate data on where people go, when they travel, the route they take, and the distance and time taken to travel. However, the GPS device is limited in what data it can collect, and it provides no information on the number of people travelling together in a vehicle, the purposes of their travel, and the costs associated with that travel. The ITLS have developed a method of collecting this additional information, called the prompted recall survey (Stopher *et al.*, 2004), which is to be conducted a week or two after the GPS data are collected (two weeks is the time limit that respondents are assumed to be able to recall travel information), and uses maps and tabular presentations, developed from the GPS records, as the basis of prompting the memory of the traveller (Stopher *et al.* 2004).

The Web based prompted recall survey was first developed as a pen and paper survey. A primary goal for developing the Web version of the survey was to provide animation of each trip measured in the initial GPS survey, and to allow the survey respondent to be able to stop the animation part way through the trip, to indicate a trip end that the analysis of the GPS data had not detected, to restart the trip animation, pause in the trip, slow down or speed up the display of the trip, and to indicate that a stop shown on the screen was only a traffic stop, and not a destination (Stopher *et al.*, 2004).

A disadvantage to this type of Web based travel survey is that it requires Java to run. Java is a complete programming language that allows programs to run from within a Web browser. Unfortunately, the Java program needs to be installed first, and it cannot be assumed that Java will be installed on all respondents' computers (Stopher *et al.*, 2004). In addition, there are numerous versions of Java and the respondent may not install the most suitable version. Therefore, to avoid this problem, a specific version of Java was selected and this required respondents to install this version (Stopher *et al.*, 2004). This led to large respondent burden, because respondents were required to install this version from a CD provided to them from ITLS, together with installation instructions (Stopher *et al.*, 2004). However, many people do not have the time, patience or computer access privileges to do this, and therefore drop out of the survey.

In addition, due the use of maps, download times were significant for dial-up modem connections (Stopher *et al.*, 2004). However, this too can be a problem for respondents on Internet plans with download or time limits. Therefore, despite the usefulness of this survey and the potential benefits of such an instrument, the present technological environment is not conducive to a large scale application of this survey. However, further testing and technological advancement will see this survey tool become more widely used in the future.

A research firm in the US designed Web based survey templates for household travel diary surveys, origin-destination surveys, travel mode choice surveys, and transit customer satisfaction surveys (The Resource Systems Group Inc., 2002). These incorporated the following components:

- The flow and design of the templates was developed to exploit the capabilities of the Web; the templates were not adapted from paper or CATI designs. This contradicts Web based survey design principles developed by Dillman *et al*, (2002), Dillman *et al.*, (1998) and Gunn (2002).
- Detailed survey based logic and consistency checks.
- Respondent interactive geocoding. This adds to respondent burden and assumes that people are able to read maps without difficulty. Again, this poses problems if the sample is drawn from the general population.
- Detailed instructions/help.
- Mutlilingual instrument options.
- Web-based administration tools to help facilitate web based survey administration processes.

Web based travel surveys are not really user friendly for novice computer users. In addition, principles of survey design, let alone principles of Web based survey design, have not been applied readily. The appearance of Web based travel surveys is often cluttered, giving the impression of a burdensome survey that is more likely to contribute to the problem of nonresponse (see Resource Systems Group Inc., 2002, for an example of such a travel survey). In this study it was interesting that none of the respondents encountered any browser problems. In contrast, such problems were encountered by some of the respondents to a Web based survey conducted by ITLS. Some respondents could not access the survey due to browser incompatibilities. This further demonstrates the coverage and measurement problems with Web based surveys in the present survey environment.

The travel survey templates are a good starting point, yet much work is needed. Refinement of the survey design and further improvements in software will lead to the development of a better Web based travel survey. At present, no studies have compared the rate of completion of Web based travel surveys to those using CATI recruitment and retrieval procedures; a very common survey mode, especially in the US.

ISSUES FOR THE FUTURE

Household travel surveys are complex instruments that try to obtain demographic and travel information from households. Obtaining all this information over the Internet is likely to lead to a relatively long survey task. This will create problems for people with limited download and time access to the Internet. In addition, anecdotal evidence suggests that respondents choosing to respond over the Internet have shorter attention spans (Schonlau *et al.*, 2001). If this is true, this has great implications for Web based travel surveys. People with shorter attention spans are therefore less likely to complete the survey or, if they do complete the survey, we cannot be sure that answers provided are in fact true answers. However, more research is required to confirm or deny this.

The present survey environment limits the use of Web based surveys, for studies of the general population, due to problems with population coverage and the fact that Internet user ability, and the type of Internet access respondents have, is unknown. Given these obstacles, Web based travel surveys should be part of mixed mode travel surveys. The Internet mode may be useful to capture traditional non-respondent groups to travel surveys, such as households that are difficult to contact. Traditional survey modes, such as mail and telephone, will capture other respondent groups better than the Internet option at this stage. In addition, the use of multimodal surveys will provide respondents with a choice as to how they would like to respond and this should increase response rates: a low response rate is a common problem encountered by most travel surveys.

There is a need to investigate Internet respondent behaviour, and to identify if any particular socioeconomic group behaves in a particular manner when responding to surveys over the Internet (Bosnjak and Tuten, 2001). This knowledge would enable the development of a better Web based survey instrument, especially in relation to Web based travel surveys. In addition, Bradley (1999) found that Web based surveys released at a particular time of day may result in a certain sample profile. However, research is required to confirm or deny this finding, especially in relation to travel surveys.

Web based travel surveys are useful but much work is still needed to improve the paper instrument let alone the Internet instrument. Web based versions of travel surveys may also require accompanying compact disks, housing maps and other relevant information, to participating households to avoid browser and download problems. Overall, much research and development is still required in relation to Web based surveys, and especially Web based travel surveys.

ACKNOWLEDGEMENTS

I would like to thank Mr. Andrew Collins, a Research Analyst, at the ITLS, for his comments on an earlier draft of this chapter.

REFERENCES

Abdel-Aty, M.A. (2003). Hybrid Distribution and Response Techniques for an Origin-Destination Travel Survey, *ITE Journal*, **73** (2), 22-27.

Alvarez, R.M. and C. VanBeselaere (2003). *Web-Based Surveys*, http://survey.caltech.edu/encyclopedia.pdf, Accessed on 20 Feb., 2004.

Arentze, T., F. Hofman and H. Timmermans (2004). Predicting Multi-Faceted Activity-Travel Adjustment Strategies in Response to Possible Congestion Pricing Scenarios Using an Internet-Based Stated Adaptation Experiment, *Transport Policy*, **11** (1), 31-41.

Bosnjak, M. and T.L. Tuten (2001). Classifying Response Behaviors in Web-Based Surveys, *Journal of Computer-Mediated Communication*, **6** (3), www.ascusc.org/jcmc/vol6/issue3/boznjak.html, Accessed on 22 Jan., 2001.

Bradley, M. (1999). Sampling for Internet Surveys; An Examination of Respondent Selection for Internet Research, *International Journal of Market Research*, **41** (4), 387-395.

Cobanoglu, C., B. Warde and P.J. Moreo (2001). A Comparison of Mail, Fax and Web-Based Survey Methods, *Int. Journal of Market Research*, **43** (4), 441-452.

Cook, C., F. Heath and R.L. Thompson (2000). A Meta-Analysis of Response Rates in Web- or Internet-Based Surveys, *Educational and Psychological Measurement*, **60**, 821-836.

Couper, M.P., M.W. Traugott and M.J. Lamias (2001). Web Survey Design and Administration, *Public Opinion Quarterly*, **65** (2), 230-253.

Couper, M.P. (2000). Web Surveys: A Review of Issues and Approaches, *Public Opinion Quarterly*, **64** (4), 464-494.

De Heer, W.F. and G. Moritz (1997). Data Quality Problems in Travel Surveys, An International Overview. In: *Transport Surveys: Raising the Standard* (P.R. Stopher and P.M. Jones, eds), II-C/1-21, Transportation Research Circular E-C008, Transportation Research Board, Washington, DC.

Dillman, D.A. (1978). *Mail and Telephone Surveys: The Total Design Method*, John Wiley and Sons, New York.

Dillman, D.A. (1998). *Mail and Other Self-Administered Surveys in the 21ˢᵗ Century: The Beginning of a New Era*, http://survey.sesrc.wsu.edu/dillman/papers.htm, Accessed on 5 Dec., 2003.

Dillman, D.A. (2000). *Mail and Internet Surveys: The Tailored Design Method*, John Wiley, New York, Second Edition.

Dillman, D.A., R.D. Tortora and D. Bowker (1998). *Principles for Conducting Web Surveys*, http://survey.sesrc.wsu.edu/dillman/papers.htm, Accessed on 5 Dec. 2003.

Dillman, D.A., and D.K. Bowker (1999). *The Web Questionnaire Challenge to Survey Methodologists*, http://survey.sesrc.wsu.edu/dillman/papers.htm, Accessed on 5 Dec., 2003.

Dillman, D.A., G. Phelps, R. Tortora, K. Swift, J. Kohrell and J. Berck (2001). *Response Rate and Measurement Differences in Mixed Mode Surveys; Using Mail, Telephone, Interactive Voice Response and the Internet*, Research Papers, http://survey.sesrc.wsu.edu/dillman/papers.htm, Accessed on 5 Nov., 2002.

Doherty. S.T. and E.J. Miller (2000). A Computerized Household Activity Scheduling Survey, *Transportation*, **27** (1), 75-97.

Ettema, D., H. Timmermans and L. van Veghel (1996). *Effects of Data Collection Methods in Travel and Activity Research*, European Institute of Retailing and Services Studies Report, www.bwk.tue.nl/urb/eirass/report.htm, Accessed on 22 Jan., 2003.

Groves, R.M., and M.P. Couper (1998). *Nonresponse in Household Interview Surveys*, John Wiley and Sons, Inc., New York.

Gunn, H. (2002). *Web-based Surveys: Changing the Survey Process*, http://www.firstmonday.dk/issues/issue7_12/gunn/, Accessed on 5 Dec., 2003.

Illieva, J., S. Baron and N.M. Healey (2002). Online Surveys in Marketing Research: Pros and Cons, *International Journal of Market Research*, **44** (3), 361-382.

Kam, H.B. and J. Morris (1999). *Response Patterns in Travel Surveys: The VATS Experience*, www.trc.rmit.edu.au/Publications/Papers/responsepatterns.pdf, Accessed on 10 Feb., 2003.

Kraan, M., H.S. Mahmassani and N. Huynh (2000). Traveler Responses to Advanced Traveler Information Systems for Shopping Trips, *Transportation Research Record No. 1725*, 116-123.

Lazar, J. and J. Preece (1999). Designing and Implementing Web-Based Surveys, *The Journal of Computer Information Systems*, **39** (4), 63-67.

Lee, M.S., S.T. Doherty, R. Sabetiashraf and M.G. McNally (1999). *iCHASE: An Internet Computerised Household Activity Scheduling Elicitor Survey* http://www.its.uci.edu/its/publications/papers/AS-WP-99-1.pdf, Accessed on 24 June 2004.

Melevin, P.T., D.A. Dillman, R. Baxter and C.E. Lamiman (1998). *Personal Delivery of Mail Questionnaires for Household Surveys: A Test of Four Retrieval Methods*,

Research Papers, http://survey.sesrc.wsu.edu/dillman/papers.htm, Accessed on 5 November 2002.

Miller, E.T., D.J. Neal, L.J. Roberts, J.S. Baer, S.O. Cressler, J. Metrik and G.A. Marlatt (2002). Test-Test Reliability of Alcohol Measures: Is There a Difference Between Internet-Based Assessment and Traditional Methods? *Psychology of Addictive Behaviors*, **16** (1), 56-63.

Myles, R. and J. Tibert (1998). Internet Surveys: Do They Work? *Institute for Social Research Newsletter*, **13** (1), http://www.math.yorku.ca/ISR/newsletter/Internet_surveys.htm, Accessed on 5 December 2003.

Resource Systems Group, Inc (1999). *Computer Based Intelligent Travel Survey System: CASI/Internet Travel Diaries with Interactive Geocoding*, April.

Resource Systems Group Inc. (2002). *Documentation for SBIR Phase II Final Report: Computer-Based Intelligent Travel Survey System, DTRS57-00-C-10030*, Prepared for the FHWA, http://www.fhwa.dot.gov/ohim/trb/sbir/sbir.htm, Accessed on 14 January 2004.

Richardson, A.J. (2000). Behavioral Mechanisms of Nonresponse in Mailback Travel Surveys, Paper presented at 79th Annual Meeting, Transportation Research Board, Paper No. P00-2551.

Schaefer, D.R. and D.A. Dillman (1998). *Development of a Standard e-Mail Methodology: Results of an Experiment*, http://survey.sesrc.wsu.edu/dillman/papers.htm, Accessed on 5 December 2003.

Schneider, K.C. and J.C. Johnson (1994). Link Between Response-Inducing Strategies and Uninformed Response, *Marketing Intelligence and Planning*, **12** (1), 29-36.

Schonlau, M., R.D. Fricker Jr. and M.N. Elliot (2001). *Conducting Research Surveys via e-mail and the Web*, http://www.rand.org/publications/MR/MR1480/, Accessed on 29 December 2004.

Stopher, P.R., A. Collins and P. Bullock (2004). GPS Surveys and the Internet, paper presented to the 27th Australasian Transport Research Forum, Canberra, ACT.

Thompson, L.F., E.A. Surface, D.L. Martin and M.G. Sanders (2003). From Paper to Pixels: Moving Personnel Surveys to the Web, *Personnel Psychology*, **56** (1), 197-227.

Woong Yun, G., and C.W. Trumbo (2000). *Comparative Response to a Survey Executed by Post, E-mail and Web Form*, http://www.ascusc.org/jcmc/vol16/issue1/yun.html, Accessed from 14 January 2004.

Zmud, J. (2003). Designing Instruments to Improve Response. In: *Transport Survey Quality and Innovation* (P.R. Stopher and P.M. Jones, eds), 89-108, Pergamon Press, Oxford.

Travel Survey Methods: Quality and Future Directions
Peter Stopher and Cheryl Stecher (Editors)
© 2006 Elsevier Ltd. All rights reserved.

33

NEW TECHNOLOGY: WEB-BASED

Patrick Bonnel, ENTPE, Lyon, France
and
Jean-Loup Madre, INRETS-DEST, Arcueil, France

INTRODUCTION

This chapter summarises the discussions of an in-depth eight-hour workshop[41], the members of which came from nine countries of four continents with a large variety of cultural and professional contexts which added to the wealth of discussion. This chapter draws conclusions about the advantages and limits of Web-based surveys with regard to different use contexts. Web-based surveys are a relatively recent development, particularly for travel surveys. We have therefore identified the main directions for research to increase their effectiveness, proposed a definition of the term Web-based survey, and given a preliminary classification of previous surveys.

DEFINITION AND CLASSIFICATION

In view of the diversity of Web-based surveys, we use a very straightforward definition that enables us to cover all past and future applications. Our definition of Web-based survey is 'any survey that can be done on the Web'. This definition requires some explanation. It refers only to the Web, thus e-mail surveys that do not involve the use of Web resources are excluded. Consequently, we can lay emphasis on an important ad-

---

[41] Members of the workshop were: Rahaf Alsnih (Australia), Patrick Bonnel (France), Linda Christensen (Denmark), Henk van Evert (Netherlands), Ruth Ditzian Haim (Israel), Antoine Haroun (Canada), Jean-Loup Madre (France), Sharon O'Connor (USA), Juan de Dios Ortuzar (Chile), Kaethe Podgorski (USA), and Tomas Ruiz (Spain).

vantage of Web-based surveys, namely interactivity. Among other things, this makes it possible to include visual aids and animation to assist the respondent, randomise questions, etc. (Alsnih, 2006). This definition is deliberately non-restrictive as regards the type of surveys, methodology, design, etc. On the contrary, all types of surveys are potentially possible. It also emphasises the specific nature of Web-based surveys that relates to the medium used to conduct the survey, as opposed to face-to-face, telephone, or postal surveys, for example. Web-based surveys can be classified with reference to three dimensions:

- Full Web-based/combined survey modes;
- Closed access/universal access; and
- Means of contact and recruitment.

The first dimension distinguishes between those surveys that use the Web exclusively and those that combine a number of survey methods. This dimension raises the issues of sample construction and of the representativeness and comparability of the data from surveys that use different media. The second dimension is important with regard to sample construction. If access is closed, the construction of the survey sample can be controlled, whereas this is much more complex, or even impossible, with universal access. Importantly, the present survey environment affects the representativeness of the sample, especially if the study is of the general population, because access to the Internet is far from universal. This dimension, therefore, relates to the control of the sample and how representative it is of the target population.

The third dimension is concerned with how contact is made with respondents: this may be by post or telephone, when it is possible to determine respondents' addresses or telephone numbers, by e-mail, if bases of e-mail addresses are available, or by the Internet (pop-ups, Websites, etc.), when sampling bases are not available. Like the first one, this dimension also raises the issues of sample construction and representativeness, but also that of comparability of the data from surveys that use different media.

We did not feel that it would be helpful to create a typology of survey types or objectives, because these would not be specific to Web-based surveys but common to surveys of all types. Finally, because use of the Web as a survey medium is still quite restricted, we have identified its main advantages and limitations in the current context.

ADVANTAGES AND LIMITATIONS OF THE WEB AS A SURVEY MEDIUM

Because the Web is a new medium it is interesting to examine the main reasons for the rapid development of Web-based surveys. However, the fact that such development has taken place should not lead us to forget the limitations of Web-based surveys in the current context, bearing in mind that some of these are likely to diminish in the future in view of the spread of Internet access and technological advances. Because these advantages and limitations are thoroughly discussed in a paper by Alsnih (2006), our coverage is fairly brief to allow us to concentrate on the consequences in terms of the quality of the output data, and on making a number of recommendations.

Principal Advantages of Web-Based Surveys

Our analysis focuses on the advantages of the Web as a medium compared to other survey media.

Low Survey Cost

The variable costs of Web-based surveys can be much lower than for surveys that are administered, because no staff are required to do this. Likewise, the variable costs are considerably lower than for postal surveys because no coding or data input is required. The situation is however more complex for fixed costs. These depend to a considerable extent on whether it is possible to re-use developments made during previous surveys and on complex aspects of the design. However, it is expected that in the future the development of Web-based survey design software should help to reduce fixed costs.

Interactivity

This advantage is shared by all computer-assisted survey media, such as telephone surveys (CATI) and increasingly face-to-face surveys (CAPI). However, only the Web would seem to extend this possibility to self-administered surveys. The Web has, nevertheless, an extra advantage over other survey media in that the central management of the survey can provide better interactivity, particularly to present questions or possible answers, in random order, so as to avoid bias resulting from systematic responses.

Availability to the Respondent at Any Time and Any Place

An important source of respondent burden is whether respondents are asked to answer the survey at an appropriate moment for them (Ampt, 2003). By 'appropriate moment' we mean a time when they are available to answer. This moment depends to a great extent on the characteristics of the individual (degree of mobility, working or not, with or without children, etc.). By its nature the person conducting the survey does not know this moment when contacting the respondent. Making an appointment to conduct the survey reduces this constraint without completely removing it: presence at home to conduct an interview limits the scope of surveys, in particular transport surveys (Madre and Armoogum, 1997). The advantage of self-administered Web-based surveys (and postal surveys) is that respondents are free to choose when they wish to answer the survey because the Internet is available twenty four hours a day and they can obtain a connection from almost anywhere. Location constraints will be even less apparent with wireless technology.

Capture of Individuals Who Do Not Respond to Other Survey Modes

People who travel the most are often more difficult to contact by administered surveys (Christensen, 2006), in particular because they are less often at home. Like postal surveys, Web-based surveys allow respondents to make contact and respond when they wish. The combination of the Web-based mode with other survey modes also provides another survey medium for individuals who refuse to answer face-to-face, telephone, or postal surveys. Thus, Web-based surveys provide a way of increasing response rates (we return to this question later, when we consider the methodological problems involved in this).

Automated Data Entry and Checking

Like other computer-assisted surveys, Web-based surveys allow real-time entry of survey data (Bonnel and Le Nir, 1998). Consistency tests and probing for clarifications or corrections can, therefore, be conducted to increase the quality of the collected data. Nevertheless, the choice of the procedure for these tests is probably more difficult than in the case of an administered survey, where the tests can be conducted using the interviewer interface. Careful programming is necessary to ensure that consistency checks and requests for clarification are placed in appropriate places in the questionnaire.

Faster Response Time

The Web provides much greater speed for processing contacts, and for sending questionnaires and reminders to respondents than postal surveys. Furthermore, no coding or keying in of questionnaires is required and the absence of survey staff means that a larger number of surveys can be dealt with at the same time. For this reason, a Web-based survey can be conducted over a much shorter time span than is usually required for other types of surveys.

Web-based surveys have many advantages over other survey media. However these advantages must not lead us to forget the limitations which still affect their use in certain applications.

Main Limitations of Web-Based Surveys

As with the advantages, we restrict our analysis to the specific limitations of the Web in comparison with other survey media.

Internet Penetration and Confidence

Even though Internet penetration is increasing rapidly in all continents, the penetration rate is still too low for the population of Internet users to be considered as representative of the population as a whole (Table 1). Even in North America, thirty two percent of the population does not have access to the Internet at their homes or workplaces. Furthermore, Internet use is highly correlated with sociodemographic variables such as age, educational attainment or income, which also have a strong influence on travel practices (Alsnih, 2006).

Table 1: Internet World Usage Statistics

World Regions	Population (2005 Est.)	Internet Usage (Year 2000)	Internet Usage, Nov. 2005	User Growth (2000-2005)	Penetration (Percent Population)
Africa	896,721,874	4,514,400	23,917,500	429.8 %	2.7 %
Asia	3,622,994,130	114,303,000	332,590,713	191.0 %	9.2 %
Europe	804,574,696	103,096,093	285,408,118	171.6 %	35.5 %
Middle East	187,258,006	5,284,800	16,163,500	392.1 %	8.6 %
North America	328,387,059	108,096,800	224,103,811	107.3 %	68.2 %
Latin America/ Caribbean	546,723,509	18,068,919	72,953,597	303.8 %	13.3 %
Oceania	33,443,448	7,619,500	17,690,762	132.2 %	52.9 %
WORLD TOTAL	6,420,102,722	360,971,012	972,828,001	169.5 %	15.2 %

Source: http://www.Internetworldstats.com/stats.htm, 11 January, 2006

Furthermore, part of the population with access to the Internet is not familiar enough with its use to be able or willing to answer a Web-based survey. Even if we have no statistics on Internet skills, we can consider that, at least for the next decade, the percentage of users who are sufficiently comfortable with the Internet to be able to answer a survey will remain insufficient to ensure that this population is representative of the population as a whole, at least for most world regions. It is, therefore, highly recommended not to conduct surveys that relate to the entire population of a conurbation or a country, with the Web as the only survey medium. However, a considerable amount of research shows that the Web is extremely helpful for specific populations (Iragüen and Ortúzar, 2004). While the Web is not to be recommended as a single mode for surveying the entire population, it nevertheless provides a possible way of obtaining responses from individuals who do not respond to more traditional types of survey.

Technical Problems

A number of problems are frequently mentioned. These include:

- Server unavailability, which may occur without the person in charge of the survey being aware of it. These interruptions can discourage respondents from answering the survey.

- The way in which the questionnaire is presented may vary depending on the browser used, which means that care must be taken to guarantee either the quality or the uniformity of survey presentation.
- Excessively long data loading times that can use up all the Internet user's connection time for some individuals, or discourage others. In either case, the nonresponse rate may increase with its associated risk of bias.

A number of recommendations can be made to deal with these problems:

- Choose a standard language, such as HTML or XML, and use only its simplest functions as far as possible;
- Use the simplest possible survey design – greater complexity is a potential source of problems, even though some studies have successfully used relatively complex designs;
- Use two servers so one is still available if the other is down; and
- As for all surveys (Stopher and Jones, 2003), it is essential to test the survey under real conditions in order to detect the principal problems.

Sample Construction

Unlike other survey modes, for which sampling bases exist (even if most of the time they are not bias-free), the construction of the sample is often more complex for a Web-based survey, because generally a sampling base of e-mail addresses from which to draw the sample is not available. When sampling bases exist, they must be checked for double counts (several addresses for the same statistical unit, i.e., individual, household, or company). The lack of an e-mail address base means that other recruitment techniques must be used (face-to-face, telephone, postal, Internet, etc.). It is, therefore, often more difficult to check that the sample is representative. The use of closed access surveys can therefore be desirable. In both cases, it is essential to analyse the representativeness of the sample with respect to the target population.

However, this limitation does not concern surveys that target specific populations, for example users on a university campus or people working for an administration, for which a sampling base may be available. In this case, normal sampling techniques can be applied in the same way as for every other survey mode. Likewise, when the Web is used to supplement other survey modes, it generally improves the representativeness of the sample because of its ability to reach individuals who do not respond to other survey modes.

Low Response Rate

Low response rates are frequently reported as with other self-administered survey modes, (Alsnih, 2006). It is also often difficult to assume that nonresponse is not correlated to the indicators that the survey is attempting to establish (number of trips or immobility rate for example). Low response rates are therefore a potential source of bias.

However, this general statement requires some qualification. As with postal surveys, some scholars have observed that fairly high response rates can be achieved if an appropriate methodology is developed and an investment made to obtain responses (Brög and Meyburg, 1983). In addition, as has been mentioned in connection with sample construction, combining the Web with other survey modes can, on the contrary, increase the response rate.

RESEARCH ISSUES

Our identification of the principal research needs has been partly based on an analysis of the advantages and limitations of Web-based surveys, but also on an analysis of their quality (Noble, 2006). Lastly, we have attempted to identify the principal current and future areas of application for Web-based surveys. As an outcome of these discussions, we recommend four main areas for research, which we present in order of decreasing importance:

- Combining survey modes;
- Sampling coverage;
- Design issues; and
- Application domains.

Combining Survey Modes

The issue of combining survey modes is not a new one (Bonnel, 2003; Morris and Adler, 2003). However, the development of Web-based surveys means this issue must be reconsidered in view of the potential benefits of combining the Web with the other survey media.

The first question that needs to be tackled in connection with combining survey methods is whether response behaviour is similar or not. Do Internet users give different answers, because no interviewer is present, or not? It may be possible that response behaviour, in this case, most closely resembles that for a postal survey, which is also self-administered. However, the comparisons that have been made (Resource Systems Group, 2002) seem to indicate that, for individual or household travel surveys, the reported travel levels are higher for Web-based surveys than for postal surveys. Notwithstanding, it was acknowledged that these results were at least partially due to respondents of higher socio-economic status responding over the Internet. Nevertheless, further analysis is required to establish that this difference is not only correlated with the socioeconomic characteristics of the respondents, which are frequently different for these two types of survey media.

It would be desirable to conduct experiments to compare behaviour, particularly travel behaviour, between Web-based surveys and surveys using other media (face-to-face, telephone, or postal surveys). However, in such comparisons it is important to control for any possible influence of respondents' socioeconomic characteristics in each survey medium. The conclusions of such research would obviously be very important for coping with the increasing rate of nonresponses encountered by the majority of urban or national household travel surveys. Last, to optimise the combination of different survey modes, it would be very useful to know individuals' preferences with regards to the different survey media.

Sample Coverage

We have already mentioned that the representativeness of Web-based survey samples is one of the limitations of these surveys, when the aim is to represent the population as a whole and when the Web is the only survey medium used. To reduce this problem, several approaches have been identified:

- The Internet penetration rate is obviously an important indicator of population coverage by the Web, but it is not the only indicator that allows us to evaluate this in the context of a Web-based survey. Many Internet users are limited in their ability to respond to a Web-based survey, either by their equipment or by their lack of Internet skills. Bradley (1999) provides a classification of users on the basis of these two dimensions. However, we have no precise knowledge about how they affect the response rate or how survey design might be able to reduce the problem.
- What are the best contact or survey sample recruitment techniques for a given target population? This question involves, on the one hand, the effectiveness of the techniques in question and, on the other, the potential they provide for controlling the representativeness of the respondent population. In particular, when certain techniques are used, it is not always possible to calculate a response rate.
- Proxy reporting is recognised as a potential source of bias (Stopher *et al.*, 2006). As with postal surveys (which are also self-administered), it is important to know, on the one hand, if there is more proxy reporting in a Web-based survey than in another type of survey and, on the other hand, if it is possible to control for the questionnaires that are answered by proxy reporting.
- The role of incentives also generated lively discussion, because of the impact of cultural differences between different countries that have led to totally different strategies. Cultural differences aside, we do not currently know how incentives affect response rates and the quality of collected data. Furthermore, consideration should also be given to the timing and form of incentives (before or after the return of the questionnaire as opposed to no incentive, a fixed amount of money versus a lottery, etc.).

- The number of reminders also merits specific consideration for the Web-based survey mode. Stopher *et al.* (2006) recommend limiting the number of reminders to five or six for telephone surveys. Can this recommendation also be applied to the Web? How do reminders affect the answers given by respondents, and what form should the reminders take? These are all questions that cannot be answered fully at the present time in connection with Web-based surveys.

Design Issues

One of the advantages of Web-based surveys is the medium's potential for interactivity. At the same time, the simplest possible design, using standard computing languages, should be recommended, because of potential technical problems. Research would, therefore, appear to be necessary to inform the trade-off that must be made between greater complexity and sophistication of the design, that are made possible by computing developments, and the need for simplification to reduce respondent burden. Also, research is needed to take account of the fact that such developments spread at various rates within the population of respondents and the fact that they may have different effects on the responses given. In particular, the research should question if it is possible to collect geocoded geographical data, trip routes, etc, from maps or other sources. If so, it should be determined if the Web is less burdensome for respondents than other media.

Self-administered surveys often result in a higher percentage of nonresponse items than administered surveys. From a technical point of view, the Web can deal with this problem by making the response to a question, or a set of questions, compulsory. Respondents may resent an obligation of this type, which means that there is a danger they may give biased responses or abandon the survey. Our current experience does not allow us to know the scale of this problem and, therefore, we cannot make recommendations about what to do in the context of different types of survey.

In a similar way, travel surveys often aim to interview each member of a household for the same given day. What should be done when one or more household members do not respond to the survey? Should it be 'compulsory' for all the individuals in the household to reply, at the risk of creating a bias in the reported composition of the household or generating survey abandonment? Should reminders be sent and if so, how many? Can incomplete households be accepted? Finally, is it really reasonable to specify that data should be collected for all household members, in particular in the case of the largest households?

Conducting a travel survey is frequently a fairly long process, and we know that survey duration can affect the response rate. It also affects the risk of abandonment in the course of the survey. This risk is fairly small in the case of administered surveys, because of the presence of the interviewer. However, we do not know the effect of survey duration on response rates in the case of a Web-based survey, although it is generally recommended that surveys should be as short as possible. This is a particularly important issue if there is an intention of combining the Web with other survey media. Can or should the same questions be used for Web-based surveys as for relatively long surveys, or should there be fewer questions with the resulting problems of comparability?

Application Domains

The importance of the Web for marketing surveys is increasing considerably and seems particularly suitable for SP surveys involving controlled samples. Even in countries where access to the Internet remains quite limited, the Web appears to be quite useful for surveying a targeted population in the context of SP surveys (Hojman *et al.*, 2004). The authors give the example of two Web-based surveys conducted in Chile to determine willingness-to-pay to reduce accident risk, which have given results very consistent with those from other studies. However, beyond these application domains, it is necessary to specify the domains and conditions in which Web-based surveys are applicable, both when it is the only survey mode used and when it is combined with other media. We can also considered the usefulness of the Web for conducting multi-day surveys, panel surveys or for in-depth analysis.

CONCLUSIONS

Use of the Web for transport surveys is likely to increase, in the same way as its use by the population. In view of the problems of coverage and Internet skills, its application as a single survey medium is for the time being restricted mainly to the study of a specific population for which the construction of the sample can be controlled. Its use as a survey mode in combination with others is very promising in view of the steady rise in nonresponses for other survey modes in many countries. Nevertheless, it is true that there is a considerable need for research concerning the comparability of the data from the different media, with reference to how the design and the survey process affect the collected data. These surveys also encounter certain specific technical problems that developments in computing should reduce in the medium term.

REFERENCES

Alsnih, R. (2006). Characteristics of Web-based Surveys and Applications in Travel Research. In: *Travel Survey Methods – Quality and Future Directions* (P.R. Stopher and C.C. Stecher, eds), 585-608, Elsevier, Oxford.

Ampt, E.S. (2003). Respondent Burden. In: *Transport Survey Quality and Innovation* (P.R. Stopher and P.M. Jones, eds), 507-521, Pergamon, Oxford.

Bonnel, P. (2003). Postal, Telephone and Face-to-Face Surveys: How Comparable Are They? In: *Transport Survey Quality and Innovation* (P.R. Stopher and P.M. Jones, eds), 215-237, Pergamon, Oxford.

Bonnel, P. and M. Le Nir (1998). The Quality of Survey Data: Telephone versus Face-to-Face Interviews, *Transportation*, **25** (2), 147-167.

Bradley, M. (1999). Sampling for Internet Surveys: An Examination of Respondent Selection for Internet Research, *Int. Journal of Market Research*, **41** (4), 441-452.

Brög, W. and A.H. Meyburg (1983). Influence of Survey Methods on the Results of Representative Travel Surveys, *Transportation Research A*, **17** (2), 149-156.

Christensen, L. (2006). Possible Explanations for an Increasing Share of No-Trip Respondents. In: *Travel Survey Methods – Quality and Future Directions* (P.R. Stopher and C.C. Stecher, eds), 315-328, Elsevier, Oxford.

Hojman, P., J. de D. Ortúzar and L.I. Rizzi (2004). Internet-based Surveys to Elicit the Value of Risk Reductions, Paper presented to the *7th International Conference on Travel Survey Methods*, Costa Rica, August 1-6, 12 pp. http://www.its.usyd.edu.au/isctsc/costarica_papers/offered/B5%20-%20Rizzi.pdf Accessed on 15 Dec., 2005.

Iragüen, P. and J. de D. Ortúzar (2004). Willingness-to-Pay for Reducing Fatal Accidents Risk in Urban Areas: An Internet-Based Web Page Stated Preference Survey. *Accident Analysis and Prevention,* **36** (4), 513-524.

Madre, J.-L. and J. Armoogum (1997). Interview et Présence au Domicile. *XIV Symposium Annuel International sur les Questions de Méthodologie.* Statistique Canada, Ottawa, Canada.

Morris, J. and T. Adler (2003). Mixed-Mode Surveys. In: *Transport Survey Quality and Innovation* (P.R. Stopher and P.M. Jones, eds), 239-252, Pergamon, Oxford.

Noble, B. (2006). Quality Assessment. In: *Travel Survey Methods – Quality and Future Directions* (P.R. Stopher and C.C. Stecher, eds), 329-336, Elsevier, Oxford.

Resource Systems Group Inc. (2002). *Documentation for SBIR Phase II Final Report: Computer-Based Intelligent Travel Survey System*, DTRS57-00-C-10030., Prepared for the FHWA, US Department of Transportation, Washington, DC. http://www.fhwa.dot.gov/ohim/trb/sbir/sbir.htm Accessed on 15 Dec., 2005.

Stopher, P.R. and P.M. Jones (2003). Summary and Future Directions. In: *Transport Survey Quality and Innovation* (P.R. Stopher and P.M. Jones, eds), 635-646, Pergamon, Oxford.

Stopher, P.R., C.G. Wilmot, C.C. Stecher and R. Alsnih (2006), Household Travel Surveys: Proposed Standards and Guidelines. In: *Travel Survey Methods – Quality and Future Directions* (P.R. Stopher and C.C. Stecher, eds), 19-75, Elsevier, Oxford.

Travel Survey Methods: Quality and Future Directions
Peter Stopher and Cheryl Stecher (Editors)
© 2006 Published by Elsevier Ltd.

34

DATA COLLECTION RELATED TO EMERGENCY EVENTS

Chester G. Wilmot, Louisiana Transportation Research Center and Department of Civil and Environmental Engineering, Louisiana State University, Baton Rouge, Louisiana, USA

INTRODUCTION

Travel surveys have concentrated primarily on urban person movement in the past. Interest is currently growing in freight travel demand, while long distance travel received a resurgence of interest in the United States with the introduction of the American Travel Survey in 1996, after the last large-scale long distance survey – the National Travel Survey – was conducted in 1977. Interest in continuing to provide data on long distance travel has been demonstrated by the collection of long distance travel in the 2001 National Household Travel Survey. However, while it is apparent that there is a diversification in the type of data being collected, there is a growing need to collect data on emergency-related events, and yet this seems to have received little attention in the past. For example, have data been collected on the travel related to the eruption of Mount St. Helens in 1980, the wildfires of California in 2003, or even the destruction of the Twin Towers in New York on September 11, 2001? We need to know how people behave in terms of travel during an emergency in order to be able to model that behaviour and develop contingency plans for the future.

Security has become a much more important issue in the US and elsewhere since 9/11. One way of improving security is understanding and being able to predict how people behave under different emergency conditions. This capability permits investigation of different scenarios and the strategies and policies that can lead to the optimum handling of people movement during emergency events. However, if we are to model human travel behaviour effectively, the first requirement is good data on human response to emergencies and the factors that influence their response. In the past, most data collected on emergency events have been collected to observe the behaviour and attitudes of people exposed to these conditions, and relatively little attention has been given to identify the factors that influence these decisions so that a modelling capability can be developed. Because developing a modelling capability of travel during emergencies is so important to achieve the maximum safety of the population, this chapter is aimed at encouraging the travel survey community to enter the realm of data collection of travel during emergency events. This is important, because of the great contribution they can make in this area from their experience in data collection for urban transport planning.

TYPES OF EMERGENCY EVENTS

There are a wide variety of events that could be classified as emergencies. Webster's dictionary defines an emergency as '...a serious situation or occurrence that happens unexpectedly and demands immediate action' or '...a condition of urgent need for action or assistance'. There are, thus, the concepts of unexpectedness, urgency, risk, and the need for action without delay. This can apply to events that provide limited warning, as well as those that occur without warning, both man-made and natural events, localised and extensive, and those that present limited danger and those that provide catastrophic danger. With such a wide variety of possible emergency events, it is useful to establish a typology that helps identify appropriate treatment for each event. For example, emergencies that provide little or no warning of their pending occurrence, do not permit pre-event evacuation as a means of mitigating their effect. Similarly, events that produce a lasting danger require post-event evacuation, whether pre-event evacuation occurred or not (e.g., a radiation release from a nuclear power plant). One typology that distinguishes among events in terms of the warning time they provide, and therefore their suitability to pre-event evacuation, is shown in Figure 1.

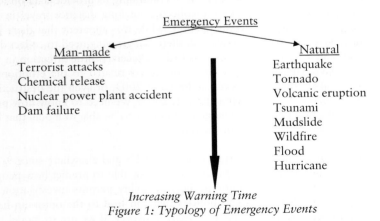

Increasing Warning Time
Figure 1: Typology of Emergency Events

Events that provide the least warning time, such as acts of terrorism or earthquakes, generate a need for travel, if a lasting danger exists for the public, and emergency response vehicles need to access the area. Examples of this are the 9/11 attack and the impact this had on the movement of people in Manhattan, or the earthquake in San Francisco in 1989, when several freeway bridges collapsed. In general, little study has been conducted on the travel implications of disasters such as these. The problem is that this class of disaster can take on so many forms that observing past disasters does not necessarily equip one for the next. However, this does not mean that the travel implications of disasters of this type should be ignored; development of contingency plans that can serve a wide variety of disasters could be extremely beneficial.

Emergencies that may provide a limited amount of warning time – e.g., chemical releases, nuclear power plant accidents, volcanic eruptions, and tsunamis – present the possibility of rapid evacuation prior to the event, and, if necessary, further evacuation after the event. This occurred with the Three Mile Island nuclear accident in Pennsylvania in 1979 where pre-event evacuation did take place but, due to being able to avert meltdown of the core, post-event evacuation was not necessary. At the Chernobyl nuclear power plant accident in the Ukraine in 1986, overheating of the core and the subsequent explosion of the reactor provided a warning of only a few seconds and only post-event evacuation was possible to remove people from areas with high levels of radiation fallout. Volcanic eruptions sometimes allow both pre-event and post-event evacuation, but, in other cases, there is virtually no warning (as in the case of Mount St. Helens) and it becomes a matter of whether the aftermath of the eruption in terms of lava flow or ash fall warrants, or is alleviated by, evacuation. Tsunamis provide pre-warning, provided seismic monitoring coupled with tsunami warning systems are in operation. The tsunami disaster in South Asia on 26th December, 2004 claimed over 200,000 lives because, while the seismic activity that generated the wave was detected, its magnitude was not immediately recognised and tsunami warning systems were not in place in the areas most affected. A tsunami wave propagates at between 500 and 1,000 kilometres per hour in the open ocean (depending on the depth), with the result that warning times of only a few hours are possible. Thus, pre-event evacuation has a very limited window in which to operate. Some scientists believe that a tsunami with even greater disaster potential, than the December 2004 tsunami, could be generated if a massive landslide should occur along a fault on the island of La Palma in the Canary Islands. It is estimated that the tsunami from this would take eight hours to cross the Atlantic and devastate the East Coast of the US for at least twenty kilometres inland.

However, it is emergencies that provide the longest warning time that are most significantly affected by travel – specifically because the negative impact of the event is mitigated by evacuation, and emergency personnel must often be able to move into, and within, affected areas. Prime examples of the type of emergency that is alleviated by pre-event evacuation are wildfires and hurricanes. Data collection for these types of emergencies is needed to understand human behaviour, to estimate models that can test alternative evacuation policies and strategies, and to monitor evacuation behaviour once a policy or strategy is introduced to test its effectiveness.

Of the data collected on emergency events in the past, much have been on human behaviour in the face of emergencies that provide relatively long warning times such as hurricanes. With long warning times, more discretion is afforded to those affected than to those that are plunged into a crisis with little warning. Because more discretion means greater opportunity to influence the decisions of the public and emergency managers to strategies and policies that will provide the greatest opportunity for safety of the population, it is in this area that this chapter suggests data collection should be directed. Data of this type will allow policy-makers to test strategies and policies that help people avoid as much of the danger of the event as possible.

The typology in Figure 1 also distinguishes between man-made and natural disasters. The distinction is made to illustrate that man-made disasters tend to provide less warning time than natural disasters, and thus less opportunity for pre-event evacuation. They may also require more emergency personnel, placing greater emphasis on transport capacity toward a disaster than is generally the case with natural disasters. However, the difference between man-made and natural disasters is not pursued in this chapter.

SURVEYS CONDUCTED IN THE PAST

Almost all of the previous surveys conducted on evacuation from emergencies have been post-event behavioural studies. That is, they have been conducted following the emergency event and have recorded the reported behaviour of individuals or households during the event. Some surveys have included questions asking respondents how they would behave under different hypothetical conditions, but full-fledged stated preference surveys of behaviour under emergency conditions are rare. One such survey was conducted in New Orleans in 2003, with 600 respondents reporting how they would react in terms of evacuation when faced with eight different hurricane scenarios. Methods of gaining information regarding evacuation behaviour from bushfires in Australia are currently also being investigated at the ITLS (Stopher *et al.*, 2004).

A large number of post-event surveys have been conducted with respect to hurricane evacuation. Baker (1991) lists fifteen such surveys conducted between 1963 and 1990 in the US. Since 1990, evacuation surveys have been conducted on all major hurricanes and, in some cases, multiple surveys have been conducted on the same hurricane. However, very few of these surveys have been conducted by transport professionals and, as a result, transport information in them tends to be sparse. For example, most do not record the time of departure of those evacuating, they do not record the occupancy of vehicles used in the evacuation, do not identify intermediate stops (if any), nor the time of arrival at the place of shelter. Most importantly, the information they do collect tends to be unrelated to time, making relating evacuation behaviour to conditions (which are constantly changing as the hurricane approaches) very difficult. If models of evacuation behaviour are going to be constructed, the data collection process must be adapted to provide the necessary data.

The preferred method of data collection for hurricane evacuation has been telephone interviews, without contact being made prior to the interview and without a printed questionnaire being issued to the respondent. These surveys have usually been conducted months, and sometimes years, after the event. The approach is similar to the initial telephone surveys conducted in the early days of urban transport planning, where respondents were asked to report on travel made, in most cases, on the most recent complete day. One of the developments that has occurred in urban travel surveys since those days, is to move from retrospective to prospective reporting, where respondents are asked to record travel performed on a prescribed day in the future, and to rely on a printed questionnaire or diary to record travel or activities during the survey day (Stopher and Metcalf, 1996). While the prospective data collection approach is clearly inapplicable to evacuation data collection, the idea of having a diary to record individual activities during the evacuation process may be useful. Particularly, the Day-timer® type of activity diaries may be very useful in capturing the temporal nature of the data important in evacuation modelling.

MODELLING EVACUATION TRAFFIC

The threat of a nuclear accident at the Three Mile Island nuclear plant in 1979 sparked interest in the development of evacuation packages that could be used to model evacuation traffic. Among the first models to be developed was NETVAC, which was specifically developed to model evacuation radially away from a point of danger, as would be the case with a nuclear accident (Sheffi *et al.*, 1982). NETVAC assumes that all households within the risk area will evacuate and, therefore, travel demand estimation is incidental in the model. Most of the accomplishment of the model was in modelling the movement of traffic through the transport network.

Several other evacuation models followed NETVAC, including DYNEV, MASSVAC, and later HURREVAC, TEDSS, OREMS, and ETIS (KLD Associates, 1984, Hobeika and Jamei, 1985, COE, 1994, Hobeika and Changykun, 1998, ORNL, 1999, PBS&J, 2000, Lewis, 2001). However, all these models either assumed that evacuation demand was given, or estimated it by means of a subjectively-based system of participation rates. These rates were based on past evacuation behaviour and assigned to evacuation zones in which evacuation behaviour was assumed to be reasonably uniform. If time-dependent travel demand was required, subjectively-defined response curves were used to distribute the total demand over time. The response curves have typically been described as three alternative ogives (S-shaped curves) of different slope to represent slow, medium, and fast evacuation. Choice of the appropriate curve has also been subjective.

The identification of evacuation zones has typically been based on areas of similar flooding potential, areas for which population data are identifiable, areas which are identifiable by verbal description (so that inhabitants can respond to calls for evacuation from their area), and areas contained within jurisdictional boundaries (Meduri, 2004). Within individual zones, participation rates are different for those living in mobile homes and among transients (tourists, visitors). Those living in mobile homes have higher participation rates in evacuation than those living in other types of homes, and transients have higher participation rates than residents.

Existing evacuation modelling procedures have modest data demands. They require information on the local topography, jurisdictional boundaries, areal descriptors (such as postcode or telephone exchange areas, subdivision names, etc.), housing type, population composition, and population totals at evacuation zone level. Generally, these data can be obtained from existing data sources such as QUAD maps, standard GIS files, land use records, tourist and business statistics, and census data. Thus, there has not been a need in the past to collect data for evacuation modelling other than to observe past behaviour in order to make good subjective estimates of participation rates and response times. However, if models are to be developed that are capable of estimating the consequences of alternative policies and strategies, then data will be required that allow the impact of policies and strategies on evacuation behaviour to be estimated. These data needs are discussed later in this chapter.

NEW MODELLING PROCEDURES

The four-step travel demand estimation process used in urban transport planning is an approach to travel demand estimation that has worked successfully for almost fifty years. It is tempting to expect that evacuation travel demand estimation can be conducted in the same way. However, evacuation from dangers such as hurricanes presents conditions that are very different from the conditions encountered in urban transport planning. For example, in urban transport planning many trips are discretionary while, in evacuation, trips are virtually mandatory. In urban transport planning, trips are relatively short while, in evacuation planning, they are long and often involve high levels of congestion. In urban transport planning, route choice is entirely discretionary while, in evacuation, it may be necessary to direct traffic along certain routes, and in some cases, even in certain directions. There is a high level of stress and anxiety present in an evacuation situation that is quite different to the stresses of everyday driving. How does this affect their behaviour and are they capable of predicting their response accurately without actually experiencing the emotions of the moment? Thus, while models have been identified that work well in urban transport planning, they may not work as well in evacuation planning because of the differences in the two situations. One area where this is particularly relevant is in traffic assignment. Static traffic assignment requires that trip travel times be shorter than the analysis period so that the assumption in the assignment process that trips traverse all links between origin and destination is fulfilled (Sheffi, 1985). It is also assumed that travel remains stable (uniform) during that period. While these assumptions are generally honoured in urban transport planning, evacuation involves trips that may extend from ten to twenty hours and flow conditions may vary considerably over this period. Having to assume uniform flow over such an extended period and forego knowledge of how speed, volume, density, delay, and travel time vary within the network over this period, is a major compromise. In contrast, dynamic traffic assignment models changing traffic conditions on the transport network over time, and therefore captures the changing condition on the network as required.

Travel demand is usually estimated for an entire day in urban transport planning; when travel demand is needed for shorter periods, time-of-day factors are typically used. The same approach has been used in evacuation planning, but the temporal behaviour in evacuation planning is likely to be more variable than the relatively stable day-to-day variation observed in urban transport planning. This is because factors such as the proximity of the storm, its path, forward speed, and intensity may change from hour to hour. This suggests that variables describing these aspects of the danger should be included in a model, so that it can respond to changes in their values. However, it is even more important that policy and strategy variables be included in the model, to assess how policies and strategies can alleviate an evacuation situation. For example, a policy variable such as the timing and type of evacuation order issued can have a considerable influence on the loading of the transport network. Similarly, if the strategy of reversing lanes, and its timing, were included in the model, this would allow estimation of the consequences of various lane reversal strategies in terms of the impact on evacuation time, the volume of people evacuated, levels of congestion, flow patterns, and so on.

Requiring variables in new models of evacuation demand that not only describe travel and the traveller (as in urban transport planning), but also reflect changing conditions related to the emergency, and allow the impact of policy directives and operational strategies to be incorporated into the model, places a considerable new burden on data collection. The collection of dynamic data (i.e., time-dependent data) in travel surveys in the past has only been accomplished by supplementing static data with dynamic information obtained from other sources. For example, Mei (2002) supplemented static data on evacuation from hurricane Andrew in southwest Louisiana with dynamic information on storm characteristics from the National Hurricane Center and evacuation order information from emergency managers in individual parishes in the region.

NEW DATA NEEDS

The challenge facing those collecting data on travel related to emergency events is primarily to move from a time-insensitive approach to a time-sensitive one. In urban transport planning, the major determinants of travel are static features of the traveller, e.g., household size, vehicle ownership, and household income. Travel data are collected with the time of travel reported, but little emphasis is placed on this temporal information and little use is usually made of it in the modelling process. Characteristics of the network, while changing during the analysis period, are assumed to remain stable in the trip assignment process. While such assumptions may work adequately for planning aimed at identifying infrastructure needs, they compromise the ability of the models to plan for more recent urban transport concerns, such as mobile emissions and congestion. However, as unsuitable as the omission of temporal considerations is becoming in urban transport planning, its omission in evacuation planning is untenable. Conditions that influence the evacuation decision change rapidly in emergency situations, and conditions on the transport network change rapidly in response to evacuation, making the assumption of stable flow quite inappropriate. Thus, it becomes imperative in evacuation planning to collect dynamic data, with attention being given to recording changing conditions and behaviour over time. This may necessitate the collection of data over more than one day, with specific attention being given to determine a time line of behaviour. Activity and time use surveys may be well suited to capture dynamic travel behaviour needed in evacuation planning. On the other hand, however, the collection of dynamic data of changing conditions introduces a totally new need in data collection.

The data that describe the development of the conditions that prompt evacuation are multifaceted. It is likely to be different for each type of emergency, although expressions of risk, urgency, and opportunities for evasion will be present in each case. Taking evacuation from an approaching hurricane as an example, the conditions that prompt evacuation have been researched quite extensively and, therefore, are fairly well known. Baker (1991) suggests that, after studying evacuations over three decades, five factors stand out as the main determinants of hurricane evacuation:

- Risk level of the area where the household resides (e.g., potential for flooding);
- Action taken by public authorities including the issuing of evacuation orders;
- Type of housing in which the household resides (e.g., mobile homes versus other more permanent structures);
- Perception of personal risk; and
- Storm-specific threat factors (e.g., storm intensity, size, and path)

Information, especially dynamic information, on these factors is likely to come from a variety of sources. First, time-dependent reports of current storm characteristics, and predictions of expected flooding and storm path are likely to be available in the US from agencies such as the National Hurricane Center and FEMA. Flooding potential is dependent on the storm intensity, forward speed, and path of a hurricane. Storm surge is caused by the wind pushing the sea toward land and having the swell accentuated by the bathymetry of the coastline. In addition, the low barometric pressure at the eye of the storm causes the water to rise even further. In the US, the Sea, Lake, and Overland Surges from Hurricanes (SLOSH) model is the official flood model used by FEMA and administered by the National Hurricane Center. Second, land use or housing inventories can be used to establish type of housing in an area. However, land use inventories are notoriously out of date, and housing records maintained by local authorities may be difficult to access and may not distinguish the type of structure in sufficient detail for the purposes of emergency planning. Third, the actions taken by local authorities in terms of issuing evacuation orders, and opening and closing lane reversal operations, can be obtained from emergency managers, provided the information has been recorded and they are prepared to divulge the information. Thus, dynamic information on the storm is likely to be available, but it would require obtaining it from a variety of agencies and merging it with the information gathered in the dynamic travel survey on evacuation behaviour.

One of the issues, surrounding the use of official records to supplement evacuation travel survey data, is that the factual data from these sources may not match what the households receive, or perception of the information may vary from household to household. For example, some households may not hear all the information that is disseminated, the wording in the message issued may be different from what was officially issued, or some people may receive information second- or third-hand and this may change in the telling (like the message sent down the trench in World War I that said 'Send reinforcements, we are going to advance', and ended up at the other end of the trench as 'Send three-and-fourpence, we are going to a dance'). Some researchers have studied the impact of the form of the message to the public in emergency conditions, and have found that considerable difference exists in response, depending on what is said, how it is said, and how it is conveyed. For example, ordering an evacuation by having state troopers go from house to house is much more effective than issuing an order by means of radio. What is said can also have a major impact. For example, when hurricane Floyd was moving up the East Coast of the US in 1999, it was likened to hurricane Andrew that, seven years earlier, had caused the greatest damage of any hurricane in US history; hurricane Floyd generated the largest evacuation in US history.

One of the interesting possibilities that can be investigated in evacuation planning is the implementation of staged evacuation. This is the sequencing of evacuation from portions of a region in such a manner that the transport network is used optimally. The idea is that policy variables, such as the type and timing of evacuation orders or the opening or closing of reverse-lane operations, are used to influence people's evacuation behaviour, to achieve the sequenced loading of the network. Data are needed to estimate people's response to these variables.

POSSIBLE NEW DATA COLLECTION PROCEDURES

The main form of data collection on evacuation has been post-event collection of revealed behaviour. While it certainly is a valid approach, it has several disadvantages that new data collection procedures could help reduce. In particular, an event must occur before a survey can be conducted. When such events are rare, this can be a severely limiting factor. Another disadvantage of the current approach is that the characteristics of the event are essentially the same for all persons affected, making it impossible to determine the influence of the event characteristics on the behaviour of the individuals. For example, if the event is a hurricane, the characteristics of the storm (e.g., its intensity, size, and forward speed), are the same for all respondents making it impossible to determine their affect on evacuation behaviour. Either data must be combined from multiple storms, or a stated preference approach must be adopted to present alternative storm scenarios to a respondent.

It is interesting to draw a parallel between data collection for emergency events and data collection for urban transport. As noted earlier, just as most of the early travel surveys for urban transport were based on the recall approach, so most of the surveys conducted on emergency events have been surveys of past behaviour. If, in the context of technological forecasting, travel surveys of urban transport are considered a leading indicator to surveys of evacuation behaviour, then the move from the recall approach to the prospective approach (where a respondent is asked to record their travel on a specified day in the future) in urban travel surveys, could be considered as a parallel move from post-event surveys to during-event emergency evacuation surveys. Similarly, SP surveys in urban transport could be considered the precursor to pre-event SP surveys in evacuation planning. If this notion of urban travel surveys playing a leading indicator role to emergency evacuation surveys is true, then during-event data collection may be the next type of survey to emerge in evacuation planning. Three possible forms of during-event data collection are suggested below.

First, there is the possibility of using cell phone activity as a measure and locator of travel intensity. New cell phones using FCC-mandated G3 technology, produce a record of the location and incidence of a call each time a call is made. Merging this information to a GIS would permit identification of calls made from vehicles. Research would be needed to match cell phone activity to traffic volumes. In addition, emergency conditions are likely to generate greater call activity than normal conditions, which would need to be accounted for. However, it is a vast resource of continuous, free data.

Linked to the above method, of obtaining estimates of traffic flow from cell phone activity, is the possibility of voluntary reporting of traffic conditions via cell phone from those in the process of evacuating. People could be invited via radio or printed evacuation material to call in and report current traffic conditions. Supplemental information, such as where they evacuated from, when they left, how many vehicles they are using, household composition, and so on, could also be gathered during the phone call. Given that up to ninety percent of traffic incidents are reported voluntarily by cell phone in some cities (FHWA, 2000), this could be a useful form of data collection. A limiting factor is that cell phone activity can become so intense during an evacuation that it fails to be an effective means of communication during the crisis (Jenkins *et al.*, 2000). In addition, a sample drawn in this manner is likely to be very biased, because of the self-selection involved, and could only be used to represent population behaviour with the appropriate weighting of observations.

Second, there is the possibility of using unmanned aircraft (drones) with on-board video cameras to capture traffic conditions (volume, speed, traffic composition, breakdowns, etc.) during an emergency event. These aircraft are used extensively in military applications, and the technology developed there could be applied to civilian applications. Real-time data collection with image processing can lead to considerable information over widespread areas. However, this technology may not be suitable for hurricanes due to high winds and low visibility although it may be useful in other emergency conditions. The information provided by this technology is limited to traffic conditions at individual locations at the time of observation and, therefore, does not provide the information typically required for evacuation planning. However, it can provide information for verification of demand estimates in the same way that traffic counts and screenlines are used to verify demand estimates in urban transport planning. Also, the observations are useful for operational management of the system, as evidenced by the use of light aircraft to monitor evacuation in some states in the past (Stubblefield, 2000). There is a great demand for real-time traffic information to assist in operational management during an evacuation (Decker, 2000).

Third, there is the possibility of adapting the self-administered questionnaire approach to emergency survey applications, in those situations where an emergency event provides sufficient warning that the survey can be issued to the respondent in advance of the event. The procedure would be initiated by recruiting potential participants over a wide area in advance, getting their agreement to participate in a survey if and when an emergency occurs. As soon as an emergency arose, recruits would be contacted to verify their continued willingness to participate in the survey. A diary would be sent out by courier or express overnight service to those who were willing to participate, together with a GPS instrument that they would switch on in the vehicle they evacuated in. If multiple vehicles were used, multiple GPS instruments would be sent out. Participants would be asked to complete the diary during the evacuation, recording information such as the type of vehicle used, any trailers or boats hauled, occupants of each vehicle, nature of the destination at any location where they stopped, etc. At the end of the emergency, the household would be asked to mail back the questionnaire and the GPS instrument(s) in a provided overnight box.

The list of latent survey participants described in the previous paragraph presents some daunting challenges for emergencies that occur over a wide area and are rare events. For example, for hurricane evacuation in the US, all inhabitants along the Atlantic and Gulf coasts would be involved, although individual communities may be impacted by a hurricane perhaps only once in ten years. However, at least two major hurricanes are projected to make landfall on the US coastline each year, offering a major potential for data collection. In addition, while maintenance of the list of latent participants requires continuous effort and needs to involve a large number of households to obtain adequate sample sizes of completed diaries, the major effort is in recruitment for a possible future event only. It is also related to an activity that people generally regard as important and about which they are generally willing to relate their personal experiences.

Pre-event surveys in the form of stated choice surveys are particularly relevant to emergency event planning, because of the rarity and limited warning time of some emergency events. However, one of the problems associated with the use of this approach in emergency planning is to be able to make storm conditions realistic enough that the respondent can make meaningful decisions. One possibility is to establish audio-visual scenarios on a DVD that portray a situation as a short television movie. Each scenario would present the emergency as it would be reported on television including news reporters on the scene, graphic footage of the impending danger, reports from experts, and so on. The video would be compiled in a TV studio using archive video material, and actors acting out fictional scenes. After viewing each scenario, respondents would be asked to indicate how they would respond.

One issue that seems to stand out, when considering data collection related to emergency events, is the need for greater passive data collection. Passive data collection reduces respondent burden in a situation where the need to collect dynamic information in emergency events increases the amount of data to be collected. Passive data collection also assists in getting accurate temporal information and in gathering information that is difficult to report such as the route taken, the speed travelled, the amount of delay experienced, and accurate total travel time. Therefore, passive data collection devices such as GPS, traffic counters, satellite imagery, and cell phone information need to be considered with renewed interest to supply the data needed in emergency planning.

CONCLUSIONS

In this chapter, it has been suggested that collection of data associated with travel generated during an emergency event is an area that provides interesting possibilities for travel survey practitioners. Expertise gained in conducting urban travel surveys will be useful, but the unique conditions that exist in emergency situations will require the development of new approaches. Of particular concern are the need to provide dynamic information, limit the respondent burden to manageable amounts, and develop new techniques whereby supplemental data can be gathered. Data that have been collected in the past do not fulfil the needs of an effective emergency modelling capability.

The data needed in evacuation planning are repeated observations over time of the looming threat, the conditions in which the potential evacuee resides, and the characteristics of the potential evacuating household. The threat is described in terms of the intensity, proximity, and projected path of the oncoming danger. The conditions relate to the particular conditions of each household and how they change over time. For example, residences located in low-lying areas are vulnerable to flooding, mobile homes are vulnerable to wind, and congested highways or crowded shelters are a disincentive to evacuation for all in the vicinity of such conditions. Non-physical conditions such as the nature and timing of official evacuation orders, the description of the danger by newscasters, and the behaviour of neighbours, also describe the conditions in which potential evacuees operate. From past studies it is known that the characteristics of the potential evacuee that are likely to influence evacuation behaviour are the convenient location of friends or relatives, the availability of vehicles, concern over the safety of their property, past evacuation experience, composition of the household, work responsibilities, and possibly the presence of pets in the household. Most of the characteristics of the potential evacuee are fixed, and therefore only need to be collected once, but some of them, such as work responsibilities or concern over the safety of personal property, can change due to new rulings or arrangements to secure property in a neighbourhood from looting or other potential damage.

The concept of repeated observations from a respondent in travel surveys is not new, but repeated observation of the same respondent over a short period of time in response to a single developing danger is a new approach. Added to this is the fact that the dangers being considered are relatively rare events and often provide little warning time, so as to permit observation during the event. As a result, virtually all surveys of evacuation behaviour have been post-event activities relying on recall of behaviour in response to a particular danger. Given that a particular threat has a fixed set of characteristics, and that these characteristics are likely to be influential in evacuation behaviour, using revealed preference data limits the variability in data needed to identify the impact of individual characteristics on evacuation behaviour. Taken together, the need for dynamic information on rare emergency events that, when occurring, have many fixed characteristics, seems to indicate that repeated-observation stated choice methods of data collection should be developed. This is an important area for future research.

Another area of research that deserves attention is the use of passive data collection during emergency events, to determine characteristics of evacuation travel behaviour that is difficult to obtain with interview-type data collection, such as route choice, location and duration of stops, destination, speed on individual links of the network, travel time, and delays experienced en route. These data should be combined with the dynamic threat, condition, and personal information suggested in the previous paragraph, to form a comprehensive data base of cause and effect data.

REFERENCES

Baker, E.J. (1991). Hurricane Evacuation Behaviour, *International Journal of Mass Emergencies and Disasters,* **9** (2), 287-310.

Baker, E.J. (2000). Hurricane Evacuation in the United States. In: *Storms: Volume 1,* (R. Pielke Jr. and R. Pielke Sr., eds), 306-319, Routledge, London.

Corps of Engineers (COE) (1994). A *Hurricane Evacuation Computer Model for Southeast Louisiana (HURREVAC Version 6.0),* Documentation and User's Guide, Prepared for the Louisiana Department of Military Affairs Office of Emergency Preparedness.

Decker, S. (2000). Data Needs for Decision Makers, Presentation at *Transportation Operations During Major Evacuations: Hurricane Workshop,* June 26-28, Westin Airport Hotel, Atlanta, GA.

FHWA (2000). *Incident Management Successful Practices: A Cross-Cutting Study: Improving Mobility and Saving Lives,* Federal Highway Administration, USDOT, FHWA-JPO-99-018, April.

Hobeika, A.G., and B. Jamei (1985). MASSVAC: A Model for Calculating Evacuation Times under Natural Disaster, *Proc. Conf. Computer Simulation in Emergency Planning,* **15** (1), 5-15.

Hobeika, A.G., and K. Chungykun (1998). Comparison of Traffic Assignments in Evacuation Modeling, *IEEE Transactions on Engineering Management*, **45** (2), 192-198.

KLD Associates, (1984). Formulations of the DYNEV and I-DYNEV Traffic Simulation Models Used in ESF, Federal Emergency Management Agency.

Jenkins, R., B. Smith, D. Goins and S. Decker (2000). Lessons Learned About Transportation Operations During Major Evacuations, Presentation at *Transportation Operations During Major Evacuations: Hurricane Workshop*, June 26-28, Westin Airport Hotel, Atlanta, GA.

Lewis, D.C. (2001). September's Great Escape: New Information System Helps Manage Hurricane Evacuations, *Roads and Bridges*, 40-42.

Meduri, N. (2004). *Developing a Methodology to Delineate Hurricane Evacuation Zones*, Master's Thesis, Department of Civil and Environmental Engineering, Louisiana State University, Baton Rouge, Louisiana.

Mei, B. (2002). *Development of Trip Generation Models of Hurricane Evacuation*, Masters Thesis, Department of Civil Engineering, Louisiana State University, Baton Rouge, Louisiana.

ORNL (1999). *Oak Ridge Evacuation Modeling System (OREMS) User's Guide*, Center for Transportation Analysis, Oak Ridge National Laboratory, Oak Ridge, TN.

PBS&J (2000). *Southeast United States Hurricane Evacuation Traffic Study: Evacuation Travel Demand Forecasting System, Technical Memorandum 2*, Final Report, Post, Buckley, Schuh & Jernigan, Inc., Tallahassee, FL.

Sheffi, Y., H. Mahmassani and W.B. Powell (1982). A Transportation Network Evacuation Model, *Transportation Research A*, **16** (3), 209-218.

Sheffi, Y. (1985). *Urban Transportation Networks: Equilibrium Analysis with Mathematical Programming Methods*. Prentice-Hall.

Stopher, P.R., and H.M.A. Metcalf (1996). *Methods for Household Travel Surveys*, Synthesis of Highway Practice 236, National Cooperative Highway Research Program, Transportation Research Board, Washington, DC.

Stopher, P.R., J. Rose and R. Alsnih (2004). *Dynamic Travel Demand for Emergency Evacuations: The Case of Bushfires*, Working Paper ITS-WP-04-16, July.

Stubblefield, H. (2000). Public Safety's Role in Contra-flow Evacuations, Presentation at *Transportation Operations During Major Evacuations: Hurricane Workshop*, June 26-28, Westin Airport Hotel, Atlanta, GA.

35

EMERGING ISSUES IN EMERGENCY EVENT TRANSPORT

Carlos Arce, NuStats, Austin, Texas, USA

INTRODUCTION[42]

Natural or man-made disasters generate travel demands and travel conditions that influence the safety of people affected by the disaster. Recent world events have brought into focus the need to develop and test options and alternative plans and policies for transport in such events. Present models used to manage evacuations and emergency services in disaster situations are not adequate for planning or testing transportation options because they are not based on an understanding of people's behaviour, but are simply operational from the perspective of police, fire, and sometimes, military officials. Such models are also static and do not respond to changes in environmental conditions. In many cases, the models are simply judgment calls of people familiar with the area.

To date, no models of travel behaviour for emergency events have been developed, because information about the travel behaviour of people in emergency events has not been collected. What data there are on emergency events have been collected by social scientists, whose interests have been on the social aspects of evacuation with relatively little attention given to travel behaviour. There is a real need for models that are responsive to changes in environmental and other conditions to help planners test policies and options and help manage the transportation aspect of emergency events. Such models must include the flow of people and vehicles out of the disaster area and the flow of emergency vehicles into the area. They must allow for the movement of au-

---

[42] Workshop members were: Carlos Arce (USA), Joost Kolkman (Netherlands), Lidia Kostyniuk (USA), John Rose (Australia), Jens Rumenapp (Germany), and Chester Wilmot (USA).

thorities in all directions, and should include the movement of people back into to area in the aftermath. The models need to take into account the types of evacuation flows, human response behaviour, perceptions of risk, communications, expectations, and group behaviours. Only then can they be used to generate flexible plans with robustness, and accommodate uncertainty.

The charge to the workshop was to identify significant research issues for emergency event transport planning and operation. The workshop's approach was to examine the common elements of emergency events, identify what behaviours should be studied, identify the type of models that might capture the behaviour for policy planning, identify methods of collecting information about the travel behaviour of people in emergency events, and brainstorm about possible funding sources for this research.

COMMONALITIES AND DIFFERENCES

The most significant commonality in emergency event planning is the goal, which in every case is to minimise injury and loss of life. Common elements in emergency events include a significant threat to human life, large movements of people (evacuation), emergency services often moving in the opposite direction of the evacuation flows, and the movement of officials moving both with and against the evacuation flows.

However, there are many differences among the emergency events, with implications for model development. The first of these is the length of time that is afforded for warning. If there is a long warning time, then evacuation will most likely follow. As warning time gets shorter, there may be little time for evacuation, and the focus will be on getting emergency services to the scene. Wilmot (2006) ordered disasters by increasing warning time available. A hurricane, for example, is a natural emergency event with a long warning time, while usually there is no warning in the case of an earthquake. Similarly, usually dam failures are well anticipated, while terrorist attacks are sudden with no advance warnings.

Another difference worth noting is the propagation or movement of the physical event, and its effects. For example, a bomb or a nuclear event would be a point event, originating from a single source, while a hurricane would be a frontal event, moving as a line across a region. Other events such as flooding could cover a large area. Bush fire propagation could be envisioned as a path with splatter. The type of propagation of the event is an important dimension in mathematical modelling of the physical aspects of the event, and also has implications for the type of evacuation and flow of emergency vehicles and services that would be required.

A third difference is cultural differences and national resources. For example, responses to hurricanes are different in various parts of world. In the US people evacuate, while in Bangladesh no one moves. A workshop member pointed out that Hamburg, Germany developed an evacuation plan following a disastrous flood in the 1960s. Now private cars are forbidden for evacuation and only public transport can be used. People learn about their assigned bus stops and routes by going to the Internet, and typing in their address. He noted that this works because people trust that they will be picked up. Other workshop members pointed out that, in the US, people insist on taking their car (with household possessions – if time permits). In fact, a family may take out more than one car and might also tow their boat. Thus, cultural aspects are an important consideration in developing models of travel behaviour for emergency events.

TOWARD AN UNDERSTANDING OF EVACUATION BEHAVIOUR

The workshop limited the scope to emergency events with enough warning time for evacuation to be a viable option. The decisions of concern, (that is, those that we need to gain an understanding of and collect information and data about) were identified as:

- To evacuate or not (go, not go);
- With whom;
- When;
- How (what mode) (what route);
- Where to go (the destination);
- What to take; and
- When to come back.

Promising approaches that are adding to the understanding of evacuation behaviour and decision making are currently being conducted in Australia by Rose and Stopher (Stopher *et al.*, 2004) and are concerned with bush fires. Rose reported that they conducted focus group studies and stated preference studies, and found that the travel decisions and behaviour of people in these situations is quite involved and complex. Rose noted that it is important to understand who is making the decision. For example, in the decision to evacuate, is it an individual, a household, or even a neighbourhood cluster that decides? Rose also noted trust in authorities is very important in these decisions.

Rose also reported that group behaviour in emergency events was very different than in ordinary travel. This includes how people cluster and form groups in evacuations, how people 'mill', that is, congregate and wait to gain information, and how people consult with neighbours to reach decisions. Rose noted that the amount and credibility of information (including sensory input), actions of others (neighbours, etc.), and evacuation orders were all important in the decisions.

A list of variables or factors that influence the decisions listed above was generated by the workshop participants. These include:

- The perception of risk;
- Post September 11 conditioning;
- Knowledge;
- Previous experience;
- Information and its credibility;
- Responsibility to others and property;
- Credibility of authorities;
- Existence (and knowledge of) evacuation plans; and
- Actions of others.

It was recognised that these are not independent of each other. Furthermore, perceptions of risk may vary by personal characteristics (locus of control and beliefs), experience with false alarms and previous disasters, and conditioning.

APPROACHES TO DATA COLLECTION

The objectives for data collection are to describe transport evacuation behaviour so that it can be modelled, and to develop capability, so that these models can assist in developing policy to improve evacuation plans. These data must be representative and statistically valid.

Interviews

One way to get information and data on emergency event behaviour is to interview subjects who recently underwent the experience. The interview questions should be about the process, and about what decisions were reached when. There is a need to 'time stamp' the decisions relative to the environmental conditions, information conditions, and other conditions. A questionnaire structure could be determined, but the interview could be a 'free form' type. so as not to traumatise the subjects. Information about departure time, route, speed, destination, arrival time is needed. There is a need to match this information with the time and environmental conditions. It was acknowledged that it may be difficult to talk to people right after the disaster in some cases. For example, it might be difficult to track down someone whose house burned down.

Stated Preference Methods

The workshop discussed the possibility of using realistic stated preference (SP) methods, using simulations, games, and virtual reality. This could be challenging because realism would require combinations of circumstances for the SP experiments. Rose noted that his research team, investigating the Australian bush fires, first conducted focus group studies to determine what was important, to get at the important terms, and to gain an understanding of how people perceive the process of evacuation for bush fires. He further noted that the perception of the emergency was absolutely critical, as was the source of the information. The studies of Stopher *et al.* (2004) of bushfire events indicate that evacuation decisions in these events were based on information clarity and credibility, instructions from authorities, cultural background, perceptions of risk, and conditioning. The workshop agreed that SP methodology could be a useful way to study various emergency events in different cultures. However, there will be a need to validate any findings from these SP studies against real situations.

Dynamic Data Collection

A third approach discussed was gathering information from real situations as they occurred. With current technology, it is possible to collect information about people going through the process. However, there is a need for caution in this approach because the data gathering should not increase the risk to subjects. For example, a sample of evacuees could be given GPS devices and small voice recorders. They would simply record what was going on, while the 'where' and 'when' would be automatically collected. However, this brought up questions of sample selection, given that we do not know where the emergency event will occur. Questions of how to get the instrumentation to the sample were also brought up.

It was suggested that once there is a national directory of cell phones, one could sample cell phone numbers. However, until that time, sampling of cell phones would be difficult. As to the question of delivery of instrumentation, it was suggested that because there is usually much lead time in the case of hurricanes, it would be possible to get the instrumentation to local authorities at the site by express delivery, and have them distribute the instruments to subjects.

Another option for collecting real time information discussed was cell-phone technology. Every cell phone has a G3 system that can be used to locate the position of the phone. Because people will be using their cell phones in an evacuation, it would be possible to follow the flow of the people through the flow of communications. It was recognised that there usually are problems with cell phone transmissions in emergency situations. However, there may be more options in the future as technology changes.

In dynamic data gathering for some near-future event, we would like to know:

- Origin - where are people at a given time;
- How many households will evacuate;
- What is their perceived risk (does it vary over time);
- When will they evacuate; and
- What are their destinations, their routes, and modes?

Other Research Questions

Several other research topics were identified by the workshop as important to understanding travel behaviour in emergency events. These include:

- *Conditioning* – People have been conditioned by the events of September 11. They now expect what was once unbelievable. Does conditioning affect their response to emergencies? How do we measure conditioning? Does spatial and temporal proximity to a disaster affect conditioning? How long does conditioning last? Does it diffuse through the population, i.e., will those conditioned condition others?
- *Information gathering* – How do people gather information in emergency events that helps them reach their decisions? There is a need to examine 'milling' behaviour for information acquisition or exchange, and how it affects traffic flow in time of evacuation.
- *Trust* - Trust appears to be an important factor in how decisions are reached. Why are some authorities trusted and some are not?

Possible Funding Sources

US – The US Department of Transportation, Federal Emergency Management Administration (FEMA), US Homeland Security.

Elsewhere – Ministry of Interior Affairs, national governments, multinational authorities (for example, in case of floods from rivers that flow through several countries).

REFERENCES

Stopher, P.R., J. Rose and R. Alsnih (2004). *Dynamic Travel Demand for Emergency Evacuations: The Case of Bushfires*, Working Paper ITS-WP-04-16, July.
Wilmot, C.G. (2006). Data Collection Related to Emergency Events. In: *Travel Survey Methods – Quality and Future Directions* (P.R. Stopher and C.C. Stecher, eds), 605-618, Elsevier, Oxford.

Travel Survey Methods: Quality and Future Directions
Peter Stopher and Cheryl Stecher (Editors)

36

SIMULATING HOUSEHOLD TRAVEL SURVEY DATA

Stephen P. Greaves, Institute of Transport and Logistics Studies, University of Sydney, Sydney, Australia

INTRODUCTION

Better (more comprehensive, higher quality, and more detailed) data on travel demand related to the sociodemographic and spatial characteristics of individuals and households are critical for modern transport planning and policy development. Provision of such data relies largely on household travel surveys (HTSs), in which a small sample of the population (usually about 2,000 to 5,000 households) records their travel patterns over some given time period. HTSs are notoriously expensive planning activities with current costs typically ranging from US$150 to US$200 per completed household, depending on the method used. Additionally, such surveys are plagued by non-participation and non- or misreporting from those who do participate – for instance, response rates of thirty to forty percent are considered about as good as can be achieved for other than face-to-face surveys (Greaves and Stopher, 2000). Given that most survey specialists maintain that any survey with less than a ninety percent response rate is potentially flawed, the implications for the quality and representativeness of the resulting data are startling.

For those regions unable to conduct original data collection, one option is to make use of existing databases, prepared for other reasons (e.g., national surveys, census journey-to-work data). In the US, for instance, the primary such source is the 2001 National Household Travel Survey (NHTS), a continuation of the Nationwide Personal Transportation Survey (NPTS) that has been conducted every five to seven years since 1969. The latest wave, conducted in 2001, included 26,000 households with a further 40,000 households from nine add-on areas. Although the format of the NHTS has become increasingly aligned to those used in a 'typical' regional household travel survey, the sample is never large enough to provide a local sample for modelling, or reporting of local area statistics.

Another approach, taken by areas with inadequate local travel survey data, is to borrow models or aggregate statistics, such as those compiled by Barton-Aschman Associates (1998). Model parameters are adjusted until the collective output of the models replicates reasonably observed aggregate travel data, such as traffic volumes in the study region. This approach has proven relatively effective if the models are borrowed from similar contexts in terms of attributes such as population size, population density, city structure, and transport infrastructure. However, if the borrowed models are developed from poor data (measurement error) or fail to incorporate key explanatory variables (specification error), these errors are typically accentuated when the models are applied in another context and then used in forecasting future travel. An additional issue with using borrowed models relates to the perception among many planners and decision-makers that local conditions militate against their use. Hence, the preference is to avoid borrowed models and use locally-estimated models whenever possible.

The high unit costs and logistical challenges of conducting HTSs have generally restricted their conduct to those jurisdictions with sufficient resources (major metropolitan regions, certain states in the US and Australia, and the national level in the US and some European nations). However, even in these cases, the costs and difficulties have reduced the feasibility of collecting even annual data sets of 3,500 to 5,000 households, as is currently done in Sydney and Perth. Added to these problems are greater demands on the coverage of HTS data to support micro-level planning for a suburb, corridor or other small area. An additional and increasingly critical issue is how to meet the extensive data needs of new disaggregate-based approaches to forecasting travel, seen by many as a necessity in replacing the current paradigm, which is ill-suited to addressing many current policy issues. The bottom line is that the data problems, outlined here, threaten to jeopardise the reliability of transport planning information and the assessment and defensibility of subsequent policy decisions for *all* areas, regardless of size and financial resources.

Against this backdrop – the cost of conducting HTSs, increasing nonresponse, issues with and resistance to using borrowed models, and the growing demands on the quality and comprehensiveness of travel data – interest is growing in developing techniques for augmenting or replacing current data collection activities with artificial or synthetic data. One recent proposition to this end is to combine local sociodemographic data for individuals or households (derivable from sources such as a census) with probability distributions of activity-travel patterns developed from other travel surveys, to *simulate* travel survey data (Greaves and Stopher, 2000). The rationale for such an approach is that it *could* provide, at a very low cost (compared to collecting HTS data), a method for generating a local sample of (potentially) thousands of households.

Such an approach, if proven successful, could have significant benefits for *all* current collectors and users of household travel survey data. For those regions relying on borrowed models, it provides the means to generate data with a local element to it, which could then be used to estimate new models. For those regions that currently conduct surveys, but then require data for micro-planning, the method could provide a local sample of sufficient size to do a range of planning and model development that is currently not possible. It is also conceivable that simulated data could form a component of current HTSs now being undertaken, and permit such surveys to reduce sample size requirements without necessarily compromising the quality of the planning activities that these data support.

While these benefits are appealing, the notion of simulating HTS data is relatively new and untested and is likely to be heavily debated. A key issue is clearly to establish a role for HTS data simulation – when is it appropriate to use and when is it not. With this in mind, the purpose of this chapter is to provide background information on this topic, with a view to triggering informed debate. The chapter covers the rationale, current approaches, and critical issues associated with simulating HTS data before providing some recommendations on potential future directions.

WHAT IS SIMULATION?

A scan of the literature suggests that *simulation* means different things to different people. Broadly speaking, it is a mathematical (some might term it a 'brute force') approach for modelling complex stochastic systems, which are difficult if not impossible to resolve analytically. The most widely-used technique for this purpose is known as *Monte Carlo simulation*. These principles have been extended to develop powerful tools for studying the risk and uncertainty of complex systems in a wide range of applications - nuclear reactor design, econometrics, stock market forecasting, etc.

While MCS is the subject of papers and entire texts, the major steps are as follows:

- *Define problem objectives:* For example, suppose we want to simulate vehicle headways for vehicles under low-flow conditions.
- *Define the probability model*: The probability model refers to the random variables and their underlying probability distribution. In this case, vehicle headway is the random variable and prior knowledge suggests that a negative exponential distribution is appropriate for describing the underlying probability distribution (May, 1990).
- *Randomly select values from the distributions*: This requires a source of random numbers, which can either be developed as look-up tables from published sources of random numbers (e.g., Rand, 1955), or using mathematically-based procedures available now in most standard statistical and mathematical software to generate *pseudo-random* numbers. For instance, Excel generates pseudo-random numbers using a linear congruential generator as follows:

a. First random number *(R1)* = fractional part of *(9821 * r + 0.211327)*, where *r = 0.5*.

b. Second random number = fractional part of *(9821 * R1 + 0.211327)*.

Pseudo-random numbers are computationally-efficient, and by controlling the starting point (seed), one can reproduce the same set of random numbers, which can be useful in scenario testing. However, it is important to ensure the numbers are truly random – for instance, Excel generates 10^6 random numbers, whereas most algorithms generate 10^9 before the cycle is repeated.

- *Numerical experimentation*: Each simulation run will give different results (assuming different random numbers are used) creating multiple scenarios from which various statistical measures can be determined. Each scenario, in effect, represents one realisation of the problem, some of which will be more probable, some less so. In fact, the accuracy of a MCS is proportional to the square root of the number of scenarios, which implies a large number of runs (typically 10,000 or more dependent on the variance), are required for the average solution to give an approximate answer to the problem (i.e., to replicate the original negative exponential distribution in this case).

- *Validation*: Compare to actual system performance, such as measured vehicle headways for this example.

Why Simulation as a Method for Generating HTS Data?

While the opening section outlined reasons why we might want to generate synthetic HTS data, attention now turns to why we might want to use simulation to achieve this. Travel behaviour is essentially the result of complex interactions and correlations between individuals, households, where they choose to live, and the transport system itself. Trying to capture the full nature of these interactions in an analytical model is particularly challenging, with the result that many of the subtleties of behaviour are suppressed or lost. Simulation (in theory) may overcome some of these problems by applying widely-used techniques to replicate observed behaviour, which implicitly encapsulates these interactions. In addition, by its nature, simulation captures the *variability* in behaviour, something which is suppressed by the traditional focus on measures of central tendency. Of course, one has to be aware that any unusual behaviour or systematic biases in the base data will also be reflected in the simulated data. While acknowledged, the same problems have always afflicted the reliability of models estimated on HTS data. The other major reason why simulation is an intuitively appealing method for generating HTS data is that it enables us (potentially) to work easily with much larger samples or in fact entire populations. This has the following advantages for the conduct of surveys and in how the data are ultimately used in forecasting:

- *Defining a 'representative' sample:* Currently, sample representation is based on pre-defined criteria, such as the categories used in the trip-production model. However, while this sample may be suited for testing one policy, it may not be for another. Data simulation enables the development of complex sampling schemes, or it might be easier to work with the entire population (Miller, 2003).

- *Mitigation of nonresponse impacts*: Currently, nonresponse is 'dealt with' after the fact by reweighting the households that did respond to try to reflect this. In theory, if demographic information on nonrespondents could be gathered either from the survey or checked against an independent source such as the census, data could be simulated for these households and the reweighting problem avoided. Clearly, a potential problem with this approach is if nonrespondents have systematically different travel patterns to respondents. In this case, it would be necessary to conduct a survey of nonrespondents to develop correction factors, something which in itself is fraught with difficulties.
- *Transferability and forecasting*: Intuition and limited empirical evidence suggest travel data could be 'more transferable' than travel-demand models (Wilmot and Stopher, 2001). Data simulation provides a method for testing this hypothesis by employing local sociodemographics directly in the travel data estimation process.
- *Replacement of current trip generation and distribution models*: By removing the sample size restrictions, the simulation of data enables greater disaggregation to be built into trip generation and trip distribution procedures. This has particular advantages for micro-level planning, where typically, there are insufficient samples for estimating models with a 'local' sensitivity to them.
- *New modelling paradigms*: A consensus now exists within modelling circles that we should be working at a *disaggregate* level (Miller, 2003). However, one of the principle difficulties of implementing such approaches is the data inputs required – detailed activity/travel data for each traveller, and some means for updating the attributes of households and land use at a disaggregate level. Microsimulation is seen as a viable (some might argue the best) solution to this problem.

Cautionary Notes

The simulation of HTS data is still a relatively new and unexplored concept and has generated doubts among some members of the transport planning community as to its merits and value. While nothing has been formally documented, the primary doubt appears to be over the logic of using statistical procedures to expand data with their existing averages, variances, and correlations for the purpose of estimating an activity/travel model, particularly if that model is to be used to predict travel in another context or location. This view may stem from some misconceptions about the purpose of simulating data and the fact that there have been insufficient and inconclusive results as to the effectiveness of the approach in research undertaken to date.

The primary motivators for simulating HTS data were presented in the introduction. While simulation is intuitively appealing, it is important to be realistic about the extent to which we could/should simulate HTS data. In the author's opinion, simulation of HTS data *will not remove the need to conduct HTSs* in the future. However, the extent to which it could form a component of future surveys and/or enrich or expand existing data sets is more open to debate. It is also important to reiterate that, by its nature, simulation is simply expanding/transferring existing data with all the inherent biases to a wider population. If the existing data do not adequately capture the behaviour of a representative sample then neither will the simulated data – we have already noted how HTSs may in reality only cover forty percent of the population.

While it is a relatively easy procedure to apply, a final cautionary note on using simulation for this purpose is that it is not straightforward to interpret results and assess their validity. Sample sizes are rarely sufficient to validate the results robustly and the nature of the procedure means different results are achieved with every cycle (assuming the random numbers change). How are these resolved in the generation of HTS data?

APPROACHES TO SIMULATING HTS DATA

Simulating Trips and Their Attributes

It is apparent that documented efforts to simulate HTS data are few and far between. In the late 1990s, a research initiative began in the US, the focus of which was to determine whether data from a national travel survey could be used to provide metropolitan regions with a low-cost option for generating travel data sets, which they could then use to estimate or update their travel-forecasting tools (Greaves and Stopher, 2000). The method began by using the Classification and Regression Tree (C&RT) method (Breiman *et al.*, 1984) to classify households in the national travel survey (the 1995 NPTS was used) into relatively homogeneous groupings with respect to pertinent travel attributes of interest – namely trip rates and purpose, mode, departure times, and trip duration in minutes. For instance, in the case of predicting home-work trip rates, the ten-category classification scheme shown in Table 1 resulted in the most parsimonious division of the data. The next stage of the procedure was to capture the variability of the trip attribute within each category as an empirical probability distribution – this would form the basis for a MCS. For instance, in the case of home-work trip rates, the ten-category scheme and associated probability distributions are shown in Figure 1.

The next step of the procedure involved subdividing households in the study region into the same categories used to develop the distributions – the US Census five percent Public Use Micro-Data Sample (PUMS) was selected as the source of the local socio-demographic data[43]. MCS was then used to select values from the appropriate distributions and assign them to the PUMS households. The process was cascading in that each

---

[43] The PUMS data provide disaggregate personal and household demographic information for five percent of households at a highly aggregated area (typically 100, 000 people) known as a Public Use Micro-data Area (PUMA) to protect confidentiality.

trip attribute was simulated conditional on household demographics and the prior simu-lated attribute; mode was dependent on trip purpose; time of day was dependent on purpose and mode; and trip length was dependent on purpose, mode, and time of day.

Table 1: Categorisation Scheme for Home-Work Trip Simulation

Trip Purpose	Categorisation Scheme	Mean	Standard Deviation
Home-Work	0 Workers	0	0
	1 Worker, 0-1 Vehicles	1.29	1.05
	1 Worker, 2+ Vehicles	1.45	1.09
	2 Workers, 0 Children (0-4), 0 Children (5-17)	2.78	1.56
	2 Workers, 0 Children (0-4), 1+ Children (5-17)	2.56	1.56
	2 Workers, 1+ Children (0-4), 0 Children (5-17)	2.14	1.40
	2 Workers, 1+ Children (0-4), 1+ Children (5-17)	2.32	1.39
	3 Workers, 0 Children (5-17)	4.12	2.05
	3 Workers, 1+ Children (5-17)	3.75	1.94
	4 + Workers	5.56	2.41

$F = 3228$; 9 degrees of freedom; $r^2 = 0.489$

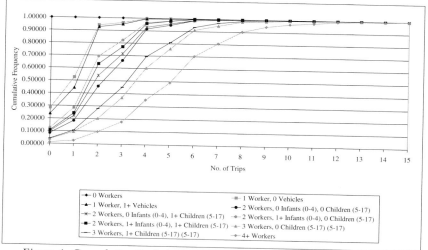

Figure 1: Cumulative Probability Distributions for Simulating Home-Work Trips

Greaves (2000) tested the concept by simulating household travel data for Baton Rouge, Louisiana, comparing the data against a 1997 HTS conducted there using a similar methodology to the 1995 NPTS. [Note that the data were drawn from Metropolitan Statistical Areas (MSAs) of a similar population to Baton Rouge (500,000 – 1,000,000) in an effort to introduce some contextual effects into the simulation]. In summarising the results, Greaves demonstrated the feasibility of the method to simulate data. He also showed it was possible to produce trip rates that were generally comparable to those derived from the actual HTS data and estimate trip-generation models that represented an improvement over the use of borrowed models and national statistics. For instance, Table 2 compares aggregate trip rates across seven purposes, showing that only home-shop trips were significantly different (over-estimated).

Table 2: Comparisons of HTS and Simulated Trip Rates per Household

Trip Purpose	HTS		Simulated Data	
	Mean	*Standard Deviation*	*Mean*	*Standard Deviation*
Home-Work	1.87	1.82	1.83	1.78
Home-School	0.69	1.47	0.74	1.46
Home-College	0.16	0.57	0.17	0.65
Home-Shop	1.17	1.66	1.32*	1.75
Home-Other	3.62	3.50	3.69	3.85
Work-Other	1.46	2.14	1.34	2.06
Other-Other	2.01	2.94	2.02	2.90
All Purposes	11.00	7.85	11.11	7.57

* Statistically significant difference in trip rates at the 95 percent confidence level (t-test for difference between two means)

Other salient trip characteristics (mode, departure time, and reported trip length) were less effectively replicated in the simulation procedure, something that was largely attributed to an inability to reflect contextual differences between regions (e.g., population size, transit service) adequately in the categorisation schemes. For instance, Table 3 shows that, in the case of mode shares in general, auto driver shares were under-estimated, while auto passengers, bike/walk, and transit shares were over-estimated. These discrepancies were attributed to the sparse public transport coverage for a city of this size and lower-than-average automobile occupancy rates.

Table 3: Comparisons of HTS and Simulated Mode Shares

Trip Purpose	Mode	HTS	Simulated Data
Home-Work	Auto Driver	91.9%	89.1%**
	Auto Pass.	6.9%	7.2%
	Transit	0.4%	2.0%**
	Bike/Walk	0.8%	1.7%*
Home-Other	Auto Driver	65.6%	61.3%**
	Auto Pass.	28.0%	31.3%**
	Transit	1.0%	2.2%**
	Bike/Walk	5.4%	5.4%
All Purposes	Auto Driver	70.4%	66.2%**
	Auto Pass.	22.3%	23.8%
	Transit	3.5%	5.1%**
	Bike/Walk	3.7%	4.8%**

* *Statistically significant at the 95th Percentile Confidence Limit*
** *Statistically significant at the 99th Percentile Confidence Limit (z-test for difference in two proportions)*

Since the original work of Greaves (2000), the transferability of the approach has been tested through application to the Dallas-Fort Worth and Salt Lake City metropolitan regions (Stopher *et al.*, 2003), Adelaide (Stopher *et al.*, 2001), and Sydney (Pointer and

Stopher, 2004). In all cases, the original categorisation schemes and 1995 NPTS distributions have been used in the simulation – note that in the Australian cases, this has been necessary because no national survey has been conducted since 1986. Socio-demographic statistics for these regions (Table 4) exhibit several characteristics that might be expected to impact travel. For instance, the larger household size and vehicles per household in Salt Lake would intuitively increase the trip rates/household, the higher rate of workers per household in Dallas would be expected to drive up the home-work trip rates, and the lower average automobile ownership rates in Adelaide would be expected to suppress trip rates and increase public transport shares.

Table 4: Sociodemographic Indicators from the Household Travel Surveys

Socio-demographic Indicator	NPTS	Baton Rouge	Salt Lake City	Dallas/Fort Worth	Adelaide
Average Age	35	33	34	35	
Average Household Size	2.63	2.71	3.14	2.47	2.46
Percent in Single Family Dwellings	74%	75%	73%	78%	
Percent Non-Car-Owning Households	8%	8%	4%	5%	
Average Vehicles Owned per Household	1.73	1.78	1.97	1.84	1.56
Percent Females in Sample	51%	52%	53%	52%	
Percent Home Owners	64%	66%	76%	68%	
Average Workers per Household	1.33	1.34	1.31	1.40	1.07

Reviews of the detailed results presented in the references on these studies may leave readers with mixed reactions about the effectiveness and value of the simulation. For instance, a comparison of trip rates (Table 5) indicates several statistically significant differences between the simulated data and the HTSs used for the various comparisons. These discrepancies (already shown to be an issue with the Baton Rouge case) are compounded in assessments of mode shares and trip lengths. What Table 5 does demonstrate, however, is the critical ability to reflect different socioeconomic characteristics in the simulated data – the significantly higher trip rates in Salt Lake and lower home-work trip rates in Adelaide being examples of this.

Several reasons may account for the differences between the simulated and HTS data, such as the choice of categories, the use of national data to derive the distributions, and differences in survey methodologies clouding comparisons. Improvements are currently under-way to address these issues, particularly in terms of how to reflect contextual factors better in the results, discussed later. This research has laid the foundation for many of the arguments for, and demonstrated the initial feasibility of, simulating HTS data from other (in this case national) data sources.

The approach followed by Greaves and Stopher (2000) simulates each trip independently of other trips made as part of the chain or tour. While this may be sufficient for meeting the needs of conventional forecasting models, it does not reflect the constraints imposed by previous trips on the generation of subsequent trips, something that is essential for incorporating behavioural realism into the simulated HTS data set. For instance, if the trip to work is made by car, then logically (but not always) the trip from work to home should be made by car. The resolution to this problem is seemingly to move away from the univariate trip to the activity/travel tour as the unit of analysis (Vaughn *et al.*, 1997).

Table 5: Comparisons of HTS and Simulated Person Trip Rates per Household

Trip Purpose	Adelaide	Baton Rouge	Dallas	Salt Lake	Adelaide		
	Simulated Mean	Simulated Mean	Simulated Mean	Simulated Mean	Diff. from Baton Rouge	Diff. from Dallas	Diff. from Salt Lake
Home-Work	1.38**	1.83	1.86**	1.83**	**		**
Home-School	0.6**	0.74	0.60	1.07*	**		**
Home-College	0.16**	0.17	0.16	0.23*		**	**
Home-Shop	1.28	1.32*	1.14**	1.38**	**		**
Home-Other	3.28**	3.69	3.19**	4.17**	**	**	**
Other-Work	1.00**	1.34	1.35**	1.33	**	**	**
Other-Other	1.95	2.02	1.86**	2.26**			**
Total	9.66**	11.11	10.17**	12.28**	**	**	**

* Statistically significant difference in trip rates at the 95 percent confidence level
**Statistically significant difference in trip rates at the 99 percent confidence level

Simulating Activity-Travel Tours

Two approaches have been followed to reconstruct (daily) activity-travel patterns at a disaggregate level, namely *sequential* and *simultaneous* approaches. Sequential approaches refer to the incremental generation of each activity in the tour and its associated attributes based on the history of activities made so far (Kitamura *et al.*, 1997; Janssens *et al.*, 2004). The approach adopted by Janssens *et al.*, constructs weighted sequential probability distributions based on the two immediately preceding activities, shown as frequencies in Table 6. Interpreting the table is fairly intuitive; for instance, if an individual sleeps then eats/drinks, it is most probable they will engage in another in-home leisure activity, and highly improbable they will go straight to work. Similarly, for those individual's travelling by car to work, it is highly probable their next activity will be a car trip.

Table 6: Frequency Distributions for Sequential Activities

1st and 2nd Element of Sequence Pair		3rd Element of Sequence Pair					
		Sleep	Eat/ Drink	Transport (car)	Work (out-of-home)	In-home leisure	...
Sleep	Eat/drink	45	5.1	250.2	0.5	397.8	...
Eat/drink	Transport (car)	1.5	4	0	274.5	8.8	...
Transport (car)	Work	11	52.7	709.3	1.3	0	...
Work	Transport (car)	24.1	166.2	0	36.8	217.7	...
Eat/drink	In-home Leisure	332.6	113.4	241.3	0	66.2	...
...	...	...	...	...	...	...	...

Source: Janssens *et al.*, 2004

The results of the work show that the simulated data compare favourably to actual survey data in terms of the number of trip tours and the variability in sequencing between different activity diaries during one particular simulation. The results for simulating mode of travel appear less conclusive. Planned extensions to the work include extending the sequential process to more than two preceding activities, as well as simulating other activity components such as the location, the duration, and with whom the activity is carried out.

Kitamura's motivation for addressing this problem comes from the data needs of disaggregate activity-based models. Under their approach, the activity-travel pattern is treated as a triple of vectors, comprising the activity types, durations, and locations. These vectors are then used to formulate conditional probabilities, which (in effect) form the basis for the sampling process. Initially, activity choice is predicted conditional on past activity engagement, duration, location, and other factors, followed by activity duration modelled conditional on activity type, and finally location, which is modelled conditional on activity type and duration.

In contrast to sequential approaches, simultaneous approaches treat the entire activity-travel pattern as the initial unit of analysis. The philosophy is similar to that espoused by Greaves and Stopher (2000), in that a household (or individual) of given socio-demographic characteristics will have a probability of exhibiting particular activity-travel patterns. While a variety of modelling approaches have been adopted for this problem, of relevance in the context of the current chapter are those which have taken a simulation-based approach to the problem in which the objective is to replicate the behaviour of observed individuals or households, not the *process* by which they schedule activities.

A simultaneous approach based on a mixture of sampling and simulation is behind the creation of household activity-travel patterns (HATPs) in the TRANSIMS framework (Vaughn *et al.*, 1997). Initially, a set of representative HATPs are defined, encompassing elements such as the number of activities, activity purposes and durations, and start and end time of tours. A multivariate C&RT approach is used to identify homogenous groupings of households (Vaughn *et al.*, 1999) – in effect this considers several dependent variables together as one measure, rather than categorising with respect to different dependent variables as used by Greaves and Stopher (2000). Ultimately, they decide on sixteen dependent variables, which reflect the total time spent in fifteen broadly classified activity types plus the total number of trips made. The procedure is available within TRANSIMS, enabling the user to develop their own scheme based on the travel survey data source(s) they have available. For instance, Table 7 shows the scheme in use for the Portland test case.

Another simultaneous approach for generating activity-travel patterns is described by Kulkarni and McNally (2001). In this case, individuals are initially segmented into three life-cycle groups: full-time employed adults, adults not employed full-time, and children. A k-means clustering algorithm is then used to identify distinct activity-travel patterns (which they term, 'Representative Activity Patterns' or RAPs) in terms of activity type, distance to home and distance between last activity for each of the three groups. Ultimately, they conclude that activity type alone is sufficient for identifying RAPs. Table 8 shows the RAPs for full-time working adults – it is notable how the variability is captured within a relatively small number of categories, something which is consistently found to be the case (Pas, 1984; Vaughn et al., 1999).

Table 7: Categorization Scheme for the Portland Test Case Application of TRANSIMS

Categorisation Scheme	No. of Households
Workers = 0, Household Size = 1, Age < 38.5	34
Workers = 0, Household Size = 1, Age > 38.5	319
Workers = 0, Household Size = 2, Age < 53.5, Income <5.5	25
Workers = 0, Household Size = 2, Age < 53.5, Income >5.5	15
Workers = 0, Household Size = 2, Age > 53.5	268
Workers = 0, Household Size > 2	32
Workers = 1, Household Size = 1	705
Workers = 1, Household Size = 2, Age 5-15 = 0	304
Workers = 1, Household Size = 2, Age 5-15 > 0	48
Workers = 1, Household Size = 3, Age 5-15 <= 1, Age <29.5	18
Workers = 1, Household Size = 3, Age 5-15 <= 1, Age >29.5	89
Workers = 1, Household Size = 2, Age 5-15 > 1	24
Workers = 1, Household Size = 4, Age 5-15 <= 1	73
Workers = 1, Household Size = 4, Age 5-15 >1	49
Workers = 1, Household Size > 4, Age 5-15 <= 2	40
Workers = 1, Household Size > 4, Age 5-15 > 2	27
Workers = 2, Household Size = 2	677
Workers = 2, Household Size = 3	248
Workers = 2, Household Size = 4, Age <5 = 0, Age 26-45 = 0	21
Workers = 2, Household Size = 4, Age <5 = 0, Age 26-45 > 0	134
Workers = 2, Household Size = 4, Age <5 > 0	69
Workers = 2, Household Size > 4, Age 5-15 <=2	49
Workers = 2, Household Size > 4, Age 5-15 >2, Housing Density <1.29	18
Workers = 2, Household Size > 4, Age 5-15 >2, Housing Density >1.29	19
Workers > 2, Household Size = 3	75
Workers > 2, Household Size = 4, Age <46.5	28
Workers > 2, Household Size = 4, Age > 46.5	24
Workers > 2, Household Size > 4	43

Source: Barrett *et al.*, 2001

The procedure continues by initially simulating the RAP for each individual. Following this, a time-dependent series of activities, durations, and general locations are simulated. The final step is to update the locations within a geographic information system (GIS). The method is applied to synthesise attributes for 100 Standard Work RAPs. For this case, the approach seems capable of generating aggregate synthetic patterns, which are similar to the RAP from which they were produced and does go further than most in dealing with location. The authors note several needed improvements, which could improve the comparability at a more disaggregate level including the incorporation of intra-household constraints, adding more detail to the activity choice set, and expanding the socioeconomic groupings.

Table 8: Representative Activity Patterns for Full-Time Working Adults

Representative Activity Pattern	Description	Proportion
Standard Work	One 8-hour work activity between 8am and 5pm	33%
Power Work	One 10+ hour work activity between 8am and late	8%
Late Work	8-hour workday starting in the afternoon	4%
Work-Maintenance	Multiple work activities	40%
Various Short Activities	Multiple short activities near home	15%

Source: Kulkarni and McNally (2001)

MAJOR ISSUES IN SIMULATING HTS DATA

What are the key issues with simulating HTS data? The framework shown in Figure 2 is used to organise this discussion. Note this is *not* intended to provide a methodology for simulating HTS data – that is up to individual researchers.

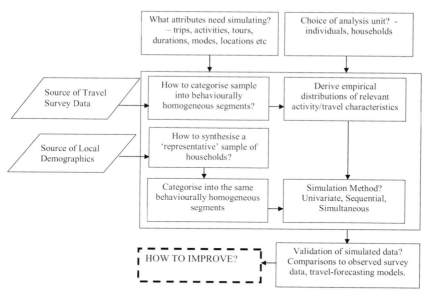

Figure 2: Major Issues in Simulating HTS Data

What are we Trying to Simulate?

The first, and perhaps most obvious, question to ask is what attributes we are trying to simulate. Clearly, this depends on the reasons for the simulation. In the work of

Greaves and Stopher (2000), the objective is to provide those data typically required for estimation of conventional forecasting models, namely trip rates by purpose for each household, then, for each simulated trip, the mode of travel used, the departure time, and the trip duration in minutes. The other approaches cited here are focused on providing the data required for implementation of disaggregate activity-based models. This involves a shift in the fundamental unit of analysis from the univariate one-way trip to a multivariate activity-travel pattern that attempts to maintain interdependencies between household members and activities made as part of a tour. In these cases, the data needs might include the following:

- Tour start and end times;
- Number of activities on the tour;
- For each activity, the purpose, duration and location; and
- For each leg of the tour, start time and end time, the mode used, and number of occupants.

The Choice of Analysis Unit – Households or Individuals

One of the most fundamental questions concerns the analysis unit for which we should be simulating data: households, or individuals within households. Arguably, if the goal of the simulation is to provide a HTS data set, that is both realistic and plausible, this (ultimately) has to be at the level of individual household members. The problem comes from the widely-acknowledged fact that individual travel behaviour is heavily impacted by constraints imposed by, and ultimately decisions made by, the household (Principio and Pas, 1997). Attempts to reflect the impact of these constraints on individual travel behaviour have proven particularly challenging, leaving researchers divided as to the relative merits of each level.

Greaves and Stopher (2000) chose to work at the household level in simulating the number of trips by purpose, then (in effect) each simulated trip becomes the unit of analysis for the subsequent attributes (mode, departure time, trip duration). Others have chosen to simulate data for individuals or groups of individuals (Axhausen and Herz, 1989; Kulkarni and McNally, 2001). Another option is to synthesise some of the data initially at the household level and then assign trip information to individuals based on the constraints imposed by the household information – such an approach is being used in the simulation of activity-travel data for the TRANSIMS project.

Data Issues – Sources and Preparation

Data needs for the simulation of HTS data include, 1) sociodemographic characteristics at the individual and/or household level, and 2) activity/travel survey data to develop the probability distributions. A popular source of sociodemographic data is the Census, which includes summary demographic characteristics for aggregate spatial areas (e.g., tracts, blocks, block groups) and micro-data for a small proportion of individuals and households within the population. These data include a number of variables known to correlate with travel such as age, gender, employment status, vehicles owned, household size, income, and housing density. For instance, in the US, micro-data (i.e., the PUMS) are typically collected for five percent of households within a highly aggregated area to protect confidentiality (typically 100,000 people) known as a Public Use Micro-data Area (PUMA). While an intuitive source for the demographic data, it is important to be aware that Census micro-data are collected for specific reasons, which are not necessarily coincident with the needs of HTSs. Among the main caveats with using such data are the following:

*   *Different sampling and recruitment regimes*: The PUMS data are generated every 10 years from the Census long form, which is distributed through a systematic sampling process to an average of one in twelve households. Most HTSs employ some pre-defined stratification for more efficient sampling.
*   *Non-coverage and nonresponse*: Because the Census is a residence-based survey, only those without a fixed address are excluded. The survey is mandatory and several face-to-face attempts are made to retrieve survey forms. In addition, because the Census is an address-based, mail-out/mail-back survey, it is not affected by reliance on the telephone as either a recruitment or retrieval device, which is used in most HTSs. All these factors result in much higher response rates for a census (typically ninety to ninety five percent) than the typical HTS, although it is acknowledged that important subgroups of the population are still under-represented.
*   *Spatial data*: The spatial aggregation of micro-data implies neighbourhood characteristics, potentially correlated with travel characteristics (e.g., residential density, proximity to transit), cannot be identified. In addition, PUMAs rarely match the planning area.
*   *Data definitions*: In the Census, some variables are provided for the family as opposed to the household (e.g., number of workers, number of persons). It is, therefore, necessary to aggregate from the person file to derive household totals, to be consistent with definitions used in HTSs.
*   *Timeliness*: While this varies by country, most censuses are decennial (Australia is every five years).

In addition to awareness of these caveats, a critical issue concerns how to use the Census data in synthesising a representative sample for simulating HTS data. One option is to draw the sample from the population, much as if one were conducting an actual HTS. In fact, to make true comparisons to observed HTS data, which is clearly one of the acid tests for the simulated data, the synthetic sample must be drawn using the same strata as those employed in the HTS, to replicate how the sample would have been drawn in the field (Stopher *et al.*, 2003).

The potential limitations of trying to define a 'representative' sample were touched on earlier, where it was noted that data simulation provides an opportunity to work with larger samples or in fact entire populations. A complicating factor here is how to re-create entire populations at a disaggregate level given that census micro-data typically only cover one to five percent of households. Various procedures have already been developed to achieve this, most notably those developed for developing synthetic populations in the TRANSIMS project (Beckman *et al.*, 1995).

Simulation by its nature is simply replicating observed travel behaviour of individuals/households at a wider level. The source of this travel behaviour is therefore a *critical* underlying factor in producing simulated data that are of a high quality. While this chapter is not focussed on efforts to improve the quality and representativeness of the collection of HTS data (this is the subject of much of this book), these issues must be kept in mind particularly when judging the value of the data.

Most of the approaches described here use existing survey data in the region of interest as the basis for the simulation (e.g., Vaughn *et al.*, 1997, 1999; Kulkarni and McNally, 2001; Janssens *et al.*, 2004). As well as being logical, if data are simulated for house-holds drawn from the sample, these can be compared directly to actual data reported for those households (at least at an aggregate level across sociodemographic indicators). Of course, one has to be careful not to include these households in the development of the original distributions, because this would clearly bias the comparison.

To the author's knowledge, the work begun by Greaves and Stopher (2000) is the only research effort to date that is positioned as a means of generating *disaggregate* travel-behaviour data in one region using data from elsewhere (in this case, US national data). They have used the 1995 NPTS, which is designed, as has previously been discussed, (primarily) to track changes in personal travel at the national level. In addition to lever-aging greater value out of national data, the appeal of using the NPTS is the large sam-ple size (around 30,000 households by the time week-end records and anomalies such as New York City are removed), making it possible to experiment with greater disag-gregation in terms of the segmentation of the population. However, the NPTS incorpo-rates several elements, which could impact comparisons, including but not limited to:

- *Spatial sampling scheme*: The survey employs a multi-stratification procedure to control sampling variation and increase coverage of transit trips. The sampling frame is stratified by nine US Bureau of the Census Divisions, metropolitan area status, the presence of subway or elevated rail systems, and the density of listed telephone numbers. The sample size is allocated to the major strata in propor-tion to estimates of the total number of households, except for twenty five per-cent over-sampling in eleven large metropolitan areas with subway/elevated rail systems to capture more transit trips.
- *Temporal sampling scheme*: Data are collected over approximately one year, which was divided into four strata to capture seasonal variations in travel. In addition, the sample was allocated equally to the seven days of the week.

- *Coverage*: Almost half the sample comes from five add-on areas, including New York State. Note, that records for New York City were not included in the development of the distributions.
- *Complete records*: The NPTS allowed records from partially responding households if more than fifty percent of adults provided responses. This issue impacts analyses at the household level because fifteen percent of households include some level of person nonresponse. In addition, one third of the data were retrieved by proxy, and over one quarter of the data retrieved without a diary available, both of which are known factors in generally reducing the amount of information provided on recall.

In terms of the various comparisons to actual HTS data in both the US (Stopher *et al.*, 2003) and Australia (Stopher et al., 2001), it is highly probable that one reason for the reported discrepancies is differing survey methodologies. The original Baton Rouge comparison (Greaves, 2000) probably fared much better, because the comparisons were to a survey conducted using identical methods to the NPTS.

Classification Scheme

The purpose of any categorisation or stratification scheme is to identify relatively homogeneous groups of households or individuals with respect to a particular attribute of interest, the aim being to minimise the intra-category variation, while maximising the inter-category variation of that attribute. This problem can be approached from the perspective either of the travel attributes (e.g., trips, activities, travel modes, number of stops on a tour, activity duration), or sociodemographic descriptors of the population, or both. For instance, in trip generation modelling, we generally stratify trips by purpose and households by demographic descriptors such as household size, vehicle ownership, income etc.

The classification scheme used is, in the author's opinion, a *critical* issue in simulating HTS data. This is argued, because the true merit of this approach is the extent to which it is sensitive to differences in travel that are attributable to sociodemographic characteristics of the population, the locations in which they reside, and the available transport system. This is particularly so, if the approach is to be used (in effect) to transfer data from elsewhere, as postulated by Greaves and Stopher (2000). Following this line of reasoning, logic suggests that the further we can subdivide the population and the dependent variables into homogeneous groups, the better chance the simulation will have of reflecting these differences ultimately.

Two broad approaches have been taken to this type of classification problem. The first is to segment the population into sociodemographic groupings based on previous studies, logic, etc., and then use these groupings as the basis for simulating the attributes of interest. This has the advantage of creating groups that are intuitive, but suffers from the fact this will not result in the most efficient segmentation of the population with respect to simulating the particular attribute of interest. The second approach is to use the travel attributes as the basis for delineating homogeneous groups. While more efficient, the pre-definition of attributes runs the risk of hiding some of the more subtle differences between activity-travel patterns.

From the discussion of approaches to simulating data, it is evident that a mix of both approaches are used. For instance, Greaves and Stopher (2000) have adopted the second approach using the C&RT method to segment the population in a multistage classification system. Vaughn *et al.*, (1999) have used a similar approach, except that they try to capture the dependent variables in a more intricate manner. Kulkarni and McNally (2001) essentially use a hybrid of both approaches, in that they initially define their life-cycle groups, and then try to identify representative activity patterns within each group. Whichever approach is used, some common factors concern the categorisation.

- *Sensitivity*: Despite the notion that greater disaggregation of the population will improve the sensitivity of the simulation procedure, the reality is that a point is reached relatively quickly where 'noise' in the data begins to cloud genuine differences in activity-travel behaviour and little is gained by further segmentation.
- *Explanatory power*: On the flip-side to the previous point, most of the variability in activity-travel behaviour goes unexplained – a reflection of the inability of current measures to capture these differences adequately.
- *Supply-side factors*: Ultimately, the data simulation must be sensitive to differences in both demand and supply. While there are many supply-side measures that intuitively impact travel (e.g., city size, public transport service, density, etc.), efforts to define and incorporate these effectively within the classification scheme have met with limited success (Greaves, 2000). An alternative approach to incorporating contextual effects is discussed in the section on data updating later in this chapter.
- *Bias*: The initial delineation of both the sociodemographic factors and the activity-attributes immediately imposes an inherent bias in the simulation, because any factors not included are implicitly excluded. This is a particular issue in simulating trip tours, where care must be taken not to exclude the great number of rare and complex chains, and hence underestimate the number of trips (Herz, 1982 cited in Axhausen and Herz, 1989).

The Simulation Method

As discussed earlier, the heart of the simulation is how to represent travel/activity in terms of probabilities. Two basic options are available; either to derive probabilities empirically or to calculate them using mathematical models. All the approaches cited here have used the former approach, the rationale being that observed data implicitly capture all the interactions and correlations, which are so complex to model. On the other hand, this does not capture the process by which people make travel decisions.

The next major methodological issue concerns whether each trip or activity should be simulated independently or dependently. While it is simpler to simulate independently, this comes at the cost of behavioural realism and is a necessity for implementing disaggregate modelling approaches. Given that the need is to simulate tours, the next decision is whether a simultaneous or sequential approach is used. On a conceptual basis, the simultaneous approach seems more appealing because it reflects better how individual's plan their travel and is more sensitive to the characteristics of the travel environment (Kitamura *et al.*, 1997). However, the initial definition of the tours could be critical as noted in the previous section. Sequential approaches appear to be less complex if the intent is just to simulate one attribute, say activity purpose. However, as the number of attributes increases, so does the probability vector, with the result that the calculations get progressively more cumbersome, particularly if conditionality is built in from more than just the previous activity in the tour.

A Particular Challenge - the Geography of Travel

A particularly challenging methodological issue concerns how to simulate the locations of activities. This actually comprises two problems: locating households and locating activities (trip-ends). As was noted previously, for reasons of confidentiality the spatial resolution of micro-data is highly aggregated. In response, various procedures have been developed to recreate households synthetically at finer scales of resolution, such as traffic zones or Census Blocks (Beckman *et al.*, 1995; Melhuish *et al.*, 2002). The basic rationale is to create a set of households that, when their demographics are viewed collectively, match the totals in the tables for the higher levels of geography, while maintaining the same overall structure as that recorded for the aggregate spatial unit for which the micro-data are provided. It could also be feasible to locate households to point locations through a random draw within the small area geography.

Logic suggests that activity location will be the last attribute to be simulated for each trip, with constraints imposed by each leg of the trip tour (e.g., trip duration, mode, time of departure) as well as potentially the total time of the tour itself. Within these constraints, each potential activity location could be assigned a probability, based on its attractiveness, which could then form the basis for the simulation. Simulation of activity locations remains a particularly difficult problem, primarily due to the difficulty of developing and maintaining disaggregate land-use databases. Geographic Information System (GIS) technology and the associated GIS databases, has undoubtedly led to improvements in the spatial dimension of this problem, but, ultimately, collecting attribute information (e.g., number of employees) is a laborious, error-prone process. It may be that we have to be satisfied (initially) with fairly coarse spatial representation in the simulated HTS data.

Validation

How can we validate the process, or put another way, how can we determine whether or not acceptable data can be produced through a simulation process? The first issue to resolve is what constitutes *acceptability*? In most studies, the primary indicator of acceptability is the statistical significance of differences between simulated data and actual HTS data across a range of attributes such as trip and activity rates, mode shares, trip lengths, etc. In most cases, despite the fact that one of the reasons we are trying to simulate data is to create (effectively) disaggregate information, the majority of comparisons are made at aggregate levels. Clearly, we cannot compare on a household-by-household basis, but comparisons across demographic segments of the population should be included to demonstrate the sensitivity of the procedure. We also may require some way to validate at finer levels of spatial resolution, particularly if the procedures are to be applied in micro-level planning studies.

These issues become pertinent when defining the validation sample. The simplest option is to hold out a sample of households from the original data source used to derive the probability distributions, ensuring, of course, that these households are not included in the sample used to develop the distributions, because this would bias results. The advantage of this approach is that comparisons are not clouded by differences in survey methodologies (something which has definitely affected the comparisons reported by Greaves, Stopher and others), and this does not require additional data collection. The disadvantage of this approach is that the original source of the HTS will rarely include more than a few observations at finer scales of spatial resolution, making it infeasible to validate the procedure at more than a regional level. If resources permit, an option to overcome this problem is to conduct targeted samples of say one or two small spatial areas (e.g., Census Block Group) within a region and simulate data for those households (Vaughn *et al.*, 1997).

Invariably in running these types of comparisons, statistically significant differences are found, even when numerical differences are very small. Should this mean rejection of the simulated data? It has been argued (Stopher *et al.*, 2003) that, given the ultimate use of the data is to estimate population statistics and travel-demand models, acceptability can only be established by building such models with simulated data and determining whether a reasonable match is obtained to traditional validation measures, such as link volumes, and public transport boarding and alighting rates. This is a *critical research need*, which has yet to be undertaken.

IMPROVEMENTS - LOCAL DATA UPDATES

Throughout this chapter, it has been stressed that, essentially, simulated data are replicating observed data on a wider level. As such the results still invariably reflect the source of that observed data and not as much of the local travel characteristics as would be desired. It was noted previously that efforts to capture these local differences through the incorporation of city contextual measures in the categorisation scheme have largely been ineffective (Greaves, 2000).

With this problem in mind, another approach is presented here in which travel survey data from a small local sample are used to adjust or update the probability distributions, which drive the simulation (Greaves, 2001). The approach involves drawing a local sample using the same categories as those used in the source HTS data. Distributions are then developed as before, which are then used to update the original distributions using a Bayesian updating procedure – similar procedures have been used in model updating (Koppelman *et al.*, 1985) and data updating (Wilmot and Stopher, 2001).

Under this procedure, an unknown parameter θ is related to its prior distribution and the likelihood function of the local data by the probability expression:

$$\begin{pmatrix} \text{Posterior probability} \\ \text{of } \theta \text{ given the local data} \end{pmatrix} \propto \begin{pmatrix} \text{prior probability} \\ \text{of } \theta \end{pmatrix} * \begin{pmatrix} \text{likelihood function of} \\ \text{the local data given } \theta \end{pmatrix} \tag{1}$$

The critical issue in Bayesian updating is to define the prior distribution of θ. The most widely used approach is to assume θ is normally distributed with mean θ_t and variance, σ_t. Similarly, the sampling distribution of the local data is assumed to be normally distributed with mean θ_s and variance, σ_s. This assumption (conjugate prior) enables data from the two sources to be combined to produce a posterior distribution that is also normally distributed with parameters θ_p and variance, σ_p that are calculated as follows:

$$\theta_p = \left[\theta_t / \sigma_t^2 + \theta_s / \sigma_s^2 \right] / \left[1/\sigma_t^2 + 1/\sigma_s^2 \right] \tag{2}$$

$$\sigma_p^2 = \left[1/\sigma_t^2 + 1/\sigma_s^2 \right] \tag{3}$$

Given that each interval is treated as a proportion, an estimate is needed for the standard error of the share – this is analogous to the standard deviation of the sampling distribution of a sample proportion. This can be derived from the following expression, although it must be noted that this requires five or more estimates for the assumption of normality to hold. This can be problematic depending on the size of the update sample and the level of disaggregation required.

$$std.error = \sqrt{\frac{p(1-p)}{n}}$$ where the sample proportion $\frac{x}{n}$ is substituted for p.

x = share, n = sample size

The approach has been tested for Baton Rouge (Greaves, 2001), Adelaide (Stopher and Pointer, 2003), and Sydney (Pointer and Stopher, 2004). *Note, for the sake of comparison, that the update sample must not be included in the HTS sample against which the comparison is being made.* In general, the use of updating has resulted in improvements in the simulation results, although the magnitude of the improvement is by no means consistent. For example, Table 9 shows the original and updated mode shares for three of the trip purposes used in the original Baton Rouge simulation based on an update sample of 200 households, where the improvement is clear.

Table 9: Mode-shares Before and After Local Updating with 200 Households, Baton Rouge

Trip Purpose	Mode	BRPTS (784 households)	Simulated Data (Original Distributions)	Simulated Data (Updated Distributions)
Home-Work	Auto Driver	92.1%	88.6%**	90.8%
	Auto Pass.	6.4%	7.6%	7.2%
	Transit	0.6%	2.1%**	0.6%
	Bike/Walk	0.9%	1.7%	1.4%*
Home-Shop	Auto Driver	77.3%	69.5%**	75.1%
	Auto Pass.	19.6%	23.7%*	21.0%
	Transit	0.1%	1.8%**	0.6%
	Bike/Walk	3.0%	5.1%*	3.3%
Home-Other	Auto Driver	65.2	60.9%**	62.9%
	Auto Pass.	28.6%	31.9%**	29.9%
	Transit	1.0%	2.3%**	1.9%*
	Bike/Walk	5.2%	4.9%	5.4%

* *Statistically significant at the 95th Percentile Confidence Limit*
** *Statistically significant at the 99th Percentile Confidence Limit*

Table 10 compares the simulation of average trip lengths for the Adelaide case (Stopher and Pointer, 2003). In all cases, the use of updated distributions results in a closer fit to the original survey data, although it does vary by trip purpose.

Table 10: Trip Duration Before and After Local Updating with 526 Households, Adelaide

Trip Purpose	AHTS	Simulation(Original Distributions)		Simulated Data (Updated Distributions)	
		Mean	Difference	Mean	Difference
Home-Work	22.85	19.38	-3.47	21.31	-1.54
Home-School	11.03	16.36	5.33	13.3	2.27
Home-College	23.01	18.9	-4.11	21.72	-1.29
Home-Shop	11.01	12.46	1.45	11.43	0.45
Home-Other	15.5	13.8	-1.7	14.64	-0.86
Other-Work	20.41	14.71	-5.7	17.61	-2.8
Other-Other	15.08	14.3	-0.78	14.9	-0.18
ALL TRIPS	16.41	14.84	-1.57	15.63	-0.78

Local data updating intuitively and practically has the potential to improve the quality of borrowed and synthetic data. However, a number of issues have been identified through both the work in the US and Australia, which must be addressed in future applications:

- *Size of update sample*: Intuition would suggest that the larger the update sample, the more accurate the results. However, in a systematic comparison of using 303, 500, and 751 households in updating data for Sydney, Pointer and Stopher (2004) found this is not always the case, something attributable to random variation within the categories used to draw the update sample.
- *Stratification of update sample*: The previous point suggests that the way in which the update sample is drawn could have (potentially) a greater impact because of the disproportionate effect of different household types on trip characteristics. For example, in the application to Sydney, using US national distributions, over-sampling of particular households to counteract the much higher rates of car-driver trips and short trip lengths should improve the situation. Another option could be to use variable weightings within the update sample scheme to try to counteract these problems.
- *Updating procedure*: For the Bayesian updating procedure to have any impact (given the discrepancies in sample size between the NPTS and update samples), the weights must be manually adjusted. This must be based on sound reasoning.
- *Other updating procedures*: One approach has been proposed and tested here. It must be established if there are other preferable approaches and whether options are available if no local survey sample data are available.

FINAL THOUGHTS

This chapter has provided the rationale for, current approaches to, and key issues associated with, simulating HTS data. The rationale is strongly rooted in the costs and difficulties of conducting HTSs, dissatisfaction with current travel-forecasting options for regions with inadequate survey data, and opening up new analytical opportunities at a disaggregate level through the expansion and enrichment of existing data sets. In addition, the use of simulation in HTSs could open up new opportunities to deal with old problems, particularly those associated with nonresponse and defining a representative sample. At the same time, some cautionary points were made about using simulation, particularly in terms of the extent to which it could replace or supplement data sets, and the realisation that it is simply expanding existing data, with all their inherent biases, to a wider population.

The various approaches to simulating HTS data, have all provided strong rationales for, and demonstrated the feasibility of, simulating HTS data. However, in the author's opinion, there is not yet sufficient proof that this method works or indeed does not work – in fact there is no consensus on how this judgement should be made. With this in mind, the following methodological issues must be addressed:

- *Unit of analysis*: Ideally, we want to be simulating data for each individual in the population. However, the difficulty of incorporating intra-household constraints into the categorisation schemes, suggests this may be problematic. Another option is the TRANSIMS framework of initially generating tour information at the household level and using this to impose constraints in simulating the more detailed activity and travel attributes at an individual level.

- *Source of the travel data*: The 2001 NHTS opens up new opportunities to assess the transferability of the approach at both an inter- and intra-regional level. However, other options exist that may be more suitable (particularly for the intra-regional case), including statewide surveys, and the large databases created through continuous surveys, such as those conducted in Sydney, Victoria (Australia), and San Francisco.

- *Classification schemes*: The classification scheme is critical for creating simulated HTS data, because the approach must be sensitive to differences in travel that are attributable to sociodemographic characteristics of the population, the locations in which they reside, and the available transport system. Evidence suggests we still cannot build in this sensitivity sufficiently, a reflection of both the complexity of travel-behaviour and the inability of current measures to explain or capture this behaviour fully.

- *Local data updating*: Following on from the previous point, we may have to look at other methods to capture these subtleties, which focus on updating or adjusting the source data. One promising approach was presented here, in which local sample data are used in a Bayesian updating procedure. Other options may be available, and there is also the issue of whether other more aggregate measures (that do not require additional data collection), could be used to update the data.

- *Simulation method*: Travel-activity tours should be the approach used in the future to maintain behavioural realism, and as an essential element for simulating the spatial characteristics of travel. Two alternatives are available – one in which the tour and its various attributes are sequentially or incrementally constructed, the other where tours are pre-defined and attributes simulated for each leg of the tour. Particular attention needs to be paid in how tours are defined to ensure parsimony without losing the inherent richness of the data. A particularly challenging issue is how to simulate spatial information.

- *Evaluating simulated data*: This should involve answering questions such as: How closely are observed survey data replicated at both an aggregate and disaggregate level? How comparable are simulated data to other available options such as borrowed models? Do forecasts from models derived from simulated data show similar sensitivities to locally-calibrated models, and do they match observed link volumes reasonably well? What is the cost saving compared to conducting surveys?

In addition to these methodological issues, it is the author's opinion that greater thought must be given as to how the notion of simulating HTS data is sold to the wider planning community. This requires more example applications of how the approach could improve the current and particularly the future transport planning decision-making process, as well as demonstrating cost savings for data collectors.

REFERENCES

Axhausen, K.W. and R. Herz (1989). Simulating Activity Chains: German Approach, *Journal of Transportation Engineering*, **115** (3), 316-325.

Barrett, C. L., (2001). *Transportation Analysis SIMulation System (TRANSIMS) Portland Study Reports— Volume Two—Study Setup: Parameters and Input Data*, Los Alamos National Laboratory report. Available from http://transims.tsasa.lanl.gov. Accessed 17 May, 2003.

Barton-Aschman Associates. (1998). *Travel Estimation Techniques for Urban Areas*. National Cooperative Highway Research Program Report No. 365, Transportation Research Board, Washington, DC.

Beckman, R.J., K.A. Baggerly and M.D. McKay (1995). Creating Synthetic Baseline Populations, *Transportation Research A,* **30** (4), 415-429.

Breiman, L., J.H. Friedman, R.A. Olshen and C.J. Stone (1984). *Classification and Regression Trees*. Wadsworth International Group, Belmont, CA.

Greaves, S.P. (2000). *Simulating Household Travel Survey Data in Metropolitan Areas*, Unpublished Ph.D. Dissertation, Department of Civil and Environmental Engineering, Louisiana State University, Baton Rouge, Louisiana.

Greaves, S.P. (2001). Local Sample Updates for Synthetic Household Travel Survey Data, *CD-ROM Proceedings of the 23rd Conference of Australian Institutes of Transport Research*, Monash University, December.

Greaves, S.P. and P.R. Stopher (2000). Creating a Simulated Household Travel/Activity Survey - Rationale and Feasibility Analysis, *Transportation Research Record No. 1706*, 82-91.

Janssens, D., G. Wets, T. Brijs, and K. Vanhoof (2004). Simulating Activity Diary Data by Means of Sequential Probability Information: Development and Evaluation of an Initial Framework, *CD-ROM Proceedings of the 83rd Annual Meeting of the Transportation Research Board*, Washington, DC.

Kitamura, R., C. Chen and R.M. Pendyala (1997). Generation of Synthetic Daily Activity-Travel Patterns, *Paper presented at the 76th Annual Meeting of the Transportation Research Board*, Washington, DC.

Koppelman, F.S., G.K. Kuah and C.G. Wilmot (1985). Transfer Model Updating with Disaggregate Data, *Transportation Research Record No. 1037*, 102-107.

Kulkarni, A.A. and M.G. McNally (2001). A Microsimulation of Daily Activity Patterns, *CD-ROM Proceedings of the 80th Annual Meeting of the Transportation Research Board*, Washington, DC.

May, A. (1990). *Traffic Flow Fundamentals*. Prentice Hall, Inc.

Melhuish, T., M. Blake and S. Day (2002). An Evaluation of Synthetic Household Populations for Census Collector Districts Created Using Spatial Microsimulation Techniques, *Proceedings of the 26th Australia and New Zealand Regional Science Association International Annual Conference*, Queensland.

Miller, E.J. (2003), Microsimulation. In: *Transportation Systems Planning: Methods and Applications* (K. Goulias, ed.),12-1 – 12-22, CRC Press, London.

Pas, E.I. (1984). The Effect of Selected Sociodemographic Characteristics on Daily Travel-Activity Behaviour, *Environment and Planning A, 16*, 571-581.

Pointer, G. and P.R. Stopher (2004). Monte Carlo Simulation of Sydney Household Travel Survey Data with Bayesian Updating Using Different Local Sample Sizes, *CD-ROM Proceedings of the 83ʳᵈ Annual Meeting of the Transportation Research Board*, Washington, DC.

Principio, S.L. and E. Pas (1997). The Sociodemographic and Travel Behaviour of Life Style Groups Identified by Time Use Patterns, Paper presented at the 77ᵗʰ Annual Meeting of the Transportation Research Board, Washington, DC.

Rand Corporation (1955). *A Million Random Digits with 100,000 Normal Deviates.* http://www.rand.org/publications/classics/randomdigits/randomdata.html. Accessed 20 Dec., 2005.

Stopher, P.R. and G. Pointer (2003). Monte Carlo Simulation of Household Travel Survey Data with Bayesian Updating, *CD-ROM Proceedings of the 21ˢᵗ ARRB/REAAA Conference,* Cairns, Queensland, Australia.

Stopher, P.R., P. Bullock and J. Rose (2002). Simulating Household Travel Survey Data in Australia: Adelaide Case Study, *CD-ROM Proceedings of the 25ᵗʰ Australasian Transport Research Forum,* Canberra.

Stopher, P.R., S.P. Greaves and P. Bullock (2003). Simulating Household Travel Survey Data: Application to Two Urban Areas, *CD-ROM Proceedings of the 82ⁿᵈ Annual Meeting of the Transportation Research Board*, Washington, DC.

Vaughn, K.M., P. Speckman and E.I. Pas (1997). Generating Household Activity-Travel Patterns (HATPs) for Synthetic Populations, Paper presented at the 76ᵗʰ Annual Meeting of the Transportation Research Board, Washington, DC.

Vaughn, K.M., P. Speckman and D. Sun (1999). Identifying Relevant Socio-Demographics for Distinguishing Household Activity-Travel Patterns: A Multi-variate Regression Tree Approach, Paper prepared for The National Institute of Statistical Sciences (NISS), P.O. Box 14006 Research Triangle Park, NC 27709-4006.

Wilmot, C.G. and P.R. Stopher (2001). Transferability of Transportation Planning Data, *Transportation Research Record No. 1768,* 36-43.

37

USING MICROSIMULATION TO GENERATE ACTIVITY-TRAVEL PATTERNS UNDER CONDITIONS OF INSUFFICIENT DATA

Harry J.P. Timmermans, Eindhoven University of Technology, Eindhoven, The Netherlands

INTRODUCTION

This chapter represents a summary of the discussions and deliberations of a workshop[44] on the topic of synthetic data. The workshop was stimulated by the resource paper prepared for it by Greaves (2006).

PROBLEMS IN SIMULATING DATA

Travel surveys are conducted to collect data or measurements of individual and household activity or travel behaviour. To the extent that the survey satisfies the assumptions underlying statistical inference theory, sample information can be used to describe activity and travel behaviour of the target population from which the sample was drawn. Lacking such sample data, activity travel patterns of a target population may still be 'predicted' or estimated, if one is willing to assume that activity or travel behaviour is transferable across time and space. Data collected in another area can then be used to predict travel behaviour of the target population in the study area of interest. Because

---

[44] Members of the workshop were: Stephen Greaves (Australia), Susan Liss (USA), Rosella Picardo (USA), Orlando Strambi (Brazil), Harry Timmermans (The Netherlands), and Dirk Zumkeller (Germany).

activity and travel behaviour are both functions of sociodemographics, spatial setting, characteristics of the transportation system and possibly other factors, it is unlikely that the sample for which information is available is representative of the target population of interest. Given however a set of variables that are assumed to influence aspects of activity-travel behaviour, and assuming that these variables are known for the target population, microsimulation can be used to predict aspects of activity-travel behaviour of the target population. One should realise that this process is very similar to the process of building, testing, and applying a model of transport demand. The main difference is that modellers often try to find the most parsimonious representation of observed distributions of travel characteristics, consistent with some underlying theory about human decision-making. Microsimulation may be more data-driven, in that often the conditional probability distributions are assumed invariant across time and space, and offers more flexibility in terms of formulating more complex assumptions.

This implies that the outcomes of these simulations are not a panacea for a lack of data:

- They do not constitute independent measurements and hence do not satisfy the assumptions underlying conventional statistical inference theory; and
- They should, in principle, not be used as input to subsequent models of travel demand, if those models are based on a different set of explicit or implicit assumptions or conditional probability distributions.

This latter caveat applies especially to the simulation of a full dataset from other sources. It may be less problematic to the construction of borrowed trip rates and, perhaps, mode split used as input for a four-step model, because these types of model do not involve complex interdependencies anyway.

The degree of transferability of any model, including these data-driven simulation models, depends on the stability of various aspects of activity-travel behaviour across time and space. Empirical evidence suggests that trip rates, time budget, and trip/tour ratios are relatively stable. At the other extreme is destination choice, which is strongly influenced by the spatial configuration of destinations. In between are aspects such as mode choice, trip distance, and activity duration. This means that considerably more additional assumptions have to be made to predict successfully destination and mode choice, trip distance and activity duration of the target population in the study area of interest, based on observations from elsewhere.

MICROSIMULATION APPROACHES

At least three different microsimulation approaches can be identified. They all assume that every individual of the target population of the area of interest can be described in terms of the selected explanatory variables. This will typically require the creation of a synthetic population. The use of synthetic populations in transport analysis has become fairly common since the 1970s. Examples include Zumkeller and Seitz (1993), Purvis (1994), Beckman *et al.* (1996), Bradley *et al.* (1999), Veldhuisen *et al.* (2000a), Veldhuisen *et al.* (2000b), Ton and Hensher (2001), Bonsall and Kelly (2003), Zumkeller (2004), to name a few. The creation of a synthetic population involves the estimation of the characteristics of each individual of the target population such that the aggregate distribution of each characteristic is consistent with observed distributions, consistent with some assumed or observed correlation structure. Monte Carlo simulation methods can be used for this purpose as well, although alternative methods, such as loglinear models, may be faster.

Once these characteristics of each individual member of the target population are known, activity-travel characteristics are added. The first possible approach implies matching the set of characteristics on the survey data set that includes the activity-travel data (Veldhuisen, *et al.*, 2000a; Veldhuisen, *et al.*, 2000b). Matching may be deterministic or probabilistic. In the case of deterministic matching, from the observations that satisfy the matching criteria, one is randomly selected and the full pattern of activity-travel characteristics is added to the simulated individual. In the case of probabilistic matching, the probability of being selected is some function of the degree of similarity between the simulated individual and the observations in the database. This process is repeated for every individual of the target population. Because full activity-travel patterns are extracted from the survey data set, all the dependencies are kept.

A second approach is, first, to conduct further analyses on the activity-travel data to find homogeneous patterns (Joh *et al.*, 2001a; Joh *et al.*, 2001b; and Joh *et al.*, 2001c). Traditionally, clustering methods have been used to classify activity-travel patterns into a smaller number of relatively homogeneous segments or types. Commonly used cluster analyses, however, are not sensitive to differences in activity sequences. If the sequence of activity patterns is relevant, multidimensional sequence alignment methods are a better alternative. Next, the relationship between sociodemographics and activity-travel type is established. The activity-travel pattern or particular aspects of this pattern of each individual of the target population are simulated by first predicting the probability that an individual with specific sociodemographics will belong to a particular segment. The probability distribution is then used to draw a specific activity-travel pattern.

Rather than analysing the effects of sociodemographics separately, it is also possible to find homogeneous groups of travellers based on their sociodemographics, spatial characteristics, and possibly other variables, typically for each facet of an activity-travel pattern separately. Various methods have been applied to this effect, including classification and regression trees (Greaves and Stopher, 2000; Stopher *et al.*, 2003), CHAID (Strambi and van de Bilt, 1998; Arentze *et al.*, 2000), association rules (Keulers *et al.*, 2001), C4.5 (Wets *et al.*, 2000; Moons *et al.*, 2002), and Bayesian networks (Janssens *et al.*, 2003). One should realise here that these classification methods differ in terms of their underlying assumptions and will not generate the same groups. If the model of transport demand also used some grouping, it is of the utmost importance that the same classification is used. In addition, new and improved methods have recently been suggested, such as parameterised action decision trees (Arentze and Timmermans, 2005). The codebooks approach presented by Janssens *et al.* (2004) represents another promising attempt to develop fast algorithms to identify basic activity sequence patterns. Because all these methods involve a reduction of the variance in the data, not all variation in the original data is kept, correlation will likely change, and the focus will be on dominant patterns. This makes this second approach quite different from the first. Finally, it is possible to estimate or build any model of transport demand from a data set and use the estimated parameters to predict activity-travel patterns in another area.

The 'geography of the study area' constitutes a special challenge in this process. It is well known that the spatial configuration of activity locations has an impact on observed travel distances and times. Hence, if one samples from such observed distributions or applies distance decay functions to a new area, it is likely that substantial errors will be made, which in turn may bias duration, route choice, traffic volumes, etc. This problem should be high on the research agenda. It is obvious that any successful approach should be relatively robust for travel times and should take dynamic choice sets or space-time prisms into consideration.

It is also not evident, *a priori*, which of these approaches will be most successful. Keeping the full details of the data may imply that a better account can be given of the variability in travel behaviour, but it may also imply that one may be capitalising too much on idiosyncratic, unlikely patterns, and possible errors. On the other hand, any analysis of the data, including the classification and fitting of equations, implies that some detail is lost. Sometimes the explained variance may be relatively low (Greaves and Stopher, 2000). Model parameters typically focus on averages, although recent developments such as random coefficient models allow one to include heterogeneity, which can and should be used in the simulations. On the other hand, apparent variation in the data can sometimes be almost perfectly accounted for by a single underlying behavioural mechanism. Hence, systematic comparative analyses are urgently needed. Such analyses may be based on numerical simulations, with the advantage that all the properties of the data are known and can be varied, or on available empirical data sets.

If the aim is to simulate, in a consistent and integral manner, comprehensive activity-travel patterns, the number of possible patterns is huge. Assume that we differentiate between 8 activities, 7 main transport modes, 1,000 destination types, 7 times of day, 7 days of the week, and 4 types of travel party, we already have 10,976,000 different patterns. If activity sequence is considered relevant, we have $8! = 40,320$ possible sequences and consequently 442,552,320,000 possible patterns. Even in a large data set, many of these patterns will not be observed. The large number of possible patterns also means that one cannot keep all the higher order interactions in the data: a sequential approach is used to simulate patterns. The problem here is that the order of decision-making is not always evident. For example, one might argue that individuals first decide on the transport mode and then on the location. However, one might also argue that, in the case of shopping, depending on the kind of products to be bought, first the location is decided, and considering the resulting travel time, transport mode is decided next. Likewise, one might conceptualise that the urgency of conducting activities of various duration evolves continuously over time, and that available time windows within some time horizon dictate which activities are conducted next, where, and how. The flexibility to conduct activities in time and space varies across activities and household types. It seems advisable to simulate the characteristics of the least flexible activities first because individuals schedule the more flexible activities around these fixed activities. The more constrained activities (i.e., the activity skeleton) dictate the space-time prism (or dynamic choice set) for conducting the remaining activities. It should be realised, however, that while some activity-based models of transport demand assume that activities such as work, school, shopping are fixed (locations are simply copied from the observations), this is not possible when the aim is to simulate patterns in another area: work, school, shopping locations also have to be predicted. For simulating the order of the choice facets, one can use a theoretical framework or base the order on the expected invariance of the facets. Unfortunately, there is a lack of systematic research into the sensitivity of simulated patterns on the sequence of simulating the various facets of activity travel patterns. Such research is urgently needed to understand better the impact of alternative sequential ways of simulating activity-travel patterns.

Another operational decision concerns the question of whether household patterns or individual patterns should be used. Based on the understanding that individual patterns are derived from household decisions, it was felt of the utmost importance that such consistency and dependency in the data were taken into consideration. For example, if a two-adult household has only one car, only one activity travel pattern can involve the car during the same time period (resource allocation). Likewise, certain activities – such as taking a child to a day care centre – only have to be completed by one household member (task allocation). These, and many other, examples illustrate the need for some mechanisms in the simulation process to capture the consistency in the data (in the case of resource allocation) and to capture the dependencies in the data (in the case of task allocation, joint activities, etc.). To date, only a few studies on household decision-making exist in the transport literature and, hence, considerably more additional theoretical and empirical research is required to identify the mechanisms that can be used to drive the simulation process.

At the final stage, the simulated activity-travel patterns need to be assigned to the transport network. Limited empirical evidence suggests here that differences in the spatial distribution of the destinations, the number and density of the residential areas, the mixture of land uses, and the supply characteristics of the transport system need further operational decisions in the simulation process to guarantee feasible patterns.

The above discussion has focused on simulating comprehensive activity-travel patterns. It is therefore felt relevant to also validate the simulation model at the various levels: pattern, tours, and trips. In some cases, it is also relevant to estimate particular statistics for the target population, e.g., trip rates. Bayesian updating methods offer an interesting approach for such types of problems because one can combine *a priori* expectations (based on data elsewhere) and small sample data of the area of interest. Alternatively, various kinds of imputation and data fusion methods may serve the same purpose. The use of such methods is to be preferred when the goal is to produce specific statistics. If multiple statistics are required, the use of simulated patterns is recommended, because this is more likely to guarantee the integrity and consistency of the data.

The discussions in the workshop illustrate that although it seems feasible to develop a more data-driven approach to simulate activity travel patterns for an area with a lack of data, the simulation soon becomes quite complex, if increased realism is built into the process. There simply is no quick fix to the problem of insufficient or complete lack of data. Even if a simulation approach has already been developed for a national travel survey or a time use data set, the work involved in applying this approach to a particular planning area may take an amount of time that may be equal to developing and applying a rather sophisticated model of transport demand. Hence, although one saves on data collection, the application of the simulation approach may still involve a considerable amount of time. If such models are considered adequate, one might, therefore, be better off collecting new survey data and calibrating the model specifically for that area. If, at the same time, authorities can be convinced that they should use more sophisticated activity-based models of transport demand, simulation approaches may be an interesting and valuable alternative. Then, the simulation can not only be used to describe activity-travel behaviour in the area, but also to predict future activity-travel patterns for at least some types of policy scenarios under the usual *ceteris paribus* conditions.

OTHER ISSUES

In addition to (data-driven) simulation, the workshop touched briefly on some alternatives, without having the time to elaborate these at length. First, rather than using a small local sample, if one exists, as the basis for estimating a model of transport demand, one can perhaps use it as a validation sample of a model derived from data collected elsewhere or in a larger area. Dependent upon the outcome of the validation, authorities may be less reluctant to rely on transferred data or models, or realise that additional local data need to be collected. Second, most travel surveys tend to be conservative in terms of sample size. Moreover, sample sizes required to estimate population parameters with the same degree of accuracy differ according to the kind of variables, their standard deviation, etc. Also, dependent upon the policy issue, required accuracies may differ. Realising that accuracy is not linearly related to sample size and standard errors, and that the costs and perhaps reliability of data obtained are not linearly related to the number of repeated contacts, it is possible to derive a more optimal sample that would maximise the information gain, subject to the available budget. Statistics derived from smaller local samples, or from samples that one believes have a higher degree of transferability, can be used to predict (smaller) expected standard errors better, generally leading to smaller required sample sizes.

Regardless of the approach taken to counterbalance increasing costs and lower response rates, the discussion illustrated that the quite common view among transportation practitioners, that valid and reliable statistics and models can be obtained only for (stratified) random samples with very high response rates, is a very limited and narrow view of survey quality. Approaches discussed in the workshop deserve further attention and elaboration, both in academic and applied research, and should be high on the research agenda.

REFERENCES

Arentze, T.A., F. Hofman, H. van Mourik, H.J.P. Timmermans and G. Wets (2000). Using Decision Tree Induction Systems for Modeling Space-Time Behavior, *Geographical Analysis*, **32**, 52-72.

Arentze, T.A. and H.J.P. Timmermans (2005). Parameterized Action Decision Trees: Incorporating Continuous Attribute Variables into Rule-Based Models of Activity-Travel Behavior, paper submitted for presentation at the Annual Transportation Research Board Meeting, January.

Beckman, R.J., K.A. Baggerly and M.D. McKay (1996). Creating Synthetic Baseline Populations, *Transportation Research A*, **30**, 415-429.

Bonsall, P. and C. Kelly (2003). Road User Charging and Social Exclusion: The Impact of Congestion Charges on At-risk Groups. In: *Proceedings of the 2003 European Transport Conference*, Strasbourg, PTRC, London.

Bradley, M., J. Bowman and T.K. Lawton (1999). A Comparison of Sample Enumeration and Stochastic Microsimulation for Application of Tour-Based and Activity-Based Travel Demand Models, Paper presented at the European Transport Conference, Cambridge.

Greaves, S.P. (2006). Simulating Household Travel Survey Data. In: *Travel Survey Methods – Quality and Future Directions* (P.R. Stopher and C.C. Stecher, eds), 641-666, Elsevier, Oxford.

Greaves, S.P. and P.R. Stopher (2000). Creating a Simulated Household Travel/Activity Survey – Rationale and Feasibility Analysis, *Transportation Research Record No. 1706*, 82-91.

Janssens, D., G. Wets, T. Bruijs and K. Vanhoof (2004). The Simulation of Activity Diary Data Using Sequential Probability Distributions. In: *Proceedings ISCTSC Conference*, August 1-6, Costa Rica (CD-Rom).

Janssens, D., G. Wets, T. Bruijs, K. Vanhoof and H.J.P. Timmermans (2003). Identifying Behavioural Principles Underlying Activity Patterns by Means of Bayesian Networks. In: *Proceedings 82nd Annual Meeting of the Transportation Research Board*, January 12-16, Washington, D.C. (CD-Rom: 20 pp).

Joh, C.-H, T.A. Arentze and H.J.P. Timmermans (2001a). Activity-Travel Pattern Similarity: A Multidimensional Alignment Method. *Transportation Research B*, **36**, 385-403.

Joh, C.-H, T.A. Arentze and H.J.P. Timmermans. (2001b). Multidimensional Sequence Alignment Methods for Activity-Travel Pattern Analysis: A Comparison of Dynamic Programming and Genetic Algorithms, *Geographical Analysis*, **33**, 247-270.

Joh, C.-H., T.A. Arentze and H.J.P. Timmermans (2001c). Pattern Recognition in Complex Activity-Travel Patterns: A Comparison of Euclidean Distance, Signal Processing Theoretical, and Multidimensional Sequence Alignment Methods, *Transportation Research Record No. 1752*, 16-23.

Keulers, B., G. Wets, T.A. Arentze and H.J.P. Timmermans (2001). Using Association Rules to Identify Spatial-Temporal Patterns in Multi-Day Activity Diary Data, *Transportation Research Record No. 1752*, 32-37.

Moons, E., G. Wets, T.A. Arentze and H.J.P. Timmermans (2002). The Impact of Irrelevant Attributes on the Accuracy of Classifier Systems in Generating Activity Schedules, *Proceedings of the Transportation Research Board Conference*, Washington, D.C., January 13-17.

Purvis, C.L. (1994). Using 1990 Census Public Use Microdata Sample to Estimate Demographic and Automobile Ownership Models, *Transportation Research Record No. 1443*, 21–29.

Stopher, P.R., S.P. Greaves and P. Bullock (2003). Simulating Household Travel Data: Applications to Two Urban Areas. In: *Proceedings 82nd Annual Meeting of the Transportation Research Board*, January 12-16, Washington, DC. (CD-Rom: 20 pp).

Strambi, P. and K.A. van de Bilt (1998). Trip Generation Modeling Using CHAID: A Criterion-Based Segmentation Approach, *Transportation Research Record No. 1645*, 24-31.

Ton, T. and D.A. Hensher (2001). Synthesising Population Data: The Specification and Generation of Synthetic Households in TRESIS. Paper presented at the 9th World Conference on Transport Research, Seoul.

Veldhuisen, K., H.J.P. Timmermans and L.L. Kapoen (2000a), Micro-Simulation of Activity-Travel Patterns and Traffic Flows: Validation Tests and an Investigation of Monte Carlo Error, *Transportation Research Record No. 1706*, 126-135.

Veldhuisen, K., H.J.P. Timmermans and L.L. Kapoen (2000b), Ramblas: A Regional Planning Model Based on the Micro-Simulation of Daily Activity Travel Patterns, *Environment and Planning A*, **32**, 427-443.

Wets, G., K. Vanhoof, T.A. Arentze and H.J.P. Timmermans (2000). Identifying Decision Structures Underlying Activity Patterns: An Exploration of Data Mining Algorithms, *Transportation Research Record No. 1718*, 1-9.

Zumkeller, D. (2004), A Socio-ecological Simulation Model of Travel Behaviour. Publication in preparation at University of Toronto, Autumn 2004. (German Version: University of Braunschweig, 1988).

Zumkeller, D. and H. Seitz (1993). Preparation of Available Data for Transport Planning Purposes as a Replacement for New Surveys (German title: Aufbereitung vorhandener Daten für Verkehrsplanungszwecke als Ersatz für neue Befragungen), Bundesministerium für Verkehr (Hrsg.), Schriftenreihe Forschung Straßenbau und Straßenverkehrstechnik, Heft 642, 1993.

38

TRANSPORT SURVEY STANDARDS AND FUTURES

Peter R. Stopher, Institute of Transport and Logistics Studies, University of Sydney, NSW, Australia
and
Cheryl C. Stecher, The Franklin Hill Group, Santa Monica, California, USA

INTRODUCTION

This chapter has two principal purposes. The first is to provide an overview and summary of the conference that was held in Costa Rica in 2004. The second is to offer a summary and conclusions of the chapters of this book, and to attempt to provide a few pointers as to where the profession should be heading in the next few years. As noted in the Preface to this book, the chapters of this book were originally among the papers presented at, or written as a consequence of the 7th International Conference on Travel Survey Methods. They have been revised since that conference, and a number were written subsequently to the conference to provide a summary of the discussions that took place in the conference. Therefore, we begin this chapter by describing the conference and what took place there.

STRUCTURE OF THE CONFERENCE

The conference was held at Playa Herradura in Costa Rica from 1st to 6th August, 2004. It attracted seventy two delegates from nineteen countries from North, Central, and South America, Europe, Africa, Australasia, and the Middle East. Conference participants were assigned to two workshops, one to discuss standards issues which met in the first half of the conference and the other to discuss future research needs in the second half. There were eight workshops in the first half of the conference and seven in the second half. Each workshop was given a specific topic and a charge. Resource papers were commissioned for each workshop, and these resource papers formed the foundation of the deliberations of the workshop. In addition, twenty one papers, written in response to a call for papers, were presented in workshops during the conference.

The conference commenced on Sunday evening with a welcome reception, and opening remarks from the Costa Rican Ministry of Transport and Public Works. On Monday morning, a plenary session was held with three keynote papers. Two of these keynote papers appear as the first two chapters in this book (Ortúzar, 2006; Stopher *et al.*, 2006). Following this opening plenary session, a second plenary session was held in which participants heard from eight commissioned paper authors, each of whom had been commissioned to write a resource paper for a specific workshop. The workshops for the first half of the conference were as follows:

Workshop A1: Survey Design

Travel survey designs vary considerably around the world. While the US gravitated toward telephone interviews in the 1970s, home interviews have remained popular elsewhere, and are, in certain countries, the dominant mode of travel survey. Telephone surveys are beleaguered by low response rates, caller ID, telephone answering machines, and 'no call' lists. At the same time, home interviews have become increasingly expensive in most countries and the issue of security remains a deterrent to their use. The time appeared ripe, therefore, to review survey designs as used around the world and in the light of current trends, good practice, and new technology, identify survey procedures that promise to improve current practice. Within each mode attention was to be given to effective means of recruitment, motivation of respondents, effective communication among participants, efficient data acquisition, and establishing means of quality control and error correction wherever possible.

Workshop A2: Sample Design

Sample design requires information on the variance in the data, levels of error in the data that would be acceptable to the user, and the certainty the user needs to know whether errors in the data are within the acceptable limits or not. Variance within the data is not known in advance of the survey and, therefore, one area of discussion was to be whether establishment of typical (or default) variances of data items would be worthwhile and useful. Another issue was what variables should be considered in establishing sample size and how should the sample sizes needed for each variable be combined to establish a common sample size. Acceptable error limits on individual variable have typically been established subjectively and yet this has been done without knowing how input errors propagate through the travel demand modelling process to model outputs. Questions to be addressed included: whether errors in input variables that are typically considered acceptable (say, ≤ 10 percent) produce output errors that are within acceptable limits; whether there is a need for sensitivity analysis to study this effect; and whether there is a need for a standardised procedure for establishing sample sizes in travel surveys.

Workshop A3: Instrument Design

Because survey instruments, and the manner in which they are used, may vary from one part of the world to the other, aspects of instrument design that are significant may vary. Issues that were to form the subject of discussion include guidelines on good practice in the design of a self-administered questionnaires (e.g., layout, font, colour, etc.) or the structure and content of a telephone-administered survey, the desirability of identifying a core set of questions to be included in all travel surveys, the value of establishing standard wording for some questions, standardization of categories on items such as education level, job classification, or income, and whether there is a desirable ordering of questions in a survey. These issues were to be discussed in the context of different international settings.

Workshop A4: Survey Implementation

Travel surveys typically run on very tight schedules and budget limits. It is therefore important that the execution of the survey be planned and administered as efficiently as possible. This involves well-administered planning and scheduling of activities, training of personnel, data checking and editing, preparation of data files, documentation, and archiving. The workshop was to investigate whether the establishment of standards in survey implementation is advisable, and if so, what aspects should be standardised. In addition, the workshop was to consider the issue of 'tailoring' respondent/interviewer contact by assigning a single interviewer to a respondent. The possibility and merit of having interviewers being able to operate in a mobile manner in CATI and other interviews were also to be discussed.

Workshop A5: Processing, Analysis, and Archiving

The processing, analysis, and archiving of travel survey data often receives considerably less attention than other aspects of travel surveys. However, it is an important part of the process that can significantly affect the quality of the data obtained and its continued accessibility and usefulness in the future. This workshop was to identify those activities that are critical to the quality of the data in this part of the survey execution, suggest standards in terms of procedures and content, and consider how to ensure that results of these activities are adequately reported in the survey documentation. Attention was to be given to the potential to establish universal standards, particularly in the area of archiving, so as to ensure the greatest value of data now and in the future.

Workshop A6: Quality Assessment

Assessing the quality of data is important because this allows users the ability to assign credibility to data. However, it is not clear how to define quality and how to measure it. This workshop was to develop a definition of data quality, suggest means by which data quality can be measured, and suggest how the results of these measurements should be interpreted in terms of data quality. Attention was to be given to the diversity of travel survey methods used throughout the world and how this would impact the assessment of data quality and whether universal measures of data quality are achievable or not. The workshop was also to consider whether the International Standards Organization (ISO) could usefully play a role in measuring, and ultimately in establishing and maintaining, travel survey data quality.

Workshop A7: Stated Preference

SP data have the advantage that they are not restricted to what has occurred, but may include a wide range of hypothetical situations. However, this versatility comes with the requirement that realistic responses are obtained. This workshop was to consider the current and possibly new ways in which hypothetical alternatives in an SP experiment can be presented to a respondent so that they have as complete and realistic an understanding of the alternatives as possible. New ways of presenting alternatives could include the use of computer-simulated virtual reality, the use of multiple graphical montages, or the use of focus groups where a clearer understanding of alternatives is achieved through dialogue. The workshop was also to consider new ways of identifying alternatives for consideration in SP experiments and identify the principles of good survey design and survey execution for SP surveys.

Workshop A8: Panel Surveys

In this workshop both true panel surveys, where the same respondents are surveyed on consecutive occasions, and repeated cross-section surveys, where the respondents are allowed to change from survey to survey, were to be considered. Panel and repeated cross-section surveys have tended to be trip-based surveys in the past, but activity-based surveys must be considered in the light of the increasing number of these surveys being conducted. Another form of survey that was to be considered was the continuous survey as implemented in the American Community Survey by the U.S. Bureau of the Census. This workshop was to consider the potential of establishing activity-based panels, repeated cross-section, or continuous surveys for urban transport planning, how the different forms of longitudinal survey would be likely to impact the periodicity and maintenance of the sample, and how the data would probably be used.

The charge to the first six workshops was to determine to what extent the proposed standards and guidelines in the paper by Stopher *et al.* (2006) could be accepted as potential global standards and guidelines, or the extent to which some of the proposed standards and guidelines would need to be modified, either to specific nations or cultures. In the event that modification would be required, it was desired that the workshops indicate the nature of the changes. Alternatively, some proposed standards and guidelines could be rejected as being not applicable, or not useful.

Following deliberations by the workshops on Monday and Tuesday, a plenary session was held with reports from the workshop chairs. Reports from the workshops were prepared subsequently and appear as chapters of this book. To start the second round of workshops, a plenary session was held at which the seven resource papers for the second round of workshops were presented. The details of these workshops are described in the following paragraphs. This group of workshops were given a threefold charge: determine the most important research issues that need current attention in the international community, determine the top two or three such issues, and suggest how such research could be funded.

Workshop B1: Freight

Relatively little attention has been given to freight surveys by travel survey researchers in the past. One of the reasons for this is that the impact of goods vehicles on urban traffic was considered negligible. However, rapid growth in the trucking industry, just-in-time delivery, and higher overall levels of congestion have changed this perception. An increase in interest in freight data collection is evident in the establishment of new committees within the Transportation Research Board, increased publications, and more research funding. However, freight surveys present their own unique challenges; shippers and carriers are reluctant to divulge details of their goods movement because of the potential value this information would have for their competitors, a wide array of participants are involved in the movement of goods (e.g., shippers, carriers, forwarders, vendors, consultants, agencies, and associations), and goods are extremely diverse in value, weight, volume, and perishability. This workshop was to set out to establish the state-of-the-art of freight travel surveys, investigate the potential of unobtrusive data collection of freight movement through technologies, such as electronic data interchange (EDI), ITS-CVO, GPS, and automated freight-handling facilities, and consider the potential of establishing a secure clearinghouse in which detailed freight data can be accumulated and processed into aggregate values that preserve the confidentiality of contributors while providing useful, dynamic information to all freight movers.

Workshop B2: Investment-Quality Surveys

Throughout the world, there is an upsurge in toll road planning and construction. This rapidly growing development is substantially the result of the failure of conventional tax financing to keep up with surface transport infrastructure needs. Tolling is a way to build and rebuild roads without having to resort to general taxation. Toll road projects rely on the capital markets for their funds and, as such, they bring highway service into the market economy. The successful planning and financing of a toll road, bridge, or tunnel project rely heavily on credible traffic and revenue forecasts. This is an integral part of the implementation process and can well be a critical factor in determining a project's financial feasibility. Recent projects have seen traffic and revenues sometimes fall significantly below forecast, while debt service obligations retain full-and-timely payment requirements. As a result, the rating agencies have raised the bar for investment-grade traffic and revenue studies, beyond the apparent statistical and modelling practices currently prevalent in the transportation planning field. This workshop was to examine the challenges and opportunities that investment-grade studies bring to travel survey design and implementation, specifically in areas of travel pattern surveys, SP surveys, socioeconomic analyses, and value pricing studies.

Workshop B3: Process versus Outcome Data

The traditional household travel survey, together with most surveys on transit, for freight, etc. measure the outcomes of decisions. Relatively little work has been done to measure the decision process leading to the outcome. However, simulation and activity models are increasingly focusing on the process as opposed to the outcome of decision making. There is relatively little experience or knowledge on how to collect process data, what types of questions would need to be asked, what survey procedures are appropriate, and what measurements need to be made. The workshop was to assess these issues and prepare a research agenda for developing good process data collection procedures, especially for person travel, but also considering issues for freight.

Workshop B4: New Technology: Non Web-based (GPS, GSM, PDA, etc.)

The last three years has seen a rapid adoption of GPS data collection for vehicle-based surveys. Recent results indicate that, by using GPS, errors of omitted trips can be reduced. For example, results from California and Ohio indicate that between twenty five and thirty percent of trips are unreported in traditional diary surveys compared to trips captured with machine-captured information. The issue of capturing non-vehicle based trips has also been explored and found to provide useful information. However, the use of GPS in vehicle-based and non-vehicle-based travel needs to be extended beyond mere comparison with data obtained by traditional survey procedures and make better use of the locational information that can be obtained from GSM technology. This workshop was to explore the potential uses of new non web-based technology in identifying travel behaviour surveys

Workshop B5: New Technology: Web-based

There is an increasing interest in the use of new technology in travel surveys and in the development of Web-based travel surveys. However, even though access to the Web is increasing in most countries there are still those that cannot be reached by this medium. Among those who do have access to the Web, familiarity with the system is highly variable and some would be uncomfortable using it to complete a survey. The workshop was, therefore, to consider issues related to the representativeness of web-based surveys, possible sampling procedures, and the quality of data that is likely to emerge from a Web-based survey. The matter of using the Web as the only means of data collection in a survey, as a supplemental mode, or for parts of a survey, was to be addressed. The use of the Web to improve contact, reduce refusal and/or offer the choice of the 'best' medium to the surveyed person was also to be considered. In all, the potential, the strengths, the weaknesses, and immediate opportunities for including Web-based travel surveys more into the mainstream of travel survey methodology were to be investigated.

Workshop B6: Emergency Events

People have become more aware that an emergency event can affect their lives. Natural or man-made disasters can generate travel demands and travel conditions that are quite atypical and can severely influence the safety of the people affected by the disaster. However, relatively little data collection has been conducted around emergency events in the past. That which has been conducted has tended to be by social scientists, whose interest has been in the social aspects of evacuation, with relatively little attention given to travel behaviour. We are currently unable to model the traffic implications of an emergency event, because data on travel behaviour under these conditions is unavailable. Thus, there is a need to identify survey procedures that would allow us to collect such information. The workshop was to establish a framework of emergency types and identify the survey approach, sampling procedures, survey instruments, and survey content that would be likely to be effective in collecting travel behaviour in each type of emergency.

Workshop B7: Simulated Travel Survey Data

There is increasing interest in simulating travel survey data, as the costs of collecting original data continue to escalate, and as nonresponse rates also rise. This workshop was to consider the potential value of simulating household travel survey data, the methods that should be researched for simulation, and especially how the geography of travel should be simulated. Issues of local updating through a small sample survey, and of sources for simulation data were also to be considered. Another issue to be considered here was what should be simulated – individual trips, tours, trip chains, activities, etc. Finally, the workshop was to consider what tests are appropriate to determine the value of simulated data, and the extent to which such data could replace or augment existing household travel surveys.

A final plenary session was held on Friday afternoon at which the results of the second series of workshops were reported to all conference participants. As noted earlier, a general call for papers was issued about a year before the conference was held, with the areas of the workshops already listed. The resulting offered papers were reviewed and those that were recommended for presentation in the conference were allocated to the workshops of most relevance.

STANDARDS AND GUIDELINES

As noted at the outset of this book, one of the principal reasons for the conference and for this book was to extend the discussion of establishing standards, guidelines, and standardised procedures for household travel surveys throughout the world. Primary motivations for examining this topic are the desire to raise the standards of household travel surveys and to increase the comparability of households travel surveys from urban area to urban area and from nation to nation. The structure of this book is to examine various steps in the design, implementation, and analysis of a survey, namely:

- Survey Design;
- Sample Design;
- Instrument Design;
- Survey Implementation;
- Processing, Analysing, and Archiving Survey Data; and
- Quality Assessment.

In this chapter, we take these in order.

Survey Design

As reported by Kurth and McGuckin (2006), a number of issues of survey design potentially may be appropriate for at least guidelines, if not standardised procedures:

1.   Guidance on the number and type of contacts was felt to be appropriate and useful, although it was noted that specific standards are not likely to be appropriate, given differences in survey methods.
2.   Use of proxy reporting is very much subject to local customs and mores, but self reporting should be encouraged.
3.   No standards were proposed for what constitutes a complete individual or household survey, but it was considered important to strive for one hundred percent completion and limited proxy reporting.
4.   In the area of item nonresponse, there was agreement on the need to minimise this problem, but no agreement on standards or guidelines with respect to item nonresponse.

Other issues that were addressed but for which no standards, guidelines, or standardised procedures were considered possible at this time included sample replacement, unit nonresponse, initial contacts, and the use of incentives. Measuring respondent burden was also considered, and it was concluded that this is difficult to measure, can possibly be assessed through other measures, and is of little interest to the clients for surveys. Survey translation was another area that was addressed, again with no concrete results, but an observation that this is potentially an overwhelming issue for some countries.

Overall, this workshop concluded that international adoption of standards and guidelines in the area of survey design seems unlikely. On the other hand, it was suggested that principles of good survey design should be developed from the material in the chapter by Stopher *et al.* (2006), and broadened to encompass other survey methods and cultures.

Sample Design

In this topic area, difficulties associated with establishing standards and guidelines were discussed and it was noted that the use of the data would, in many cases, dictate the choice of the sample design variables. It was also felt that general guidance on the size of variances for possible design variables would not be useful, but that pilot surveys would provide the information required on a case-by-case basis.

Following from this, it was felt that the recommended standardisation of pilot surveys and pretests should be adopted, with the note that the minimum sample sizes specified by Stopher *et al.* (2006) be considered guidelines not standards. It was also proposed that verification should be considered a standard tool to complement pilot surveys and pretests (Picardo, 2006).

Instrument Design

In a somewhat similar conclusion to Survey Design, it was concluded (Cohen, 2006) that, rather than standards and guidelines, a 'good practice resource' should be developed, providing advice on the best ways to undertake various design tasks, while also warning of the pitfalls that should be avoided. Possible constituent elements of such a resource were developed and are to be found in Table 2 of Cohen (2006). Two of these were discussed in detail and a number of suggestions put forward as to what the content might be. This also led to the development of research questions relating to the first topic areas. The discussion also addressed the recommended minimum questions put forward by Stopher *et al.* (2006), where agreement with twenty one of the twenty eight questions was indicated, with four being considered inappropriate as global standards and three being considered questionable.

Survey Implementation

In the area of survey implementation (van der Reis and Harvey, 2006), there was considerable agreement with many of the standards and guidelines put forward by Stopher *et al.* (2006), with the following results:

1. Ethics: there was broad agreement with the proposed ethical standards, but with a note that those standards dealing with anonymity, when households can be contacted, and the minimum age for interviewing without parental consent may need adaptation to specific cultures. It was also suggested that mobile phone costs should not be borne by respondents, and that this should appear as a standard. The workshop also identified three additional candidates for inclusion in the list of ethics standards.

2. Mailing materials: these proposed standards were considered to be generally acceptable. It was noted that similar standards need to be developed for other survey methods than ones that entail mailing, such as for show cards, diary covers, etc. in face-to-face interviews.

3. Respondent questions: these recommended standards were also found acceptable, and some additional guidelines were offered from the discussion.

4. Caller ID: The workshop concurred with the proposed standard in this area.

5. Answering machines and repeated call-back requests: the proposed standards should be extended to cover face-to-face interviewing. It was also noted that these standards may not be applicable in all cultures and will need some modification according to local mores and customs.

6. Incorrect reporting of non-mobility: these standards were considered to be particularly relevant for proxy reports. In the area of both non-mobility reporting and proxy protocols, the workshop recommended additional standards.

7. Reporting time of day: the recommended standards were accepted as valuable.

8. Time of day to begin and end reporting: rather than specify a particular time, which might need to vary from culture to culture, the recommendation is to replace this standard with one specifying that the start and end time must be clearly designated for all surveys.

9. Missing standards: additional standards were proposed in the areas of survey personnel training, scheduling of the survey process, and handling hard-to-reach populations.

In addition to these specific areas, several research topics were also identified, specifically:

1. Development of flexible protocols on interview/interviewer and respondent tailoring;

2. Data freshness;

3.   Combining data from different sources;
4.   Effect of call-back delays on data retrieval;
5.   Implications of mobile telephone use; and
6.   Response comparability over different survey modes.

Processing, Analysing, and Archiving Survey Data

Strambi and Garrido (2006) report that there was considerable agreement with many of the standards proposed by Stopher *et al.* (2006) in the area of processing, analysing, and archiving survey data. Additional standards and guidelines were also suggested in this area. In the area of Data Processing, the issues addressed were:

1.   Database construction: the principal issue discussed here was that of confidentiality and availability of data. No standards were proposed, but research into ways to maintain confidentiality while also releasing useful data were clearly surfaced.
2.   Questionnaire response editing: it was recommended that '...a well conceived version control system...' should be a requirement.
3.   Coding: the proposed standards relating to missing data, coding binary variables, and using hierarchical coding systems on certain complex categorical variables were all accepted as appropriate standards for surveys. Geocoding was also discussed, and the proposed standards for geocoding were also largely agreed to.
4.   Data imputation: a point of significance raised in the discussions was the idea that information obtained by recontacting households or persons should be regarded as another case of data imputation. There was agreement with the standard to flag all imputed values. Several other issues were also discussed and are documented in Strambi and Garrido (2006).
5.   Weighting: there was general acceptance of the proposed weighting standards and guidelines, with additional recommendations. These included recommendations to look at the distributions of weighting factors, to weight using demographic variables first and to do trip correction as a last resort only, to keep weighting and expansion factors separate, and to document fully the development of weights.

In the area of Data Analysis, the principal issue addressed was that of validation. While the recommendations of Stopher *et al.* (2006) on validation were accepted, the workshop added a recommendation that audits should also be undertaken, where the audit is performed by a third party. In essence, the audit determines whether or not procedures were followed, and verifies all procedures used in data collection. In addition, the workshop recommended that results should always be presented with statistical significance and confidence information.

In the area of Documentation and Archiving, the discussion largely ignored the recommended standards and, instead, developed some recommended basic archiving architecture. This architecture consists of seven elements:

1.   Document description;
2.   Study description;
3.   File description;
4.   Variable description;
5.   On-line Help;
6.   An accessibility hierarchy that handles confidentiality of the records; and
7.   Version control.

Finally, the workshop addressed issues of harmonisation or consistency, observing that this may raise problems for users of data who have different goals and restrictions on their use of the data. Nevertheless, it was suggested that harmonisation has four principal advantages: economies of scale, ease of use, ease of validation and comparison, and quality standards.

Quality Assessment

The discussions of this workshop were focused in three areas: defining data quality, suggesting how it could be measured, and suggesting how the results of measurement should be interpreted (Noble and Holroyd, 2006). In the area of definition of quality, the workshop contribution was to suggest that this is measured by 'fitness for purpose', while also admitting that this may itself be difficult to define because of its dependence on the use to which the data are put, where this may not be known until after the survey is completed.

To measure data quality, the workshop proposed four issues, in priority order:

1.   Validation and comparison to other relevant independent data;
2.   Representativeness of the sample;
3.   Procedural issues; and
4.   Headline indicators.

Under the first issue – validation and comparison – it was stressed that novel findings from a survey should first be suspected of being an artefact of the survey design, rather than an indication of a major departure in behaviour. A number of parameters were suggested for comparison, largely mirroring those proposed by Stopher *et al.* (2006) as transport measures of quality, including trip rates, immobility rates, time spent travelling per day, distance travelled per day, and trends in data.

Under the second issue, the workshop considered three elements, representativeness over time, representativeness over space, and representativeness of the population. Representativeness over time relates to the period of time of interest to the user of the data, such as weekdays versus weekends, time of the year, etc. Representativeness over space refers to geographic coverage and its relation also to the needs of the user. Representativeness of the population should be measured by demographics, car ownership, incomes, education levels, and another relevant characteristics.

Under procedural issues, the recommendations relate mainly to documentation of the procedures used, so that it is easy to determine where procedures have changed. Such indicators as allowance of proxy responses, survey burden, whether pretests and pilot surveys were conducted, training and motivation of interviewers, and how participants were motivated were suggested as important items to document in this respect.

The principal headline indicator discussed was the response rate. While the workshop acknowledged the recommendation of Stopher *et al.* (2006) to use the AAPOR formula, the workshop suggested that an existing standardised formula from the country of the data collection may possibly be preferred. Detailing how the response rate was calculated was deemed more important than standardising a specific method of calculation. The workshop also discussed some issues of survey documentation.

Conclusions

There was remarkable consensus on the applicability of the standards recommended by Stopher *et al.* (2006) across all of the workshops. Workshop participants agreed that there could and should be global standards for issues such as:

- Need for self-reporting;
- Need for pilot surveys and pretests;
- Ethical standards for data collection;
- The wording of certain respondent questions;
- Reporting of certain quality indicators, such as:
  - Response rates (using either standard or local formulas);
  - Reporting of non-mobility;
- Hierarchical coding system for complex categorical variables;
- Need to flag any imputed data;
- Documentation; and
- Data archiving;

There were additional recommendations for standards, or suggested modifications to the proposed standards that would render them more suitable for global application, including:

- Requiring the start and end time of the travel reporting period to be clearly designated (instead of using the same start and end times for all surveys);
- In weighting data, to use demographic variables first and to do trip correction as a last resort; and
- Provide full documentation of the development of weights.

There was also consensus on the areas in which local mores and culture would render global standards meaningless. These areas included:

- Use of incentives;
- Sample replacement;
- Unit non-response;
- Initial contacts;
- What constitutes a complete household;
- Use of answering machines; and
- Instrument design, in general.

There was general consensus that the issues relating to design are more varied from culture to culture and nation to nation, making the idea of global standardisation in these areas more difficult to achieve and possibly even not relevant.

This conference did indeed move the practice of travel surveys further along the path towards defining standards for household and person travel surveys. In the design area, it may be that the global community can best be assisted by a compendium of good practices in travel survey designs, whilst a number of standards could be promulgated for survey implementation, data processing, analysis, documentation, archiving, and quality assessment.

RESEARCH DIRECTIONS

The two remaining workshops from the first half of the conference and the seven in the second half of the conference were charged to focus on research agendas. In this section, we summarise the research issues identified. To the extent that the workshops prioritised these issues to the top two or three and suggested potential ways of funding the research, we also document those. However, a number of workshops became so involved in the definition of research that they never tackled these last two questions. The topics that were identified for these workshops are:

- Stated preference surveys;
- Panel surveys;
- Freight data collection;
- Investment-quality surveys;
- Process data;
- Application of no-Web technologies to travel surveys;

- Application of Web-based technologies to travel surveys;
- Data Collection for emergency events; and
- Simulation of travel survey data.

These are discussed below in order.

Stated Preference Surveys

The workshop on Stated Preference surveys (Jones and Bradley, 2006) identified seven priority areas for research, but did not further prioritise these, nor suggest sources of funding for the research. The seven areas are:

1. Determining criteria for success and validity. While these issues apply to all surveys, the workshop identified that there are additional issues specifically for SP surveys that need to be addressed and that require research.
2. Information provision and survey framing. This issue has to do with the potential of biasing survey responses through the information provided and the way in which the survey is presented to respondents.
3. The influence of presentation formats. This has to do with such issues as the use of photos, sounds, and other information that may impact the way in which people undertake the SP task. It also concerns the amount of detail provided on the attributes of interest in the study.
4. The influence of interview media and survey location. There are many locations that are used for SP surveys as well as alternatives of pencil and paper, laptop, and other media, the influence of which on the SP results are quite unknown.
5. The treatment of complex choices. Most SP experiments focus on a single event or situation and do not consider complex choices. How a complex choice should be framed and presented is a matter requiring research.
6. Temporal dimensions to SP choices. There are two temporal issues that require research – the temporal stability of the preferences expressed in a SP survey and the time frame within which choices expressed in a SP survey might be expected to be realised in practice.
7. An international cross-discipline review of evidence should be undertaken, building on the advantages found in this conference of hearing from people with a variety of experiences in different countries and contexts.

Panel Surveys

Both the chapter on panel surveys that was commissioned for the conference (Zumkeller *et al.*, 2006) and the chapter on the workshop discussions (Murakami *et al.*, 2006) represent very valuable resources on the design and conduct of panel surveys and the alternative definitions of such surveys. Like the preceding workshop, this workshop put forward a research agenda, but did not get to the point of selecting the top two or three issues in priority, nor in addressing the funding of research. The ten recommended research areas were:

1. Documentation of the benefits of panels. This should include both comparisons between panels and cross-sectional data and also a synthesis of the state of practice in transport panels.
2. Training on applying the statistical methods for panels.
3. Learning about qualitative research techniques that apply to panels, such as biographic studies.
4. Comparison of the addition of retrospective questions to a cross-sectional survey with the use of a panel.
5. Potential to use existing general purpose market research panels for transport purposes.
6. Determining the optimal spacing between waves for a panel survey. Most transport panels have used one year, but it is not known what the optimal period might be.
7. Exploring the effects of conditioning, especially as it applies to effects on the travel of panel members.
8. Use of panels to observe the process rather than solely the outcomes.
9. Inclusion of attitudinal questions in panel surveys, especially to track how attitudes may change over time.
10. Inclusion of questions about why respondents stay in the panel.

Freight Transport Data Collection

This workshop developed a list of twelve research issues, but did not prioritise them nor propose sources of funding to undertake the research (Meyburg and Garrido, 2006). The issues were:

1. Develop understanding of the decision processes of those involved in the freight transport task;
2. Develop an understanding of the fundamental issues in the freight transport task;
3. Develop an understanding of the group decision processes involved in the freight transport task;
4. Investigate the feasibility of a public and private data clearinghouse;
5. Investigate different approaches to understand freight flows;
6. Develop guidelines rather than inflexible standards to guide freight survey design and execution;
7. Exchange information on best freight survey practices;
8. Identify the limitations for non-invasive data collection technologies in freight;

9.	Develop guidance on how to specify unambiguously the purposes of freight studies;
10.	Adopt the concept of a National Freight Data Programme;
11.	Investigate the practical implementability of the national freight data framework; and
12.	Form an international committee on freight forecasting data and models.

Investment-Quality Surveys

The area of investment-quality surveys is a very new area of concern for transport professionals (Zmud, 2006). As a result, the workshop discussions produced a listing of nine categories of key issues that need to be tackled through research. These are:

1.	Value of time. About eight research topics were identified in this area.
2.	Route choice. This is particularly important for toll road decisions, and current modelling of route choice generally ignores cost elements. Four specific topics were listed in this area.
3.	Social impacts of tolling. Social impacts have largely been ignored to date. Four specific research topics were listed in this area.
4.	Criteria of financiers. This has to do with the models used to evaluate risks by the banks and others who finance investments. Six topic areas were identified.
5.	Relationship between finance and quality. The issue here relates to how accurate the forecasts need to be and the influence this has on financing. Two research topics were identified here.
6.	Heavy vehicles. As with freight in general, there is little knowledge about choice of trucking routes in relation to toll and non-toll facilities. Seven research topics were identified in this issue area.
7.	Market segmentation. This relates to segmenting the sample to obtain values of time, for which four research topics were identified.
8.	Modelling issues. Models are generally used to forecast volumes of use and revenue streams. The workshop identified six research topics in this issue area.
9.	Quality guidelines. What constitutes an investment-grade survey is as yet ill-defined. However, the workshop felt that it is timely to begin formulating criteria for what this is. Eight research topics were identified in this area.

Process Data

Process data have not been a focus of previous conferences on travel survey methods. In this workshop (Pendyala and Bricka, 2006), considerable time was spent in defining process data and discussing how to measure processes as opposed to outcomes. The workshop defined seven research topics:

1.   Determining the most effective method to administer the survey;
2.   Determining the appropriate balance and use of open-ended and closed-ended questions for determining process information;
3.   Determining if it is possible and how to include a process survey in a larger sample survey;
4.   Determining the impact of administering a process survey in a group setting as opposed to an individual one;
5.   Determining the impact of different survey methods and question designs on respondent burden, conditioning, and bias;
6.   Determining the impact of different survey methods and question designs on interviewer burden, training, and bias; and
7.   Determining how to minimise respondent conditioning.

With respect to funding, the workshop felt that agencies interested in travel data should be made aware of the benefits of obtaining process data, and may be willing to fund such data collection. However, the workshop also recognised that the research mentioned above is of a fundamental nature, and suggested a number of potential funding sources for such data. A substantial number of funding avenues were proposed by workshop members and can be found in the chapter by Pendyala and Bricka (2006).

Non-Web Technologies

The workshop discussed all new technologies except those using the Internet for travel surveys (Lee-Gosselin and Harvey, 2006). In a slightly different approach, each workshop member was asked to give their two highest priority research areas, from which a list of four research topics emerged. The four topics are:

1.   Generic pilot surveys of location/time aware devices (LAD), including determining sample sizes, timing issues, and use in mixed-mode survey settings;
2.   Evaluation of the prompted recall method of obtaining additional data from LADs;
3.   Comparing the benefits and problems of LAD surveys with other travel surveys; and
4.   Developing and testing post-processing techniques both with and without the use of GIS.

An additional four topics were also suggested and may be found in the chapter by Lee-Gosselin and Harvey (2006). Among the sources of funding suggested for research in this area are agencies concerned with ITS and pricing or tolling systems, the European Commission, and health agencies, among others.

New Technology: Web-Based

The workshop on this topic first defined the technologies covered in this area, and then discussed the advantages and disadvantages of using Internet or Web-based surveys (Bonnel and Madre, 2006). The workshop then defined four broad areas of research that were needed, but did not prioritise these further. The four topics are:

1. Combining survey modes. The principal issue here is the extent to which the survey mode influences and changes the responses provided. Comparisons between different modes, whilst controlling for such differences as sociodemographic characteristics and availability of and familiarity with the Internet, are desired for this topic.
2. Sample coverage, which is largely an issue not only of Internet penetration, but also of the type of Internet service and familiarity with using the Internet. Several subtopics of research were suggested for this topic.
3. Design issues. A number of design issues were raised by the workshop members, including that of the complexity of the survey and the computing language used, the effect of making answers to questions compulsory, the issue of having all household members complete a survey, and the effect of survey duration on the response rate.
4. Application domain. This has to do with the topics for which a solely Web-based survey could be used and those where mixed modes are required to cover the population adequately.

The workshop concluded that Web-based surveys are currently somewhat restricted in sole use, but are very promising in mixed-mode situations. Comparability of the data from different media remains the greatest concern for the future of these surveys.

Data for Emergency Events

The discussions on the topic of data for emergency events were restricted to those types of emergency where enough warning is able to be given to enable evacuation to take place, so that the focus of the data collection is to provide information about the evacuation behaviour of people and households (Arce, 2006). A clear research agenda did not emerge from this workshop. It is clear, however, that a major area for research concerns the methodology to use for gathering data about evacuation behaviour. The workshop discussed several alternative approaches, concluding that there were merits and difficulties in each. Therefore, one research issue would clearly be that of determining the comparative advantages and disadvantages, as well as feasibility of different methods to survey populations that may be in the process of evacuation, may have evacuated recently, or may have to consider evacuating at some unspecified time in the future. Three other research questions were put forward:

1.   To what extent are people conditioned by previous emergency events, how long does such conditioning last, and how does it diffuse through the population?
2.   How is traffic flow in an evacuation affected by the way in which people gather information on emergency events?
3.   Why are some agencies or authorities trusted with respect to evacuation orders and related information, and others are not?

The workshop also identified some potential funding agencies for pursuing research in this area, especially government agencies concerned with security and emergency management.

Simulation of Travel Survey Data

Discussion focused initially on problems in simulating data (Timmermans, 2006), and then examined alternative approaches to microsimulation. These discussions did not result, however, in a list of research issues for a research agenda. This appears to be a topic in which there are substantial arguments for and against the process, and more research is clearly needed into the merits of using simulation as opposed to collecting small sample data in an area. The workshop warned that the situation could arise in which the amount of time and effort (and, therefore, money) that might need to be expended in doing a realistic job of data simulation, for an area with no data, may be as much or more than that required to collect data for the local area. Also, when microsimulation of travel data is attempted, there are several different methods that could be used – the workshop enumerated three of these – and research is needed to determine which method works best and under what specific circumstances.

CONCLUDING REMARKS

As so often happens with conferences of this type, some progress is clearly evident, but much remains to be done. In the area of standards, guidelines, and standardised procedures, as already noted in this chapter, some real progress appears to have been made, thanks in large part to the work completed under NCHRP Project 8-37, and encapsulated in the chapter by Stopher *et al.* (2006) in this book. At the same time, areas have clearly been identified where it is unlikely that cultural differences will permit global standards and guidelines to be developed, but where a best practice resource might provide the information that would achieve an improvement in quality and comparability of household and person travel surveys.

In the research topics discussed in this conference, a number of research issues were identified, some of which have been identified in previous conferences, while others have emerged for the first time in this conference. Perhaps the largest problem is the continuing lack of research funding to tackle these problems. For various reasons, the different agencies around the world that possess research funds seem little inclined to fund research of this nature. One may speculate that there are at least three reasons for this. First, many of the research topics identified here require the collection of real data to illuminate them. Such data collection is often expensive, and many funding agencies have little interest in seeing funds spent in such activities. Second, the case for improving data collection is not an easy one to make, unless one is extensively involved in the use and collection of data. Very often, data are used primarily to inform policy and to build models. Those who ultimately use the results from the data collection are far removed from the survey activity and frequently do not appreciate the impact of the data on the modelling and policy information. Third, the research issues are fairly pragmatic in nature, and do not seem appealing to those agencies interested in funding theoretical research. On the other hand, the agencies that are the clients for the improved data collection often lack research funds that can be used to improve data collection activities.

Probably, a key to future funding of such research will be to broaden the appeal of travel survey technology to other areas of endeavour. Clearly, with trends in obesity within developed countries increasing at an alarming rate, health agencies are becoming more and more interested in how people move around and what exercise they might get. Issues relating to evacuation behaviour are becoming more pressing as global warming appears to be generating more severe and more frequent natural emergency events (hurricanes, cyclones, and typhoons; tornadoes; floods; fires; etc.), and emergency management agencies should be more and more interested in understanding and planning evacuations. The list of potential agencies outside the usual small group of research agencies and transport agencies could continue on. This is a direction that must be pursued for the future, if we are to succeed in tackling many of these research issues.

REFERENCES

Arce, C. (2006). Emerging Issues Related to Emergency Events. In: *Travel Survey Methods – Quality and Future Directions* (P.R. Stopher and C.C. Stecher, eds), 619-624, Elsevier, Oxford.

Bonnel, P. and J.-L. Madre (2006). Web Based Technologies Research Needs. In: *Travel Survey Methods – Quality and Future Directions* (P.R. Stopher and C.C. Stecher, eds), 593-603, Elsevier, Oxford.

Cohen, T. (2006). Instrument Design Standards and Guidelines. In: *Travel Survey Methods – Quality and Future Directions* (P.R. Stopher and C.C. Stecher, eds), 161-173, Elsevier, Oxford.

Jones, P.M. and M.A. Bradley (2006). Stated Preference Surveys: An Assessment. In: *Travel Survey Methods – Quality and Future Directions* (P.R. Stopher and C.C. Stecher, eds), 347-361, Elsevier, Oxford.

Kurth, D. and N. McGuckin (2006). Survey Design Standards and Guidelines. In: *Travel Survey Methods – Quality and Future Directions* (P.R. Stopher and C.C. Stecher, eds), 95-109, Elsevier, Oxford.

Lee-Gosselin, M.E.H. and A.S. Harvey (2006). Non-Web Technologies. In: *Travel Survey Methods – Quality and Future Directions* (P.R. Stopher and C.C. Stecher, eds), 561-568, Elsevier, Oxford.

Meyburg, A.H. and R. Garrido (2006). Issues Related to Freight Transport Data Collection. In: *Travel Survey Methods – Quality and Future Directions* (P.R. Stopher and C.C. Stecher, eds), 451-455, Elsevier, Oxford.

Murakami, E., S.P. Greaves and T. Ruiz (2006). Moving Panel Surveys from Concept to Implementation. In: *Travel Survey Methods – Quality and Future Directions* (P.R. Stopher and C.C. Stecher, eds), 399-412, Elsevier, Oxford.

Noble, B. and S. Holroyd (2006). Quality Assessment. In: *Travel Survey Methods – Quality and Future Directions* (P.R. Stopher and C.C. Stecher, eds), 317-324, Elsevier, Oxford.

Ortúzar, J. de D. (2006). Travel Survey Methods in Latin America. In: *Travel Survey Methods – Quality and Future Directions* (P.R. Stopher and C.C. Stecher, eds), 1-18, Elsevier, Oxford.

Pendyala, R. and S. Bricka (2006). Collection and Analysis of Behavioural Process Data: Challenges and Opportunities. In: *Travel Survey Methods – Quality and Future Directions* (P.R. Stopher and C.C. Stecher, eds), 511-530, Elsevier, Oxford.

Picardo, R. (2006). Sample Design. In: *Travel Survey Methods – Quality and Future Directions* (P.R. Stopher and C.C. Stecher, eds), 139-142, Elsevier, Oxford.

Stopher, P.R., C.G. Wilmot, C.C. Stecher and R. Alsnih (2006). Household Travel Surveys: Proposed Standards and Guidelines. In: *Travel Survey Methods – Quality and Future Directions* (P.R. Stopher and C.C. Stecher, eds), 19-74, Elsevier, Oxford.

Strambi, O. and R. Garrido (2006). Processing, Analysing, and Archiving Standards and Guidelines. In: *Travel Survey Methods – Quality and Future Directions* (P.R. Stopher and C.C. Stecher, eds), 271-278, Elsevier, Oxford.

Timmermans, H.J.P. (2006). Using Microsimulation to Generate Activity-Travel Data Under Conditions of Insufficient Data. In: *Travel Survey Methods – Quality and Future Directions* (P.R. Stopher and C.C. Stecher, eds), 651-658, Elsevier, Oxford.

Van der Reis, P. and A.S. Harvey (2006). Survey Implementation. In: *Travel Survey Methods – Quality and Future Directions* (P.R. Stopher and C.C. Stecher, eds), 213-222, Elsevier, Oxford.

GLOSSARY OF ABBREVIATIONS

AADT	Annual Average Daily Traffic
AAPOR	American Association of Public Opinion Research
ACASI	Audio Computer-Assisted Self Interviewing
ADEME	(France) Agency for Environment & Energy Management
ADM	(Germany) Arbeistkresis Deutscher Market und Sozialforschungsinstitute
AET	Association of European Transport
A-GPS	Assisted Global Positioning System
AQS	Association for Qualitative Research
ASC	Association for Survey Computing
ASCII	American Standard Code for Information Interchange
ATIS	Automatic Traveller Information System
AVV	(Netherlands Transport Research Centre) Adviesdienst Verkeer en Vervoer
BBR	(Germany) Federal Office for Building & Regional Planning
BMRA	British Market Research Association
BMVBW	(Germany) Bundesministerium Für Verkehr, Bau- Und Wohnungswesen
BOT	Build Operate Transfer
BPCC	Bakwena Platinum Corridor Concessionaire
BSI	British Standards Institute
BTS	Bureau of Transportation Statistics
C & RT	Classification and Regression Trees
CAITR	Conference of Australian Institutes of Transport Research
CAPI	Computer Assisted Personal Interview
CASRO	Council of American Survey Research Organisations
CATI	Computer Assisted Telephone Interview
CBD	Central Business District
CD	Compact Disc
CHAID	Chi-Square Automatic Interaction Detection
CHASE	Computerised Household Activity Scheduling Elicitor
CMOR	(USA) Council for Opinion & Market
CORBA	Common Object Request Broker Architecture
COE	Corps of Engineers
DATELINE	Design & Application of a Travel Survey for European Long Distance Trips on an International Network of Expertise
DCS	Data Cleaning Statistic
DDF	Data Description File
DDI	Data Documentation Initiative
DEST	Department of Economics & Sociology of Transport

DIF	Data Interchange Format
DIW	German Institute of Economic Research
DLR	Deutsches Zentrum für Luft- und Raumfahrt eV (German Aerospace Centre)
DNTS	Danish National Travel Survey
DOT	(USA) Department of Transportation
DR	Dead Reckoning
DRCOG	Denver Regional Councils of Government
DTD	Document Type Definition
DYNEV	Dynamic Evacuation Model
ECHO	Enquête Envois Chargeurs Opérateurs
ECHP	European Community Household Panel
EDI	Electronic Data Interchange
EDR	Event Data Recorders
ELMIS	European Long-Distance Mobility Information System
EPHRAMO	European Federation of Associations of Market Research Organisations
ESOMAR	European Society of Opinion & Market Research
ESRC	Economic and Social Research Council
ETC	Electronic Toll Collection
ETH	(Switzerland) Federal Institute of Technology
ETHTDA	Eidgenossische Technische Hochschule Travel Data Archive
EUROSTAT	Statistical Office of the European Communities
EX-ACT	Extended Activity
FAQs	Frequently Asked Questions
FASTER	Flexible Access to Statistics Table & Electronic Resources
FCC	(USA) Federal Communications Commission
FCSM	Federal Committee on Statistical Methodology
FEMA	(USA) Federal Emergency Management Agency
FHWA	(USA) Federal Highway Administration
FOMT	Federal Office for Motor Traffic
FONDECYT	National Fund for Scientific & Technological Development
FPC	Finite Population Correction
FTA	(USA) Federal Transit Administration
FTF	Face-To-Face
GBR	Geographic Basic Register
GEV	General Extreme Value
GIS	Geographical Information System
GMA	Greater Metropolitan Area
GPS	Global Positioning System
GSHC	Gauteng Super Highways Consortium
GSM	Global System for Mobile Communication
HATP	Household Activity Time Patterns
HATS	Household Activity and Travel Simulator
HTS	Household Travel Survey

HURREVAC	Hurricane Evacuation Computer model for Southeast Louisiana
IA	Information Acceleration
IATBR	International Association of Travel Behaviour Research
IATUR	International Association of Time Use Research
ICC	International Chambers of Commerce
I-CHASE	Internet-Computerised Household Activity Scheduling Elicitor
ICPSR	Inter-University Consortium of Political Science Research
IID	Identically and Independently Distributed
INE	(Spain) Instituto Nacional de Estadística
INEGI	Instituto Nacional de Estadística Geografía & Informática
INFAS	(Germany) Instituto fur angewandte Sozialwissenschaft
INRETS	(France) National Institute of Research on Transport & Safety
IPUMS	Integrated Public Use Microdata System Series
IQCS	Interviewer Quality Control System
ISA	(Swedish) Intelligent Speed Adaptation
ISCTSC	International Steering Committee for Travel Survey Conferences
ISO	International Standards Organisation
ITRD	International Transport Research Documentation of the OECD
ITLS	(Australia) Institute of Transport and Logistics Studies
ITS	Intelligent Transport System
ITSA	International Travel Survey Archive Project
IVS	(Germany) Institut fur Verteilte Systeme
IVT	Institute for Transport Planning & Systems
JICA	Japanese International Cooperation Agency
JIT	Just in Time
KID	(Germany) Kraftfahrzeugverkehr in Deutschland
LADS	Location/time Aware Device
LATS	London Area Transport Survey
LDV	Light Duty Vehicle
LOC	Local Organising Committee
LPG/LNG	Liquid Petroleum Gas / Liquified Natural Gas
LVO	(Netherlands) Longitudunaal Verplaatsingsonderzoek
MASSVAC	Massachusetts Institute of Technology Evacuation Model
MEET	Methodologies for Estimating Emissions from Air Traffic
MID	Mobilitat in Deutschland
MIT	Massachusetts Institute of Technology
ML	Mixed Logit (Model)
MNL	Multinomial Logit (Model)
MON	(Netherlands) Mobiliteitsonderzoek Nederland
MOP	(Germany) Mobilitaespanel (German Mobility Panel)
MPO	Metropolitan Planning Organisation
MRA	(USA) Market Research Association
MRI	Magnetic Resonance Imaging
MRQSA	Market Research Quality Standards Association
MRS	Market Research Society

MSA	Metropolitan Statistical Areas
MTC	(Colombian) Ministry of Transport
MTC	Metropolitan Transportation Council
MTSA	Metropolitan Travel Survey Archive
MTUS	Multinational Time Use Study
NAD	North American Datum
NCES	National Centre for Educational Statistics
NCHRP	(USA) National Cooperative Highway Research Program
NCL	NESSTAR Light Client
NESSTAR	Networked Social Science Tools & Resources
NETVAC	Network Evacuation Model
NGA	National Geospatial Intelligence Agency
NHAI	National Highways Authority of India
NHTS	National Household Travel Survey
NIMA	National Imagery & Mapping Agency
NKD	New Kontiv Design
NOVG	Nieuw Onderzoek Verplaatsingsgedrag
NPTS	Nationwide Personal Travel Survey
NSF	National Science Foundation
NTS	National Travel Survey
O-D	Origin Destination
OECD ITRD	Organisation for Economic Co-Operation and Development Information Technology Research and Development
OMB	Office of Management & Budget
ONS	(UK) Office of National Statistics
OVG	Onderzoek Verplaatsingsgedrag
PAPI	Paper and Pencil Interview
PCA	Principal Components Analysis
PDA	Personal Digital Assistant
PMRS	(Canada) Professional Market Research Society
PPP	Public Private Partnership
PPS	Probabilities Proportional to Size
PSID	Panel Survey of Income Dynamics
PSTP	Puget Sound Transportation Panel
PSU	Primary Sampling Units
PUMA	Public Use Micro-Data Area
PUMS	Public Use Micro-Data Sample
QA/QC	Quality Assurance/Quality Control
RAP	Representative Activity Patterns
RDD	Random Digit Dialling
RDF	Resource Description Framework
RFID	Radio Frequency Identification
RMSE	Root Mean Square Error
RP	Revealed Preference

RV	Recreational Vehicle
SANRAL	South African National Roads Agency
SATURN	Simulation & Assignment of Traffic to Urban Road Network
SC	Stated Choice
SDA	Survey Documentation & Analysis Software
SECTRA	Executive and Technical Secretariat of an Inter-Ministerial Commission for Urban Transport
SLOSH	Sea, Lake, and Overland Surges from Hurricanes
SMASH	(Netherlands) Simulation Model of Activity Scheduling Heuristics
SMS	Short Message Service
SNCF	(France) Société Nationale des Chemins de Fer
SOEP	(Germany) Socioeconomic Panel
SP	Stated Preference
SR	Stated Response
SRA	Social Research Association
SRS	Simple Random Sample
SUV	Sports Utility Vehicle
TASTI	Time Assignment Travel and Income
TAZ	Traffic Analysis Zone
TCRP	Transit Cooperative Research Program
TDA	Time Difference of Arrival
TIGER	Topologically Integrated Geographic Encoding and Referencing
TMIP	Travel Mode Improvement Program
TRANSIMS	Transportation Analysis Simulation System
TRB	(USA) Transportation Research Board
TRM	(France) Transports Routiers de Marchandises
TTS	TeleTravel System
TUS	Time Use Survey
TxDOT	Texas Department of Transportation
UMTS	Universal Mobile Telecommunication System
UNECE	United Nations Economic Commission for Europe
UNFCCC	United Nations Framework Convention on Climate Control
USDOT	United States Department of Transportation
UTSG	University Transportation Studies Group
VATS	Victoria Activity and Travel Survey
VKT	Vehicle Kilometres Travelled
VNF	(France) Voies Navigable de France
VOT	Value of Time
VTTS	Value of Travel Time Savings
W3C	World Wide Web Consortium
WAPOR	World Association of Public Opinion Research
WCTRS	World Council on Transport Research Society
XML	Extensible Markup Language